MW01035366

POLITICIZING THE BIBLE

POLITICIZING THE BIBLE

The Roots of Historical Criticism and the Secularization of Scripture 1300-1700

Scott W. Hahn and
Benjamin Wiker

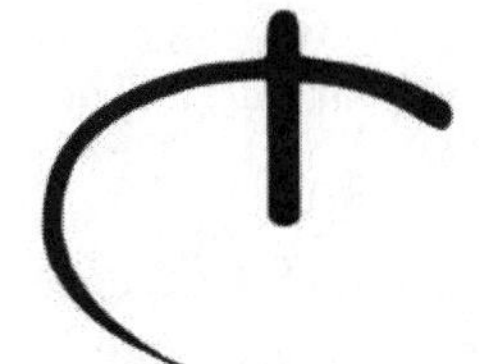

A Herder & Herder Book
The Crossroad Publishing Company
New York

The Crossroad Publishing Company
www.CrossroadPublishing.com

Printed in the United States of America in 2013.

ISBN 978-0-8245-9903-4 (alk. paper)

Library of Congress Control Number: 2013941247

Cover design by George Foster

"A Herder & Herder book".

PRAISE FOR *POLITICIZING THE BIBLE*

"Pope John Paul II notably observed that the connection with Greek philosophy helped the Church avoid the danger of falling into the mistakes of either 'divinizing nature' or falling into superstition. The Church moved with two wings, faith and reason. But it has been part of the project of Modernity to offer a constricted notion of 'reason' that pushes religion—and God—into the domain of the irrational or what Hobbes called the 'fantastical': mere beliefs, untethered, detached from any 'truths' that can reliably be 'known.' In this way, writers on politics sought to remove from political life that vexing 'problem of God' and the way of life that would spring from His laws. The problem of politics could be solved by removing religious conflict, and that conflict would be removed by consigning religion to the domain of things largely beside the point, put safely under political control. In this manner, Scott Hahn and Benjamin Wiker argue, religion has been 'politicized' in a way that degrades both politics and the public understanding of religion.

"The central figure, drawing on the currents of the past, and carving out the paths for the future, was Spinoza. And the treatment of Spinoza reflects the deep strengths of this book. With Spinoza, as with all of the other writers dealt with in the book, Hahn and Wiker tell his story, place him in the currents of his time with other writers, and then home in on his teaching with a reading of the work that is not only close but penetrating. Hahn and Wiker have not only given us a notable work in theology, but one of the most compelling histories of political philosophy. I cannot recall any book that achieves that combination as arrestingly as this one. It is, altogether, the most remarkable of works."

—**Hadley Arkes**, Edward N. Ney Professor of Jurisprudence and American Institutions, Amherst College

"Hahn and Wiker show how the study of Scripture was transformed by centuries of conflict over the fundamentals of Western civilization. They demonstrate their thesis in minute detail. The Bible clearly emerges as the foundational document of Western civilization and its academy."

—**Jacob Neusner**, research professor of religion and senior fellow of the Institute of Advanced Theology, Bard College

"Years ago, then Cardinal Ratzinger called for a thoughtful critique of biblical criticism, and this book is the sort of study I believe he had in mind. As Hahn and Wiker demonstrate, historical criticism did not appear fully formed in the nineteenth century, and its problems are not primarily exegetical, but philosophical. Its intellectual roots reach back to the Nominalism of the late Middle Ages, when subtle philosophical missteps set into motion alternate ways of reading Scripture that were alien not only to the Church and her tradition, but to the classical ways of interpreting texts. Historical criticism has its own history, and its development should be subject to the scrutiny of historical method, as it is in these pages."

—**Archbishop Augustine DiNoia,** secretary of the Congregation for Divine Worship, consultor to the Congregation for the Doctrine of the Faith

"In this magisterial work of intellectual history, Hahn and Wiker have tackled the overwhelming bias of modern textual criticism of the Bible by going straight to the Gordian knot of its fractal agenda and cutting through it in a fashion reminiscent of the clarity of the Apostles themselves. As St. Paul (1 Thess. 2:13) put it in his own context, the issue is whether the text is to be received by the Church merely as 'the word of men' or 'as it is in truth, the word of God.' In taking us back to the late Middle Ages for the roots of the secularizing agenda of the discipline, they give us a far more telling analysis of motive and ideological agenda than we could have without these pre-Enlightenment foundations for the long attempt to secularize and thus marginalize the distinctive claims of Revelation. This is essential reading, and not just for biblical scholars."

—**Prof. David Jeffrey**, Baylor University, editor, *The King James Bible and the World It Made*

"Biblical scholarship has long been regarded as something scientific and thus neutral and objective. Recent decades, however, have seen a rising awareness that scholarship is anything but objective as ever more attention is paid to the fact that scholarship is always situated and serves certain ends. In their well-researched, thoughtful, and painstaking study, Hahn and Wiker make a particular and necessary contribution to the history of the Bible in going back not to nineteenth-century Germany or to Martin Luther but rather deep into the Middle Ages and Renaissance, showing that the deliberate Erastian project of subjugating the Bible and with it Christian faith to the power of the State has deeper roots than often assumed. A must-read for those concerned with the place of the Bible and Christian faith in contemporary culture."

—**Prof. Leroy A. Huizenga**, University of Mary, coeditor, *Reading the Bible Intertextually*

"Scott Hahn and Benjamin Wiker have produced a scholarly masterpiece. *Politicizing the Bible* is the most important work to date on the history of modern biblical criticism. Several features single this book out from the rest of the scholarly literature in the field. First and foremost, it is commonplace for historians of historical criticism to begin in the eighteenth century; this book thus ends where most begin, at the close of the seventeenth century. Hahn and Wiker demonstrate how the roots of modern biblical criticism go back to the late medieval period (the fourteenth century), even prior to the Renaissance and Reformation. In the process, each chapter offers a clear and thorough discussion of the key intellectuals and the role they played in the gradual secularization of Scripture. Refreshingly, Hahn and Wiker place each of the biblical interpreters within their cultural, political, and philosophical context, providing a rare in-depth glimpse into the wider world that gave shape to their intellectual work.

"One of the great contributions of *Politicizing the Bible* is how it shows the inextricable link between these philosophical, political, and theological cross currents, and the scholarly shape and direction taken by each exegete in their critical readings of scripture. Hahn and Wiker examine a host of figures over the first 400 years of the rise and development of biblical criticism. Their names are well known to historians of early modern thought, but rarely enter into discussions of the history of biblical interpretation: Marsilius of Padua, William of Ockham, Wycliffe, Machiavelli, Luther, Henry VIII, Descartes, Hobbes, Spinoza, Locke, John Toland, and others. These key figures and developmental stages are often missed or neglected by scholars in the field. Indeed, Hahn and Wiker bring to light an entire history that is virtually unknown to biblical scholars. Another major component in this history is the influence of Islamic Averroism and how it provided a philosophical framework that powered the early intellectual engines of biblical criticism. By showing how these early critical readings of Scripture reflected and reinforced the 'secularization' of modern thought, this work will also have far-reaching implications for how the Bible is read in universities and seminaries, and how it is preached in pulpits and parishes.

"The impressive combination of breadth, depth, and clarity achieved in this book is unrivaled in the field. Moreover, Hahn and Wiker's lucid and crisp prose will make this book more than a must-read for scholars and students of the history of biblical interpretation; predictably, it should prove to be accessible and profitable for anyone interested in understanding the roots of historical criticism. Despite its size, readers will have a hard time putting this book down—for the story that Hahn and Wiker tell is gripping, with political intrigue and the violent conflicts of throne vs. altar that gave rise to the Protestant Reformation and the so-called 'wars of religion,' all of which contributed to the rise of the modern secular nation-state. In sum, students, informed laity and scholars alike, will want to have *Politicizing the Bible* on their shelves to be read and referred to again and again. This book is a rare gem."

—**Jeffrey Morrow**, professor of theology, Seton Hall University

"*Politicizing the Bible* is an impressive and provocative account of the unrecognized political presuppositions of historical criticism. It disentangles the legitimate tools and achievements of this method from its various political aims. No theologian, regardless of his denominational tradition, can afford not to pay attention to this sophisticated, clearly written, and engaging book."

—**Ulrich L. Lehner**, director of undergraduate studies and professor of theology, Marquette University

"Decades ago Richard Weaver penned a small monograph entitled *Ideas Have Consequences*. According to Weaver, our beliefs about metaphysics and epistemology, though seemingly isolated from our other beliefs, are so foundational to the way we view the world that they have the power to shape, and eventually change, many of these other beliefs. It is only in retrospect that we realize what has happened. In a much more comprehensive fashion, Hahn and Wiker make the case that biblical criticism and how we interpret Scripture has been shaped by philosophical and political ideas that are intrinsically hostile to Christian faith. This is an important work that will force its readers to readjust, and in some cases totally reject, what they had been taught about the objectivity and neutrality of contemporary approaches to God's Word."

—**Francis J. Beckwith**, professor and resident scholar at the Institute for Studies of Religion, Baylor University

"Like the contrast between the 'Jesus of History' and the 'Christ of Faith,' the criticism of the Bible by historical experts has been regarded as neutral and 'scientific' over against the naïve piety of the faithful. While some have challenged this assumption, situating the tradition of criticism in its own modern context, the authors of *Politicizing the Bible* reach back further to uncover the deeper roots. Readers may not agree with every interpretation, but the massive research and analysis is well worth the investment."

—**Michael Horton**, J. Gresham, Machen Professor of Systematic Theology and Apologetics, Westminster Seminary California, and author of *The Christian Faith: A Systematic Theology for Pilgrims on the Way*

To Michael Waldstein.

TABLE OF CONTENTS

CHAPTER 1

GETTING TO THE ROOTS OF THE HISTORICAL-CRITICAL METHOD

It is commonplace to see the historical-critical method described as an objective or neutral method. In his discussion of the roots of historical criticism, John Barton explains that "historical criticism was meant to be value-neutral, or disinterested. It tried, so far as possible, to approach the text without prejudice, and to ask not what it meant 'for me,' but simply what it meant. . . . The historical critic's calling was to be a neutral observer, prescinding from any kind of faith-commitment in order to get at the truth."[1]

It is one thing to make the standard acknowledgment that such an ideal can never be fully attained. It is important to take the next step and note that many scholars assert that such objectivity was rarely the stated goal of real historical critics. For example, James Barr asks the pointed question "But where are these claims to be value-neutral and value-free?" and then proceeds to use Julius Wellhausen as a case in point, showing how Wellhausen's work was not an attempt to be objective or neutral.[2]

Yet Wellhausen himself clearly argued that biblical criticism was independent and prior to philosophical commitments. For example, he wrote, "Biblical criticism, however, did not in general develop under the influence of philosophical ideas. . . Philosophy does not precede, but follows. . . ."[3]

Which is it, then? A neutral, objective method, or a method largely defined by some prior philosophical commitment (a commitment that can and should be the subject of critical analysis)? We argue that it is the latter, and we hope that our account of the history of historical criticism's roots will clarify the philosophical

---

1 John Barton, *The Old Testament: Canon, Literature and Theology* (Aldershot: Ashgate, 2007), pp. 203–204. See also Barton, *The Nature of Biblical Criticism* (Louisville: Westminster/John Knox Press, 2007), p. 3, where Barton even uses a mathematical analogy to describe his own argument: "Rather like a mathematician covering many pages with calculations in order to show that a theorem is in fact self-evident, I shall have to spend a great deal of detailed discussion to show that such an apparently banal conclusion [that biblical criticism comes down to attention to the plain meaning of the biblical text] holds. . . ." In Barton's defense, although he sees biblical criticism as a method which is in some way objective, he recognizes limits to this objectivity, and especially in the way in which the method has been practiced (p. 6).

2 James Barr, *History and Ideology in the Old Testament: Biblical Studies at the End of a Millennium* (Oxford: Oxford University Press, 2000), p. 48.

3 Quoted in Craig G. Bartholomew, "Uncharted Waters: Philosophy, Theology and the Crisis in Biblical Interpretation," in Craig Bartholomew, Colin Greene, and Karl Möller, eds., *Renewing Biblical Interpretation* (Grand Rapids, MI: Zondervan, 2000), p. 17.

and (even more important) political commitments inherent in the core foundations of the method itself.

That is the task of this present volume. But before taking up that task, since we are proposing a different account of the history of the historical-critical method, we must first offer a word about the current status of the history of biblical scholarship. We do not wish to burden the reader with a long account of the many histories of scriptural scholarship, but some attention will help situate our book and make clear its particular contribution. There are many such histories; we focus briefly on just a few.

Werner Kümmel's *The New Testament: The History of the Investigation of Its Problems* remains an important overview of the development of the historical-critical method.[4] He sets the real origin of the modern historical-critical approach well into the eighteenth century. As he says, "Scientific study of the New Testament is indebted to two men, Johann Salomo Semler and Johann David Michaelis, for the first evidences of a consciously historical approach to the New Testament as a historical entity distinct from the Old Testament."[5] Of course Kümmel realizes that earlier figures had prepared the way for Semler and Michaelis, and so he devotes two chapters to important predecessors, in which (affirming Theodore Zahn's assessment) he denotes Richard Simon as "'the founder of the science of New Testament introduction.'"[6] He also notes the importance of "English Deism and Its Early Consequences," covering such key figures as John Locke, John Toland, Matthew Tindal, Thomas Chubb, Thomas Morgan, and others, but goes into very little detail.[7] Amazingly, he fails even to mention Thomas Hobbes or Benedict Spinoza, both of whom are elsewhere credited with being, in their own ways, founders of the modern historical-critical approach to Scripture, and whose efforts predate Semler's and Michaelis's by about a century.[8]

The very first sentence of volume I, chapter 1 of William Baird's *History of New Testament Research* is "The critical study of the Bible began in the eighteenth century."[9] Baird's history is a fine, two-volume study, but one that needs to be supplemented by a close analysis of important earlier works. He does provide a quick sweep over the Renaissance, Reformation, and early Enlightenment, giving several pages to Richard Simon, of whom he also notes, "If any individual can be named as the founder of modern biblical criticism, that person would have to be Richard Simon."[10] But Baird passes completely over Spinoza, even though Spinoza's arguments provided a significant part of the context for Simon's work. Moreover, Baird fails even to mention Hobbes, whose efforts predate Spinoza's. While Baird rightly attends to English

4 Werner Kümmel, *The New Testament: The History of the Investigation of Its Problems*, translated by S. McLean Gilmour and Howard C. Kee (Nashville, TN: Abingdon Press, 1972).

5 Kümmel, *The New Testament*, III.1, p. 62.

6 Ibid., II.1, p. 41.

7 Ibid., II.2.

8 This is already noted, for example, in Hans-Joachim Kraus, *Geschichte der historisch-kritischen Erforschung des Alten Testaments* (Neukirchen: Kreis Moers, 1956), p. 57.

9 William Baird, *History of New Testament Research, Vol. I: From Deism to Tübingen* (Minneapolis, MN: Fortress Press, 1992), p. 3.

10 Ibid., p. 17.

Deism—focusing on such figures as Locke and Toland[11]—only a few pages are given to each as background figures for the real critical approach to the Bible that begins in earnest in the mid-eighteenth century.

Much the same is true for Rudolph Smend's *From Astruc to Zimmerli: Old Testament Scholarship in Three Centuries.*[12] While a fine study, it begins with Jean Astruc, famous for having differentiated the divine names in Genesis and using them for discerning distinct literary sources. Smend thereby leaves the reader with very little indication of intellectual predecessors, and hence gives the impression that the roots of modern biblical scholarship reach back only to the mid-eighteenth century.

Our analysis ends where these studies begin. We commence in the early fourteenth century with Marsilius of Padua and William of Ockham; move through John Wycliffe, Niccolò Machiavelli, Martin Luther, Henry VIII and the English Reformation; consider the philosophical revolution of Descartes; and conclude with the earliest acknowledged fathers of modern biblical criticism—Hobbes, Spinoza, and Simon. We treat each of them in much more detail than is almost invariably the case with those surveys that hurry through the fathers of the historical-critical method in order to discuss their more famous sons in the latter half of the eighteenth century, or the heyday for modern biblical criticism in nineteenth-century Germany. In extending the story back to the later Middle Ages, we hope to get a deeper and clearer understanding of the "fathers," and hence, of the patrimony they bequeathed to the great biblical critics of the latter eighteenth, nineteenth, and early twentieth centuries such as Semler, Michaelis, W.M.L. de Wette, Hermann Reimarus, Johann Griesbach, Johann Eichhorn, Friedrich Schleiermacher, D. F. Strauss, F. C. Baur, Johannes Weiss, Heinrich Ewald, Bruno Bauer, Julius Wellhausen, Rudolph Bultmann, and Hermann Gunkel.

As several newer studies show, we are (thankfully) not alone in our desire to illuminate more fully the centuries leading up to the Enlightenment. Henning Graf Reventlow has been something of a pioneer in shifting the focus from nineteenth century Germany to much earlier developments. James Barr, in his foreword to Reventlow's *The Authority of the Bible and the Rise of the Modern World,*[13] has likewise noted the deficiencies of most historical overviews, asserting (with Reventlow) that

> modern histories of biblical scholarship, in so far as they give any attention at all to the period of English Deism and early biblical criticism, have done so

---

11 As well as Matthew Tindal, Anthony Collins, Thomas Woolston, Peter Annet, Thomas Morgan, and Thomas Chubb. Ibid., ch. 2.

12 Rudolph Smend, *From Astruc to Zimmerli: Old Testament Scholarship in Three Centuries,* translated by Margaret Kohl (Tübingen: Mohr Siebeck, 2007).

13 Henning Graf Reventlow, *The Authority of the Bible and the Rise of the Modern World,* translated by John Bowden (Philadelphia: Fortress Press, 1985). The original German title gives a much better "picture" of Reventlow's argument: *Biblical Authority and the Spirit of Modernity: The Significance of the Biblical Understanding for the Intellectual History and Political Development in England from the Reformation to the Enlightenment* (*Bibelautorität und Geist der Moderne, Die bedeutung des Bibelverständnisses für die geistesgeschichtliche und politische Entwicklung in England von der Reformation bis zur Aufklärung*).

> only tangentially: they have noted here and there various points at which these early days showed an anticipation of later critical ideas or results. But on the whole they have not tried to enter into the profounder setting in life in which these new ideas came to birth: the reasons why new questions were asked, the nature of the problems which were encountered, the concerns which animated the scholars as they thought and wrote.[14]

Recovering the deepest roots of the historical-critical method is, for Reventlow, necessary precisely because of the "considerable decline in the significance of biblical study with the general framework of Protestant theology as it is practiced in universities and church colleges and as it affects the work of local church communities." The decline is in part caused by the "failure of exegetes to reflect adequately on their methodology and the presuppositions, shaped by their view of the world, which they bring to their work."[15] Reventlow regards it as ironic (given the critical and historical focus on the Bible by contemporary scholars) that "Reflection on the presuppositions of historical criticism appears only by way of exception. . . ." In the rare instances that it does occur, "it immediately becomes clear that this method cannot be detached from a quite specific understanding of the world and reality,"[16] a point seconded by Gerhard Ebeling.[17] Hence to understand historical criticism not as some ideal, neutral method but as a methodology shaped by a particular view of the world, Reventlow maintains that "it is desirable that I should dig deeper and uncover the ideological and social roots to which more recent biblical criticism owes its origin, its deeper impetus and the direction of the answers which it gives," thereby undertaking "the task of looking back at the beginnings of biblical criticism" so as "to uncover the motives, the intellectual presuppositions, the philosophical assumptions, and last, but not least, the developments in church politics, which have led to the conclusions at which it arrived."[18]

We agree wholeheartedly, and offer the present work as a complement to *The Authority of the Bible and the Rise of the Modern World*. Reventlow set about diligently uncovering the roots of the historical-critical method as they stretch all the way into the Middle Ages and Renaissance, and (rather than solely focusing on Luther) he consequently made readers much more aware of the significant contributions made by the "Left Wing of the Reformation." Moreover, he has pressed home the importance of early theological, political, and philosophical developments in England, paying much more attention to the Puritans and Deists. Reventlow's newly translated *History of Biblical Interpretation* (four volumes) is

14 James Barr, foreword to Reventlow, *The Authority of the Bible*, p. xii.

15 Ibid., p. 1.

16 Ibid.

17 Gerhard Ebeling, "The Significance of the Critical Historical Method for Church and Theology in Protestantism," in Ebeling, *Word and Faith*, translated by James Leitch (Philadelphia: Fortress Press, 1969), pp. 17–61; especially pp. 42–43.

18 Reventlow, *The Authority of the Bible*, p. 2.

likewise a much-needed contribution to a broadened treatment of the history of biblical scholarship.[19]

As much as we admire Reventlow's work, we believe that further and deeper reflection on the intellectual presuppositions and philosophical assumptions of historical criticism are in order, especially as these are formed and informed by politics in the broadest sense—both secular and Church politics, including the political philosophy and political aims of those who most profoundly defined the intellectual presuppositions and philosophical assumptions of modernity. That goal entails our spending time on figures that Reventlow either passes over too quickly or does not treat at all—such as Marsilius of Padua, Ockham, Machiavelli, England's Henry VIII, and Descartes—and bringing out a much different emphasis in figures he does treat, such as Wycliffe, Luther, Hobbes, Simon, Spinoza, Locke, and Toland.

Two other notable efforts in recovering the deeply buried presuppositions of the modern historical-critical method have recently been published in English. The first is John Sandys-Wunsch, *What Have They Done to the Bible? A History of Modern Biblical Interpretation*,[20] and the multivolume work under the editorial guidance of Magne Sæbø, *Hebrew Bible/Old Testament: The History of Its Interpretation*—the second volume, *From the Renaissance to the Enlightenment*, being the most important for our consideration.[21]

Half of Sandys-Wunsch's book is dedicated to sketching out the thinkers in the centuries before the high Enlightenment, and so readers are made much more aware of how the foundations for biblical scholarship in the nineteenth century were laid much earlier. While his treatment is admirably broad, he cannot provide much depth under the constraints of such a short history.

The scholars gathered by Sæbø show an unusual breadth in their accounts of the historical, philosophical, theological, and political developments of the centuries that prepared for the full flowering of the historical-critical method, and the bibliographies well represent the best scholarship available. Clearly, Sæbø's work is the finest survey history of Old Testament interpretation now available, and will be the standard for many years to come. But the treatment often suffers under the constraints of its format. Any survey that deals with so many figures over so many years must sacrifice depth for breadth; and a collection of different scholars, each treating only a few figures, makes intense intellectual integration of the entire volume exceedingly difficult. As is the case with Reventlow, we believe that a more detailed account of key figures will provide a needed complement to Sæbø's fine efforts.

---

19 Henning Graf Reventlow, *History of Biblical Interpretation*, 4 vols., translated by Leo G. Perdue (Atlanta, GA: Society of Biblical Literature, 2009–2010). Volume 1 is entitled "From the Old Testament to Origen," volume 2 is entitled "From Late Antiquity to the End of the Middle Ages," volume 3 is entitled "Renaissance, Reformation, Humanism," and volume 4 is entitled "From the Enlightenment to the Twentieth Century."

20 John Sandys-Wunsch, *What Have They Done to the Bible? A History of Modern Biblical Interpretation* (Collegeville, MN: Liturgical Press, 2005).

21 Magne Sæbø, ed., *Hebrew Bible/Old Testament: The History of Its Interpretation*: Vol. II, *From the Renaissance to the Enlightenment* (Göttingen: Vandenhoeck & Ruprecht, 2008).

More recently, Pierre Gibert published his fine treatment of the history of modern historical biblical criticism, *L'invention critique de la Bible*, which has emphasized the important role of seventeenth-century scholars more than other similar treatments have done.[22] Admirably, Gibert's work delves earlier than most studies, including a very brief treatment of Luther and the contribution of others to modern biblical criticism prior to the seventeenth century, but the focus of his attention (approximately 150 pages of his 377-page book) is on Spinoza and Simon. Indeed, although he mentions nearly 50 important figures within this history, on some he spends only a few sentences, and the overwhelming majority of his text is focused on the developments from Spinoza through the eighteenth century. Gibert's work likewise fails to treat adequately the philosophical and political undercurrents that gave rise to the very methods whose development he describes.

Roy Harrisville and Walter Sundberg have provided another survey, *The Bible in Modern Culture: Baruch Spinoza to Brevard Childs*, especially welcome because it digs deeper than most into the presuppositions of the historical-critical method that have resulted in what the authors call "the Agony of Historical Criticism," the "serious tension [that] exists between historical criticism and the church."[23] For Harrisville and Sundberg, there is an essential "theological and doctrinal conflict between historical criticism and the dogmatic tradition of the church." They "consider this tension to be nothing less than a war between two worldviews of faith: the worldview of modern critical awareness originating in the Enlightenment and the inherited Augustinian worldview of the Western church."[24] Harrisville and Sundberg understand the source of this tension to be Benedict Spinoza's *Theological-Political Treatise* (1670), of which they remark that "the *Tractatus* is clear evidence that [the] historical-critical method originated in politically engendered hostility to the claims of faith."[25]

Others have recognized that key figures like Spinoza who contributed to the development of the historical-critical approach were less than orthodox. But having noted that, little if anything is said about the effect unorthodox motives may have had on the development of the historical-critical approach.[26] In contrast, Harrisville and

22 Pierre Gibert, *L'invention critique de la Bible: XVe-XVIIIe* (Paris: Éditions Gallimard, 2010).

23 Roy Harrisville and Walter Sundberg, *The Bible in Modern Culture: Baruch Spinoza to Brevard Childs* (Grand Rapids, MI: Eerdmans, 2002), 2nd ed., pp. 2, 10.

24 Harrisville and Sundberg, *The Bible in Modern Culture*, p. 5.

25 Ibid.

26 See, for example, Edgar Krentz, *The Historical-Critical Method* (Philadelphia, PA: Fortress Press, 1975), who notes that Spinoza's efforts in biblical interpretation were spent "to discredit the appearance of supernatural authority," but then makes no attempt to examine Spinoza's universally acknowledged influence on the development of the historical-critical method (pp. 13–14). This parallels a larger omission, where Krentz asserts that the rise of historical criticism "introduced into biblical interpretation a new method based on a secular understanding of history," but then makes no further inquiry into the origins of the secular assumptions and aims that defined the method (pp. 1, 30, 48). We are simply informed, after a brief history of its rise, that "Today historical criticism is taken for granted; we cannot go back to a precritical age" (p. 33). Having said that, Krentz remarks that theologians should "ask that historians be as critical of philosophical assumptions as they are of theological ones" (p. 69), but does not himself follow his own advice.

Sundberg explore this very connection, focusing in part on the politicized aspects of the method. Obviously, from the title of the book, we also believe that the historical-critical method is somehow essentially defined by political aims.

While we share much of the assessment of Harrisville and Sundberg of the "agony" of historical criticism (again, their treatment of Spinoza is particularly well done),[27] we believe that the source of the tension lies historically much further back than the Enlightenment, and that defining the conflict in terms of the "Augustinian worldview" is too narrow. The late-eighteenth-century Enlightenment is not the beginning of the conflict, but the culmination of several centuries of a slowly building new, (it's not a new secular as opposed to the old secular) secular worldview.[28] The tension that exists has its causes far deeper and broader than Augustinianism (of whatever stripe).

Other scholars besides Harrisville and Sundberg have called attention to the political aspects embedded in the historical-critical method, especially insofar as the sustained use of the method has a particular political effect upon its adherents. As Wilfred Cantwell Smith noted over thirty years ago, biblical studies programs "are on the whole calculated to turn a fundamentalist into a liberal."[29]

The term "liberal" here was not used by Smith in the rather crude, popular form of contemporary political discourse, but in the more technical form used in the history of ideas: beholden to the presuppositions and goals of modern liberalism, a particular political-intellectual movement that stretches back far beyond nineteenth-century Germany. Yet there is a connection between the popular meaning of liberalism and the more technical meaning. Liberalism even in the popular arena is associated with either the abandonment of religious beliefs (especially the exclusive beliefs in Judaism and Christianity) or the dissolution of theological dogma into mere moral precepts. But the more technical sense is well captured by Jon Levenson, taking up Smith's point:

> Smith's use of the term "liberal" to designate historical-critical scholarship on the Bible is thus more than conventional: it is also profoundly appropriate. For historical criticism is the form of biblical studies that corresponds to the classical liberal political ideal. It is the realization of the Enlightenment project in the realm of biblical scholarship.[30]

---

27 Harrisville and Sundberg, *The Bible in Modern Culture*, ch. 2.

28 There is a growing scholarly trend to emphasize the theological roots of secular modernity. Eric Nelson, *The Hebrew Republic: Jewish Sources and the Transformation of European Political Thought* (Cambridge: Harvard University Press, 2010); Michael Allen Gillespie, *The Theological Origins of Modernity* (Chicago: University of Chicago Press, 2008); David Sorkin, *The Religious Enlightenment: Protestants, Jews, and Catholics from London to Vienna* (Princeton: Princeton University Press, 2008), and Charles Taylor, *A Secular Age* (Cambridge: Harvard University Press, 2007). These represent very important contributions to the study of modernity, but they fail to recognize the secularity implicit in the theological and philosophical movements they describe, as well as the politics such theologies served. Our present volume will unmask the secular politics underpinning these theological movements, from Nominalism to Gallicanism, which did indeed assist in the birth of modernity.

29 Wilfred Cantwell Smith, "The Study of Religion and the Study of the Bible," *JAAR* 39 (1971), 132.

30 Jon D. Levenson, *The Hebrew Bible, the Old Testament, and Historical Criticism* (Louisville, KY: Westminster/John Knox Press, 1993), p. 118.

Note that Levenson is saying more than what is often admitted about the historical-critical method, as, for example, by Edgar Krentz, that "Historical method is the child of the Enlightenment."[31] Going beyond this commonplace insight, Levenson considers the method itself to be an intrinsic part of the attempt to achieve a particular political vision, the "classical liberal political ideal," undertaken as a kind of intellectual, social, religious, and political "project," the Enlightenment project.

For Levenson, as with Reventlow, professional exegetes seem not to be sufficiently aware of the Enlightenment project *as* a project, but rather assume its characteristic presuppositions and goals as incorporated into a methodology to be the true and proper cure of dogmatic, ill-formed, and unscientific biblical fundamentalism. In assuming the truth of the Enlightenment project, Levenson warns, biblical scholars fall into professing "a secular equivalent to fundamentalism," held with equally dogmatic tenacity, which "though it subjects all else to critique, it asserts axiomatically its own inviolability to critique."[32]

Such inviolability to critique would indeed seem to be a mark of a kind of intellectual fundamentalism. If turnabout is indeed fair play, it would be fair to subject the presuppositions of the historical-critical method to the same intense scrutiny as its proponents exercise on the biblical text, "suspecting the hermeneuts of suspicion," to use Levenson's apt phrase.[33] Levenson's desire that we be suspicious of the historical-critical method itself (that is, to be both more historical and more critical, especially of its original intellectual and political presuppositions and aims) is shared by other scholars of the history of biblical interpretation, such as J. C. O'Neill and David Dungan.[34] This desire was also expressed by then Cardinal Joseph Ratzinger, now Pope Benedict XVI, in his famous Erasmus Lecture of 1988, "Biblical Interpretation in Crisis," wherein he too asserted that "What we need might be called a criticism of criticism," that is, "a self-criticism of the historical method. . . ."[35]

Some attention may now be paid to our title, *Politicizing the Bible: The Roots of Historical Criticism and the Secularization of Scripture 1300–1700*. Obviously, we intend more than a mere chronology of ideas; we hope to contribute to a critical and historical understanding of the historical-critical method itself. Our argument, to put it all too simply, is that the development of the historical-critical method in biblical studies is only fully intelligible as part of the more comprehensive project of secularization that occurred in the West over the last seven hundred years, and that the politicizing of the Bible was, in one way or another, essential to this project. By politicization, we mean the *intentional exegetical reinterpretation of Scripture so as to make it serve a*

31 Krentz, *The Historical-Critical Method*, p. 55.

32 Levenson, *The Hebrew Bible, the Old Testament, and Historical Criticism*, p. 117.

33 Ibid., p. 116.

34 J. C. O'Neill, *The Bible's Authority: A Portrait Gallery of Thinkers from Lessing to Bultmann* (Edinburgh: T. & T. Clark, 1991); David Laird Dungan, *A History of the Synoptic Problem: The Canon, the Text, the Composition, and the Interpretation of the Gospels* (New Haven: Yale University Press, 1999).

35 Joseph Cardinal Ratzinger, "Biblical Interpretation in Crisis: On the Question of the Foundations and Approaches of Exegesis Today," in Richard John Neuhaus, ed., *Biblical Interpretation in Crisis: The Ratzinger Conference on Bible and Church* (Grand Rapids, MI: Eerdmans, 1989), pp. 1–23; quote, p. 6.

merely political, this-worldly (hence secular) goal. Since this effort was largely undertaken by those who embraced a new secular worldview, the effect was to subordinate the method of interpreting Scripture to secular political aims. This subordination was essential in the early development of the modern historical-critical method.

We do not mean to claim, of course, that there is nothing more to the history of the development of modern scriptural scholarship than is outlined in the present work or that there is nothing of the historical-critical method that developed apart from the attempt to politicize exegesis. Yet we are convinced that the attempt to politicize the biblical text for quite secular purposes by such figures as (among others) Marsilius of Padua, Machiavelli, Hobbes, Spinoza, Locke, and Toland is a largely untouched dimension in the accepted understanding of the historical development of the modern approach to Scripture, and yet this insight sheds much needed light on the formation of the historical-critical method *and* its effects.

A sign of the importance of this approach is the overlap that exists between the fatherhood of the modern historical-critical method and the fatherhood of modern political philosophy. At least two of the just-mentioned figures (Hobbes and Spinoza) are generally held as fathers of modern scriptural scholarship, and four (Machiavelli, Hobbes, Spinoza, and Locke) are deemed fathers of modern political philosophy—that is, of political liberalism. The overlap is not accidental, and lends credence to Levenson's assertion that "historical criticism is the form of biblical studies that corresponds to the classical liberal political ideal."

But again, it has become clear, in ferreting out the historical connections, that we needed to go back much further even than the foundations of modern political thought in the sixteenth and seventeenth centuries. Modernity's roots are deeper than most imagine, having their source in theological, philosophical, and political conflicts that arose in the late Middle Ages. That is why we begin the analysis with a chapter on Marsilius of Padua and William of Ockham.

Before beginning an historical analysis of the earliest roots of the historical-critical method, we must give some kind of definition to the method under consideration, although we shall find that ultimately the best definition of the historical-critical method will slowly be revealed in the painstaking investigation of its origins.

If we might return to the relationship between the historical-critical method and its effects, we will better understand what it is as a cause. Here we wish to make clear again that we are not condemning the historical-critical method, but attempting to bring to light *why* it has particular characteristic effects that undermine or radically transform religious belief and *how* these effects are related to the method itself.

In Edgar Krentz's now standard short account of the historical-critical method, he states matter-of-factly in regard to its effects that "The method tends to freedom from authority and criticism of tradition. It treats biblical material in a different manner than theological thought had done for centuries, and in the process questions the validity of theological method."[36] As for defining the method itself, Krentz points to

---

36 Krentz, *The Historical-Critical Method*, p. 4.

Ernst Troeltsch's famous authoritative essay "On Historical and Dogmatic Method in Theology"[37] (1898) as the text that "formulated the principles of historical criticism."[38]

Of course, as Troeltsch himself admitted, he did not formulate the principles of historical criticism himself, but gathered them from the approach taken by *"the historical method as such,"* a method developed over the previous several centuries, and coming to full fruition in the nineteenth. He summarized rather than formulated.

For Troeltsch, the necessary effect of applying the historical method to Scripture was and is "the disintegration of the Christian world of ideas. . . ." "Once applied to the scientific study of the Bible and church history," declared Troeltsch, "the historical method acts as a leaven, transforming everything and ultimately exploding the very form of earlier theological methods."[39] The reason for this disintegration (or explosion), according to Troeltsch, is the irreconcilable difference that exists between the earlier dogmatic method, which presupposes certain historical facts, like the Resurrection, that stand outside a purely secular understanding of history, and the modern historical method, which assumes "secular history reconstructed by critical historiography."[40] Secular history assumes that miracles cannot happen or at least such miracles cannot be verified by the historical method. More accurately, secular history assumes that all alleged supernatural beings or events can be explained in natural terms.[41]

Since according to Troeltsch the historical method is essentially opposed to the dogmatic, then application of the historical method to Scripture can only result in treating it from the secular point of view—as one would any other artifact in the history of religions. The result would seem to be a complete relativizing of Christianity that, Troeltsch claimed, would indeed be "the consequence of the historical method only within an atheistic or a religiously skeptical framework." Troeltsch, a liberal Protestant, asserted that he was seeking "to overcome this relativism through the conception of history as a disclosure of the divine reason," wherein revelation is replaced by a "philosophy of history."[42]

We do not need to assess the adequacy of Troeltsch's idealism in rescuing Christianity from the historical method, except to remark that it depends upon the reality of inevitable historical progress discernable with the secular historian's eyes, *and* that it was uttered just prior to the devastation of that notion of progress by World War I.[43] For our purposes, it is enough to have his admission that without some such

37 Ernst Troeltsch, "On Historical and Dogmatic Method in Theology," in Troeltsch, *Religion in History*, translated by James Adams and Walter Bense (Minneapolis, MN: Fortress Press, 1991), pp. 11–32.

38 Krentz, *The Historical-Critical Method*, p. 55.

39 Troeltsch, "On Historical and Dogmatic Method in Theology," p. 12.

40 Ibid., pp. 20–21.

41 In Troeltsch's words, the historical method must always postulate an "analogy" between our contemporary experience and all experience. In the latter, all "phenomena" are "knit together in a permanent relationship of correlation . . . in which everything is interconnected and each single event is related to all others." Ibid., pp. 13–14, 20–22.

42 Ibid., pp. 27–28.

43 For the radical way in which the experience of World War I affected the discipline of history (especially in the U.S.), see Peter Novick, *That Noble Dream: The "Objectivity Question" and the American Historical Profession* (Cambridge: Cambridge University Press, 1988).

attempt, the historical method leads to skepticism or historical relativization of all dogmatic belief and also inclines to use by atheists and skeptics for the purposes of dissolving dogmatic belief.

Troeltsch's essay therefore vindicates the assessment of Harrisville and Sundberg of the essential tension that exists between the historical-critical method and Christian dogma, and Troeltsch well represents the accepted assumptions of the most important nineteenth-century exegetes of the historical-critical method. Krentz provides an apt summary of the effects:

> It is difficult to overestimate the significance the nineteenth century has for biblical interpretation. It made historical criticism *the* approved method of interpretation. The result was a revolution of viewpoint in evaluating the Bible. The Scriptures were, so to speak, secularized. The Biblical books became historical documents to be studied and questioned like any other ancient sources. The Bible was no longer the criterion for the writing of history; rather history had become the criterion for understanding the Bible.[44]

Troeltsch's seminal essay, which so accurately sums up the assumptions and effects of the historical-critical method, allows us to see that what is significant about the method is not its appreciation for textual variants and literary forms, or its delving into historical context and comparative philology, but rather its premise: that *if history is to be scientific, it must exclude or reinterpret the supernatural.* The systematic exclusion of the supernatural and the consequent attempt to give natural explanations for events like miracles, theophanies, and other alleged irruptions of the divine or angelic effectively secularizes Scripture, making it one among many other manifestations of religious belief without verifiable substance. It relativizes and privatizes belief, or simply eliminates it as unscientific. In doing so, it removes Christianity as a political force, making of it at best a bearer of nondogmatic moral teachings that undergird the political order. There is no doubt that this transformation of Christianity accords nicely with the modern secular political aims. The question we pose here is: Did this happen by accident or design?

Let us return to Levenson's assessment that "historical criticism is the form of biblical studies that corresponds to the classical liberal political ideal." If Levenson is even close to the mark—and we think he has hit the bull's-eye—then we have a good reason to suspect that the historical-critical method is, in significant aspects, defined by motives other than the laudable desire to get at the truth of the biblical text using every available and appropriate means. According to Levenson, the historical-critical approach has an intrinsic aim, not found in Scripture itself, of *producing the beliefs that accord with modern secular political aims,* where religion is either reduced to mere private belief unsupported or rejected by reason and science, or made to serve as a moral prop for a particular kind of political order. The defining secular political aim is to keep religion from disturbing or significantly

44 Krentz, *The Historical-Critical Method,* p. 30.

determining public life—an understandable aim, given that the modern historical-critical method was largely forged during and just after the great "wars of religion" that so disturbed political order in the late 1500s and a large portion of the 1600s.[45] But to say that it is an understandable aim only highlights the fact that it was an alien one, forced upon the text, rather than derived from it.

The two already-named presuppositions that contribute the most to achieving this aim through exegetical method are the bias against the supernatural and the notion that the core of Christianity is moral rather than dogmatic. A critical approach and a deeper knowledge of history do not produce these presuppositions, we shall argue. Rather, the presuppositions determine the way that exegetes are critical and the way that they use history. We hope to make this clear to the reader as the following chapters unfold.

Making these distinctions allows us to separate the tools used by the method from what might be called the guiding spirit that uses the tools. There is nothing intrinsically detrimental to belief in the actual resurrection of Jesus Christ in the attempt to establish as accurate a scriptural text as possible using every available manuscript; in the minute examination of the Hebrew or Greek language; in an in-depth historical analysis of ancient Palestine and first-century Rome; or in the investigation of literary forms and editorial layers in the New Testament. But the modern secular assumption *that the supernatural must be excluded* obviously makes belief in the Resurrection impossible. If that assumption becomes the guiding spirit that uses the tools of textual, philological, historical, literary, form, and redaction criticisms, then the critical use of the tools is defined by a secularizing aim. This union of tools with secularizing presuppositions constitutes what is almost invariably meant by the historical-critical method.

Obviously this thesis is controversial, and therefore we wish to argue for it with extreme care and with great attention to detail. We ask the reader in advance to be patient, for the argument must be substantiated by close analysis of seminal texts in modern political thought, philosophy, and theology, as well as treating in detail those pre-Enlightenment and early-Enlightenment figures now recognized as contributing directly to providing the foundations for the modern approach to Scripture. Moreover, all of this must be set in the proper historical and political contexts so as to make amply clear the importance of the nexus of political aim and exegetical method.

We begin this volume in the early fourteenth century with Marsilius of Padua and William of Ockham, whose biblical interpretation cannot be separated from the politics that gave it shape. Marsilius and Ockham both became party players in Ludwig of Bavaria's conflicts with Pope John XXII; although Ockham's goals appear to have been

45 The work of William Cavanaugh has challenged greatly the notion that these so-called wars of religion were primarily concerned with doctrinal disputes; they were, rather, the final stages of the birth of modern centralized European states. See especially William T. Cavanaugh, *The Myth of Religious Violence: Secular Ideology and the Roots of Modern Conflict* (Oxford: Oxford University Press, 2009), pp. 123–180; and Cavanaugh, "'A Fire Strong Enough to Consume the House': The Wars of Religion and the Rise of the State," *Modern Theology* 11 (1995), 397–420.

spiritual, Marsilius's were patently secular. The philosophy of Averroës is important here, because Marsilius imbibed Averroist philosophy, which elevated reason over revelation (and hence, for Marsilius, the rational state over religion). Marsilius, by his own design, and Ockham, inadvertently, placed the Bible in the hands of the state, which, coupled with Marsilius's naturalization of supernatural revelation and Ockham's denial of universals, paved the way for modernity and the modern secular state.

Our next chapter examines the work of John Wycliffe, a figure rarely included in studies of the history of historical criticism. As we explain, Wycliffe is an intermediary figure in the secularization of Scripture, connecting Marsilius to ideas that will emerge in the sixteenth and seventeenth centuries in more explicit and overt ways. Despite Wycliffe's opposition to Ockham's thought, and notwithstanding the fact that he would have disagreed with Marsilius's wholesale subordination of the Church to the state, Wycliffe's proposal remained Marsilian in significant regards: He argued for theologians to serve the crown and upheld both disendowing the Church and a view of the monarch as an absolute ruler by divine right. His thought would thus prepare England to embrace the work of Marsilius in the English Reformation.

After Wycliffe, we turn to Niccolò Machiavelli, almost universally ignored in histories of modern biblical criticism (with the rare exception of Sæbø's one-thousand-plus-page volume that, unfortunately, devotes but a single paragraph to Machiavelli[46]). With Machiavelli we find an animus toward tradition, priesthood, and in general any otherworldly aims that deflected from the glory and power of secular power—an animus that played itself out in very clear ways in later centuries, contributing immensely to the pure secularization of politics. Significantly, Machiavelli interprets Scripture through a very specific secular framework, helping set the stage for the use of worldly philosophical and political frameworks as the means of exegesis. Thus, for Machiavelli, only the truly "enlightened," that is, those with his secular framework, can understand Scripture properly.

We next come to our examination of Martin Luther and the Protestant Reformation. We do not pretend to be exhaustive in our treatment of this movement, but we think an examination of Luther's place is instructive, especially in the ways in which the Reformation continued the political and secularizing trends that came before. First, Luther used the state as a force to counteract the power of the papacy, and thereby put enormous theological power into the hands of the state. Luther also self-identified as a follower of Ockham, thus helping to carry philosophy forward to its modern secular form. Moreover, his upholding of Scripture as a sole authority, in a more explicit and simple form than Wycliffe, provided the catalyst for the splintering of Christendom, which would invariably preclude theological resolutions and thus provided the occasion for political ones. The violent conflicts that subsequently engulfed Europe became the ostensible rationale for the creation of a scientific exegesis, a critical exegesis, that would aim at taming the fires of faith so as to achieve political peace.

From Luther we turn to King Henry VIII and the Reformation in England. Henry VIII's Reformation combined the philosophical and political strains from Marsilius,

46 Sæbø, ed., *Hebrew Bible/Old Testament*, Vol. II, p. 102.

Wycliffe, and Machiavelli in a very practical subordination of theology and scriptural interpretation to the needs of the state. Henry's reign thus paved the way for Hobbes's political and exegetical work that gave the philosophical rationale for the complete subordination of scriptural interpretation to the political sovereign. The England that Henry VIII reshaped became a seedbed for the biblical scholarship launched by Hobbes and others like him that would eventually be replanted and thrive in the Germany of the eighteenth and nineteenth centuries.

After Henry VIII, René Descartes is the next figure we explore. Descartes's work became fundamental for the biblical exegesis that followed in his wake. In significant ways, Descartes assisted the birth of modernity through the banishment of the supernatural. But Cartesian philosophy also entered biblical scholarship directly, primarily but not exclusively through the efforts of Spinoza and his followers. Moreover, the emphasis Descartes placed on method (defined, for him, by the rigor and form of mathematics) itself became a key factor in the development of biblical criticism and led to pretensions of methodological neutrality. Cartesian skepticism, his methodic doubt, was the critical link in the progression of thought that ended in the contemporary ideal: the ostensibly objective biblical interpreter, no longer an exegete but a quasi-scientific investigator whose method is significantly defined by skepticism of its subject matter.

The political philosopher Thomas Hobbes is the focus of our next chapter. Many of the same philosophical currents and political aims that preceded him—especially in Marsilius, Machiavelli, Henry VIII, and Descartes—came together in Hobbes's work. In it, the secular aims of Marsilius and Machiavelli combined with an Ockhamist Nominalism. Hobbes's biblical exegesis followed suit, justifying the absolute subordination of the Church to the state. Hobbes's method—which consisted of sifting through Scripture and positing earlier naturalistic and this-worldly origins to later, allegedly artificial theological and supernatural layers—set the tone for future biblical critical projects. For Hobbes, the point of his new method was to support the political ideal of the English polity, where the sovereign was head of both Church and state. This political agenda gave shape to his method, even as it was developed by later scholars who did not share Hobbes's political motives.

With our next chapter, we come to the figure of Baruch Spinoza, whose *Tractatus Theologico-Politicus* sought to present a scientific method for biblical interpretation. Influenced by Machiavelli, Spinoza's political project was likewise Marsilian in his attempt to ensure the Church became nothing more than a purely suasive and politically subordinate association. Spinoza built upon the work of Hobbes and Descartes, bringing Cartesian skepticism fully into the realm of biblical interpretation. One point we emphasize in this chapter is the way in which Spinoza does not stand alone, but rather was a significant member of a circle of intellectuals, a complex web of skeptical associations of the Radical Enlightenment united in their attempts to deconstruct Scripture to serve a host of related political and philosophical ends. Through the Radical Enlightenment's embrace of Spinoza, and the many eighteenth-century responses to Spinoza, we can see the influence Spinoza's work had on future generations of scriptural scholars.

The next father of historical criticism we discuss is Father Richard Simon. Simon responded to the skepticism of Hobbes and Spinoza, but in his response followed their exegetical program, albeit with more philological sophistication (thereby carrying forward what he intended to criticize). Simon's historical-critical project was aimed at defending Catholic tradition against Protestant claims of *sola scriptura*, but what he did was inadvertently ensure that Spinoza's approach to Scripture would continue into the eighteenth century and beyond.

Our penultimate chapter deals with John Locke, a significant figure too often omitted from studies of the history of biblical scholarship.[47] Locke's work is patently indebted to that of Hobbes, Spinoza, and Simon, whose works he assiduously studied, and like Marsilius and Machiavelli, Locke's biblical interpretation was at the service of the political order. His own exegesis was in the service of his Whig politics. Significantly, Locke provided core principles for judging the Bible historically, and because of his enormous international philosophical stature, these principles had a correspondingly enormous intellectual effect. Precisely because he was less overtly radical than either Hobbes or Spinoza, Locke's appropriation of their methods—along with Simon's—was carried into more mainstream circles in England, and furthered the development of biblical criticism in the seventeenth and eighteenth centuries.

Our final full-length chapter is on John Toland and his role in the history of modern biblical criticism. In Toland, Spinoza's and Simon's works especially came together in his devastating deistic criticism of Scripture and Christianity. In this chapter we hope to show that the Deism represented by Toland was not a slow incremental enlightenment, but rather a very conscious subversion of traditional Christianity, one that demanded a corresponding subversion of Scripture. Toland's purpose was to domesticate Christianity in order to support his secular politics.

Finally, in our conclusion, we hint at some of the ways the history we have recounted in the previous chapters continued into eighteenth and nineteenth centuries, with figures including Hermann Samuel Reimarus, Gotthold Lessing, Johann Salomo Semler, Johann Gottfried Eichhorn, Wilhelm M. L. de Wette, David Friedrich Strauss, and Julius Wellhausen. Our point here—in ending where most histories of scriptural scholarship begin—is to recast our whole understanding of the work of these famous, explicit proponents of the historical-critical method. In this account we do not wish to be partisan. Although we are Catholic scholars, we are not reading the history of biblical criticism in an apologetical spirit. It is true that most of the figures we examine found themselves in opposition to popes, or attacked the Catholic Church more broadly. But we make clear, especially in our chapters devoted to Machiavelli and Spinoza, that there existed real problems—at times even at the highest levels of Church authority—and the misdeeds of popes, prelates, and other Christians doubtless helped provoke the animus whose trajectory we trace. What we have attempted

47 There are a few notable exceptions to this general neglect. See the fine treatments of Locke's role in the rise of modern biblical criticism in Reventlow, *History of Biblical Interpretation*, Vol. 4, pp. 51–65; Dungan, *History of the Synoptic Problem*, pp. 261–286; and Reventlow, *The Authority of the Bible*, pp. 243–285.

to do in this volume is uncover the fourteenth to mid-eighteenth-century roots of the historical criticism that emerged in the later eighteenth, nineteenth, and twentieth centuries, and thus expose the secularization of Scripture that has walked through the halls of the academy and classrooms across the globe in the dress of objective science, impervious to critique. This inquiry should prove of the greatest interest to everyone, whatever his creed, concerned with the secularizing effects of the historical-critical method. In short, we have attempted a criticism of criticism, deracinating historical criticism's origins so that scholars might be able to assess more clearly the method's values, limits, and detriments.

But as we have made clear, even in this short introduction, in order to do this, we must begin with a look at the fourteenth-century political and philosophical context in which the process began; a process that would come to fruition five centuries later.

CHAPTER 2

THE FIRST CRACKS OF SECULARISM: MARSILIUS OF PADUA AND WILLIAM OF OCKHAM

We first examine the two figures who, by their use of Scripture, initiated a radical break with antecedent tradition, and set the West on the *via moderna*, that distinctive path that led to modern scriptural scholarship.[1] In regard to Scripture, this break occurred through the effort—especially by Marsilius of Padua—to politicize the biblical text. William of Ockham's contribution consisted not so much in consciously as in *accidentally* politicizing the text.

The relationship between the two figures is complex. As a Franciscan friar involved in the poverty controversy with Pope John XXII, Ockham's main goal was to preserve the distinction between *use* and *ownership* that allowed the Franciscans to continue as scholars, priests, and mendicants faithful to the order's charism. In pursuing this project, Ockham ran headlong into John XXII, and became convinced that John was acting heretically, that the Avignon papal court was itself debased by luxury, and that the papal claims to superiority over temporal rulers entailed absolute power that exercised a degrading influence. For Ockham, John XXII's claim of the right to overrule his predecessor's decisions, and the papalist assertion that the spiritual realm rules the secular, had a common source—the corrupting desire for absolute power. But in arguing so fervently against papal supremacy, Ockham inadvertently aided Marsilius's far more radical case for the complete subordination of the Church, theology, and Scripture to the secular political order.

It is precisely this subordination of the spiritual to the secular order that puts the West on the centuries-long march to complete secularization. On this *via*, this road, we shall find, slowly unfolding, the distinctively modern approach to scriptural scholarship.

Maintaining that the desire for secularization is the historical root of modern biblical scholarship will no doubt strike many as a contentious argument. Few would deny, however, that modern scriptural scholarship, especially the historical-critical method, contributed significantly to the secularization of the West in the nineteenth century and beyond. If this is granted, then we only ask readers' patience in making

1 We would like to thank Vasileios Syros for his many helpful comments and bibliographical suggestions.

the case that the "fruit" of secularization, including the secularization of Scripture, was present in seed form many centuries before.

As is well known, Ockham is also considered to be one of the great intellectual precursors of modern philosophy (and by some, of modern science). But even here, we will find significant ambiguity, since the great shift effected by Ockham philosophically was in the service of a decidedly premodern theological goal: the affirmation of God's absolute, free power. Whatever his motives, the effect of Ockham's revolution was to shift the West onto intellectual paths leading to modern philosophy, thereby contributing to the larger intellectual transformation in which the subordinate development of modern historical-critical scholarship developed.

These abstract assertions will remain unconvincing until we descend to our analysis of the particulars. This is always a daunting undertaking, and the historical context that makes the disputes that embroiled Marsilius and Ockham is no exception. It is well worth our effort to spend some time setting up this context in some detail because this period helps to define the theological and political developments that will unfurl in the sixteenth through the eighteenth centuries (and beyond). Understanding this political-theological context will illuminate why and how Scripture would become politicized.

The Avignon Papacy and the Politics of Empire

It is in the context of the Avignon papacy and the ongoing political machinations of imperial and papal politics in Germany and Italy that we encounter the first sustained modern, or protomodern, contributions to the formation of modern scriptural scholarship.

With the death of the notorious Frederick II in 1250, the Holy Roman Empire came to an effective end (despite its many ineffective centuries to come). Although his grandson Conrad IV ruled until 1254, the real power now lay not in a German emperor but in the German electors and nobility (a political situation that is essential for understanding the politics of the Reformation almost three centuries later). After the death of Conrad, the seven great electors saw no reason to elevate anyone to the imperial crown. They were more than satisfied to enjoy their increasing power. The other, lesser noble houses of Germany likewise welcomed their freedom from imperial rule. We thus have an imperial interregnum from 1254 until the election of the next emperor in 1273, Rudolf of Habsburg of the house of Austria. On the larger historical-geographical scene, we therefore see a diffraction of power in Germany—and just the opposite in France and England, where power was successfully being centralized in the monarchy against the nobility.

When Rudolf was elected in 1273, imperial authority was consequently weaker in comparison to the power of its Germanic electors, weaker than royal authority as exercised in France and England, and weaker in regard to the papacy. It was precisely this situation that Ludwig the Bavarian (or Louis IV, his imperial title[2]) of the

2 We will use his German name Ludwig, rather than Louis. The title Louis IV was, of course, his imperial title, which he was never able to make good.

powerful Wittelsbach house hoped to reverse when Emperor Henry VII (ruling from 1308) died in 1313, leaving the imperial office open for a successor. At Henry's death, the most prominent factions in Germany's dynastic struggles were the Wittelsbachs (Bavaria), the Habsburgs (Austria), and the Luxembourgs (Bohemia). The Wittelsbach and Luxembourg houses allied against the Habsburgs, and the result was a double election in October 1314. The Wittelsbach-Luxembourg alliance elected Ludwig, and the Habsburgs elected Frederick I.[3] The contested election took place in a papal vacuum, since Pope Clement V had died in the spring of 1314 and no successor would be named until 1316. There was a double coronation in different cities, and the two "emperors" were soon at war. Seeing the confusion of this election and its aftermath as an opportunity, the newly-elected Pope John XXII (1316–1334) in his bull *Si fratrum* (1317) called on both Ludwig and Frederick to abdicate within three months or face excommunication, and claimed the right to rule Germany himself in the meantime during imperial vacancy.[4]

To fully appreciate this conflict, especially its pervasive political aspects, one need only look at a map. Imperial German designs were constantly focused on Italy (especially insofar as it seemed easier to control and milk for funds, as opposed to recalcitrant Germany), while the popes were continually trying to extend their territory further north to create a buffer against imperial or other foreign dominance. Continual discord among Italian states was a papal preoccupation, especially as enflamed by Guelph and Ghibelline, pro-papal and pro-imperial, factions. Northern Italy was therefore a kind of battleground. In H. S. Offler's words, "At the root of Lewis' [Ludwig's] controversy with the papacy lay this clash of interests in Italy. To it, the religious issues arising from Lewis' choice of methods and allies were only consequential."[5] That is certainly true in regard to Ludwig, whose motives seem entirely political.

But we must not forget that this fateful link of Germany and Italy was not merely geographical. "The German empire was linked to the papacy like no other European power; it was after all the German kings alone who had been crowned emperors by the pope since the revival of Charlemagne's empire by Otto I in 962."[6] Going all the way back to Pope Innocent III (1198–1216), the popes had considered the rule of the empire

---

3 Adding to the irony and confusion, "The coronation was equally disputed: Frederick was crowned by the duly qualified archbishop of Cologne with the true insignia but in the wrong place (Bonn), Lewis [Ludwig] in the right place (Aachen) but by the archbishop of Mainz (who had no authority to do so) and without the lawful insignia." Peter Herde, "From Adolf of Nassau to Lewis of Bavaria, 1292–1347," in *The New Cambridge Medieval History*, Vol. VI, ed., Michael Jones (Cambridge: Cambridge University Press, 2000), p. 537.

4 As Herde notes, "On the basis of a decretal of Innocent III, issued in an insignificant lawsuit in the Papal State, the popes considered themselves vicars of the empire during imperial vacancies, a right they claimed and tried to make good in Italy above all, in view of the almost total breakdown of imperial power there." Peter Herde, "From Adolf of Nassau to Lewis of Bavaria, 1292–1347," p. 538.

5 H. S. Offler, "Empire and Papacy: the Last Struggle," in Offler, *Church and Crown in the Fourteenth Century*, A. I. Doyle, ed., (Aldershot: Ashgate, 2000), II, p. 25.

6 Herde, "From Adolf of Nassau to Lewis of Bavaria, 1292–1347," p. 522.

to be at the behest of their spiritual power, and that meant oversight and approval of the imperial elections via the German prince electors.[7]

Ludwig ignored the call for his abdication, and in pursuit of his crown, finally subdued his rival, Frederick, in 1322, imprisoning him for three years, and then releasing him only to make him joint (but honorific) king in 1325. The papacy issued a declaration against Ludwig in October 1323, threatening his excommunication for daring to assume power without papal approval, and for aiding the excommunicated Giovanni Visconti of Milan, an enemy of the papacy.

Ludwig responded to Innocent's threats by calling for a general council to judge the claim of the necessity of papal sanction for imperial election, and further, by publishing the Sachsenhausen Appeal in 1324, a resounding indictment of papal abuses (including a charge of heresy), which included the call for a general council. At almost the same moment, the pope formally excommunicated Ludwig. Ludwig's response was momentous both for history and especially the history of scriptural scholarship. He soon took under his protection (in 1326) two fellow fugitives from the papacy—Marsilius of Padua and John of Jandun—who would provide Ludwig with the philosophical and theological justification for imperial supremacy.[8]

At the request of the pro-imperial Ghibellines, Ludwig undertook an Italian expedition in 1327–1329, marching into Rome for his coronation in January 1328, a city that had been deserted by the papacy (now at Avignon). "The fact that Lewis [Ludwig] was prepared to do so was the result in no small part of the arrival of Marsilius of Padua and his friend John of Jandun at his court in 1326. In June 1324 Marsilius, a supporter of the Ghibellines in his native city, then master and rector at Paris university, finished the *Defensor Pacis* (Defender of Peace) which laid him and his assumed co-author, John of Jandun, open to accusation of heresy and forced them to flee."[9] Again, they fled to Ludwig, a refuge that made sense, given the radical subordination of the spiritual to the temporal power advocated in the *Defensor Pacis*. Now both Marsilius and John of Jandun were at Ludwig's side, in every sense, at the imperial coronation.

Ludwig was crowned at St. Peter's on January 17, and four days later, without having learned of the coronation, John XXII called for a crusade against Ludwig. Upon

---

7 In regard to the supremacy of the papacy, Pope Innocent III (1198–1216) is usually taken to express the height of papal power. Innocent offered an allegory from Scripture, reaffirming the superiority of his spiritual office over earthly kings. "Just as the founder of the universe established two great lights in the firmament of heaven, a greater one to preside over the day and a lesser to provide over the night, so too . . . he instituted two great dignities, a greater one to preside over souls . . . and a lesser one to preside over bodies. . . . These are the pontifical authority and the royal power. Now just as the moon derives its light from the sun and is indeed lower than it in quantity and quality, in position and in power, so too the royal power derives the splendor of its dignity from the pontifical authority," Brian Tierney, *The Crisis of Church & State, 1050–1300* (Englewood Cliffs, NJ: Prentice-Hall, Inc., 1964), p. 132.

8 For a discussion of difficulties and disagreements in discerning the historical particularities of Marsilius's connection to Ludwig, see Frank Godthardt, "The Philosopher as Political Actor—Marsilius of Padua at the Court of Ludwig the Bavarian: The Sources Revisited," in Gerson Moreno-Riaño, ed., *The World of Marsilius of Padua* (Turnhout: Brepols, 2006), pp. 29–46.

9 Herde, "From Adolf of Nassau to Lewis of Bavaria, 1292–1347," pp. 540–541.

hearing news of the ceremony, John declared the coronation void on March 31, and to return the favor, Ludwig then deposed John XXII, naming him a "Destroyer of the Peace" on April 18 (a move obviously done "under the influence of Marsilius"[10]). On May 13, Ludwig elected his own pope (a Franciscan friar, Peter of Corbara, or Corvara, who took the name Nicholas V), and subsequently had himself reaffirmed as emperor by his new pope. Marsilius was appointed the spiritual vicar of Rome, and immediately set about the persecution of all of John XXII's supporters. Ludwig's own support was not strong, however—especially among his own troops, whom he had continual trouble paying. He therefore withdrew from Italy, and returned to Munich. During his return, a group of Franciscans fleeing from John XXII joined Ludwig; one of them was William of Ockham. Under Ludwig's protection, both Marsilius and William would champion imperial over papal power.

We must add another layer of complexity—the great disputes about poverty between the Franciscans and Pope John XXII that brought William of Ockham to Ludwig. As we shall see, Ludwig was shrewd enough to use Franciscan opposition to John XXII as a purely political tool to resist the papacy.

The Sachsenhausen Appeal mentioned above included the charge of heresy against John XXII—specifically, the charge that he had wrongly condemned the radical Franciscan claim of the total poverty of Christ and his disciples. Since there were not as yet any Franciscans at Ludwig's court when the appeal was made (1324), news of the controversy must have arrived with his ambassadors from Avignon.[11] It was certainly reaffirmed with Marsilius of Padua and John of Jandun (since the poverty dispute appears prominently in the *Defensor Pacis*).

Briefly, the poverty dispute arose from the radical affirmation of poverty by St. Francis himself. Because of the very success of St. Francis, his order grew tremendously, but with expansion came compromise, especially in regard to the nature of poverty. Those who sought some pragmatic easement of Franciscan poverty formed the party of the Conventuals; those who embraced St. Francis's austerity literally were called the Spirituals (or Zealots). The Conventuals were not engaged in diluting their order's ideals, so much as applying them prudently. Entailed in St. Francis's own charism was the demand to preach. Preaching in turn demanded education (especially as the order attracted more educated brothers); education, books; books, libraries; libraries, buildings to contain them, and so on.

A solution of sorts was finally hammered out, one that was clever but not convincing. The Franciscans declared that, while they might *use* such things as books and buildings, they did not *own* them—a view given papal sanction in Pope Gregory IX's bull *Quo elongati* (1230).[12] This view was reaffirmed by Pope Nicholas III in *Exiit qui seminat* (1279), in which Nicholas declared that things given to the Franciscan

10 Ibid., p. 541.

11 Ibid., p. 539.

12 The immediate point of the bull was, more famously, to declare that St. Francis had no right to demand obedience to his "Testament," a document written near the end of his life, expressing his desire that the friars return to radical poverty.

Order for use could be considered the property of the papacy, thereby relieving the conscience of the friars. As the disputes seemed endless, Nicholas also forbade any glosses on, or further disputation about, the matter. This distinction between use and ownership was again affirmed by Pope Clement V in *Exivi de Paradiso* (1312). In *Exivi*, Clement also dealt with the divisions still festering between the Conventuals and Spirituals, the latter bent on pulling the order back to its founder's mode of complete poverty, the former arguing that in doing so they were pulling the order apart. The Spirituals maintained that the distinction between use and ownership of goods allowed many Franciscans to live in (relative) luxury while declaring that they still owned nothing; but in their zeal for poverty, the Spirituals pushed against their vow of obedience to their superiors.

In 1316 John XXII was elected pope, and Michael of Cesena was elected the Minister General of the Franciscan Order. Each had as his goal reining in the Spirituals. John's bull *Quorumdam exigit* (1317) ordered all Franciscans to obedience. But beyond this, and against Nicholas's *Exiit*, the pope reopened the debate about the use-ownership distinction, which he considered disingenuous. When certain Franciscans argued that Nicholas had forbidden further discussion, John issued *Ad conditorem canonum* (1322), which declared that as reigning pope he did indeed have the right to overrule decisions of his predecessors. As if to illustrate, he proclaimed that the papacy did *not* own goods that the Franciscans used; the Franciscans who used them owned them. The Sachsenhausen Appeal, issued in response from Ludwig's court in May 1324, declared John XXII a heretic for rescinding the decision of a previous pope. There is good reason to believe that the Appeal was influenced both by Marsilius and by certain unknown Franciscans. John's subsequent *Quia quorundam* (1324) simply reaffirmed his right to rescind.

John XXII's position may seem like a common-sense readjustment of the questionable use-ownership distinction, but seen in context, we can perceive how inflammatory it was. For the papacy to declare suddenly that the Franciscans owned the vast resources they had been using was spiritually debilitating, a blow at the heart of St. Francis's most distinctive attribute and the order's most prized aspiration. Conversely, the Franciscan argument for the use-ownership distinction was always couched in terms of the superiority of the life of poverty as a direct imitation of Christ and his Apostles. The rich papal court at Avignon could hardly miss the point.

By 1328, John XXII was at odds with Michael of Cesena, the conflict serious enough that Michael fled with a number of fellow Franciscans, including William of Ockham—who had previously been summoned to Avignon on charges of heresy. They fled into the arms of Ludwig, who was all too happy to use their dispute with the papacy to his own political ends.

Obviously, from all of the above, we have some appreciation of how extraordinarily political the entire situation is. But because the poverty dispute ultimately turned on questions concerning Christ and the Apostles, it centered upon Scripture—whose exegesis could not help but be thoroughly politicized, as will become clear in our analysis of the work of Marsilius and Ockham.

Marsilius's Averroistic Revolution

A Paduan by birth, Marsilio dei Mainardini (c. 1275–1342), or Marsilius (or Marsiglio) as he is known to us, probably studied medicine at the University of Padua (which later became strongly Averroist, especially among the faculty of medicine), and was rector of the University of Paris at about the time (1313) Ockham was studying theology at Oxford.[13] The University of Paris was also a stronghold of Averroism, and it was there that Marsilius was further influenced by the Averroist John of Jandun.

Averroes (or Ibn-Rushd, c. 1126–1198) was a Muslim philosopher,[14] influenced by both Plato and Aristotle. In a Muslim culture that took the Koran to be the absolute and unquestionable revealed truth, Averroes's devotion to philosophy, especially pagan philosophy, made his situation at times uncomfortable. Despite this, he wrote extensively, his commentaries on Aristotle being of especial note precisely because certain conclusions according to the reasoning of Aristotle were incompatible with the Koran (such as the eternality of the world and doubts about personal immortality). In an effort to deal with contradictions between philosophy and theology, Averroes argued in his *On the Harmony Between Religion and Philosophy* that there is indeed one truth, but it is known according to the capacity of the knowers: at the bottom are those open only to rhetorical persuasion, in whom appeal is made to the imagination and the passions; above these are those capable of dialectic, who are satisfied with the probable arguments of theology; and finally, at the top and fewest in number, are the philosophical men who demand rigorous rational demonstration. Needless to say, the hierarchical ranking entails a superiority of the truths of natural reason to those of revelation, but it also includes the notion of control of the masses by the philosophers using the myths of religion.[15]

---

13 For a detailed account of this period see William Courtenay, "University Masters and Political Power: The Parisian Years of Marsilius of Padua," in Martin Kaufhold, ed., *Politische Reflexion in Der Welt Des Späten Mittelalters/Political Thought in the Age of Scholasticism* (Leiden: Brill, 2004), pp. 209–223. For a recent overview of the state of scholarship see Cary Nederman, "Marsiglio of Padua Studies Today—and Tomorrow," in Moreno-Riaño, ed., *The World of Marsilius of Padua*, pp. 11–25.

14 For a more extensive analysis see Gregorio Piaia, "*Averroisme politique: Anatomie d'un mythe historiographique*," in Albert Zimmermann and Ingrid Craemer-Ruegenberg, eds., *Orientalische Kultur und europäisches Mittelalter* (Berlin/New York: de Gruyter, 1985), pp. 288–300; idem, "*L'averroismo politico e Marsilio da Padova*," in Carlo Giacon, ed., *Saggi e ricerche su Aristotele, Marsilio da Padova, M. Eckhart, Rosmini, Spaventa, Marty, Tilgher, Omodeo, metafisica, fenomenologia ed estetica* (Padua: Antenore, 1971), pp. 33–54.

15 See Averroes, *The Book of the Decisive Treatise: Determining the Connection Between the Law and Wisdom*, translated by Charles Butterworth (Provo, UT: Brigham Young University Press, 2001), ch. III, and *Averroes' Tahafut Al-Tahafut*, Volumes I and III, translated by Simon Van Den Bergh (Cambridge: Cambridge University Press, 1987), 580–588 ("About the Natural Sciences," Fourth Discussion, pp. 359–363). For a solid, short discussion in the context of the wider history of such political use of religion see Vasileios Syros, "Simone Luzzatto's Image of the Ideal Prince and the Italian Tradition of Reason of State," in *Redescriptions: Yearbook of Political Thought and Conceptual History* (Münster: Verlag, 2005), pp. 157–182, especially his short discussion of Averroes with bibliography in footnotes, pp. 160–163.

When Averroes's commentaries accompanied Aristotle's works into the West, the difficulty that had beset Islam fell upon Christians: What should be done when the philosophical arguments of Aristotle contradicted the truths of Christian faith? Aristotle could be rejected (the radical Augustinian approach); Aristotle could be corrected and worked into a synthesis (St. Thomas); or the truths of his philosophy could stand, in contradiction, alongside the truths of faith, creating a kind of double, incompatible set of truths, the truth according to reason and the truth according to revelation (the "Latin Averroist" approach of, among others, Siger of Brabant)

Such Averroism imbued Marsilius's thought, especially his most famous work (allegedly coauthored with John of Jandun[16]), the anti-papal treatise *Defensor Pacis* (1324), a work that the great historian of medieval thought Etienne Gilson aptly calls "as perfect an example of political Averroism as one could wish for."[17]

Before publishing the *Defensor Pacis*, Marsilius had actually been in the good graces of John XXII, with the pope offering him a canonry in Padua in October 1316, and reserving him a vacant Paduan benefice in April 1318.[18] Marsilius was soon after to be found at Paris, lecturing in philosophy and practicing medicine. Sometime during this period, he was working on the *Defensor Pacis*. Although it was finished in the summer of 1324, Marsilius's authorship became public only in 1326. Once he was known as the author of the shocking treatise, he and John of Jandun (the alleged coauthor[19]) found that they had to flee, seeking refuge with the enemy of John XXII, Ludwig of Bavaria. In October 1327, the pope issued the bull *Licit iuxta*, proclaiming Marsilius and John heretics. He considered their threat so grave that he widely publicized the errors of the pernicious book, sending a letter of warning, *Certum processum*,

---

16 While it is almost certain that John of Jandun influenced the writing of the *Defensor Pacis*, that he was truly the coauthor has not been established beyond doubt. Thus, we shall generally refer to Marsilius as the author. For further details see N. Valois, "*Jean de Jandun et Marsile de Padoue auteurs du* Defensor pacis," *Histoire littéraire de France*, XXXIII (Paris 1906), pp. 528–623. For a convincing revision of this assumption, see Alan Gewirth, "John of Jandun and the *Defensor Pacis*," *Speculum* XXIII (1948), pp. 267–72, and C. Dolcini, "*Marsilio da Padova e Giovanni di Jandun*," D. Quaglioni, ed., *Storia della chiesa* v. 9: *La crisi del Trecento e il papato avignonese (1274–1378)* (Cinisello Balsamo: San Paolo, 1994), pp. 435–46.

17 Etienne Gilson, *History of Christian Philosophy in the Middle Ages* (New York: Random House, 1955), p. 526. For a solid overview of the contours of Marsilian scholarship see George Garnett, *Marsilius of Padua and "The Truth of History"* (Oxford: Oxford University Press, 2006), Introduction.

18 An outline of Marsilius's life can be found in the Introduction to Alan Gewirth, *Marsilius of Padua and Medieval Political Philosophy*, Volume 1 (New York and London: Columbia University Press, 1951). J. Miethke, *De potestate papae. Die päpstliche Amtskompetenz im Widerstreit der politischen Theorie von Thomas von Aquin bis Wilhelm von Ockham, Spätmittelalter und Reformation*, N. R., 16 (Tübingen: Mohr Siebeck, 2000), 204ff.; C. Pincin, *Marsilio*, Pubblicazioni dell'Istituto di Scienze Politiche dell'Università di Torino, 17 (Turin: 1967), pp. 21–54; C. Dolcini, *Introduzione a Marsilio da Padova, I filosofi*, 63) (Bari: Laterza, 1995); J. Haller, "*Zur Lebensgeschichte des Marsilius von Padua*," *ZKG* 48 (1929), pp. 166–199 [*wiederabgedr. in: ders., Abhandlungen zur Geschichte des Mittelalters* (Stuttgart: Verlag, 1944), pp. 335–368].

19 As noted above, there is controversy on this point, but it seems highly likely that the allegation of coauthorship was more rumor than fact. See Garnett, *Marsilius of Padua and "The Truth of History*," pp. 14–17, with attendant bibliography.

to his bishops.[20] It is famously (but apocryphally) reported that when Ockham later fled to Ludwig, he declared, "I will defend you with my pen, if you will defend me with your sword." For Marsilius the chronology was reversed. Ludwig was happy to protect Marsilius, because the *Defensor Pacis* already championed Ludwig.

But the *Defensor Pacis* is not merely a political tract aimed at a particular political situation. It is, in the deepest sense, revolutionary, a landmark philosophical document in the secularization of the West that enjoyed a wide circulation from the very beginning; indeed the very thoroughness of repeated condemnations ensured that the substance of Marsilius's argument would become well known.[21] As Alan Gewirth notes, going far beyond the immediate needs of Ludwig, Marsilius' political Averroism provides a self-conscious foundation for a secular revolution.

> The specifically political feature of Marsilius's Averroism consists in his completely secular approach to all aspects of the state, including those connected with religion, theology, and the church. The Averroist method meant that problems could be investigated by rational procedures alone in complete independence of faith and of the theological tradition founded upon faith. Marsilius attains this result by setting up a politics based upon reason alone in Discourse I, omitting the consideration of eternal life and divine causation on the plea that they are not amenable to reason. To be sure . . . he proceeds in the second Discourse to "confirm" by revelation the rationally established conclusions of the first. But the salient point of this procedure is that it permits the establishment of the central doctrines of a political philosophy in complete disregard of the supernatural order. Hence when revelation is invoked in the second Discourse to "confirm" the first, a complete rational, non-supernatural political system lies already at hand, *and the texts of Scripture can be so selected and interpreted as to support that system.*[22]

This politicized selecting and interpreting of text has, for Gewirth, a larger secular aim that defines it. For our purposes, it is essential to see how Marsilius treated Scripture to support his secular goal in his *Defensor Pacis*.

Defending Earthly Peace: The Birth of the Secular State

The entirety of Marsilius's *Defensor Pacis* is designed, at least ostensibly, for curing a particular "disease" of the civil body, one that "[n]either Aristotle nor any other philosopher of his time or before" could have recognized because it was rooted in "a certain perverted opinion . . . which came to be adopted as an aftermath of the miraculous effect produced by the supreme cause long after Aristotle's time; an effect

20 Garnett emphasizes the wide-scale response of John XXII that scholars have neglected: Garnett, *Marsilius of Padua and "The Truth of History,"* pp. 19–20.

21 On this important point, see Garnett, Introduction.

22 Gewirth, *Marsilius of Padua and Medieval Political Philosophy*, Volume I, p. 43. Emphasis added.

beyond the power of the lower nature and the usual action of causes of things."[23] The miraculous effect, the reader assumes, is the resurrection of Jesus Christ, and the perversion is, as Marsilius makes quite clear, the papal claim to a spiritual power to rule over secular, political life. At least on the surface, the *Defensor Pacis* is one, long anti-papal diatribe.

If that summed up the entirety of Marsilius's work, it would be of little importance for our understanding the history of modern scriptural scholarship. But far deeper things are going on in the *Defensor Pacis*. Although Marsilius is evidently concerned with undermining papal authority in the political realm, his ultimate concern is the radical reordering of secular and sacred authority, so that the priesthood is firmly subordinated to political power—a task that entails the biblical justification of political power and the subordination of biblical interpretation to it. This subordination is seen quite clearly in the very title of the work. As he notes in the very last chapter, the treatise is called *Defensor Pacis* "because it discusses and explains the principal causes whereby civil peace or tranquility exists and is preserved, and whereby the opposed strife arises and is checked and destroyed." It aims at civil peace or tranquility, or more accurately, it aims to teach the *defender* of peace both what civil peace is, and against whom and how to defend it. Marsilius therefore speaks not to the ecclesiastic but to "the ruler." [24]

Marsilius is not concerned with civil peace as one worthy goal among many; rather, civil peace becomes for him *the* defining aim, the greatest good. Marsilius therefore lowers the aim of the "greatest good" from supernatural to natural or civil peace, turning away from the heavens and the city of God, toward the earth and the city of man. His primary concern, then, is "the truth which leads to the salvation of civil life," adding almost incidentally that it "also is of no little help for eternal salvation."[25]

Thus, from the opening paragraph, Marsilius praises first of all "the tranquility or peace of civil regimes" as "the greatest good of man," or more accurately, he praises such tranquility for the sake of "sufficiency of life, which no one can attain without peace and tranquility."[26] Furthermore, this "greatest good" does not need revelation for its illumination. As Marsilius reveals quite soon, this earthly political goal, sufficiency of life, is based not on revelation but on reason, in particular, on a *modified* version of Aristotle's reasoned account of the end of political life.[27]

We must be especially clear about this last point. Marsilius did not embrace Aristotle's entire argument, but a peculiarly blunted form of it.[28] In Aristotle, there is

---

23 Marsilius of Padua, *Defensor Pacis,* translated by Alan Gewirth (Toronto: University of Toronto Press, 1980), I, 1.3.

24 Ibid., III, 3.

25 Ibid., I, 1.5.

26 Ibid., I, 1.1.

27 Ibid., I, 2.3.

28 On this important point see Vasileios Syros, *Die Rezeption der aristotelischen politischen Philosophie bei Marsilius von Padua: Eine Untersuchung zur ersten Diktion des* Defensor pacis, *Studies in Medieval and Reformation Traditions,* p. 134 (Leiden/Boston: Brill, 2007); idem, "Marsilius of Padua's Classical Sources," in Cary J. Nederman and Gerson Moreno–Riaño, eds., *The Life and Thought of Marsilius of Padua* (Leiden/Boston: Brill, in press).

always a certain tension between political and philosophic life. We are indeed political animals by nature,[29] but precisely because our nature, our form, is defined by rationality, the life of contemplation properly and ultimately defines our perfection, our *telos*, our final cause.[30] For this reason, the political life is, properly speaking, subordinate to the contemplative life, that is, to the contemplation of eternal truths. Such a philosophic life, argued Aristotle, is

> above that of a man, for a man will live in this manner not insofar as he is a man, but insofar as he has something divine in him; and the activity of this divine part of the soul is as much superior to that of the other kind of virtue [i.e., ethical-political virtue] as that divine part [i.e., the rational part of the soul] is superior to the composite soul of man [consisting of the divine-like rational part, animal-like sensitive part, and the plant-like vegetative part]. So since the intellect [*nous*] is divine relative to a man, the life according to this intellect, too, will be divine relative to human life.[31]

For this reason, Aristotle asserted, we must not follow the recommendation of those who say that "men should think only of human things and that mortals should think only of mortal things. . . ." Rather, "we should try as far as possible to partake of immortality and to make every effort to live according to the best part of the soul in us; for even if this part be of small measure, it surpasses all the others by far in power and worth."[32]

The analysis of the human good in terms of formal and final causes guides Aristotle's hierarchical ordering of political life, allowing him to rank different kinds of political regimes in accordance with their orientation toward the final cause, the proper perfection of human nature.[33] The flawed regimes (tyranny, oligarchy, and democracy) distort our nature; the good regimes (monarchy, aristocracy, and polity) order political life toward the proper perfection, the *telos*, of our nature.[34] The paradox, of course, is that in ordering political life toward the best part of the soul, we would be orienting political life beyond "human things and . . . mortal things" to divine things. The highest, defining political goal, the suprapolitical goal for any human being would be to live in a "manner not insofar as he is a man, but insofar as he has something divine in him."

To be sure, Aristotle was quite aware that most human beings and most regimes fall far short of perfection. So, even while the best regimes, monarchy and aristocracy, properly embody the *telos* of human nature (or at least approximate it as closely as

29 Aristotle, *Politics,* 1253a2–5; *Nicomachean Ethics* 1097b7–12, 1162a16–18, 1169b17–22; *Eudemian Ethics,* 1242a23–28.

30 *Nicomachean Ethics,* 1097a15–1097b21, 1177a12–1178a8.

31 Ibid., 1177b27–32. Translation from the edition by Hippocrates Apostle.

32 Ibid., 1178b32–1178a2.

33 Cf. J. Miethke, "*Marsilius von Padua. Die politische Philosophie eines lateinischen Aristotelikers des 14. Jahrhunderts,*" in H. Boockmann, B. Moeller, K. Stackmann, eds., *Lebenslehren und Weltentwürfe im Übergang vom Mittelalter zur Neuzeit: Politik–Naturkunde–Theologie* (Göttingen: 1989), p. 56.

34 *Politics,* 1278b6–1279b10.

possible), Aristotle spends a significant part of the *Politics* discussing oligarchy and democracy, since experience proves that these regimes are far more likely to occur. Although a true political science takes its bearings from the best regimes, it must also instruct as to how to live as well as possible in the actual, degraded regimes in which we are far more likely to find ourselves.

It is not difficult to see that this subordination of body to soul would weigh in favor of the affirmation of the superiority of the spiritual to the temporal by Pope Gregory VII, Hugh of St. Victor, Innocent III, and John XXII.[35] As a consequence, Marsilius could not simply adopt Aristotle's arguments intact. He therefore provides a truncated view of politics, one without any upward thrust, designating civil peace and not contemplation as the highest and defining good. This truncated view signals the origin of secularism in the peculiarly modern sense.

Marsilius begins with the Aristotelian distinction between living and living well—that is, between biological necessity (which is both common to and desirable by all human beings) and theoretical speculation (which, as Aristotle readily admits, is sought only by a few). This distinction between living and living well, the practical and the theoretical, defines two distinct ends, one that is "temporal or earthly," and the other "eternal or heavenly." This "latter kind of living, the eternal," remarks Marsilius, "the whole body of philosophers were unable to prove by demonstration nor was it self evident," but in regard to the earthly life, "the glorious philosophers comprehended [it] almost completely through demonstration."[36]

Heaven is obscure; earth is clear. Since politics cannot be built upon speculative obscurity, it must be confined to practical, biological necessity. Marsilius therefore lowers the aim, or final cause, of politics, confining it tightly within the lower two parts of the soul, the vegetative and the sensitive, the plantlike and animal-like aspects of our nature. As Gewirth points out, this results in a stunted account of politics that departs from both Aristotle and St. Thomas because it focuses exclusively on the needs and desires of the body:

---

35 To cite an example of their reasoning, in a letter to the Bishop of Metz in 1081, Pope Gregory VII (1073–1085) set out the proper relationship of the spiritual to the temporal powers, stating that " . . . every Christian king when he approaches his end asks the aid of a priest as a miserable suppliant that he may escape the prison of hell, may pass from darkness into light and may appear at the judgment seat of God freed from the bonds of sin. But who, layman or priest, in his last moments has ever asked the help of any earthly king for the safety of his soul? And what king or emperor has power through his office to snatch any Christian from the might of the Devil by the sacred rite of baptism, to confirm him among the sons of God and to fortify him by the holy chrism? Or—and this is the greatest thing in the Christian religion—who among them is able by his own word to create the body and blood of the Lord? or to whom among them is given the power to bind and loose in Heaven and upon earth? From this it is apparent how greatly superior in power is the priestly dignity. Or who of them is able to ordain any clergyman in the Holy Church—much less to depose him for any fault? For bishops, while they may ordain other bishops, may in no wise depose them except by authority of the Apostolic See. How, then, can even the most slightly informed person doubt that priests are higher than kings? But if kings are to be judged by priests for their sins, by whom can they more properly be judged than by the Roman pontiff?" Cited in Tierney, *The Crisis of Church & State, 1050–1300*, p. 70.

36 Marsilius, *Defensor Pacis*, I, 4.1–3.

> As was to be expected from the biological context in which he places his politics, the "natural" as he conceives it is always the primitive, not the perfected; it consists in man's material endowment, physical and biological, not in his rational powers or virtues. Thus man's "natural" desire for the sufficient life is a desire which man shares with "every genus of animals." [37]

Since Marsilius confines politics to the needs and desires of the body, to animal existence, his analysis contains no ranking of regimes in accordance with the Aristotelian notion of the perfection of our rational nature. Doing so would obviously leave a large door open to papal arguments about the superiority of the spiritual to the temporal realm. Instead, he focuses merely on the *efficient* causes of this-worldly peace in the context of a view of politics confined to *material* needs and desires. As we shall see, this focus on efficient and material causes, at the expense of formal and final causes, will fit well with the modern concept of nature developed in the sixteenth and seventeenth century.[38]

What part, then, does Scripture play in all of this? A quite subordinate one, to say the least: Scripture serves the secularizing aim of Marsilius's politics: Heaven serves earth, the spirit serves the body. Marsilius quotes Scripture to support his argument about "the greatest good of man" being defined according to the body, using both the Old Testament (e.g., Job 22:21, "Be at peace, and thereby thou shalt have the best fruits") and citing many instances from the New Testament that emphasize peace, including the greeting of the heavenly choir in Luke 2:14 announcing the birth of Christ ("Glory to God in the highest: and on earth peace to men of good will") and Christ's own post-Resurrection words to his disciples in John 20:19, Mark 9:50, and John 14:27 ("Peace be to you," "Have peace among you," and "Peace I leave with you: my peace I give unto you").[39]

Obvious tensions arise in thus bending the heavenly to earthly purposes. Could Christ *really* be referring to civil peace in these passages, especially as defined by Marsilius—the same Christ who says in Luke 12:51, "Do you think that I have come to give peace on earth? No, I tell you, but rather division . . . "? Could such civil peace be the same peace of which St. Paul speaks in Philippians 4:7, "the peace of God, which passes all understanding"? This tension is found throughout the entire *Defensor Pacis*, and in fact defines its very structure. Part I of the treatise deals with "living well" according to what is "temporal or earthly," and Part II with living well according to what is "eternal or heavenly." But as Gewirth rightly noted, the second half of the treatise is subordinate to the first; the heavenly serves the earthly, and religion must be redefined accordingly.

---

37 Gewirth, *Marsilius of Padua and Medieval Political Philosophy*, Volume I, p. 55. The quote at the end, which Marsilius includes in his text (I, 4.2) comes from Cicero, *De Officiis*, I, 4.11.

38 Again, see Syros, *Die Rezeption der aristotelischen politischen Philosophie bei Marsilius von Padua: Eine Untersuchung zur ersten Diktion des* Defensor pacis, passim.

39 Marsilius, *Defensor Pacis* I, 1.1.

The Civil Religion of Philosophers

Marsilius does not wait until Part II to discuss religion. In Part I, he addresses it from the "temporal or earthly" perspective. According to Marsilius, there is a natural place for religion in civil communities, a place that (unlike revealed religion) *does* contribute to political tranquility. Religion's place is natural because it is not founded by God through revelation for the sake of heavenly bliss, but by philosophers for the sake of civil tranquility.[40] Marsilius's words are well worth quoting at length, for it will become a familiar form of reasoning among those who follow:

> [T]he philosophers, including Hesiod, Pythagoras, and several others of the ancients, noted appropriately a quite different cause or purpose for the setting forth of divine laws or religions [*sectae*]—a purpose which was in some sense necessary for the status of this world. This was to ensure the goodness of human acts both individual and civil, on which depend almost completely the quiet or tranquility of communities and finally the sufficient life in the present world. For although some of the philosophers who founded such laws or religions did not accept or believe in human resurrection and that life which is called eternal, they nevertheless feigned and persuaded others that it exists and that in it pleasures and pains are in accordance with the qualities of human deeds in this mortal life, in order that they might thereby induce in men reverence and fear of God, and a desire to flee the vices and to cultivate the virtues. For there are certain acts which the legislator cannot regulate by human law, that is, those acts which cannot be proved to be present or absent to someone [i.e., those acts no one other than the doer witnesses], but which nevertheless cannot be concealed from God, whom these philosophers feigned to be the maker of such laws and the commander of their observance, under the threat or promise of eternal reward for doers of good and punishment for doers of evil. Hence, they said of the variously virtuous men in this world that they were placed in the heavenly firmament; and from this were perhaps derived the names of certain stars and constellations. These philosophers said that the souls of men who acted wrongly entered the bodies of various brutes; for example, the souls of men who had been intemperate eaters entered the bodies of pigs, those who were intemperate in embracing and making love entered the bodies of goats, and so on, according . . . the proportions of human vices to their condemnable properties. So too the philosophers assigned various kinds of torments to wrongdoers, like perpetual thirst and hunger for intemperate Tantalus. . . . The philosophers also said that the infernal regions, the place of these torments, were deep and dark; and they painted all sorts of terrible and gloomy pictures of them. For fear of these, men eschewed wrongdoing,

40 For an extremely insightful detailed analysis of the political use of religion in Marsilius and Maimonides see Vasileios Syros, "Did the Physician from Padua Concur with the Rabbi from Cordoba? Marsilius of Padua and Moses Maimonides on the Political Utility of Religion," forthcoming.

> were instigated to perform virtuous works of piety and mercy, and were well disposed both in themselves and toward others. As a consequence, many disputes and injuries ceased in communities. Hence too the peace or tranquility of states and the sufficient life of men for the status of the present world were preserved with less difficulty; which was the end intended by these wise men laying down such laws or religions.[41]

This is a revealing passage.[42] As Gewirth points out, many other sources known to Marsilius set forth this notion of the invention of religion "for its this-worldly social utility"—such as Aristotle, Averroes, St. Augustine, St. Albert the Great, and St. Thomas Aquinas—but "whereas all these thinkers *except Averroes* treat this conception of religion with disparagement or indignation, Marsilius's lengthy exposition of the idea is integrally connected with his naturalistic politics as a whole."[43] Following Averroes's positive assessment of the political use of religion,[44] Marsilius makes very clear that philosophers—"wise men," as he designates them—fashioned religion for the sake of civil tranquility, knowing all the while that it was not true, but feigning belief for the sake of controlling men who could not be governed otherwise.[45] Even more telling, the philosophers pretended that God was the author of their merely human laws or commandments, and heaven (but especially hell) were fictions designed to lure nonphilosophers into civil obedience with eternal rewards, or failing that, frighten them with the specter of eternal punishments.

The attentive reader cannot help but ask the obvious question: Is Marsilius also a wise philosopher who feigns belief, or is he truly a believer? Given the assumptions and mode of his argument, it is impossible to tell. After this passage he does indeed say that "correct views concerning God were not held by the gentile laws or religions

---

41 Marsilius, *Defensor Pacis*, I, 5.11.

42 See Vasileios Syros, "Did the Physician from Padua Concur with the Rabbi from Cordoba? Marsilius of Padua and Moses Maimonides on the Political Utility of Religion," forthcoming.

43 Gewirth, *Marsilius of Padua and Medieval Political Philosophy,* Volume I, p. 83. Emphasis added.

44 For example, Averroes's comments on Aristotle's *Metaphysics* 1074b1–14. See Charles Genequand, *Ibn Rushd's Metaphysics: A Translation with Introduction of Ibn Rushd's Commentary on Aristotle's Metaphysics, Book Lām* (Leiden: Brill, 1986), 1687–1690. Averroes's point in this section seems to be that the ancient Chaldaeans were wise men whose philosophic sayings, over time, were presented as mythic symbols (such as the celestial bodies being gods). To these, additional layers of myth were accreted, argues Averroes, such as the gods being like men or in the form of animals, that "contain no truth at all" but were "aimed at persuading the people to improve their morals and (to do) that which is best for them; this is what is intended [in Aristotle] by 'benefit of the laws.'" The difference with Aristotle is instructive. Aristotle actually asserts that "the ancients" were not wise men, or philosophers, but themselves offered the myth that the heavenly bodies were gods. But, in contrast, Averroes presents these ancient Chaldaeans as having "Wisdom" and that their ancient wise sayings were purposely re-presented over time in myths or symbols. Thus, in Averroes's account, unlike that of Aristotle, the ancient wise men act as philosophic founders of popular religion, which is designed to control the masses.

45 Cf. Richard C. Taylor, "Averroes: God and the Noble Lie," in R. E. Houser, ed., *Laudemus viros gloriosos: Essays in Honor of Armand Maurer, CSB,* (Notre Dame: University of Notre Dame Press, 2007), pp. 38–59.

and by all the other religions which are or were outside the catholic Christian faith or outside the Mosaic law which preceded it . . . in general, [correct views were not held] by all those doctrines which are outside the tradition of what is contained in the sacred canon called the Bible."[46] But it is difficult to know what to make of such an assertion. Marsilius has just informed us that philosophers, wise men, feign belief, and Marsilius is clearly an intellectual disciple of the pagan philosopher Aristotle, or more accurately, of the "Averroistic" reading of Aristotle. And again, Averroes (unlike Aristotle) was not concerned with the truth or falsity of religion, but only with its utility. Although Marsilius's intentions may have been entirely unambiguous, his presentation was bound to arouse suspicion. Marsilius's account of law, which firmly subordinates the interpretation of Scripture to the state, only adds to the ambiguity.

Law, Legislator, and Sola Scriptura

Marsilius puts forth four senses of the word "law." The third sense "means the standard containing admonitions for voluntary human acts according as these are ordered toward glory or punishment in the future world. In this sense the Mosaic law was in part called law, just as the evangelical law [revealed in the New Testament] in its entirety is called a law." A Christian would understand the evangelical law to be in a class by itself, but in his consideration of this third sense of the law, Marsilius includes "all religions [*sectae*], such as that of Mohammed or of the Persians," adding that "among these only the Mosaic and the evangelic, that is, the Christian, contain the truth."[47]

The problem with this exemption is that, according to the "Averroist" Marsilius, its truth cannot be demonstrated. As he states elsewhere concerning the founding of the Mosaic law, "we can say nothing through demonstration, but we hold it by simple belief apart from reason."[48] This "simple belief" amounts to a kind of fideism, rationally indistinguishable from the fideism of other religions, and it is precisely because it is indistinguishable that Marsilius can consider both Judaism and Christianity as *sectae* along with other *sectae* such as "that of Mohammed or of the Persians." From the perspective of reason, one cannot distinguish between them in regard to truth or falsity.

The problem of distinguishing between true and false revealed religions is made all the more difficult in Marsilius's discussion of Christianity in Book II, one which bears directly on Scripture. Because he does not want to allow any argument that gives power to the Church hierarchy—especially the pope—Marsilius sets forth a kind of pre-Reformation doctrine of *sola scriptura*, asserting that "for salvation it is necessary for us to believe in or to acknowledge the certainty or truth of no statements or writings except those which are called canonic, that is, those which are contained in the

---

46 Marsilius, *Defensor Pacis*, I, 5.14.

47 Ibid., I, 10.3.

48 Ibid., I, 9.2.

volume of the Bible. . . ."[49] By this maneuver, Marsilius hopes to nullify the authority of any and all papal bulls, decretals, and other pronouncements.

But how do we know the "certainty or truth" of the Bible? His only answer is, to say the least, both unsatisfying intellectually and pejorative in tone: "That the holy Scriptures must be firmly believed and acknowledged to be true is assumed as self-evident to all Christians; but since it could be proved only by the authorities of these Scriptures themselves, I have omitted such proof for the sake of brevity." In lieu of this much-needed proof of the truth of Scripture, Marsilius simply intones repeatedly that its alleged divine inspiration "must be piously held,"[50] but the piety is based on a curious circularity. The truth of Scripture is self-evident to those who already take it to be true, so that its truth can be proved as true only from Scripture. As much (or as little) could be said of any believing Moslem and the Koran.

But Marsilius's peculiar doctrine of *sola scriptura* goes far beyond merely wresting authority from the pope. It is carefully designed to serve the merely political end of the *Defensor Pacis*. Spiritual authority resides in the Bible, *not* in the ecclesial hierarchy; yet Marsilius places the authoritative *interpretation* of the Bible ultimately in the hands of the civil legislator, the *legislator humanus*. He argues that the power to interpret doubtful passages of Scripture resides not in the pope or any other bishop, but in a general council, one whose members are ultimately determined by human legislators.[51] The outline of his "plan" for such a council is illuminating.

Marsilius suggests that "all the notable provinces or communities of the world, in accordance with the determination of their human legislators whether one or many . . . elect faithful men, first priests and then non-priests, suitable persons of the most blameless lives and the greatest experience in divine law." These men will represent "the whole body of the faithful by virtue of the authority which these whole bodies have granted to them," and they are "to settle those matters pertaining to divine law which have appeared doubtful, and which it seems useful, expedient, and necessary to define." Their power extends beyond the interpretation of Scripture, to "such other decrees with regard to church ritual or divine worship as will be conducive to the quiet and tranquility of the believers."[52]

Hence the legislator has the ultimate power, since it is he who elects the members of the worldwide council. According to Marsilius, "the legislator . . . is the people or the whole body of citizens, or the weightier part thereof," and it is they who make the laws.[53] Furthermore, it is they who appoint both priests and bishops.[54] The result—and happily so, for Marsilius—is that the papacy can no longer control secular affairs through the appointment of bishops and priests. The power to "invest" ecclesiastical offices is placed firmly in the hands of secular powers.

49 Ibid., II, 28.1. See also II, 19.1.

50 Ibid., II, 19.1–3, 10.

51 Ibid., II, 19.3.

52 Ibid., II, 20.2.

53 Ibid., I, 12.3.

54 Ibid., II, 17.8–9.

Following upon this, no pope (be he Innocent III or John XXII) may quote Scripture to support his aims, for the legislators through their council representatives would determine the meaning of every contested passage. If there is a conflict between the Church and the State, the papacy and the empire, the State will obviously elect representatives who will vote for an interpretation in its favor. And as a safeguard against excommunication, Marsilius also bestows upon the legislators the power to compel a rebellious priest or bishop to administer the sacraments.[55]

By placing the power to determine the meaning of Scripture in the legislator, Marsilius effectively subordinates the interpretation of Scripture to politics, and he vindicates his position by a politicized exegesis. As Gewirth notes, Marsilius proves his position through a quite selective scriptural exegesis. In the early Church (as reported in Acts 6:1–6), Marsilius argues, we find that the Apostles, overburdened with the administration of charity, appealed to the disciples to choose seven men to take over the task of the distribution of alms to widows—and by "disciples," Marsilius argues, the text means the entire number of believers. This proves that the appointment of all ecclesiastical offices "pertains only to the human legislator or the multitude of the believers."[56] In regard to the powers of the priesthood to administer the sacraments, and to bind and loose sins, every priest has these powers equally—as is proved from Luke 22 in which Christ commands all his disciples to offer the Eucharist. "Christ did not address these words to St. Peter more than to the others."[57] As for binding and loosing, John 20:22–23 (where Christ gives the power of forgiving or retaining sins to all the disciples) takes interpretive precedence over Matthew 16:19 (where Christ seems to give the power especially to Peter).[58] That Peter (and hence the Roman pontiff) has no intrinsic superiority is also seen quite clearly, argues Marsilius, from the equal dignity of Paul, who was an "'Apostle, not of men, neither by men, but by Jesus Christ, and God the Father,'" and who further corrected Peter in regard to circumcision (Galatians 1:1–12, 2:6–11; Acts 15).[59] Given that all priests are equally priests, there is no preeminence contained in the office of bishop or pope. On the contrary, they are purely administrative offices, with no coercive power at all.[60] The power to elect priests and bishops, the power to interpret Scripture and define doctrine and worship, and the power to coerce, are all vested in the legislator.

It is no accident that all the passages just quoted are from the New Testament. In order to demonstrate this position from Scripture more securely, Marsilius dismisses the Old Testament as irrelevant on the grounds that with the advent of the New Law, the Old has become obsolete and nonbinding.[61] As with his doctrine of *sola scriptura*, the motivation is entirely political. As Gewirth asserts:

---

55 Ibid., II, 17.12.

56 Ibid., II, 17.9–10.

57 Ibid., II, 16.2.

58 Ibid., II, 15.3.

59 Ibid., II, 16.3–5.

60 Ibid., II, 15.6–7.

61 Ibid., II, 9.10.

> The motivation of this removal [of the Old Testament from consideration] is to be found in the fact that the Old Testament was an outstanding source not only of papal "decretals" but also of papalist arguments: the exercise of judicial functions by Moses, Melchisedech, Samuel, and others was frequently cited as proof that priests were, and should be, kings or superior to kings, by direct appointment of God. In refusing to deal with the Old Testament, Marsilius is thus denying the relevance of one of the primary foundations of the papalist position.[62]

In contrast to the Old Testament, the New Testament provides Marsilius with scriptural ammunition to support the complete obedience of all believers—whether laymen or priests—to the secular power. In perfect harmony with Marsilius's political aims, Christ is said to have handed over full political power to secular authority. According to the Old Law, Moses as priest had coercive powers, but:

> [S]uch commands were not given by Christ in the evangelic law; rather, he took for granted the commands which were or would be given in human laws, and he commanded every human soul to observe these and to obey the men who ruled in accordance with them, at least the commands which were not opposed to the law of eternal salvation. Hence in the twenty-second chapter of Matthew and the eleventh of Mark: "Render unto Caesar the things that are Caesar's," by "Caesar" signifying any rule. So too the Apostle said in the thirteenth chapter of Romans, and it bears repeating: "Let every soul be subject to the higher powers." So too in the first epistle to Timothy, last chapter: "Even to infidel lords". . . . From all these it is quite evident that Christ, the Apostle, and the saints held the view that all men must be subject to the human laws and to the judges according to these laws.[63]

The same political motivation drives Marsilius to reject all allegorical and typological exegesis of Scripture; that is, his Averroist aim even reaches and reformulates the *method* of biblical exegesis. As Marsilius asserts, the papal plenitude of power has often rested upon "certain fictitious and foreign interpretations" of the Bible.[64] In order to make their case, the papalists must stray from the literal interpretation of the text, giving "wandering expositions of Scripture" that are "gladly accepted when such expositions seem to savor of their corrupt opinion and perverted emotions."[65] That is, Marsilius maintains that papalists invoke nonliteral expositions when literal ones do not suit their needs; therefore, all allegorical or typological readings are inherently suspect as being politically motivated. That is not to say that Marsilius never has recourse to a nonliteral meaning of the text, when the literal one would too obviously undermine his secularist purposes. For example, in regard to the "two swords" passage

62 Gewirth, *Marsilius of Padua and Medieval Political Philosophy,* Volume I, pp. 72–73.

63 Marsilius, *Defensor Pacis,* II, 9.9.

64 Ibid., II, 1.3.

65 Ibid., II, 28.24.

used by popes to affirm the papal use of the sword, Marsilius states that "Christ was speaking metaphorically when to his disciples' words, 'Behold, here are two swords,' the Lord replied, 'It is enough.'" And so, rather than taking the two swords passage literally, "it is apparent that Christ's words had [only] a mystical meaning. . . ." This interpretation is confirmed when Christ elsewhere "said to Peter: 'Put up again thy sword into its place,' or, 'into the sheath,' wherein he showed that he had not commanded the Apostles to defend him by such swords, but rather had been speaking mystically."[66] However, such occasional use aside, Marsilius casts a pall of suspicion over nonliteral interpretation—one that will be reinforced in Reformation debates. Obviously, given his arguments as outlined above about the subordination of scriptural interpretation to the legislator, little allowance will be made for deviating from the literal meaning of the text, except when it will serve secularizing political ends.

We must turn to one last aspect of the law and legislators as understood by Marsilius that has indirect, but very important, implications for the politicizing of Scripture. It was a commonplace of medieval political thought prior to Marsilius that unjust laws were not laws at all; that is, the measure of any human law was the Natural Law, one written into human nature itself by the Eternal Law, God Himself.[67] Marsilius deviates—or perhaps better, shifts—from this standard, arguing instead that human law is to be defined not by natural justice but as "a command coercive through punishment or reward to be distributed in the present world . . . considered in this way it most properly is called, and is, a law." Thus, against the notion that an unjust law is no law at all, Marsilius maintains that "sometimes false cognitions of the just and the beneficial become laws," indeed sometimes they are based upon "absolutely unjust" cognitions. But rather than being no laws at all, Marsilius classes them as "not absolutely perfect," for they *do* have the "proper form, that is, a coercive command," even while "they lack a proper condition, that is, the proper and true ordering of justice."[68] As we have seen above, Marsilius has already removed the consideration of divine law and justice from the political realm. Here, he severely qualifies any appeal even to natural standards of law and justice, offering a near prototype (as we shall see in later chapters) of the Machiavellian and Hobbesian notions of law defined as simply whatever the sovereign commands. Precisely because Marsilius has already given the power to interpret Scripture into the hands of the legislator, unbridling the power of the legislator cannot but have ominous implications for the subordination of Scripture to a thoroughly secularized, and even quite brutal, notion of politics.

The Defender of Peace and Ecclesiastical Poverty

The arguments of the *Defensor Pacis* were not intended by Marsilius to remain merely theoretical, as should be clear from Marsilius's influence on Ludwig of Bavaria.

66 Ibid., II, 28.24.

67 See, for example, St. Thomas, *Summa Theologiae*, I–II, 93–95.

68 Marsilius, *Defensor Pacis*, I, 10.4–5.

Marsilius himself participated in Ludwig's Italian expedition of 1327–1328, in his crowning as emperor in St. Peter's on January 16, 1328, his imperial deposition of John XXII on April 18, 1328, in the election of Ludwig's own candidate for pope (Nicholas V), and in the subsequent persecution of John XXII's supporters in Marsilius's capacity as Imperial Vicar. The *Defensor Pacis* was written to be put into action. The papacy must be subordinated to the imperial crown, the sacred to the secular, and no one can doubt Marsilius's decisive influence upon Ludwig's actions during the Italian campaign. But the pope in Avignon was able to muster antagonism to the alien German presence in Rome, and Ludwig found it necessary to withdraw from Rome in the late summer of 1328, making his desultory way back up to Germany, finally reaching it by the end of 1329.

But there were more subtle ways to subordinate the sacred to the secular, and do Ludwig a good turn. One in particular tied Marsilius to William of Ockham—who, himself fleeing persecution, would meet Ludwig while he was still in Italy. Marsilius obviously wished to deprive the popes of their temporal power. The poverty dispute provided an additional argument to help accomplish this. Arguing on behalf of the absolute poverty of Christ and the Apostles through appeal to the New Testament, Marsilius sought to strip the papacy of temporal power so that a secular ruler could establish a purely secular rule.

For Ockham, the same argument for poverty had a much different end, the integrity of the Franciscan charism. Yet the more fervently Ockham argued his case, the stronger the inadvertent support he supplied for Marsilius and his radical politicizing of the Bible. This seemingly symbiotic relationship was actually parasitic.

Marsilius had not met Ockham before writing the *Defensor Pacis*, but most likely learned of the great poverty dispute while he was teaching at Paris, and hence knew of it while writing the *Defensor Pacis*. In line with his political Averroism, Marsilius argued that "Christ separated the office of priest or bishops from that of rulers," and that Christ came "to teach humility and contempt for this world, as the way to deserve eternal salvation." This "utmost humility and contempt for the world" is "poverty," and hence the embrace of poverty is the only way to follow Christ's call to perfection" (as is evidenced in Matthew 19:16–21, Mark 10:17–21, and Luke 18:18–22, where the rich young man is told, if he would be perfect, "sell all that thou hast and distribute unto the poor, and thou shalt have treasure in heaven").[69] This disavowal of all worldly goods and embrace of poverty represents the supreme perfection, and hence is called "supreme poverty."[70] Marsilius provides ample support from Scripture: Luke 14:33 ("so likewise, whosoever he be of you that forsaketh not all that he hath, he cannot by my disciple"[71]); Matthew 6:21 ("Where your treasure is, there will your heart be also"[72]); Matthew 13:22 ("the deceitfulness of riches chokes the word"[73]); Luke 6:20

69 Ibid., II.11.2.
70 Ibid., II.13.22.
71 Ibid., II.13.23.
72 Ibid., II.13.24.
73 Ibid., II.13.24.

("Blessed are the poor"[74]), Luke 9:23 ("If any man will come after me, let him deny himself"[75]); and Matthew 6:34 ("Take therefore no thought for the morrow: for the morrow shall take thought for the things of itself").[76]

Marsilius thereby put John XXII, ensconced at the rich papal court in Avignon, on the defensive: poverty "befits every perfect man, especially the disciple and successor of Christ in the pastoral office; indeed, it is almost necessary for the man who must urge upon others contempt for the world, if he wished to succeed in teaching and preaching."[77] Pope John XXII, the cardinals, and bishops display no such contempt for the world; in fact, to Marsilius and many others, they seemed all too worldly.

> For they who are teachers or pastors of others, and who possess such riches, do more to destroy men's faith and devotion by their contrary deeds and examples than they do to strengthen them by their words. . . . For if the future just judgment of God in the world to come is indeed believed in by most of the Roman pontiffs and their cardinals and the other priests or bishops . . . then by what conscience in accordance with God—let them answer, I beg—do they seize or steal, at every opportunity, all the temporal goods they can, which devout believers have bequeathed for the sustenance of gospel ministers and other poor persons, and donate or bequeath them to their relatives, or to any other persons not in need, obviously despoiling the poor thereby? And again—let them answer, I beg—by what conscience in accordance with the Christian religion do they consume the goods of the poor on so many unnecessary things—horses, estates, banquets, and other vanities and pleasures, open and concealed—when according to the Apostle in the first epistle to Timothy, last chapter, they ought to be content with food and shelter for ministering the gospel.[78]

Rather than following Christ, and in contradiction to the Apostles whose successors they claim to be, "bishops and almost all other priests in modern times practice in almost every instance the opposites of the Gospel teachings whose observance they preach to others. For they have a burning desire for pleasures, vanities, temporal possessions, and secular rulership, and they pursue and attain these objectives with all their energies, not by rightful means, but by wrongdoing, hidden and open."[79] By such words, Marsilius tapped into the widespread (and well-earned) discontent with the all-too-worldly Avignon papacy.

Against the Church hierarchy, and in defense of the Franciscans, Marsilius then argued against John XXII that the embrace of supreme poverty allows for the

---

74 Ibid., II.13.25.

75 Ibid., II.13.27.

76 Ibid., II.13.27.

77 Ibid., II.11.3.

78 "There is great gain in godliness and contentment; for we brought nothing into the world, and we cannot take anything out of the world; but if we have food and clothing, with these we shall be content" (1 Timothy 6:6–8). Marsilius, *Defensor Pacis*, II.11.4.

79 Ibid., II.11.6.

use of temporal goods—even buildings and real estate—and that this use does not entail *ownership*.[80] Since Christ obviously fulfilled supremely his own counsels for perfection,[81] argued Marsilius, then he must have embraced poverty perfectly; yet Christ did make use of things, from the food he ate and the clothes he wore, to the money that Judas was keeping as a common fund;[82] therefore, Christ must have used these things without owning them.[83] And indeed, the use of such things is necessary both for sustenance and for carrying on the exigencies of preaching the Gospel. From this reasoning, "it clearly follows of necessity that it is insane heresy to assert," as John XXII did in his bull *Ad conditorem canonum,* "that a thing or its use cannot be had apart from the aforesaid ownership. For he who says this thinks nothing other than that Christ's counsel [of perfection] cannot be fulfilled; which is an open lie and . . . must be shunned as vicious and heretical."[84]

In arguing against the widespread and widely-known abuses of the Church hierarchy and affirming the Franciscan use-ownership distinction, Marsilius was far more concerned with subordinating the sacred to the secular than with reforming the Church. This is especially clear when Marsilius came to discuss who owns the goods of which the Franciscans claim use but not ownership. We recall that Pope Nicholas III's *Exiit qui seminat* (1279) declared that things given to the Franciscan Order for use could be considered the property of the papacy. Since that would only buttress the power of the papacy, Marsilius asserted instead that "the ownership of temporal things which have been set apart for the support of gospel ministers belongs to the legislators or to deputies appointed for this purpose either by the legislator or by the donors. . . ."[85] (The ripple effect of this assertion will be seen in the chapters on John Wycliffe and Henry VIII.)

Despite the initial success of the Italian campaign, Ludwig and his entourage (including Marsilius) were unable to effect anything so radical as the reduction of the papacy to apostolic poverty. The papacy, secure at Avignon, had no inclination toward Marsilius's demand to divest itself of its royal splendor in imitation of Christ and the Apostles, and even less to hand over its wealth to the imperial coffers. In the decade after Ludwig returned to Germany, Marsilius seemed to fade from view even while Ockham's star was rising. Yet the *Defensor Pacis* was destined to have its historic influence on other kings, as later chapters will show.

William of Ockham

In the same year that Marsilius's *Defensor Pacis* was written, 1324, William of Ockham left England for Avignon, having been summoned by the papal court to answer charges

80 Ibid., II.12.13–16; II.13.3–37.

81 Ibid., II.13.33.

82 Ibid., II.13.34–35.

83 Ibid., II.13.36.

84 Ibid., II.13.6–7.

85 Ibid., II.14.8.

that his writings were heretical (charges made by his fellow Englishmen, especially John Lutterell and Walter Chatton), the principal worries being Ockham's alleged Pelagianism and his Eucharistic theology.[86] About a year after Marsilius entered Rome with Ludwig, the head of the Franciscan Order, Michael of Cesena, also at Avignon, broke into open, heated disagreement with John XXII in regard to the poverty dispute. In May 1328, Michael of Cesena, William of Ockham, and some other Franciscans fled from Avignon to the protection of Ludwig of Bavaria, who was in Pisa at the time, making his way slowly back up the Italian peninsula to Germany. Ockham was excommunicated on June 6, 1328, for leaving Avignon without permission. From Pisa, Michael of Cesena issued appeals to John XXII (which Ockham signed) criticizing the pope's bulls. The pope's response was *Quia vir reprobus*, which simply reaffirmed John XXII's position and accused Michael and his fellow rebellious Franciscans of being heretical. Against John XXII, Ockham would take up his pen, and then soon enough turn to a defense of Ludwig against John as well, to spend his exile in Germany writing polemical treatises against John XXII and his successors, Benedict XII (1334–1342) and Clement VI (1342–1352).

As one might suspect, given that they were together in the court of Ludwig and had a mutual enemy in the papacy, there are connections between Ockham's political arguments and those of Marsilius. Unlike Marsilius, Ockham does not subordinate the ecclesiastical powers to the political powers; rather, he attempts to reinstate, against later papal pretensions, the generally accepted medieval view that the sacred and the secular are two distinct powers. Inadvertent support is given to Marsilius in the *way* that Ockham argues for the distinction, and the force by which he attacks any temporal claims of the papacy.

The Work of Ninety Days

Sometime between 1332 and 1334 Ockham wrote the *Opus nonaginta dierum* (*The Work of Ninety Days*, its title, coming from Ockham having written it in that amount of time[87]). It is an enormous work that, after the manner of disputation, sets out both sides of the argument in the poverty dispute because "all things are examined and tested more effectively and 'truth hardpressed shines more into light' when arguments are strongly and sharply advanced on both sides of a disagreement."[88] The work proceeds as a debate on the text of John's *Quia vir reprobus*. Given the formal neutrality of the

86 See the extensive bibliography in regard to John Lutterell and Walter Chatton in William Courtenay, "The Role of English Thought in the Transformation of University Education in the Late Middle Ages," in James Kittelson and Pamela Transue, *Rebirth, Reform and Resilience: Universities in Transition, 1300–1700* (Columbus, OH: Ohio State University Press, 1984), pp. 146–147, fn 7.

87 In his Epilogue, Ockham states, "This work of ninety days I have completed, although hastily and in a completely undecorated style, yet with much labor." William of Ockham, *The Work of Ninety Days* (2 volumes), translated by John Kilcullen and John Scott (Lewiston, NY: Edwin Mellen Press, 2001), vol. II, Epilogue, p. 848.

88 Ibid., I, Prologue, p. 47.

presentation, Ockham's own opinions do not appear explicitly,[89] even though we are well aware that Ockham took the side of the Michaelists (the followers of Michael of Cesena) against John XXII in the poverty dispute. In this work at least, Ockham's focus is not defending Ludwig against John XXII, but the Franciscan distinction between use and ownership, for to deny this distinction "does destroy and confound every religious order which has a vow renouncing ownership of all temporal things" and "especially destroys and confounds the Order of blessed Francis."[90]

Yet insofar as Ockham presents his case on behalf of the Franciscans against John XXII, he is duplicating and inadvertently reinforcing Marsilius's earlier arguments on behalf of poverty from the *Defensor Pacis,* which Marsilius made in order to support Ludwig and the subordination of the sacred to the secular. Needless to say, much ammunition for Marsilius and Ludwig was supplied by Ockham's charge that, in rescinding the use-ownership distinction affirmed by previous popes, and in declaring that the Apostles did own things, John XXII was a heretic.[91]

Ockham also supplied indirect support for Marsilius's politicization of the Bible. For example, Ockham's use of Matthew 19:21 ("If you wish to be perfect, go, sell all you have, and give to the poor"[92]) or Matthew 8:20 ("Foxes have holes, the birds of the air have nests, but the Son of Man has nowhere to lay his head"[93]) in the service of his defense of poverty lent indirect support to Marsilius's politicized use of these very same passages of the New Testament.

But Ockham provided more direct support as well. Both Ockham and Ludwig wished to strip the papacy of all temporal claims, even though for quite different reasons. Ockham argued quite reasonably that John 18:36 ("My kingdom is not of this world") means that "the kingdom of Christ as man was not a temporal kingdom," and charged John XXII with a distorted interpretation of this passage, "dragging the divine Scripture—most clearly resisting—to his own sense" in order to assert that Christ did indeed have temporal lordship.[94] At first glance, this charge of manipulation is convincing, for John XXII asserted that Christ's statement "My kingdom is not of this world" should be interpreted in light of his immediate clarification to Pilate, "my kingdom is not *from* here [i.e., this world]" (John 18:36). "He did not say, 'It is not here,' but 'It is not from here,' as if to say, 'I do not have my kingdom from the world.'"[95] In short, the papacy's claim to temporal lordship, even over the emperor, comes from heaven, thereby making the pope's claims all the more compelling.

89 In his Epilogue, Ockham remarks, "What I myself think of all these things, however, I will attempt to explain if God grants grace, as far as the poverty of my talent permits for the time, in a certain thorough work upon all the constitutions of his [i.e., the bulls of John XXII] that others have attacked." Ibid., I, Epilogue, p. 849.

90 Ibid., I.8, p. 157.

91 Ibid., I.9, pp. 165–168.

92 Ibid., I.11, 201.

93 Ibid., I.11, p.203.

94 Ibid., II.93, p. 583.

95 Ibid., II.93, pp. 576–577. Emphasis added.

It is easy to suspect, with Ockham, that John XXII is quibbling over words, twisting Scripture to his own dubious ends. But our judgment should be made in light of the larger political and theological context, and significant parts of that context are the arguments of Marsilius and the actions of Ludwig, both aimed at stripping the papacy of all temporal claims so that Christianity would serve the secular realm. Such servitude could not help but politicize the text. This will become startlingly clear, as we shall see, when, two centuries hence, England's Henry VIII will put Marsilius's arguments into action.

A Letter to the Friars

In the spring of 1334, Ockham wrote a far more personal work, the *Epistola ad Fratres Minores in capitulo apud Assisium congregatos* (*A Letter to the Friars Minor Gathered in Chapter at Assisi*), explaining why Michael of Cesena, Ockham himself, and other Franciscans had broken with John XXII—a most serious action, given St. Francis's adamant demand for the Friars' obedience to the papacy. Writing in his own person, Ockham states, "Know, then, and may all Christians know, that I stayed in Avignon almost four whole years before I recognized that the one who presided there had fallen into heretical perversity," and that, upon reading John XXII's arguments, "I found a great many things that were heretical, erroneous, silly, ridiculous, fantastic, insane, and defamatory, contrary and likewise plainly adverse to orthodox faith, good morals, natural reason, certain experience, and fraternal charity," and indeed, that John's arguments were "manifestly heretical."[96] As a result, "I gladly left Avignon to devote myself, in my small measure, to attacking that heretic and his heresies."[97] "For against the errors of this pseudo-pope 'I have set my face like the hardest rock,'" declared Ockham, using the words of the prophet Isaiah (50:7). And before he would ever affirm John's "errors as compatible with the faith, I would think that the whole Christian faith, and all Christ's promises about the Catholic faith lasting to the end of the age, and the whole Church of God, could be preserved in a few, indeed in one. . . ."[98]

A Dialogue: The Birth of the Modern Exegete

Ockham's devotion, under the protection of Ludwig's court, to "attacking that heretic and his heresies," produced several important works during the period from 1334 to 1347, among them *Dialogus (A Dialogue)*, *Octo quaestiones de potestate papae*

96 William of Ockham, *A Letter to the Friars Minor* in William of Ockham, *A Letter to the Friars Minor and Other Writings,* Arthur McGrade and John Kilcullen, ed., and translated by John Kilcullen (Cambridge: Cambridge University Press, 1995), pp. 3–4, 6.

97 Ibid., p. 8.

98 Ibid., p. 13.

(Eight Questions on the Power of the Pope), the *Breviloquium (Short Discourse)*,[99] *De imperatorum et pontificum potestate (On the Power of Emperors and Pontiffs)*, and, interestingly enough, a defense of the English king Edward III (1327–1377) against the papacy, *An Princeps*.[100]

In the *Dialogus*, which takes the form of a dialogue between a student and master and that was influenced directly by Marsilius's arguments,[101] Ockham again presents both sides of the argument,[102] but his own position is easy to discern as he ever more thoroughly undermines the claims of the papacy. Especially notable for both the Reformation and the long-term secularization of the West that would mark the centuries ahead, is Ockham's assertion that

> some believe that all the dissensions, wars, fights, and battles and the destructions and devastations of cities and regions and the countless other evils which have occurred in Italy for many years past, and still do not cease, have resulted from the riches of the Roman Church; it would have been beneficial for the whole Church of God if the Roman Church had in fact and deed imitated the Apostles' poverty and their way of living, putting at a distance all display in respect of vessels, clothes and furnishings generally, guards and every other kind of servant, and all sorts of other things.[103]

In this, Ockham links the scriptural affirmation of poverty to civil peace in such a way that civil peace would seem to be assured if only the religious dispute can be resolved. In doing so, he prefigures the Enlightenment assertion made in the seventeenth and eighteenth centuries that religious dissension was the primary if not the only cause of war and civil discord (a view lent great support by the horrors of the Thirty Years' War).

Unlike Marsilius, Ockham's concern with the temporal power of the pope was not only the ill effects it has on civil peace. Temporal power also magnifies the effects of heresy, and "if a pope became a heretic, especially a pope with temporal

---

99 The full title of the last could hardly be more pointed: *Breviloquium de principatu-tyrannico super divina et humana, specialiter autem super Imperium et subiectos imperio, a quibusdam vocatis summis pontificibus usurpato* (*A Short Discourse on the Tyrannical Government Over Things Divine and Human, but Especially Over the Empire and Those Subject to the Empire, Usurped by Some Who Are Called Highest Pontiffs*.)

100 For an analysis of this latter treatise on behalf of the English king—which was written by Ockham, an Englishman in Munich pining for his homeland about 1338—see Michael Wilks, "Royal Patronage and Anti-Papalism from Ockham to Wyclif," in Anne Hudson and Michael Wilks, *From Ockham to Wyclif* (Oxford: Basil Blackwell, 1987), pp. 135–163.

101 That does not mean, of course, that there was not some friction between Marsilius's and Ockham's arguments. See Garnett, *Marsilius of Padua and "The Truth of History,"* pp. 30–34.

102 "[I]n this tract, as in the whole of the dialogue, we will not say anything except in reporting. . . . In this tract. . . I will not indicate at all which of the reported opinions I think should be approved." William of Ockham, *A Dialogue*, in William of Ockham, *A Letter to the Friars Minor and Other Writings*, Part III, Tract II, Prologue, pp. 236–237.

103 Ibid., III, Tract I, Book 2, Chapter 2 (hereafter, III:I.2.2), p. 130.

power or temporally powerful adherents, it must be feared that he would infect almost all Christians with heretical wickedness."[104] Ockham's zeal to remove temporal power from the papacy was therefore doubled, given his belief that John XXII was indeed a heretic.

Going beyond criticizing John XXII in particular, Ockham offers reasons (quite compatible with Marsilius's call for a general council to rule the Church) that "It is beneficial . . . for the whole congregation of the faithful to be ruled by many," i.e., a general council, "rather than by one," i.e., a pope,[105] and further that "if the Church notices that the Church is ruled perversely or less usefully because of the fact that one by himself [i.e., the pope] rules over all, it is beneficial for it to have power to change such a regime into another that will be more useful for the time."[106]

Of course, the papacy could easily cite Scripture about the primacy of Peter against such a change. But Ockham argues that necessity and utility trump even divine commands found in Scripture. Thus Ockham asserts that

> for the sake of necessity it is permissible to act against a divine commandment, even one that is explicit, in things not evil in themselves but evil only because they are prohibited. Therefore, also, for the sake of the common utility it is permissible to act against a commandment of God and an ordinance of Christ. Therefore, even if Christ had ordained that one highest pontiff should be set over all the faithful, it would be permissible for the faithful, for the sake of common utility, to establish some other regime, at least for the time.[107]

Overriding a divine command has scriptural warrant, maintains Ockham, in the example that Christ himself teaches in Matthew 12:4 and Luke 6:4, wherein "David and those who were with him licitly ate the loaves of offering against a divine commandment, for God explicitly commanded that no one except a priest should eat that bread." This is an important example in regard to Ockham's situation. Implied here, was the power of a king to override the authority of a priest in cases of necessity, a scriptural lesson not lost on Ludwig.

To drive home the point Ockham points out that King David himself "appointed several highest pontiffs" (I Chronicles 24:5).[108] In his own time, this would entail a change, effected by the emperor, of the Church from a monarchy to an aristocracy (as manifested in the council). This change would not be done lightly, but is called for because of the extraordinary need for reforming the Church, for "there is one rule of living in a time of peace and another in a time of persecution," so that similarly, "notwithstanding Christ's commandment, there is one rule of living in a case of necessity and utility and another outside the case of necessity and utility. . . ."[109]

---

104 Ibid., III:I.2.30, p. 206.
105 Ibid., III:I.2.2, p.131.
106 Ibid., III:I.2.20, p. 173.
107 Ibid., III:I.2.20, p. 176.
108 Ibid., III:I.2.20, p. 177.
109 Ibid., III:I.2.22, p. 183.

Yet even a general council is not immune from error: it "can begin with a bad beginning . . . since the pope can sin and be damned and can err against the faith with a bad and corrupt purpose—indeed, he can assemble a general council with the purpose of defining something contrary to Catholic truth. . . ."[110] More important for our purposes, a council's decisions may or may not be properly guided by Scripture. Councils "have decided questions of faith arising out of the Scriptures by means of the sacred Scriptures." In doing so, "those present in a general council . . . rely on human wisdom and virtue, because they rely on the expertise concerning the Scriptures that they have and can have by careful thought. But error can be found in all things that rely on human wisdom and virtue; therefore members of a general council can err in deciding a question of faith."[111]

This brings Ockham to examine the question of scriptural interpretation, the "power to interpret a commandment of God or of Christ."[112] Here Ockham makes a decisive move; in light of the later history of scriptural scholarship, a seismic shift. He appeals to the authority of the experts (*periti*) over the papacy and Church councils (or for that matter, over the entire *traditio*).

Interpretation is necessary, argues Ockham, when words are *ambigua* (doubtful, ambiguous, uncertain). "Interpretation therefore pertains to anyone who knows the true meaning of what has to be interpreted" (*qui scit verum intellectum illius quod interpretandum est*).[113] Ockam asserts:

> But many experts [*multi . . . periti*] know the true meaning [*verum intellectum*] of the commandments of God and Christ. They can interpret those commandments to those who do not know, because such interpretation is nothing but an exposition, clarification, or making manifest of the true meaning of God's commandments [*nisi expositio vel declaratio seu manifestatio veri intellectus preceptorum Dei*]. And thus Christians have power [*potestatem*] sometimes to interpret a divine commandment, namely when they know its true meaning [*verum intellectum*].[114]

The "Christian experts" (*Christiani periti*) are empowered to interpret such commands and ordinances—including those in regard to the status of poverty and about appointing the pontiff—because interpretation is not a matter of office, divine sanction, charism, or tradition, but "can be known through reasoning and the Scriptures" (*sciri potest per rationem et Scripturas*).[115] Although he may intend it, Ockham makes no specific mention of conformity with doctrine or of the personal holiness of the *periti*. Expertise is sufficient authority alone.

---

110 Ibid., III:I.3.8, p. 211.

111 Ibid., III:I.3.8, p. 210.

112 Ibid., III:I.2.24, p. 185.

113 Ibid., III:I.2.24, p. 186.

114 Ibid., III:I.2.24, p. 186.

115 Ibid., III:I.2.24, pp. 186–187.

Ockham does not leave the reader in doubt that the authority of the *periti* can override that of the pope because it is they who properly interpret the meaning of Scripture:

> [I]t is not permissible for the pope to interpret the words of God or Christ otherwise than it is for another, nor do we have to believe him in such matters more than any other wise man—indeed, in such matters those more expert than the pope [*magis periti quam papa*] should be preferred to the pope himself . . . [so that] in explaining the divine Scriptures those who treat of the divine Scriptures are preferred to the highest pontiffs [*quod divinarum scripturarum tractatores in sacrarum scripturarum expositionibus summis pontificibus preferuntur*].[116]

The councils fare no better against the experts. Like popes, councils have no guarantee keeping them free from error. Thus they too must be judged according to their Catholicity and that means according to Scripture. But the appeal to Scripture, for Ockham, is really an appeal to the experts:

> If it is asked who is to judge whether they [the general councils] were held in a Catholic way, it is answered that because they did not define anything except what can be drawn out from the divine Scriptures [*quod potest elici ex scripturis divinis*], therefore it is for experts in the Scriptures [*periti in scripturis*], and those having sufficient understanding of the other written sources [*aliarum sufficientem intelligentiam scripturarum*], to judge in the manner of firm assertion that the things defined by them are defined in a Catholic way.[117]

While the appeal to Scripture may seem to some, especially non-Catholics, both innocent and obvious, Ockham's particular mode of making it represents an immense shift of authority, one that, in many respects, is far greater and far more modern than the turn to *sola scriptura* of the Reformation. The shift of authority is not from the pope and council to the text itself, but from the pope and council to the *expert* in interpreting the text.

Herein lie the first awakenings of the modern biblical exegete. In regard to the order of authority, we are far closer in these passages to the nineteenth- and twentieth-century understanding of the role of the professional scriptural scholar than we are to the sixteenth-century attempt to root authority in the biblical text as against the papacy. The "expert" stands in authoritative judgment not just above Church councils and the papacy, but also above the inexpert who are the vast majority of the faithful. He even stands above the text itself, insofar as it is *his* expertise that unlocks its definitive meaning.

Of course, it was not Ockham's intention to create the modern academic exegete—although one must add that, as is clear from reading his works, Ockham was a

116 Ibid., III:I.2.24, p. 187.

117 Ibid., III:I.3.9, p. 213.

thoroughgoing academic, a man of the university. But we can see the importance of attending to the larger political context for understanding the rise of modern biblical scholarship: it was Ockham's wranglings with the papacy, and the consequent disagreements concerning scriptural interpretations of poverty and Petrine authority, that brought him to elevate the exegetical expert to a position of authority characteristic of later modern biblical scholarship. We must now turn to another important aspect of Ockham, his highly influential approach to philosophy that helped put the "modern" in modern philosophy, thereby creating the intellectual context for historical-critical scholarship.

Ockham's Nominalism?

In regard to philosophy, William of Ockham is most famous for denying the reality of universals. That is, he argued that when we utter the quite ordinary sentence "That sheep is good natured" or the more philosophical "Socrates is a man," the words "sheep" and "man" do not refer to any reality *inside* or *outside* that particular sheep or Socrates. In other words, according to Ockham, the species name, the universal noun, has no foundation in nature. In nature there are only particulars.

If such universals are not in nature, from whence do they come? The notion of universals arises because we human beings class together particular things that *appear* to be similar to each other. Based upon this appearance of similarity, Ockham argued, the abstracting intelligence creates general concepts that are then reflected in the universal names "sheep" and "man." Since these universal terms are not rooted directly in reality, but are really only names, Ockham's philosophical position was later given the name nominalism (from the Latin *nomen*, name).[118] This way of approaching philosophy would become known by the fifteenth century as the *via moderna*, and would be self-consciously defined against another approach, the *via antiqua* associated most famously with the realist philosophy of St. Thomas. Adherents of the two schools were also known (respectively) as the *nominales* or *moderni* and the *reales*.[119]

118 According to Marilyn Adams, "Ockham regarded the view that universals are real things other than names as 'the worst error of philosophy.'" Marilyn McCord Adams, *William Ockham*, Vol. I, (Notre Dame: University of Notre Dame Press, 1987), p. 13.

119 This terminology can sometimes generate more confusion than clarity. First of all, as has been pointed out by others, the appellations are relative even during the later Middle Ages, wherein the use often depended on what a particular person thought was original and venerable, and what an innovation and hence modern. Ockham believed that he was restoring the truth against the innovations of the radical Aristotelians, yet he is taken to be the founder of nominalism, the school of thought that scholars now agree defines the *via moderna*. See Heiko A. Oberman, "*Via Antiqua* and *Via Moderna*: Late Medieval Prolegomena to Early Reformation Thought," in Oberman, *The Impact of the Reformation* (Grand Rapids, MI: William B. Eerdmans Publishing Company, 1994). Following upon this, the *via antiqua* obviously does not represent the united front of all ancient thinkers (it includes Aristotle but certainly not Democritus, Epicurus, or the Pyrrhonists) nor is it truly defined in terms of antiquity, since the most eminent proponents of the *via antiqua* were St. Albert and St. Thomas Aquinas. The terms are best understood in regard to their respective intellectual assumptions and methods, rather than relative age.

Such is the standard picture of Ockham and his influence, which, under intense scrutiny by scholars, has become more and more blurred (or at least stands in need of further clarification). To begin with, while it is clear that Ockham denied the extra-mental reality of universals, he did not regard them as purely fictional (in a way that we find later in Hobbes). Is Ockham, then, really a nominalist?

In regard to nominalism as a school, scholars have uncovered a surprising and daunting diversity in the century and a half after Ockham of those who may be classed as nominalists,[120] but depending on the criteria used, the lines of descent from Ockham have been drawn, erased, and redrawn so variously that the picture has become less and less distinct.[121] Given this, some have even despaired of using the term "nominalist" at all (as if to vindicate the nominalist disparagement of universals and affirm the existence of sheer intellectual particularity). Some have whittled down the number of true nominalists to a handful, excluding Ockham himself! To this development in scholarship, Charles T. Davis whimsically replied, "There is a certain irony in the fact that nominalism, the great dissolvent, is being dissolved itself."[122] Even more ironically, this dissolution would seem to shrink Ockham's signal contribution to philosophy

---

We may take them, then, as they come to be defined in the 1400s, as distinct schools of thought, the *via antiqua* identified principally with St. Albert Magnus, St. Thomas Aquinas, and Giles of Rome, and the *via moderna* identified most eminently with Ockham, but also Jean Buridan, Marsilius of Inghen, and others of similar approach. Nor would we want to read back into this controversy, the later ancients versus moderns, Aristotelians versus anti-Aristotelians, debates. Both the *via antiqua* and *via moderna* in the fifteenth century were largely defined by their respective approaches to reading Aristotle, each school having "its preferred reading of the *corpus aristotelicum*." The debate was largely over which side was properly interpreting Aristotle, or perhaps more accurately, which interpretation of Aristotle was in accordance with the faith. See Maarten J.F.M. Hoenen, "*Via Antiqua* and *Via Moderna* in the Fifteenth Century: Doctrinal, Institutional, and Church Political Factors in the *Wegestreit*," in Russell Friedman and Lauge Nielsen, *The Medieval Heritage in Early Modern Metaphysics and Modal Theory, 1400–1700* (Dordrecht: Kluwer Academic Publishers, 2003), pp. 11, 13–16. See also William Courtenay, "The Academic and Intellectual Worlds of Ockham," in Paul Vincent Spade, ed., *The Cambridge Companion to Ockham* (Cambridge: Cambridge University Press, 1999), especially pp. 28–29. For clarification of when the terms came to be applied with determinate consistency, see Neal Ward Gilbert, "Ockham, Wyclif, and the '*Via Moderna*,'" in Albert Zimmermann, ed., *Antiqui und Moderni: Traditionsbewußtsein und Fortschrittsbewußtsein im späten Mittelalter* (Berlin: Walter De Gruyter, 1974), pp. 85–125. For an insightful history of contemporary attempts to define the *via moderna*, see John Bossy, "Met on the *Via Moderna*," in Peter Biller and Barrie Dobson, *The Medieval Church: Universities, Heresy, and the Religious Life: Essays in Honour of Gordon Leff* (Woodbridge, Suffolk: The Boydell Press, 1999), pp. 309–324.

120 For an assessment of the difficulties see Alister McGrath, *The Intellectual Origins of the European Reformation* (Grand Rapids, MI: Baker, 1993), pp. 70–75; William J. Courtenay, "Nominalism and Late Medieval Religion," in Charles Trinkaus and Heiko Oberman, *The Pursuit of Holiness in Late Medieval and Renaissance Religion* (Leiden: Brill, 1974), pp. 26–59.

121 For a good introduction to the difficulties inherent in the diverse approaches to tracing Ockham's influence see William Courtenay, "Was There an Ockhamist School?" in Maarten Hoenen, J. J. Josef Schneider, and Georg Wieland, eds., *Philosophy and Learning: Universities in the Middle Ages* (Leiden: Brill, 1995), pp. 263–292.

122 Charles T. Davis, "Ockham and the Zeitgeist," in Trinkaus and Oberman, *The Pursuit of Holiness in Late Medieval and Renaissance Religion*, pp. 59–65; quote from p. 60.

considerably, and hence undermine in important respects the very attention scholars have lavished upon him and as well as upon nominalism.[123] Such are the confusions

123 To give an example, William Courtenay has done as much as Heiko Oberman to rehabilitate Ockham, and notes that the result of the combined research of Erich Hochstetter, Paul Vignaux, Philotheus Boehner, Ernest Moody, and Oberman himself "has been to establish the orthodox, non-radical character of the thought of Ockham and [Gabriel] Biel, and, by extension, [Pierre] d'Ailly," as opposed to the radical nominalism of Robert Holcot, Adam Wodeham, Nicholas of Autrecourt, and John of Mirecourt. But he then argues that recent research has also found that even the radical nominalists weren't radical nominalists, and in fact Nicholas of Autrecourt may be the only true nominalist left—although that may be due to scantiness of texts. See Courtenay, "Nominalism and Late Medieval Religion," pp. 50, 54–57. He also notes the semi-Pelagianism of Ockham's soteriology, citing Oberman as source, as if semi-Pelagianism is somehow within the domain of orthodoxy. But Boehner states—seemingly to the contrary of the near-dissolution of nominalism under scholarly scrutiny—that Ockham's nominalism was epoch-making: "Almost all his predecessors had maintained that natures and essences considered in themselves had some kind of generality or commonness; in order to become numerical units or individuals or singulars, natures had to be individualized by a principle of individuation. Ockham's predecessors had thus approached this problem from the side of the universal; Ockham attacked it from the side of the individual; a change of outlook almost as epoch-making as the Copernican revolution in astronomy." See Philotheus Boehner, O.F.M., *Ockham: Philosophical Writings* (Indianapolis, IN: Hackett, 1990), p. xxvii. If it was indeed epoch-making, then it should not dissolve under scholarly scrutiny. Yet Alister McGrath cites Boehner's account of Ockham's epistemology (which Boehner denotes "realistic conceptualism") as vindication that ascribing nominalism to Ockham is "an anachronism." See Philotheus Boehner, O.F.M, "The Realistic Conceptualism of William Ockham," in E. M. Buytaert, *Philotheus Boehner, O.F.M., Ph.D.: Collected Articles on Ockham* (St. Bonaventure, NY: The Franciscan Institute, 1958), pp. 156–174, and McGrath, *The Intellectual Origins of the European Reformation*, pp. 71–72. One is left to wonder: If Ockham's contribution was epoch-making, and it was not nominalistic, what was the Copernican revolution he initiated? Boehner himself is not clear. He argues that Ockham inspired not so much disciples as followers of a general trend called nominalism, united not around Ockham himself but "united at least against the realism of the older scholastics." And this loose band, united by opposition to realism, are rightly called proponents of the *via moderna*, "not so much a school as a trend of thought." See Boehner, O.F.M., *Ockham: Philosophical Writings*, p. li. But then it would seem odd of Boehner to think Ockham's thought epoch-making and also call Ockham's epistemology "*realistic* conceptualism." Boehner's explanation of this designation is as follows. It is conceptualism because of Ockham's "affirmation of universals in the mind and by the denial of any universality outside the mind," but it is realism because of Ockham's "affirmation of a correspondence or similarity between concepts and reality . . ." See Boehner, O.F.M, "The Realistic Conceptualism of William Ockham," p. 163. Assuming its accuracy, Boehner's Ockham reminds one of something like the modern idealism of Fichte or Kant: Universals are not in things, nor are they fictions in the imagination; rather, "the concept or universal involved in a cognition is identical with the very act of abstractive cognition, hence it is a psychical entity . . ." See Boehner, O.F.M., *Ockham: Philosophical Writings*, pp. xxviii–xxix. Boehner vehemently denies that this is "idealism" in his "The Realistic Conceptualism of William Ockham," on the grounds that idealism demands a divorce of thought from reality. But in calling it idealism, we are indicating the similarity to, e.g., Kant in affirming that universals are derived from the mind's mode of knowing rather than from things, for while the similarity existing in individuals is real, and we have, argues Ockham, a true intellectual knowledge of the singular (*notitia intuitive intellective*), the universality still comes from the mind directly. It is on the basis of Ockham's affirmation of the intellectual, intuitive knowledge of the singular that brings Boehner to deny that Ockham is really an idealist. It is interesting to note that Ockham himself made two attempts at the formulation of universals. The original formulation of the status of universals, the so-called *fictum* theory, assumed that universals were in the imagination rather than in the intellect. In the revised theory, the *intellectio*-theory, they are in the intellect. According to Boehner, there was a greater dissimilitude between things

of scholarship. Perhaps the best way to sort things out would be to take another tack, and focus on the theological reasons for Ockham's assertions.

God's Absolute and Ordained Power

Given the effect of nominalism upon later philosophy, it would be reasonable to assume that Ockham's rejection of the reality of universals, of common natures, was at heart philosophical. But strange as it may sound, Ockham's philosophical nominalism was at heart theological. Ockham rejected the reality of universals because he believed that those who asserted their reality were somehow binding God's omnipotence to His creation. This notion of binding of God's omnipotence had two related sources in the Middle Ages, Islam and Averroism.

To set things out in the most general way, earlier Islamic thinkers (oddly enough, somewhat like Ockham) had desired to assert the fullest sense of God's omnipotence, and argued that God *immediately* caused the physical order to be the way it was, re-creating and sustaining it at every moment with no causal connections in time at all. They relied on a particular atomistic view of nature to sustain this theological view of God's absolute omnipotence, since they could imagine that things being made of atoms—created in particular configurations on the spot, so to speak—would eliminate the notion that common natures (i.e., universals like dog, cat, sheep, etc.) existed over time. Their reasoning: such common natures, if allowed to exist, would themselves provide the structure and continuity of reality, rather than having reality directly and continually depending upon God.

Against this view, Islamic thinkers—the most prominent being Avicenna (980–1037) and especially Averroes (1126–1198)—argued that God is bound to the order of creation (as elucidated by Aristotle), and so does not act like a kind of oriental tyrant in regard to natural things.[124] As we said above, on the Christian side of things those

---

and universals as *ficta* than things and universals as concepts in the intellect. Even so, Boehner makes the curious statement that in the "*intellectio*-theory . . . universals are real beings (that is real accidents of the mind)" and so this grants "more similarity between concept and reality. . . ." See Boehner, O.F.M, "The Realistic Conceptualism of William Ockham," pp. 162, 169–174. Marilyn Adams uses the earlier and later theories as "objective-existence theory" and the "mental-act theory," which undoubtedly confuses most readers, given that we associate "objective" with real. But for Ockham, the nonreal mode of existence is called "objective." See Marilyn McCord Adams, *William Ockham*, Vol. I, pp. 73–75. It would seem that the universal had its origin in the *name* that we give to our abstractive cognition, a cognition that has its origin in the mind's comparison of similarities of individuals. As Boehner states, "Universality, therefore, is simply a manner in which a sufficiently generalised abstractive cognition is predicable, and thus it exists wholly within the mind. On the side of the individuals that are known, there exists only individuality and the similarity of individual natures." See Boehner, O.F.M., *Ockham: Philosophical Writings*, p. xxviii. But this fits the classic definition of nominalism well enough to wonder why we should join McGrath in thinking that ascribing nominalism to Ockham is "an anachronism." We seem to be back at our starting point, with the standard definition of nominalism.

124 E. Grant, "Science and Theology in the Midle Ages," in D. C. Lindberg and R. L. Numbers (Hgg.), *God and Nature: Historical Essays on the Encounter between Christianity and Science* (Berkeley/Los Angeles/London 1986), pp. 49–113; "The Condemnation of 1277: God's Absolute Power and Physical Thought in

later Islamic thinkers informed the West's incorporation of the philosophy of Aristotle. For some, the Aristotelian approach was so lucid that they began to place the philosophy of Aristotle (as mediated especially through the commentaries of Averroes) above revealed truth.

Such an elevation of the philosophy of a pagan above the revelation of Christ raised Ockham's ire to defend the omnipotence of God against *any* philosophical attempts to mitigate His absolute will. For Ockham, any binding of God's will was an unconscionable violation of God's sovereignty and a direct contradiction to His omnipotence (*potentia Dei absoluta*). Ockham hoped to deny the "Greco-Arabian necessitarianism"[125] (to use William Courtenay's phrase) of Averroism by asserting that universals were merely names. If universals were actually in things, then not only would creation be determined by them, but also it would seem that God's actions as creator would be restricted by their existence and necessary relationships. Against this, Ockham argued that nature as it presents itself to us is merely one among the infinite number of possible expressions of God's creative will and power, and that God's power itself is so absolute that it is bound by nothing at all except the principle of noncontradiction. Thus, nature as it *happens* to be is entirely contingent, ordained by God as one among countless possibilities, although once God has so determined the order—expressed as His *potentia ordinata*—he binds Himself to that decision in a kind of covenant (*pactum*). For Ockham, the same reasoning applied to the *ordinata* of redemption. God could save by any means according to his *potentia absoluta*. Christ could be incarnated as a stone, a block of wood, or even an ass, or more importantly, God could justify sinners directly without creating any specific habit in the individual. [126] But in both cases, God has indeed chosen a particular *ordinata*.[127]

Ockham's position had important implications. Since ultimately nothing can be read from nature (which was merely a particular expression of God's power) about His actual, inscrutable nature defined by His absolute power, then there could be no philosophical climbing from the contingent creation to an understanding of any necessary metaphysical principles or to God Himself. The only real connection that can be made is from the side of God, through revelation, and even here God's power is absolute and His ways ultimately inscrutable. He could have ordained any number of ways for our salvation as long as they weren't self-contradictory. Thus, the supernatural does not presuppose and build upon the natural; rather, the two are radically separate. The long-term tendency will be to make philosophy entirely independent of the truths

the Late Middle Ages" *Viator* 10 (1979), pp. 211–244. Cf. also D. Perler and U. Rudolph, *Occasionalismus: Theorien der Kausalität im arabisch-islamischen und im europäischen Denken* (Göttingen: 2000).

125 Courtenay, "Nominalism and Late Medieval Religion," pp. 40–41.

126 Alister McGrath, *The Intellectual Origins of the European Reformation* pp. 21, 79–80.

127 It is important to understand that Ockham affirms that this distinction between the *potentia absoluta* and *potentia ordinata* does not mean that there are in God two actual, distinct powers. The distinction is one in our intellect, in conceiving the difference between what God has in fact ordained, and what He could do (anything that is not contradictory). See Armand Maurer, *The Philosophy of William of Ockham in the Light of Its Principles* (Toronto: Pontifical Institute of Mediaeval Studies, 1999), pp. 257–259, 265.

of revelation, and the truths of revelation themselves to be understood fideistically. Both tendencies reinforce Marsilian thought. Philosophy supports the secular order as the independent authority in natural affairs, and defines reason entirely since faith is entirely above reason. But in so radically disassociating supernatural revelation from creation, Ockham's thought tends toward faith understood as irrational fideism—exactly the assessment of Averroes and Marsilius. Ockham's argument seems to imply that about revelation (to reuse a quote from Marsilius) "we can say nothing through demonstration, but we hold it by simple belief apart from reason."

Ockham's philosophical revolution would also have long-term effects that are essential to grasp for what will occur later in regard to modern scriptural scholarship. First, it sets up for a law-based understanding of the cosmos that will eventually yield a natural philosophy in which the miraculous is impossible. How this happened is rather complex.

For Ockham, philosophy grasps only the contingent order of creation. Therefore, of the three greatest theoretical sciences as enumerated by Aristotle—metaphysics, mathematics, and physics—Ockham's analysis severely deflates the pretensions of two, metaphysics and physics, leaving only mathematics unscathed (an important result, we shall see, in regard to the development of modern science). In their stead, Ockham (albeit unintentionally) raised the merely instrumental science of logic, the tool by which we examine what is or is not self-contradictory. Some reflection will be necessary to bring out the implications.

In rejecting universals, nominalism rejected Aristotelian forms, and this rejection, we recall, was theological at root. The forms, even understood as ideas in the Divine Mind, seemed to Ockham to limit God's will. But the elimination of forms left reality as a collection of essentially unrelated particulars, each of which, presumably, could then be an object of empirical scrutiny.[128] Yet empirical examination of sheer particularity as such is notably difficult. The human mind understands more by similarity than difference. Rather than being left with an intractable mass of particulars, natural philosophers such as Galileo, Descartes, and Newton would substitute mathematical forms as the new universals, the ideal forms that define the shape and activity of passive or inert matter. For most theologians in the seventeenth century, these mathematical forms were taken to be impressed by God according to His will; they were the "forms" of His commands, or laws, of nature. Since for these theologians the laws had their origin in God's will, the laws could be otherwise, and so, presumably, would the mathematical forms they took.[129] But again, the theological belief in the ultimate contingency of the laws was short-lived. Within a century, the inner necessity of

128 In Francis Oakley's words, "The tendency [of the *via moderna*] . . . was to set God over against the world he had created and which was constantly dependent upon him; to view it now as an aggregation of particular entities linked solely by external relations, comprehensible . . . each in isolation from others, and, as a result, open to investigation only by some form of empirical endeavor." See Francis Oakley, *Natural Law, Laws of Nature, Natural Rights: Continuity and Discontinuity in the History of Ideas* (New York: Continuum, 2005), p. 53.

129 See Francis Oakley, "Christian Theology and the Newtonian Science: The Rise of the Concept of the Laws of Nature," *Church History* (1961), Vol. 30, pp. 433–457 (especially pp. 436–437).

mathematics was identified with the laws of nature, and nature came to be governed by its own laws, the result being that the "necessitarianism" of mathematics drove out the possibility of divine action (and soon enough, the Divine).

Again, we must be careful about what charge we lay against Ockham. Ockham's denial of universals allowed for, but did not of itself cause, the replacement of Aristotelian forms with mathematical forms. The most accurate characterization might be that Ockham's nominalism left a vacuum that would be filled by another kind of universal. If the modern account of the laws of nature did indeed have its origin in Ockham's desire to safeguard God's omnipotent will,[130] these laws would soon enough break away from the will of God (in the late eighteenth and nineteenth centuries), and come to be considered self-subsisting causal powers that either limited or excluded divine action. One can hardly downplay the importance of this development for the judgment of nineteenth-century German scriptural scholars that the miraculous had to be excised from Scripture or be reduced to the mythological.

It is also fair to say that Ockham's denial of universals led to, or at least contributed to, a kind of reductionism in physics that favored materialism, another important development for setting the context of the development of modern scriptural scholarship. While Ockham seems to have remained something of an Aristotelian, he qualified it in such a way as to support the development of atomism.[131] In addition, insofar as nominalism focused on particularity as the source of intelligibility, it would lend itself to the notion that particular parts are more essential than wholes. As will become apparent in later chapters, the acceptance of a reductionist mode of science will lead (by imitation) to an exegetical focus on the parts of the text at the expense of the whole. Further, the materialist assumptions of modern science will cause spiritual aspects of the biblical text to become more and more suspect. Again, Ockham did not cause these developments directly, but he did prepare the way for them.

There is another related and important effect of Ockham's philosophical-theological arguments. As should be clear, much of Ockham's analysis depends upon the

---

130 We might call this the Oberman-Oakley thesis, after two of its most significant recent proponents, Heiko Oberman and Francis Oakley. See the already-mentioned works by Oakley, and the works by Oberman mentioned below. As Peter Harrison has pointed out in some detail, there are other significant problems with Oberman-Oakley thesis about the relationship of Ockham's nominalism and voluntarism to modern science. See Peter Harrison, "Voluntarism and Early Modern Science," *History of Science* 40 (2002), pp. 63–89. While it has some merit—more, we think, than Harrison seems to indicate—there are serious flaws and oversimplifications. As a generalization, it seems safest and most accurate to say that Ockham prepared the way for later developments, but other contributing factors must be taken into account. The pertinent question, of course, is how all this bears on our understanding of modern scriptural scholarship.

131 See André Goddu, "Ockham's Philosophy of Nature," in Paul Vincent Spade, *The Cambridge Companion to Ockham* (Cambridge: Cambridge University Press, 1999), pp. 143–167. The more radical nominalist Nicholas of Autrecourt (1300–1350) soon made the implicit sympathy to atomism explicit. This is all the more interesting because he did it through a revival of atomism as found in Democritus and Epicurus. It was more likely his association with Epicurus, rather than nominalism, that brought about the condemnation of his writings. See Bernard Pullman, *The Atom in the History of Human Thought* (Oxford: Oxford University Press, 1998), pp. 99–100.

distinction between God's *potentia absoluta* and the merely contingent expression of God's *potentia ordinata*. In the expression of God's *potentia ordinata* in nature we are faced with a myriad of particulars, and there is no way, through analysis, to reach beyond the created effect to the metaphysical cause, God. There is no *analogy of being* connecting creator and creature.[132] This will contribute to the displacement of typo-

---

132 More recent assessments of nominalism, especially by Heiko Oberman, have counted this as a gain. For Oberman, the old Thomistic charge that nominalism introduced an arbitrary God defined by an untethered will, misreads the distinction intended between the *potentia absoluta* and *ordinata*. "As far as the fourteenth-century intention of the distinction between the *potentia absoluta* and the *potentia ordinata* is concerned, there exists a firm scholarly consensus: it marks the voluntary self-limitation of the omnipotent God and hence the non-necessary contingent nature of the established order of creation and redemption. The older view of the nominalist God as the arbitrary tyrant by whose whim the present order can be suddenly overturned seemed discredited once and for all." See Oberman, "*Via Antiqua* and *Via Moderna*: Late Medieval Prolegomena to Early Reformation Thought," in Oberman, *Impact of the Reformation*, p. 20. For Oberman, nominalism of the *via moderna* is a boon for the development of modern science, for it "not only intended to establish the contingency of the created order but also to free physics from the embrace of metaphysics so as to allow the investigation of the world by means of reason and experience." See Oberman, "*Via Antiqua* and *Via Moderna*: Late Medieval Prolegomena to Early Reformation Thought," p. 11. Oberman would seem to tie this boon to the destruction of analogy, and his words are worth quoting at length because the issues presented are central to the analysis of the present book.

> If God is no longer tied to creation by "deterministic" causation but related to it by volition, that is, by his personal decision, then all metaphysical arguments based on necessary causal links—as is indeed typical of the cosmology of Aristotole and the *via antiqua* of Aquinas—lose their cogency, if not their credibility. The actual situation is the exact reverse of what the modern critics of nominalism argue: it is not God who is arbitrary but rather human beings in their explanations of problems in natural philosophy, when these are not tested and supported by experience and experiment. . . .
>
> In theology a parallel advance is achieved. Whereas in the realm of natural philosophy physics is freed from the shackles of metaphysics, in the realm of theology metaphysics is shown to be sheer speculation when not verifiable in God's self-revelation, which for the later Middle Ages means Scripture and tradition. If there does not exist a metaphysically necessary ladder along which the first cause has to "connect with" the second cause, the laws of nature can be derived no longer from illuminating the physical world from "above," but from this world itself. The same applies to theology, but vice versa. The truth about God can no longer be derived from "below": the second causality does not erect a Jacob's ladder which allows us to transcend the natural phenomena by reasoning back to the first cause, God. Not the reliability but the predictability of the established order is in doubt.

Oberman, "*Via Antiqua* and *Via Moderna*: Late Medieval Prolegomena to Early Reformation Thought," pp. 10–11. See also his "Luther and the *Via Moderna*: The Philosophical Backdrop of the Reformation Breakthrough," contained in Oberman, *The Two Reformations: The Journey from the Last Days to the New World* (New Haven: Yale University Press, 2003), especially pp. 22–23, 27, 33. While no one can gainsay the important work that Oberman has done to deepen and clarify our understanding of nominalism, one can take significant issue with parts of his analysis. To begin, we should distinguish between "Greco-Arabian necessitarianism" (to use Courtenay's phrase again) such as one would find in Averroism and the doctrine of the analogy of being as found in Aquinas. Averroism displaced revelation by exalting Aristotelian philosophy, so that the God of revelation had to conform to the god of philosophy as understood through a particular reading of the Peripatetic, one that was, arguably, designed to render revelation innocuous. But to conflate Averroism with Thomism in this regard is

logical, allegorical scriptural interpretation, a more profound displacement than may at first appear.

For St. Thomas,[133] since universal names do refer to the universal forms in real things, there is a real relationship when we signify a thing by a word. This bears an *analogy* to the Divine relationship of word and thing in regard to the biblical text, even while the Divine relationship remains qualitatively superior: "The author of Holy Writ is God, in whose power it is to signify His meaning, not by words only (as men can do) but also by things themselves," so that "the things signified by the words have themselves also a signification."[134] Thus, for St. Thomas, "the things signified by the words can be themselves *types* of other things."[135] Such was the foundation of biblical typology.

This distinction between the way human beings and God can signify allowed for the twofold distinction between the literal and the spiritual sense: the "first signification whereby words signify things belongs to the first sense, the historical or literal"; and the second "signification whereby things signified by words have themselves also a signification is called the spiritual sense, which is based on the literal, and presupposes it." (St. Thomas, following St. Augustine, maintained that "allegory . . . stands for the three spiritual senses."[136])

Both human beings and God can signify according to the historical or literal sense, but only God, properly speaking, can signify in the spiritual sense for only He can create real things that signify other things. The spiritual sense is, therefore, ontologically rooted. As Peter Harrison notes, it was this "representative power of natural objects" that allowed things, in allegory, to stand for other things, and "provided the world with its intelligibility."[137] God wrote allegories into creation itself before He wrote them into the Bible; the allegorizing of the biblical exegete had divine mandate.

Nominalism first of all severed the real connection between universal names and things, because it severed the real connection between the similar appearance of natural kinds and the actual species-universal in things (which God uses to signify other things, e.g., the nature of lion as a species, and not just a particular thing we happen to call lion by its appearance of similarity). Moreover, nominalism's rejection of the doctrine of analogy and its affirmation of the created order as completely contingent meant that *natural* things do not bear inherent spiritual meanings directing the human

---

much the same as to conflate Ockham with later nominalists such as Nicholas of Autrecourt and John of Mirecourt (or perhaps in light of what we say below, to conflate Ockham with later, more acceptable forms of nominalism, such as one finds in Gabriel Biel). Thomas's doctrine of the analogy of being is not meant to limit God, but to express the necessary relationship between the goodness of the Creator and the goodness of creation.

133 We do not imply, of course, that allegorical reading began with St. Thomas. Such readings can be traced back to Origen and St. Augustine.

134 St. Thomas, *Summa Theologiae*, I.1.10.

135 Ibid.

136 Ibid., ad 2.

137 Peter Harrison, "The Bible and the Emergence of Modern Science," *Science & Christian Belief*, vol. 18, No. 2 (2006), pp. 115–132, especially p. 118.

mind to God (although, by contrast, particular things revealed in Scripture may).[138] Spiritual interpretation, in whatever form it may occur (the spiritual had been famously subdivided into the allegorical, moral, and anagogical senses[139]), would then need to be downplayed or transformed (a development that will become apparent in later chapters). This is important for understanding why, in part, modern scriptural scholarship came to emphasize the literal-historical sense. Since the natural world no longer is analogically symbolic, the second way of signifying (the "signification whereby things signified by words have themselves also a signification . . . called the spiritual sense") of which only God is capable, must drop out, leaving only one kind of signification for both God and humanity: the "first signification whereby words signify things belongs to the first sense, the historical or literal." The result is that Holy Scripture itself comes to be understood as signifying *in the same way* as any humanly written book.

The End of Ockham and the Beginning of Ockhamism

Ockham died of the plague in 1347, but even before his death his work had gained a foothold on the continent in Paris. The works of Ockham were prohibited (but not condemned) at Paris by the Arts Faculty in 1339 and 1340.[140] In the statue of 1339 the prohibition had to do with the works of Ockham not being customarily read and officially approved, yet despite this, "some have presumed to dogmatize [*dogmatizare*] the doctrine of William called Ockham publicly and privately [*occulte*] by holding small meetings on this subject in private places. . . ."[141] This was not merely a neutral decree, but promulgated to protect the Arts Faculty from intellectually dangerous ideas, specifically hearkening back to the famous decree of 1277 condemning Averroism.[142] An oath was demanded of the English-German nation at Paris in October 1341 that demanded that they reveal any persons secretly supporting the *secta Occanica*. At about the same time, the Arts Faculty of Paris instituted an anti-Ockhamist oath against the *scientia Okamica*, and admonished its members instead to uphold (irony of ironies, in light of the edict of 1277) the "*scientiam Aristotelis et sui Commentatoris Averrois et aliorum commentatorum antiquorum in expositorum dicti Aristotelis*," unless,

138 On these implications, especially as they play out in the Reformation and in early modern science, see Peter Harrison, "The Bible and the Emergence of Modern Science" and also his "Fixing the Meaning of Scripture: The Renaissance Bible and the Origins of Modernity," *Concilium* 294 (2002), pp. 102–110.

139 According to St. Thomas (*Summa Theologiae*, I.1.10), the allegorical sense is applicable "so far as the things of the Old Law signify the things of the New Law," the moral sense "so far as things are done in Christ, or so far as things which signify Christ, are types of what we ought to do," and the anagogical sense "so far as they signify what relates to eternal glory. . . ." As noted above, the term allegory could stand for all three.

140 On these statutes see Courtenay, "Was There an Ockhamist School?" in Hoenen, Schneider, and Wieland, eds., *Philosophy and Learning*, pp. 276–284.

141 Ibid., "Was There an Ockhamist School?" p. 276.

142 Ibid., p. 279. There is, of course, an interesting irony here, given that the edict of 1277 would go a long way in preparing for Ockham's rejection of Aristotle and use of the *potentia absoluta*.

of course, they are *"contra fidem."*[143] Despite all this, by 1343 Ockham was cited often and positively by the Italian scholar Gregory of Rimini at Paris (even given his differences with Ockham), and by 1345 Paris seemed enthralled by English thought.[144] Interestingly enough, the flow of Ockham's thought into Paris in regard to theology was, largely, by way of Italy.[145] And so, just before Ockham's death, his thought was set to spread all over Europe, a point that we can understand, given the special academic place of Paris. Since Paris was the principal continental university granting theological doctorates, knowledge of Ockham and those influenced by him spread to all nations who sent students for this degree. It was at Paris (or at least from contact with Paris) as early as the 1340s that German students learned of the new English thought, although some Germans went directly to Oxford for study during this period and would pick it up there.[146] And so, Ockham and nominalism, however we may trace the complex lineage, would have a significant hold in Germany by the time of Luther a century and a half later.

Conclusion

We began with the assertion that Marsilius politicized the exegesis of scripture directly, and Ockham, indirectly or accidentally. Marsilius's direct politicizing must be understood in terms of his secularizing goal; Ockham's theological-philosophical and political arguments, which he meant to serve a higher cause, overlapped with and hence reinforced those of Marsilius. It is not the last time that we will see this kind of symbiosis.

Keeping the symbiotic nature of the arguments in mind, we may end by highlighting the specific contributions of each to the future development of the modern approach to Scripture that comes to define the historical-critical method. Much could be said, but at least the following points should be emphasized.

The first and most obvious—seen clearly in Marsilius—is the steering of the West toward secularization, toward a this-worldly focus that regards belief in the next world with suspicion if not contempt. In this view, religion is regarded as subrational, at best a step toward the perfection of reason in philosophy. We should not then be surprised that this common theme ties together—in form, if not by pedigree—Averroism and the Enlightenment disdain for revealed religion so characteristic of the late seventeenth and eighteenth centuries. We might even see a link to the Hegelianism that sees history itself as an unfolding from the bottom to top of the hierarchy, moving from those

143 Ibid., p. 284.

144 Courtenay, "The Role of English Thought in the Transformation of University Education in the Late Middle Ages," in James Kittelson and Pamela Transue, *Rebirth, Reform and Resilience: Universities in Transition, 1300–1700*, pp. 121–122. As Courtenay has pointed out, scholarship now points to a closer affinity between Ockham and Rimini, even though Rimini criticized the Pelagian tendencies of Ockham. Ibid., pp. 129–133.

145 Ibid., pp. 125–126.

146 Ibid., pp. 104, 137–145.

defined by their imaginations and passions and moved only by poetry and rhetoric, to the theologians moved by probable arguments, and finally culminating with the philosophers moved only by reason. According to this type of schema, wherever it occurs, the goal of scriptural exegesis will be either to rationalize Scripture for everyone's sake, or as Marsilius desired, to politicize it by reinterpreting Scripture to serve a merely moral function, keeping the unphilosophic masses orderly and happy with their lot in civil society. But ultimately it simply means leaving revelation behind for the maturity of philosophy. As a consequence, at least for the enlightened, the biblical text is of interest only historically.

A second theme in Marsilius, which he emphasized by innuendo, likewise leads to ever more thorough politicization of the Bible by modern exegetes, and so we can call it by a more modern name, the hermeneutics of suspicion. Marsilius implied that revealed religion always has a natural cause: at its best, the philosophic few who use religion to control the unruly masses for the sake of good political order; at its worst, the cagey priests who dupe the masses to fill their own coffers. Since Marsilius provides a rather tepid defense of Scripture in this regard, the reader is left wondering whether the Bible itself might be (along with *other* ancient religious texts) simply another example of such clever manipulation, either by the characters in it, or the editors of it.

On the less theoretical level, Marsilius placing in secular hands the ultimate interpretation of the Bible (along with Ockham's inadvertent support) will have immediate ramifications for the political use of Scripture, a use that, since it is bent to the particulars of political situations, cannot help but politicize interpretation. We will soon discover the ill effects of such bending in the chapters on Machiavelli and Henry VIII.

Turning now to Ockham in particular, nominalism and voluntarism will bear much and varied fruit over the next centuries. Although Ockham did not consider himself un-Aristotelian, his rejection of the reality of universals could not help but undermine formal and final causation, and hence prepare the way for the anti-Aristotelianism inherent in the new materialist reductionist science. In addition, his voluntarism would at least indirectly influence those who put forth the new mathematical law-based account of nature. Both aspects—materialist reductionism and mathematization—would help drive Divine activity out of the cosmos, and hence require its excision from the biblical text.

We have also noted the effect of the destruction of the analogy of being on allegorical biblical interpretation. If nature can no longer act in a real symbolic way, then traditional typology becomes more and more difficult to maintain, either disappearing so that only the historical sense is finally tenable or becoming entirely rarified as merely spiritual or literary. Because the human kind of signifying is the only type that remains, the biblical text will more and more be approached according to the mode of a human artifact.

Ockham's emphasis on the authority of "experts" in Scripture seems to lift exegetes out of the context of the Church and into an entirely academic realm, making it a kind of activity unto itself (in much the same way that, through his nominalism, Ockham lifts up logic out of the context of a much broader understanding of philosophy, and into an art in itself). The tendency once this is done—and it is certainly beyond Ockham's intention—is to make exegesis an independent skill that can be practiced by anyone with the requisite intellectual abilities and training, whether or not the exegete believes the Bible is revealed (in the same way that, say, an atheist electrician can competently wire a church building).

Finally, Ockham's assertion that the faithful have a right to reject anything deemed unnecessary to salvation prepares the way for a future wrestling over the boundaries of the essential and adiaphorous, first in regard to theology using the Bible as authoritative (in the Reformation), and then sorting through the Bible itself to separate the wheat from the chaff (in the Enlightenment). In either case, the task of exegesis has turned from illuminating the fullness of the faith in light of the fullness of the revealed text, to delineating the essential from the adiaphorous within the text.

The history of Ockhamist and Marsilian thought is, to say the least, complex. We will now trace its effects in the latter fourteenth century in John Wycliffe's England, where this famous reformer adds further important dimensions to the politicization of Scripture that will help set up both for the Reformation. But perhaps even more important for purposes of tracing the history of scriptural scholarship, Wycliffe will help prepare England for the Henrican revolution, which in turn sets the stage for the political and intellectual transformations that eventually lead to Deism, the takeoff point of most histories of modern biblical scholarship.

CHAPTER 3

JOHN WYCLIFFE

John Wycliffe (c. 1330–84) is usually given an honorary place in histories of the Reformation as a predecessor, a "morning star" as the popular designation would have it, a title given first by John Bale (1495–1563)—*stella matutina*—but made more famous by John Foxe (1516–1587) in his Protestant *Book of Martyrs*. Wycliffe, we are often told, is the man who first translated the Bible into English and trumpeted the doctrine of *sola scriptura*. Little else is said of him, as the histories hurry on to the explosive sixteenth century. But if with less haste, we linger and look more closely at Wycliffe, we do indeed find that the explosions of the sixteenth century were detonated from long fuses lit in the fourteenth, even if the legends surrounding Wycliffe himself prove inaccurate.

In regard to the arguments of the present work, Wycliffe is important for the way that he politicizes Scripture, acting as an historical intermediary, as it were, between Marsilius and the full subordination of Scripture that will be found later in political fact, in Henry VIII's Reformation, and in theory, in Thomas Hobbes's *Leviathan*. Needless to say, Wycliffe's subordination of the Church to civil power also foreshadows what will occur in Luther's Germany. As with our previous figures, the more concrete our understanding of the political situation, the more thoroughly we will grasp that nature of the politicizing of Scripture.

Wycliffe's Early Life and Education

John Wycliffe (or, variously, Wyclif, Wyclyf, Wicluf, Wykliff, etc.) was born some time near the end of the 1330s near Richmond, Yorkshire, England, the son of Roger (a sheep farmer) and his wife, Catherine. They resided in Wycliffe Manor, part of the holdings of the Earl of Richmond, John of Gaunt, the son of England's King Edward III. The number of John's siblings is not known. He must have been at least the second son, since he was not to inherit the manor, but had to find a place in the Church as a parish priest. John began his studies at about seven, and went off to Oxford in his mid-teens around 1345, a bit over twenty years since Ockham had left. Ockham's influence was strong at Oxford, and Wycliffe would soon set himself in direct opposition to it, disparaging Ockham as one of the *moderni* who turned away from the only sources of wisdom, Scripture and the Fathers, to dabble in logic. Wycliffe soon received the tonsure of a subdeacon, a secular clerk studying to be a parish priest, and began his studies among his peers and, with some friction, monks and friars. As was the way at the time, his study consisted primarily of Holy Scripture, Peter Lombard, and Aristotle.

Wycliffe hoped to stand for his bachelor of arts in 1349, but the Black Death intervened (killing Ockham in Germany) and Oxford was nearly deserted. By 1351, Wycliffe had been ordained a priest, but would not stand for his bachelor's until around 1356, after the denizens of Oxford finally returned. Upon passing, he moved from Balliol to Merton College. He was especially influenced by the writings of Robert Grosseteste, and became fascinated with the study of light and optics. Wycliffe became a master of arts in 1360, receiving one of the fellowships provided by John de Balliol in penance for attacking the bishop of Durham,[1] and hence a Master of Balliol College. From here, Wycliffe went on to take a position as parish priest for about two years in Fillingham, Lincolnshire, a living provided in association with Balliol.

In 1361 the plague swept through again. When it subsided in 1363, Wycliffe would return to the life of an Oxford scholar. "It seems a fair inference that Wyclif did not find parish life completely satisfying, for it was not long before he was making plans to go back to Oxford and study for the higher degree which would eventually make him a doctor of theology."[2] To fund this, Wycliffe engaged in a common practice of the time, and applied for several absentee "livings" at parishes.[3]

Wycliffe took up study for his bachelor of theology, being especially enamored with the study of St. Augustine. During the first half of the 1360s, he composed books on logic. In the meantime, both his father and any rival heirs for Wycliffe Manor had died. John became its head, but chose to remain at Oxford. There he would be appointed warden of Oxford's Canterbury College, but soon lost the appointment as a result of ongoing squabbles between seculars and members of religious orders. Wycliffe appealed to the pope at Avignon, but the appeal was refused. Losing this living, Wycliffe would have to scratch out money to pay his bills, which he did, in part, by juggling his several existing parish appointments.

Contra Ockham: Wycliffe's Metaphysical Realism

From the mid-1360s until 1372, Wycliffe devoted himself to questions of metaphysics, writing his *De Universalibus* near the end of this period. That does not mean that his attention was diverted from theology, since, as Ian Levy rightly points out, "Wyclif was convinced of the inexorable connection between realist metaphysics and theological orthodoxy. His positions on a whole host of topics, not the least of which being Scripture and the Eucharist, are scarcely comprehensible apart from his metaphysical realism. . . . [E]ven in places where his metaphysical realism may not have been the overriding factor it was always an integral factor."[4]

1 G. R. Evans, *John Wyclif: Myth & Reality* (Downers Grove, IL: InterVarsity Press, 2005), p. 89. Evans's biography, the newest, has been our authoritative source for Wycliffe's life.

2 Ibid., p. 94.

3 Ibid., pp. 94–95.

4 Ian Christopher Levy, *John Wyclif: Scriptural Logic, Real Presence, and the Parameters of Orthodoxy* (Marquette, WI: Marquette University Press, 2003), p. 47.

Wycliffe's arguments were formed directly against the threat of nominalism and its attendant skepticism about reason, and like Ockham's arguments, they have a direct bearing on his understanding of politics, ecclesiology, and Holy Scripture itself. Certainly he was influenced both by his reading of St. Augustine and Wycliffe's fellow Oxford realists (especially Grosseteste), but he claimed that his position came ultimately from Scripture.[5] For Wycliffe, realism strikes at the heart of relativism or sophism, i.e., any attempt to say that human language and knowledge are merely matters of convention—a claim also incompatible with the Scriptures. As he states in *On Universals*, "nor will it do to say that human convention constitutes genus and species, because then there would be no genus and species before human convention, which is against holy Scripture, Genesis 1. . . ."[6]

For Wycliffe, the eternal logos or exemplar idea in God [*ratio vel idea exemplaris aeterna in Deo*] is the cause of individual things that exist and in which the universal exists as well.[7] There is, then, a real identity of the universal in God's mind and the universal in the thing,[8] and this identity is expressed most clearly, for the faithful, in Scripture's revelation that the Son is the Word through Whom all things were created (John 1:3–4) and that Jesus Christ is "*omnia in omnibus*" (1 Corinthians 15:28).[9] That is precisely what "*Ockham et multos alios doctores signorum*" fail to understand.[10]

---

5 Speaking of his "conversion" to realism in his *De Dominio Divino* I, ix, 63, Wycliffe states that "It was a long time before I understood that judgment from Scripture concerning ideas [*ex Scripturis intellexi istam sentenciam de ydeis*], however, when, illumined by God, I carelessly [*perfunctorie*] discovered it, I gave joyful thanks to God, with his servant Augustine and others whom God eternally ordains as his ministers to help me to this." By *perfunctorie,* Wycliffe seems to mean that he happened upon it, rather by accident, which at the same time he took to be the result of overarching Providence. On this see Beryl Smalley, "The Bible and Eternity: John Wyclif's Dilemma," included in Smalley, *Studies in Medieval Thought and Learning from Abelard to Wyclif* (London: Hambledon Press, 1981), pp. 405–406. See also Levy, *John Wyclif,* p. 4. The parallel between St. Augustine's realism, forged against Academic skepticism, and Wycliffe's extreme realism, forged against the skepticism engendered by nominalism, is worth noting. In addition to Augustine, Wycliffe was also influenced by the realism in Grosseteste, as he makes clear in his *Tractatus de Universalibus,* II.59; Latin text quoted in Levy, p. 54. The same position is also enunciated in his *De Universalibus*: "this philosophical truth helps us to understand the holy Scripture. For when that outstanding philosopher and prophet Moses said, in the first chapter of Genesis, 'let the earth produce a living soul in its kind, beasts of burden and reptiles and the beasts of the earth according to their kind' he did not mean by 'kind' or 'species' a term or human concept [as the nominalists profess], but universal natures . . . shared by many supposits [i.e., individuals of the species]. And so with the other sayings of holy Scripture." See John Wyclif, *On Universals,* translated by Anthony Kenny (Oxford: Clarendon Press, 1985), II, 382–389.

6 Wyclif, *On Universals*, XV, 24–27.

7 From *De Universalibus* II, 165–177, as provided in Anthony Kenny, "The Realism of the *De Universalibus*," in Kenny, *Wyclif in His Times* (Oxford: Clarendon Press, 1986), pp. 17–29, p. 23. Translating *ratio* as *logos* obviously seems to be a step back, Latin to Greek, but doing so allows us to grasp the connection between Christ the Word/Logos and the logos, the rational structure and definition, of a created thing. Wycliffe sets out five kinds of universals, first and foremost those in God's mind, those in created things being the third kind, and last, and least important, those signs in the human intellect, the very ones that nominalists claimed to be mere names. Ibid., p. 23–24.

8 Levy, *John Wyclif,* p. 55–56, with Latin from *De dominio divino* I, ix, 62–63: "*et hoc [i.e., racio exemplaris] est ista creatura: et tamen ista creatura non est Deus, sed idem Deo in racione exemplari. . . .*"

9 Ibid., pp. 56–57, with Latin from *De Dominio Divino* I, vi, 39.

10 Ibid., pp. 57–58, with Latin from *De Universalibus*, II,65. The entire passage is worth quoting [from Kenny's translation, *On Universals*, II, 297–307]:

Wycliffe concludes against Ockham and the other "doctors of signs," that "the theologian begins from intelligible being [*ab esse intelligibili*]" and proceeds through the faith of Christ [*per fidem Christi*] to the existence of the creature."[11] It would be hard to imagine a more radical denial of Ockham's unbridgeable gap between God's *potentia absoluta* and His *potentia ordinata*.

The reality of universals also had moral import for Wycliffe, for the love of the more universal is the love of that which is closer to God, a greater rather than a lesser, particular or private good. "Thus," declares Wycliffe, "beyond doubt, intellectual and emotional error about universals is the cause of all the sin that reigns in the world. That more universal goods are better than private goods is clear from this, that what is more universal is prior by nature to its inferior. The inferior is ordained for the maintenance of the universal. . . ."[12]

Realism also supported a return to the original biblical languages. Already in Robert Grosseteste, for whom Wycliffe showed the greatest admiration and emulation, there was an emphasis on learning Greek and Hebrew because (against nominalism) human language, through its use of universals, has a real relationship to God's wisdom writ in creation. If the Latin Vulgate, a translation, participated in such divine wisdom, how much more insight could be gained from the Hebrew and Greek.[13]

Although Wycliffe himself never learned either Hebrew or Greek, he seized upon the importance of realism for the understanding of Scripture. In his zeal, Wycliffe's realism appears to go beyond the *analogy* of being (affirmed in the "moderate" realism of St. Thomas, and rejected by Ockham) to an *identity* of being that seems to collapse the Divine Logos and the created logos.[14] A strange effect of this was Wycliffe's asser-

---

> Metaphysicians . . . know that before a common nature is shared in effect, it is thought of by God at an earlier stage in the order of nature as common to many supposits. And in this way universality or metaphysical truth does not depend on any created intellect, since it is itself prior, but it does depend upon the uncreated intellect which uses its eternal intellectual knowledge to bring everything into effective existence.
>
> Ignorance of this interpretation made Ockham and many other doctors of signs, through the weakness of their understanding, give up real universals.

11 Levy, *John Wyclif*, p. 58 (our translation) from *De Dominio Divino* II, v, 198.

12 Wyclif, *On Universals*, II, 162–167.

13 As Beryl Smalley states, "Both Augustine and Grosseteste had contributed to make him [Wycliffe] a realist metaphysician. He looked back to the past to find that certainty which skepticism and terminism had dissolved. His two guides account for another strand in his thought. Grosseteste restated the Augustinian thesis that Scripture, since it contained all truth, should be the theologian's supreme study. . . . This was one motive for his pioneer work on Greek and encouragement of Hebrew studies. God, the author of Scripture, had given names to things in accordance with their properties. Hence to know the name in the original tongue would enable the student to penetrate mysteries hidden in the natures of things as denoted by their names." Smalley, "Wyclif's *Postilla* on the Old Testament and his *Principium*," *Oxford Studies Presented to Daniel Callus* (1964), pp. 253–296, p. 279.

14 J. I. Catto makes the interesting comment in this regard: "It was a notion perilously close to pantheism, and Wyclif would almost maintain that the word of scripture, an eternal entity, was God indeed 'transposed into writing.'" J. I. Catto, "Wyclif and Wycliffism at Oxford, 1356–1430," in J. I. Catto and Ralph Evans, eds., *The History of the University of Oxford: Vol II, Late Medieval Oxford* (Oxford:

tion that the universal in the created thing could not be destroyed. As Gordon Leff makes clear, the assertion of the identity of the eternal universal in God's mind and the universal in the created thing had odd ramifications.

> All being was accordingly indestructible in virtue of its intelligible being in God, from which all other being derived and in which its true nature resided. That was the principal legacy of Wyclif's metaphysics to his theology. . . . [T]he belief in an eternal archetype in God as the indestructible essence of everything in the world, independently of its temporal manifestations, provided the philosophical framework for Wyclif's concepts of the Bible, the Church and the Eucharist.[15]

Wycliffe on Dominion and Disendowment

By 1372, Wycliffe had finally—after almost three decades—achieved his doctorate in theology at forty-three years of age, and thence became a doctor and regent-master of Oxford. Not long after, he began producing revolutionary works rooted in his extreme realism—works that were written forms of lectures given to his eager students—*De Dominio Divino* (*On Divine Dominion*, 1373–1374) and *De Civili Dominio* (*On Civil Dominion*, 1375–1376).

Wycliffe's arguments have some very important resemblances to those of Marsilius and Ockham, even if they may have had distinct theoretical roots in his extreme realism. Like Ockham, Wycliffe argues that private property, ownership, is the result of the fall, and that with Christ, our original disassociation with private property is restored by grace. Thus, the Church—which should live according to this *ecclesia primitiva*

Clarendon Press, 1992), pp. 175–261, pp. 190–191. As examples of quasipantheistic remarks, Wycliffe comments in his *De Veritate Sacrae Scripturae* that "truth can be understood just as one understands the relationship between existent things and their principal being. In this way every truth is God, just as every existent thing is God . . ."; "every truth, just as every existent thing, is God himself, according to the principal reason of truth . . ."; and finally, quoting his own *On Ideas* [circa 1368, unpublished], "every creature according to its intelligible being is God himself, in keeping with that passage in John 1:1–2, 'That which was made, in him was life.'" See John Wyclif, *On the Truth of Holy Scripture*, translated by Ian Christopher Levy (Kalamazoo, MI: Medieval Institute Publications, 2001),I, xv, pp. 207–208. Page numbers will correspond to those of Levy's translation.

15 Gordon Leff, "The Place of Metaphysics in Wyclif's Theology," in Anne Hudson and Michael Wilks, *From Ockham to Wyclif* (Oxford: Basil Blackwell, 1987), pp. 217–232, p. 224. It is worth noting that Wycliffe's inference about indestructibility may well have been the result of his accepting what Ockham had deemed the impossible consequences of the belief in real universals in things. In Ockham's *Summa Totius Logicae*, he remarks that if one holds that universals exist in singulars, "It would follow that God cannot annihilate one singular of a given substance without annihilating all the others; for if he annihilated the singular thing he would annihilate that which is the essence of the singular in question, and consequently would annihilate the universal that is in it and in other singulars of the same substance and so they would not remain [in these other singulars] either." Quoted in Maurice Keen, "Wyclif, the Bible, and Transubstantiation," in Kenny, *Wyclif in His Times*, pp. 1–16, p. 9. Rather than reject Ockham's conclusion as absurd, Wycliffe embraced it heartily, and this acceptance, as we shall see, led to his heretical views on the Eucharist.

we find in the New Testament, rather than being steeped in worldly wealth—must be divested of its temporal holdings for its own good, a holy task that Wycliffe assigns to the secular power. That does not mean, as we shall see, that Wycliffe embraced something like Marsilius's secular state. In fact, quite the reverse. Wycliffe advocated a kind of theological polity—or political theology—in which the king was to be advised by theologians as to how to govern the realm according to Christ's law.[16]

To help understand this more fully, we now turn to important political events that occurred between (and overlapping) the time that Wycliffe was writing *De Dominio Divino* and *De Civili Dominio*. It is difficult, if not impossible, to sort out the causal relationship between the events and the tracts. Since Wycliffe advocated (in his lectures, disputations, and whatever of *De Dominio Divino* and *De Civili Dominio* had come to the attention of the king's court) that reform of the sacred could only be achieved if the Church's riches and temporal power were taken away by the civil secular sword, his works received a ready hearing among those in the royal court, for the king had every desire to control and divert payments flowing from England toward Avignon.[17]

The immediate context that drew in Wycliffe was the demand by the papacy that England pay papal back-taxes originally incurred because King John had ceded his kingdom to Pope Innocent III in 1211 to end a general excommunication of England. As a result, the English king was thereby under the papacy as its feudal holding and hence owed taxes, which had not been paid since 1333.[18] Wycliffe was not entirely disinterested on the question of taxation, since he himself had more than one living, and "he was a poor payer of taxes due from his livings in later years."[19]

In July 1374, Wycliffe was made part of a commission that was to meet with a papal delegation at Bruges on the matter of the taxes due. The main question at issue was whether the English king could hold back such taxes in time of national need, in this case, the Hundred Years' War with France (1338–1453).[20] Wycliffe, of course, argued in the king's favor. An essential part of Wycliffe's argument, developed fully in *De Dominio Divino* and *De Civili Dominio*, was that dominion (*dominium*) was granted by God on condition that the one exercising dominion is righteous.[21]

---

16 For a more in-depth account, see Lowrie J. Daly, *The Political Theory of John Wyclif* (Chicago, IL: Loyola University Press, 1962), Ch. 3. We will treat Wycliffe's account in more detail below as it was developed in later treatises.

17 We should not misconstrue the situation, however, either in regard to the king or Wycliffe himself. The English king did not want papal subsidies and tithes to cease, since in practice they were collected by royal officials who skimmed off half to three-quarters for the royal treasury. Evans, *John Wyclif*, p. 140.

18 Wycliffe argued in his subsequent *Determinatio* that, even if the pope were feudal lord of England, lordship was nullified by sin, and since the last two centuries of popes had manifestly committed sin, they had thereby given up all rights to papal taxes. See Louis Brewer Hall, *The Perilous Vision of John Wyclif* (Chicago, IL: Nelson-Hall, 1983) pp. 85–86. On the whole political-ecclesiastical situation at the time of Wycliffe in regard to this papal tax see Evans, *John Wyclif*, Ch. 8.

19 Evans, *John Wyclif*, p. 141.

20 Ibid., p. 129.

21 This was an argument that had developed out of the Franciscan poverty controversies, and that had recently been stated at Oxford by Richard FitzRalph in his *De Pauperie Salvatoris*, 1355–1356. Evans,

Wycliffe distinguished two kinds of dominion, civil and evangelical (a distinction that will find echoes in Luther's doctrine of two kingdoms, over a century and a half later). Civil dominion comes about because of sin, and is indeed given as a remedy for sin. Here Wycliffe leaned on Romans 13:1–7, the Pauline passage that admonishes all to be subject to the governing authorities, who *non sine causa portant gladium*, who do not bear the sword in vain.

But those falling under evangelical dominion—ecclesiastics from parish priest to pope—must forsake all civil dominion. In support, Wycliffe quotes Luke 22:24–26, where Christ admonishes his disciples, "The kings of the nations dominate them and they who have power over them are called benefactors: for you, however, it is not thus."[22] It is precisely because the clergy are held to a higher law that they should not exercise civil dominion, for given that civil dominion was made necessary because of sin, its exercise now involves at least venial sin.[23]

This leads to Wycliffe's argument for disendowment of the clergy. According to Wycliffe, the king can and should take away possessions of ecclesiastics if they are misusing them, or if the possessions themselves are inordinate, on the grounds that the unrighteous have no right of dominion—and further because disendowing the clergy returns them to their proper condition of Christlike poverty. But as Gordon Leff points out, the unhappy effect of his zealous desire to reform the Church was the back-hand, seemingly unlimited affirmation of civil authority: "Whereas Wyclif effectively denuded the Church hierarchy of any authority, he insisted upon universal submission to the king and lay lords. A pope could be deposed, disobeyed and corrected; but even a tyrant must ordinarily be obeyed."[24] The one exception (provided in a later work) seems to be heresy, about which Wycliffe says that, "when any person of the Church, whether pope, emperor, king, priest, or temporal lord, falls patently into heresy," the "whole Church" (*tota ecclesia*) should rise up against him.[25]

These were, for the most part, the arguments that Wycliffe had formed when he was sent with the commission to meet with the papal representatives. Whether or not Wycliffe proved a royal asset, his meeting "got him engaged with a trail of implications which carried him along to the end of his life. It was to prove an intellectual turning point for him, the most significant of his life."[26]

John Wyclif, pp. 154–157. We should note that FitzRalph's angle on the controversy was, as a secular clergyman, the difficulty in controlling the friars, and the power they had while under no diocesan control. For context, see Catto, "Wyclif and Wycliffism at Oxford, 1356–1430," pp. 180–182.

22 "*Reges gencium dominantur eorum et qui potestatem habent super eos benefici vocantur*: *vos autem non sic*." Our translation of Wycliffe's Latin is meant to bring out the important connections to his theory of dominion that would be lost in the normal English translation. Latin in Daly, *The Political Theory of John Wyclif*, p. 73, from John Wycliffe, *De Civili Dominio* (London: Trübner & Co., 1885–1904), I, xi, 75. On the intricacies of Wycliffe's theory of dominion see Daly, Ch. 3.

23 Ibid., pp. 74—80.

24 Gordon Leff, *Heresy in the Later Middle Ages: The Relation of Heterodoxy to Dissent c. 1250–1450* (New York: Barnes & Noble, 1967), 2 vols.: II, p. 544. For a textual analysis of Wycliffe's position, see Daly, *The Political Theory of John Wyclif*, pp. 120–126.

25 Daly, *The Political Theory of John Wyclif*, p. 144–145 and *De Civili Dominio*, II, iv, p. 34.

26 Evans, *John Wyclif*, p. 144.

The National Church and Holy War

But there was more than money involved. This was the century of the Hundred Years' War between England and France, and England had developed a notion of itself fighting a holy war as the new Jerusalem. As Michael Wilks notes:

> During the course of the fourteenth century, inspired by an allegedly holy war and the need for propaganda, English political theology under royal patronage forged a most intimate connection between the Church and the land, between Eng-*land*, the national community, and the idea of the regional Church as an *ecclesia terrae Angliae*, an *eglise d'Angle-**terre***. It was the outcome of deliberate adoption of the Old Testament . . . for the benefit of the English people as the new chosen race, the heirs of the promised land.[27]

The notion of England as the chosen nation was, somewhat ironically, a mantle taken over from the French, who had previously formed their own tradition of a holy and chosen nation led by a most Christian king (who was reputed to have miraculous powers).[28] The Hundred Years' War, in great part, represented the dynastic struggle of the English king to wrest this coveted title from the French monarch.

The Hundred Years' War began over dynastic struggles exacerbated by the disputed duchy of Gascony in southwestern France, still held as a fiefdom by the English monarch. In 1328, the great centuries-long Capetian dynasty in France was extinguished with the death of the heirless Charles IV (ruling France, 1322–1328), himself the last remaining son of France's Philip IV the Fair, who had died in 1314. Although Philip had left no more sons, he did have a daughter, Isabella, who had married England's Edward II (1307–1327). Edward III (1327–1377), the son of Edward II and Isabella, thought that he, as the grandson of France's Philip the Fair, should inherit France upon the death of Charles IV. The struggle over Gascony provided a pretext for Edward III to claim the French crown for England. France, not wanting to be absorbed into England, gave the crown to the Frenchman Philip VI, a cousin of Charles IV. Hence, the dynastic battle known as the Hundred Years' War. Adding fuel to this struggle was Edward III's desire to claim the French king's status as Most

---

27 Michael Wilks, "Royal Patronage and Anti-Papalism from Ockham to Wyclif," in Hudson and Wilks, *From Ockham to Wyclif*, pp. 135–163, p. 151.

28 See the excellent J. W. McKenna, "How God became an Englishman," D. J. Guth and J. W. McKenna, eds., *Tudor Rule and Revolution: Essays for G. R. Elton* (Cambridge: Cambridge University Press, 1982), pp. 25–43; Joseph R. Strayer, "France: The Holy Land, the Chosen People, and the Most Christian King," contained in Strayer, *Medieval Statecraft and the Perspectives of History* (Princeton: Princeton University Press, 1971), pp. 300–311; and Marc Bloch, *The Royal Touch: Sacred Monarchy and Scrofula in England and France* (London: Routledge, 1973). It is worth noting that the papacy helped to build the French notion of a holy nation. Clement V's Bull *Rex Gloriae* (1311) referred to the French as, "just like the Israelite people . . . a peculiar people elected by the Lord in execution of the mandates of heaven. . . ." From Strayer, *Medieval Statecraft and the Perspectives of History*, p. 313, footnote 51, our translation.

Christian King, and the dynastic struggle thereby became a holy war to decide which nation was the new Israel.[29] Hence the propaganda battle, wherein

> late-medieval English publicists sought to usurp this French status of most favored nation [by God]. Edward III, who claimed the French crown itself, intensified a rivalry with the French kings over the mystical attributes of regality. In so doing he laid the foundation for a distinctively English political theology which could support and underlay both Henrician [i.e., Henry VIII's] assertions of autonomous national sovereignty and Elizabethan assurances of Britannic godliness. [30]

It is not difficult to imagine how politicized Scripture would become in this context. Helping to buttress national pride was a newly developing English vernacular literature, and transition from French to native English as the official language of business. As John McKenna remarks, "When the publicists of Edward III added to this repertoire with new claims of English national piety, it was the English who became godly as God became an Englishman."[31] Again, this was a co-opting of the French tradition of being the new Israel, headed by a Davidic, Christlike king.

> The old French royal myth had been created to unify the kingdom and rival the Empire; its English counterpart was conceived and sustained to rival the French. Just as the French "religion of nationalism" grew from a cult of monarchy, so the new English reputation for divine sanction sprang from wholly dynastic pretensions grounded on the tradition of exalting royalty but soon infused with the abundant elements of patriotism and xenophobia. A purloined ideology of mystical kingship underlies the first great age of vernacular English political and literary patriotism and the new language of nascent English nationalism.[32]

Given this context, one can easily guess the negative effects on the English mind of having a series of French popes during Edward III's reign. (In full cognizance of the

---

29 Like Israel, England gauged its favor with God by how well the battles with the enemy were going. For example, in the Parliament of 1377, presided over by Richard II, the heir to Edward, the chancellor's opening address included the stirring claim (still in court French, ironically), that Richard, the heir presumptive, was sent to them as God had sent Christ into the world, the long-awaited heir proclaimed by Simeon in the Temple: "And thus you have that which Scripture tells us, '*Pacem super Israel*,' peace over Israel, because Israel is understood to be the heritage of God as is England [*pur quel Israel est a entendu l'eritage de Diue, q'est Engl*]. For I truly think that God would never have honored this land in the same way as He did Israel through great victories over their enemies, if it were not that He had chosen it as His heritage." Context and quote in McKenna, "How God became an Englishman," p. 31.

30 McKenna, "How God became an Englishman," p. 27. We should note that before Henry VIII broke with Rome, he sought the coveted status of most Christian king through alliance with the papacy. Hence his chase after the title of *Defensor Fidei*, which would be granted by Pope Leo X for Henry's tract against Luther. Ibid, pp. 41–42. The full irony of this title will become evident in our chapter on Henry VIII.

31 McKenna, "How God became an Englishman," p. 27.

32 Ibid., pp. 29–30.

English attempt to take upon itself the status of the new Israel, a French joke at the time proclaimed "the pope has become French and Jesus has become English."[33]) As a consequence, this nationalist vision was united to Edward's very practical policy of looking after the needs of the realm against the claims made by the Church at Avignon. As Wilks points out, Edward III consistently denied papal jurisdiction throughout his reign, taxed the clergy, denied papal authority without royal consent, seized papal letters and carriers, restricted papal taxation and appeals to Rome, and in the *Statue of Provisors* of 1351 asserted that "the holy Church of England [*sainte eglise d'Angleterre*] had been founded by the king and his ancestors, and the counts, barons and nobles of his kingdom and their ancestors, for the purpose of teaching them and their people the law of God and to do good works . . . a document so extreme that by implication it deprived all clerics of all rights altogether."[34] Perhaps more famously, Edward issued the *Ordinance and Statute of Praemunire* in 1353 that forbid appeals to Rome over English courts—a statute that would later be used to great effect by Henry VIII.

This complex context shows the implicit political import of Wycliffe's mission to meet the papal delegation, his own assertions about the supremacy of the English king over the priesthood and over the pope himself, and even his desire to have the Bible translated into the vernacular.

Moreover, the notion of England's being the promised land in continuity with ancient Israel added a new dimension to the existing arguments of Ockham and Marsilius for civil control of ecclesiastical affairs. There is a shift from imperial to national political power, from the notion of a Holy Roman Empire that complements the universality of the Church, to a particular holy nation (a shift expressed in Wycliffe's argument that English law is better than Roman law[35] and that England is not under the jurisdiction of the empire[36]). As Wilks notes:

> [U]nlike earlier fourteenth-century upholders of lay supremacy [centered on imperial power], Wyclif did not need to deal in terms of Roman law or natural rights like Marsilius of Padua or William of Ockham: it was enough to equate Edward III with Old Testament kingship, to make him lord of the promised land, a land-lord of the realm, the only person from whom the English clergy could derive their rights and possessions, and who correspondingly enjoyed the power of a Solomon or an Ezra to appoint, depose or dispossess them. Priests have no rights of possession of their own in Israel, for as Ezekiel said, they have God for their inheritance.[37]

33 Quoted in ibid., p. 30.

34 Wilks, "Royal Patronage and Anti-Papalism from Ockham to Wyclif," p. 147.

35 Evans, *John Wyclif*, p. 131.

36 Daly, *The Political Theory of John Wyclif*, p. 133. England was outside the empire's jurisdiction both because of the empire's failures to uphold the law of Christ, and from the fact that England was historically and geographically outside of the empire's ambit.

37 Wilks, "Royal Patronage and Anti-Papalism from Ockham to Wyclif," pp. 150–151. It is important to realize that this notion was not confined to France and England, and, in fact, the widespread notion of linking national destiny to salvation history through a particular kind of biblical exegesis inevitably

And so, when Wycliffe was hired to defend England's cause, he was in part enlisting to advocate a national messianic-political vision, united with a sustained political policy of rebuffing papal claims, both of which required theological defense. Wilks continues, "what Edward III needed was a justification of his right to act as a supreme ecclesiastical overlord on a biblical basis—not the Bible recognising natural right [as with Ockham]—but the Bible as specifically the book of the *ecclesia Anglicana* . . . and that was what Wyclif gave him."[38]

We also mention, against the tide of hagiographical treatments of Wycliffe, that he did have expectations of further preferment as a member of the commission; in particular, it is likely he had an eye on the See of Worcester. In failing to receive it, he was disappointed and embittered, as he would be in 1375 when the rich living of Caistor (promised to Wycliffe by Pope Gregory XI himself in 1373) was given instead to another priest, Sir John Thornbury.[39] Rather ironically, it was at this time that Wycliffe was writing his *De Civili Dominio* (1375–1376). Again, central to this work was Wycliffe's claim that the Church, in imitation of Christ's poverty, should not own property. It is unclear exactly how Wycliffe reconciled his own desire for ecclesiastical preferment with his call for enforced poverty of clerics.

Also part of *De Civili Dominio* was Wycliffe's arguments that the English crown had the right to control property without interference from the Church, either in England or from Rome; and that the Roman pope was only "the head of a particular Church" (*Romanus pontifex sit caput particularis ecclesie*).[40] He would eventually reject the papacy, and "say that the very papal office was of Caesar's foundation: there was no foundation for it in scripture, and no one was pope before Silvester received the Donation from Constantine: that is, no one before him claimed 'to be Christ's vicar on earth, to have pre-eminent power in both spiritual and temporal things, and to be above all other bishops.'"[41] While not going so far at this point, Wycliffe did deny the validity of papal bulls and the power of binding and loosing from sins, both on the grounds that the powers claimed could only be legitimate *if* the pope "conformed to the law of Christ."[42]

---

linked the rise of nationalism with the rise of national churches in the Reformation. "Something approaching the full Jewish principle of the landed church could only be restored when the Christian church began to come to terms with the principle of nationalism and national sovereignty in the later Middle Ages, and equated a church with a regional area, with a specific geographical, territorial unit. In the course of the fourteenth and fifteenth centuries this equation of *ecclesia* and *terra*, church and land, spread to most parts of Europe. . . . The result was that the Reformation became a virtual inevitability as Europe came to accept this territorial doctrine of the Church as being essentially a collection of 'lands', of independent Israels. And this new—or rather, very old—conception of a church as a territory, as a defined geographical area, was bound to be inherently anti-papal." Ibid, p. 152.

38 Ibid., pp. 147–148.

39 Evans, *John Wyclif*, p. 145.

40 *De Civili Dominio*, I, 382, quoted in Edith C. Tatnall, "John Wyclif and *Ecclesia Anglicana*," *Journal of Ecclesiastical History*, Vol. 20, No. 1, April 1969, pp. 19–43, quote from p. 21, n. 1.

41 Howard Kaminsky, "Wyclifism as Ideology of Revolution," *Church History*, Vol. 32 (1963), pp. 57–74, pp. 60–61.

42 Tatnall, "John Wyclif and *Ecclesia Anglicana*," p. 27.

In the Service of the State

In local political-ecclesiastical affairs, Wycliffe was summoned in the fall of 1376 by the same John of Gaunt, son of the king, who had been lord of Wycliffe Manor. John of Gaunt's older brother, the Black Prince, had died in the summer of that same year, leaving the Black Prince's son, Richard, as heir presumptive at only ten years old. John of Gaunt, who was jockeying for the exercise of royal power, was far less interested in the theological reasons Wycliffe would give for disendowment of the Church than he was for a chance at its riches and a reduction of ecclesiastical power. One of the first missions, then, for Wycliffe was preaching in the many churches of London that the Church should embrace poverty, yielding its riches to the poor.[43] But this reform message had an essential political element. "Here in London, Wyclif repeated his demand that the Church return to the age of purity, demonstrate its social responsibility, and give back its wealth to help the poor of London. And if the Church would not help the poor, the civil government had the right to force it to do so. Only in this way would the Church ever embrace holy poverty."[44] Possessions were appropriate for the secular power not the sacred power, "and Wyclif's favorite name for the clergy who enjoy secular power and wealth is *clerus cesareus*, Caesar's clergy."[45] Yet, high-sounding as these and his other complaints were, as L. J. Daly rightly remarks, "It must be remembered . . . that Wyclif did not live up to his complaints! As has been noted, this constant critic of pluralities, of nonresidence, and of the clergy engaged in politics, was 'himself a pluralist, had been cautioned for being away from his cure, and had spent several years in the service of the crown.'"[46]

As Wycliffe was the agent of John of Gaunt and directly attacking the Church, he was soon summoned by William Courtenay, bishop of London. To make matters more confusing, John of Gaunt, on behalf of the crown's interest, was in the process of trying to transfer the government of London to the crown, a move that gave the independent Londoners great offence. Apparently, while the bishop was gracious, John of Gaunt was quite rude, and his brashness incited the crowd. In the tumult that followed, he and Wycliffe had to flee.

Condemnation by the Papacy

At this time, Wycliffe's unorthodox opinions became known to the papacy as it was finally moving from Avignon back to Rome—Gregory XI having been prodded by St. Catherine of Siena—thereby ending its Babylonian captivity. The Benedictine monk Adam Easton had examined Wycliffe's writings, as well

---

43 Hall, *The Perilous Vision of John Wyclif*, p. 90, and Catto, "Wyclif and Wycliffism at Oxford, 1356–1430," p. 204.

44 Hall, *The Perilous Vision of John Wyclif*, p. 93.

45 Kaminsky, "Wyclifism as Ideology of Revolution," p. 60.

46 Daly, *The Political Theory of John Wyclif*, p. 81. Daly is quoting from Joseph Dahmus, *The Prosecution of John Wyclyf* (New Haven, CT: Yale University Press, 1952), p. 81.

as reports of his opinions from his lectures to students, and submitted a list of about fifty heresies (most from Book I of his *De Civili Dominio*).[47] In May 1377, Pope Gregory XI condemned eighteen (or nineteen, sources differ) propositions in five bulls, and sent word to England that Wycliffe was to be "seized and jailed on our authority."[48] The bulls explicitly identified Wycliffe's teachings with those of Marsilius of Padua and John of Jandun of "damned memory" whose errors "attempt to subvert and enervate the *status* of the whole Church and even the secular *politia*,"[49] although it is a matter of debate whether Wycliffe had actually read the *Defensor Pacis*. But Adam Easton certainly had, and he was able to draw up rather arresting parallels for papal scrutiny.[50] Such parallels were not the work of Easton's imagination. As historian A. G. Dickens notes, Wycliffe "shared most of the bold anticlerical and Erastian doctrines for which, very shortly before his birth, Marsiglio of Padua had been excommunicated."[51]

The bull sent to the University of Oxford was met with typical polite obfuscation, neither condoning nor condemning, a political move that was obviously designed to protect the university from outside interference even by the papacy. The university also asserted that "they should not imprison 'a man of the King of England' [*hominem Regis Angliae*] on the orders of a Pope. That would be to allow the Pope royal powers in the kingdom of England."[52] In a disputation at this time or a little after, Wycliffe identified himself "as the King's 'special' [*peculiaris*] clerical apologist [*Regis clericus*] and it is in that capacity that he 'puts on the habit' of a responder and defender and

47 Easton's own dialogue, *Defensorium Ecclesiastice Potestatis*, is written in part against Wycliffe's *De Civili Dominio*. Evans, *John Wyclif*, pp. 164–165, and Margaret Harvey, "Adam Easton and the Condemnation of John Wyclif," *English Historical Review* 118 (1998), pp. 321–334. As Harvey notes, Wycliffe was "quoted regularly" during the latter half of the text, referred to as "a certain new master John." Harvey, "Adam Easton and the Condemnation of John Wyclif," p. 323.

48 Quoted in Hall, *The Perilous Vision of John Wyclif*, p. 104. For a summary of the condemned propositions see Evans, *John Wyclif*, p. 172.

49 George Garnett, *Marsilius of Padua and "The Truth of History"* (Oxford: Oxford University Press, 2006), pp. 43–44.

50 Harvey, "Adam Easton and the Condemnation of John Wyclif," pp. 326–327, 331. Apropos of this similarity, Kaminsky remarked that "It has in fact been suggested by [Ephraim] Emerton [in his *The Defensor Pacis of Marsiglio of Padua*, 1920] that Wyclif had the *Defensor Pacis* open on his desk as he wrote his own works, and although the hypothesis has not yet been proven, its attraction will be felt by anyone who reads Wyclif immediately after reading Marsilius." See Kaminsky, "Wyclifism as Ideology of Revolution," p. 59.

51 A. G. Dickens, *The English Reformation*, 2nd edition (University Park, PA: Pennsylvania State University Press, 1991), p. 46.

52 Evans, *John Wyclif*, p. 174. Evans's comments are worth noting: "The subtle blending of considerations of truth and considerations of the politics of the real world manifested in Oxford's reply was already the usual academic way six hundred years ago. The decision [of the university] neither condemned nor approved of Wyclif, and the Regent Masters regretted that it was beyond their power to act as the Pope wished, when their duty to the King of England went against it. So the University formulated its response to the Bull in an equivocal manner entirely in keeping with the combination of political sophistication and pusillanimity characteristic of the academic mind." Some things, it seems, never change.

persuader of the view that the King may justly rule the kingdom of England and refuse to pay tribute to the Roman Pontiff."[53]

Ecclesia Anglicana

Books II and III of *De Civili Dominio* were written when Wycliffe had at least received news of the condemnation, for they take a more radical position against Rome and in favor of England. It is notable (as Edith Tatnall remarks) that, "while Wyclif began his pattern of reference to English law and custom in Book I, it is in Book II that he attempted to build a complete case based on English law. . . . In fact, the English Church-nationalism that Wyclif so clearly expressed in Books II and III may be seen as an answer to the pope's condemnation of him, by denying the pope's right to such jurisdiction over an English priest."[54] However that may be, his denial was part of a larger argument that the jurisdiction that the Church enjoyed through owning so much property in England violated both the Gospel mandate for Christian poverty for clergy and the right in times of war of the crown to use the property of the realm against the nation's enemy (the latter substantiated by an appeal to English law).[55] It is also notable that not too long before, the Commons in Parliament had complained that money was flowing out of England through benefices held by those outside the realm, money that was needed for the king to wage war against France.[56]

In addition to the need for war funds, the need for reform was also on the national mind, and not just on Wycliffe's. In another Parliament, the Commons complained of the unworthiness of clerics with concubines, which was met with a threat from the king to remove offenders and allow their benefices to revert to secular control.[57] This power of the king to correct unworthy clergy and seize their property was a matter of precedent, argued Wycliffe, and he cited previous actions by the crown (running all the way from William the Conqueror's taking of money from monasteries, to Richard II's appropriation of English benefices to carry on the war with France).[58] Even more, the power of the king to correct clergy and seize property would restore England's Church to its golden era: "Wyclif had an idea of a kind of primitive state of innocence and virtue in the English Church, to which the temporal lords could return it by taking from it the large accretions of temporal property that had caused its fall."[59] This English primitive Church was (according to the Venerable Bede, upon whom Wycliffe was relying) itself an imitation of the Apostolic Church.[60] In apostolic times, as St. Paul makes clear in Romans 13:1–7, the Church did not lord it over the state, but Christians

53 Ibid., p. 168.
54 Edith C. Tatnall, "John Wyclif and *Ecclesia Anglicana*," p. 22.
55 Ibid., p. 24.
56 Ibid., p. 25.
57 Ibid., pp. 25–26.
58 Ibid., pp. 32–34.
59 Ibid., p. 34.
60 Ibid., p. 36.

were to obey the ruler. In the case of England, Wycliffe surmised, the ruler himself was Christian, indeed the most Christian king, so that the subordination of the Church to the state had both biblical-apostolic and national-historical sanction.

Reaching back into the Old Testament, the height of Israel's existence was during David's rule, a rule that included directing the Levitical priesthood and Israel's religious life. Given that all three—David's kingship, the early Church, and England's halcyon past—represented golden eras free of corruption, Wycliffe believed that a return was warranted for the sake of reform. In Wilks's words:

> [T]here was absolutely no reason why the lay ruler should not revert to the position approved by the primitive Church. On the contrary there was a positive obligation on him to do so: and the teaching of the *Ecclesia primitiva*, the early Church, on the matter of jurisdiction, as laid down in the New Testament, was naturally essentially the same as that to be found in the Old Testament [where the king, e.g., David or Solomon, ruled over the clergy], since any conflict between the two testaments was unthinkable. In other words, it was now the duty of the lay prince to convert, or reconvert, the kingdom of England into the condition of a Jewish landed Church, an *ecclesia terrae*. It was to become a king's Church, an *ecclesia regis*, since there should be no aspect of the realm which was exempt from the king's peace, the *pax regis* being the *pax Christi*. There should be a *reformatio*, a great re-forming of the ecclesiastical structure so that the English Church might return to its pristine condition of purity. . . .[61]

On the Truth of Holy Scripture

Sometime around his condemnation or soon thereafter (1377–1378) Wycliffe was also writing his *De Veritate Sacrae Scripturae* (*On the Truth of Holy Scripture*), a work of obvious importance for our purposes.[62] His understanding of Holy Scripture conforms to his extreme realism, the true Word of Scripture being Christ Himself, the Divine Word, the Exemplar who informs the written sacred page in somewhat the same way that exemplar universals in the Divine Mind inform particular, physical individuals. This distinction between the Word and the written word in a biblical manuscript allows Wycliffe, in important respects, to bypass the problem of the variances and corruption of manuscripts that will so vex later exegetes.

This is clearly seen in his presentation of the five levels of Scripture, where Wycliffe makes vivid the distinction between the first and proper level (Christ Himself) and the fifth (the physical, corruptible manuscripts). The intervening levels are patterned after his realist metaphysics. The second level of Scripture is "the truths inscribed in the Book of Life, according to their intelligible being," which does not

61 Wilks, "Royal Patronage and Anti-Papalism from Ockham to Wyclif," pp. 157–158.

62 John Wyclif, *On the Truth of Holy Scripture*, translated by Ian Christopher Levy (Kalamazoo, MI: Medieval Institute Publications, 2001). Page numbers will correspond to those of Levy's translation.

differ essentially "but rather according to reason" from the first level, Christ Himself; that is, the second level consists of the divine ideas. The third level focuses on these exemplar ideas as causative of things outside the divine mind: "the truths which are to be believed in their proper genus . . . inscribed in the Book of Life according to existence and effect." The fourth level accords with ideas as understood in the soul of human beings: "Scripture in light of the truth which must be believed as it is inscribed in the book of the natural man, that is, in his soul." [63] Some fleshing out of these levels, their interaction, and the implications will be helpful.

In regard to the first level, Wycliffe argues that the Incarnate Christ is Himself "the Scripture that cannot be destroyed, 'whom' the Father sanctified and sent into the world" quoting from John 10:35, *"non potest solvi scriptura 'quem' Pater sanctificavit et misit in mundum."*[64] According to Wycliffe, in this passage the Holy Spirit ordained in the correct manuscripts [*de scriptura vitali*] the masculine personal relative pronoun *'quem'* (referring to the Son) and not the impersonal feminine *quam* (referring only to *scriptura* itself). In this first level, Christ is indeed the Book of Life (Revelation 20–21), and "God the Father sent this book into the world in order to save the world . . . "[65] By contrast, "That Scripture which is perceptible through voices and manuscripts"—i.e., the fifth level—"is not Holy Scripture, except in an equivocal sense, just as we might say the picture of an image of a man is called a man on account of its resemblance to the actual man."[66]

If a physical Bible were itself considered to be Holy Scripture, "then all Holy Scripture could be damaged by a leather-worker, authorized by a scribe, torn apart by a dog, and corrected by a buffoon, as if it were liable to such defilement."[67] But that would make salvation dependent upon the corruptible work of human hands making impermanent human-made books, which cannot be the case. "For in Mark 13:31, Christ says, Heaven and earth will pass away but my words will not pass away."[68] "Since the works of Christ are not ultimately dependent upon the works of men, such as parchments, engravings, voices, manuscripts, or other handiworks, one must grant that this [i.e., Christ Himself, the Word made Flesh] is the superior Scripture, of which those sensible scriptures are but images."[69] Thus, "when it comes to the substance of the faith, individual manuscripts are of no greater value than the beasts from which they are made. Their true worth rests in the sense and truth which they signify." If it were otherwise, "then were they [i.e., the manuscripts] burned or otherwise destroyed

63 Ibid., I, vi, p. 97.

64 Emphasis added. Ibid., p. 98. The full context in the Vulgate: *Respondit eis Iesus, "Nonne scriptum est in lege vestra quia 'ego dixi dii estis'? Si illos dixit deos ad quos sermo Dei factus est et non potest solvi scriptura quem Pater sanctificavit et misit in mundum vos dicitis quia blasphemas quia dixi Filius Dei sum"* (John 10:34–36). Whatever the merits of Wycliffe's point here, readers will realize that the grammar of the sentence allows for a different rendering.

65 Ibid., I, vi, p. 98.

66 Ibid., I, vi, p. 99.

67 Ibid.

68 Ibid., I, vi, p. 100.

69 Ibid., I, vi, p. 101.

the faith would perish."[70] In a striking passage, which would be entirely alien to the Reformation's tendency to focus on the visible book as opposed to the visible Church hierarchy, Wycliffe even declares:

> Under no circumstances is it [the physical, biblical manuscript] deemed sacred, except for the fact that it functions as a guiding process which leads the faithful into the knowledge of the heavenly Scripture. For this reason it is considered holy in an even more remote fashion than vestments and other priestly ornaments are said to be holy. . . .
>
> As such, one may conclude that the Scripture which is perceptible to the senses is called holy insofar as it is the means by which one is directly led to see by faith the will and order of God, which is itself the most sacred Scripture of all.[71]

Connected to this, and equally alien to the Reformation's tendency to elevate the biblical text above the Church, was Wycliffe's assertion that the Church itself was the locus of authority in correcting manuscripts: "Concerning the manuscripts, one must comprehend them as they have been corrected by the sense and authority of the Church."[72] Wycliffe attributes the presence of uncorrected manuscripts—manuscripts with discrepant readings—to two sources: "sin on the Church's part"[73] and what might be called inspired "verbal discrepancy" that occurs "so that we would come to realize that words and manuscripts are only the signs of Holy Scripture, which is the knowledge of the Holy Spirit."[74] In either case, the Church is properly the guardian of the sense of Scripture: "it is essential that the Catholic faith abide with the entire Mother Church, since Christ's petition could not have been vain when he prayed that the faith of Peter would not fail (Luke 22:32)."[75]

But the Church is also the locus of authority in regard to interpretation, as is seen in Wycliffe's account of the proper mode of understanding the sense of the biblical text. The fifth level, that of physical manuscripts, consists of the signs by which the truth is gathered by the mind (i.e., the fourth level) in conformity with the intended sense of the divine author, Christ Himself (the first level), "For Holy Scripture is an aggregate formed from the manuscript and the sacred sense or meaning, which the Catholic gathers from the material element, just as from a sign."[76]

---

70 Ibid., I, xi, p. 159.

71 Ibid., I, vi, p. 102. See also I, ix, p. 140.

72 Ibid., I, xi, p. 156. Wycliffe provides the example of St. Augustine's determining the proper reading of different manuscripts of Matthew 27:9, in which a prophetic passage attributed to Jeremiah actually comes from Zachariah. Ibid., I, ix, pp. 143–144.

73 Ibid., I, xi, p. 158. Wycliffe is unfortunately not clear about what this might mean.

74 Ibid., I, x, p. 152.

75 Ibid., I, xi, p. 158.

76 Ibid., I, ix, p. 139. In regard to the distinction between the manuscript and the sense, Wycliffe cites St. Jerome. Ibid., II, xvi, pp. 231.

> That mental intellection [the fourth level] is more truly Scripture than the line upon the parchment [the fifth level], for the latter is only counted as Scripture on account of its relationship to it. Nor is the Scripture existing in the mind sacred except through that objective Scripture which it perceives [the first level]. That one by which all Catholics communicate is primarily sacred, since it is the one common faith of the whole Church.[77]

Clearly, from this last sentence, Wycliffe did not imagine that faith consisted in a solitary union of a believer, the text, and Christ. For Wycliffe the believer's mind must be formed according to the "catholic sense," the sense that "has been revealed" according to "the signification of terms defined by the Church."[78]

Yet Wycliffe does not envision a dual source of authority, the Church *and* Scripture, for "Holy Scripture . . . is itself the Catholic faith."[79] Indeed, both the historical rise and fall of the faith are seen, by Wycliffe, in terms of the unfolding and corruption of the five levels of Scripture. While the "Christian religion arose from faith all the way from the aforementioned first level of Scripture to its fifth level," the "infidelity of our own so-called Christians begins with their corruption of the aforementioned fifth level of Scripture and leads, step by step, all the way up to a denial of the first," Christ Himself.[80] Obviously, this allows, even demands, criticism of the papacy—for no one, not even the pope, can turn Scripture away from its proper sense, which is Christ Himself.[81]

As we have just seen, Wycliffe's affirmation of the Church is defined in terms of his complex account of Scripture, one that views ecclesiology entirely in terms of his realist metaphysics in which the Church is, or should be, somehow a kind of manifestation of Christ Himself understood as, and through, Scripture. It is accordingly very difficult to grasp, and we might add, all too amenable to reduction into a simple formula in which the Church is derived from the Bible, the physical manuscript in the believer's hands.

Given the primacy of Christ as Scripture and Wycliffe's downplaying of the importance of the written biblical text, one might wonder how important the text really is, or if the revelation of Christ could not just come straight to the believer with no mediation of the written word. Wycliffe's answer is illuminating, especially in regard to claims by some Reformers after Luther of direct, complete inspiration that made even the Bible unnecessary: "[I]n order to prevent some pseudo-disciples from pretending that they have received their understanding directly from God, God established a com-

77 Ibid., I, ix, p. 140.

78 Ibid., I, xii, p. 177; xiii, p. 181.

79 Ibid., II, xxiv, p. 304.

80 Ibid., I, xi, p. 166.

81 Thus, "it does not appear to fall within the domain of Lord Pope's plenitude of power to render conclusions heretical . . . by forcing Holy Scripture to signify a heretical meaning after he has dismissed the prior [proper] sense." Ibid., I, ix, pp. 138–139.

mon Scripture which is perceptible to the senses, by means of which the catholic sense should be comprehended."[82]

Again, this common Scripture was not an end in itself, but a means by which its incorruptible exemplar, the archetype of the Bible as a universal in God's mind, came to be known. Thus, to quote Leff, "The truth of the Bible was therefore metaphysical; and the conclusion Wyclif derived from it was precisely that it represented an ever-present state of reality, eternally true in God," and therefore, "Wyclif accordingly reinforced the self-sufficiency of Scripture as metaphysical truth as well as revealed truth."[83] We must keep constantly in mind—since we can feel the undertow toward later Reformation ideas—how deeply philosophical Wycliffe's account of Scripture is.

In that regard, it is important to note that Wycliffe's defense of Scripture as Christ Himself, rather than the physical Bible, was not forged primarily as a weapon against the authority of the papacy or tradition. His main target was closer to home, his own academic colleagues. Taking Wycliffe's presentation of the problem at face value, his complaint seems to be against a caviling professorate that takes great pleasure in chipping away at the faith of students through logical acrobatics (even if they do attempt to build it back up again in the lecture's finale).[84] But there is more to his complaint. Wycliffe's ire was aroused against the quasi-Averroist position of the day,[85] related to nominalism's focus on logic as an independent tool exploring the realm of pure possibility,[86] that something in Scripture could be logically (hence philosophically)

82 Ibid., I, xv, p. 203.

83 Leff, "The Place of Metaphysics in Wyclif's Theology," pp. 224–225.

84 Hence Wycliffe's statement that "some object that it is not unfitting for Holy Scripture to be false"; his caricature of brash students who say, "Today I learnt in the lecture halls that one ought to concede that there are contradictions found within the Sacred Page"; and his complaint of "our own theologians [who] walk into the lecture hall one day dressed as sheep with the purpose of commending the law of Scripture, and all of a sudden acquire the teeth of foxes, adding to this the tail of a viper. They say that Holy Scripture is for the most part impossible and even blasphemous when read according to the literal, verbal, and fleshly sense." Wycliffe is not assuaged by claims that "they later annul the accusations they have made against Holy Scripture when they go on to bestow the catholic sense upon it," for since God gave it the literal sense in which they think they find contradiction, they must simply be wrong about the literal sense, rather than Scripture itself containing an actual contradiction. See Wyclif, *On the Truth of Holy Scripture*, I, vi, p. 97; I, ii, p.54; and I, xii, pp. 172–173. See also Evans, "Wyclif on Literal and Metaphorical," in Hudson and Wilks, *From Ockham to Wyclif*, pp. 259–266, esp. 260–263, and Evans, "Wyclif's *Logic* and Wyclif's Exegesis: the Context," in Katherine Walsh and Diana Wood, eds., *The Bible in the Medieval World: Essays in Memory of Beryl Smalley* (Oxford: Basil Blackwell, 1985), pp. 287–300.

85 Wycliffe's denial of Averroism can be seen in his assertion that "I am quite certain that it is not truly philosophical to deny the creation of the world and all of its parts. . . ." Wyclif, *On the Truth of Holy Scripture*, I, ii, p. 60.

86 In saying this, we are not blaming *only* nominalists for the "logic-chopping" that had become so popular in university disputation. The importance of disputation itself as the means by which the academic ladder was climbed can be blamed as well. That having been noted, we must give a fair hearing to Wycliffe's complaint that the effect of nominalism's playing out every manner of noncontradictory possibility in God's *potentia absoluta* fueled the attention already paid to logic as a kind of independent formal art, and turned disputation into an exercise that tore down rather than built up the faith.

false but, as understood by faith, spiritually true. This was a false use of logic, a "logic used by the modern doctors to falsify Scripture."[87]

It may seem a contradiction to assert that tendency was somehow related both to Averroism and nominalism, since the latter arose in antagonism to the former. Some explanation is in order. The Parisian condemnation of Ockham in 1340 included for especial censure those who declared something to be false *de virtute sermonis*—literally, according to the power of the word, but less confusingly, according to the literal word—without taking into account the intention of the author.[88] The danger, so they warned, was that the same method could be applied to the Bible, so that propositions in the text, taken out of context, could likewise be considered false, "which is dangerous."[89] While this mode of approach is not genealogically tied to Averroes but to Ockham, it does duplicate a kind of double truth, where something (according to strict logic) is deemed false that Scripture affirms to be true. And so there was more at stake than mere academic disgruntlement. For Wycliffe, through its misuse of logic, nominalism led both to philosophical and religious skepticism.[90]

Yet even though he was primarily pitting his extreme realism against nominalism, he was also setting the Word (Christ Himself as Scripture understood according to the first level) against the aberrations existing in the ecclesiastical hierarchy. This has immense implications. As we shall see, these aberrations were a sign that the visible Church was not an image of the *exemplar Church* of the elect in God's mind. But since the Bible was the image of its exemplar, *the Bible became the default authority against the Church*. That meant, of course, that Wycliffe's ecclesiology—complex and nuanced as it may have been—depended entirely upon the peculiar mode of his interpretation of the Bible. As Leff remarks:

> For independently of how he might interpret the Church, he could do so only through the Bible. Hence his interpretation of the Church depended upon his interpretation of the Bible. For the Bible as God's word was true in itself; it therefore sufficed—properly understood—for knowledge of God's dispensation for this world. The Church, on the other hand, in its unchanging archetypal nature, was to be sought not in its temporal form as it appeared in this world but as God had eternally conceived it outside space and time in its intelligible being in him. . . . Since, however, only the Bible, as God's eternal word, revealed his eternal design,

87 Ibid., I, xv, 205. "Nor can one pretend that the logic of Scripture is compatible with that logic used by the modern doctors to falsify Scripture, when in fact they are completely at odds with one another." Ibid., xv, p. 205.

88 Neal Ward Gilbert, "Ockham, Wyclif, and the 'Via Moderna,'" in Albert Zimmermann, ed., *Antiqui und Moderni: Traditionsbewußtsein und Fortschrittsbewußtsein im späten Mittelalter* (Berlin: Walter De Gruyter, 1974), p. 93.

89 " . . . *quia pari ratione propositiones Bibliae absoluto sermone essent negandae, quod est periculosum.*" Latin in Gilbert, "Ockham, Wyclif, and the 'Via Moderna,'" p. 93.

90 In Beryl Smalley's like assessment, "The rot had set in with terminism [the nominalist mode of logic], the casting of doubt on the reality of universals, and the use of God's *potentia absoluta* to dissolve the whole divine order. Now the skeptics had turned upon their own last refuge against anarchy, faith in Scriptures." See Smalley, "The Bible and Eternity: John Wyclif's Dilemma," p. 401.

> it must be taken to provide the norm for the Church in its temporal existence just because its true nature . . . could not be known in this world.[91]

The Need for Divine Logic

Given the emphasis on logic in the curriculum at Oxford and Wycliffe's own intellectual dedication to logical clarity, it is not surprising that he believed that bad logic must be driven out by good logic[92] so that the proper exegesis of Scripture has to be done according to a Divine Logic.[93]

So it is that Wycliffe argued for something higher than the various "foreign logics" of the schools—the Divine "Logic of Scripture" itself,[94] rooted in the Divine Word, according to which Scripture is "true in all its parts according to the intended literal sense [*de virtute sermonis*]"[95]—a position for which he continually cites St. Augustine as authority.[96] For Wycliffe, this legitimate exegetical goal had been lost, and logic had taken on a life of its own among the Oxford nominalists, detached from

91 Leff, "The Place of Metaphysics in Wyclif's Theology," p. 226.

92 The understanding that a thorough knowledge of logic is necessary for exegesis did not, of course, originate with Wycliffe, as the copious application of logical analysis to Scripture by previous medievals attests. As Evans states, "The assumption which underlies these exercises is that since Scripture cannot contradict itself in reality (if it is wholly true), something has been misread or misunderstood if it appears to do so. The art of resolving contradictions is therefore close to the art of spotting the fault of fallacious argument—not because Scripture is deceitful, as are the arguments of the sophists, but because human fallibility fails to see clearly what is being said." See Evans, "Wyclif's *Logic* and Wyclif's Exegesis: the Context," p. 296.

93 Reading his analysis, it is quite clear that Wycliffe is at home in scholastic disputation, even if he believes that that home must be put back in good order. As Evans notes, "Where the scholars of the Reformation sometimes reject a scholasticism wholly in decay, Wyclif merely asks for a proper application of scholastic methods." Ibid., p. 300.

94 Wyclif, *On the Truth of Holy Scripture*, I, I, p. 44. According to Wycliffe, the many logics proliferating in the Oxford of his day represent a falling away from the proper human use of dialectic, and this in turn must be distinguished from the true "exemplar" logic as manifested in Scripture: "For we are unable to obtain so perfect a logic or eloquence as Scripture possesses, but instead possess only a humble derivative, one which is made more perfect the more it conforms to it." Ibid., I, i, p. 44. Thus, Wycliffe confirms the importance of Aristotle, even while asserting that he is to be corrected "by means of the philosophy of Scripture . . .," as in, for example, the eternity of the world. Yet "that philosophy which the Christian piously learns from the books of Aristotle is not studied because it is Aristotle's, but instead, because it belongs to the authors of Holy Scripture." Ibid., I, ii, p.59, and see I, iii, p. 66. Thus, "the greatest philosopher is none other than Christ, Wisdom itself, our God. Consequently, it is by following and studying him that we too become philosophers, while in learning various falsehoods we are straying away from the authentic understanding of the saints, who are the true philosophers." Ibid., I, ii, p. 60. A double sign of his own time's corruption for Wycliffe was "linguistic novelties in matters of logic" that were then applied to Scripture. Ibid., I, xiii, pp. 180–181.

95 Ibid., I, i, p. 41. As Wycliffe notes here, he affirms that Scripture is "true in all its parts" repeatedly.

96 St. Augustine is, apart from the "authors of Holy Scripture . . . the foremost among all the doctors of Holy Scripture," even though "Augustine is not infallible, since Augustine himself was capable of committing errors," although "very few in number." Ibid., I, ii, p. 61–62; I, xiii, pp. 181–182.

the goal of understanding Scripture, and bent on exacerbating, rather than resolving, apparent contradictions in the biblical text. This decay led to plurality, a proliferation of logics, and as Gilbert rightly notes, "From the standpoint of 'the Eternal,' the succession of logics at Oxford ('They change every twenty years,' remarked Wyclif) could hardly be anything but an invention of the Devil, designed to shake the confidence of simple students in the authority of God's Word."[97]

According to Wycliffe "one must learn a new grammar and a new logic when attempting to explicate or understand Holy Scripture," a burden he places on "every Catholic theologian."[98] Given that the first and proper sense of Scripture is Christ Himself, the Word, this new grammar and logic can only be had by devoting our "attention to the sense of the author" of Scripture, so that we might ultimately "gaze upon the unveiled Book of Life,"[99] the Word Who is the Exemplar of the words in Scripture. The true author is not, then, the human author, such as, say, Matthew or Luke, just as the true Scripture is not the parchment with ink. "By faith, it is surely God, for he is the immediate author of every suitable sense in our manuscripts."[100] And thus, "it is only right that one comprehend Scripture in its wholeness, as it pertains to the sense of the author,"[101] for "each part of Holy Scripture is true according to the divinely intended literal sense [*de virtute sermonis divini*]."[102] But the literal sense *is* Christ, or we might say, the typological reading *is* the literal reading, for the entire Bible is written as pointing to Him as the Truth.[103]

There is then a complete parallel of scriptural exegesis and metaphysics, for "nothing can be true unless it is the First Truth, or participates in it. . . . The First Truth is itself the first cause by which every created thing is known. . . . Truly then, since Christ is the true light which illuminates every person (John 1:9), it is evident that it is absolutely impossible for a person's sense to be illuminated such that he could know anything at all, unless he is first enlightened by him."[104] In regard to the exegesis of Scripture, this literal sense, the correct sense, the "sense of the author," is equated with "the catholic sense."[105] And, in parallel to his moral claims about metaphysical realism noted above, Wycliffe declares that "all human evil arises from a failure to venerate and understand Scripture correctly."[106]

The Need for True Philosophy

None of this suggests that Wycliffe considered the Bible easy to understand. As he made clear in his doctoral *Principium*, three things were necessary so that one "may reach

97 Gilbert, "Ockham, Wyclif, and the 'Via Moderna,'" p. 103.

98 Wyclif, *On the Truth of Holy Scripture*, I, iii, p. 65 and I, xv, p. 205.

99 Ibid., I, iii, p. 65.

100 Ibid., I, iii, p. 66. Wycliffe asserts that "Scripture has a three-fold author, namely God, the humanity of Christ, and their proximate scribe," the latter being "the lowest author . . ." Ibid., I, xv, p. 210.

101 Ibid., I, iv, p. 80.

102 Ibid., I, v, p. 93.

103 Ibid., I, x, pp. 152–155.

104 Ibid., I, ix, pp. 146–147.

105 Ibid., I, ix, p. 137.

106 Ibid., I, ix, p. 138.

due knowledge of the Scriptures": a good moral disposition, experience in studying philosophy, and the practice of virtue based upon a good moral disposition. There is quite a bit included in the study of philosophy as a prerequisite for the study of Scripture, as much as was included in Wycliffe's own education at Oxford before he took up theology proper: grammar, dialectic, rhetoric, natural philosophy, and moral philosophy.[107] Wycliffe accordingly argues a position seemingly at odds with at least the popular presentation of Luther's animosity to Aristotle and philosophy.[108] Good philosophy, as a prerequisite, is needed to combat bad philosophy. As Beryl Smalley remarks, "Wyclif saw his realist metaphysics as the one infallible means to save Scripture from the destructive criticism of the hateful sophists and terminists," i.e., those indebted to Ockham.

> Instead of exalting Scripture at philosophy's expense, he [Wycliffe] goes far beyond St. Augustine's permission to "spoil the Egyptians," to the point of asking how anyone ignorant of pagan ethics can hope to penetrate the meaning of Scripture even superficially; the natural philosopher has learnt metaphysical truths which alone can give him insight when he turns to the Bible.[109]

The Literal Sense

Getting at the literal sense required all these academic tools wielded by one who subscribed to the proper philosophy, as becomes clear in exploring further what Wycliffe meant by the literal sense of Scripture. Whatever sense the Divine Author intends—whether it is expressed as history, figuratively, in parables, mystagogically, tropologically, anagogically, analogically, metaphorically, or allegorically—*is* to be counted the literal sense,[110] a position for which he cites St. Thomas Aquinas but which was also found in Nicholas of Lyra and Richard FitzRalph.[111] This "mystical

107 See Smalley, "Wyclif's *Postilla* on the Old Testament and his *Principium*," pp. 272–276.

108 As we shall see in the Luther chapter, the truth is more complex.

109 Smalley, "Wyclif's *Postilla* on the Old Testament and his *Principium*," p. 278.

110 Wyclif, *On the Truth of Holy Scripture*, I, iv–v, pp. 72–96. These are the terms used by Wycliffe in the aforementioned passages, but as he notes later, these all may be reduced to the traditional four senses, "namely the literal, allegorical, tropological and anagogical . . ." I, vi, p. 104.

111 Ibid., I, iv, pp. 77–78, citing St. Thomas, *Summa Theologiae*, I.1,10. As its presence in St. Thomas and elsewhere attests, Wycliffe's argument here is not revolutionary. As Evans notes, "In the late twelfth and thirteenth centuries some knowledge of Hebrew and an increasing technical expertise in the analysis of the grammatical structure of language and its signification made the study of the literal sense much more interesting to scholars. In light of new insights into the way signification works, it began to seem that where the figure is clearly being used deliberatively, and there is no question of the interpreter's 'reading' of a figurative usage where none is intended, the literal sense could be taken to include the figurative. The literal sense thus becomes the 'primary' meaning." See Evans, "Wyclif on Literal and Metaphorical," p. 261. In Wycliffe's words, "Although any sense which the letter possesses can fittingly be called the literal according to the intended literal sense [*de virtute sermonis*], the doctors commonly call the literal sense that sense of Scripture which the Holy Spirit primarily intends so that the faithful soul would journey upwards to God." See Wyclif, *On the Truth of Holy Scripture*, I, vi, p. 104.

equivocation,"[112] where one word may have several senses, dissolves what appears to be contradictory in the text and reveals the unified, intended meaning of the Divine Author.[113] Such equivocation is deciphered according to the proper, literal sense, which points to Christ.

Contradictions therefore only arise when the reader does not understand the sense intended by the Divine Author. "For what seems uncultured and contradictory to us, actually proves to be wise . . . so long as we do not ignore the equivocation and the reason why Scripture equivocates."[114] One must therefore be a skilled theologian, and "have a thorough knowledge of the logic of Scripture. Otherwise the reader could end up falsifying Scripture. . . . It is fitting, therefore, that the theologian become acquainted with the logic of Scripture, so that he does not find himself overwhelmed by its language."[115]

And so, when (for example) Christ says "I am the door" (John 10:7), if "door" is understood in the wrong sense, what *we* might naturally be tempted to call the "literal" sense, it is obviously a contradiction: Christ is not a physical, wooden door. But, according to mystical equivocation, Christ "properly called himself the door"[116] as the only one through Whom salvation is possible, and so (quoting St. Augustine) "'None of us may properly call himself the door, for he has properly retained this for himself.'"[117] There is, then, no contradiction, and since this is the meaning intended by the Divine Author, this meaning of "door" *is* the literal sense of the passage.

Metaphysical Realism and Scriptural Logic

We stress again how thoroughly grounded in his metaphysical realism Wycliffe's mode of exegesis is, and how deeply he understood his main enemy to be nominalism. This is especially clear in his explication of the first two of the five kinds of weapons in the "heavenly logic . . . by which the Catholic can demolish all the javelins and insults of the sophists. . . ." The first, acting as the "helmet of salvation," "assigns to God the co-eternal ideas, which are those reasons or exemplars subsisting within him by which the universe was created, according to John 1:3–4, 'What was made, in him was life.'" The second weapon, "the breastplate," "assigns an actual reality to universals beyond signs. For according to Genesis 1:21, 'So God created every living and moving creature, which the waters bring forth in their species, and every flying thing according to its genus.'" Wycliffe's fundamental antagonism to the nominalists is here

112 Ibid., I, i, p. 50.

113 "It is granted that every part of Holy Scripture's character is true, having been assigned many different senses, insofar as God is the first and last sense of every creature. And according to those senses, the other parts of Scripture are truths advancing, piece by piece, toward that ultimate truth upon which all individual truths converge." Ibid., I, iv, pp. 85–86.

114 Ibid., I, ii, p. 57.

115 Ibid., I, ix, p. 142.

116 Ibid., I, i, p. 46.

117 Ibid., I, iii, p. 64.

unmistakable. Quoting St. Anselm, he argues that "those who deny such universals are 'heretical logicians.'" There is for Wycliffe a direct connection between the nominalist denial of universals and heresy: the literal sense of Scripture demands the reality of the common things to which it alludes, and even more, "there is no fallacy regarding the Trinity or the Incarnation which cannot be detected proportionally in the matter of universals."[118]

Scriptural Logic grounded in metaphysical realism is the real and true logic, the standard by which all other "logics" are to be judged, for indeed, "it is precisely the fall from this logic to which we are principally indebted that so savors of sin and its resulting divisions and quarrels. This is why Peter and Paul commanded everyone to speak the words of God in one voice."[119] And indeed, "I have often said that all the evil which was introduced into the human race stems from the erroneous perception of the sense of Scripture, insofar as it is the Catholic faith itself."[120]

In the context of his own day—that is, amidst the highly contentious debates and disagreements at Oxford,[121] the dire need for reform among the clergy and religious orders, and the divisions created by the schism—Wycliffe was putting forth Scriptural Logic as the cure. A pertinent example of Wycliffe's applied Scriptural Logic:

> I have adduced from Scripture that the priests of Christ should humbly minister to the Church by means of the sacraments, the sacramentals, and the teaching of the gospel of peace. . . . Thus they should live a poor life, devoid of property, thereby imitating Christ in this way. For having been placed in a wicked world, it is that much more necessary. Neither the change in times, nor a papal dispensation, excuses priests of Christ from this duty, but rather it serves to accuse them if they abandon it. I have selected for this purpose Luke 22:25–26, "The kings of the Gentiles lord it over them, though not so with you." By the faith of Scripture I have proven that the way of life of Christ and his Apostles conforms to this sense, such that life is the best interpreter of Scripture.[122]

---

118 The third weapon "maintains that things which belong as much to one species as to another, although they might be separated by time and space, really form one totality, according to John 1:3, 'The world was made through him.'" Given that a universal represents something real in things, all things that share that universal can be understood under that universal, regardless of being separated by time and space, such as the Church being referred to as one body. The fourth weapon, "a protective shield," is "the lofty metaphysic declaring that all things which once had been, or will be in the future, exist now in the presence of God." The fifth weapon, "a wide belt embracing all these things," is a "thorough knowledge of the equivocation of terms belonging to Scripture . . ." Ibid., I, viii, pp. 122–126.

119 Ibid., I, iii, p. 67.

120 Ibid., I, vi, p. 109. See also I, ix, p. 138.

121 As opposed to the logic of Scripture that "stands eternally," "[o]ther logics can be recognized for being sporadic and excessively numerous. Sporadic, because, as is evident at Oxford, a foreign logic endures for barely twenty years. And they change so often, since however many masters of logic there are, there are that many logics being rearranged given their craving for conceited distinction." Ibid., I, iii, p. 71. See also I, v, p. 91.

122 Ibid., I, vii, pp. 114–115.

The Scriptural Logic is Christ Incarnate, and "it was Christ's intention that by coming in the flesh his own manner of living would serve as an example in condemning earthly things. . . ."[123] The example of Christ's life, *as* Scripture and as it is reported *in* Scripture, has authority over both any "unskilled grammarian" and even more over the pope. Thus, "it does not appear to fall within the domain of Lord Pope's plenitude of power to render conclusions heretical or even make Holy Scripture heretical, against which he is said to have the power to legislate."[124]

The Reform of the Church by the State

As should be clear, the primary instance of heresy that concerned Wycliffe in his day was twisting Scripture so that it supported the riches and endowments of the papacy and lesser clergy. In making his criticisms, he claimed that he was "not throwing the Church into disarray, seeking to separate the members from their head, and striving to destroy the privileges of the Roman Church," but instead was goading "Christ's Church" to "destroy the sin of scandal," and "if this means creating division among the ranks of the enemies of the cross of Christ then so be it. One does this for the sake of securing the true peace of Mother Church, even if it results in disquieting bodily pain. For as Christ says in Matthew 10:34–35, 'I have not come to bring peace to the earth, but a sword.'" So that it is not he who is a heretic, but "clerics . . . married to the world and thus to riches. . . ."[125]

Wycliffe's exegesis becomes inextricably political because he infers that "the world would be wise to withdraw material alms from such men. . . ."[126] thereby returning the Church to its original, pristine condition, i.e., without property, when it most clearly imitated Christ's poverty. Wycliffe marks the downfall of the Church with the Donation of Constantine, in which the emperor had supposedly given Pope Sylvester I (314–335) not only ecclesiological dominion but political dominion over all Italy.[127] Since then, "Holy Mother Church is intent upon gaining prosperity through temporal power . . ."[128] Having property also entails continual entanglement in human law rather than focusing on divine law, but such human laws "would be of no use to them unless they were intent on securing their ecclesiastical possessions which have been introduced over and above the gospel."[129] "It would certainly be better," remarks

---

123 Ibid., I, vii, p. 117.

124 Ibid., I, ix, pp. 138–139. See also I, xii, p. 171.

125 Ibid., I, xiv, pp. 194–196. As the text makes clear, Wycliffe's defense is quite personal—he speaks of fearing for his life in being summoned "before Lord Archbishop"—and at the same time includes his followers, referring in his defense to "the growth of our faction . . ." Ibid., p. 197, 194.

126 Ibid., I, xiv, p. 196.

127 Ibid., II, xx, pp. 271, 281, 284.

128 Ibid., II, xx, p. 275.

129 Ibid., II, xx, pp. 280–281.

Wycliffe, "that such an eye be plucked out and thrown away from the person of the Church."[130]

Given that the Donation was the signal cause of the Church's corruption, plucking out the eye that offends meant, for Wycliffe, a return to the condition in which the state rules over the Church, so that "all of this leads one to conclude that clerics should be ruled under civil dominion."[131] For its own good, the Church must be disendowed: "while the world hates to hear it, I tell you that the laity are permitted in some cases both to withdraw and to carry away the Church's property from their ecclesiastical superiors."[132] That would leave priests free to perform their most sacred duty, "preaching God's word," which for Wycliffe, given the ultimate identity of Christ and Holy Scripture, "is a more solemn act than consecrating the sacrament, since only one person receives the word of God when accepting the body of Christ." The "preached word is the truth, it is essentially God himself."[133]

Not surprisingly, Wycliffe brings forth scriptural support for disendowment. The priestly class should be like the Levites, without property but supported by the laity: "God thus ordained that secular lords, artisans, and laborers would receive spiritual offerings from their priests and, having obtained these, would then gladly give them material offerings in return."[134] The implication, for Wycliffe, was that if the priests did *not* give spiritual offerings, then material offerings should be withdrawn. If, therefore, a cleric "fails notoriously in this task, the layman has the right to lay claim to such property."[135] Wycliffe offers more specific scriptural support for condemnation of wayward clerics (1 Samuel 2:12–36; Ezekiel 34:1–10); the lay judgment of clerics (King Solomon's judgment of the priest Abiathar in 1 Kings 2:26–27, and the refusal of the officers of the Pharisees to arrest Christ in John 7:45–46); and the lay seizure of religious property (1 Kings 2:26–27 again).[136]

But Wycliffe presses his case even further, arguing that "not only is it lawful" for the laity to disendow "in some cases, but they are in fact damned and excommunicated by heavenly justice if they fail to exercise the power the Lord has bestowed upon them."[137] In this regard, he quotes St. Isidore approvingly: "Secular princes should recognize . . . that they will have to give account to God on behalf of the Church which Christ has given them to defend."[138] This is not an act of vengeance or for private gain, but "spiritual assistance," a "work of love," an "act of almsgiving" that the laity do "by charitable intention" for the good of the clerics themselves.[139]

130 Ibid., II, xx, p. 285.

131 Ibid., II, xxiv, pp. 304–305.

132 Ibid., II, xxv, p. 306.

133 Ibid., II, xxi, pp. 286–287.

134 Ibid., II, xxiv, p. 306.

135 Property should be understood in the widest sense: "the Church's belongings are understood to be the possessions donated to the Church as either perpetual or temporary alms." Ibid., II, xxv, p. 307.

136 Ibid., II, xxiii, pp. 296, 298; xxv, pp. 307, 309; xxvi, pp. 314–315; xxxi, p. 344.

137 Ibid., II, xxvii, p. 320.

138 Ibid., II, xxvii, p. 316.

139 Ibid., II, xxvi, p. 312.

Without doubt, a layman bent on disendowment of the clergy under Wycliffe's precise conditions would have to be a saint himself, since he is both judge and executor of the clerics. Granting the sorry state of the clergy and the papacy at the time, Wycliffe seems to have been unduly optimistic about the character and motives of laymen, especially rulers.

Trial Before the Bishop and the Great Schism

When Wycliffe appeared at Lambeth Palace in the spring of 1378 for his trial before the attendant English bishops, the bishops were informed by Sir Lewis Clifford (an envoy of the widow of the Black Prince, Joan of Kent[140]) that the secular arm would not carry through any ecclesiastical sentence. This time the crowd sided with Wycliffe.[141] The most the bishops could do was prohibit him from discussing the topics proscribed by the Inquisition, a prohibition that Wycliffe ignored.

Because Wycliffe was under the protection of John of Gaunt and the crown, he could not refuse his services when requested. One such case was the defense of the crown in regard to the violation of sanctuary, when in the fall of 1378 the crown's agents hacked to death one Robert Hauley (or Haule), a fugitive from the Tower of London seeking sanctuary in Westminster Abbey Church. This was Wycliffe's last direct pleading on behalf of the government. During preparation for the defense, Wycliffe heard of the election of the new pope, Urban VI (1378–1389), a pope whose holy and simple ways greatly appealed to Wycliffe. In his work-in-progress at the time, *De ecclesia*, Wycliffe writes, "Blessed be the Lord our Mother [i.e., the Church], who provides in these days a Catholic Head, a man of the Gospel, Urban VI."[142] In the same treatise, Wycliffe referred to the Hauley affair as expressing his principle that the pope had no jurisdiction in England, not only because the Church had no jurisdiction over the secular realm but also because English law trumped both canon law and civil Roman law—a double affirmation of the superiority of the particular over the universal, a sign that the nation was displacing the empire at the same time that the national Church was displacing the transnational. Part of Wycliffe's argument, interestingly enough, was that England had never fallen under imperial rule and consequently could not have been "donated" to the Church by Constantine.[143]

The fact that Urban VI was Italian rather than French (as Gregory XI had been) appealed to an England still at war with France. But any hope in the papacy was soon dispelled when, during his defense of the crown in the Hauley affair, a messenger arrived with the startling news that another pope, an antipope and Frenchman, had been elected, taking the name Clement VII. So began the great Western schism, following upon the already bruised heels of the Avignon papacy. In a later chapter of *De*

140 She was now acting as Queen Mother, given that her son Richard, the heir, was too young to rule.

141 Hall, *The Perilous Vision of John Wyclif*, pp. 111–113.

142 Quoted in Evans, *John Wyclif*, p. 216.

143 Tatnall, "John Wyclif and *Ecclesia Anglicana*," p. 22, 27–28.

ecclesia, obviously written after the news, Wycliffe speaks of the "schism which now pullulates between the two pretend-monks."[144]

Not surprisingly, whatever hope Wycliffe held out for the papacy and the visible Church immediately vanished in this scandal. Instead, he turned to the completely invisible Church, the exemplar Church. The position of Wycliffe in *De ecclesia*, already outlined in his *De Civili Dominio*, portrayed the true Church as the predestined elect, a foreknown exemplar of the real Church in God's mind, a divine idea that had no real connection to the corrupted visible Church, which is itself a mixture of those predestined to election and those predestined to damnation.[145] A direct inference of Wycliffe's "realism" was that no one can know whether the pope himself is among the elect, but since virtue is a surer sign of election than vice, the contemporary popes are more likely among the damned.[146]

The Reform of Religious Orders and the National Church

But there was another implication of his ecclesiology that we have already mentioned above. While the visible Church only presents a mix of the elect and damned, and therefore cannot serve as an image of the archetype in God's mind, Scripture is an image of the archetype and hence can be authoritative where the Church itself cannot. As Leff remarks:

> it was in relation to the Church, also conceived metaphysically, in its true archetypal nature outside space and time as the exclusive body of the elect, that the full impact of the independent reality of scriptural truth lay. For he used the Bible to fill the void which resulted from the distinction between the Church in its archetypal nature and in its temporal form as a mixed body not confined to the elect. . . . [and] it provided an added metaphysical justification for his condemnation of the contemporary Church as unscriptural and, by the end, its hierarchy and the religious orders as members of Antichrist.[147]

We should also note Wycliffe's especial animus against the religious orders. For Wycliffe, the religious orders, with their vast holdings, came to symbolize the corruption of the Church. The preaching clergy—and by this, Wycliffe would seem to mean the secular clergy doing their duty in the parish rather than the preaching orders—could present the Scriptural truth, but the monks seemed to Wycliffe to be both rich and irrelevant. Thus:

> By 1376 Wyclif had established the line of attack from which he never wavered: monks squander their goods to the detriment of Christians in

144 Quoted in Evans, *John Wyclif*, p. 216.

145 Tatnall, "John Wyclif and *Ecclesia Anglicana*," pp. 22–23.

146 Kaminsky, "Wyclifism as Ideology of Revolution," p. 60–61. See also Wyclif, *On the Truth of Holy Scripture*, I, xiv, p. 192–193.

147 Leff, "The Place of Metaphysics in Wyclif's Theology," p. 225.

> general, the poor in particular. He deprives the religious state of any intrinsic merit. Almost in passing he notes that the monastic *vita* is a private religion which has wandered from the law of Christ. Monastic possessions, moreover, inevitably lead to avarice, discord, and soft living. Wyclif hints that monasteries might have to be disendowed in view of their flagrant mishandling of their goods.[148]

As Thomas Renna also makes evident, the present condition of the monasteries of England inevitably stamped the monks as among the reprobate, and, by contrast, the preaching secular clergy as the elect.

> Although Wyclif admitted that the chosen could not be recognized, he implies that they will be known by their good deeds. His unshakable assumption that the preaching clergy will save the Church compelled him to identify (by implication at least) the elect as being among these good clergy. So too, it was obvious that most monks were not among the predestined, for their worldly behaviour proved their exclusion. Wyclif never argued solely from the alleged immorality of the monks; he preferred to dwell on their irrelevance. As he became more convinced of the urgent need for an effective diocesan priesthood, the routine of the cloister seemed a total waste of time.[149]

Thus, from his extreme realism coupled with his desire to reform the Church, Wycliffe laid the groundwork that would prepare for the metaphysically much simpler doctrine of *sola scriptura* championed by the Reformation, and the focus on preaching rather than monastic contemplation. This, in turn, would throw support behind the development of national churches, and hence further advance politicization of Scripture as nationalism itself advanced historically.

Since the preaching religious orders, both Dominican and Franciscan, had vast holdings in England and primary allegiance to Rome rather than (as with the secular clergy) to the English bishops, Wycliffe's entire reforming hope was set upon the king, his bishops, and the diocesan clergy. The anti-monastic call for disendowment lent immediate support for a national Church. According to Renna:

> Tied to his [Wycliffe's] arguments for disendowment of excess possessions is his demand for total dispossession in the interest of the English Church and the English nation. As it happened, Wyclif quickly emerged as the most effective critic of monasticism in the fourteenth century. His diatribes became commonplaces because they were simple, moralistic, passionate, polemical, and well suited for exploitation by ambitious laymen and zealous reformers alike. . . . Wyclif stands at the close of medieval antimonasticism. For in the century and a half after him the monks' critics focus almost entirely on the immoral behaviour

148 Thomas Renna, "Wyclif's Attacks on the Monks," in Hudson and Wilks, *From Ockham to Wyclif*, pp. 267–280, p. 273.

149 Ibid., pp. 274–275.

> within the monasteries. . . . Just as Bernard of Clairvaux had been a prophet for the monastic way, John Wyclif was a prophet against it. The antimonastic forces had found their Isaiah.[150]

This monastic emphasis will be asserted in full force in the Reformation, both in Henry VIII's savage disendowment of monastic orders, and construction of the Church of England, and in Luther's Germany, where preaching clergy under the direction of the state take the place of useless monastics allied to Rome. More connections will come to light as we examine Wycliffe's developing account of the subordination of the Church to the state.

On the Duty of the King

During 1379, Wycliffe wrote *De Officio Regis* (*On the Duty of the King*), a work comparable to (but not identical with) Marsilius of Padua's *Defensor Pacis* in its subordination of the Church to the state. Quoting Aristotle's *Nicomachean Ethics*, it asserts that the king, in his care for his subjects, is a kind of *pastor ovium* [of sheep] in acting as a *pastorem populorum*.[151] But Wycliffe is not using Aristotle (as Marsilius did) to secularize the state, but rather to demonstrate that the king (like David or Solomon) must have the religious care of the realm foremost in his mind.

In support, Wycliffe argues that the two natures of Christ, divine and human, relate to kingly and priestly rule respectively because Christ was a king forever but a priest only while on earth.[152] Obviously, this put great power in the hands of the king. As Gordon Leff notes:

> Wyclif was the champion of royal authority. His treatise *De Officio Regis* was devoted to exalting the king's supremacy over all mankind, including the priests. Whereas the king's power was fashioned in the image of Christ as God, that of the priest was to be compared with Christ's humanity. The king was God's vicar and he stood apart from the rest of men, who were his servants. To resist him was to sin. Even tyrants were ordained of God and had to be suffered, provided that the evil done was to men and not to God.[153]

---

150 Ibid., p. 280.

151 Latin in Daly, *The Political Theory of John Wyclif*, p. 63. Aristotle, *Nichomachean Ethics*, 1161a10–18.

152 This argument was not original, but was stated much earlier by the so-called Anonymous of York (c. 1100) who asserted that since Christ was king from eternity, and only a priest through the incarnation, that kingly rule was superior to priestly rule. Furthermore, Christ established only a temporal priesthood, and did it for the sake of his everlasting kingdom. "For everywhere in the Scriptures he promised the kingdom of heaven to the faithful but nowhere the priesthood. It is clear, therefore, that in Christ the royal power is greater and higher than the priestly in proportion as his divinity is greater and higher than his humanity." Inherent in this position was the belief that kings were not merely secular rulers, but God's anointed ones who "receive in their consecration the power to rule this church," not for their own ends, but "in accordance with the discipline of the Christian law . . ." Quoted in Brian Tierney, *The Crisis of Church & State, 1050–1300* (Englewood Cliffs, NJ: Prentice-Hall, Inc., 1964), pp. 76–77.

153 Leff, *Heresy in the Later Middle Ages*, II, p. 543.

For Wycliffe, the king had power directly from God, from Christ's kingly power, and "Christ, according to his deity, gave to the king as His vicar that office before there was a Roman Church."[154] The "pope ought to instruct kings"—as, of course, any theologian could—"on what way he ought to use his power to honor God and for the edification of the Church," but if the pope "strives to tear away that sacred power given singularly by God, the king with his own people ought to resist him just as if he were the most evil anti-Christ about which the truth prophesied in Matthew twenty-four."[155] Luther will set forth similar assertions in his doctrine of the two kingdoms.

Although Wycliffe does speak in terms of two vicars, one temporal and one spiritual, he refers for the most part, not to the emperor and the pope, as had been the case in the previous centuries' debate about the two powers, but to king and priest in accordance with a national Church.[156] Indeed, Wycliffe argues that, however worthy the idea of a Holy Roman Empire is in theory, the universality is impracticable because the vast geographical distances and obstacles (such as mountains and seas) and diversity of languages and customs make such rule impossible; therefore, "the terrestrial Empire ought to be dissolved" [*oportet quod terrenum imperium dissolvatur*].[157] Given its unlikely dissolution, Wycliffe admonishes the emperor, "who is lord of our pope" [*qui est dominus pape nostri*], to subordinate the pope to himself, for "the pope ought, as he formerly was, to be subject to Caesar . . ." [*papa debet, sicut olim, esse subjectus Cesari*].[158] The parallels to Marsilius are obvious.

As we have noted above, this political restoration to a previous, better situation, which Wycliffe suggests should be writ large in the empire, is exactly what Wycliffe envisions will bring about the needed reformation in England. Previous English kings had "irreligiously and foolishly endowed the Church" [*irreligiose et stulte dotarunt ecclesiam*] causing it to fall from the English Church's golden age, but now the king should set things aright and "recall his own Church . . . to the pristine state of perfection" [*ecclesiam suam . . . ad statum perfeccionis pristinum revocare*].[159]

It is no surprise, then, that Wycliffe (in *De Civili Dominio*, Book III) interpreted the "two swords" passage along the same lines as did Emperor Henry IV against Pope Gregory in 1076—that is, not in accordance with some modern separation of Church and state, but like Henry, as a union of distinct spiritual and temporal powers in one Church militant, an ecclesiastical polity in which the spiritual sword was purely spiri-

---

154 "*Christus enim secundum deitatem dedit regi vicario suo illud officium antequam fuit romana ecclesia.*" Latin in Daly, *The Political Theory of John Wyclif*, p. 64, and in A. W. Pollard's and C. Sayle's edition of Wycliffe's *Tractatus de Officio Regis* (London, 1887), pp. 244–245. Our translation.

155 "*Papa ergo debet instruere quomodo debent ad honorem dei et edificacionem ecclesie uti huiusmodi potestate; quod si nitatur potestatem illam tam sacram a Deo singulariter datam diripere, rex cum gente sua debet sibi resistere tamquam pessimo anticristo de quo veritas prophetavit Matth.xxiv.*" Latin in Daly, *The Political Theory of John Wyclif*, p. 64, and *Tractatus de Officio Regis*, pp. 244–245. Our translation.

156 In his own words, "*in ecclesia duos vicarios, scilicet regem in temporalibus et sacerdotem in spiritualibus.*" Latin in Daly, *The Political Theory of John Wyclif*, p. 83, and *Tractatus de Officio Regis*, p. 13.

157 Daly, *The Political Theory of John Wyclif*, p. 134, and *Tractatus de Officio Regis*, p. 261.

158 Daly, *The Political Theory of John Wyclif*, pp. 134–137, and *Tractatus de Officio Regis*, pp. 213, 237.

159 Daly, *The Political Theory of John Wyclif*, p. 134, and *Tractatus de Officio Regis*, p. 213.

tual and the temporal sword exercised all temporal power (for Christ tells Peter, who represented the spiritual power, to put his sword back in his scabbard, John 18:11).[160] In fact, in arguing for the superiority of the king to the priest, Wycliffe asserts that the priest has no claim for superiority because he can administer the sacraments, since the king can command the priest to administer the sacraments.[161] Another advance of Marsilian thought, and a great weapon forged for Henry VIII.

As we have already seen adumbrated in his *De veritate sacrae scripturae*, the unsheathed sword of the temporal power is not merely for punishing thieves, murderers, etc., but also (among other things) to keep the clergy from grasping at the temporal sword or inordinate temporal holdings.[162] Such is the case precisely because Wycliffe does not envision a secular or purely natural state, but one where the king is "to rule the men of his own kingdom according to divine law."[163] This made it necessary that the king employ theologians—"doctors and worshipers [*cultores*] of the divine law"—to help him discern the divine law properly, a position that, no doubt, Wycliffe thought he was filling through his service to the crown. Such "court theologians" are necessary precisely because the truth of Scripture is *not* easily discerned, and was all too easily misconstrued (as the endless debating in Wycliffe's Oxford amply proved), hence his claim that these men wrestle with "difficulties reserved to theologians alone."[164]

Certainly Wycliffe thought that such theologians lead (rather than be led by) the royal court and its interests; moreover, he held fast to the distinction between priests and laymen. In contrast to Luther's later priesthood of all believers, Wycliffe provides a hierarchical ranking of society with the "priests or praying men" [*sacerdotes vel oratores*] on top, followed by the "secular lords or defenders" [*seculars dominos vel defensores*], and finally the "plebes or laborers" [*plebeos vel laboratores*] on bottom.[165] But it is not difficult to imagine that kings would appoint pliant rather than obstinate theologians for the task. Since the theologian's work of discerning revelation is focused on Scripture, the political interpretation of Scripture would almost inevitably flow from the theologian's pen. The fruit of the seeds planted here, and coming into maturity under Henry VIII, would no doubt taste bitter to Wycliffe. The same pattern of derailed reforming intentions will be seen in the implementation of Lutheranism in the various German states.

Yet, for Wycliffe, this arrangement had biblical support. The civil arm is charged with being "especially solicitous about the state and morals of the clerics,"[166] and this "solicitude" is based in the Old Testament, which extended civil oversight even to

160 Daly, *The Political Theory of John Wyclif*, p. 84, and *De Civili Dominio*, III, xix, p. 397.

161 Daly, *The Political Theory of John Wyclif*, pp. 116–117, and *De Officio Regis*, p. 138.

162 Daly, *The Political Theory of John Wyclif*, pp. 85–86, and *De Civili Dominio*, II, xvii, p. 254.

163 [*P*]*atet quod Regis est regere secundum legem divinam homines regni sui . . .*" Daly, *The Political Theory of John Wyclif*, p. 108 and *De Civili Dominio*, I, xxvi, 188–189.

164 Daly, *The Political Theory of John Wyclif*, p. 111, and *De Officio Regis*, pp. 48–49.

165 Daly, *The Political Theory of John Wyclif*, p. 115, and *De Officio Regis*, pp. 58–59.

166 Daly, *The Political Theory of John Wyclif*, p. 85, and *De Civili Dominio*, II, viii, 77.

the punishment of the high priest, and under the New Testament, to the pontiffs.[167] However Wycliffe intended such punishment of a pope to be carried out (presumably by the imperial arm), we are not surprised to find that on English turf, English bishops were obligated first of all to the English king, as were all the clergy under them. All in the realm were subject to the realm, and there was neither historical support (given that England was not included in the Donation of Constantine) nor scriptural support for papal interference.[168]

Again, this is not a Marsilian bid for a secular state (even though it offers inadvertent support). Repeating his earlier arguments, Wycliffe contends that since the civil power is responsible for the condition of the Church within the realm as part of its concern for justice,[169] the ecclesiastics for their own good should be reduced to their proper Christlike poverty. Consequently, disendowment became a civil responsibility by which the Church was forced to reform. Such reform was no merely spiritual, indefinite aspiration. As Gordon Leff remarks:

> To achieve his aim [of disendowment of the Church] Wyclif turned to the king and the lay lords; they were to expropriate the Church and withdraw its civil rights. Instead of living on endowments those of its priests who were worthy were to be supported by voluntary offerings and tithes; the rest were to be dispossessed. Such in essence was the course which Wyclif, with the inevitable inconsistencies, advocated for the spiritual regeneration of the Church. By making its implementation depend upon the lay power he turned an indefinite aspiration into an immediate programme; in place of the prophetic expectations of the Franciscan Spirituals and Joachists, which he explicitly rejected, he put political action. It was this which made him an heresiarch where they remained primarily heterodox. Unlike them, his conception of Antichrist as a palpable presence at work within the Church called forth palpable measures for its destruction; where they looked to a new spiritual order and the end of the present age, Wyclif looked to the strength of the secular arm and the consummation of the existing state.[170]

Thus, the English nation was a positive reforming entity endowed with semi-mystical, providential status. The strange thing about this doctrine, as Leff remarks

167 "*Item, reges veteris testamenti habuerunt potestatem se extendentem ad castigacionem summi pontificis . . . Sed . . . potestas regum novi testamenti sufficit ad castigandum eciam pontifices obvios legi Christi. . . .*" See Daly, *The Political Theory of John Wyclif*, p. 85, and *De Civili Dominio*, II, xii, p. 137.

168 Tatnall, "John Wyclif and *Ecclesia Anglicana*," p. 28–29. This type of argument was used by John of Paris in regard to France. See Daly, *The Political Theory of John Wyclif*, p. 15.

169 In his *De Civili Dominio*, Wycliffe argues that the justice of the king consists of four elements, the first to sanction just laws consonant with the laws of God, the second to destroy laws against the divine worship [*divino cultui contraria*], the third, to compel the people to be pleasing to God, and fourth, to pacify the people internally and externally. From these, it is not difficult to imply the power to make ecclesiastics pleasing to God by returning them to Christlike poverty. See Daly, *The Political Theory of John Wyclif*, p. 109, and *De Civili Dominio*, I, xxvi, p. 189.

170 Leff, *Heresy in the Later Middle Ages*, II, pp. 542–543.

elsewhere, is that "metaphysically there was no more means of knowing whether a King was damned or saved than a priest. Wyclif's doctrine of royal power, in his *De Officio Regis*, thereby effectively superseded his earlier doctrine of dominion, in *De Civili Dominio*, dating from 1376, that only grace could confer temporal lordship." According to *De Civili Dominio*, kings (at least in theory) could be denied the rights of ownership because of sin, but in *De Officio Regis* this proviso seems to drop out, with the result that "On the one hand the Church was excluded from civil and spiritual jurisdiction on metaphysical and biblical grounds. On the other, kings and secular lords, to whom the doctrine of dominion and grace could have applied with most force, were expressly endowed by Wyclif with divinely ordained authority, the sanction for which he found, not surprisingly, in Scripture with everything else."[171]

In regard to is focus on the state, Wycliffe repeated the claim in *De Officio Regis* that the *leges regni Anglie* were more excellent than the *leges imperiales*, thereby denying the superiority of Roman law to English national law. He drew the conclusion that the king, and not the pope, should judge cases of heresy (hardly a disinterested position).[172] He also wrote *Dialogus sive speculum ecclesie militantis* and *De potestate pape*. "It is from this group of treatises," Tatnall remarks, "that we may derive the concept of *ecclesia anglicana* as Wyclif seems to have synthesised it in his own mind from 1377 to 1379."[173] We are drawing ever closer to the England of King Henry VIII.

The Wycliffite Bible

As seemingly every popular historian tells it, Wycliffe was the first to translate the entire Bible into any vernacular, much less into English. Both aspects of the truism are false. Translating Scripture into the vernacular was not a notion invented by Wycliffe, as the case of King Richard II makes clear. Born in France but arriving in England at four, Richard was the first king to speak English as his native language rather than Anglo-Norman. (A dialect of French, called Anglo-Norman or Norman French, had been the language of the ruling class in England since William the Conqueror four centuries prior.) Richard's personal Bible, which he had inherited, was in French. When Anne of Bohemia came to England to be the bride of Richard, she brought with her two vernacular Bibles, in Czech and German. Even in regard to England itself, as we have mentioned above, the latter fourteenth century was a time of cultural transition from French to English as the official language of court, business, and even teaching. And so the plan to put the Bible into the vernacular was not fundamentally revolutionary, but part of a larger cultural shift occurring in England at the time from French to English.

171 Leff, "The Place of Metaphysics in Wyclif's Theology," p. 229.

172 Tatnall, "John Wyclif and *Ecclesia Anglicana*," p. 29–30.

173 Ibid., p. 23.

Secondly, it is almost certain that Wycliffe did not do the translation credited to him, although he evidently desired it.[174] The Wycliffite Bible was a protracted effort made sometime during the last two decades of the fourteenth century by a team of Oxford-trained scholars sympathetic, even devoted, to Wycliffe's views.[175] The drawn-out nature of the project reflects the kind of scholarship that made the translation possible: "the text falls into two versions, the earlier and more literal succeeded first by an overall revision and then by an idiomatic, though careful version; stages which were not truly distinct, but which punctuate a long process of piecemeal revision." In the course of their considerable efforts, "the translators developed a sophisticated technique, recognizing the problems of a literal rendering and eventually evolving, in the later version, a smooth and idiomatic English style."[176]

Whoever was responsible—scholars have pinned down only one Nicholas of Hereford—they confronted a number of variations in several Latin texts, as well as interpolations and careless errors by scribes. In doing so, the translation team had to mull over many variations before coming to decisions, and this often brought them to consult commentaries of earlier theologians such as Jerome, Ambrose, Augustine, Venerable Bede, Gregory, Peter Comester, the Victorines, and Thomas Aquinas for biblical quotations against which they could check their several Latin versions.

As should be clear, they faced all the basic translation difficulties that would form the jumping off point of modern scholarship at its watershed three hundred years hence, difficulties that would render the principle of *sola scriptura* problematic a century and a half before Luther. This is an important point, given that often histories of scriptural scholarship make it seem as if the discovery of such difficulties only occurred in the seventeeth century, and initiated modern historical-critical scholarship. The problems, however, were known significantly earlier, and much worried over. As the Prologue humbly states, "a symple creature hath translatid the Bible out of Latyn into English."

---

174 See the discussion in Anne Hudson, *The Premature Reformation: Wycliffite Texts and Lollard History* (Oxford: Clarendon Press, 1988), pp. 240–242, and Anne Hudson, ed., *Selections from English Wycliffite Writing* (Toronto: University of Toronto Press, 1978), p. 162. The belief that Wycliffe did indeed do the translation, or at least part of it, arose very early, in Henry Knighton's *Chronicon,* written sometime before 1395. Even more authoritative was John Hus's assertion that Wycliffe was the translator. Hudson, *The Premature Reformation,* p. 240. As it turns out, it is not at all clear that he put any of his writings at all into English. See Evans, *John Wyclif,* p. 228–230. This calls into question Wycliffe's reputation as, with Chaucer, defining the English written vernacular. Certainly Chaucer did, but it would be more accurate to say that Wycliffite writings coupled with Chaucer ushered in the age of written English. See Evans, p. 243.

175 On the Wycliffite Bible see Hudson, ed., *Selections from English Wycliffite Writing* and *The Premature Reformation,* H. Hargreaves, "The Wycliffite Versions," in *The Cambridge History of the Bible* (1969), and "Popularizing Biblical Scholarship: The Role of the Wycliffite Glossed Gospels" in W. Lourdaux and D. Verhulst, eds., *The Bible in Medieval Culture* (Louvain, 1979), and J. Forshall and F. Madden, eds., *The Holy Bible . . . Made from the Latin Vulgate by John Wycliffe and His Followers* (Oxford: Oxford University Press, 1850)

176 Catto, "Wyclif and Wycliffism at Oxford, 1356–1430," p. 222. See also Hudson, *The Premature Reformation: Wycliffite Texts and Lollard History,* pp. 238–247.

> First this symple creature hadde myche travaile with diverse felawis [fellows] and helperis to gedere [gather] manie elde biblis, and othere doctouris and comune glosis, and to make oo [one] Latyn bible sumdel trewe [some deal true]; and thanne to studie it of the newe, the text with the glose [gloss], and othere doctouris as he mighte gete, and speciali Lire [Nicholas of Lyre] on the elde testament that helpide ful myche in this werk. The thridde [third] tyme to counseile with elde gramariens and elde dyvynis [divines] of harde wordis and harde sentencis, hou [how] they mighten best be undurstonden and translatid. The fourthe tyme to translate as cleerli as he coude to the sentence, and to have manie gode felawis and kunnynge [knowledgeable] at the correcting of the translacioun.[177]

This leads to the deflation of a further aspect of the "myth" of Wycliffe's Bible: the notion that the Wycliffite Bible (in accord with Wycliffe's spirit, and as carried out by his Lollard followers) represented a stripping away of all the unnecessary academic-scholastic accretions, glosses, logical wranglings, disputations, etc., and a return to the unmediated text. As should be clear from Wycliffe's account of the Logic of Scripture, his mode of exegesis demanded a thorough familiarity with logic, grammar, and realist metaphysics, and the team of translators themselves used every available academic aid, including glosses and commentaries, to help them sort out the Latin variants and settle on the English translation. Wycliffe's "rebellion is not predicated on a simple and facile rejection of the premises and the superstructures of [his] contemporary academic study of the Bible," argues Kantik Ghosh. "What he instead attempts is a transformation, a reclamation of even academia from its present corrupt state into what it ideally should be: a devoted handmaiden serving the Word."[178] Thus, concludes Ghosh, the fallout heresy that developed from Wycliffe, Lollardy, is not essentially "an anti-intellectual heresy advocating a fundamentalist return to the Bible, though anti-intellectualism does form one of its major facets; it is equally an *intellectual* heresy. . . ."[179] Indeed, the Lollard achievement consists in "converting into popular vernacular currency ideas traditionally confined to an academic Latinate mint."[180] And so, "What needs to be kept in mind always, therefore, is the academic nature of the Lollard heresy, and its embeddedness in traditions of self-conscious intellectual endeavour."[181] Simply put, without Oxford, there would have been no Wycliffe or Wycliffite Bible.

This leads us to another aspect of the Wycliffite Bible that remains generally underappreciated. It was translated by followers of Wycliffe; that is, the textual decisions were made by those who adhered to Wycliffe's interpretation of the text. That is not to claim an entirely personal and peculiar translation, so that the adjective "Wycliffite" entirely modifies the noun "Bible." As we have seen, the translating team

177 Prologue to Wycliffite Bible in Hudson, ed., *Selections from English Wycliffite*, pp. 67–68.

178 Kantik Ghosh, *The Wycliffite Heresy: Authority and the Interpretation of Texts* (Cambridge: Cambridge University Press, 2002), p. 2.

179 Ibid., p. 2.

180 Ibid., *The Wycliffite Heresy*, p. 2.

181 Ibid., *The Wycliffite Heresy*, p. 15.

relied upon a wide variety of commentators, both ancient and modern, to help them sort out passages.

That having been said, we should not underestimate the transforming effect of the adjective. This suspicion is strengthened by realizing that his Oxford followers also produced (almost simultaneously) the *Floretum* (and its abbreviated version, the *Rosarium*), what amounted to a "Lollard theological dictionary" of some 3,000 pages,[182] meant for preachers as a theological guide: "it comprised, in the longest version, under some 509 topical headings, short quotations of and detailed references to the relevant passages in scripture, the fathers, later theologians, canonical authorities and Wyclif's own writings." Written between 1384 and 1396, the *Floretum* contained much of the scaffolding behind the construction of the Wycliffite Bible, and was intended as a guide to the interpretation of Scripture. Obviously, it too was an academic work, one that bore the stamp of Wycliffe's influence. J. I. Catto continues: "If one notable feature [of the *Floretum*], the range of citation from Wyclif's works, here elevated to equal status with those of the fathers, determines the Lollard origin of the compilation, another, the meticulous references and comprehensive sweep of topics, shows that its anonymous authors were scholars. Probably working in co-operation, and certainly having access to rich library resources, they produced a work comparable to that of the compilers of the glossed gospels; . . ."[183] A telling comparison, for it implies that one gloss had been replaced by another.

As to the subject of glosses, the Wycliffite circle also produced the so-called *Glossed Gospels*.[184] As the name suggests (and in contrast to the notion that Wycliffe and the Lollards were adverse to glossing), these were detailed commentaries on the four Gospels that made ample use of traditional authorities like Bede, Jerome, Augustine, Chrysostom, Ambrose, and Thomas Aquinas, among others. They were elaborately typological rather than plain and simple, and occasionally betrayed a Wycliffian slant. An illuminating example can be found in the glossed Gospel commentary on Luke 15:22–24, which shows not only a heavy-handed typological treatment of the parable of the prodigal son but also Wycliffe's bent toward preaching as primary. Upon seeing his wayward son return, the father orders the servants to "brynge ye a fat calf and slee yee, and eete we and make we feeste," which the commentary treats allegorically: the calf "is the Lord Iesu Crist" and the order "to bringe the calf and sle is to preche Crist and to shew his deeth, for thanne he is slayn as freshe to ech man whanne he bileveth hym slayn." Bede and Augustine are treated as authorities for this interpretation.[185] But the larger point should not be missed: The glosses were shaped by the spirit of Wycliffe's understanding of the text and his general concerns, even if they did not venture into heterodoxy. Apparently, the Wycliffite commentaries on the Psalms were even more heavy-handed, especially in condemnation of the clergy.[186]

182 The estimate of Hudson, *The Premature Reformation*, pp. 106–107.

183 Catto, "Wyclif and Wycliffism at Oxford, 1356–1430," 223.

184 For details see Hudson, *The Premature Reformation*, pp. 247–264.

185 Hudson, ed., *Selections from English Wycliffite*, pp. 49–50.

186 See Hudson's assessment in *The Premature Reformation*, pp. 257–264.

Another interesting piece of evidence supporting the Wycliffite slant of the translation was that in 1401 "the question of biblical translation could be debated openly, without accusations of heresy . . . and without identification of the proponents of translation as *Wycliffistes*."[187] But a little over half a decade later, given the success of the Lollard movement with its Bible and *Floretum*, Archbishop Thomas Arundel issued an edict "forbidding the possession of vernacular scripture unless the owner had received prior permission from his bishop, and unless the translation were one dating from *before* the time of Wyclif."[188]

At issue was not simply the fear of vulgarization, of putting the Bible (along with commentaries) into common hands.[189] Even more, there was a profound disagreement among scholars of the time about language, signification, and translatability. "The Franciscans, tracing their own tradition of biblical scholarship back to Robert Grosseteste, still regarded their order as the chief guardian of textual criticism. They recognized the errors that Purvey and his helpers discovered. They claimed that these errors would appear in the translation with more errors added, for English, they said, was not as exact a language as Latin. The errors upon errors would lead the uneducated English readers to heresy."[190] As Archbishop Arundel argued, "it is dangerous, as St. Jerome declares, to translate the text of Holy Scripture out of one idiom into another, since it is not easy in translations to preserve the same meaning in all particulars."[191] The problem strikes at the heart of the shared desire to get at the literal meaning—literal even in the broadest sense, as set forth by St. Thomas and affirmed in modified form by Wycliffe himself. As Rita Copeland notes, "If the literal sense, which is what the author intended, includes the idiomatic particulars of . . . [a] language, then it would be impossible to translate from one language to another without losing the literal sense."[192] Even more to our point, wherever there is ambiguity, decisions must be made, and there can be little doubt that in the Wycliffite Bible, decisions were made in accord with the *Floretum*.

Wycliffe obviously rejected the notion that there was any insurmountable difficulty in translating into the vernacular, pointing out that "Moses heard God's law in his own tongue, so did Christ's Apostles. Latin is the mother tongue of Italy as Hebrew

187 Hudson, "The Debate on Bible Translation, Oxford 1401," in Anne Hudson, *Lollards and Their Books* (London: The Hambledon Press, 1985), p. 83. Emphasis added.

188 Hudson, ed., *Selections from English Wycliffite*, pp. 163–164.

189 As one chronicler warned: "By this translation the scriptures have become vulgar, and they are more available to lay, and even to women who can read, than they were to learned scholars, who have a high intelligence. So the pearl of the gospel is scattered and trodden underfoot by swine." Quoted in Hall, *The Perilous Vision of John Wyclif*, p. 150.

190 Ibid., p. 150. Obviously, Hall still accepted the later efforts of translation to the headship of Purvey.

191 Rita Copeland, "Rhetoric and the Politics of the Literal Sense in Medieval Literary Theory: Aquinas, Wyclif, and the Lollards," in Piero Boitani and Anna Torti, eds., *Interpretation: Medieval and Modern* (Cambridge: D. S. Brewer, 1993), pp. 1–23; Arundel's quote from pp. 17–18.

192 Ibid., p. 18. We have dropped the confined term "rhetoric"—without doing violence to her meaning, we hope—because the point is valid beyond the confines of the rhetorical aspects of language to which she has confined her analysis in the essay.

is for the Jews."[193] And, of course, to accuse Wycliffe of heresy in this regard would, as he pointed out, implicate Queen Anne with her Czech and German Bibles.[194] His followers added:

> the trouthe of God stondith not in oo [one] langage more than in another, but who so lyveth best and techith best plesith moost God, of what langage that evere it be, therefore the lawe of God writen and taught in Englisch may edifie the commen pepel, as it doith clerkis in Latyn. . . . And Crist comaundid the gospel to be prechid, for the pepel schulde lerne it. . . . Whi may we not thanne writ in Englische the gospel and al holy scripture to edificacioun of cristen soulis. . . . For, if it schulde not be written, it schulde not be prechid.[195]

The command to "preche it to alle pepelis" demanded translation into "that langage that the pepel used to speke [i.e. the vernacular of each particular people], for thus he [Christ] taught himself."

> And here is a rule to cristyne folke of what langage so evere thei be: it is an highe sacrifi[c]e to God to knowe holy write and to do theraftur, wher it be taught or writen to hem in Latyn or in Englisch, in Frensche or in Duche, or in ony other langage after the pepel hathe understandynge.[196]

Surely, part of this confidence about complete translatability is attributable to Wycliffe's metaphysical realism, and not merely optimism about common "cristyne folke." If the human mind truly grasps universals, and these universals are ultimately in God's mind, then language, any language, merely serves as a sign of the understood universal. Indeed, it is God that first moves our mind "toward simple apprehension. . . . This Wisdom is the foremost active intellect," Wycliffe had earlier argued, "I ask you, what does it matter which sensible signs Uncreated Wisdom chooses to employ when illustrating her meaning, whether it is by adapting the words of so many languages to her logic, or more efficaciously instructing us through her works, or even most effectively through her internal inspiration?"[197] Every language, so it seems, should be completely adaptable to Scriptural Logic, and hence fully and equally able to translate the literal meaning of Scripture from its original languages.

But the translators go further, and claim that the intended sense—that is, the "literal" sense—of the text can be captured even better in English, not in a word-for-word translation, but one that captures the meaning: "the beste translating is, out of Latyn into English, to translate aftir the sentence [sense, meaning] and not

193 Quoted in Hall, *The Perilous Vision of John Wyclif*, p. 150.

194 Ibid., p. 151.

195 Hudson, ed., *Selections from English Wycliffite*, p. 107.

196 Ibid., p. 108.

197 Wyclif, *On the Truth of Holy Scripture*, I, ix, pp. 147–148.

oneli aftir the wordis, so that the sentence [sense, meaning] be as opin either openere [clear or clearer] in English as in Latyn, and go not fer from the lettre. . . ."[198] The shift from word-for-word translation to the sense of the passage is reflected in the presence of the *two* versions of the Wycliffite Bible. As Anne Hudson remarks, the two versions differ substantially: "one [the earlier] is a very literal, stilted, and at times unintelligible rendering; the other [the later] is a fluent, idiomatic version, and is found far more commonly [i.e., in terms of the number of manuscripts] than the other." The second was undertaken "in the realization that only those with the Latin beside the English could make sense of the first rendering, and that more concessions were needed to the vocabulary and fixed word order of English."[199] Speaking on behalf of the latter, the author of the Prologue claims he "purposede with Goddis helpe" to make the translation "as trewe [true] and open [clear] in English as it is in Latyn, either [or] more trewe and more open than it is in Latyn." And if anyone find fault with the "truthe of [this] translacioun, let him sette in the trew sentence and open [true and clear meaning] of holi writ. But loke that he examine truli his Latyn bible, for no doute he shal funde ful manye bibles in Latyn ful false, if he loke manie, namely newe. And the comune Latyn bibles han more need to be corrected, as manie as I have seen in my life, than hath the English bible late translatid."[200]

Finally, the writer of the Prologue chides the "worldi clerkis" who criticize the translation. If they had only read their "croniclis and bookis," they would have discovered that Bede and King Alfred had translated the Bible into Saxon, and Frenchman into their "modir [mother] langage." So "Whi shulden not English men have the same in here modir langage?" His answer: "I can not wite [know], no but [unless] for falsnesse and necligence of clerkis, either [or] for oure puple [people] is not worthi to have so greet grace and gifte of God, in peyne of here olde synnes. God for his merci amende these evele causis, and make oure puple to have and kunne [know] and kepe truli holi writ to lijf [life] and deth!"[201] Given the primacy of Scripture *as* Christ even over the Eucharist, this was a rallying cry to God—and, following Wycliffe, to the secular arm—to amend the evil causes by removing the false and negligent "clerkis." The assumption seems to be that *only* worldliness, deviance from apostolic poverty and holiness, would lead a cleric to question the translation. And whatever the old sins of the English people, the cure was having Scripture in the vernacular.

Enough has been said about the translation to affirm that it was a thoroughly academic undertaking, made by Wycliffe's followers who were well aware of significant textual variations and corruptions in the Latin, and fully confident that, by grace and effort, they could in many places improve on the Latin. Given what we know of the

198 Hudson, ed., *Selections from English Wycliffite*, p. 68.

199 Hudson, *The Premature Reformation*, pp. 238–239.

200 Hudson, ed., *Selections from English Wycliffite*, pp. 68–69.

201 Ibid., pp. 70–71.

rise of messianic English nationalism, as mentioned above, it seems a fair assumption that the Prologue writer's passion for an English Bible is animated in no small part by the vision of England as the new Israel.

Although Wycliffe did not translate the Bible, by 1379 he had completed a commentary on both Testaments.[202] The commentary was quite ordinary, even formulaic, for the most part.[203] Occasionally, he adds his own peculiar twist, such as in his interpretation of the "great image" with head of gold, breast and arms of silver, legs of iron and feet of iron and clay in Daniel 2:31–35. The fourth "kingdom" of iron and clay Wycliffe thought represented the secular power and the Church respectively, the clay signifying the Church weakened after its endowment.[204] But however ordinary it was for the most part, the passion behind the commentary was peculiarly Wycliffe's. In J. I. Catto's words, "Wyclif had fastened upon scripture the status of an idea. It was not 'lines on a parchment' but 'understanding in the mind' or 'a glass in which all truths are reflected'; here above all was the face of God turned upon man."[205] The inference was picked up by one of Wycliffe's most cogent detractors, William Woodford, who himself wrote a *Postilla super Matthaeum*, a bit after Wycliffe's. If Scripture contained all truth, asserted Woodford in a consequent lecture, then the Church would be superfluous; but many truths—such as the dogmas and creeds—were not in Scripture directly; the Church and doctrine preceded the written text; and tradition was necessary for the proper interpretation of Scripture.[206]

Eucharistic Heresy

While others were working on the translation in the last two decades of the fourteenth century, in the final years of his life Wycliffe was driving himself into heresy with his *De Eucharistia*. By the spring of 1381, Wycliffe's view, which he had been teaching publicly,[207] that (against the doctrine of transubstantiation) the substance of the bread and wine that exist before consecration, remain after consecration, was condemned as heretical by an Oxford University council. At

202 On Wycliffe's commentary on the Old Testament, see Smalley, "Wyclif's *Postilla* on the Old Testament and his *Principium*," mentioned above and also Smalley, "John Wyclif's *Postilla super totam bibliam*," *Bodleian Library Record*, iv (1953), pp. 186–205. Although it may seem impossible that Wycliffe could have produced so great a work in so short a time, we must recall that Wycliffe was already engaged lecturing on the entire Bible between 1371 and 1376, and that much of the material in the lectures and written commentary is based on previous authors.

203 As Smalley relates, with some whimsy, the formula was quite simple: "use [Pierre] Auriol's *Compendium* [*totius Biblie*] as a mould, pour in [Nicholas of] Lyre, flavour with Augustine, and sprinkle with [Robert] Grosseteste." Smalley, "Wyclif's *Postilla* on the Old Testament and his *Principium*," p. 256.

204 Ibid., pp. 264–265.

205 Catto, "Wyclif and Wycliffism at Oxford, 1356–1430," p. 196.

206 Ibid., pp. 196–197, 205.

207 It seems that his controversial position might have been formulated as early as 1379. G. R. Evans, *John Wyclif*, p. 186.

issue for him (as he made clear in his *Confessio de Sacramento Altaris*, 1381) was the philosophical explanation.[208] While accepting that the self-same Body of Christ that suffered on the cross was resurrected and is now in heaven was really in the sacramental host, Wycliffe could not allow the supernatural realm to conflict with the natural realm in a way that violated his extreme realist metaphysics. As we noted above, his realism could not allow for the annihilation of a substance (in this case, the substances of bread and wine), nor could it allow for accidents (in this case, of bread and wine) to exist without their proper subject (since accidents without a subject would be, for Wycliffe, the lowest thing in nature, less than mud).[209] Wycliffe attempted a novel explanation, based in part on his earlier fascination with light and optics, a light metaphysic in which the Body of Christ was present sacramentally like the reflection of a body in a mirror.[210]

An appeal to John of Gaunt for protection was met with a personal visit in which the duke advised, if not commanded, Wycliffe to keep silent. Wycliffe would thence give up teaching at Oxford and retire to Lutterworth in 1381, but not before firing off three quite bitter treatises *De Simonia*, *De Apostasia*, and *De Blasphemia*, the first attacking religious endowments and property, the second Petrine authority and religious orders, and the third the papacy and transubstantiation.

The Peasant Revolt, Condemnation, and Death

The same year that Wycliffe retired to Lutterworth brought the great Peasant Revolt, which has been blamed by some on the teaching of Wycliffe. Whatever the connection, Wycliffe writing afterward in his *De Blasphemia*, chastises the peasants only insofar as "they acted a little beyond the law." But the clergy received less violence than was due them, for the cause of the revolt was the temporal riches of the clergy.[211] The animus of the common folk was directed, not at the king, but at the nobility, whom they regarded as bleeding them dry, and even more at the great monasteries that held many around them as tenants in the conditions of

208 Evans, *John Wyclif*, pp. 189–190.

209 See Catto "John Wyclif and the Cult of the Eucharist," in *The Bible in the Medieval World: Essays in Memory of Beryl Smalley* (Oxford: Basil Blackwell, 1985), pp. 269–286.

210 Catto explains, quoting Wycliffe: "In the sacrament the *figura* of Christ, a kind of mirror image of the Body of Christ in heaven, was present on the altar: as he explained in the language of optics: 'To understand how the body of Christ is sacramentally, not dimensionally, present in this venerable sacrament, consider the view of the optical philosophers who tell us that when a clean mirror is placed proportionately opposite a shape, a full likeness of that shape is present in every point of that mirror, although one man may see it in one point and another man in another point, depending on where the mirror falls and reflects.'" See Catto, "John Wyclif and the Cult of the Eucharist," p. 273. The belief that Wycliffe simply rejected the Eucharist as a sacrament, or denied that Christ was truly present, most likely came from his excoriations of what he considered to be idolatrous practices of Eucharistic devotion. See Ibid.

211 On this, see Hudson, *The Premature Reformation*, pp. 68–69.

serfs.[212] Especially an enemy to the people was Wycliffe's old protector, John of Gaunt, who for the rioters signified the nobility that stood in the way between the people and their good and sympathetic king, Richard II. Or so they thought. Even though Richard momentarily granted the rebels' requests, upon being able to gather his knights, he suppressed them savagely.

Wycliffe's continual attacks on the riches of the Church and monasteries and his call for their disendowment and forced return to poverty at the hand of civil power, had appealed to the king's desire to lessen papal interference, but had also ironically proven a source for insurrection against the nexus of the state's comfortable political-economic-ecclesiastical arrangements. Again, the problem, for the king and nobles, was not ecclesiastical riches gained through taxes, tithes, and fines, but the flow of these riches out of England to Rome. Thus to the civil power Wycliffe represented both a boon and a threat.

The latter would soon be dealt with. William Courtenay had recently been elevated from bishop of London to Canterbury, and in the year after the Peasant Revolt, 1382, heresy proceedings were initiated against Wycliffe at the Blackfriars Synod in London, where twenty-four heretical propositions were listed. Wycliffe was still only a priest at Lutterworth, but was continually busy preaching and publishing his doctrines. With the uprising, the king and nobles were now alarmed at the implications of Wycliffe's doctrines. As if to certify divine displeasure, a great earthquake hit England that year, followed by another outbreak of the plague. Wycliffe's books were confiscated from Oxford, his followers were prohibited from teaching or preaching his condemned doctrines, and Archbishop Courtenay condemned ten of Wycliffe's propositions as heretical and fourteen as erroneous. Wycliffe himself suffered a stroke in November of that same year, and was rendered partly paralyzed. His sermons and writings had already turned bitter, and were laced with personal outbursts.[213] It was during this time that he wrote his summary work, the *Trialogus*, a dialogue between Truth (*Alithia*), Falsehood (*Pseustis*) and the interlocutor representing Wycliffe, Wisdom (*Phronesis*). This work would be his most popular, and the first to be printed (in 1525) rather than hand-copied.

In December 1382, a crusade was called against the antipope Clement VII—in effect, a crusade against France for supporting him. As England had already been warring intermittently with France in the Hundred Years' War since 1337, Pope Urban

212 The monasteries charged tenants a pound for the privilege of marrying daughters ($200–$300 by today's standards); tenants had to use the monastery's grain mill (private grinding stones had been confiscated) and its wool processing facilities; tenants had to work sometimes three quarters of their year on monastery lands at the expense of their own; and finally they had to endure a multitude of other taxes and fines. See Hall, *The Perilous Vision of John Wyclif*, Ch.18.

213 "A considerable number of little choleric works came from Wyclif's pen during these last few years in Lutterworth. Like his revisions to earlier works, these were not the products of an intellectual maturity but of a disappointed old age. They lack any coherence but that lent by his obsessive anger. This was not the saintly old age of hagiographical convention but a raging against the dying of the light, and against anything else which came in his way. He took the criticism of his ideas extremely personally." See Evans, *John Wyclif*, p. 204.

VI's call fit conveniently with existing royal aims. Wycliffe, who had already consigned both popes as antichrists to hell, inveighed against the crusade.

In January 1383, the young king Richard II married Anne of Bohemia, thereby providing a momentous geographical connection of Wycliffe's ideas to the distant East European nation. Wycliffe himself would suffer his second stroke while hearing Mass on December 28, 1384, and die three days later. Queen Anne would die ten years hence, much to the sorrow of her devoted husband Richard. Wycliffe's influence would not end with his life, partly due to Anne of Bohemia, and partly due to his native English followers, the Lollards.

The Lollards

As mentioned above, the followers of Wycliffe in England came to be called Lollards, although in what exact sense they can be considered followers of Wycliffe is much debated. However the notion that reigned in modern scholarship for some time, that there is no connection between Wycliffe and Lollardy, has been overthrown in the past quarter century. The best estimation seems to be that Lollardy was "a heresy that began as a product of academic speculation but that moved out of the academic world to become a popular movement."[214]

The first use of "Lollard" in regard to Wycliffe's disciples seems to have been as a term of abuse by an opponent, the Cistercian Dr. Henry Crumpe in 1382.[215] The term "lollard" appears to have come from the Dutch *lollen*, to mumble, a term "used for any kind of vagabond or religious eccentric."[216] Already during Wycliffe's lifetime, his views were being spread. Part of this is certainly due to his sermons, of which it was complained that he did not preach his views circumspectly, but "*nude et aperte*" "nakedly and openly."[217] Wycliffe's own stress on preaching could not help but to inspire followers, beginning with his academic circle referred to above in their translation of the Bible and dispersion of his *Floretum*.

As an example of the penetration of Wycliffism in academia, Robert Rygge, chancellor at Oxford and very sympathetic to Wycliffe's views, invited two other avid followers of Wycliffe, Nicholas Hereford and Philip Repingdon, to give sermons at Oxford's St. Frideswide's Church in late spring of 1382. Both delivered their sermons in the vernacular, inveighed against the wealth of the clergy, and called for disendowment, while Hereford rather forthrightly affirmed the Peasant Revolt.[218]

214 Hudson, *The Premature Reformation*, p. 62. She continues: "Academic heresies were, of course, numerous in the period, heresies of popular origin no less so; but Wycliffism both in its English and its Bohemian manifestations seems to be the only case of a progression between the two worlds." Ibid. See also, Dickens, *The English Reformation*, pp. 46–56.

215 Catto, "Wyclif and Wycliffism at Oxford, 1356–1430," p. 216.

216 Hudson, ed., *Selections from English Wycliffite Writing*, "Introduction," p. 7–8.

217 Quoted in Hudson, *The Premature Reformation*, p. 65.

218 Hudson, *The Premature Reformation*, pp. 70–72.

From Oxford, the appeal to the laity radiated outward to London, then Leicester, Coventry, Bristol, Northampton, and beyond, first by the preaching of Oxford academics, and then by those from outside academia whom they influenced. Wycliffe's ideas were also disseminated by books, pamphlets, broadsheets, and laymen, especially of certain gentry (the so-called Lollard Knights) among the court of Henry IV (1399–1413).

The height of Lollard influence during this period was the Disendowment Bill presented to Parliament in 1410. The Bill is almost stunning in its attempt to "sell" the king and nobles on disendowment, the first three quarters of it being merely a matter-of-fact dollars and cents (or pounds and shillings) listing of the riches to be gained by the crown and nobles in disendowing particular monasteries, bishoprics, and temporalities. It then ends with the rationale for disendowment, pointing the finger at "thes worldely clerkes, bisshopes, abbots and priours" who do not live as "trewe curates," "helpe nat the pore," "lyve nat in penaunce ne in bodily travaylle as trew religious shulden by here p[rog]ession."[219] It was an ominous foreshadowing of what was to come about a century later under Henry VIII.

Ensuring this connection, Lollard texts also stressed the primacy of royal over ecclesial power, echoing Wycliffe's argument (again, hearkening back to the Anonymous of York) that kings represented the divine, kingly power of Christ, while priests only represented Christ's temporary human and priestly power. The "state of seculere lordis" is as "vicars of the godhead," while "the state of prestisis" was merely as "vicaris of his manhede."[220] As caretakers of order, "kyngis and lordis schulden wite [know] that thei ben [they are] mynystris and vikeris of God to venge synee and ponysche mysdoeris," and that included especially the clergy who did not live up to their holy vocation. In addition, Lollards followed Wycliffe's affirmation of St. Paul (Romans 13:1–7) that subjection to temporal rulers was subjection to God.[221]

Suppression of Wycliffe's doctrines began, as we have seen, even during his life, and persecution continued afterward against Lollardy in the early 1400s. In 1401 *De Heretico Comburendo* was passed under King Henry IV, prohibiting the ownership or production of a translation of the Bible and proscribing the death penalty for heresy. Archbishop Arundel's *Constitutions* issued in 1408 against Wycliffe's doctrines helped dampen but not extinguish Lollardy. Additional political animus against Lollardry occurred with another rebellion. Sir John Oldcastle—made famous later in Shakespeare as Falstaff in *Henry IV*—was arrested for Lollardy in 1413 and convicted, but escaped only to head up what has been called Oldcastle's Revolt. He was finally caught and hanged in December 1417. From then on, although there are records of trials for heresy, Lollardry seems to have gone largely underground until the last quarter of the 1400s; however, records of investigations during this period show that evident continuity existed between Lollardry at the beginning of the 1400s and identifiably

219 Hudson, ed., *Selections from English Wycliffite Writing*, pp. 135–137.

220 Quoted in Hudson, *The Premature Reformation*, p. 363.

221 Ibid., p. 364–367.

Lollard opinions arising with "ever-increasing frequency" at the end of the century and leading up to the reign of Henry VIII.[222]

If we might offer a general pattern of the historical transition from Wycliffe to his followers during this period, it would be fair to say that the very academic and philosophical nature of Wycliffe's thought dissipated as it spread. A seemingly arcane philosophical quibble about the terms of transubstantiation of the Eucharist soon became an outright rejection of the sacrament as anything but a symbol. Wycliffe's worries about pilgrimages, icons, and statues turned to scorn and iconoclasm. Wycliffe's complex foundation of philosophical realism that regarded Christ Himself as Scripture and offered a sophisticated Scriptural Logic, soon enough became the quite simple cry of *sola scriptura* as interpreted by anyone who could read (and many more who were illiterate but had memorized parts of Scripture).[223] And finally, as we shall see in our chapter on Henry VIII, Wycliffe's call for disendowment by the secular ruler for the sake of holiness and reform soon offered support for the control of the Church by a king for purely political purposes.

From England to Bohemia: the Hussites

Wycliffism did not stay in England, but traveled to Bohemia, and became the foundation of the Hussite movement, named after John Hus. How that happened is rather complex, and amply demonstrates how entwined were politics and theology. Marsilius's champion Ludwig of Bavaria had died in October of 1347, the victim of an accident while on a bear hunt. The imperial title, which had never been properly affirmed, was empty again. But another claimant was already in the offing, the future Holy Roman Emperor Charles IV. Charles was born Wenceslaus in Bohemia.[224] As heir to Luxembourg and Bohemia, Charles was an imperial elector who was himself elected as King of Germany in 1346, thereby displacing Ludwig as imperial designate a year before the latter's death. In 1355, he became Holy Roman Emperor, and made Prague the imperial capital. One of his great achievements was founding the University of Prague in 1348, the first university in central Europe.

How did Wycliffe's doctrines get to Prague? As noted above, Edward III's son, the Black Prince, died before him, the Black Prince's son Richard II inherited the English crown in 1377 at age ten. By dynastic arrangement Richard would marry Anne of Bohemia, the eldest daughter of Holy Roman Emperor Charles IV, in 1382. Anne would bring to England a train of Bohemians, including Bohemian scholars who then studied at Oxford—where they eagerly picked up the doctrines of John Wycliffe. The connection between Oxford and the University of Prague was thereby established, and

222 Dickens, *The English Reformation*, pp. 49–56.

223 For a detailed analysis see Hudson, *The Premature Reformation*, Ch. 10.

224 His father was King John the Blind of Luxembourg and Bohemia, who died as a mercenary to the king of France in the Hundred Years' War, at the Battle of Crécy (1346). King John was commanding the first French division, his horse strapped to the horses of some of his other men, so that he, a blind leader, could be led into battle.

that is how Master John Hus of Bohemia became a zealous propagator of Wycliffe's doctrines.

But it would be a mistake to assume that Wycliffe's writings, by themselves, were the sole cause of the Bohemian reformation or revolution. The reform movement in Bohemia went back to the 1360s, to the Prague priest Jan Milíč, who embraced both poverty and a zealous reforming spirit, chastising the clergy for luxury and immorality and setting up a reform center called Jerusalem in the center of the red-light district of Prague. At the core of his reform was the Eucharist, which he and his followers understood to be the very heart of renewal. Fr. Milíč, stressed frequent communion, and this emphasis would become transformed over the next half century, to the characteristic focus on communion in both kinds for the laity (*utraquism*). Milíč would die in Avignon in 1374, having been summoned on charges of heresy.[225] The reform movement in Bohemia would grow, even though directly opposed by the archbishop of Prague.

A new center of renewal, the Bethlehem Chapel, was founded in Prague in 1391, and in 1402 Jan Hus would become its rector. Wycliffe's writings had already appeared prior to this time, but Hus (along with the Czech faculty at the University of Prague) pushed his writings to prominence.

From Prague they would spread through the empire. Charles IV modeled the University of Prague after the great University of Paris, and sought great scholars from all over his territory to populate the academic halls of his new university. (In fact, Prague was the first German language university in Europe.) Bohemia itself held a mixture of German and Czech population, and the struggle between Germans and Slavs was played out between German and Czech faculty at the University of Prague.[226]

As with other medieval universities, Prague was divided into nations, in this instance four with voting rights, Saxon, Bavarian, Polish and Czech (the Czech nation being made up of Bohemia, Moravia, Hungary, Croatia, Transylvania, and Spain). In voting, the Saxon, Bavarian, and Polish nations acted as a German nation, continually outvoting the Czech nation three to one.[227]

By 1403, Wycliffe's writings had gained much popularity, principally, among the Czech nation. That very year the university masters espousing Wycliffe's realism were accused of heresy by the masters espousing nominalism, in an interesting divide pitting Czech versus German, Wycliffe versus Ockham, realist versus nominalist, and *via antiqua* versus *via moderna*. A German master, Johannes Hübner, declaring Wycliffe heretical, gathered together the twenty-four articles condemned at the Blackfriars Synod in London in 1382 along with another twenty-one, and these forty-five articles became the basis of his later condemnation.[228] This was a difficult and contentious act by the Germans, given that John Hus himself had just been dean of the faculty of arts,

225 Thomas Fudge, *The Magnificent Ride: The First Reformation in Hussite Bohemia* (Aldershot, England: Ashgate, 1998), pp. 48–51.

226 Ibid., pp. 29, 63–64, 69–70.

227 Ibid., p. 69.

228 Ibid., p. 64.

and was then rector of the university. It was he who had translated Wycliffe's masterwork, the *Trialogus*, into Czech nearly two years before the condemnation, and he was not about to withdraw his support.

At this time, the king of Bohemia was King Wenceslaus IV (in Czech, Václav IV), the son of Emperor Charles IV. (Wenceslaus himself was never able to make good on his claim to follow his father as emperor, and, in fact, was officially deposed by the German electors.) Hus cleverly used King Wenceslaus IV's opposition to Pope Gregory XII, one of the two popes claiming authority in the Great Schism. In the disputes in regard to legitimacy of the papal claimants during the Great Schism, the three non-Czech nations had sided with Pope Gregory XII, whom Wenceslaus IV opposed. Knowing this opposition, Hus was able to extract from Wenceslaus the "Kuttenberg Decree" (1409) that gave the Czech nation *three* votes and the other three nations combined only *one* vote in the university's affairs, thereby giving the Czechs a victory over the Germans. Obviously, Hus's goal was to overturn the condemnation of Wycliffe's doctrines, but this cannot be understood apart from nationalist conflicts. The immediate effect, however, was the mass emigration of the German professors and students from Prague to the University of Leipzig in the spring of 1409, a kind of intellectual disembowelment of the University of Prague from which it never really recovered, but which allowed it to become the intellectual center of the Hussite revolution.

Warned by the archbishop of Prague, Pope Alexander V (elected at the Council of Pisa, to take the place of the two popes it deposed, Benedict XIII and Gregory XII) was soon aligned against the Hussites as well, and a papal bull was issued in December 1409. The archbishop used the forty-five heretical propositions as the basis of his investigation. Alexander V would die in May, and (the putative) John XXIII would take his place, but as there were still rival popes, settling the schism would await the Council of Constance.

Hus remained intransigent, boldly proclaiming in Bethlehem Chapel his continued support for Wycliffe and reform.

> This pope who has just died, whether he is in heaven or hell I cannot say, has written to the archbishop on his asses's skins that the books of Master John Wyclif should be burned. But there are many good things in these books. Behold, they say in their bulls that they desire to uproot the false teachings of Wyclif which have become heresy in the hearts of many people in Prague.

At this point, it is reported that the great crowd at the Chapel cried out, "They lie, they lie," to which Hus replied:

> Yes they lie, and I tell you, while thanking God, that I have never seen a Czech heretic. Behold, I have appealed against the mandate of the archbishop and again I will appeal. Will you stand with me?

And they replied, "We will, and we do." To which Hus made the fateful response, "The time has come for us, just as it did for Moses in the Old Testament, to take up our swords and defend the law of God."[229] Wycliffe's books were publicly burned in July of 1410.

For political reasons, King Wenceslaus IV originally sided with the reformers, but when political opportunities changed, so did his support. The occasion is of some interest, in light of what would happen soon enough in Luther's Germany. John XXIII was ousted from Rome by the King of Naples, and in turn he called for a crusade against the king, complete with indulgences. As he would get a significant portion of the indulgence money, Wenceslaus backed John XXIII, even while Hus spoke out against it, vehemently criticizing the pope's bull of indulgence. Now the pope and Wenceslaus were aligned against Hus, and the king ordered Bethlehem Chapel destroyed in 1412. Hus went into exile for two years, but did not remain silent.

While Wenceslaus IV of Bohemia could not secure the imperial crown, his younger half-brother Sigismund would become emperor, ruling from 1410 to 1437, and it was he who would help convene the Council of Constance in the fall of 1414 both to hear the case of Hus, and more importantly to settle the Great Schism. Forty-two articles from Hus's *De Ecclesia* (itself based heavily on the writings of Wycliffe) were considered as heretical, the panel of judges for his case including the great nominalists, Pierre d'Ailly and Jean Gerson. The charges were finally whittled down to thirty, but Hus refused to recant because he denied holding them. He was condemned and burned at the stake in July 1415, thereby galvanizing a Hussite League to carry on reform *and* revolution, with Hus as its martyr. Given the condemnation of Wycliffe and Hus, nominalists could now portray "the realists as defenders of John Wyclif, whose teachings had been condemned at Oxford, Prague, and at the Council of Constance."[230]

The cause of the Hussites soon united Church reform, radical social reform, communion in both kinds, and apocalypticism. It thereby became more of a danger to the state. King Wenceslaus IV was unable to stop the movement. Pope Martin V, newly elected at the Council of Constance to heal the Schism, issued a crusade bull in March 1420. The heir to the Bohemian throne and the emperor-to-be, Sigismund, answered the call with a host of other German princes, but the Hussites would achieve victory after victory, marching under the sign of the chalice and the inspiration of their saint, Jan Hus. The Hussites not only fought on their own native turf, but struck out at all those countries that supplied Germany with soldiers. Needless to say, the Germans saw the Hussites (and hence, Wycliffe and even philosophical realism) as a most serious political danger. One could hardly imagine a greater entanglement of theology, Scripture, philosophy, and politics—but there is more to come.

229 Quoted in ibid., p. 72.

230 Maarten J. F. M. Hoenen, "*Via Antiqua* and *Via Moderna* in the Fifteenth Century: Doctrinal, Institutional, and Church Political Factors in the *Wegestreit*, in Russel Friedman and Lauge Nielsen, *The Medieval Heritage in Early Modern Metaphysics and Modal Theory, 1400–1700* (Dordrecht: Kluwer Academic Publishers, 2003), p. 21.

The Ongoing Battle between the Via Antiqua *and* Via Moderna

The German exodus from the University of Prague amounted to what might be characterized as a philosophical migration, but one that could not help but become part of the larger political turmoil as it unfolded. The University of Leipzig was founded that same year (1409) by the Elector of Saxony, Frederick I, for the very purpose of receiving the exodus from Prague. Frederick would spend great energy fighting the Hussites, so that for Frederick and much of Germany, Wycliffe, Hus, realism, and the *via antiqua* were doubly distasteful as tainted by heresy and linked to political rebellion.

The effect of this association was far-reaching for the ongoing battle between the *via antiqua* and *via moderna*. The University of Paris condemned nominalism in 1474, a condemnation issued by King Louis XI in his capacity as "most Christian king" responsible for purity of France's faith. Hence, the works of Ockham, John of Mirecourt, Gregory of Rimini, Jean Buridan, Pierre d'Ailly, and others, known as *nominales* or *terministae* (but not specifically *moderni*), were proscribed.[231] This did not stop the battle, as a private letter of the following year attests: "The nominalists and realists are warring in a ridiculous fashion as gladiators."[232]

It is of some interest that that the Parisian nominalists' manifesto, written in self-defense after the condemnation in the same year, proudly claimed Ockham as "*primus*" among nominalists, and noted that it was nominalist doctors who successfully brought about the condemnation of the heretic John Hus at the Council of Constance.[233] The manifesto also issued a complaint that nominalists had been unjustly persecuted three times, the first when Ockham himself was persecuted, and the second by the Hussites in Bohemia who forced the nominalists to leave Prague and migrate to Leipzig, and the third when the University of Paris was dispersed (after the murder of a duke in 1407), and the Albertists took over, throwing out the doctrines of the nominalists.[234] In any case, nominalism did not disappear from Paris. The king lifted the ban on nominalist works in 1481, and thereupon nominalism prospered at Paris, the most popular being associated with Jean Buridan.[235]

Just to add to the confusion of names and doctrines brought about by the condemnation of Wycliffe, in the last quarter of the fourteenth century followers of St. Albert and St. Thomas attempted to identify themselves by the term *via antiqua*, rather than the more general term *reales*, precisely to distinguish themselves from the heretical John Wycliffe and the Wycliffites.[236] It seems that the University of Louvain attempted

---

231 Ibid., p. 31; Gilbert, "Ockham, Wyclif, and the '*Via Moderna*,'" p. 93–94; and Astrik Gabriel, "'*Via Antiqua*' and '*Via Moderna*' in the Fifteenth Century," in Albert Zimmermann, ed., *Antiqui und Moderni*, pp. 446–447.

232 The letter is by Robert Gaguin, February 1475. Quoted in Gabriel, "'*Via antiqua*' and '*via moderna*' in the Fifteenth Century," p. 447.

233 Gilbert, "Ockham, Wyclif, and the '*Via Moderna*'," pp. 95–96.

234 Gabriel, "'*Via Antiqua*' and '*Via Moderna*' in the Fifteenth Century," p. 449.

235 Ibid., pp. 453–454.

236 See Gilbert, "Ockham, Wyclif, and the '*Via Moderna*,'" p. 106.

to follow this distinction in 1447, restricting interpretations of Aristotle to those of Albert and Thomas, and prohibiting the mode of approach found in Wycliffe, Ockham, and their followers, all who are called *nominales* or *terministae*.[237] The faculty of arts at Louvain had forbidden the teaching of "*Buridanum, Marsilium* [i.e., of Inghen], *Ockam, aut eorum sequaces*" twenty years earlier.[238] The University of Heidelberg, founded in 1386, was nominalist from the beginning, Marsilius of Inghen having been instrumental in its founding. To stop the flow of the Wycliffian heresy from Prague, a statute in 1412 prohibited not only Wycliffe's works but any doctrines of realism. Heidelberg would later begrudgingly accept proponents of the *via antiqua* at mid-century. Just before the end of the century, there was a proud revival of Marsilius of Inghen's doctrines.[239]

We can see the wisdom of Maarten Hoenen's assessment that, while the philosophical roots of nominalism reach back to Ockham, the "*via moderna* was a typical product of the fifteenth century, closely related to the proliferation of new universities in the German Empire and the dangers of Hussitism."[240] For the same reason, the *via antiqua* was, by this time, not a simple presentation of the orthodox views of St. Thomas or St. Albert, but was enmeshed in contemporary assessments with Wycliffe, Hus, and official council condemnation, and through guilt by association, social revolution in Bohemia that threatened to spill over into Germany.

The confusions and complexities did not remain merely philosophical and political, but focused on methods of exegesis as well. In 1340, the Faculty of Arts at Paris issued a statute warning against the use of logic detached from faith, specifically in regard to scriptural interpretation. Logic detached from the subject matter of the Bible, they warned, could result in showing the biblical texts were contradictory.

This, of course, sounds exactly like Wycliffe's later diatribe against the nominalists at Oxford. But Wycliffe's designation of nominalism as the enemy was not unchallenged, as a later document (1388) makes clear, written by the nominalist Cardinal Pierre d'Ailly against Johannes de Montesono, a Thomist. Writing on behalf of the University of Paris, Pierre d'Ailly makes the above charge against Johannes that, as Hoenen reports, "Thomas Aquinas was a clear example of a theologian who illegitimately used philosophical arguments in theology and thus came to conclusions that were almost heretical—an accusation which was repeated in the fifteenth and sixteenth centuries."[241] It was the nominalist Pierre d'Ailly, we recall, who helped condemn Hus at the Council of Constance.

---

237 Hoenen, "*Via Antiqua* and *Via Moderna* in the Fifteenth Century," p. 21. The list of the approved doctors is much longer—including Aristotle, Averroes, Duns Scotus, and Bonaventure—and they are referred to as *Doctorum Realium*. Among those included in the condemnation of the "Renewing Doctors" (*Doctorum Renovatorum*) are John of Mirecourt, Gregory of Rimini, Jean Buridan, Pierre d'Ailly. Gilbert, "Ockham, Wyclif, and the '*Via Moderna*,'" p. 94.

238 Ibid., p. 91.

239 Gabriel, "'*Via Antiqua*' and '*Via Moderna*'in the Fifteenth Century," pp. 459–464.

240 Hoenen, "'*Via Antiqua*' and '*Via Moderna*' in the Fifteenth Century," p. 12.

241 Ibid., pp. 23–24.

But countercharges of heresy were forthcoming, in an important early instance by Jerome of Prague, who along with Hus, was an avid propagator of Wycliffe's views at the University of Prague. When Jerome visited the University of Heidelberg for a debate in 1406, he defended the Wycliffian position that denying the reality of universals led ineluctably to heresy, and so nominalists such as Ockham, Jean Buridan, and Marsilius of Inghen were *heretici diabolice*. Witnesses at the debate, specifically the nominalists at Heidelberg, would later testify at the Council of Constance, thereby ensuring that Jerome was burned at the stake a year after Hus, another early martyr for the Hussite revolution.[242]

Again, the association of the *via antiqua* with the Bohemian revolution would mean that the *via moderna* would therefore be allied with social conservatism, especially to the nearby German princes. The German elector princes wrote a letter to the city of Cologne in 1425, warning that it had better compel the university to abandon its allegiance to the *via antiqua* since the writings of Albert and Thomas, whatever their merits, were confusing to young minds and associated with the heresy condemned at Constance. Better to stick to the *magistri moderniores*, John Buridan, and Marsilius of Inghen.[243] Cologne had started off on a nominalist foot, but soon held to the *via antiqua*. The Cologne master politely but firmly asserted the superiority of the *via antiqua*, but noted that students were permitted to study the *via moderna*.[244] This connection between social and theological conservatism in the German electors' minds remains part of the context of Luther, less than a century hence, and accounts for Luther's ambiguous relationship to Wycliffe.

The Importance of Wycliffe

Readers are certainly aware by now that the real John Wycliffe is considerably more complex than the "morning star" of legend, especially in regard to the politicization of Scripture. Although Wycliffe was a declared enemy of Ockham, insofar as he set forth an almost Marsilian argument he had the unintended effect (as did Ockham) of reinforcing the secularizing, politicizing thrust of Marsilius's thought. And so, even while Wycliffe obviously would not approve of Marsilius's rather ruthless subordination of the Church and scriptural interpretation to the state, in calling for disendowment, in advocating the necessity of "court theologians," and in gathering from Scripture almost unqualified support for the king as a kind of Davidic figure, Wycliffe's solution to the problem of Church reform fit all too well with Marsilius's politicizing plan. This unintended synergy between Marsilius and Wycliffe would prove to be decisive for Henry VIII's policies: Marsilius's *Defensor Pacis* was read and put into practice by Henry's closest advisors; the English soil was prepared for Marsilian thought by over a century of distillation of Wycliffe through Lollardy.

---

242 Hoenen, "'*Via Antiqua*' and '*Via Moderna*' in the Fifteenth Century," pp. 25–26.

243 Ibid., p. 28.

244 Gabriel, "'*Via Antiqua*' and '*Via Moderna*' in the Fifteenth Century," pp. 465–466.

Intimately related to this, Wycliffe's participation in English messianic nationalism lent tremendous weight to the establishment of a national Church, one (again) in which the king ruled, in the style of David and Solomon, the priesthood. Since the focus is on the nation, the English nation, Wycliffe's exegesis in support of a national Church could not help but involve a politicization of Scripture. If England is the new Israel, salvation history as found in Scripture must be reinterpreted with English history as its culmination.

Of course, as noted above, this shift of focus from empire to nation is not found solely in England; in fact, we offer Wycliffe and England as an example of the politicization of Scripture that of necessity accompanied the rise of nationalism. England was neither the first nor the last case of messianic nationalism. And although Wycliffe himself did not translate the Bible from Latin to English, the labors of his followers in this regard cannot be understood apart from this larger context. For the Bible to pass from Hebrew to Greek to Latin and finally into English represented the march of Providence through political history.

We repeat that especially for Wycliffe this was a very practical and hence political transformation, one in which salvation history had to be actively produced rather than passively awaited. Wycliffe was not calling for general spiritual renewal and leaving the rest up to God; he was demanding that the state put the Church back into the position of the *ecclesia primitiva*, the apostolic, pre-Constantinian Church as Wycliffe drew it from Scripture, which was the faithfully followed template for the mythical *ecclesia terrae Angliae* of England's golden age. Certainly, Wycliffe himself seemed to believe that, in his service to the state, he was fulfilling his duty as court theologian, as r*egis clericus*. But he also appears dangerously naïve in regard to the real motives of his political masters, John of Gaunt and Edward III. In failing to account fully for the threat of political manipulation, his attempt to take the Church back to apostolic purity or an Anglican golden age would all too easily lead it forward to the complete political manipulation of Henry VIII's *Anglicana Ecclesia*, wherein the adjective threatens to swallow the noun.

There are other no less important connections to future politicization that are more indirect. We have been at pains to distinguish Wycliffe's philosophically and theologically sophisticated presentation of Scripture from the much simpler later doctrines of *sola scriptura*. If readers have had difficulty in keeping that distinction intact, they have inadvertently duplicated the history of Wycliffe's doctrine in the century after its espousal.

For Wycliffe, Scripture alone could only mean Christ alone, for He and He alone is the "Book of Life," the "Scripture that cannot be destroyed." The difficulty with this position is that the high-flying metaphysical realism that makes it intelligible cannot easily pass into common coin (and, indeed, becomes suspect anyway with the condemnation at Constance). The "decay" of the position into a simple notion of *sola scriptura,* in which the individual reader of the text claims immediate access to its truth, was inevitable, and indeed occurred in Lollardry. In fact, it was inherent in Wycliffe's original argument. Where else was Christ to be known but through the Scripture? And if the Church and the hierarchy were not only corrupt, but likely among those damned by predestination, then all authority of interpretation was thrown back upon the individual believer. Since multiple interpretations will then naturally arise, the confusion will call for an authoritative clarification. Wycliffe would have this done by properly trained theologians, but since they are in service to the state, the remedy for clarification falls to the secular power. The practical effect will be for the state to settle theological disputes arising from multiple interpretations according to exigencies of state.

Our chapters on Luther, Henry VIII, Thomas Hobbes, Rene Descartes, and Benedict Spinoza will follow the consequences of having the state settle biblical disputes for the early development of modern biblical scholarship. That the state should be vitally interested in settling theological disputes during and after the Reformation should come as no surprise, since we have seen that with both Wycliffe and the Hussites, political and social revolution seemed to go hand in hand in the two centuries prior to the Reformation. This pattern will continue in Luther's Germany.

We must now turn to a thorough analysis of Luther and the Reformation in Germany. Here we will discover other similarities between Wycliffe and Luther. Luther's reliance on Scripture as the sole arbiter of theological conflict is, of course, well known, although it is much more simple and direct than Wycliffe's complex metaphysical realism. Like Wycliffe, Luther saw the reform in light of a providential return of the Church to its pre-Constantinian purity, only for Luther the *ecclesia primitiva* was Germanic, not English. While Luther originally attempted to divide the sacred from the secular, the practicalities and pressures of reform, as well as the unexpected and early divergence among reformers, brought him to rely more and more on the state. But before we turn to Luther, we must examine the complex figure of Niccolò Machiavelli, who pursued Marsilius's project of secularization with even more candor than his forebear.

CHAPTER 4

MACHIAVELLI

It might seem odd to turn to the "infamous" Niccolò Machiavelli (1469–1527) to shed light upon on the assumptions of modern biblical exegetes.[1] Machiavelli is legendary as a teacher of evil, a man who counseled princes to cast away all notions of right and wrong and do whatever furthers their political causes, no matter how brutal or duplicitous. Furthermore, although he is generally accorded the status of being one of the founders of modernity, Machiavelli was a political theorist, not a biblical exegete, and so attending to his thought would appear to be fruitless for the present endeavor.

But as the reader will soon realize, Machiavelli was *deeply* concerned with the interpretation of the Bible insofar as it served his purposes. It is central to his project, as a self-conscious founder of "new modes and orders," that he must treat Holy Scripture in a most unholy way. The reason for this treatment is profoundly political, or to say it another way, fundamentally secular. In *The Discourses on the First Ten Books of Titus Livy,* Machiavelli asserts that, in contrast to the ancient, pagan vigorous and manly love of freedom, Christianity makes citizens effeminate and hence incapable of the rigors of true political freedom.

> Thinking then whence it can arise that in those ancient times peoples were more lovers of freedom than in these, I believe it arises from the same cause that makes men less strong now, which I believe is the difference between our education and the ancient, founded on the difference between our religion and the ancient. For our religion, having shown the truth and the true way [John 8:32, 14:6], makes us esteem less the honor of the world, whereas the Gentiles, esteeming it very much and having placed the highest good in it, were more ferocious in their actions. . . . Our religion has glorified humble and contemplative men more than active men. It has then placed the highest good in humility, abjectness, and contempt of things human; the other [i.e., the Gentiles] placed it in greatness of spirit, strength of body, and all other things capable of making men very strong. And if our religion asks that you have strength in yourself, it wishes you to be capable more of suffering than of doing something strong. This mode of life thus seems to have rendered the world weak and given it in prey to criminal men, who can manage it securely, seeing that the collectivity of men, so as to go to paradise, think more of enduring beatings than of avenging them. And although the world appears

1 We would like to thank Vasileios Syros and Paul-Erik Korvela for their very helpful comments.

> to be made effeminate and heaven disarmed, it arises without doubt more from the cowardice of the men who have interpreted our religion according to idleness and not according to virtue.[2]

In order to break the spell of Christianity on the imagination, so that he can bring a common this-worldly benefit, Machiavelli must somehow get men to *see* in a new way, and this involves a new reading of Scripture, one that is inherently political and admittedly in accord with those Gentiles whom he singles out for praise. Machiavelli must give a secular reading of the sacred text.

If we are to understand this reading, and the implications it will have upon modern scriptural scholarship, we must place Machiavelli's assessment of Christianity within the context of his own turbulent times. Witnessing the civil strife that afflicted the Italian city-states of his own day, and the consequent corruption (especially of the ecclesiastical hierarchy at Rome) will help us comprehend Machiavelli's use of Christianity for political ends. This context will also acquaint us with the conditions that would ignite the Reformation and, a century and a half later, contribute to Enlightenment skepticism about religion in general and Christianity in particular.

The Cradle of Corruption

Niccolò was born in Florence, Italy, on May 3, 1469, the son of Bernardo di Niccolò di Buoninsegna and his wife, Bartolemea de' Nelli. He had two sisters, Primavera and Margherita, and a younger brother, Totto. The family was respectable but not rich, the father being a lawyer with a great love of classical literature, a love he passed on to Niccolò.

Italy of the time was not a single nation but divided into five regions, Florence, Venice, Milan, Naples, and the Papal States. The rulers of these regions—including the Papal States—treated their dominions as personal family possessions, and so conflicts and wars in Italy were often affairs of great rival families. Political intrigue, corruption, viciousness, and contempt for religion were the rule rather than the exception, and in view of the notorious doings of the papacy and Church hierarchy during this period, religious hypocrisy had gone from being a scandal to an art. The damage done to the faith of the Church by the popes during Machiavelli's lifetime is incalculable. In Barbara Tuchman's words:

> Over a period of sixty years, from roughly 1470 to 1530, the secular spirit of the age was exemplified in a succession of six popes—five Italians and a Spaniard [leaving out two short-lived popes, Pius III and Adrian VI]—who carried it to an excess of venality, amorality, avarice, and spectacularly calamitous power politics. Their governance dismayed the faithful, brought

---

2 Niccolò Machiavelli, *Discourses on Livy*, translated by Harvey Mansfield and Nathan Tarcov (Chicago, IL: University of Chicago Press, 1996), II.2.2, pp. 131–132.

> the Holy See into disrepute, left unanswered the cry for reform, ignored all protests, warnings and signs of rising revolt, and ended by breaking apart the unity of Christendom and losing half the papal constituency to the Protestant secession. Theirs was a folly of perversity, perhaps the most consequential in Western history, if measured by its result in centuries of ensuing hostility and fratricidal war.[3]

Two years after the birth of Niccolò, a Franciscan, Francesco della Rovere, was elected to the papacy as Sixtus IV (largely owing to the influence of the unscrupulous Cardinal Rodrigo Borgia, who would become Pope Alexander VI in 1492[4]). Of Sixtus, Machiavelli would later say he was a "spirited pope"[5] who "was the first who began to show how much a pontiff could do and how many things formerly called errors could be hidden under pontifical authority."[6]

Austere before election, Sixtus soon engaged in nepotism on a grand scale. "Sixtus IV's dominating idea was the desire to advance his family and obtain for it a leading position in Italy. Other popes had engaged in nepotism, some out of family loyalty, others from political considerations: but under him it became the chief influence in papal policy."[7] Two nephews would be given the cardinal's hat; one of them, Giuliano della Rovere, would later become Pope Julius II. The other, Piero Riario, would largely dictate his uncle's policies until the cardinal's early death in 1474. But it was the purchase of land for Cardinal Riario's brother Girolamo[8] that would cause a conflict between the pope and the great Medici family, and leave a black mark upon the papacy of Sixtus that would deeply impress Machiavelli's assessment of Christianity.

The great Medici family were the real rulers of Florence, Machiavelli's native town. Pope Sixtus's purchase of the district of Imola for his nephew Girolamo Riario brought his ongoing conflict with the Medici to a head. Given the papal animosity to the Medici, the purchase was sponsored by another leading banking family, rival to the Medici, the Pazzi. The Pazzi family, powerful and rich though it was, felt overshadowed and threatened by the even more powerful Medici, who had a virtually complete grip on Florence since 1434 (through the unscrupulous actions of Cosimo de' Medici the Elder). Girolamo, the Pazzi family, and the archbishop of Pisa, Francesco Cardinal Salviati—with the knowledge and consent of Sixtus—plotted to rid Florence

3 Barbara Tuchman, *The March of Folly: From Troy to Vietnam* (New York: Alfred A. Knopf, 1984), p. 52.

4 Marion Johnson, *The Borgias* (New York: Holt, Rinehart and Winston, 1981), p. 72.

5 Niccolò Machiavelli, *The Prince*, translated by Harvey Mansfield (Chicago, IL: University of Chicago Press, 1985), XI, p. 46.

6 Niccolò Machiavelli, *Florentine Histories*, translated by Laura Banfield and Harvey Mansfield (Princeton: Princeton University Press, 1990), VII.22, p. 301.

7 Eric John, *The Popes: A Concise Biographical History* (New York: Hawthorn Books, Inc., 1964), pp. 300–301.

8 Machiavelli points out that "Piero and Girolamo . . . according to what everyone believed, were his [Sixtus'] sons . . ." Machiavelli, *Florentine Histories*, VII.22, p. 301.

of Medici rule.[9] Although it has not been proven that Sixtus approved of murder—he was reported to have said to the conspirators, "I do not desire the death of any man, but only a change in the government. . . . Go and do as seems good to you, but no one's life is to be taken"[10]—his consent was enough to stain his papacy indelibly.

The Pazzi conspiracy unfolded on Sunday, April 26, 1478, and Machiavelli himself would later write about it in his *Florentine Histories*. The place and time of the murder was Sunday Mass at Florence's cathedral, Santa Reparata. The "signal for action" was the "taking of communion by the priest."

> The appointed hour came; [Pazzi conspirator] Bernardo Bandini . . . pierced the breast of Giuliano [de' Medici], who after a few steps fell to the ground; Francesco de' Pazzi threw himself on him, filled him with wounds, and struck him with such zeal that, blinded by the fury that transported him, he wounded himself gravely in the leg. Messer Antonio and Stefano . . . attacked Lorenzo [de' Medici] and, after aiming many blows at him, struck him with one light wound in the throat. Lorenzo [escaped and] shut himself in the sacristy of the church.[11]

Medici revenge was prompt. Quite soon, the archbishop, decked out in the finery of his ecclesiastical position, dangled by the neck from a window of Florence's Palazzo Vecchio for all to see. The Florentines sided with the Medici and threw themselves into hunting down the conspirators. Soon "the limbs of the dead were seen fixed on the points of weapons or being dragged about the city, and everyone pursued the Pazzi with words full of anger and deeds full of cruelty."[12]

In response, Sixtus issued a bull of excommunication against "that son of iniquity and foster-child of perdition, Lorenzo de' Medici, and those other citizens of Florence, his accomplices and abettors,"[13] a move that merely underlined his personal involvement with the conspiracy. Having escaped, Lorenzo de' Medici would live on as Lorenzo the Magnificent, ruling Florence in power and splendor until his death in 1492. Giuliano de' Medici, although struck down with a knife, would live on in another way through his mistress, Fioretta Gorini. One month after Giuliano's murder, his illegitimate son, Giulio, was born—"filled with virtue and fortune that in these

---

9 On the Pazzi conspiracy see Lauro Martines, *April Blood: Florence and the Plot against the Medici* (Oxford: Oxford University Press, 2004); See John, *The Popes: A Concise Biographical History*, p. 301; Tuchman, *The March of Folly*, pp. 59, 64; Maurizio Viroli, *Niccolò's Smile: A Biography of Machivelli*, translated by Antony Shugaar (New York: Hill and Wang, 2000), p. 14; Sebastian de Grazia, *Machiavelli in Hell* (New York: Vintage, 1994), pp. 9–14; Ludwig Pastor, *The History of the Popes* (St. Louis, MO: Herder, 1902), Vol. IV, pp. 300–312; and Christopher Hibbert, *The Rise and Fall of the House of Medici* (New York: Penguin, 1979), Ch. 10.

10 Pastor, *The History of the Popes*, Vol. IV, p. 305; Hibbert, *The Rise and Fall of the House of Medici*, pp. 132–133.

11 Machiavelli, *Florentine Histories*, VIII.6, p. 324.

12 Ibid., VIII.9, p. 326.

13 Hibbert, *The Rise and Fall of the House of Medici*, p. 148.

present times all the world recognizes. . . ."[14] Giulio would become Pope Clement VII in 1523, and Machiavelli's *Florentine Histories* was dedicated to him. Clement was the reigning pope when Machiavelli died on June 21, 1527; he was also the pope who denied Henry VIII's request to divorce Catherine of Aragon.

When the Pazzi conspiracy took place Machiavelli was only nine years old, living about three blocks from where the archbishop hung by his neck. "Even if he did not see Archbishop Cardinal Salviati hanged from the windows of the Palazzo Vecchio, or the limbs of the defeated and murdered Pazzi raised high on the points of lances or dragged through the streets, he certainly heard people talking about these events for years afterward, accounts that made a profound impression on him."[15]

Cardinal Rodrigo Borgia was another ignoble influence on Machiavelli's assessment of Christianity. Cardinal Borgia had more than a few illegitimate children, the mothers of the first three (Pedro Luis, Isabella, Girolama) being unknown. He then had four children with Vannozza dei Cattanei (one of his many mistresses). The four children—Giovanni (Juan), Cesare, Goffredo (Jofré), and Lucrezia—were born between 1474–1482, and were openly acknowledged by Cardinal Borgia, who used his power when he became Pope Alexander VI to lavish gifts and honors upon all. "Alexander VI never did anything, nor ever thought of anything, but how to deceive men,"[16] Machiavelli would later relate, and praised him as a prince of the Church in quite a different manner than is usually meant by the phrase: "of all the pontiffs there have ever been he showed how far a pope could prevail with money and forces."[17] In fact, Machiavelli would single Alexander out as a sterling example of the principle that a prince must learn to be "a great pretender and dissembler," so that "he should appear all mercy, all faith, all honesty, all humanity, all religion." And, Machiavelli adds, "nothing is more necessary to appear to have than this last quality." But a prince—especially a "new prince" like Alexander VI—"cannot observe all those things for which men are held good, since he is often under a necessity, to maintain his state, of acting against faith, against charity, against humanity, against religion." Such a one must "know how to enter into evil, when forced by necessity."[18]

While he was pope, Alexander's passion soon fell upon Giulia Farnese, a beautiful woman already married to Orsino Orsini. She would move into a palace next to the Vatican (staying with the pope's illegitimate daughter Lucrezia). She claimed a daughter, Laura, by the pope, and would remain his mistress until around 1500.

Through Giulia's influence, Alexander VI would make her brother Alessandro a cardinal, and Alessandro would later become Pope Paul III in 1534 (and go on to call the great reforming Council of Trent). Alexander hoped that Giovanni would advance the Borgia cause militarily as captain general of the papal forces, but he was murdered when not yet twenty-five. Alexander's son Cesare was made a bishop of Pamplona at

14 Machiavelli, *Florentine Histories*, VIII.9, p. 327.
15 Viroli, *Niccolò's Smile*, p. 15.
16 Machiavelli, *The Prince*, XVIII, p. 70.
17 Ibid., XI, p. 46.
18 Ibid., XVIII, p. 70.

age fifteen, and cardinal at the age of eighteen. He resigned in 1498, the year after his brother's murder, and disburdened from the cares of the cardinalate, Cesare would take up his brother's torch. Machiavelli would make Cesare a prime example of the kind of ruthless cunning needed by a prince (and blessed by a pope).[19]

At the behest of Alexander VI, Lucrezia was betrothed to Giovanni Sforza, to make an alliance with the powerful Milanese family, but when a better chance for political alliance came up, Alexander VI granted her an annulment (allegedly on grounds of Giovanni's impotence, which made things all the more delicate since Lucrezia had become pregnant in the meantime, rumors circulating that it was by her brother Cesare). Lucreza's second husband, Alfonso of Aragon, was strangled by order of Cesare, and Alexander arranged a third marriage to Alphonso d'Este.

Enough has been said about the political-ecclesiastical context of Machiavelli's early life to appraise how easily the hypocrisy and frankly political machinations of the ecclesiastical hierarchy would give rise to widespread cynicism about the papacy and even some skepticism about Christianity itself. In Machiavelli, this cynicism and skepticism take a particular form, defined well in biographer Maurizio Viroli's description of Machiavelli's personality as "mischievous; irreverent; gifted with an exceedingly subtle intelligence; unconcerned about questions of soul, afterlife, or sin; fascinated by practical affairs and great men."[20]

This mischievous and erudite cynicism, nurtured by the corruptions in ecclesiastical politics, is born from one central insight, a momentous illumination nourished by his insatiable appetite for classical pagan literature: Christianity is *just one more religion*, and as such can be treated with the same detached curiosity as the ancient pagan religions were treated by ancient sages. For Machiavelli—partly from his own character but also from witnessing the morally decrepit state of the lives of churchmen—this detached curiosity assumes that religion is a false but politically necessary and powerful tool for irreligious rulers to control their subjects. This is as true for popes as it is for great religious leaders (such as Moses) who appear in Holy Scripture.

The actions of Alexander VI in particular are so illuminating for Machiavelli because in Alexander one finds a man with the brutal grandeur of a Gentile ruler who sees his only and highest good in this-worldly power and honor, acting in everything against Christianity's assumption that the "highest good [is to be found] in humility, abjectness, and contempt of things human," and using religion as a means to his own secular glory.

As with the lives of Renaissance popes, so also with the lives of those biblical: the underlying desire for political power must be discerned below the level of appearances, below the surface of the text. Machiavelli therefore politicizes his exegesis of the Bible because he assumes that all religion of any type is a façade for power, or can be made a façade for power. Of course, this must all be borne out through an analysis of his life and works. Given his emphasis on this-worldly political reality against otherworldly

19 See especially *The Prince*, VII.

20 Viroli, *Niccolò's Smile*, p. 4.

theories and aims, we should have some notion of Machiavelli's own immersion in the politics of his day, for this, too, will have their effect on his approach to Scripture.

Machiavelli, the Young Republican

Machiavelli did not come from a rich family, and so did not benefit from the education offered to the aristocracy. But young Niccolò early on developed a love of the classics through his father, a love that so thoroughly defined the intellectual air of the Renaissance. He absorbed Aristotle, Cicero, Virgil, Ovid, Thucydides, Tacitus, Livy, Plutarch, Polybius, and Lucretius, whose *De Rerum Natura* he "not only read but diligently copied, perhaps to improve his Latin but, more likely, to have a copy to read and reread when he liked."[21] As one can see from this list, it is heavy on historians, especially those who treat pagan religion according to what could rightly be called the sociology or history of religion—as one more phenomenon to be explained by the historian. The focus on Lucretius is important as well, for Niccolò could hardly have missed the Roman Epicurean's well-drilled lesson that religion is a merely social fabrication, and a pernicious one at that. All these pagan authors would effect a great transformation in Machiavelli's assessment of Christianity.

Not just books, but life was full of lessons, and Machiavelli, although still young, had his eyes wide open. Less than two years after the Pazzi conspiracy, Lorenzo de' Medici became the hero of Florence by saving it from the combined forces of Sixtus IV (angered at the failure to bring down the Medici in the Pazzi conspiracy) and Ferdinand of Aragon, king of Naples. The pope threatened Florence not only with destruction by the sword, but eternal destruction as well by continued excommunication. The bishops of the region, meeting at the cathedral of Florence, issued their own counter-excommunication of the pope, *Contrascommunica del clero Fiorentino fulminate contro il summo Pontifice Sisto IV*—a move that had the complete support of Lorenzo.[22] The Medici was able to avoid defeat through a grueling ten-week negotiation with the king of Naples, and returned to Florence in triumph and to secure his family's hold on its politics. Lorenzo would continue to thwart the pope's political ambitions.

Sixtus died in the fall of 1484, furious that his nephew Girolamo Riario had been bested in negotiations with Lorenzo. The latter successfully ingratiated himself with the next pope, Innocent VIII (Giovanni Battista Cibo), whose papal name, given the number of illegitimate children he fathered, was hardly appropriate. He was elected largely through the efforts of Sixtus's nephew, the cardinal Giuliano della Rovere, who would dominate Innocent's policies and would himself become Pope Julius II in 1503. Lorenzo assured his good relations with Innocent by marrying his daughter Maddalena to one of Innocent's sons, Franceschetto Cibo.[23]

21 Ibid., p. 9.

22 Hibbert, *The Rise and Fall of the House of Medici*, p. 150.

23 Ibid., p. 162.

In the summer of 1489, there would be another invasion of Florence of quite a different sort, carried out from the pulpit by the Dominican preacher Girolamo Savonarola (1452–1498). Savonarola attacked both moral and ecclesiastical corruption without care for the status of those chastised, be they noble, bishop, cardinal, or pope. Many in Florence were swept up in his reforming fervor, except for Lorenzo de' Medici (the chief target of Savonarola's jeremiads against evil and corrupt rulers) and Machiavelli himself, who heard his sermons but took from them quite different lessons than Savonarola intended.[24]

In the spring of 1492, lightening struck the dome of the very church, Santa Reparata, that had witnessed the blasphemous murder of Lorenzo's brother fourteen years earlier. Rubble fell down near the Medici home. Both Savonarola and Lorenzo himself took it as an omen of Lorenzo's death, and, indeed, Lorenzo would die at the beginning of April at age forty-three, making his last confession to Savonarola himself.[25]

While the omen was ill for Lorenzo, it heralded a great change for Florence and even more for Machiavelli. Lorenzo's son, Piero, proved incapable of stepping into his father's shoes, and when the French king Charles VIII invaded Italy in 1494, Piero disgraced Florence in the course of negotiations, then fled. Florence, rid of Medici rule, became a republic under the guidance of the preacher Savonarola, and was ruled by the Great Council. That same council would later turn against the Dominican reformer, in no small part because of the pope's ire at his criticisms, and instigate heresy proceedings that ended in Savonarola being burned at the stake on May 23, 1498. Machiavelli had just heard him preach at the first of March, an assignment of the Florentine ambassador to the Holy See. Five days after Savonarola's execution, Machiavelli (then twenty-nine years old) was appointed Secretary of the Second Chancery, and began his political service to the new Republic of Florence. His mother had died two years earlier, his father would die two years hence, and Niccolò would marry Marietta Corsini the year after.

By this time the pope was Alexander VI, and Machiavelli spent a significant amount of his time dealing directly with his ambitious and ruthless son, the ex-cardinal Cesare Borgia. As Borgia continually threatened Florence, the new republic and Machiavelli its representative could not help but be at odds with the papacy.

Alexander would die in August 1503, followed by the short-lived Pius III. Machiavelli would travel to Rome to witness the conclave, finding out even before the official announcement that the Borgias had decided to help elevate an old enemy, Giuliano della Rovere, who took the name Julius II. Julius soon broke the Borgia power, and Cesare faded from political importance.

---

24 For an interesting analysis, see Alison Brown, "Savonarola, Machiavelli and Moses," in Brown, *The Medici in Florence: The Exercise and Language of Power* (Perth: University of W. Australia, 1992), Ch. 8.

25 Viroli, *Niccolò's Smile*, pp. 17–18. Hibbert does not note that Savonarola was present, but only a priest. Hibbert, *The Rise and Fall of the House of Medici*, pp. 173–174.

Early on in his duties Machiavelli set about to convince Florence to arm itself, rather than rely on treaties and powerful friends. One of the great problems he faced was that the Florentines were not the sturdy warlike folk extolled by the ancient Roman historians as the backbone and life of a republic. The Florentines, made soft by commerce and luxury and suspicious even of their own people, were neither soldiers nor would they trust arming the lower classes, whom they oppressed. Machiavelli's efforts to raise an army were interrupted in the summer of 1506 by someone already quite successful in the endeavor: the warrior pope Julius II, himself determined to exercise greater political control over Italy.

Machiavelli was chosen to go to the papal court in the midst of Pope Julius's military campaign against Perugia and Bologna in the fall of 1506. While this failed to produce diplomatic fruit, Machiavelli found sustenance in closely watching Julius on campaign, quite eager for "the chance to follow a pope who rode at the head of an army (Julius scorned the more customary sedan chair). This was a unique opportunity to study the actions of an unusual prince, who brandished a sword in one hand and the scepter of Saint Peter in the other."[26]

Machiavelli would soon be called away to another great task. The Holy Roman Emperor at the time was Maximilian I (1493–1519). Maximilian was a Habsburg born in Austria, a man of grand designs, which included mastering both Italy and the papacy. Florence wanted him on its side as a foil against Julius II and the French king. After many months of bickering among the Florentines—the aristocrats were quite opposed to sending a commoner—Machiavelli set off for Germany in December 1507 (the very year Martin Luther, a faithful monk, was ordained a priest). Machiavelli was quite impressed with the Germans, insofar as they were frugal and used their money to arm themselves, but considered Maximilian only a mediocre ruler, weakened by his fateful dependence on the German electoral princes. He returned in June 1508, only to rush off and orchestrate the successful reduction of Pisa by military siege to Florentine control (ending with surrender in June 1509). This victory would be his crowning achievement, and through the jealousy of the Florentine nobles, part of the cause of his downfall.

Machiavelli did not stay in Florence long, but was soon off to deliver a payment to Emperor Maximilian, busy at war against Venice. This provided a lesson for Machiavelli, as the Venetian populace fought under the emblem of Saint Mark, substituting a sword for a book in their lion banner. "The book Saint Mark holds in the traditional depiction is his Gospel. By replacing the Gospel with a sword, the Venetians demonstrated, in Machiavelli's view, that they understood this principle: in order to preserve a state, especially in war, one must set aside the principles of Christian morality." In Machiavelli's understated comment at the time, for the preservation of states, "study and books are insufficient," even (and especially) if the book in question is the Gospels.[27]

26 Viroli, *Niccolò's Smile*, p. 91.

27 Ibid., p. 112.

In the summer of 1510 Machiavelli was off to try to make the best for Florence in the war between King Louis XII of France (a fairly noncommittal ally of the Republic of Florence) and Pope Julius II, who was bent on tearing down the republican government and bringing the Medici back to power. In Florence, the Medici faction was gaining strength, given the direct aid of Giovanni Cardinal de' Medici (soon to be Pope Leo X). In 1511, Julius formed the Holy League, bringing Europe's most powerful rulers (Spain, Venice, the emperor, and England) with him against Louis XII of France. The tide would soon turn to the papacy. At the direction of Julius, the Holy League turned upon Florence, and it hastily capitulated. On November 7, 1512, Machiavelli was relieved of his duties as Secretary of the Second Chancery. Power had passed back to the Medici again.

Out of Power, Deep in Thought

By the second week of February 1513 Machiavelli was in prison, suspected as a conspirator in a plot to overthrow the Medici (based on a list of potential conspirators found upon one of the ringleaders). Cruelly tortured himself, he also had to listen to the screams and executions of others. A quite interesting twist of fate brought his release after a month. Pope Julius died on March 11, and Cardinal de' Medici was elected as Pope Leo X. The jubilant Medici party in Florence pardoned Machiavelli, and he was released the following day. Shut out of politics, he soon moved out into the country home willed to him by his father.

Removed from power and living his life among the crude rustics, Machiavelli would have more effect on world history than his post in Florence ever could have yielded. In his famous letter of December 10, 1513, to Francesco Vettori, Florentine ambassador to Rome and long-time friend, Machiavelli described "what my life is like."[28] He gets up "in the morning with the sun," and for two hours oversees woodcutting on his property, a not very successful way of alleviating poverty for a man who spent fifteen years directing the republic and negotiating in person with kings, princes, cardinals, and popes. He reads love poetry—Dante, Petrarch, Tibullus, Ovid—and "I remember my own and enjoy myself for a while in this thinking."[29] Machiavelli's amours would have provided much food for reverie, given his countless mistresses before and after marriage, the frequency of his visits to brothels, and his appetite for unusual and (so it was alleged) unnatural sex acts.[30] He then stops by an inn for the news of the day, goes home to eat with his family, then comes back to the inn and "become[s] a rascal for the whole day," playing games and cursing with the host, a butcher, a miller,

---

28 The letter, "Niccolò Machiavelli to Francesco Vettori, Florence, December 10, 1513" is contained in *The Prince,* translated by Harvey Mansfield, pp. 107–111.

29 Ibid., p. 109.

30 Viroli, *Niccolò's Smile,* throughout the entire biography, but especially ch. 16.

and two bakers to "scrape the mold off my brain and . . . satisfy the malignity of this fate of mine . . ."[31]

> When evening has come, I return to my house and go into my study. At the door I take off my clothes of the day, covered with mud and mire, and I put on my regal and courtly garments; and decently reclothed, I enter the ancient courts of ancient men, where, received by them lovingly, I feed on the food that alone is mine and that I was born for. There I am not ashamed to speak with them and to ask them the reason for their actions; and they in their humanity reply to me. And for the space of four hours I feel no boredom, I forget every pain, I do not fear poverty, death does not frighten me. I deliver myself entirely to them. And because Dante says [in his *Paradiso*, V, 41–42[32]] that to have understood without retaining does not make knowledge, I have noted what capital I have made from their conversation and have composed a little work *De Principatibus*, where I delve as deeply as I can into reflections on this subject, debating what a principality is, of what kinds they are, how they are acquired, how they are maintained, why they are lost.[33]

This little book *De Principatibus*, *On Principalities*, is better known to us under the title *The Prince* as one of the most influential of all books in political philosophy, one that helped to form the modern mind.

The Prince of This World: Machiavelli's Via Moderna

In his most famous work, *The Prince*, Machiavelli seems artfully intent on shocking the reader. This tactic is necessary to awaken us to see reality for what it is—the way Machiavelli experienced it firsthand as a child, and then as Secretary of the Republic—rather than what pious fiction would make it. Machiavelli uses scandal as a kind of weapon, to break the spell of Christianity on the minds, and hence the actions, of princes, and to teach them to view things in an entirely new way. Shock makes the unthinkable thinkable.

Machiavelli is explicit that he is charting a new path. In speaking of the "modes and government of a prince," he asserts that "in disputing this matter I depart from the orders of others," meaning both the ordering of society and, even more profoundly, of the reader's very thoughts.

> But since my intent is to write something useful to whoever understands it, it has appeared to me more fitting to go directly to the effectual truth of the thing than to the imagination of it. And many have imagined republics and

31 "Niccolò Machiavelli to Francesco Vettori, Florence, December 10, 1513," p. 109.

32 Importantly, in the *Paradiso*, it is Beatrice, taking Dante ever higher up into the realms of heaven, who utters these words. By contrast, Machiavelli uses them for the opposite goal of planting us firmly upon earth.

33 "Niccolò Machiavelli to Francesco Vettori, Florence, December 10, 1513," pp. 109–110.

> principalities that have never been seen or known to exist in truth; for it is so far from how one lives to how one should live that he who lets go of what is done for what should be done learns his ruin rather than his preservation. For a man who wants to make a profession of good in all regards must come to ruin among so many who are not good. Hence it is necessary to a prince, if he wants to maintain himself, to learn to be able not to be good, and to use this and not use it according to necessity.[34]

The subsequent history of political philosophy would reveal the full import of Machiavelli's revolution, one that defines the very nature of modern secularism, the *via moderna* that is more familiar to us than—but not unrelated to—the *via moderna* we have traced from Ockham.

As with Ockham, Machiavelli's *via* is constructed specifically against the *via antiqua*, in particular, against the kind of political reasoning one finds in Plato, Aristotle, and Cicero. According to these ancient philosophers, politics should conform to the standards of right reason and justice. In the new political reasoning Machiavelli introduced, which would contribute to the foundation of the later doctrine of "reason of state," the political goal is the preservation of power. The new political science, therefore, consists in the "knowledge of the means of preserving domination over a people,"[35] rather than conformity to independent rational or moral principles.

In regard to the later doctrine of reason of state, both reason and state take on a new meaning. The "state" is not some impersonal entity, but (connected to the term "status") an expression of the power of someone or some group over others, so that as Maurizio Viroli points out, the reason of *state* is "the art of preserving a state, in the sense of a person's or group's power and control over public institutions (for instance, the *stato* of the Medici)."[36] The *reason* of state emphasizes that political reasoning is not theoretical, but is in the service of securing and maintaining political control.[37] That is the sum and substance of Machiavelli's *The Prince*, dedicated to "the Magnificent Lorenzo de' Medici."[38] It is the take-home lesson of his political experience.

The literary context for Machiavelli's *Prince* is illuminating. The political *via antiqua* was well represented in the literature written as advice to princes and kings, taking the form, especially in Machiavelli's Italy, of Ciceronian advice on properly ruling a republic according to right reason and true justice.[39] But written, public advice was different from private counsel. "The principles of the art of ruling the republic were publicly discussed and recommended in scholarly works; the rules of the art of the state [as in "reason of state"] were almost exclusively whispered in restricted

---

34 Machiavelli, *The Prince*, XV, p. 61.

35 Maurizio Viroli, *From Politics to Reason of State: The Acquisition and Transformation of the Language of Politics, 1250–1600* (Cambridge: Cambridge University Press, 1992), p. 2.

36 Ibid., p. 3.

37 Ibid., pp. 3–4.

38 "Dedicatory Letter," Machiavelli, *The Prince*, p. 3.

39 See Viroli's in-depth discussion in *From Politics to Reason of State*, Chs. 1–2.

gatherings or couched in private letters and memoranda."[40] Machiavelli's great innovation consisted in saying publicly, in writing, what others had dared only to whisper, and in giving political advice according to how princes actually act in the real world, especially those who are most successful at gaining and maintaining power. He revealed what has been called the "mysteries of state," the *arcana imperii*, the secrets spoken by rulers and advisors to rulers behind closed doors.[41]

But Machiavelli was not simply setting down a how-to manual; he was undertaking a thoroughgoing revolution that made a decisive break with the *via antiqua*, one that entailed a radical reformulation of Christianity as well. To understand this, we must make a short excursion into Plato's *Republic*, where we find the most famous of "imagined republics."

Cities and Republics Not of This World

In the *Republic*, Socrates and his interlocutors, Glaucon and Adeimantus, construct, not a real city, but a city in speech, a city built in the imagination.[42] Machiavelli is quite obviously at odds with Plato, whose Socrates uses the idea or form (in Greek, *eidos*) of justice to fashion the city in speech, and further, understands justice as a standard by which one may judge any actual political regime. (Again, we find a parallel to Ockham insofar as Machiavelli attacks the notion of form as a universal existing in things, or as a supramundane causative principle existing above the visible world.)

Even greater than the idea of justice, for Socrates, is the "idea of the good" that "provides the truth to the things known and gives the power to the one who knows." The idea of the good is not a mere idea but the very cause of "existence and being," and even more astonishingly, "the good isn't being but is still beyond being, exceeding it in dignity and power."[43]

But do ideas build real cities? Near the end of Plato's *Republic*, it becomes clear both to the interlocutors and to the reader that the city in speech exists *only* in speech, and further, seems to be useless for founding actual cities. As Glaucon notes, "the city whose foundation we have now gone through . . . has its place in speeches,

---

40 Ibid., p. 133.

41 On the "mysteries of state," see Peter Donaldson, *Machiavelli and Mystery of State* (Cambridge: Cambridge University Press, 1988), Preface.

42 Plato, *Republic*, 368e–369b. Part of the context of Machiavelli's concern with the *Republic* is the revival of Platonism in Italy in the mid-fifteenth century, a half-century before he wrote the cold words of *The Prince*. The early phase of the Platonic revival was focused on the *Republic* as a template for political reform, but by the dawn of the sixteenth century the attention to Plato was largely transformed from practical and political, to philosophical and theological attempts at forging a new Christian neo-Platonic mystical system. This occurred especially under the guidance of Marsilio Ficino (1433–1499) and in the spirit of the founder of neo-Platonism, the third-century AD pagan philosopher, Plotinus (whose work had so influenced, via Dionysius the Pseudo-Areopagite, medieval theologians and mystics). See Viroli, *From Politics to Reason of State*, pp. 109–122.

43 Plato, *Republic*, 508d–509c. *The Republic of Plato*, translated by Allan Bloom, second edition (New York: Basic Books, 1968).

since I don't suppose it exists anywhere on earth."[44] To which Socrates replies, "But in heaven," I said, "perhaps, a pattern is laid up for the man who wants to see and found a city within himself [i.e., in his soul] on the basis of what he sees [by philosophy]. It doesn't make any difference whether it is or will be somewhere. For he would mind the things of this city alone, and of no other."[45]

For Machiavelli, minding the things of imaginary cities is a tragic waste of time; that is, it is a primary cause of this-worldly tragedy. Such "imagined republics and principalities," he reminds us, "have never been seen or known to exist in truth." Only real cities exist "in truth." The source of Socrates' confusion lies in standing on the wrong side of an unbridgeable gap between "how one lives" and "how one should live." Socrates foolishly built an imaginary city based on "how one should live," and therefore was forced to confess, ironically, that it doesn't make any difference "whether it is or will be somewhere." Machiavelli turns us away from imaginary cities in heaven, toward how people *actually* live, and this means that "how one should live" as defined by the idea of the good must be let go so that one may embrace the "effectual truth" of the real world, this world. Embracing the effectual truth is a denial of the primacy of goodness, a severe demotion of the exalted position of the idea of the good from both the cause and measure of all things, to (at best) a mere tool for use or neglect, "according to necessity."

Machiavelli's *Prince* is, therefore, the manual by which one unlearns Plato's *Republic*. But we notice that Machiavelli does not mention this most famous work in the above-quoted passage. His critical scope is much wider because his argument is directed against all those ancient philosophers, partisans of the *via antiqua*, such as Plato, Aristotle, or Cicero, who shared the common belief that moral goodness, the perfection of the soul entailed in the task of becoming virtuous, should define political life. But for Machiavelli, imagined "oughts" should not define the "is." Rather, what is—the real world, *this* world—should define the "ought." At its deepest level, even below the moral level, Machiavelli's *via moderna* provides the entire rationale of modern secularism insofar as it calls for a turn from the supramundane to the mundane. (In this, of course, it is at odds with Ockham's *via moderna*, which was put at the service of theology.)

On Heavenly Kingdoms

It doesn't take much imagination to see that Machiavelli's criticisms of Plato and pagan philosophers like him are *a fortiori* criticisms of Christianity.[46] In the Bible, Jesus Christ claims to be king of a kingdom "not of this world."[47] And just to prove Machiavelli's

44 Ibid., 592a–b.

45 Ibid., 592b.

46 On Machiavelli's antagonism to Christianity see Vickie Sullivan, *Machiavelli's Three Romes* (DeKalb, IL: Northern Illinois University Press, 1996), and Paul-Erik Korvela, *The Machiavellian Reformation: An Essay in Political Theory* (Jyväskylä: University of Jyväskylä, 2006).

47 John 18:36.

point, Jesus came to "ruin among so many who" were "not good," and did so in a much more gruesome way and at a much earlier age than Socrates.

The problem with Jesus—if we take Machiavelli's view—is that, while He came to ruin, out of that ruin a religion sprang up that focuses solely on the imaginary kingdom, and thus turns men, including princes, away from the "effectual truth." Such is the substance of his complaint against Christianity quoted at the beginning of this chapter. Christianity has historically come to define everything, even and especially the political world, according to "how one should live," which is itself defined according to a kingdom not of this world. The result is a "mode of life" that "seems to have rendered the world weak," because Christianity places the "highest good in humility, abjectness, and contempt of things human" as compared to the pagans who placed the highest good "in greatness of spirit, strength of body, and all other things capable of making men very strong." This essential difference, we recall, is caused by a difference in focus between Christians and pagan religion: "our religion, having shown the truth and the true way [John 8:32, 14:6], makes us esteem less the honor of the world, whereas the Gentiles, esteeming it very much and having placed the highest good in it, were more ferocious in their actions." But the problem is not just in the emasculation of citizens. In focusing princes' attentions on another world and binding their wills by the idea of the good, Christianity makes them ineffectual rulers, and therefore renders them unable to do what is necessary—be it good or evil—to keep the peace and make nations visibly, tangibly glorious. Clearly, learning how "not to be good" demands a revolution in worldview, one that goes beyond good and evil precisely by defining good solely in terms of effectiveness in bringing about this-worldly peace and glory.

Machiavelli's New Exegesis

To accomplish his goal, Machiavelli must effect a fundamental shift in the treatment of Scripture. Implicit in his rejection of kingdoms not of this world is a questioning of the divine goal and origin of Scripture, one that occurred in a time and place where questioning Scripture could be very dangerous. We must then be prepared for more than a little circumspection on Machiavelli's treatment of Holy Writ.

In Chapter VI of *The Prince*, the title of which is "Of New Principalities That Are Acquired through One's Own Arms and Virtue," Machiavelli claims that he will be examining the "greatest examples" of those who "are altogether new both in prince and in state," that is, of those who are the founders of new principalities. He then lists the "most excellent" examples, "Moses, Cyrus, Romulus, Theseus, and the like."[48]

This inclusion of Moses would give readers a bit of a jolt, for they would not expect to find Moses listed among pagans as one of a number of *political* leaders, of great *princes* who have founded principalities. To consider him *as* a merely political leader would seem a kind of profanation since the Bible treats Moses as having been called by God to lead the Israelites. It is especially interesting to treat Moses as a prince

48 Machiavelli, *The Prince*, VI, p. 22.

since, as we have seen above, Machiavelli deems it "necessary to a prince, if he wants to maintain himself, to learn to be able not to be good, and to use this and not use it according to necessity." But that cold advice actually occurs later in *The Prince*, and only the most alert reader would remember, nine chapters later, that Machiavelli considers Moses to be an exemplary prince.

Obviously Machiavelli is aware of the discomfort caused in the reader by his inclusion of Moses in his list of the greatest princes, for he says immediately that "although one should not reason about Moses, as he was a mere executor of things that had been ordered for him by God, nonetheless he should be admired if only for that grace which made him deserving of speaking with God."[49] But no sooner does Machiavelli exempt Moses from consideration on seemingly pious grounds, than he proceeds to consider him. Machiavelli notes first that if we "consider Cyrus and the others . . . [in] their particular actions and orders . . . they will appear no different from those of Moses, who had so great a teacher."[50] How, we might ask, could that be, *if* Moses' teacher is God? Perhaps Moses had another teacher? Perhaps Machiavelli wants to teach us something different about Moses.

In order to understand Machiavelli's intent, we must do that which is forbidden and, following Machiavelli's lead, "reason about Moses." We must treat Moses' actions as we would those of Cyrus, Romulus, Theseus, and any other merely human, merely historical example. To do so, we must read the Bible *alongside* other ancient historical accounts, in the same kind of historical-critical treatment as one would any other historical work. This implies that one is considering the Bible's author as one among equals with Livy, Polybius, Plutarch, Xenophon, Herodotus, Thucydides, Tacitus, and other eminent ancient pagan historians.

It is difficult to overemphasize the momentous effect of this great shift in the consideration of the Bible. The recovery of ancient texts in the Renaissance—in the deepest sense of recovery: a reading of pagan authors on their own terms, a consideration of what pagan sages said independently of Christianity and even in antagonism to it—contributed far more as a catalyst to modern secularization than many historians would lead us to believe. Our concern with Machiavelli in particular is the way he uses pagan authors as guides to reading the Bible as one would any other historical work, a mode of approach that contributes to the later historical-critical assumption that the Bible must be treated as one text among others. The assumption in both instances is that faith in the Bible as revealed actually *obscures* its real meaning, so that its real meaning can only be recovered, or better uncovered, by laying aside faith and deferring to history as known by reason. Machiavelli provides a template, an exercise in exegesis, which works to alert Christianized minds to long-buried pagan truths.

To return to *The Prince*, Machiavelli begins his reasoning about Moses in a particular context, that of a discussion of virtue and fortune. The list of princes provided above is qualified as "those [princes] who have become princes by their own virtue and not by fortune," or more exactly, those who did not have "anything else from

49 Ibid., VI, p. 22.

50 Ibid., VI, pp. 22–23.

fortune [other] than the opportunity."[51] That is, they did not receive divine aid. While the opportunity may be given to them by fortune, it is their virtue that enables "them to introduce any form they pleased" in fashioning their principality. The first prince treated is Moses, then Romulus, Cyrus, and Theseus.

"It was necessary then for Moses to find the people of Israel in Egypt, enslaved and oppressed by the Egyptians, so that they would be disposed to follow him in order to get out of their servitude,"[52] asserts Machiavelli. No mention of God is made, as if one could somehow equate the opportunities supplied by fortune with the actions of God (or as if the Israelites themselves confused the two, taking good fortune for Providence). Machiavelli does not answer any questions he raises in the attentive reader's mind, but instead hurries the reader to a consideration of the other princes in the list as well. This list is not haphazardly made. In lumping Moses, Theseus, and Romulus together, Machiavelli gives us the founding princes of the three great civilizations of the West, each centered ultimately on a different city: Jerusalem, Athens, and Rome.

But why is Cyrus included in the list? Interestingly, Cyrus the Great is the only prince in the list found in *both* sacred and secular sources, both in the Old Testament (primarily in the prophets Isaiah and Ezra) and also, most notably, in Xenophon's *Cyropaedia*.[53] That gives the reader a chance to compare the two accounts. In Isaiah, God declares Cyrus to be His shepherd, chosen and anointed to fulfill His purposes, in particular to crush Babylon, Israel's oppressor, and send the Jews back from captivity to build His temple.[54] Ezra begins by declaring that "In the first year of Cyrus the King of Persia, that the word of the Lord by the mouth of Jeremiah [Jeremiah 29:10] might be accomplished, the Lord stirred up the spirit of Cyrus king of Persia" to proclaim: "'The Lord, the God of heaven, has given me all the kingdoms of the earth and he has charged me to build him a house at Jerusalem, which is in Judah.'"[55]

But Machiavelli remains silent about the Bible's narrative, and instead gives us an account based largely upon Xenophon. Therefore, he says nothing of the providential machinations of the God of Israel in raising Cyrus to power for His purposes, but mentions only that Cyrus was fortunate in finding "the Persians malcontent with the empire of the Medes, and the Medes soft and effeminate because of long peace."[56]

In Xenophon's profane version, Cyrus makes no mention of the God of the Israelites but rather devotes himself to Zeus and other gods. The military campaign that will end in the destruction of Babylon is not undertaken at the command of the God of the Israelites, but begun by appeal to Zeus and the gods. When Babylon is cap-

51 Ibid., VI, p. 22.

52 Ibid., p. 23.

53 Herodotus has a fairly extensive account of Cyrus, primarily in Book I of his *History*. On Xenophon's understanding of the ideal prince see Wolfgang Knauth and Sejfoddin Nadjmabadi, *Das altiranische Fürstenideal von Xenophon bis Ferdousi* (Wiesbaden: Steiner, 1975).

54 Isaiah 44:23–45:25.

55 Ezra 1:1–2. RSV.

56 Machiavelli, *The Prince*, VI, p. 23.

tured, Cyrus offers the first fruits and spoils to the gods through the magi, the priests who instruct him in polytheistic worship and sacrifice.[57]

Apparently, Machiavelli considers the profane history of Xenophon to be more reliable in finding the "effectual truth," and hence a corrective of the biblical account. To understand why Machiavelli might think a corrective is needed, we may turn again to Plutarch, one of the ancient historians upon whom Machiavelli also continually relies, who also provides an ancient source for the lives of two princes on the list, Theseus and Romulus. Plutarch considers Theseus and Romulus men who are just beyond the reach of real history, although not quite in the realm of myth, in which there is nothing but prodigies (or miracles or omens) and tragic drama, a realm inhabited not by philosophers and historians but by poets and myth-writers.[58]

To include Moses in a list with Theseus and Romulus is therefore to indicate (however obliquely) that while all three *may* be historical figures, the accounts we have of them are an uncertain mixture of myth and history, a gray area at best. To assert that Moses, Theseus, and Romulus inhabit the indistinct borderline between myth and history is also to imply, perhaps, that the Old Testament can be divided between the realm of myth (say, Genesis) and the realm of real, or at least more reliable history (perhaps the Book of Joshua and following). In between we have Exodus, Leviticus, Numbers, and Deuteronomy, which occupy the borderline and tell us of Moses the semimythical founder of the Jewish nation, the equivalent of Theseus and Romulus.

But Plutarch, as an historian, was not satisfied to leave a mixture of myth and history, and so he offered a corrective for understanding Theseus and Romulus that prefigures aspects of the modern historical-critical method. By it, Plutarch hoped to "to purify (or cleanse) the myths by compelling them to submit to reason, and thereby to take the appearance of histories."[59] In his attempt to reduce the many legends of Theseus and Romulus to something at least "likely," Plutarch had recourse to an army of corrective sources, from poets to historians, taking what appeared least like the drama written by the tragedians,[60] and when there was conflict among historians, taking what the greater part of the historians write or what seemed more likely. Plutarch mentions, among his many sources, Hesiod, Archilochus, the writers of Megara, Euripides, Aristotle, Simonides, Philochorus, Homer, Ion, the Naxians, Pherecydes, Hellanicus, Herodorus, Menecrates, Clidemus, Pindar, Aeschylus, Dicaearchus, Hereas, Ister, and Diodorus. Even with this great army at his side, Plutarch admits that it is difficult to bring order out of disorder, and separate fact from fiction.

This opens up for the reader's consideration a startling difference between Plutarch and the Bible. It should be quite obvious—as it must have been to Machiavelli—that the Bible's account of Moses does not read like Plutarch. That is, it does not appear to be the result of a careful sifting of multiple views of the same events, but presents itself simply as reporting what happened to Moses and the Israelites in their escape

57 Xenophon, *Cyropaedia* VI, i.1, 3, 6, 10; VI, v.35; VIII, i.23.

58 Plutarch, *Lives*, Vol. I, Theseus, I.1.

59 Ibid., 1.3.

60 Ibid., p. 2.

from Egypt and long trek to the Promised Land. Thus, the way is opened for exegetes to treat the Bible according to the mode of Plutarch. The sacred history must submit to a purification by reason, set critically against other historical sources. But in so doing, one can no longer treat it as sacred.

Again, Machiavelli has a goal beyond secularizing the text. To reason about Moses means to draw from Moses the lessons that Machiavelli wanted to teach prospective princes. The lesson is quite startling:

> [A]ll the armed prophets conquered and the unarmed ones were ruined. For . . . the nature of peoples is variable; and it is easy to persuade them of something, but difficult to keep them in that persuasion. And thus things must be ordered in such a mode that when they no longer believe, one can make them believe by force. Moses, Cyrus, Theseus, and Romulus would not have been able to make their peoples observe their constitutions for long if they had been unarmed, as happened in our own times to Brother Girolamo Savonarola.[61]

We note the shift in his presentation, from calling Moses, Cyrus, Theseus, and Romulus princes to calling them *prophets*—the better to focus on them as religious founders of their respective "constitutions." We also cannot fail to bring to mind, not only the list of Old Testament prophets who being unarmed came to ruin, but even more, Jesus Christ Himself, who explicitly rejected the use of arms because His kingdom was not of this world. In contrast to Jesus who would not take up the sword, Moses ordered the slaughter of three thousand rebellious worshippers of the golden calf at Mt. Sinai, and those who carried out the deed, the sons of Levi, were thereby "ordained . . . for the service of the Lord, each one at the cost of his son and of his brother. . . ."[62] The Levitical priesthood begins with a quite astonishing act of bloodshed, one that can be understood in Machiavellian terms.

One might make the objection that Machiavelli can't *really* be treating Moses and the other great princes as Machiavellian. After all, the entire Chapter VI of *The Prince* praises their virtue. The difficulty with this objection is that it doesn't take account of the new way that Machiavelli uses the word "virtue" (*virtù*, in his tongue), a way that suits the new modes and orders he wishes to introduce. As *The Prince* unfolds, it is clear that virtue, for Machiavelli, does not mean moral goodness but the manly use of effective force.[63] While virtue in the old sense was intrinsically related to morality, a prince having virtue in the new sense must choose to be good or evil depending upon which is most effective. That is why he does not focus on what we would call the moral qualities of Moses, Cyrus, Theseus, and Romulus in Chapter VI, but instead, in praising their virtue, he praises their use of *force* as armed prophets.

The effective use of force to impose order, then, is the great virtue of the prince, the virtue that allows him to use the opportunities that fortune provides him. The

---

61 Machiavelli, *The Prince*, VI, p. 24.

62 Exodus 32:25–28. RSV.

63 For a thorough treatment of Machiavelli's startling concept of virtue, see especially Harvey Mansfield, *Machiavelli's Virtue* (Chicago: University of Chicago Press, 1996).

newness of Machiavelli's approach can be seen quite clearly in his very short discussion of "good laws," one that he must have meant to apply to Moses, who brought the law to the Israelites: "The principal foundations that all states have, new ones as well as old or mixed, are good laws and good arms. And because there cannot be good laws where there are not good arms, and where there are good arms there must be good laws, I shall leave out the reasoning on laws and shall speak of arms."[64]

It might appear to be bad logic to equate good laws with good arms, since it would seem obvious that a tyrant might be exceedingly well armed, and enforce wicked laws. But we must remember that the most important question according to Machiavelli's new political teaching is whether a prince's force is effective, not whether it is considered (according to ancient philosophy, Christianity, or common opinion) to be morally good. Reasoning about Moses, we must conclude that if he was indeed one of the greatest princes, then the laws given on Mt. Sinai can be called "good" only insofar as Moses used effective force to make the Israelites believe them.

Although written in 1513, Machiavelli's most famous work was not published until 1532, five years after he died. But it did circulate in handwritten copies, and Machiavelli's reputation as a teacher of evil soon circulated with it. He had originally intended to dedicate *The Prince* to a nephew of Pope Leo, Giuliano de' Medici, who was powerful in the court of Rome, but ended up dedicating it, as noted above, to another nephew of Leo, Lorenzo de' Medici (grandson of Lorenzo the Magnificent), thereby hoping to raise himself up again in Florence. But that did not happen, at least right away. Even though *The Prince* did not achieve its immediate aim, it soon became a widely known and influential work throughout Europe, and produced a spawn of "reason of state" literature, beginning with Machiavelli's friend Francesco Guicciardini and his *Dialogo del Reggimento di Firenze* (*On the Government of Florence*) (written between 1521 and 1525).[65] In it, Guicciardini coins the term "reason of state" that will pass into common currency in the coming centuries.

The context of the minting is instructive, as Viroli notes: "If we want to preserve states [argued Guicciardini], we must then leave aside the imperatives of moral conscience, cease to think as Christians, and think in the terms of the 'reason' and the customs of the states (*'secondo la ragione e uso degli stati'*). The term that embodies the new idea of politics appears here for the first time," and it is meant to convey the notion that "besides moral reason, there is another reason, the reason of the states, that must at times guide the actions of the political man."[66] Implicit in this advice, especially in this context, is the very Machiavellian view that the maintenance of political power demands the subordination of theological reasoning to the reason of state. And since theological reasoning is concerned with scriptural interpretation, then reasoning about Moses must conform to reason in "reason of state." We shall follow the stream

---

64 Machiavelli, *The Prince*, XII, p. 48.

65 For an account of Guicciardini and subsequent Italian works on reason of state, see Viroli, *From Politics to Reason of State*, Chs. 4–6.

66 Ibid., p. 194.

of Machiavelli's influence in later figures, beginning with the reign of Henry VIII in England.[67]

More Discoursing on Ancient Wisdom

After finishing *The Prince*, Machiavelli was still kept from the center of politics during the remaining second decade of the 1500s. He spent time reading and writing, producing plays (the comedies, *Andria* and *Mandragola*) and some poetry (notably, "The Ass"). Sometime during this period of political inactivity—probably between 1513 and 1517—Machiavelli wrote another classic of political philosophy, the *Discorsi sopra la Prima Deca di Tito Livio*, (*Discourses on the First Ten Books of Titus Livy*), a sustained reflection on the very same themes of *The Prince* but focused on recovering the wisdom of ancient, pagan philosophy for the sake of building a stable, prosperous republic (such as he had always hoped Florence would be). Again, we remind readers that Machiavelli was recovering only certain aspects of pagan philosophy, not those parts of Plato, Aristotle, and Cicero that had proven to be compatible with Christianity, but tenets of pagan philosophy that had been left behind. As Machiavelli asserted in the *Discourses*, the recovery of ancient wisdom for the sake of republican virtue demands a sustained criticism of Christianity, and Machiavelli uses Livy, among others, to bring out those pagan teachings that most conflict with Christian ethics. Importantly, this critique takes the form of the analysis of a pagan historical work, one that allows Machiavelli to treat Scripture from the perspective of a pagan historian.

At the beginning of the *Discourses* Machiavelli makes it even more clear than in *The Prince* that he is setting out a new way, a new *via*, new "modes and orders." In his famous words:

> [D]riven by that natural desire that has always been in me to work, without any respect, for those things I believe will bring common benefit to everyone, I have decided to take a path as yet untrodden by anyone, and if it brings me trouble and difficulty, it could also bring me reward through those who consider humanely the end of these labors of mine.[68]

---

67 On the spread of Machiavelli's ideas, especially in regard to reason of state, see Friedrich Meinecke, *Machiavellianism: The Doctrine of* Raison d'Etat *and Its Place in Modern History*, translated by Douglas Scott (New York: Frederick A. Praeger Publishers, 1965); E. A. Rees, *Political Thought from Machiavelli to Stalin* (New York: Palgrave Macmillan, 2004); Paul Rahe, ed., *Machiavelli's Liberal Republican Legacy* (Cambridge: Cambridge University Press, 2005); Vickie Sullivan, *Machiavelli, Hobbes, and the Formation of a Liberal Republicanism in England* (Cambridge: Cambridge University Press, 2004); Victoria Kahn, *Machiavellian Rhetoric from the Counter-Reformation to Milton* (Princeton: Princeton University Press, 1994); and Leo Strauss, "Three Waves of Modernity," in Hilail Gildin, ed., *An Introduction to Political Philosophy: Ten Essays by Leo Strauss* (Detroit, MI: Wayne State University Press, 1989), pp. 81–98.

68 Machiavelli, *Discourses on Livy*, I, Preface, 1, p. 5.

As Machiavelli makes immediately clear—and here, we are a witness to, at least, the partial birth of modern historical consciousness, and hence the modern historical-critical method—that the great labor is the recovery of history (or better, the pagan wisdom about history) shorn of the Christian overlay and interpretation. The difficulty, which Machiavelli seeks to solve by going back to the pagan Roman historian Livy, is caused by "not having a true knowledge of histories, through not getting from reading them that sense nor tasting that flavor that they have in themselves."[69] The original sense and flavor of the pagan histories is unavailable until one can set aside one's Christian presuppositions and think like a wise pagan. To help this transition to occur in the reader, Machiavelli enlists not only the aid of Livy, but Polybius, Plutarch, Tacitus, Sallust, Suetonius, Herodotus, Thucydides, Diodorus Siculus, and Xenophon as well. Yet the recovery of ancient, pagan wisdom is not an end in itself; it is a means of stripping away the alien influences of Christianity. For this reason, it must be directed at Holy Scripture itself.

We are not surprised, then, to find that Machiavelli continues his reflections on Moses, emphasizing once more the disjunction between effective force and goodness. Again, he reasons about Moses just as he reasons about every other ancient political ruler in the pagan historians, just as Titus Livy might have done if he had had occasion. Moses is considered as one among other founders of regimes. Since Livy is Machiavelli's main source in the *Discourses,* we should turn to Livy's history of Rome for clarification.

As with Plutarch, we find a recognition in Livy that in discussing Rome's founders, he is dealing more with the adornment of poetic fables than a solid account of real history. Yet he offers this excuse on behalf of the poets: "[I]t is a pardonable fault of the ancients to mix divine things with human things to make the beginnings of cities more august."[70]

One cannot help but wonder about Moses, or at least about Machiavelli's assessment of Moses, as just such a founder—especially since the infants Romulus and Remus were ordered by the wicked king Amulius to be exposed *in a basket floating in the Tiber River,* only to run aground and be rescued and suckled by a nearby she-wolf, then taken by the shepherd of the king's flock, Faustulus, to his home to raise.[71] An interesting parallel, to say the least.

But even more telling, Machiavelli discusses the necessity of a single individual being the founder of a republic, and takes for consideration none other than Romulus, "who killed his brother [Remus],"[72] a deed that is excusable, Machiavelli tells us,

69 Ibid., Preface, 2, p. 6.

70 Livy, I, Preface, 6–7.

71 Ibid., I, iv.1–9.

72 Machiavelli, *Discourses on Livy*, I.9.1. Machiavelli also mentions that Romulus "consented to the death of Titus Tatius, the Sabine, chosen by him as partner in the kingdom. . . ." The episode with the Sabines is also instructive for Machiavelli's case. According to Livy, Romulus hoped to intermarry with the surrounding peoples so as to increase Rome's population and cement alliances, but all the surrounding peoples spurned the Roman request for intermarriage. Romulus thereby contrived to lure the surrounding peoples to celebratory games in Rome. After they arrived, at a signal from Romulus,

because it allowed Romulus to be the sole founder of Rome, and "a prudent orderer of a republic . . . should contrive to have authority alone." But while "the deed accuses him, the effect excuses him; and when the effect is good, as was that of Romulus, it will always excuse the deed; for he who is violent to spoil, not he who is violent to mend, should be reproved."[73] The ends justify the means.

In the paragraph *immediately following* these words, Machiavelli remarks that "One could give infinite examples to sustain the things written above, such as Moses, Lycurgus, Solon, and other founders of kingdoms and republics who were able to form laws for the purpose of the common good because they had one authority attributed to them; but I wish to omit them as things known."[74]

Things known? Or things implied? Was Moses really offended by idolatry at Mt. Sinai on behalf of God, or did he merely order the slaughter of those Israelites who opposed his rule? Was Moses really guarding the priesthood in opposing the rebellion of Korah (Numbers 16), or eliminating his political opposition? Machiavelli later informs the reader, "whoever reads the Bible judiciously will see that since he [Moses] wished his laws and his orders to go forward, Moses was forced to kill infinite men who, moved by nothing other than envy, were opposed to his plans."[75]

As Machiavelli also lets it be known, mere force is not enough. Romulus had sufficient virtue (in the Machiavellian sense) to apply effective force so that Rome could have its beginning, but in order to continue, Rome needed something beyond mere physical force to maintain that order. Happily, the next king after Romulus, Numa Pompilius, "turned to religion as a thing altogether necessary . . . to maintain a civilization." Religion is not true, but necessary to maintain order. While subjects cannot always be persuaded to obey on rational grounds alone, "wise men who wish to take away this difficulty have recourse to God. So did Lycurgus; so did Solon; so did many others who have had the same end as they."[76] In agreement with Marsilius, Machiavelli considers the utility of religion for keeping peace to be a matter of political prudence, and that utility is not restricted to pagan religion. We note the familiar names Lycurgus and Solon, among whom Machiavelli had previously listed Moses as well.

According to Machiavelli, Numa "pretended to be intimate with a nymph who counseled him on what he had to counsel the people." Fleshing out Machiavelli's account with Livy, we find that Numa believed he could not rule his subjects in times of peace (that is, without the unifying effect that an external enemy had on the Romans). The "most effective" way of dealing with them was "putting into them the

---

their women (including those of the Sabines) were taken away. When the Sabines, the strongest of the surrounding tribes, later declared war on Rome, it was the captured women themselves, who had grown to love their captors (in great part through bearing them children), who ran amidst the Romans and Sabines and begged them not to fight. As part of a treaty, Romulus and the Sabine King Titus Tatius became joint kings, but when Titus Tatius was later killed by a mob, Romulus refused to seek revenge, thereby making himself sole ruler. Livy, I, ix.1–xiv.3.

73 Machiavelli, *Discourses on Livy*, I.9.2.

74 Ibid., I.9.3.

75 Ibid., III.30.1

76 Ibid., I.11.1–3.

dread of the gods," and this required that he "feign some miracle," that "miracle" being the nocturnal meeting with the nymph Egeria.[77] Plutarch adds that it is quite possible—at least the thought shouldn't be taken lightly—that "Lycurgus and Numa and such like others" who had "to deal with hard-to-control and unappeasable multitudes and to impose great innovations in constitutions . . . should pretend to have a vision from the god. . . ."[78] If Moses is to be included in their company, shouldn't we, following where Machiavelli leads, be hermeneutically suspicious about what *actually* occurred on Mt. Sinai? After all, no one else went up with Moses.

From his discussion of Numa, Machiavelli is able to subtly reform the reader's mind, from considering religion as either true or false, to (in accord with Marsilius) thinking of it as *useful*, indeed necessary, if one is to maintain political order. This is obviously a major historical step forward in politicizing religion, and hence the Bible. Machiavelli may well have read Marsilius, but he was far more likely to have gotten this notion from the historian Polybius, upon whom he so frequently relies.

One great sign of Rome's superiority, Polybius asserts, is its "grasp of the gods." By this, Polybius means its political use of *deisidaimonia*, a word that means god-fearingness but with a connotation of superstition. Since the masses are ignorant, irrational, and violent, Polybius tells us, they must be controlled by the "invisible terrors" of religion—a thing that would not be necessary "if the regime [or state] could be composed of wise men." The elite therefore wisely maintain all the pomp of civil religion in public and private life, and over and above that, invoke the horrors of Hades as an extra incentive. Of these things, Polybius remarks, the "ancients did not act rashly and by chance in secretly introducing among the masses notions of the gods and Hades," rather, "those who now cast out these things are most rash and irrational."[79]

Again, it is important to understand that like Marsilius, Machiavelli considers this to be applicable, not just in ancient times, but in modern as well; that is, the lesson must be applied to Christianity as one more religion useful for keeping order in the state. This aspect of Machiavelli's new *via*, borrowed from the ancients to domesticate Christianity, has an important commonality with Ockham's: Both put the power of governing the church in the hands of the state, albeit for radically different reasons. That will make it all too easy as the streams of the two *viae* flow forth for the Marsilian-Machiavellians to make use of the Ockhamists.

Like Ockham's, Machiavelli's approach to religion does concern itself with reform, but for an entirely different reason. In the chapter immediately following his discussion of Numa, Machiavelli reasons about the Catholic Church, not as being either true or false, but as being well or poorly used by princes to maintain order. He begins by considering religion as such, then the "Gentile religion," and finally Christianity. His advice to princes is as follows.

77 Livy, I, xix, 4–5.

78 Plutarch, *Parallel Lives*, Numa, iv.7–8.

79 Polybius, *Histories*, VI, 56.6–13.

> Those princes or those republics that wish to maintain themselves uncorrupt have above everything else to maintain the ceremonies of their religion uncorrupt and hold them always in veneration; for one can have no greater indication of the ruin of a province than to see the divine cult disdained. This is easy to understand once it is known what the religion where a man is born is founded on, for every religion has the foundation of its life on some principal order of its own.[80]

Religion provides political order, but political order is always particular, founded on particular soil with a particular people and with particular religious beliefs and rituals. What is essential, Machiavelli notes, is not the truth or falsity of each religion, but the power of its particular historical formation on a people, and the prudent prince should do everything he can to maintain it.

> All things that arise in favor of that religion they should favor and magnify, even though they judge them false; and they should do it so much the more as they are more prudent and more knowing of natural things. Because this mode has been observed by wise men, the belief has arisen in miracles, which are celebrated even in false religions; for the prudent enlarge upon them from whatever beginnings they arise, and their authority then gives them credit [literally, faith] with anyone whatever.[81]

It is not overly difficult to see adumbrations of the later doctrine of *cuius regio, eius religio*. But we also see another important modern conviction that begins to permeate scriptural scholarship in the Enlightenment: that particular or positive religions often have their origin in alleged miracles, events that wise men, who are "more prudent and more knowing in natural things," doubt. But falsity is no bar to utility. Prudent princes will *use* the credulity of the unwise for the sake of strengthening the controlling hold of religion on the masses.

To return to the *Discourses*, Machiavelli launches directly into an account of Christianity in the light of utility. "If such religion had been maintained by the princes of the Christian republic as was ordered by its giver," Machiavelli remarks, "the Christian states and republics would be more united, much happier than they are." Machiavelli is not clear on *who* the giver is, especially since he fails to consider the Resurrection, the greatest and most miraculous claim of Christianity. Instead, he focuses on the corrupt ecclesiastical hierarchy, "those who are closest to the Roman church, the head of our religion," who actually have "less religion." Because of the "wicked examples of that court, this [Italian] province has lost all devotion and religion—which brings with it infinite inconveniences and infinite disorders. . . ."[82] The problem is not that they are wicked, but as we know from *The Prince*, in imprudently

80 Machiavelli, *Discourses on Livy*, I.12.1.

81 Ibid.

82 Ibid., I.12.1–2.

making their wickedness public, thereby ruining the power of religion over the masses. That is why he praised Pope Alexander VI as "a great pretender and dissembler."

Machiavelli's *Discourses* did nothing at the time to lift him from political exile to political power, but like *The Prince*, it initiated a particular line of republican thought that was extraordinarily influential, and helped to disseminate Machiavelli's mode of reasoning about Scripture and religion.[83] To all of this we shall return in later chapters.

The Last Years

Lorenzo de' Medici, to whom Machiavelli had dedicated *The Prince*, died in late spring of 1519. The Medici family in Rome was determined not to let rule slip from their hands. Giovanni de' Medici (Leo X) was still on the papal throne, but it was Cardinal Giulio de' Medici who came to Florence to assess the situation. One of the important outcomes was a papal commissioning on November 8, 1520, of Machiavelli to write the history of Florence, which Machiavelli would not complete until after Cardinal Giulio de' Medici would become Pope Clement VII. Such was the beginning of better fortunes for Machiavelli. Another favorable outcome was that Machiavelli became a consultant for the Medici family on the proper government of Florence, but as it turns out, they ignored his advice.

Much to his dismay, Machiavelli's new opportunities did not return him to the days of glory he had enjoyed as Secretary of the Republic of Florence. In the fall of 1521, he published *Dell' arte della Guerra (The Art of War)*, in which he extolled the virtues needed for a strong republic—those, we assume, that Christianity does not provide—and offered concrete military and political advice as well. The work was well received, printed seven times that very century, and translated into other languages.

In December of that same year, Pope Leo X died, and once again the question of the government of Florence became a concern of the Medici. Machiavelli was again asked for his advice. But the aims of the Medici were about to be upset by disturbances elsewhere. The Reformation, sparked by Martin Luther in 1517, was now in full flame, and the embarrassment of papal scandal, especially the control of the papacy as a family possession by the less-than-holy Medici, began to exert pressure on business as usual in Rome. A German, Adriaan Florenszoon Boeyens, born in Utrecht (now in the Netherlands), was elected by near-unanimous result, taking the name Adrian VI. In contrast to the Medici and many others firmly entrenched in the Roman Curia, Pope Adrian was bent upon reform. He did not live long enough to see his efforts bear

83 The accounts of the influence of Machiavelli's republican teaching are numerous, and significant disagreement exists among scholars about the substance of this teaching. See J.G.A. Pocock, *The Machiavellian Moment: Florentine Political Thought and the Atlantic Republican Tradition* (Princeton: Princeton University Press, 1975); Gisela Bock, Quentin Skinner, and Maurizio Viroli, *Machiavelli and Republicanism* (Cambridge: Cambridge University Press, 1990); and the above mentioned Paul Rahe, ed., *Machiavelli's Liberal Republican Legacy* and Sullivan, *Machiavelli, Hobbes, and the Formation of a Liberal Republicanism in England*.

fruit, dying on September 14, 1523. The Medici returned to power with the election of Cardinal Giulio de' Medici to the papal throne on November 19.

Machiavelli continued to work on the *Florentine Histories* as far more consequential events rolled forward in Reformation Europe, the papacy now threatened both by Protestantism and imperial ambitions. He completed the commissioned project in early March 1525, but waited until May to deliver it in person to Pope Clement (who would give him 120 gold ducats for his trouble). Machiavelli gave advice to Clement on how to deal with the impending military threat of the emperor, Charles V, but Clement decided to try to save his skin by other means, hoping to rely on France and what military might and allegiances might be gathered in Italy.

Clement did make use of Machiavelli in 1526 in regard to fortifying Florence, which was a key strategic point in the defense of Italy. Meanwhile, Clement formed the Holy League, allying the papacy with France, Florence, and Venice against Emperor Charles V. The league was too disunited to be effective. As a now-elder statesman, Machiavelli was pressed into service in a variety of ways, but all to no avail. On May 6, 1527, Rome was viciously sacked by imperial forces, consisting of both Spanish and German troops. The German mercenary soldiers were Lutherans who had little mercy on the city they believed represented the Whore of Babylon. The rape (a favorite target being nuns), torture, murder, and destruction went on for three days. Clement fled to the protection of the Castel Sant'Angelo, and later bought his freedom for 400,000 ducats.

The humiliation of the pope brought an effective end to Medici power, and Florence was restored as a republic. But Machiavelli, the champion of the republic, was not restored to power. He had two counts against him. First, he had been closely allied with the Medici for over a decade, and the Medici party was now despised in Florence. But even more, because of his writings (especially *The Prince*, circulating in handwritten copies and by rumor), Machiavelli had already earned a reputation as an evil counselor in his own native city. Worn out by a hard life and the sorrows of invasion and rejection, Machiavelli died on June 21, 1527. That same year, a bit earlier, England's Henry VIII became convinced that he had Scripture on his side in his desire to rid himself of Catherine and marry Anne Boleyn, and later that same year, a second child, Elizabeth, would be born to Martin Luther and his wife, Katherine. By this time the reformers had split into several irreconcilable factions over questions of biblical interpretation.

Conclusion

Even aside from Machiavelli, the impact of the all-too-evident hypocrisy of the ecclesiastical hierarchy of Rome was inestimable. Given the moral caliber of popes and cardinals, their use of Scripture to justify their indulgences, indiscretions, immorality, and naked political ambitions was an egregious, even epic, example of politicization—one that was clear to all of Europe. This hypocrisy not only stained the Roman Curia and brought about the splintering of Christianity in the Reformation (which had its own politicizing effects upon Scripture), but even more, served for centuries to come as an exemplar illustrating the alleged fundamental duplicity of all priests and all "organized" religion. In regard to modern scriptural scholarship, the effects will be multiple: the rejection, downplaying, or downgrading of the Old Testament priesthood as a corruption of the true religion (the true religion either embedded in a submerged layer of the Old Testament, or contained only in the New Testament); the exegetical excision of all nonmoral aspects of the Old and New Testament as harmful accretions, in an effort to purify Christianity of its harmful historical accidents; and finally, the treatment of the Bible itself, by those who have given up their faith entirely, as an earlier illustration of the corruption found in the Renaissance Roman Curia.

Machiavelli himself clearly exemplifies the shaking of foundations that occurred with the Renaissance recovery of ancient, pagan thought. For some, like Erasmus, this yielded a wisdom compatible with and perfected in Christianity. For others, like Machiavelli, pagan literature offered wisdom incompatible with Christianity, which must be detached from its Christianized presentation and examined on its own. Pagan literature functioned for Machiavelli much the same way it functioned for Marsilius, but for Machiavelli the "awakening" is more thorough. There is little doubt that reading Livy, Polybius, Plutarch, and other ancient authors "opened" Machiavelli's eyes, allowing him to see, through the eyes of pagan wisdom, the "true" nature of Christianity as *one more* religion (or one more *secta*, to use Marsilius's words). This revelation is at the heart of the great modern intellectual transformation of theology to religious studies that signifies the demotion of Christianity to one particular example of a species, "religion."

As we shall see, this same eye-opening experience occurs again and again, as moderns read the pagan philosophers anew, not as precursors to be judged by Christianity as compatible or incompatible with divinely revealed truth, but as wise men revealing forgotten truth, truth obscured by Christianity but known clearly by the philosophers of Greece and Rome. Pagan philosophy reveals what Christianity conceals. Some will blame the obscurity on the stupidity or arrogance of the priestly class, but maintain that the founder of Christianity Himself held this now-forgotten philosophical truth (perhaps in its most elevated, pure form). Others will regard the entire enterprise of Christianity from its founder on as misbegotten. In either case, if there is any truth in the Bible, it is insofar as it confirms the favored pagan philosophical view.

Hypocrisy had further effects. The gap between the appearance of holiness and the underlying reality of corruption in the Curia became, for Machiavelli, the paradigmatic form of princely deception. As we saw in his treatment of Moses, Machiavelli inferred that the same gap exists in the Biblical text itself. His discovery of the "key" to the underlying motives of biblical figures created a new mode of exegesis, and Machiavelli therefore can rightly be considered as one of the earliest, and certainly the most influential, sources of the hermeneutics of suspicion. Even aside from Machiavelli, this suspicion defines itself against tradition. Since the orthodox treatment of the text assumes a unity of appearance and reality, orthodoxy itself becomes suspect, and the hermeneutics of suspicion thereby defines its exegetical approach against the *traditio* of interpretation. In doing so, it follows Machiavelli's lead.

This suspicion is not pure or merely neutral. As we have seen, Machiavelli's own philosophy determines what it means to read the Bible "judiciously," and hence what is hidden under the surface of the text. Appearances to the contrary, Moses is *really* affirming Machiavelli's counsels; that is, the biblical text contains a largely hidden message that only the wise can see, or at least that Machiavelli has seen and is now revealing. But once we are enlightened then we too can interpret the text correctly.

Such enlightenment begins by focusing on particular key passages that contain the hidden wisdom most clearly, and then proceeds by interpreting the rest of the text in light of those passages. The problem with this approach is that soon enough one runs into passages that can only fit the interpretation according to the alleged "key" by ever-more elaborate hermeneutical reconstructions that have the effect of ever-more completely undermining the integrity of the text. The passage in Exodus 32:25–29 in which Moses has three thousand men slain for idolatry seems to fit Machiavelli's teaching, but what of the rebellion of Korah in Numbers?

According to the text, the rebels were miraculously destroyed, when at the word of God and then Moses, the earth split open and swallowed them (Numbers 16:20–33). *If* such a miraculous punishment actually happened, *then* Moses would be a real prophet of a real God, and not a merely political prince using religion to maintain his power. But that would obviously undermine Machiavelli's entire teaching; therefore to reason about Moses with Machiavelli means to offer an account of what really happened, appearances or reports in the text to the contrary. Perhaps Moses secretly had a trap dug near the rebels' tents and then carefully covered it, or knowing the rebels' designs, he contrived to have them camp upon fragile ground that had been washed out by an underground stream—or even more likely, later writers could simply have made the story up to cow anyone who challenged the priesthood. Any such explanation will do as long as it supports Machiavelli's philosophy and shuns the miraculous.

In future biblical exegesis, Machiavelli's mode of procedure is repeated, but in the service of other philosophies, such as Stoicism, Deism, Hegelianism, Liberalism, or Marxism. The pattern set is one in which the philosophy, no matter how far removed it is from the assumptions of the biblical text, becomes the secret knowledge that allows the exegete to wield the exegetical threshing tool. Passages that fit become the key to illumination; passages that do not must either be reinterpreted against the apparent meaning, or inferred to have some less than noble source. In Machiavelli's case, he can attribute anything miraculous either to the cleverness of the wise who "feign some miracle" or "pretend to have a vision from the god," or to the stupidity of the masses, or to both. The task of the enlightened exegete, then, is to ferret out all the "real" passages—the ones that fit the philosophy—and reinterpret the rest, giving some *other* explanation for their appearance in the text.

For this reason, *it is ultimately misleading to designate the historical-critical method as historical and critical, since history is understood according to the critical framework of a quite particular philosophy*. Machiavelli's treatment of Scripture as a history according to the mode of Livy is the founding paradigm.

This mode of procedure appears again and again in modern scriptural scholarship. As we shall see, an especially notable trait of modern biblical exegesis is its adherence to some quite practical, this-worldly political or moral system that defines the exegetical framework by which the enlightened hermeneut parses the text. Using this framework, he finds (at the end of his labors) that some key figure in the Bible (be it Moses, Jesus Himself, or St. Paul) is *really* a Stoic, a common sense Englishman, a Deist, a Hegelian, an existentialist, or a Marxist revolutionary. All the passages that seemingly contradict such a surprising interpretation can be put down to the cleverness or benevolent condescension of the key figure in hiding his true identity, or the stupidity of the masses as manifested in the key figure's disciples (who being unable to grasp the truth, embrace and then embellish a religion built upon a mythologized account of the key figure, complete with miracles).

Returning to our consideration of Machiavelli's own thought, given that his philosophy is pointedly secular, focusing on kingdoms of *this* world, his exegesis must be decidedly political. As with Marsilius, the goal of exegesis is to yield a political lesson, and Scripture must be politicized accordingly. Obviously, Machiavelli is not interested in theology; indeed, the focus on theology takes our mind from this world, to "imagined republics and principalities" that "have never been seen or known to exist in truth." But rather than discard religion as false, Machiavelli counsels (with Polybius) that it is wiser to understand religion as *useful*, so that rulers may use it well rather than poorly. This is necessary because the unwise masses are irrational in both senses, passion-filled and ignorant. Thus Machiavelli repeats the Averroistic pattern laid down by Marsilius.

This, of course, has an immediate effect on how one comes to consider the Bible. The Bible could be considered a book written in all sincerity by men both unwise and irrational. However that may be, since it has become enshrined as the culture's holy book, it can be used as a tool of wise rulers to control the masses *if* they control its interpretation. Deepen your suspicion, and the Bible could appear as a book of hidden political wisdom that illustrates how the wise, or at least the powerful, use religion to dupe the irrational masses. True exegetical illumination occurs only for those who carefully separate the hidden political wisdom from the religious fictions. In either case, the text will be politicized.

How does Machiavelli's *via moderna*, his new path, relate to the complexities of the *via moderna* issuing from Ockham? This Latin, technical phrase is, in the scholarly literature, almost entirely connected to the rise and variations of nominalism. However, the direction modernity took is much more closely associated with people like Machiavelli, and later philosophers like Descartes, Hobbes, Spinoza, than with the theological Ockham—however he might have helped prepare the way for them. Machiavelli's "new modes and orders" puts the definitive stamp upon modern modes of thinking. Moving forward, Descartes is not usually associated with the invention of new modes of scriptural analysis, but Hobbes and Spinoza are rightly considered fathers of modern scriptural scholarship. To understand in what way each of these thinkers is modern, we must keep in mind, as we proceed in our analysis, the separate streams of the "modern way" that flow into them.

For Marsilius and Machiavelli, the project of secularization, including its approach to biblical exegesis, was never meant to remain merely theoretical. To be truly revolutionary, it must be put into practice. And so it would be.

CHAPTER 5

LUTHER AND THE REFORMATION

As many have rightly said, it is not sufficient to treat the Reformation as if it were defined by just one man, Martin Luther. However, Luther's centrality in that movement cannot be denied, and to treat in detail the entire Reformation with all its personalities and permutations is beyond our scope. So let us examine the main principles and implications of the Reformation insofar as they are connected to the politicization of Scripture, using Luther's life as a loose framework upon which to hang the intellectual developments in the early sixteenth century that helped set the context for the fathers of modern scriptural scholarship almost two centuries later.

Early Life, Early Education, Early Nominalism

Martin Luder was born on November 10, 1483, in Eisleben, in the county of Mansfeld in Saxon Germany, the son of Hans and Margarete Luder. He was named Martin after St. Martin of Tours (c. 316–397), on whose feast day he was baptized. Later, at the University of Erfurt, he added an "h" to enhance his name, Ludher. The year after nailing his famous ninety-five theses to the door of the Wittenberg Castle Church in 1517,[1] he took the spelling familiar to us today, Luther.

Martin was the second son of the Luders, one of many children, perhaps eight, of whom only one brother and three sisters lived to adulthood. Hans Luder, the son of a successful peasant farmer, started out as a miner, but was able to lease a copper pit, and therefore, as its master, become fairly prosperous. Margarete (or Hanna) was not from the peasantry, but from the more elevated Lindemann family of the burgher class, a family that included those educated at universities, town leaders, lawyers, doctors, even a mayor and a university professor.

Given the status of the Lindemann side of the family, it is understandable that Martin was sent, not to the mines, but after schooling in Mansfeld, Madgeburg, and Eisenach, to the University of Erfurt in 1501 for a bachelor's (1502), a master of arts (1505), and then on to Erfurt's law school. Erfurt was dominated by the *via moderna*[2]

1 The "fact" that Luther actually nailed the theses to the Wittenberg door has been challenged. The report or story, whichever it may be, seems to have arisen in Philipp Melanchthon's biography written just after Luther died. See Richard Marius, *Martin Luther: The Christian between God and Death* (Cambridge, MA: Belknap Press, 1999), pp. 137–138.

2 The dominance was gained only in the latter half of the fifteenth century. Martin Brecht, *Martin Luther: His Road to Reformation, 1483–1521*, translated by James Schaaf (Philadelphia, PA: Fortress Press, 1985), p. 28.

(the Ockhamist, not the Machiavellian strain), and Luther would soon consider himself a philosophical disciple of Ockham, asserting "My master Occam" to be "the greatest dialectician," and the Ockhamists "my own school . . . which I have absorbed completely."[3]

As with all universities of the time, there was much Aristotle in the curriculum, and so Luther would have learned the *via moderna*'s approach to Aristotle. Luther most likely did not read Ockham directly, but studied in the general atmosphere of the more traditional thinkers of the *via moderna,*[4] as led by two of his influential teachers, Jodokus Trutfetter and Bartholomäus Arnoldi von Usingen, who were heavily influenced by nominalist Gabriel Biel.[5] As we have seen, given the condemnation of Wycliffe and Hus at Constance and the fear of Hussitism in Germany, nominalism would have appeared, at least to some, as a theologically and politically conservative intellectual position, rather than a radical one.

Luther's well-known affirmation of nominalism does not by itself tell us of what branch of nominalism he considered himself a disciple, nor what relationship (positively or negatively) the tenets of nominalism may have had to his theological doctrines. It is important to understand that the adherents of nominalism were scattered across a broad spectrum, from those who used the principles of the *via moderna* to support the faith and the general contours of scholastic thought's appreciation of reason, such as Gabriel Biel (1410–1495); those more radical proponents who seemed to undermine them, such as Nicholas of Autrecourt and John of Mirecourt; and those more difficult to classify, such as Robert Holcot.[6]

Although during this early period he was not acquainted with the works of Wycliffe the archrealist, Luther shows a nominalist's zeal in condemning realism, which he soon associated with Aristotle. But in linking the condemnation of realism

---

3 Luther was later asked by a Saxon prince to make clear the differences between the *via antiqua* and the *via moderna* (the latter also known by its logical approach, terminism).

> "Terminists" was the name of one sect of the university to which I, too, belonged. They take a stand against the Thomists, Scotists, and Albertists, and were also called Occamists after Occam, their founder. They are the very latest sect and the most powerful in Paris, too. The dispute was over whether "humanitas" and words like it meant a common humanity, which was in all human beings, as Thomas and the others believe. Well, say the Occamists or terminists, there is no such thing as a common humanity, there is only the term "homo" or humanity meaning all human beings individually, the same way a painted picture of a human being refers to all human beings.

Quotes in Heiko Oberman, *Luther: Man between God and the Devil*, translated by Eileen Walliser-Schwarzbart (New Haven: Yale University Press, 1989), p. 120, 169–170.

4 Richard Desharnais, "Scholasticism, Nominalism, and Martin Luther," in John Ryan, ed., *Studies in Philosophy and the History of Philosophy* (Washington, DC: Catholic University of America Press, 1969), Vol. 4, p. 218.

5 Brecht, *Martin Luther: His Road to Reformation, 1483–1521*, pp. 34–36.

6 For discussions of the branches of nominalism in relationship to Luther see Desharnais, "Scholasticism, Nominalism, and Martin Luther," pp. 207–228. See also Heiko Oberman's assessment of Robert Holcot in his "*Facientibus Quod in se Est Deus non Denegat Gratiam*: Robert Holcot O. P. and the Beginnings of Luther's Theology," in Steven E. Ozment, *The Reformation in Medieval Perspective* (Chicago: Quadrangle Books, 1971), Ch. 5.

to a condemnation of Aristotle, Luther would be signaling a break with his nominalist professors (notably, Trutfetter at Erfurt[7]). In early February 1517 he would write that "Should Aristotle not have been a man of flesh and blood, I would not hesitate to assert that he was the Devil himself."[8] These words were written prior to his *Disputation against Scholastic Theology* (early September, 1517). By then, Luther considered the *via moderna*'s commentaries on Aristotle as no more salvageable than those of the *via antiqua* because both gave too much honor to the pagan philosopher. In this reaction, we have the seeds of the modern critical notion that the purity of faith demands the de-Hellenization of the biblical text.

Yet it would be more accurate to say that it was not Aristotle's particular philosophical arguments that Luther rejected, but philosophy as such, or more exactly, the encroachment of philosophy, of reason, into the domain of revelation. This, too, could be traced to the influence of nominalism, at least in part. While nominalism was quite friendly to Aristotle, it contained an inner antagonism to philosophy insofar as it stressed the distance between God and creation, even to the point of denying any analogy between Creator and creature. If there is no real analogy, then revealed theology must likewise be completely distanced from natural philosophy.

But nominalism did not necessitate the denigration of philosophy in its own domain. Luther himself admitted, at times, that reason could function on the natural level (for example, in regard to secular government[9]) as long as it did not transgress the supernatural boundary.[10] But the overwhelming movement of Luther's thought would be more and more against the utility of reason, and hence against the pretensions of even his early nominalist teachers.

Ironically, in setting reason free in its own domain, nominalism contributed to its secularization, therefore duplicating the quasi-Averroist framework found in Marsilius of Padua. Whereas a truncated version of Aristotelianism defined the domain of secular reason for Marsilius, a century after Luther entirely different philosophies would defeat and displace Aristotelianism, and secularized reason would consequently define itself more sharply against revelation. A new form of Averroism was born; same framework, different philosophies. Of course, Luther could not have foreseen this development, even as he may have inadvertently contributed to it.

We may also assess the effect that nominalism had on Luther in two other, related ways. First, Luther accepted the distinction stressed by nominalism between God's

7 See Heiko Oberman, *Luther: Man between God and the Devil*, pp. 120–121.

8 Quoted in ibid., p. 121. See Luther's *Disputation against Scholastic Theology* in Helmut Lehmann, ed., *Luther's Works*, Vol. 31, *Career of the Reformer I* (Philadelphia, PA: Muhlenberg Press, 1957), numbers 40–44.

9 See the extended praise of secular wisdom in Martin Luther, *Commentary on Psalm 101*, in Jaroslav Pelikan, ed., *Luther's Works*, Vol. 13, *Selected Psalms II* (Saint Louis: Concordia Publishing House, 1956), pp. 198–201, and Duncan Forrester, "Martin Luther and John Calvin," in Leo Strauss and Joseph Cropsey, eds., *History of Political Philosophy*, second ed. (Chicago: University of Chicago Press, 1981), pp. 305–307.

10 On this see Lewis Spitz, "Luther as Scholar and Thinker," in his set of collected essays, *Luther and German Humanism* (Brookfield, VT: Variorum, 1996), VI, pp. 91–94.

potentia absoluta and *ordinata* as between the unknowable God and God as revealed in Christ.[11] Of the former, we could know nothing; of the latter, all could be found in the Scriptures.[12] Since Scripture is a divine given, aside from and even against reason, there is again an inadvertent duplication of the Marsilian Averroist doctrine that in regard to revelation "we can say nothing through demonstration, but we hold it by simple belief apart from reason." Luther allowed reason to function on the natural level, but in a way isolated from revelation. That very isolation would permit, even encourage, the development of a more self-consciously secular philosophy, one that would soon come to define what was a reasonable approach to Scripture.

Second, in emphasizing the difference between God's *potentia absoluta* and *ordinata*, nominalism stressed "a belief in the absolute power of God so strong that it did not allow for the effective activity of any intermediate sacred being," whether person or thing, so that it had a marked tendency to destroy "belief in Sacramentals, and even in the Sacraments themselves."[13] Some of this must have flowed into Luther's de-emphasis of the sacraments, and his focus on the direct relationship to God, with no sacerdotal or sacramental mediation. Ironically, Luther would use the distinction to combat those other reformers who, accepting his theology of justification by faith alone, declared the sacraments to be merely symbolic, and perhaps unnecessary. Against them, Luther argued that the sacraments were part of God's *potentia ordinata*, and were therefore not dispensable.[14] This tendency toward desacramentalizing had two important effects: it reinforced secularizing tendencies by "disenchanting" the world; and it contributed decisively to cutting the scriptural continuity between the priestly and sacrificial elements in the Old Testament and the New. Both contribute to what may be called Luther's dialectical treatment of the New against the Old Testament (which we shall analyze below).

In sum, Luther's thought was definitively marked by nominalism, whatever aspects of it he rejected.[15] The importance of this will become clear as his story unfolds.

The Plague, a Storm, and a Vow

In the summer of 1505, one of the successive waves of the Black Plague that had pummeled Europe since the mid-fourteenth century was surging through the area, and

11 See Heiko Oberman, "*Via Antiqua* and *Via Moderna*: Late Medieval Prolegomena to Early Reformation Thought," in Oberman, *Impact of the Reformation* (Edinburgh: T. & T. Clark, 1994), pp. 13.

12 Heiko Oberman, "Luther and the *Via Moderna*: The Philosophical Backdrop of the Reformation Breakthrough," in Oberman, *The Two Reformations: The Journey from the Last Days to the New World* (New Haven: Yale University Press, 2003), p. 41.

13 R. W. Scribner and C. Scott Dixon, *The German Reformation*, second ed. (New York: Palgrave Macmillan, 2003), p. 14.

14 Oberman, "*Via Antiqua* and *Via Moderna*: Late Medieval Prolegomena to Early Reformation Thought," pp. 15–16.

15 See Oberman, "Luther and the *Via Moderna*: The Philosophical Backdrop of the Reformation Breakthrough." The "break" with some aspects of nominalism may have come as early as 1509. Ibid., p. 40.

would soon claim two of Martin's brothers. The unshakable scourge would later break out in Wittenberg in 1527, 1535, and 1539. To all believers, the plague was an evident sign of the wrath of God. Nature spoke for God's displeasure. It would speak to young Martin in a particularly vivid way, but not through the plague. Coming back from visiting his parents in Mansfeld on July 2, with only four miles to go until arriving at Erfurt, Luther was caught in a storm and knocked to the ground by a thunderclap. So frightened was he, that he appealed to St. Anne, mother of the Virgin Mary and the patroness both of miners and of those caught in thunderstorms. As he later recounted, "Suddenly surrounded by the terror and the agony of death, I felt constrained to make my vow." And so he uttered the famous words: "Help me, St. Anne; I will become a monk!"[16] Luther made it through the thunderstorm, and true to his vow—even though he immediately regretted it, and his father was vehemently opposed—on July 17 he entered the Order of the Hermits of St. Augustine in Erfurt (an order that, ironically, owed its origin to the papal decree of Alexander IV[17]).

Just as much has been made of the sternness of Luther's parents and its possible effect on Luther's doctrine of justification by faith, so also much has been made of the suddenness of Luther's vow (both the inappropriateness of monastic life for his character and the opposition of his father) and his later theological rejection of monasticism. It may or may not be that the sternness of his parents acted as an image of the wrathful God who could not be pleased by human efforts, driving Luther to embrace a works-free doctrine of righteousness.[18] Luther may indeed have deeply resented a vow given under duress and against his father's wishes.[19] This much is certain: Given his personal character, Luther would not feel able to sunder this vow without rejecting the entire theological-ecclesiastical structure on which it rested.

When Luther entered the monastery in the summer of 1505, he intended nothing other than to become an exemplary monk; he did not intend to reform the Church but himself—indeed, he would not use the term Reformation in the way that has now, for better or worse, become commonplace.[20]

Early Work on Romans, Theological and Political

Luther was ordained in the spring of 1507, lectured on Aristotle's *Ethics* at the new University of Wittenberg (founded by Frederick the Wise in 1502) in the winter semester of 1508–1509, and visited Rome on behalf of his order in the winter of

16 See Marius, *Martin Luther: The Christian between God and Death*, pp. 44–45, and Brecht, *Martin Luther: His Road to Reformation, 1483–1521*, pp. 48–49.

17 Ibid., p. 52.

18 For a sober analysis of the evidence of Luther's relationship to his parents see Marius, *Martin Luther: The Christian between God and Death*, pp. 21–24.

19 Although Luther's father did attend Martin's first Mass, bringing along twenty friends and twenty gulden for the monastery, Hans rejoiced when Luther finally left the Augustinians. Ibid., pp. 52–53.

20 For a quick but insightful overview (with bibliography) of the ambiguities of the term "Reformation" and the myths about Luther's place in it, see Scribner and Dixon, *The German Reformation*, Ch. 1.

1510–1511.[21] He was put in charge of the academic training of the young men of his order in 1512, and later that same year received his doctor of theology degree, becoming professor of biblical theology at Wittenberg.[22] Frederick the Wise himself put up the fifty gulden (guilder) fee on the condition that Luther would remain as professor of biblical studies his entire life.[23] He lectured on the Psalms from 1513 to 1515,[24] and then on St. Paul's Epistle to the Romans from the spring of 1515 to the early fall of 1516. This somehow acted as a preparation for his revelatory moment that would yield a first formulation of his reforming principle. However, his actual lectures of the time reveal no indication of any such revelatory moment.[25] In his own words, written as a reminiscence in 1545:

> I had . . . been captivated with an extraordinary ardor for understanding Paul in the Epistle to the Romans. But . . . a single word in Chapter 1, "In it [the gospel] the righteousness of God is revealed," that stood in my way. For I hated that word "righteousness of God" . . . Though I lived as a monk without reproach, I felt that I was a sinner before God with an extremely disturbed conscience. I could not believe that he was placated by my satisfaction. I did not love, yes, I hated the righteous God who punishes sinners. . . . At last, by the mercy of God, meditating day and night, I gave heed to the context of the words, namely, "in it the righteousness of God is revealed, as it is written, 'He who through faith is righteous shall live.'" There I began to understand that the righteousness of God is that by which the righteous lives by a gift of God, namely by faith. . . . Here I felt that I was altogether born again and had entered paradise itself through open gates. There a totally other face of the entire Scripture showed itself to me.[26]

---

21 This trip was undertaken on behalf of those Observant Augustinian houses that did not wish to be under the control of Johannes von Staupitz, who was trying to bring all the Augustinian monasteries of Saxony under one head. Very soon, Luther would consider Staupitz a kindly father figure and spiritual guide. Ironically, while in Rome, Luther was quite passionate about freeing his relatives from purgatory, especially his grandfather—celebrating Masses and undergoing penances, saying Mass daily at St. Sebastian's, and climbing the Santa Scala on his knees. Far from being edified in Rome, Luther was famously scandalized by the impiety and corruption he found there. See Marius, *Martin Luther: The Christian between God and Death*, pp. 79–83, and Brecht, *Martin Luther: His Road to Reformation, 1483–1521*, pp. 100–104.

22 Brecht makes the interesting assertion that "Precisely at Luther's time, expert scholars were beginning to claim an independent, rival authority over against those who possessed ecclesiastical and secular power." Hence, we see intimations of the extraecclesial authority on Scripture in academia. Brecht, *Martin Luther: His Road to Reformation, 1483–1521*, p. 127.

23 Marius, *Martin Luther: The Christian between God and Death*, p. 84.

24 Also in 1515, he was given even more responsibility as vicar over ten Augustinian monasteries.

25 On this see Marius, *Martin Luther: The Christian between God and Death*, Ch. 7, and Martin Luther, *Lectures on Romans*, translated and edited by Wilhelm Pauck (Philadelphia: Westminster Press, 1961).

26 Martin Luther, "Preface to the Complete Edition of Luther's Latin Writings," in John Dillenberger, ed., *Martin Luther: Selections from His Writings* (New York: Doubleday, 1961), pp. 10–11.

Although he may not have "entered paradise" through Romans 1:17 during his three-semester course on this epistle (his lecture on this passage certainly adumbrates his later position on justification, but does not highlight it as a defining, earth-shattering insight[27]), he did offer far more extensive and revealing commentary on Romans 13, dealing with submission to political authority. In the gloss, he asserts "in contrast to the Jewish conception, he [St. Paul] teaches that they must submit also to evil and unbelieving rulers. As it is also written in I Peter 2:13 ff. . . . Even though the rulers are evil and unbelieving, the order of government and their power to rule are nevertheless good and from God. . . . Christians should not refuse, under pretext of religion, to obey men, especially evil ones."[28]

We should also be aware that Luther's admonition takes place in the context of a lecture that contains an extended digression on the evils of ecclesiastics in usurping temporal rule and enjoying worldly pleasures and prestige.[29] In light of their misconduct, Luther declares, "I am not sure, but I am inclined to think that the secular powers fulfill their office better and more happily than the ecclesiastical ones do," and that because of such intractable ecclesiastical corruption, "it would be much safer if the temporal affairs also of the clergy were placed under the control of the secular rulers."[30] Had he been able to secure one of the handwritten copies of Machiavelli's *The Prince*, penned less than two years prior, Luther might have formed a different opinion of secular rulers.

Parting Ways with Pelagian Nominalism

After Romans, Luther took up Galatians in October 1516, lecturing on it until March 1517.[31] In September, Luther set forth his *Disputation against Scholastic Theology*, in which he made a definitive attack on Aristotle and break with nominalism, singling out not only Ockham himself, but nominalists Pierre D'Ailly and Gabriel Biel.[32] The objections seem to be made, not against nominalism as such, but against any affirmation of the human will or reason aside from grace. Luther was objecting to what he regarded to be a Pelagian tendency that had shown itself among certain nominalists, one rooted in nominalism's positive affirmation of nature, its tendency to view theological problems from the vantage point of God's *potentia absoluta* (so that, e.g., for Ockham God *could* accept someone as meriting eternal salvation

27 Luther, *Lectures on Romans*, pp. 17–19.

28 Ibid., p. 358, fn. 1.

29 Ibid., pp. 360–364.

30 Ibid., p. 362.

31 What is extant is Luther's revised version of these lectures published in 1519, and so they undoubtedly bear the marks of the conflict aroused by his ninety-five theses of 1517.

32 For an assessment see Paul Vignaux, "On Luther and Ockham," in Ozment, *The Reformation in Medieval Perspective*, Ch. 4, and in the same volume, Oberman's assessment of Robert Holcot in his "*Facientibus Quod in se Est Deus non Denegat Gratiam*," pp. 130–134. For general biographical context see Brecht, *Martin Luther: His Road to Reformation, 1483–1521*, pp. 172–174.

without grace),[33] and its assertion (by Ockham, Gabriel Biel, and Robert Holcot) that God has indeed willed, according to his *potentia ordinata*, to give grace to all who do all they can naturally.[34] Alister McGrath has even suggested that "it could be argued that Luther's theological protest against the church of his day was the consequence of his improper identification of the theological *opinions* of the *via moderna* concerning man's justification before God (opinions that he came to regard as Pelagian) with the official teaching of the church."[35] It is also questionable how new Luther's doctrine of justification really was, given that it had clear antecedents in the *schola Augustiniana moderna*, which had "developed a strongly—occasionally ferociously—anti-Pelagian theology of justification."[36] Whatever the source, Luther's *Anfechtungen*, his struggles to become holy, his intense scrupulosity and doubt about his redemption, and his overwhelming fear of God as a harsh judge, all contributed to his animosity to any perceived Pelagian elements,[37] and to his fierce affirmation of justification by faith alone.

The Political Context of the Reformation

Before delving into Luther's call to reform the Church, we must have some notion of the political complexities that would contribute to bringing about the Reformation. What makes Luther's challenge historically significant is the combined force of his particular theological reformulation and the peculiar political context of his time. As some historians have remarked, if not for that political context, Luther's challenge would likely have remained a merely local affair, quickly contained and diffused by the joint efforts of the emperor and the pope, and with the help of the German electors.[38]

As R. W. Scribner and C. Scott Dixon rightly note, it is clear that "From the very beginning, the question of religious reform was so inextricably linked to political issues

33 Vignaux, "On Luther and Ockham," pp. 114–115.

34 Oberman, "*Facientibus Quod in se Est Deus non Denegat Gratiam*, pp. 125–126.

35 Alister McGrath, *The Intellectual Origins of the European Reformation* (Grand Rapids, MI: Baker, 1993), pp. 24–25, 26–28. This assessment, for McGrath, becomes plausible in light of the great confusion that arose in the fifteenth century about exactly what was the official dogma of the Church. Part of the difficulty, it seems, is that Pelagianism was originally condemned at the Council of Carthage (418), but that condemnation was given much greater clarity and precision at the Second Council of Orange (529). Apparently, the more precise statements of Orange were unknown until the Council of Trent, and reliance on Carthage alone was insufficient guidance to avoid Pelagianism. Hence, Pelagianism could grow within nominalism, until it seemed to Luther to be the general approach of the Church. We will return to this point below.

36 Ibid., p. 26.

37 On Luther's struggles in the monastery, see Brecht, *Martin Luther: His Road to Reformation, 1483–1521*, pp. 63–82.

38 Oberman, *Luther: Man between God and the Devil*, pp. 8, 20–24, 29, 34–35, 49; Hajo Holborn, *Ulrich von Hutten and the German Reformation*, translated by Roland Bainton (Westport, CT: Greenwood Press, 1965), p. 15.

that it could never give rise to an unpolitical Reformation."[39] Nor to an unpolitical exegesis of Scripture.

The Holy Roman emperor at the time was the Habsburg Maximilian I, whom Machiavelli had judged ineffectual, but who nevertheless had political ambitions of lording it over Italy and the papacy itself. The tension between the emperor and electors ran all the way back, in a modified form, to the conflicts between the king of the eastern portion of the empire and his electors after the breakup of the Carolingian empire in the ninth century, and were quite pronounced even under the first German emperor, Otto I. While the power of the emperor had been declining since at least the early fourteenth century, the power of the German electors had risen accordingly, thus "German politics were determined by polycentricism and factionalism, as Machiavelli observed shrewdly in 1508, commenting that neither the cities nor the princes wished the emperor to be great or strong because he would dominate and reduce them to an obedience not dissimilar to that exercised by the King of France over his subjects."[40] In this context, the use of religion by the electors as a counterforce to imperial power would be a great temptation.

Given the long history of wrangling between pope and emperor, it is not surprising that imperial-papal conflicts involved the electors as well. Intertwined with all this was the fact that three of the seven designated electors were archbishops (of Mainz, Cologne, and Trier) and the remaining four were secular sovereigns of their respective territories (of Bohemia, Palatinate, Brandenburg, and Saxony). The archbishops had been given power by earlier emperors to offset the power of the secular princes, and as a consequence had themselves become feudal lords jealously protecting the privileges of their own territory, thereby causing ecclesiastical-political entanglements not unlike the popes' in the Papal States.[41]

Luther's soon-to-be protector, Frederick III (the Wise), was Elector of Saxony from 1486 until his death in 1525. As an elector, he had local (Saxon), national (Germanic), and imperial power (as an elector and potential candidate for emperor). As the prince of Saxony, he considered himself to be a sovereign whose responsibility extended over both the temporal and eternal welfare of his subjects; that is, as with nearly all medieval sovereigns, he considered the Church in his territory to be rightfully under his charge. As Heiko Oberman rightly states, "The supreme ecclesiastical authority of the German prince was not a result of the Reformation, as often claimed: it preceded the Reformation and provided the cradle for its early emergence and ultimate survival."[42]

39 Scribner and Dixon, *The German Reformation*, p. 35. And Brecht: "From the very beginning in Wittenberg the monk Martin Luther was in a powerful political arena, even though at first he knew nothing about it. That he himself became a factor in this arena had religious and theological reasons. From the very moment when Luther appeared, speaking and acting independently, his involvement in a concrete political and social context also became inevitable." See Brecht, *Martin Luther: His Road to Reformation, 1483–1521*, p. 113.

40 Robert Scribner, Roy Porter, and Mikuláš Teich, *The Reformation in National Context* (Cambridge: Cambridge University Press, 1994), p. 6.

41 Holborn, Ulrich von *Hutten and the German Reformation*, pp. 16–17.

42 Oberman, *Luther: Man between God and the Devil*, p. 20.

Interference from the papacy was foreign interference. Papal taxes and indulgences were revenues siphoned from Frederick's own royal coffers.

Conflict between Saxony and the papacy was not new. Frederick II, Elector of Saxony from 1428 to 1464, had restricted the right of the pope to sell indulgences in his domain. The Turks had captured Constantinople in 1453, and Pope Calixtus III (1455–1458) called for a crusade with indulgences for support. Frederick II allowed indulgences as long as he could receive half the proceeds.[43] In 1502, Frederick III had confiscated indulgence money, following the precedent of Frederick II.[44]

Also, Frederick III was struggling against the power of his own bishops, which itself was part of his struggle as a prince against the nobles. For the most part, the great sees were in the hands of the nobles, and unfortunately provided an "outlet" for younger sons of varying caliber and questionable religious sincerity.[45] Independently of his protection of Luther, we should therefore not be surprised to find that Frederick III was "at the forefront when it came to throwing off the yoke of ecclesiastical power," even while he struggled to control his own territory against the claims of the nobles.[46]

Frederick's political desire to throw off ecclesiastical power did not imply sympathy with Luther's theological cause, at least initially. Behind the very door of the Castle Church of Wittenberg upon which Luther posted his ninety-five theses was one of the greatest collections of relics in Christendom—and Frederick, its owner, was proud of the indulgences these relics made available, and jealous of the monetary benefits that accrued from their sale.[47] (Ironically, the "relics" of both Luther and Frederick remain there today, both entombed within the Church).

In addition to all these sources of tension, conflicts between the papacy and the German electors were experienced in nationalist terms, representing Italian versus Germanic interests, so that Frederick and the other elector princes would view control by the papacy as a ruse by an Italian prince to have his political way in Germany. Indeed, the nationalism of Germany was, if anything, more intense than England's in Wycliffe's day. The electors chose the emperors, and Frederick was for a time a candidate. In fact, after Emperor Maximilian died in 1519, Pope Leo X (1513–1521) who would later excommunicate Luther, at one point avidly supported Frederick, even bestowing on him the Golden Rose.[48] The Habsburgs alone spent over a million gulden in the successful election of Charles V; the French, in their hope to elect Francis I, did not fall far behind in largesse; the papacy also spent lavishly, and also offered various ecclesiastical offices as rewards.[49]

---

43 Ibid., pp. 16–17.

44 Ibid., pp. 17–18.

45 Holborn, *Ulrich von Hutten and the German Reformation*, pp. 22–23.

46 Oberman, *Luther: Man between God and the Devil*, p. 14.

47 Brecht, *Martin Luther: His Road to Reformation, 1483–1521*, p. 118.

48 The Golden Rose was an honorary gift given by popes to illustrious and devout persons, usually monarchs. Its origins stretch back to the late first millennium, sometime after Charlemagne. Henry VIII would receive three, from Popes Julius II, Leo X, and Clement VII—all to no avail.

49 Oberman, *Luther: Man between God and the Devil*, pp. 26–27.

Since he remained the holdout vote among the seven electors, Frederick the Wise's power as elector was suddenly and considerably enhanced. The future emperor Charles V, who desired Frederick's vote, had previously negotiated a secret marriage alliance with his sister Catherine to the bachelor Frederick's nephew and heir to the electorship of Saxony, John Frederick.[50] Pope Leo X was quite wary of Charles being elected, considering an emperor with such considerable power a real threat to the independence of the Papal States. Charles was duke of Burgundy, but even more important, as the grandson of Ferdinand and Isabella of Spain, the king of Spain, and even more uncomfortably, king of Naples-Sicily. Therefore, wariness at the possible ascent of the Habsburg Charles made Leo equally wary of stepping on the toes of Frederick the Wise. All of this would work to Luther's advantage.

Fateful Indulgence

We now come to another political entanglement, one that leads to the famous episode with Luther over indulgences. In 1513 Frederick's younger brother, the archbishop of Magdeburg, had died, and the ambitious Albrecht of Brandenburg, of the rival political Hohenzollern house, was able to secure his appointment to the archbishopric. From there, he soon gained (by devious means) the archbishopric of Mainz, thereby becoming one of the seven electors. Archbishoprics were lucrative once gotten, but expensive in the getting, and Albrecht's success came with huge debts to the famous Fugger bank (coupled with the still-unpaid debts of his predecessors). Albrecht, being only twenty-four at the time, needed a special dispensation by the pope to exercise his office, which Pope Leo X (in typical Medici fashion) was only too willing to give him—for a price. The entire negotiated amount for him to assume the episcopal office was almost thirty thousand gulden. Leo wanted to finish the basilica of St. Peter, and needed money. In exchange for Albrecht's dispensation, the young archbishop of Mainz agreed to allowing a sale of indulgences in his territory, a deal to the benefit of both since they would split the indulgence money evenly (estimated, they hoped, at a bit over seventy thousand gulden).[51]

Like Frederick the Wise, Archbishop Albrecht was a great collector of relics—having almost nine thousand—and these carried with them countless years of indulgences. But since a papal indulgence sold better and he would get a 50 percent cut, Albrecht was only too happy to acquiesce to Leo, who proclaimed the sale in 1515.

Frederick refused to permit the sale of these particular indulgences in his territory, but not out of any moral or theological scruple. Like many Germans, he resented the flow of indulgence money out of his own land and into Rome. Worse, he was not getting a share, and the more revered papal indulgences competed against his own church's. Things came to a head when the now infamous Dominican Johann Tetzel

50 Ibid., pp. 34–35.

51 Brecht, *Martin Luther: His Road to Reformation, 1483–1521*, pp. 178–179.

came to Jüterbog in the summer of 1517, just outside the border of Saxony, but close enough to Luther's Wittenberg to attract buyers.[52]

Challenging Indulgences to Challenging Doctrines

By the fall of 1517, the Augustinian monk did indeed mean to reform the Church when he posted his famous ninety-five theses on the door of the Castle Church at Wittenberg. In calling for reform, even in regard to indulgences, Luther was not being revolutionary. Continual calls for reform had been echoing throughout Europe for several centuries. The entire poverty controversy, for example, arose in the context of great anguish about the Avignon papacy, and the Franciscans themselves as an order arose from a crisis of holiness in the Church to which St. Francis, with the blessings of Pope Innocent III, was called as a cure. John Wycliffe's outcry for reform was directed just as much (if not more) at the clergy in England as at the papacy in Rome, and the same was true for Hus in regard to the Bohemian clergy. Luther's own religious order, the Augustinian Hermits, was part of the century-and-a-half-old Observant movement in monasticism that, against the perversions and laxity of the religious orders, strove to follow the original founders' holy rigor. Even the attack on the selling of indulgences was not peculiar to Luther, but had been going on for over a half-century.

What will distinguish Luther from these previous calls for reform is this: Luther insisted that his focus was not on reforming the morality of the papacy and clergy, admonishing them to return to a standard of Christlike poverty, humility, and holiness, but on an entire reformulation of doctrine. In his later words, "Life is as evil among us as among the papists, thus we do not argue about life but about doctrine. Whereas Wyclif and Hus attacked the immoral lifestyle of the papacy, I challenge primarily its doctrine."[53] Or to put it in a more startling way, even if the ecclesiastical hierarchy had been exhibiting exemplary holiness at the time, Luther would, it seems, have attacked its doctrine as fundamentally flawed.

In regard to the particulars of the Reformation's most famous document, if Martin Luther's criticisms of the Church had remained as they appeared in his ninety-five theses (properly called the *Disputation on the Power and Efficacy of Indulgences*), there would likely have been no Protestant Reformation (or at least not one associated with Luther). Witness thesis 91: "If . . . indulgences were preached in accordance with the spirit and mind of the pope, all these difficulties [mentioned among the previous 90 theses] would be easily overcome, and, indeed, cease to exist."[54]

52 See Marius, *Martin Luther: The Christian between God and Death*, pp. 128–129, 134–137.

53 Quoted in Oberman, *Luther: Man between God and the Devil*, p. 55. From *D. Martin Luthers Werke: Kritische Gesamtausgabe, Tischreden* [*Table Talk*], I. No. 624; 294, 19–23; autumn 1533.

54 The ninety-five theses are contained in John Dillenberger, ed., *Martin Luther: Selections from His Writings*, pp. 489–500.

Indeed, Luther's concern was originally with the *abuse* of indulgences.[55] There is, to be sure, characteristic sharpness, such as thesis 86: "Since the pope's income today is larger than that of the wealthiest of wealthy men, why does he not build this one church of St. Peter with his own money, rather than with the money of indigent believers?" And premonitions of what would later become central: "The true treasure of the church is the Holy Gospel of the glory and the grace of God" (62). But Luther's main enemy at this time was, quite clearly, the local hawkers of indulgences (like Johannes Tetzel), and not the papacy.[56]

The ninety-five theses made Luther immediately famous, given the new power of the printing press. In a little over a month, they were translated into German and spread like a brushfire all over the empire. Notoriety also brought immediate criticism, given that critics were inclined to ferret out the worst from Luther's often ambiguous statements. In turn, Luther's defense, coupled with his own rather tempestuous temperament, brought sharpness to his replies that soon cut closer and closer to essential doctrinal reformulation.[57]

In April 1518 Luther traveled to Heidelberg as a kind of celebrity under the protection of Frederick, to join a student in debating theses written up by Luther. He took the occasion to make clear his rejection of Aristotle, especially the Paduan reading of him that denied the immortality of the soul,[58] and to drive home, in no uncertain terms, his new theology of justification, declaring that, "Although the works of men always seem attractive and good, they are nevertheless likely to be mortal sins. Like everything that happens outside grace and faith, they are condemned by God."[59] As a consequence, Luther set forth his characteristic antithesis between Law and Gospel that would yield his later dialectical treatment of the Old and New Testament.

By early August, a summons had arrived in Wittenberg, notifying Luther of accusations of heresy, and hence, the necessity to appear before an ecclesiastical court (meaning, of course, in Rome). Luther and Frederick both wanted any examination to be in Germany. For Luther, it was a matter of safety; for Frederick, it was a matter of asserting his sovereignty against the foreign power of Rome.

German Discontent and German Nationalism

An imperial diet was convened in October of that same year at Augsburg, not for the express purpose of considering the Luther affair, but as housekeeping for the

---

55 Thus, he could say (in thesis 69) that, "Bishops and curates . . . must receive the commissaries of the papal indulgences with all reverence" but add in the very next, "But they are under a much greater obligation to watch closely and attend carefully lest these men preach their own fancies instead of what the pope commissioned." "Let him be anathema and accursed who denies the apostolic character of the indulgences," states thesis 71, but in 72, "let him be blessed who is on his guard against the wantonness of license of the pardon-merchants' words."

56 See especially theses 27–28, 38, 41–42, 50–51, 53, 73–74, 81.

57 See Brecht, *Martin Luther: His Road to Reformation, 1483–1521*, pp. 202–221.

58 Marius, *Martin Luther: The Christian between God and Death*, p. 154.

59 Quoted in Brecht, *Martin Luther: His Road to Reformation, 1483–1521*, p. 232.

German emperor, the ailing Maximilian, and the German princes. The diets themselves, so prominent during the first half of the sixteenth century, were a sign that the emperor had to give a hearing to the powerful German princes and other nobility.[60] The Germans were far more interested in venting their anger at the actual encroachments of Rome rather than worrying about the potential advance of the Turks (the advance of Islam was taken to be a punishment for the sorry state of the Church). These complaints against the practices of Rome—the so-called *Gravamina Nationis Germanicae*—went back at least a hundred years to the Council of Constance.[61]

Many enlightening examples of the *Gravamina* could be cited,[62] but we must bring to view another cause, beyond clerical abuse, of so many complaints: unlike France and England, Germany had so far been unable to establish a kind of national church in which the monetary benefits remained largely within the realm. As Scribner notes:

> In the wake of the fifteenth-century conciliar movement, many lands established national churches, either through exploiting papal weakness in the wake of the Great Schism, as did England and France, or by rebellion and assertion of the rights of an independent national church, as occurred in Bohemia. But Germany had nothing similar to the Concordat of Bologna of 1516, which formally conceded to the King of France the right to nominate to nearly all the bishoprics, abbacies and major benefices in the kingdom. Instead, German lands were a rich picking ground for foreigners seeking ecclesiastical benefices, especially Italian favourites at the papal court or those able to tap into the network of patronage whose centre was Rome and the Curia.[63]

---

60 Holborn, *Ulrich von Hutten and the German Reformation*, pp. 12–13.

61 To cite an example, in 1457 Martin Mair, chancellor to the archbishop of Mainz, wrote to Enea Silvio Piccolomini (who would become Pope Pius II the following year), "The Archbishop, my master, receives daily accusations and complaints against the Roman pontiff [Calixtus III] . . . who . . . despises the German nation and seems bent on sapping it of its strength and substance." Mair then goes on to list abuses almost identical to those catalogued by Luther over sixty years later in his *An Appeal to the Ruling Class of German Nationality*, including the complaint that "New indulgences are approved day after day for one purpose only: their profits to Rome." Even more ominous, Mair warns the future pope that "our proud nation," having been "subjected to humiliating exactions" by Rome, is preparing for action: "Now, however, our leaders have been, so to speak, awakened from their sleep and have begun to ponder what means they might take to oppose their misfortunes, shake off their yoke, and regain the ancient freedom they have lost. Consider what a blow it will be to Rome if the German princes should succeed in their design!" The future pope replied that "the grievances and burdens catalogued by Mair either do not exist or are trivial." As for indulgences, "their purchase is voluntary; why should this be condemned? You are jealous of the money going to Rome; there you have the root of your accusation. 'All your lamenting is about money!'" Martin Mair's letter, along with Enea Silvio's response, is contained in Strauss, *Manifestations of Discontent in Germany on the Eve of the Reformation* (Bloomington, IN: Indiana University Press, 1971), pp. 37–40. See also A. G. Dickens, *The German Nation and Martin Luther* (London: Edward Arnold, 1974), Ch. 1, for the broader context, reaching all the way back beyond the Council of Constance, to the fourteenth century.

62 See Strauss, *Manifestations of Discontent in Germany on the Eve of the Reformation*.

63 Scribner, Porter, and Teich, *The Reformation in National Context*, p. 10.

Hence, the "tradition" of complaint was in no small part caused by not being able to establish a national church wherein church revenues would stay in Germany; or to put it the other way around, the *Gravamina* contain an implicit desire for a national church, and so for the Germans, "Desire for reform was thus powerfully bound up with a desire for a national church."[64] Without this political impetus, it is likely that "Luther's emergence would probably have remained a provincial event instead of gripping as it did the whole nation in a few months."[65]

Decisive Debates and Sola Scriptura

Such is the broader context of the famous Diet of Augsburg in 1518. At the diet Luther would meet another, equally avid reformer, Jacopo di Vio de Gaeta, Cardinal Cajetan, who had already taken the clergy in his own jurisdiction to task, had upbraided Pope Leo X's warlike predecessor Julius II, and would later be instrumental in the election of Adrian VI. Cajetan's mission to Augsburg, as papal legate, was to gather (via a crusade tax and indulgence) political and financial support for a crusade against the Turks, who had been advancing ever closer since the sack of Constantinople in 1453. Failing to find support at the diet, he quite naturally blamed Luther's attack on indulgences as a cause for his rebuff by the Germans. At the diet, Frederick himself called the proposed crusade indulgence "false" and "blasphemous."[66]

Cajetan's demand that Luther recant was met with Luther's refusal and his epic insistence on proof from Scripture rather than papal decree or canon law. Luther also put forth the possibility of calling a general council. Suggesting a council in his dealings with Cajetan put Luther in the position of resurrecting conciliarism, and at the same time affirming the Council of Constance's decision to condemn Wycliffe and burn John Hus (even though Luther himself would soon embrace the example of Hus). Luther, convinced that he would suffer the same fate as Hus, slipped away from Augsburg at night on October 16.

In January 1519, Emperor Maximilian died, temporarily throwing the spotlight off Luther and directly onto the imperial succession. Charles V would be elected on June 28, just as Luther would begin to debate with Johannes Eck at Leipzig.[67] The debate would last until July 16, and it proved to be decisive. Both driving himself and being pushed by Eck, Luther declared that some of the beliefs of the condemned Hussites were "most Christian and evangelical," and that, consequently, both popes *and* general councils could err. All were under the judgment of Scripture.[68] It was also during this debate that Luther denied the canonicity of the book of Maccabees as a

64 Ibid., p. 10.

65 Holborn, *Ulrich von Hutten and the German Reformation*, p. 15.

66 Oberman, *Luther: Man between God and the Devil*, p. 195.

67 The debate was actually arranged between Eck and Andreas Bodenstein von Karlstadt (Carlstadt), with Eck's aim being to draw Luther into debate.

68 Marius, *Martin Luther: The Christian between God and Death*, Ch. 11.

means to show that, although the doctrine of purgatory might be true, it had no solid scriptural support.

The End of Traditio *and the Need for Method*

The Leipzig debate marks the definitive moment when reformers rejected the dual authority of Church *traditio* and Scripture, and located sole authority in Scripture. It thereby also ushered in the monumental difficulty of establishing the authoritative interpretation of Scripture from Scripture itself *as a text,* helping to lay down the essential matrix in which modern scriptural scholarship would arise.

We mean this not only in the obvious sense that a new and passionate attention would now be focused on the biblical text, and consequently on sifting through layers of manuscripts trying to arrive at the "original," but also in another, more profound way that will become apparent upon consideration of Thomas Hobbes and Benedict Spinoza. Contrary to Luther's intention, differences in interpretation arose almost immediately, and just as quickly translated themselves into conflicting political divisions. As it became increasingly clear that the principle of *sola scriptura* was not sufficient to resolve these differences in interpretation, a search began for an infallible *method* of exegesis to function as a substitute for the claimed infallibility of Catholic *traditio.* But as we shall see, Hobbes and especially Spinoza would be concerned to construct such a method for an entirely different end—not to establish the true meaning of the text, but to control the political divisions.

Because of the printing press, both the Leipzig debate and its aftermath were quite public. Just after the debate, Luther was contacted by a Hussite from Prague, congratulating him as a kindred spirit, and Luther would read Hus's works with approval the following spring. This convinced him, all the more that the Council of Constance was in error. Quite soon, Eck's report reached Rome, and in the early spring of 1520, at the behest of Eck as well, the faculties of theology at Louvain and Cologne condemned Luther's doctrines. Condemnation would have the effect, in Luther, of developing these doctrines in a number of treatises, three of which we will examine in some detail below. But before doing this, we must look at the peculiar intellectual, cultural, and social context in which these treatises were written.

German Messianic Nationalism and Humanism

In addition to its long-standing *Gravamina Nationis Germanicae* against Rome, the Germans were afflicted (if that is the right word) by a kind of inferiority complex in comparison to Italy, an affliction that German humanists attempted to heal by elaborate accounts of Germany's noble and heroic pedigree.[69] They competed, one

69 See the excellent W. Bradford Smith, "Germanic Pagan Antiquity in Lutheran Historical Thought," *Journal of the Historical Society* IV:3 (2004), pp. 351–374.

might say, with the elaborate nationalist testimonies of the *ecclesia Anglicana* as *ecclesia primitiva* circulating since Wycliffe's time.

Classical literature was obviously filled to overflowing with references to Rome. What, then, of the Germans? Had they merely been barbarians until their late introduction to Christianity and classical culture? Albertus Krantz (d. 1517) wrote a history of Saxony that contained the dubious claim that the Germans were actually descended from a fourth son of Noah, Tiusco, who was conceived after the flood, and whose name, slightly varied, yielded the Teutsch, hence proving the ancient lineage of the Teutonic peoples.[70] Johannes Nauclerus (c. 1425–1510) repeated the story of the Tiusco pedigree in his *Chronicles of Memorable Things of Every Age and All Peoples*, deriving from it the lesson that the Germans were the Ur-folk of Europe, meant for world rule. "God chose you before others," he declared to the German princes, "and gave you the monarchy of the world [i.e., the imperium] so that you should rule all nations."[71]

A more secure foothold in history for Germany was provided by the publication of a new edition of the ancient Roman historian Tacitus in 1515, complete with recently discovered chapters from his *Annals* that focused on the noble Germanic chieftain Arminius.[72] Tacitus thereby provided an ancient source for Germanic pride, especially insofar as he stressed the decadence of the Roman caesars Tiberius, Caligula, Claudius, and Nero.[73] Ulrich von Hutten (1488–1523), a German noble and nationalist, thereupon took to transforming Tacitus's Arminius into a mythic national hero.[74] The effect of this rediscovery of Tacitus should not be underestimated. As A. G. Dickens states, "Altogether the discovery and popularization of Tacitus contributed strongly to the self-confident, not to say aggressive attitudes of German intellectuals and their half-educated followers."[75] In 1518 Franz Friedlieb (1495–c. 1559), also known as Irenicus, tried

70 Ibid., pp. 355–356. Such dubious pedigrees continued. For the centenary of Luther's initiation of the Reformation, one Paul Reinel penned a history claiming that Lucius Cyrenaeus (mentioned in Acts 13:1) was sent to preach the Gospel, and ended up founding the German town of Selb, which preserved the pure Gospel truth through all the many centuries of the rule of the Antichrist. Ibid., pp. 366–369. See also Dickens, *The German Nation and Martin Luther*, pp. 23–24.

71 Quoted in Dickens, *The German Nation and Martin Luther*, pp. 38–39.

72 For the importance of Tacitus, especially for Germany, see Donald Kelley, "*Tacitus Noster*: The *Germania* in the Renaissance and Reformation," in T. J. Luce and A. J. Woodman, eds., *Tacitus and the Tacitean Tradition* (Princeton: Princeton University Press, 1993), Ch. 8.

73 Tacitus, *Annals*, I:55–68; II:9–17, 44–46, 88. One passage in particular stands out, Tacitus's praise of Arminius who for so long successfully fought against Rome for German freedom: "He was unmistakably the liberator of Germany [*liberator . . . Germaniae*]. Challenger of Rome—not in its infancy, like kings and commanders before him, but at the height of its power—he had fought undecided battles, and never lost a war. He had ruled for twelve of his thirty-seven years. To this day the tribes sing of him. Yet Greek historians ignore him, reserving their admiration for Greece. We Romans, too, underestimate him, since while we extol ancient things, we are negligent [*incuriosus*] of the more recent." Translation modified from Tacitus, *The Annals of Imperial Rome*, translated by Michael Grant, rev. ed. (New York: Penguin, 1989), II.88 (p. 119).

74 Strauss, *Manifestations of Discontent in Germany on the Eve of the Reformation*, p. 75.

75 Dickens, *The German Nation and Martin Luther*, p. 36. Dickens adds, "There arose and spread that appealing image of teutonic integrity which ended by capturing the impressionable Machiavelli and, alongside his more factual admiration for the orderly government and civic spirit of German cities, served to reinforce his charges of decadence against the Italians."

to make up the deficit even further by publishing his *Exegesis Germaniae*, an exhaustive exaltation of Germanic history gotten by combing through every classical writer available, and providing definitive proof that the Germans were not barbarians.[76]

Clearly nationalism was not merely in the air in some vague or primitive way when Luther appealed to the Germans against the papacy and the Italians. Luther, himself indebted to the German humanists, was playing to the most learned men in Germany. As Dickens notes, "Nourished thus by truth and fable alike, ultra-patriotic literature continued to gush forth during the years immediately preceding the revolt of Martin Luther." Dickens concludes that the "phenomenal expansiveness of Lutheranism" within Germany was thus preceded by "the expansiveness of a teutonic humanism, turning ever more from the Latin to the German language." German humanists not only "sharpened the resentment of the [German] nation against Rome long before Luther made his appeal," but became the educators of the next generation of civil bureaucrats filling important positions in the various administrative posts all over Germany. [77]

Of these humanists, Ulrich von Hutten deserves special attention because it was he who offered to help and protect Luther in 1520, and he represents, in one person, an important type in Germany—a nobles at odds with the elector princes, a romantic German humanist, a man imbued with "ferocious anticlericalism," and an avid pamphleteer.[78] Hutten allows us to see how Luther's zeal for reform was co-opted for nationalist use.

Hutten was convinced that the German empire was the rightful heir of true Roman virtue and the emperor "the embodiment of the virtues of the German people." His encounter with the just-published *Annals* of Tacitus at this time deeply reinforced his notions of German destiny, and he would write his *Arminius*, in which Arminius, now in the underworld, argues the case (buttressed by Tacitus's authority) for being included among the great military commanders of history.[79] Hutten's goal, of course, was to raise up the ancient German rebel against Rome as "a symbol of the German character."[80]

In congruity to that goal, Hutten ran upon another decisive text in his travels, Lorenzo Valla's work exposing the *Donation of Constantine* as a fraud,[81] and he resolved

76 Strauss, *Manifestations of Discontent in Germany on the Eve of the Reformation*, pp. 72–75.

77 Dickens, *The German Nation and Martin Luther*, pp. 37, 41, 48, 50.

78 Ibid., pp. 46–47. Thus Dickens's conclusion: "In the transition from humanism to Lutheranism, no figure was more influentially—or more debatably and ambivalently—concerned than Ulrich von Hutten." Ibid., p. 45. Others well worthy of study would be Sebastian Brant (c. 1458–1521), author of *The Ship of Fools*; Jacob Wimpfeling (1450–1528), author of the *Epitome of Germanic Affairs*, which traced Germany's history back to Tacitus; and perhaps most of all, Conrad Celtis (1459–1508). See Ibid., pp. 25–36, and Lewis Spitz, *Conrad Celtis: The German Arch-Humanist* (Cambridge: Harvard University Press, 1957). On the importance of popular pamphleteering, see Dickens, *The German Nation and Martin Luther*, ch. 5.

79 See Strauss, *Manifestations of Discontent in Germany on the Eve of the Reformation*, pp. 75–82.

80 Holborn, *Ulrich von Hutten and the German Reformation*, pp. 74–76.

81 A useful bibliography in regard to Valla is contained in John O'Malley, Thomas Izbicki, and Gerald Christianson, *Humanity and Divinity in Renaissance and Reformation: Essays in Honor of Charles Trinkaus* (Leiden: Brill, 1993), pp. 287–301.

to get it in print in Germany,[82] a plan that would fit into his larger design of printing a series of anti-papal texts from previous centuries.[83] Hutten early on expressed amused interest at the controversy stirred up by Luther at Wittenberg, seeing it as a fight among monks. "One faction attacks the authority of the pope, the other vindicates papal indulgences. There is great excitement and heated controversy with the monks as captains on both sides." As Hutten's only wish was to undermine Italian ecclesial authority, he could state blithely, "I devoutly hope that our enemies will cockfight to the last feather."[84] German humanism and German imperial power (which he saw in nationalist-messianic terms) would rise triumphant from the dust of such devouring. Hutten soon met the most powerful German knight of the day, Franz von Sickingen, whom he would enlist in his cause and offer his powerful aid to Luther.

In draping the emperor with quasi-messianic qualities, Hutten was not alone. A much larger, popular expectation of a great reforming emperor reached, in its obscure origins, all the way back to the prophecies of Joachim of Fiore in the twelfth century.[85] This essentially Germanic belief in a emperor-deliverer is seen quite clearly in the *Gamaleon* (written sometime in the first half of the fifteenth century), which prophesied an emperor who would exalt Germany, destroy its political enemies, remove the Roman clergy, and move the seat of ecclesiastical power (now under imperial control) to Mainz. There was also the more famous *Reformatio Sigismundi* (c. 1439), a messianic prophecy put in the mouth of Emperor Sigismund (who presided over the condemnation of Hus at the Council of Constance). This prophecy predicted a great reforming messianic priest-king, Emperor Frederick, who would strike down the greedy prelates and merchants, and perform a top-down revolution of society benefiting Germany's poor.[86] As Dickens points out, "Luther himself quoted this tract, and the points of agreement suggest that, when in [Luther's *Appeal to the*] *Christian Nobility* he came to excogitate his own social programme, he may have been affected by some of its proposals."[87] There was also the *Book of a Hundred Chapters* (c. 1500), by the so-called "Revolutionary of the Upper Rhine," which likewise predicted a messianic Emperor Frederick, who will lead a new brotherhood (the Brethren of the Yellow Cross) out of Germany's Black Forest and massacre sinners, from the pope and priests to nuns and friars at a rate of 2,300 per day for four and a half years (nearly 4,000,000 in sum). The emperor and the brotherhood will then reform Germany's society, turning it back by force to its Teutonic primitive simplicity, where all things would be held in common,

82 Holborn, *Ulrich von Hutten and the German Reformation*, p. 81.

83 Another treatise of particular importance was one that extolled the pious Emperor Henry IV against the evil Pope Gregory VII in the investiture controversy. See John D'Amico, "Ulrich von Hutten and Beatus Rhenanus as Medieval Historians and Religious Propagandists in the Early Reformation," in John D'Amico, *Roman and German Humanism, 1450–1550* (Brookfield, VT: Variorum, 1993), XII, pp. 11, 16–25.

84 Holborn, *Ulrich von Hutten and the German Reformation*, p. 102.

85 See Dickens, *The German Nation and Martin Luther*, pp. 8–9.

86 Norman Cohn, *The Pursuit of the Millennium: Revolutionary Millenarians and Mystical Anarchists of the Middle Ages*, rev. ed. (New York: Oxford University Press, 1970), pp. 118–119.

87 Dickens, *The German Nation and Martin Luther*, pp. 10–12.

thereby finally shaking off the centuries-long contamination of Rome. This revolution represented a return to its true Christian roots, since Germans (not Jews or Romans) were the true chosen people, and the real Ur-language prior to the Tower of Babel had indeed been German. (Hebrew arose *after* Babel.) As with the *Gamaleon*, a new, truly German messianic emperor would rule all Christendom from its spiritual capital in Mainz.[88] The importance of this extraordinary document is not its publication—since it has never been published—but (as Norman Cohn points out) its presentation of "the influences which he [the author] underwent and registered"[89] as representative of messianic expectations circulating among the German lower classes, which had their parallel among the nobles like Hutten.

To return to Hutten, it was about this time, 1520, that he began to see Luther as "a welcome comrade in the war against Rome"[90] in his opposition to the papacy. In February 1520, he conveyed to Luther an offer of protection from Rome by the powerful Sickingen, an offer orchestrated by Hutten himself.[91] It was near the end of February as well that Luther read Hutten's edition of Lorenzo Valla's exposure of the Donation of Constantine as fraudulent, a discovery that so shocked Luther that he was galvanized to write his *An Appeal to the Ruling Class of German Nationality*.[92] This was precisely the kind of reaction Hutten intended to create.[93] As with Wycliffe, Luther would then date the corruption of the Church at its rise to power over secular rulers.

The moral and spiritual downfall of the Church meant that the papacy should be torn down. About this time, Luther read Sylvester Prierias's *Epitoma responsionis ad Lutherum*. In response to Prierias's apology for papal supremacy, Luther wrote (in the

---

88 Cohn, *The Pursuit of the Millennium*, pp. 119–126, and Dickens, *The German Nation and Martin Luther*, pp. 15–16. See also Chapter 2, "The Germanic Christ," in Alan Davies, *Infected Christianity: A Study of Modern Racism* (Kingston, Ontario: McGill-Queen's University Press, 1988).

89 Cohn, *The Pursuit of the Millennium*, p. 125.

90 Holborn, *Ulrich von Hutten and the German Reformation*, p. 117. Perhaps Hutten first really noticed Luther as a potential ally because of Luther's performance at the Leipzig debate in the summer of 1519. Ibid., p. 118.

91 Ibid., p. 122.

92 Oberman, *Luther: Man between God and the Devil*, p. 42. Luther wrote a letter at the time to Georg Spalatin, expressing his outrage, which was, in A. G. Dickens's words, "one of the most violent letters on the Anti-christ of Rome." Dickens, *The German Nation and Martin Luther*, p. 62. We should note that Lorenzo Valla applied his philological skills to the New Testament as well, and, in fact, heavily influenced Erasmus in his critical approach. Valla's main emphasis was on showing the inferiority of the Vulgate to the original Greek, although his Greek manuscripts were not of the highest quality. See Jerry Bentley, *Humanists and Holy Writ: New Testament Scholarship in the Renaissance* (Princeton: Princeton University Press, 1983), Ch. 2. See also Jerry Bentley, "Biblical Philology and Christian Humanism: Lorenzo Valla and Erasmus as Scholars of the Gospel," *Sixteenth Century Journal* (1977) 8, no. 2, pp. 9–28.

93 As John D'Amico states, "In his edition Hutten affixed a satirical prefatory letter to Leo X. Casting the Donation as a touchstone of the evils of the medieval papacy, Hutten labeled all those popes who had accepted the Donation as *pseudopontifices*, false pastors, tyrants, and wolves. Through Valla's text Hutten hoped to expose the historical falsity of the papal claims to temporal dominance, and the evils which resulted from this forgery for Germany through the centuries. The success can be seen in Luther's enthusiastic response to the text that he believed proved the pope to be the Anti-Christ." D'Amico, *Roman and German Humanism, 1450–1550,* p. 11.

words of Richard Marius) "one of the most ferocious and bloodthirsty cries ever written against the papacy."

> It truly seems to me that if this fury of the Romanists should continue, there is no remedy except that the emperor, kings, and princes, girded with force and arms, should resolve to attack this plague of all the earth no longer with words but with the sword. . . . If we punish thieves with the gallows, robbers with the sword, and heretics with fire, why do we not all the more fling ourselves with all our weapons upon these masters of perdition, these cardinals, these popes, and all this sink of Roman sodomy that ceaselessly corrupts the church of God and wash our hands in their blood so that we may free ourselves and all who belong to us from this most dangerous fire?[94]

Hutten would soon declare his open support for Luther in a pamphlet, *To All Free Germans*, and he and Luther began regular correspondence by May 1520. "I will stand by you whatever comes," he wrote to Luther. "Let us vindicate the common freedom; let us liberate the fatherland, so long oppressed."[95]

Although Luther's goal was, without doubt, theological, Hutten's was unabashedly political: the subordination of the papacy to the imperial power (which he still understood as essentially Germanic), and the control of the church by the civil government. Hutten therefore gives us a clear picture in himself of the significant Marsilian spirit that was from the very beginning allied with Luther's attempts to reform the Church, and the success and character of the German Reformation cannot be understood without acknowledging it.

Insofar as we can speak of Hutten's theological aims, he envisioned a reform—somewhat along the lines of Wycliffe's—wherein the clergy would be reduced to their original, pure simplicity, a condition that exemplified the specifically Germanic (versus Italian) virtues evidenced in Tacitus's accounts. As Hajo Holborn remarks, "The restoration of Christian piety and of primitive German manliness went hand in hand for Hutten," although we must be clear that "the emphasis here was not on primitive Christian piety, but on primitive German virtue."[96] Unsurprisingly, Hutten "seized the idea of the priesthood of all believers with avidity. He was one of the first to follow Luther in saying that the Church needed no head, for Christ is her head. The political implications of the idea interested Hutten more than the theological premises."[97] Such a priesthood immediately leveled any ecclesiastical pretensions of the spiritual power to dominate the temporal power.

The papal bull *Exsurge Domine*, warning Luther of excommunication and giving him sixty days to recant, was officially published in Rome in mid-June 1520, just two days after Luther's *Appeal to the Ruling Class of German Nationality* was sent to the printer, and by August, when the *Appeal* came out, Luther knew the dire contents

94 Quoted in Marius, *Martin Luther: The Christian between God and Death*, pp. 282–283.

95 Holborn, *Ulrich von Hutten and the German Reformation*, p. 125.

96 Ibid., pp. 126–127, 131.

97 Ibid., p. 130.

of the bull (although he tried, for some months, to believe that it was all concocted by Eck). On October 6, Luther's *Babylonian Captivity of the Church* followed from the press, and in November, *Freedom of a Christian*. With the *Appeal*, these constitute the three definitive writings of Luther.

Appealing to the Christian Nobility of the German Nation

Luther's aim in his Appeal was "the amelioration of the condition of Christendom"[98] through the hands of secular authority, that is, through the emperor and the German princes. Luther's turn to secular authority was for him (as it had been for Wycliffe) a return to the proper and original relationship of the secular to the sacred power that had been subverted when the great reforming popes Leo IX and Gregory VII wrested the Church from lay control in the eleventh century. But this appeal was made in the context of the messianic nationalism and humanism that so deeply imbued Germany.

As we have seen, ecclesiastical control was a double affront to Germany, against the German princes and the Germanic Holy Empire.[99] On this count, Luther consistently cast the conflict in terms of Germans versus "Romanists," so that papal power would be seen as serving the interest of Italians rather than the Church. Luther also turned to the secular power because he believed that the Church left to itself would not reform, the reason being (as Wycliffe earlier had claimed) that it was under Satanic influence, if not headed by the Antichrist himself: "[W]e must be clear that we are not dealing permanently with men in this matter, but with the princes of hell who would fill the world with war and bloodshed. . . ."[100]

To dismantle the power of the Romanists, Luther argued that three "walls" that they have built around themselves must be torn down: the first, "that secular force" has "no jurisdiction over them," and that the "spiritual" is "superior to the secular"; the second, "that no one except the pope" is "competent to expound Scripture"; and third, that "no one but the pope could summon a council."[101] Since our concern is to understand how Luther's strategy for breaking down these walls will be effected through Scripture and how this will in turn affect the interpretation of Scripture, we concentrate on the first two walls.

In regard to the first wall, Luther completely undermined the claim of superiority by sacred over secular power by declaring that "our baptism consecrates us all without exception, and makes us all priests," a position vindicated by appeal to I Peter 2:9 ("You are a royal priesthood and a realm of priests") and Revelation 5:9 ("Thou hast

98 All quotations from Martin Luther, *An Appeal to the Ruling Class of German Nationality as to the Amelioration of the State of Christendom* in Dillenberger, ed., *Martin Luther: Selections from His Writings*, p. 404.

99 We note Luther's praise of "emperors Frederick I and II, and many other German emperors, [who] were shamelessly trodden under foot and oppressed by the popes whom all the world feared." Ibid., p. 405.

100 Ibid., p. 406.

101 Ibid., pp. 406–407.

made us priests and kings by Thy blood").[102] Since baptism effects consecration, and "Those who exercise secular authority have been baptized like the rest of us," it follows that emperor, kings, and princes (and indeed *all* the laity without distinction) may each claim that "he has already been consecrated priest, bishop, or pope . . ." Thus, "there is, at bottom, really no other difference between . . . religious and secular, than that of office or occupation. . . . All have spiritual status, and all are truly priests, bishops, and popes." Or as he puts it in terms of its effect, "Christ has not two bodies, nor two kinds of body, one secular and the other religious. He has one head and one body."[103]

In an important way, the secular ruler has undergone a demotion. He, like the officiating priest, is a kind of officeholder with a defined task, rather than an anointed king. Yet in another respect, his status has risen. The ruler is "ordained by God to punish evil-doers and to protect the law-abiding . . ." Hence rulers should "exercise their office freely and unhindered and without fear, whether it be pope, bishop, or priest with whom they are dealing," and whatever canon law says to the contrary (which, echoing Wycliffe, is merely "Romish presumptuousness and pure invention"). In support, Luther paraphrased Romans 13:1–4, adding his own interpretive interjection, "Let every soul (I hold that includes the pope's) be subject to the higher powers, for they bear not the sword in vain"; and I Peter 2:13–15, "Be subject unto every ordinance of man for God's sake, whose will is that it should be so."[104] In his office, it seems as if the secular ruler is the head, rather than the body, but since all the baptized are spiritually equal, it is unclear why the peasants could not claim to rule as well. The "priesthood of all believers" contained, then, a fundamentally revolutionary undertow in the direction of the lower classes. As was Wycliffe, Luther will be blamed when the revolutionary implications become real.

Even aside from the dangers of revolution from below, the doctrine of the priesthood of all the baptized had far-reaching political implications for the power of the German princes whom Luther addressed. Most obviously, it immediately severed any spiritual obedience of a secular prince to Rome, thereby making disobedience inconsequential ("whether they," i.e., bishops and the pope, "denounce or excommunicate to their hearts' desire"[105]).

The destruction of the second wall pertains directly to Scripture, and follows from the destruction of the first. Since "each and all of us are priests because we all have the one faith, the one gospel, one and the same sacrament; why then should we not be entitled to taste or test, and to judge what is right or wrong in the faith?" Indeed, "it is the duty of every Christian to accept the implications of the faith, understand and defend it, and denounce everything false." Luther brings for support I Corinthians

102 The RSV version of the same: "But you are a chosen race, a royal priesthood, a holy nation, God's own people . . ." and "thou . . . hast made them a kingdom and priests to our God. . . ."

103 Martin Luther, *An Appeal to the Ruling Class of German Nationality*, pp. 408–409.

104 Ibid., pp. 409–411.

105 Ibid., p. 411.

2:15 ("He that is spiritual judges all things and is judged by none") and II Corinthians 4:13 ("We all have the one spirit of faith").[106]

Although Luther may have meant to include only preachers, princes, and nobles among the "we," his doctrine of baptism clearly makes all the faithful judges. In the immediate context, Luther wanted to keep the papacy from claiming sole power to determine the meaning of Scripture as justification for its worldly use of power. But in conferring the power to interpret Scripture on all the laity, he inadvertently gave to secular sovereigns the kind of power over Scripture advocated by Marsilius and German nationalist humanists like Hutten, and also empowered multiple theological revolutions from below without a *traditio* to constrain them. As we noted above, this will not only put immense pressure on each sect's exegetes to derive their respective positions from the text alone, but will also lead to the kind of theological-political fractioning that will all too easily play into the hands of Hobbes and Spinoza in their designs to subordinate scriptural exegesis to the secular sovereign for the sake of civil peace.

Luther followed up his analysis with a very practical political program for the German princes and the new emperor, Charles V. This included stemming the flow of cash out of Germany by disallowing the creation of new cardinals by the pope (who would be Italians financially supported by Germans[107]), stopping Rome from taking the annates (first year earnings) of benefices in Germany or giving German benefices to Italian candidates,[108] rejecting the control of Roman ecclesiastical courts in favor of German secular courts,[109] and having Germans take back the investiture of bishops from Rome.[110] He also calls for an interior reform of the Church at the hands of the pope, but since by baptism all are pope including the secular rulers, it amounts to a call for reform by lay rulers. Among such reforms, Luther includes disallowing pilgrimages,[111] forcibly reducing (if not eliminating) the number of mendicant orders,[112] allowing priests to marry,[113] abolishing feast days,[114] reforming the universities, and in particular, driving out the study of Aristotle.[115]

Luther's suggestions, by no means put forth meekly, were accompanied by stirring rhetorical appeals to German nationality and the duties of the German princes. Luther was more animated than Wycliffe in his appeal to national honor, in no small part due to the greater strength of messianic nationalism in fifteenth- and sixteenth-century Germany. A sampling: "How has it come about that we Germans have to tolerate such

106 Ibid., pp. 414–415.
107 Ibid., pp. 419–420.
108 Ibid., pp. 421–423.
109 Ibid., pp. 434–435.
110 Ibid., pp. 438–439.
111 Ibid., pp. 443–445.
112 Ibid., pp. 445–447, 460–461.
113 Ibid., pp. 447–450.
114 Ibid., pp. 454–455.
115 Ibid., pp. 470–472. Luther allows for the retention of Aristotle's *Logic*, *Rhetoric*, and *Poetics*. Ibid., p. 471.

robbery, such confiscations of our property? If the kingdom of France has resisted it, why do we Germans let the Romanists make fools and apes of us in this way?" "The German nation, including their bishops and princes, should remember that they too are Christian. They should protect the populace whom it is their duty to rule. . . ." "O my noble princes and lords, how long will you let these ravening wolves range at will over your land and people?" "My own purpose is to stir up, and give food for thought to, those who can and will help the German people to regain their Christian faith, and to liberate themselves from the wretched, pagan, and unchristian régime of the pope."[116]

To these, Luther added a kind of rhetorical demonization of the papacy. While he did allow, however grudgingly, some place for the papal office,[117] he all but claimed several times that the pope was the Antichrist.[118] The duty to reform, mixed with wounded German pride and resentment at ill-treatment by Italians, combined with a messianic call to unseat the diabolical papacy, would all help to overcome any scruples about political action against the pope. But in order to be effective, the call for reform needed a new kind of justification, one that Luther spelled out in more detail in his *The Babylonian Captivity of the Church*.

Depaganizing, Desacramentalizing, and Dialectical Hermeneutics

The Pagan Servitude of the Church[119]—more popularly, the *The Babylonian Captivity of the Church*—spells out the effect that Luther's doctrine of justification by faith, and

116 Ibid., pp. 420, 422, 424, 435–436. And more: The Romanists "must think the German Christians are, to a greater extent than any others, the household of fools of the pope and papacy, for doing and suffering what no one elsewhere will suffer or do." Ibid., p. 438. "We [Germans] have the title of empire, but the pope has our goods, our honour, our bodies, lives, souls, and all we possess. . . . How beautifully have we Germans been taught our German! While we supposed we were to become masters [by gaining the empire] we have become serfs of the most cunning tyrant. We have come into possession of the name, the titles, and the coat of arms of empire; but the treasures, the powers, the rights, and the liberties of it remain the pope's. So the pope eats the nut while we play with the empty shell. . . . Let the pope give us the Roman empire and all it means, but let our country be free from his intolerable taxes and frauds. Give us back our freedom, our power, our honour, our bodies and souls; and let us be an empire as an empire ought to be, and let there be an end of his words and claims." Ibid., pp. 478–480.

117 "It is not fitting for the pope to arrogate to himself superiority over the secular authorities, except in his spiritual functions such as preaching and pronouncing absolution." Ibid, p. 439. "It is enough for the pope to be his [the emperor's] superior in divine affairs, i.e., in preaching, teaching, and dispensing the sacraments." Ibid., p. 480.

118 "Of a truth, I fear it is possible to call the pope 'the man of sin.'" Ibid., p. 434. "The pope seems almost the Counter-Christ, called in Scripture the Antichrist." Ibid., p. 439. "If there were no other insidious device [papal legates in Germany taking money for various questionable acts, such as dissolving vows and agreements] making it clear that the pope was the true Antichrist, this particular example would prove it. Do you hear that, O pope, you who are not most holy, but most sinful? Would that God in heaven immediately destroyed your throne, and sent it into the abyss of hell!" Ibid, p. 464.

119 All quotations from Martin Luther, *The Pagan Servitude of the Church,* are from Dillenberger, ed., *Martin Luther: Selections from His Writings*.

the consequent declaration of the priesthood of all the baptized, would have upon the seven sacraments recognized by the Catholic Church. In it, Luther did not merely reduce the number of sacraments from seven to two or three—Luther kept baptism and "the Lord's Supper," and in a nominal way, penance[120]—but called for an entire reformulation of the very meaning of sacraments so radical that, as Luther himself realized, it demanded "almost the whole form of church life, should be changed and done away with. Entirely different rites and ceremonies would have to be introduced, or rather reintroduced."[121] As we should expect, since the "whole form of church life" had for centuries interpenetrated political life in the west, the political ramifications would be momentous as well.

Luther's radical reformulation is seen most clearly in his discussion of "the Lord's Supper." Here we find the full import of his belief that "the righteousness of God is that by which the righteous lives by a gift of God, namely by faith." As Luther realized, the doctrine of justification by faith would reveal "a totally other face of the entire Scripture. . . ." For Luther, the "promise" of justification by faith alone, i.e., that "life and salvation are promised without price; they are given to those who believe in the promise,"[122] would become the interpretive key to Scripture. The notion of promise, then, would become *the* exegetical typology.[123]

According to Luther, the Old Testament is full of promises: to Adam was given the promise of "the woman who was to bruise the serpent's head"; to Noah that God would not curse the ground again or destroy every living thing, which was accompanied by a "sign . . . the rainbow of the covenant"; to Abraham "that all the nations should have blessing in his seed"; and then "to Moses and the children of Israel, and especially to David, He plainly made the promise of Christ. . . ." Of course, "the most perfect promise" is "that of the new testament." The difference between the promises of the Old and the New Testaments is "that the older testament, mediated through Moses, was not a promise of remission of sins, or of eternal life, but of temporal things, to wit, the land of Canaan."[124] In either case, the interpretive focus is solely on what God says (His words) in the form of a promise, and the human response, belief or faith that God will do as He promises. And so, "these two, promise and faith, are necessarily yoked together. No one can believe if there is no promise. If there is no faith, a promise is useless, because faith is its counterpart and completion."[125]

For Luther, this interpretive key unlocks the true meaning of "the words with which Christ instituted this sacrament" of "the Lord's Supper." When Christ said at the

120 Luther initially argues for all three, but in the end asserts that "strictly speaking, there are but two sacraments in the church of God: baptism and the Lord's supper. . . ." Luther, *The Pagan Servitude of the Church*, pp. 256, 357.

121 Ibid., p. 271.

122 Ibid., p. 275.

123 On the development of promise as the interpretive key for Luther, see James Preus, *From Shadow to Promise: Old Testament Interpretation from Augustine to the Young Luther* (Cambridge: Harvard University Press, 1969), esp. pp. 184–199, 267.

124 Luther, *The Pagan Servitude of the Church*, pp. 274–275.

125 Ibid., p. 277.

Last Supper "'Take and eat: this is my body which is given for you.' And taking the cup, He gave thanks, and gave to them saying: 'All ye drink of it. This cup is the new testament in my blood which is poured out for you and for many for the remission of sins'" (Matthew 26:26–28), it is:

> as if He had said, "Lo! Thou sinful soul, out of the pure and free love with which I love thee, and in accordance with the will of the Father of mercies, I promise thee with these words, and apart from any deserts or undertakings of thine, to forgive all thy sins, and give thee eternal life. In order that thou mayest be most assured that this my promise is irrevocable, I will give my body and shed my blood to confirm it by my very death, and make both body and blood a sign and memorial of this promise."[126]

Luther thereby interprets what appears to be the language of sacrifice as if it were distinguishing between promise and a sign of the promise. With this great shift, the promise or word is essential, and the sign or sacrament becomes accidental.[127] Hence, "these promises of Christ . . . truly constitute the mass itself," so much so that, "I am able daily, indeed hourly, to have the mass; for, as often as I wish, I can set the words of Christ before me, and nourish and strengthen my faith by them. This is the true spiritual eating and drinking."[128]

What makes this interpretation possible is Luther's treatment of "testament" in the Last Supper passage from Matthew.[129] The Greek *diathēkē* bears a double meaning, both a will or testament (according to its secular Greco-Roman meaning) and covenant (according to its Septuagintal meaning), a doubleness played upon by St. Paul in Galatians 3:15–18. The Septuagint uses *diathēkē* as the equivalent of the Hebrew word for covenant, and this usage is reflected throughout the New Testament in general, with the possible exception of Galatians 3:15–18. The Vulgate uses *testamentum* in the above-quoted passage in Matthew. The Latin primarily means a last will or testament, derived from the verb *testari*, to bear witness, make known, or declare. The Vulgate New Testament consistently chooses *testamentum* to render the Greek *diathēkē*, such as in Hebrews 9:20 ("'This is the blood of the covenant which God commanded you.'"),

126 Ibid., pp. 272, 275.

127 Ibid., p. 279.

128 Ibid., pp. 276, 279. Luther asserts that the Eucharistic passage in John 6 may "be totally set on one side, on the ground that it does not utter a syllable about the sacrament. The sacrament was not yet instituted [since this passage occurs prior to the Last Supper]; and more to the point, the chapter is plainly and obviously speaking about faith, as is shown by the warp and woof of the words and thoughts." Thus, Jesus "was speaking of spiritual eating," for "No sort of eating gives life except eating in faith. This is the true eating, the spiritual." Ibid., pp. 256–257.

129 For a full account of the problems on proper translation of *diathēkē* especially as focused on the passage in Hebrews 9:15–22 see Scott Hahn, "A Broken Covenant and the Curse-of-Death: A Study of Hebrews 9:15–22," *Catholic Biblical Quarterly* 66 (2004), pp. 416–436. For an account of Luther's exegesis of Hebrews see Kenneth Hagen, *The Theology of Testament in the Young Luther: The Lectures on Hebrews* (Leiden: Brill,1974).

which recalls the words of Moses to the Israelites in Exodus 24:7–8, and therefore intends it to bear the covenantal meaning of *diathēkē*.

Luther takes *testamentum* solely in terms of its primary Latin secular meaning, rather than the covenantal meaning of the Greek *diathēkē*—rather a surprise, given his emphasis on returning to the original Greek: "Without question, a testament is a promise made by a man in view of his death." Thus:

> when He [Christ] says: "This is my blood which is given. This is my blood which is shed." He names and designates the bequest when He says, "In remission of sins." Similarly, He appoints the heirs when He says, "For you and for many," i.e., those who accept, and believe in, the promise of the testator. Faith here makes men heirs. . . .[130]

Consequently, rather than the Mass being a sacrifice somehow related to the Old Testament sacrificial covenants, "what we call the mass is a promise made by God for the remission of our sins; a promise which was confirmed by the death of the Son of God."[131] Luther even asserts that the Old Testament use of covenant should be understood, typologically, in the same way, not as a sacrificial binding oath but a promise:

> Now Christ's death was foreshadowed in all the promises of God from the beginning of the world. Indeed, whatever value the ancient promises had, depended on that new promise in Christ which lay in the future. Hence the very frequent use in Scripture of the words, "covenant," "compact," "testament of the Lord." Their meaning was that God would die at some future date; because, before a testament comes into effect, the testator's death must take place (Hebrews 9). But it was God who made the testament, and therefore He needs must die. But He Himself could not die unless He became man. Therefore the one comprehensive word, "testament," envisages both the incarnation and the death of Christ.[132]

Luther was thereby able to narrow the entire exegetical endeavor of Old and New Testaments and the celebration of the Mass to a very sharp point: "the mass is a part of the gospel, nay the sum and substance of the gospel; for the whole gospel is simply the good news of the forgiveness of sins."[133]

This exegetical approach yielded Luther's famous law-gospel dichotomy that characterized his dialectical approach to the Old and New Testaments: "the whole of Scripture is concerned to rouse faith in us, now urging us with commandments or retributions [i.e., law], and again encouraging us with promises and consolations [i.e., gospel]. In fact, the whole of Scripture consists of either precepts [i.e., laws] or

---

130 Luther, The Pagan *Servitude of the Church*, p. 273.

131 Ibid.

132 Ibid.

133 Ibid., p. 290.

promises. The precepts make demands which humble the haughty, whereas the promises lift up the lowly by forgiving their sins."[134]

In this dialectical hermeneutic, the Old Testament serves a largely negative function as law, rather than serving as the priestly, sacrificial foundation to be fulfilled in the New Testament. Or to focus on the positive, the Old Testament foundation is limited to promise (a limitation that shears away the now unnecessary cultic elements of the covenant), and the New Testament is limited to fulfillment of that promise, so that cultic elements in the New Testament must either be exegetically downplayed or eliminated completely as Judaizing reversions to the law. The first option we have just seen in Luther's presentation of the Mass as a testament. By it, Luther will initiate the detaching of scriptural exegesis from the liturgy.[135] The second option (which we will examine in later chapters) will enjoy a long history in various stages of modern scriptural scholarship, and it will complete the divorce of exegesis from liturgy.

This dialectical hermeneutic was indeed revolutionary in other ways as well. It allowed Luther to reinterpret the traditionally understood two senses of Scripture, the literal and the spiritual (the latter, we recall, subdivided into the allegorical, moral, and anagogical senses, hence the twofold is fourfold), as "letter and spirit" now understood by him to be equivalent to law and gospel, Old and New Testament. Letter and spirit could then be set against each other dialectically.[136] Luther's rather complex reinterpretation is monumentally important, and worthy of more careful analysis.

In a treatise written in 1521 as a reply to the anti-Lutheran Jerome Emser,[137] Luther explicitly criticized the traditional fourfold manner of interpreting Scripture. Emser cited II Corinthians 3:6, "the letter kills, but the Spirit gives life," as justification for taking a spiritual reading (allegorical, moral, or anagogical) over a literal reading. As we would expect, Luther's ire is raised against those who found affirmations of the papacy and its powers (via spiritual exegesis) in the passages of the Gospels. But also at issue in this treatise was Luther's avowal of the priesthood of all believers, which he took to be enjoined by I Peter 2:9: "'You are a royal priesthood and a priestly kingdom.' With this saying I proved that all Christians are priests."[138] Emser asserted, contra Luther, that here the letter kills, for "St. Peter speaks of the inward spiritual priesthood which all Christians possess, and not of the consecrated priesthood."[139]

134 Ibid., p. 357.

135 On the centrality of liturgy to exegesis, see Scott Hahn, *Letter and Spirit: from Written Text to Living Word in the Liturgy* (New York: Doubleday, 2005).

136 See Scott Hendrix, "Luther against the Backdrop of the History of Biblical Interpretation," in Hendrix, *Tradition and Authority in the Reformation* (Brookfield, VT: Variorum, 1996), I, pp. 236–237.

137 Emser's treatise was entitled *Against the Un-Christian Book of the Augustinian Martin Luther, Addressed to the German Nobility* and Luther's response was *Answer to the Hyperchristian, Hyperspiritual, and Hyperlearned Book by Goat Emser in Leipzig—Including Some Thoughts Regarding His Companion, the Fool* [Thomas] *Murner*.

138 Luther, *Answer to the Hyperchristian, Hyperspiritual, and Hyperlearned Book by Goat Emser in Leipzig—Including Some Thoughts Regarding His Companion, the Fool Murner* in Lehmann, ed., *Luther's Works*, Vol. 39, p. 152.

139 According to Luther's report. Luther, *Answer to the Hyperchristian, Hyperspiritual, and Hyperlearned Book by Goat Emser in Leipzig*, p. 152.

Against this, Luther argued for the primacy of the literal, the "letter." If the literal or historical meaning "kills," remarked Luther caustically, one would have to "condemn the whole Scripture and to prefer the devil's lies or fables [the propapal spiritual exegesis] to the holy words of God, especially since it [Scripture] has no other meaning that counts but the one you teach as deadly [i.e., the literal] and to be avoided."[140] Luther then offers an account of the Scripture that, while remaining somewhat loyal to St. Augustine's account of the fourfold meaning of Scripture, has taken on the anti-analogical (and hence anti-symbolic) aspects inherent in Ockham's nominalism.

> The Holy Spirit is the simplest writer and adviser in heaven and on earth. That is why his words could have no more than the one simplest meaning which we call the written one, or the literal meaning of the tongue. But [written] words and [spoken] language cease to have meaning when the things which have a simple meaning through interpretation by a simple word are given further meanings and thus become different things [through a different interpretation] so that one thing takes on the meaning of another. This is true for all other things not mentioned in Scripture because all God's creatures and works are sheer living signs and words of God, as Augustine and all the teachers say. But one should not therefore say that Scripture or God's word has more than one meaning.[141]

Curiously enough, Luther affirmed the *root* of the allegorical, moral, and anagogical senses of Scripture (that, unlike human beings who can only signify things with words, God can make things living symbols of other things), but allowed it to apply only to nature, not Scripture.[142] In Scripture, so his argument seems to go, words can only signify things (that is, according to the historical or literal sense). The traditional fourfold senses of Scripture, Luther then asserted, arose out of the confusion among the Church Fathers. "Some people, out of ignorance, therefore, attributed a fourfold meaning to Scripture: the literal, the allegorical, the anagogical, and the tropological [i.e., moral]. But there is no basis for it."[143]

Yet these last words must be considered as a rhetorical overstatement. Although Luther strongly affirms the priority of the literal (an affirmation not peculiar to Luther, but stretching back several centuries[144]), he was by no means entirely adverse to allegory or a spiritual interpretation. The question for Luther, then, was not so much wheth-

140 Luther, *Answer to the Hyperchristian, Hyperspiritual, and Hyperlearned Book by Goat Emser in Leipzig*, p. 178.

141 Ibid., pp. 178–179.

142 Luther lived a century before the rise of the anti-Aristotelian, reductionist (or materialist) view of nature that would render any symbolic view of it untenable.

143 Luther, *Answer to the Hyperchristian, Hyperspiritual, and Hyperlearned Book by Goat Emser in Leipzig*, pp. 180–181.

144 Hendrix, "Luther against the Backdrop of the History of Biblical Interpretation," p. 232. See, for example, Beryl Smalley's treatment of Hugh and Richard of St. Victor in *The Study of the Bible in the Middle Ages* (Notre Dame, IN: University of Notre Dame Press, 1964), Ch. III.

er allegory was being used (thus, Luther could interpret Psalm 3 Christologically[145]), but *how* it was being used. "For Luther it was not a matter of choosing one level of meaning (i.e., literal or spiritual) over another but of choosing the meaning of the text which best fit the significance of the words, the historical circumstances, and his own theological perspective."[146]

With Luther, the significance of the words was defined by his theology of justification by faith alone, and hence according to his dialectical framework of letter and spirit, law and gospel, and promise and faith, rather than according to the traditional four senses.[147] Thus, it was possible for the literal meaning to be spiritual (if it supported justification by faith alone), and an allegorical or moral interpretation to represent the "letter that kills" (if it supported a rival theological view).[148] "Letter," therefore, no longer meant literal, but that which stands in dialectical antithesis to the "Spirit" as defined in accordance with his theology.

It is misleading, then, to assume that the importance of Luther as an exegete is his focus on the literal account of Scripture; rather, his importance consists in substituting the dialectical mode of exegesis for the traditional fourfold meaning of Scripture. That having been said, Luther does tend to hold that the literal meaning is the one that supports his theology, a position that brought him into conflict with other Reformers, for whom the plain meaning of the text led elsewhere, thereby causing the theological-political fractioning of the various reformers.

If we may now return to *The Pagan Servitude of the Church*, we can see this tendency—along with its attendant ambiguity—in Luther's account of the Eucharist itself, which he takes to be based on a literal reading. Luther asserted that, based on a literal reading of Scripture, the laity should freely partake of both the bread and the wine—a position that he acknowledges is associated with the Hussites, but accords with Scripture nonetheless.[149] Even more pointedly, Luther self-consciously accepts something like the Wycliffian Eucharistic doctrine against the Catholic doctrine of transubstantiation, again based upon what he takes to be a literal interpretation on Scripture.[150] This provides the context for his assertion that "the word of God does not need to be forced in any way by either men or angels. Rather, its plainest meanings are to be preserved; and unless the context manifestly compels one to do otherwise, the words are not to be understood apart from their proper and literal sense, lest occasion

145 Hendrix, "Luther against the Backdrop of the History of Biblical Interpretation," I, p. 232.

146 Ibid., I, p. 234.

147 Luther, *Answer to the Hyperchristian, Hyperspiritual, and Hyperlearned Book by Goat Emser in Leipzig*, pp. 182–186.

148 Hendrix, "Luther against the Backdrop of the History of Biblical Interpretation," I, p. 237.

149 Since, for Luther, communion in both kinds is supported in Scripture, he remarks, "These considerations have kept me from condemning the Bohemians, who, whether in the right or the wrong, have certainly the words and works of Christ on their side." And more strongly, "If any are to be called heretics and schismatics, it is neither the Bohemians, nor the Greeks, who take their stand on the gospel; rather, you Romanists are heretics and impious schismatics, who presume on your figments alone, and fly contrary to plain passages in divine Scripture." Luther, *The Pagan Servitude of the Church*, p. 260–262.

150 "Here I shall be called a Wycliffite and six hundred times a heretic. But what does it matter?" Ibid., pp. 265–267.

be given to our adversaries to evade Scripture as a whole."[151] According to Luther, the introduction of "transubstantiation" was an aberration based upon the introduction of the "specious philosophy of Aristotle" that diverted the church from orthodoxy.[152] But Scripture speaks otherwise, for:

> [T]he evangelists plainly record that Christ took bread and blessed it; the book of Acts and the Apostle Paul call it bread; therefore we are intended to understand it means real bread; and so also true wine, and a true chalice. . . . Since, therefore, it is not necessary to assume that divine power effected a transubstantiation, this must be regarded as a human invention, because it is not supported by Scripture or reason. . . .[153]

Luther therefore took Wycliffe's heretical view that the substance of the bread and wine that exist before consecration also remain after consecration. Again, he believed this to be in accord with the plain sense of Scripture; Wycliffe himself took it to be a necessity of his realist metaphysics, the Logic of Scripture, rather than a literal reading of the text.

As will soon become evident, however, a literal reading of the same texts would lead other reformers to assert that the bread and wine were *all* that was there, a position that Luther vehemently denied. These fundamental differences of interpretation in regard to the literal sense would yield both theological and political fault lines among the reformers, increasing the impetus for a secular resolution that would yield civil peace.

We find much the same pattern in Luther's treatment of the other sacraments. Luther understands baptism—"the prime sacrament, the foundation of them all"[154]—in much the same way as the Lord's Supper. It is a sign that itself effects nothing, but merely accompanies an act of faith. This would seem to bring Luther to reject infant baptism since "when infants are baptized, they cannot receive the promises of God," but he asserts that "infants are helped by vicarious faith: the faith of those who present them for baptism."[155] In regard to all the sacraments, the "whole of their effectiveness lies in faith, and not in anything that is done. He who believes in them, fulfils them, even if nothing is done."[156] The other sacraments alleged by Rome—confirmation, matrimony, ordination, and extreme unction—are not sacraments since, for Luther, they are either not scriptural or contain no promise.[157] Even in regard to the sacraments that remain, since their efficacy is entirely centered on the faith of the hearers in the words of promise, a distinct sacerdotal function is rendered entirely unnecessary—an effect that accorded well with his declaration of the

151 Ibid., p. 266.
152 Ibid., p. 207.
153 Ibid., p. 267.
154 Ibid., p. 294.
155 Ibid., p. 307.
156 Ibid., pp. 299–300.
157 Ibid., pp. 324–356.

priesthood of all believers. From this, three results follow, one exegetical, one political, and one exegetical-political.

First, to repeat our point above, in regard to exegesis, especially of the Old Testament, either the priesthood must be treated dialectically as something merely of the Old Law (and hence there is no typological connection to the New Testament for priesthood and sacrifice), or the priesthood must somehow be exegetically muted or transformed.

Second, in regard to society, the priesthood can no longer function as a distinct, essential class (a point that Luther makes abundantly clear in his rejection of ordination, or rather his transformation of it[158]). Since the sacrament of baptism makes all equally priests, as Luther asks rhetorically, "What function, then, is left for you as a priest which is not equally appropriate for a layman?"[159] Obviously, for those who might benefit by eliminating ecclesial power rooted in the specific sacramental claims of priesthood, Luther's mode of exegesis would prove attractive. Luther's intention, of course, was not to play into the hands of someone inspired by Machiavelli or Marsilius, or even Hutten, but by a great revolution to deprive the Romanists of the specific claims to sacramental power that they had abused so unashamedly.[160] Yet for our purposes, we must trace both intended and unintended consequences to their cause.

Third, Luther's definition of a sacrament, in making the hearing of the word/promise central, seems to undermine keeping any sacraments even in name, and to affirm instead simply holding to the primacy and sufficiency of the Bible. Again, such would be the inference of other nonsacramental reformers in Luther's own generation, especially the Anabaptists (who would embrace Luther's teaching on faith and reject his notion of vicarious faith in regard to infant baptism), but also his "closer" allies like Zwingli (who would take Luther's denial of the efficacy of the signs, bread and wine, to its logical conclusion, completely rejecting "the Lord's Supper" as a sacrament).

Such disagreements about the proper literal interpretation will set forth an historical-political dynamic that will directly and indirectly affect the development of modern critical scholarship. Fundamental disagreements will result in multiple interpretations, diverse reforming sects, and hence political divisions. Ever greater exegetical energy will be spent in vindicating positions through close textual analysis, and since the ensuing controversies are necessarily tied to political divisions, exegesis cannot help but become politicized. Those of a secular bent who want to be rid of the theological-political conflict will seek a mode of exegesis that either makes theological conflict impossible or renders it politically innocuous.

---

158 Ibid., p. 345.

159 Ibid., p. 348.

160 "But, you will say: What is this? Surely your contentions will overturn the practices and purposes of all the churches and monasteries, and destroy those by which they have waxed rich for many centuries, since they have been founded on masses at anniversaries, intercessions, 'applications,' 'communications.' You will deprive them of their largest incomes. My answer is: That is the very thing which led me to write that the church has been taken prisoner. For this sacred testament of God has been forced into the service of impious greed for gain by the opinions and traditions of irreligious men." Ibid., p. 284.

The theological-political situation will be rendered even more volatile by Luther's declarations about the freedom from law in *The Pagan Servitude of the Church*. Luther maintained that "it is not possible for either men or angels rightfully to impose even a single law upon Christians except with their consent; for we are free from all things."[161] This declared freedom, aimed originally at Church law, had immediate socio-political implications. As Luther declared concerning the various Church-based laws forbidding marriages on grounds of consanguinity: "There is no hope of a cure unless the whole of the laws made by men, no matter what their standing, are repealed once for all. When we have recovered the freedom of the gospel, we should judge and rule in accordance with it in every respect. Amen."[162] As an example of such judgment, Luther recommended that a woman married to an impotent man should be allowed the freedom either to divorce or "with her husband's consent . . . she should have coition with another man, say her husband's brother . . . keeping this 'marriage' secret, and ascribing the children to the putative father. . . ." The reason he gives is that "the harshness of the law does not allow divorce; yet by the divine law the woman is free, and so cannot be forced to remain continent."[163] That is not to say that Luther was an advocate of divorce. "For my part, I have such a hatred of divorce that I prefer bigamy to divorce, yet I do not venture an opinion whether bigamy should be allowed."[164]

As it turns out, he did venture his opinion later, illustrating a particularly interesting entanglement of exegesis and politics. Luther advised in 1539 the great militant Protestant protector Landgrave Philip of Hesse to marry a second wife (Margarethe von der Sale), without divorcing the first (Christina, daughter of Luther's assiduous enemy, Duke George of Saxony).[165] Philip was one of the first of the German princes to declare himself Protestant after the Peasant War of 1525—he had apparently converted in 1524[166]—and he soon became the primary source of political unity among the various reformers. In theology, especially in regard to the great Eucharistic controversies among Protestants, Philip sided with the reforming opponents of Luther, but tended to see the matter as of little consequence compared to the broad-based political unity needed against Catholicism.[167] He well understood, to quote Hillerbrand, that "the unresolved differences over the proper interpretation of communion between Zwingli and Luther hung like a millstone around the neck of Protestants,"

161 Ibid., p. 306.

162 Ibid., p. 336.

163 Ibid., p. 337.

164 Ibid., p. 339.

165 Philip declared of Christina, "from the time I first took here, I neither desired nor wished her because of her unattractive appearance, disposition, and reputation, and besides she was subject to spells of excessive intemperance, as her court-mistress, maids, and many other people know." Quoted in Hastings Eells, *The Attitude of Martin Bucer toward the Bigamy of Philip of Hesse* (New Haven: Yale University Press, 1924), p. 58. For a general account of the whole affair see Brecht, *Martin Luther: The Preservation of the Church, 1532–1546*, translated by James Schaaf (Minneapolis, MN: Fortress Press, 1993), pp. 205–215.

166 Hans J. Hillerbrand, *Landgrave Philipp of Hesse, 1504–1567: Religion and Politics in the Reformation* (Saint Louis, MO: Foundation for Reformation Research, 1967), p. 6.

167 Ibid., pp. 13–14.

and so unlike the reformers themselves, Philip saw "political unity at any cost as the call of the hour."[168] For this reason, at the great Marburg Colloquy of 1529, while the reformers (including Luther himself, Zwingli, Bucer, and Melanchthon) tried unsuccessfully to agree about the nature of communion, Philip "defined the theological affirmations so broadly that they presented no serious infringement on their utilization for practical politics."[169] Luther and Zwingli proved irreconcilable, their rival positions both appealing with equal earnestness to Scripture. The political unity Philip sought through softening up the theological edges proved fruitless. Although Philip's policy failed in the short run, the latitudinarian theological approach would bear significant fruit in a little over a century, and it too found its way into the very methods of scriptural scholarship.

When the Augsburg Diet of 1530 brought an ultimatum to Protestants from the emperor, Philip became the political force uniting reformers in a theological-political alliance for protection that culminated in the League of Schmalkald, with Luther's blessing. It was in his capacity as the locus of political unity of the Protestantism that Philip turned to the reformers to settle his marriage "problem," first of all to Martin Bucer, and through Bucer, to Luther and Melanchthon. Apparently, Philip's "difficulty" was much like Henry VIII's—a voracious sexual appetite. He had been unfaithful to Christina from the start, and in his sexual indulgence, Philip had contracted syphilis, a disease that racked his frame and convinced him that his continuing indulgence made him unworthy to receive the sacraments. This guilt was magnified by his zealous reading of Scripture.[170]

Interestingly enough, when Henry VIII was canvassing for opinions in regard to his desire to marry Ann Boleyn, Luther remarked, "Before I should approve of such a repudiation, I would rather let him marry a second queen."[171] "It might be permitted," he advised Henry, "that the king should take another wife according to the example of the patriarchs, who had many wives even before the law, but it is not right that he should exclude her [Catherine, Henry's first wife] from the royal family and from the name of English Queen."[172] Melanchthon was less circumspect, declaring that Leviticus 18:16 was no longer binding, and noting that "it is certain that polygamy is not prohibited by divine law."[173] In response to the request made by Bucer on behalf of Philip in December 1539, Luther and Melanchthon wrote a joint statement of approval, known as the Wittenberg Rathschlag. In it, they declared scriptural sanction for bigamy in case of sufficient need, as long as it was kept secret to avoid scandal, asserting that "whatever is permitted in marriage by the Mosaic law, is not forbidden by the gospel, and . . . it will restore once again the depraved nature."[174]

168 Ibid., pp. 23–24.

169 Ibid., p. 25.

170 Eells, *The Attitude of Martin Bucer toward the Bigamy of Philip of Hesse*, pp. 58–60.

171 Quoted in Oberman, *Luther: Man between God and the Devil*, pp. 284–287.

172 Eells, *The Attitude of Martin Bucer toward the Bigamy of Philip of Hesse*, p. 35.

173 Ibid., pp. 35–36.

174 Quoted in ibid., p. 81.

With Christina, Philip had ten children, three of them after he married Margarethe.[175] As Philip's sister Elisabeth counseled him, in regard to Luther's and the other reformers' advice, it would be better to "take *one* bedmate instead of the *many* whores." "Elisabeth knew what she was talking about," Heiko Oberman notes. "The unmarried Elector Frederick the Wise, her father-in-law George's cousin, had his 'bedmate' Ann Weller and, though discreet, made no secret of their relationship."[176]

Whether or not Luther knew of his protector Frederick's indiscretions, his advice to Philip has always raised eyebrows, and there can be no doubt whatsoever that the political pressure to sanction Philip's bigamy was significant and significantly felt. As Philip warned Bucer early on, if the reformers would not grant him dispensation, he would seek one from the Catholic emperor and the pope. The same pressure brought the new Elector of Saxony, John Frederick, to approve as well.[177]

All three reformers were loath to let the bigamy become public, and did all in their power to conceal it, admonishing Philip to deal with rumors by telling a "holy lie," such as Abraham did when he said that his wife was his sister.[178] Philip consistently refused, and pushed for defense of a public declaration. Luther also refused to budge, continuing to counsel private, scriptural approval and public deception.[179] Later, the reformers would fall out with Philip over bigamy. Anxious to resolve the legal implications of his bigamy, the Landgrave would turn to the emperor anyway in a treaty of 1541 that effectively removed Philip as the militant protector of the Protestant cause.[180]

Even so, one must not underestimate Philip's part in reforming the Reform. As Hillerbrand notes, "More clearly than anyone else among the contemporaries he perceived . . . the concrete political implications of this fact," that implementation of Protestantism "meant a modification of the ideals as originally propounded by the Protestant reformers." Philip's

> contribution to the cause of the Protestant Reformation must be seen in this setting—that he resolutely sought to implement its inevitable political necessities. Thereby he aided both in the formation as well as the survival of the political Protestantism that was to characterize the Reformation. The conviction that politics was the means—perhaps the only means—to perpetuate the cause of the Protestant faith dominated his thinking and explains his contribution.[181]

Clearly, politics and theology were entwined in Philip's headship of the Protestant cause in Germany, and the infamous bigamy scandal was part of this entire complex

175 Oberman, *Luther: Man between God and the Devil*, p. 284. Hillerbrand, the earlier source, puts it at nine. Hillerbrand, *Landgrave Philipp of Hesse*, pp. 16–17.

176 Oberman, *Luther: Man between God and the Devil*, p. 286.

177 Eells, *The Attitude of Martin Bucer toward the Bigamy of Philip of Hesse*, pp. 68, 76, 83–84.

178 Ibid,, pp. 120–121.

179 Ibid., pp. 132–133.

180 Hans J. Hillerbrand, *Landgrave Philipp of Hesse*, pp. 17–19.

181 Ibid., p. 36.

web. Returning to our consideration of Luther's arguments in his *Pagan Servitude of the Church*, the case of Landgrave Philip's bigamy makes abundantly clear that Luther's claim of freedom to judge the law included the moral law and not just ceremonial Church laws; that he (with Bucer and Melanchthon) provided scriptural support for Philip; and that political pressures and ramifications played a significant role in what Luther and the others counseled. The private affirmation of polygamy was never meant by them to go beyond the specific rulers in question; it was not a general approval of polygamy[182] but a sanction for certain kings or princes only made as an exception in the privacy of the confessional. But it was a *moral* and *scriptural* sanction nonetheless.

We end this section noting that Luther himself understood that his claims for freedom from the law would sound revolutionary to the keepers of political order, and that is why he immediately followed up his *Babylonian Captivity*, with *The Freedom of a Christian*, which proclaimed two seemingly contradictory propositions: "A Christian is a perfectly free lord of all, subject to none" and "A Christian is a perfectly dutiful servant of all, subject to all."[183]

Gospel for the Soul, Law for the Body

Perhaps the most startling theological move in *The Freedom of a Christian*, one that had enormous ramifications for the political realm, was Luther's exegetical substitution of the individual soul for the Church as the bride of Christ in the marriage passage of Ephesians 5:21–33. The passage speaks primarily of the relationship of husband to wife, but also, importantly, of the analogous bridegroom-bride relationship of Christ to the Church. Luther used the passage to illustrate his doctrine of justification by faith, wherein "faith . . . unites the soul with Christ as a bride is united to her bridegroom," so that "as the Apostle teaches, Christ and the soul become one flesh."[184] In this "royal marriage," the soul receives Christ's full righteousness, without any works on its part. And so, declares Luther, "a Christian has all that he needs in faith and needs no works to justify him; and if he has no need of works, he has no need of the law; and if he has no need of the law, surely he is free from the law."[185] And that is *The Freedom of a Christian*.

This substitution of the individual soul for the Church—which does indeed follow from his doctrine of justification by faith alone—eliminated in one stroke the necessity of the Church as the essentially distinct counterpart to the state, and by consequence, allowed the state to assume the structure of ecclesiastical authority over

182 Johannes Lening did publish a pamphlet that, on Philip's behalf and with his approval, made the case for polygamy as morally indifferent (March 1541), and Luther attacked it vehemently. See Brecht, *Martin Luther: The Preservation of the Church, 1532–1546*, pp. 213–214.

183 All quotations from Martin Luther, *The Freedom of a Christian* in Dillenberger, ed., *Martin Luther: Selections from His Writings* (propositions from p. 53).

184 Ibid., pp. 60–61.

185 Ibid., p. 58, 61.

the individual believer-citizens. In *Babylonian Captivity*, Luther made the sacramental system of the Church unnecessary; in *The Freedom of a Christian* he removed the ontological, theological structure of the visible Church itself. In March 1521, as part of a reply to criticisms leveled against him by Ambrosius Catharinus, Luther argued that the true church was the invisible company of faithful whom God alone knows (thereby restating Wycliffe's ecclesiology, albeit without his realist metaphysics).[186] In Luther's alternative ecclesiology, in which there is no real distinction between priest and lay,[187] the Church as a necessary, permanent, and divinely intended body of Christ that visibly mediates salvation has been made secondary and derivative to what becomes the primary relationship of salvation, the promises of God known through the biblical text to the individual soul.

Without this move, the characteristic privatization of religion in modernity, and hence its increasing removal from the public realm, would not have been possible, and even more, the religious affirmation of modern individualism, which gave it such strength as it arose in the seventeenth century, would have been far less powerful. But the most important effect was the removal of the Church as a visible entity, which allowed the state to fill the vacuum.

The way that Luther distinguished faith from works in terms of the soul from the body is also important because of the dualistic tendencies that will later be brought out in the enormously influential philosophy of Rene Descartes.[188] These dualistic tendencies will manifest themselves in the new Averroism, where faith will be confined to the purely spiritual realm, the interior realm of the individual believer, the subjective realm, and (in place of the Aristotelianism of the earlier Averroism) the new philosophical materialism, and science will rule unchallenged and triumphant over a completely self-contained material, objective world. Since the self-contained world will act in accordance with its own inviolable laws, divine activity will eventually be excluded. This exclusion will reach its fulfillment in biblical scholarship in the nineteenth century, where miracles will be systematically relegated to myths, and faith will of necessity be redefined as entirely interior to keep it free from the mechanical-material world.

Of course, Luther could not have foreseen all of this, but since there are genealogical connections to later developments, Luther's dualistic tendencies must be thoroughly explored. On his account, righteousness through faith pertains only to the soul, to "the inner man," as distinguished from the "outer man," and hence from the

186 See Marius, *Martin Luther: The Christian between God and Death*, pp. 283–284.

187 "You will ask, 'If all who are in the church are priests, how do these whom we now call priests differ from laymen?' I answer: Injustice is done those words 'priest,' 'cleric,' 'spiritual,' 'ecclesiastic,' when they are transferred from all Christians to those few who are now by a mischievous usage called 'ecclesiastics.' Holy Scripture makes no distinction between them . . ." Yet, for the sake of good order, Luther adds, "Although we are all equally priests, we cannot all publicly minister and teach. We ought not to do so even if we could." Luther, *The Freedom of a Christian*, p. 65.

188 In addition to fueling the dualist tendencies, one might also point out that Luther's disjunction between the invisible inner man and the visible outer man reinforces a kind of skepticism in regard to the senses also prevalent in Descartes.

body or any works done by the body.[189] Faith and works therefore correspond to soul and body respectively, such that "no good work helps justify or save an unbeliever," and "no evil work makes him wicked or damns him. . . ."[190] This dichotomy is so absolute—based upon the absolute demand that faith in the promises of Christ alone fully justifies—that there exists, it would seem, no real connection between the two. The "inner man cannot be justified, freed, or saved by any outer work or action at all, and . . . these works, whatever their character, have nothing to do with this inner man. On the other hand, only ungodliness and unbelief of heart, and no outer work, make him guilty and a damnable servant of sin."[191] This dichotomy—or we may even say dialectic—between soul and body, faith and works, has direct implications for the distinction between sacred and secular, and between the Old and New Testaments (reinforcing and further clarifying what Luther had said in *Babylonian Captivity*).

In regard to sacred and secular, Luther intends a kind of inversion of our expectations based upon what we see, as if the invisible world of the inner man and the visible world of the body, corresponding to the sacred and secular, are essentially detached. Certainly the hypocrisy of much of the ecclesiastical hierarchy at the time reinforced this inversion.

> It does not help the soul if the body is adorned with the sacred robes of priests or dwells in sacred places or is occupied with sacred duties or prays, fasts, abstains from certain kinds of food, or does any work that can be done by the body and in the body. . . . On the other hand, it will not harm the soul if the body is clothed in secular dress, dwells in unconsecrated places, eats and drinks as others do, does not pray aloud, and neglects to do all the above-mentioned things which hypocrites do.[192]

Yet the ultimate reason for this inversion of appearance and reality, of secular and sacred, is not the all too evident misdeeds of popes, cardinals, bishops, and priests, but the fact that *faith alone saves*. Since it does, and the promises faith believes are found in Scripture, it is true that "the soul can do without anything except the Word of God and that where the Word of God is missing there is no help at all for the soul."[193] The locus of faith is even more narrowly defined, for (as Luther quotes St. Paul), "If you confess with your lips that Jesus is Lord and believe in your heart that God raised him from the dead, you will be saved" (Romans 10:9).[194]

---

189 "Man has a twofold nature, a spiritual and a bodily one. According to the spiritual nature, which men refer to as the soul, he is called a spiritual, inner, or new man. According to the bodily nature, which men refer to as flesh, he is called a carnal, outward, or old man. . . . Because of this diversity of nature the Scriptures assert contradictory things concerning the same man, since these two men in the same man contradict each other, 'for the desires of the flesh are against the Spirit, and the desires of the Spirit are against the flesh,' according to Gal. 5 [:17]." Luther, *The Freedom of a Christian*, p. 53.

190 Ibid., p. 70.

191 Ibid., p. 56.

192 Ibid., p. 54.

193 Ibid.

194 Ibid., p. 55.

By thus defining salvific faith, Luther strongly reaffirmed in *The Freedom of a Christian* the dialectical (rather than typological) relationship of the Old to the New Testament. As we recall, for Luther "the entire Scripture of God is divided into two parts: commandments and promise." On the one hand, "the commandments show us what we ought to do but do not give us the power to do it. They are intended to teach man to know himself, that through them he may recognize his inability to do good and may despair of his own ability. That is why they are called the Old Testament and constitute the Old Testament." Once we have despaired, "the second part of Scripture comes to our aid, namely, the promises of God," and "the promises of God belong to the New Testament. Indeed, they are the New Testament."[195] Although it sounds like Luther is making a simple identification of the New Testament text with the promise, we shall see below that such is not quite the case.

Of course, this dichotomy between Old and New Testaments, since it is built upon the distinction between works and faith, corresponds to Luther's distinction between body and soul, outer and inner man. With the combination of entirely Christological typology focused on promise, and the dialectic of New against Old Testament in regard to Gospel and law, we might well be tempted to say, with James Preus, that Luther's "hermeneutical theory . . . is merely bypassing the Old Testament text in its grammatical, historical sense," and that therefore the "Old Testament history is utterly devoid of theological relevance in the interpretation. . . ."[196] It would be more accurate to say, however, that Old Testament has been reduced to a dialectical foil for the New Testament promise.

Burning Bulls and the Diet of Worms

Now that we have Luther's main theological position, in all its intricacy, we may return to our account of the political implications as they would unfold. When the papal bull *Exsurge Domine* finally arrived in December 1520, Luther himself threw it on a pyre near the gate of Wittenberg. His break was then complete. Pope Leo issued the official declaration of Luther's excommunication on January 3, although it was not immediately published.

The diet opened on January 27, and high on the agenda were the familiar *Gravamina Nationis Germanicae*.[197] Luther would arrive at Worms on April 16, and questioning began the next day, the only question being whether a great pile of books before them were his (they were), and would he recant (he asked time to consider). The next day he replied that, since his works were of diverse kinds, he could not offer a simple yes or no. Some were quite orthodox by anyone's standards, so they could not

---

195 Ibid., pp. 57–58.

196 This is the assessment of Preus, *From Shadow to Promise: Old Testament Interpretation from Augustine to the Young Luther*, p. 147.

197 On sale at the time was a popular placard showing Luther and Hutten, the former with a book and the latter in armor with the title, "To the Champions of Christian Liberty." Dickens, *The German Nation and Martin Luther*, p. 47.

be recanted. Some listed the offenses of the papacy, descried by nearly everyone (especially the Germans). And finally, some were heated attacks on individuals in which, Luther admitted, he may have gone too far rhetorically. In any case, since he was a sinner, he could err, and he would recant *if his errors could be proven by Scripture—and plain reason.*

> Unless I am convicted by scripture and by plain reason (I do not believe in the authority of either popes or councils by themselves, for it is plain that they have often erred and contradicted each other) in those scriptures that I have presented, for my conscience is captive to the Word of God, I cannot and I will not recant anything, for to go against conscience is neither right nor safe. God help me, Amen.[198]

At popular instigation, another form of help made its presence known at the diet: placards appeared, warning that four hundred armed knights stood ready to attack any who would harm Luther.[199] Luther left Worms on April 26, accompanied by an imperial herald, and twenty horsemen sent by Sickingen via Hutten. He was "kidnapped" according to a secret plan of Frederick the Wise, and went into hiding at Wartburg Castle.

Charles issued an imperial edict in May, declaring Luther a heretic and enemy to the empire, but he had to rely on the elector princes to carry it out. Not only was the emperor obliged to respect their power in their own territories, but Charles was about to go to war against France, the Turkish threat still loomed, and a revolt in Spain continued to get bloodier. Luther was saved by the larger imperial concerns, but would now face a rebellion of his own.

Rebellion from Within: Mr. Everybody and the Word

About this time dissent within the reform movement was bubbling up, and it would have enormous political as well as theological implications, both affecting the fate of Scripture. Luther's seclusion at Wartburg in 1521 proved both painful and productive. During this period he not only wrote popular homilies, but also specific treatises elaborating his principles.[200] One of these homilies deserves special mention, "The Gospel for the Festival of the Epiphany."[201]

---

198 Quoted in (among many places) Marius, *Martin Luther: The Christian between God and Death*, p. 294. The famous rhetorical flourish, "Here I stand; I can do no other," was added in a later printed version at Wittenberg.

199 Ibid., p. 295.

200 Such as his *Martin Luther's Judgment on Monastic Vows* (1522), in which he made such vows nonbinding and also proclaimed that his own had been the result of Satan, and *On Confession* (dedicated to Sickingen), in which he declares that Christians need only confess to each other and not priests. Ibid., Ch. 17.

201 Martin Luther, "The Gospel for the Festival of the Epiphany," in Lehmann, ed., *Luther's Works*, Vol. 52, *Sermons*, pp. 159–286. As Hillerbrand points out in the Introduction, these sermons were not actually preached by Luther, but intended to provide homiletical material for preachers, p. ix–x.

In the midst of a "spiritual" interpretation of Scripture (wherein Herod signifies "a spiritual government which does not rule people by faith and the gospel, but by works and human doctrines," in short, "Herod is the pope and his spiritual realm"[202]), Luther makes the following rather surprising assertions that the New Testament is primarily and originally not a text but "oral and public preaching" that was "an uncovering and a revelation of the Old Testament. . . ." The written New Testament represents a kind of decline:

> That is why Christ did not write his doctrine himself, as Moses did his, but transmitted it orally, and also commanded that it should be orally continued giving no command that it should be written. Likewise the Apostles wrote little, and not all of them at that, but only Peter, Paul, John, and Matthew. . . . Those who did write, do no more than point us to the old Scripture. . . . So it is not at all in keeping with the New Testament to write books on Christian doctrine. Rather in all places there should be fine, goodly, learned, spiritual, diligent preachers without books, who extract the living word from the old Scripture and unceasingly inculcate it into the people, just as the Apostles did. For before they wrote, they first of all preached to the people by word of mouth and converted them, and this was their real apostolic and New Testament work. . . .
>
> However, the need to write books was a serious decline and a lack of the Spirit which necessity forced upon us; it is not the manner of the New Testament. For when heretics, false teachers, and all manner of errors arose in the place of pious preachers giving the flock of Christ poison as pasture, then every last thing that could and needed to be done, had to be attempted, so that at least some sheep might be saved from the wolves. So they began to write in order to lead the flock of Christ as much as possible by Scripture into Scripture.[203]

It might seem ironic that Luther himself was penning this written homily as an aid to his German translation of the New Testament. On his behalf, he obviously considered himself to be, as with the Apostles of old, forced into writing books because of the errors of his own time—not just those of the papacy, but as we shall soon see, those of other reformers.

Luther's demotion of the status of the written New Testament is worth noting. In some respects, it repeats Wycliffe's primacy of Christ the Word over the biblical text. In other respects, it sets up for later distinctions made in scholarship between the central proclamation of Christ (known by faith) and the biblical text as the object of historical-critical inquiry (known by reason). According to this distinction, the exegete's task is twofold: to recover the original proclamation, and to map the decline, in the scriptural text itself, from a pure preaching to the written word. In the latter task, the New Testament text is not a unified theological whole into which the parts harmoniously fit, but a kind of inadvertent record of historical decline. It is in map-

202 Ibid., p. 204.

203 Ibid., pp. 205–206.

ping the decline that the exegete becomes, primarily, historical-critical: the critical aspect deriving from the assumption of distance between the real proclamation of Christ and the text, and the historical aspect deriving from the attempt to recreate the decline from within the text.

While Luther was in seclusion, a new spirit had arisen in his Wittenberg, one that claimed allegiance to Luther's principles but took them where Luther did not wish to go. At first Luther strongly supported the "Wittenberg Movement" (in fact, he said he was pleased when he happened to make a quick visit in December 1521), but did an about-face very early in 1522.[204] While Luther generally advocated a more gradual reform in accordance with his doctrines, Andreas Bodenstein von Karlstadt (who had been with Luther at the Leipzig debate) and others did not.

Karlstadt advocated immediate and far-reaching reforms, playing out the full consequences of the equality of all as priests, *sola scriptura*, and *sola fide*.[205] It is of no small consequence, moreover, that he was one of the earliest figures to cast doubt on the Mosaic authorship of the Pentateuch (although, as John Calvin was soon to make clear, such doubt also came from scurrilous sources[206]). While Luther was hidden at Wartburg, Karlstadt was summoned to Denmark by King Christian II, who saw in the Lutherans a theological weapon that would help him win his political battles against the clergy and nobility—an early and important case of a ruler seeing the purely political potential of Luther's theological doctrines—but the attempted reform aborted and Karlstadt was back in Wittenberg in six weeks.[207]

Even more radical than Karlstadt were the so-called Zwickau prophets, Nicholas Storch, Marcus Stübner, and Thomas Drechsel, who claimed immediate revelation from God, and even more unpleasant for Luther, argued that infant baptism had no scriptural justification. Storch, the leader, may even have rejected adult baptism.[208] Luther's response to the rejection of infant baptism revealed it as a known sore spot: "I always expected Satan to touch this ulcer. But he did not wish to do it through the papists. It is among ourselves and among our own that this grave schism is set in motion, but Christ truly will quickly crush it under our feet."[209]

Luther's confidence was misplaced. The rejection of infant baptism, and indeed of all the sacraments, would define entire branches of the Reformation. Luther consid-

204 On the Wittenberg movement as well as Luther's relationship to all the "false brethren," see Mark Edwards, *Luther and the False Brethren* (Stanford, CA: Stanford University Press, 1975).

205 For a useful translation of some of Karlstadt's main works, see E. J. Furcha, ed., *The Essential Carlstadt* (Waterloo, Ontario: Herald Press, 1995) and Ronald Sider, ed., *Karlstadt's Battle with Luther: Documents in a Liberal-Radical Debate* (Philadelphia, PA: Fortress Press, 1978).

206 "I know what certain rascals bawl out in corners in order to display the keenness of their wit in assailing God's truth. For they ask, Who assures us that the books that we read under the names of Moses and the prophets were written by them? They even dare question whether there ever was a Moses." John Calvin, *Institutes of the Christian Religion*, translated by Ford Lewis Battles (Philadelphia, PA: Westminster Press, 1960), I:viii.9. According to the note 14 on I.vii.4, this may have been a group centered around Rabelais in Paris just prior to mid-sixteenth century.

207 See Marius, *Martin Luther: The Christian between God and Death*, p. 319.

208 John Oyer, *Lutheran Reformers against Anabaptists* (Hague: Martinus Nijhoff, 1964), pp. 10–11.

209 Quoted in Marius, *Martin Luther: The Christian between God and Death*, p. 325.

ered this a rebellion from within, and the rebels themselves satanic.[210] The difficulty was (as Luther himself was forced to admit by appealing to the *tradition* of infant baptism) that Scripture was ambiguous. Luther did, of course, point to Scripture, e.g., such passages as I Corinthians 7:14 (where Paul argues that an unbelieving spouse is consecrated through a believing spouse, and then adds "Otherwise, your children would be unclean, but as it is they are holy.") and Matthew 19:14 (where Christ says "'Let the children come to me, and do not hinder them; for to such belongs the kingdom of heaven'"). But such appeals could only be decisive to those already convinced because they were far from clear affirmations of infant baptism.[211]

From this ambiguity and his appeal to tradition to settle the matter would arise a twofold effect for scriptural exegesis: first, a redoubling of efforts by disagreeing parties to comb the Scriptures by all available means to substantiate rival positions (using those exegetical tools and methods developed previously by the humanists); and second, a turning to tradition that was (as opposed to a Catholic understanding of *traditio*) really a focus on the earliest history of Christianity to determine by a combination of biblical exegesis, the Fathers, and other historical documents, what the practices of the first Christians really were. One can see, then, in the earliest disagreements among Protestant Reformers a violent quickening of the seeds of the historical-critical impulse initially sown by the humanists.

The problem was not confined to one or two doctrinal points, but lay in the development of an entirely different outlook than Luther's. Zwickau prophet Nicholas Storch is an important case in point. He was a disciple of Thomas Müntzer, a reformer who himself had already caused a storm in Zwickau, arriving in May 1520 only to be driven out in April 1521.[212] Müntzer had come, through his connections to Luther, to take up a temporary preaching post. He believed that revelation was not confined to Scripture, but continued even today, and indeed was surpassed by private revelations, revelations of the inner Word, in relation to which the merely written text of the Bible was a dead letter.[213] But more famously, Müntzer did not mind inciting violence for the sake of reform.[214]

Storch claimed to have continual conversations not only with angels, but directly with God, and said that the angel Gabriel himself had revealed a vision of a new church, with Storch as leader, that would finish what Luther had only begun.[215] As noted above, he rejected infant (and possibly adult) baptism. The same rationale led him to reject original sin, because the same infant incapable of faith was also incapable of sin.[216] Storch was

210 Edwards, *Luther and the False Brethren*, pp. 22–23.

211 Oyer, *Lutheran Reformers against Anabaptists*, p. 29.

212 On Müntzer in Zwickau see Susan Karant-Nunn, *Zwickau in Transition, 1500–1547* (Ann Arbor, MI: Edwards Brothers, 1992), pp. 95–106.

213 Oyer, *Lutheran Reformers against Anabaptists*, p. 7–8, 10.

214 Such as inciting his hearers in a sermon to run a Catholic priest, Nicolaus Hofer, out of the church, pelting him with stones and mud, Hofer later being murdered by one of Müntzer's followers, Karant-Nunn, *Zwickau in Transition, 1500–1547*, p. 98.

215 Oyer, *Lutheran Reformers against Anabaptists*, pp. 9–10.

216 Ibid., p. 11.

a social as well as theological radical, appealing directly to the lower classes, preaching to them the same message that Luther had preached to the Germans, except for Storch it was the Germanic upper classes who were the oppressors rather than the "Romanists." While Luther adamantly retained class distinctions, Storch stirred the unhappy masses with utopian notions of revolution that would produce a society where all was shared in common. The appeal to a Messianic nationalism already seen in *Reformatio Sigismundi* and *Book of a Hundred Chapters* had now taken on class attributes.

Pushing Luther's freedom from the law in regard to marriage, Storch asserted that the marriage bond was not permanent, and that polygamy was a positive good (rather than, with Luther, a last resort).[217] In fact, "Storch was said to be unchaste himself and to advocate abstaining from marriage but having the sexual favors of as many women as one wished." (This was an odd offshoot of Müntzer's teachings about marriage, which brought married woman to deny sex to their husbands on the grounds that they belonged now to Christ.[218])

One further aspect of Storch and Stübner must be mentioned: even though they considered the Bible to be inferior to private revelation of the inner Word, their command of Scripture was phenomenal, Stübner's (it was said) surpassing even that of Melanchthon.[219] They did not argue their position from ignorance of Scripture.

Needless to say, the more conservative members of Zwickau, generally the upper classes, were alarmed at the ideas of the Zwickau prophets. Fearing political persecution by the "conservative" Lutheran faction, Storch, Stübner, and Drechsel left for Wittenberg, arriving two days after Christmas 1521, and hoping to find Luther's home base more amenable to their ideas.

Luther would soon refer to these radicals collectively as the *Schwärmer*, the fanatics. But for many in Wittenberg, their radical message was welcome. As a consequence, Wittenberg was experiencing something of an uproar while Luther was away, with rioting of students, attacks on the traditional Mass, and an attempt by Karlstadt (who had come under the influence of Stübner) to push through reforms via the Wittenberg city council, including the destruction of images and the institution of communion in both kinds (in which the consecrated bread and wine were simply passed from person to person rather than administered by the priest).

Karlstadt's reforms, so he thought, were taken directly out of the Old Testament, and this was backed by a particular exegetical stance, at odds with Luther, that the Old Testament was still in force precisely because Christ was its fulfillment in the New: "Nor did Christ break the smallest letter in Moses," proclaimed Karlstadt. "Further, he did not make one addition to or subtraction from the law of Moses. Briefly, Christ did not pull down anything which pleased God in the old law."[220] As David Steinmetz notes, Karlstadt's "reformation program was a mixture of wise and overdue plans for

217 Ibid., p. 12.

218 Karant-Nunn, *Zwickau in Transition, 1500–1547*, p. 104.

219 Oyer, *Lutheran Reformers against Anabaptists*, pp. 10, 13.

220 Quoted in Ronald Sider, *Andreas Bodenstein von Karlstadt: The Development of His Thought, 1517–1525* (Leiden: E. J. Brill, 1974), p. 110.

reform together with shrill and utopian cries for the immediate restoration of Eden. Christians are bound by the law of Moses, which forbids graven images in worship. The absolute demands of the Old Testament must be put into effect immediately without faithless worrying about the consequences."[221] As we might suspect, Frederick the Wise was not pleased by a utopian revolution in his domains, and Luther would be pressed to do something.

Luther came back to Wittenberg for good in March 1522 to restore order, and took the reins of reformation from Karlstadt and the prophets. Luther would meet with all three of the prophets over the next few months, finally dismissing them as satanic. As for Karlstadt, his impatient reforming fervor went directly against Luther's pastoral tendencies to move ahead slowly, but even more, Karlstadt's legalism rubbed against Luther's fundamental declaration of Christian freedom from the law.

Frederick the Wise soon had enough as well, banishing Karlstadt from his territories. In his exile, he would write a dialogue about the Eucharist that asserted (against Luther and Catholicism) that it was merely a reminder of an historical event with no sacramental qualities at all—declaring that the New Testament nowhere supported any notion either of transubstantiation *or* (as Luther held) the Real Presence. This helped make Karlstadt influential among Luther's later enemies, Müntzer, Zwingli, and the Anabaptists.

When at Karlstadt's request, he and Luther met at the Black Bear Inn at Jena in 1524, the meeting ended with Luther challenging Karlstadt to write against his understanding of the Eucharist publicly and openly: "If you do, I will present you with a gulden for it."[222] Karlstadt accepted, "thereby serving public notice that the two men were henceforth to be regarded as enemies."[223]

As if a portent of things to come, the next day Luther preached in a church outside Jena, in which to get to the pulpit he had to step over a large crucifix that had been smashed by Karlstadt's iconoclasts. By the time Luther arrived back at Wittenberg, he changed his mind about a war of words with Karlstadt, and advised the prince to expel Karlstadt from Saxony, and by mid-September, the order was issued.[224] Luther could no longer sit back and let the Word do the work; political means had to be used to support his evangelical ends, for the interpretation of Scripture had clearly gotten out of hand.

Political expulsion did not bring silence; and, in fact, the number of adherents to Karlstadt's cause rose. Luther felt compelled to answer Karlstadt and the Zwickau prophets, publishing his *Against the Heavenly Prophets in the Matter of Images and Sacraments* (1525). In it, he proclaimed that "Doctor Andreas Karlstadt has deserted

221 David Steinmetz, *Reformers in the Wings: From Geiler von Kayserberg to Theodore Beza*, second ed. (Oxford: Oxford University Press, 2001), p. 127.

222 An accurate, contemporary account of the exchange can be found in Sider, ed., *Karlstadt's Battle with Luther*, pp. 38–48, the quote being from p. 47.

223 Steinmetz, *Reformers in the Wings*, pp. 128–129. According to Steinmetz, Karlstadt's attempt to justify his argument about the Eucharist hinged on obscure and unconvincing grammatical exegesis of the eucharistic passages, that was so tendentious that it never enjoyed wide support. See also Oyer, *Lutheran Reformers against Anabaptists*, pp. 24–27.

224 Marius, *Martin Luther: The Christian between God and Death*, pp. 403–404.

us, and . . . become our worst enemy" because he "seeks to destroy it [the gospel] with cunning interpretation of Scripture."[225] By this, Luther meant that Karlstadt, in his exegesis, was in the service of Satan.[226] At the "bottom of it all" was the irony that Karlstadt and the Zwickau prophets used Luther's focus on Scripture to revive the centrality of the Mosaic Law. Asserting his own dialectical stance toward the two Testaments, Luther cried out:

> [T]hese teachers of sin and Mosaic prophets are not to confuse us with Moses. We don't want to see or hear Moses. How do you like that, my dear rebels? We say further, that all such Mosaic teachers deny the gospel, banish Christ, and annul the whole New Testament. I now speak as a Christian for Christians. For Moses is given to the Jewish people alone, and does not concern us Gentiles and Christians. We have our gospel and New Testament.[227]

For the true Christian, the law has only one use, the spiritual, dialectical use: it must be preached to bring to a head the conviction of sin, so the Christian may embrace the justifying grace of Christ. Yet, declared Luther, "we ought to proclaim the law and its works, not for the Christians, but for the crude and unbelieving." The law is a necessary stick, and

> among the crude masses, on Mr. Everyman, we must use it bodily and roughly, so that they know what works of the law they are to do and what works ought to be left undone. Thus they are compelled by sword and law to be outwardly pious, much in the manner in which we control wild animals with chains and pens, so that external peace will exist among the people. To this end temporal authority is ordained, which God would have us honor and fear (Romans 13; I Peter 3).[228]

What then of the Ten Commandments, the very heart of the law? Luther answers that in one sense, they have been abrogated because "out of the Ten Commandments flow and depend all the other commandments and the whole of Moses." But in another sense, they remain, "Where . . . the Mosaic law and the natural law are one, there the law remains and is not abrogated externally, but only through faith spiritually, which is nothing else than the fulfilling of the law (Roman 3)." We must keep the Ten Commandments because "the natural laws were never so orderly and well written as by Moses."[229]

The ramifications of Luther's position may not strike us straightaway. He seems to be offering a simple affirmation of the natural law as ensconced in a particular part of the Mosaic Law, the Ten Commandments, but jettisoning the rest as merely ceremonial (e.g., circumcision and dietary laws). But the title of the treatise makes

225 Martin Luther, *Against the Heavenly Prophets in the Matter of Images and Sacraments,* in Sider, ed., *Karlstadt's Battle with Luther,* p. 94.

226 Edwards, *Luther and the False Brethren,* p. 51.

227 Luther, *Against the Heavenly Prophets in the Matter of Images and Sacraments,* p. 100.

228 Ibid., pp. 96–97.

229 Ibid., pp. 100–102.

clear the difficulty. If having images is idolatrous, and idolatry is strictly forbidden by one of the Commandments, then Karlstadt's iconoclasm would seem entirely justified. But Luther objected to smashing images for two reasons: first, reform had to proceed slowly, "by first tearing them [images] out of the heart through God's Word and making them worthless and despised. . . . For when they are no longer in the heart, they can do no harm when seen with the eyes";[230] and second, image smashing whipped the rabble into a frenzy, and hence the iconoclastic spirit was always associated for Luther with rebellion of the "crude masses." For "to do away with images in a Karlstadtian manner, [is] to make the masses mad and foolish, and secretly to accustom them to revolution."[231] It was no accident, Luther surmised, that the "crude masses" were the very ones on whom Karlstadt and the Zwickau prophets spent their reforming zeal. But the masses are not to be trusted: "Give a rogue an inch and he takes a mile. For why do we have sovereigns? Why do they carry the sword, if the masses are to rush in blindly and straighten things out themselves."[232]

Further, iconoclasm cannot go unpunished by the secular arm. If Karlstadt's preaching goes unhindered, "disorder will gain in momentum, and the masses will have to kill all of the wicked. For Moses, when he commands the people to destroy images (Deuteronomy 7), also commands them to destroy without mercy those who had such images in the land of Canaan." The Bible in the hands of the masses is a dangerous thing, Luther warned.

> Suppose Dr. Karlstadt won a large following, which he thought he could assemble on the Saale [River], and the German Bible alone was read, and Mr. Everybody began to hold this commandment (about killing the wicked) under his own nose, in what direction would Dr. Karlstadt go? How would he control the situation? Even if he had never intended to consent to something like that, he would have to follow through. The crowds would mutiny and cry and shout as obstinately, "God's Word, God's Word, God's Word is there. We must do it!" As he now cries against images, "God's Word, God's Word!" My dear lords, Mr. Everybody is not to be toyed with. Therefore God would have authorities so that there might be order in the world.[233]

This was a startling admission by Luther, especially in light of his notion of the priesthood of all believers and his earlier hopes that translating the Bible into the vernacular would finish the work he had begun. Luther was not the only one worried about Mr. Everybody. A magistrate's report given during the Hanseatic Diets of 1525 complained that "everybody, and above all the uneducated, even women, dare to preach the Gospel and the Word of God . . . and using Christian freedom as a pretext, they live according to their own will and fancy, disregarding the ordinances and regulations. . . ." At the heart of the problem was exegesis: the "everybodies" were

230 Ibid., p. 98.
231 Ibid., p. 99.
232 Ibid., p. 103.
233 Ibid., pp. 103–104.

interpreting the words of the Gospel wrongly, twisting them "from what they really meant in order to please the common people . . . and this would lead to carnal freedom, which would be followed by revolts against the magistrates and bring about the ruin of towns."[234]

Exegesis soon became a widely recognized political and a theological problem. This is made quite clear in the debate between Luther and Karlstadt in regard to images. The direct implication of Luther's position is that proper interpretation of the commandment against idolatry, and more important, its enforcement, must necessarily become a civil matter for "we are under our princes, lords, and emperors," and "we must outwardly obey their laws instead of the laws of Moses."[235] It is not surprising that exegetical divergences from Luther would soon be politically suppressed, and the proper interpretation politically impressed.

The same pattern arose in regard to the proper interpretation of the Eucharist, the sacrament at issue in the treatise's title *Against the Heavenly Prophets in the Matter of Images and Sacraments*. In a series of five incendiary tracts published in 1524, Karlstadt argued from Scripture that the Eucharist was not a sacrament, but a "remembrance." When Christ spoke his words at the Last Supper, "This is my body, etc.; this is my blood, etc.," he was actually indicating his body and blood in the one-time sacrifice of the cross, an event to come, not a miraculous transformation of bread and wine at that time or thereafter. The Lord's Supper is merely a celebratory event that helps believers spiritually discern the one-time event in retrospect and respond in faith now.[236] As Ronald Sider notes, "Directed primarily against Luther, these five tracts contain the first published Protestant enunciation of a symbolic eucharistic doctrine. They constitute, in fact, the first salvo in a long, bitter intra-Protestant battle over the meaning of the Eucharist."[237] For Karlstadt, Luther's doctrine of the Real Presence led to idolatry, the seeming worship of bread and wine as if God were somehow really present in them.

Karlstadt would end up taking refuge in Switzerland with Zwingli, one of Luther's bitterest enemies in regard to how Protestants should interpret scriptural passages regarding the Eucharist. Against Karlstadt, Luther replied:

> [S]ince his spirit is bent on making spiritual what God wants to be bodily, he has to treat the discernment in this way, making recognition and remembrance a spiritual discernment, inward in the spirit, when God intends a bodily discernment, between bread and the body of Christ. . . . I have often asserted

234 Quoted in Heinz Schilling, "Alternatives to the Lutheran Reformation and the Rise of Lutheran Identity," in Andrew Fix and Susan Karant-Nunn, *Germania Illustrata: Essays on Early Modern Germany Presented to Gerald Strauss* (Ann Arbor, MI: Edwards Brothers, 1992), pp. 99–120; quote, p. 111.

235 Luther, *Against the Heavenly Prophets in the Matter of Images and Sacraments*, p. 99.

236 The clearest of the five tracts is *Concerning the Anti-Christian Misuse of the Lord's Bread and Cup, Whether Faith in the Sacrament Forgives Sins; and Whether the Sacrament is an Arrabo or Pledge of the Forgiveness of Sin. Exegesis of the Eleventh Chapter of the First Epistle of Paul to the Corinthians, Concerning the Lord's Supper*, in Sider, ed., *Karlstadt's Battle with Luther*, pp. 74–91.

237 Ibid., p. 72.

> that the ultimate goal of the devil is to do away with the entire sacrament and all outward ordinances of God. Then as these prophets teach, all that would count would be for the heart to stare inwardly at the spirit.[238]

Luther is quite prophetic here, as developments over the next century would make clear. For some, such as Sebastian Franck[239] (1499–1542) and later and more famously the Quakers of the seventeenth and eighteenth centuries, the inner illumination of the Spirit would soon displace the need for any outward observances, and indeed, teeter on rendering superfluous the revelation of Scripture itself.

Leaving aside later developments for now, our proximate point is this: the "long, bitter intra-Protestant battle over the meaning of the Eucharist" that arose so early—not even a decade had passed since Luther nailed up his ninety-five theses—could not help but have political implications. Again, the other reformers used Luther's own principles to arrive at divergent conclusions. If idolatry violates a commandment, and the Eucharist really is mere bread and wine, then treating it as if somehow Christ is really present would be a case of supreme idolatry, and hence should be suppressed by the sword. But if Christ is truly present as Luther argued, then treating the Eucharist as mere bread and wine would be blasphemy, and hence also punishable by the secular sword. The very bitterness of the battle ensured that, for the sake of civil peace, civil power would have to attend to the interpretation of the scriptural passages at issue. To turn again to the Hanseatic Diets for an example, in the Diet of July 1535, a resolution was passed proclaiming that "a Hanseatic town afflicted with the heretical doctrine of the Anabaptists or Sacramentarians [i.e., those holding the merely symbolic view of Karlstadt or Zwingli] should be suspended from all rights and privileges of the [Hanseatic] League until it should refrain from its error."[240]

One obvious solution to the problem caused by divergent, politically divisive interpretations of Scripture would be simply to mandate the proper interpretation of all hotly contested scriptural passages by law. This would be achieved by determining politically the kind of Christianity allowed. Since political decentralization had been occurring for some time, the mandate would be accomplished according to the decentralized principle of *cuius regio, eius religio* that would soon be accepted out of frustration at the Peace of Augsburg in 1555.

This solution came to be called *erastian,* after the Swiss theologian Thomas Erastus (1524–1583), but it is important not to forget its Marsilian roots (even as we look forward to its most thorough exponent, Thomas Hobbes). In such a view, Church officials are appointed and controlled by civil power, the state exercising both complete civil and religious jurisdiction. Luther embraced this alternative—perhaps more out of frustration than principle—as he chastised Karlstadt for taking a pastoral position in Orlamünde as a minister elected by his congregation but not sanctioned by the

238 Luther, *Against the Heavenly Prophets in the Matter of Images and Sacraments,* p. 119.

239 On Franck see Patrick Hayden-Roy, *The Inner Word and the Outer World: A Biography of Sebastian Franck* (New York: Peter Lang, 1994).

240 Quoted in Schilling, "Alternatives to the Lutheran Reformation and the Rise of Lutheran Identity," p. 112.

prince. Here, Luther was forced to deny his earlier assertion that, on the basis of all being priests, each congregation should elect its priest. Doing an about-face, Luther now argued that

> the princes of Saxony sit as governing authorities ordained by God. The land and the people are subject to them. What kind of a spirit then is this that despises such a divine order, proceeds with headstrong violence, treats princely possessions and rights as though they were his own, and doesn't even once recognize the prince or confer with him about it. . . . Should not a good spirit fear God's order a little more, and *since the estate, the pastorate, and the land belong to the prince,* first humbly beg permission to leave and resign one position, and beg the favor of being installed in another?[241]

But an even more radical solution might be set forth. One might declare that all such theological differences remain merely verbal, and that those with differences live and let live according to some shared, but merely moral, foundation. This second solution will be offered down the line with Benedict Spinoza and John Locke, and will become the foundation for the modern liberal solution to the religious "problem."

Whichever the case, the preferred solution either will have to be enforced by brute civil power, or much more benignly, will *itself* have to be vindicated through an exegesis of Scripture. If it is vindicated through exegesis, an appropriate method will arise, implicitly or explicitly, from the mode of exegesis, and since the method has political ends, there must of necessity be a politicization of both the method of exegesis and Scripture itself.

We are not yet at the point, with Luther, of designing a particular method of exegesis, and so the question of method proper will be taken up in succeeding chapters. Thomas Hobbes will provide the mode of exegesis that established erastianism, but on an entirely novel foundation, radical materialism. Spinoza and Locke will provide the mode of exegesis that grounds the liberal solution in Scripture itself. Luther's attempts lay the first groundwork for the establishment of both modes.

Readjusting the Canon

To return to the spring of 1522, Luther received at that time a German translation of a treatise by none other than Henry VIII, king of England, whom Luther thought might come over to his cause. Unfortunately for Luther, Henry's *Assertio Septem Sacramentorum* was a direct repudiation of Luther's reduction of the sacraments from seven to two in his *Babylonian Captivity*. Luther was both enraged and disappointed, hurling invectives at Henry in a manner that helped to bring Erasmus against him full force.

---

241 Luther, *Against the Heavenly Prophets in the Matter of Images and Sacraments*, pp. 106–107. Emphasis added.

> Here I stand, here I sit, here I remain, here I glory, here I triumph, here I contemn Papists, Thomists [he referred to Henry as a "vainglorious Thomist"], Henricians, sophists, and all the gates of hell all the more in that they are led astray by the sayings of holy men or customs. God's word is over all. The divine majesty works with me, and I do not care if a thousand Augustines, a thousand Cyprians, a thousand churches of Henry stand against me. God cannot err or fail; Augustine and Cyprian like all the elects can err, and they did err.[242]

Whereas Luther previously had claimed the primacy of Scripture (which cannot err) against pope and council (both of whom could), now he added that even the Church Fathers, including his beloved Augustine, could err. His ire was aroused precisely because the Fathers were being quoted against his particular doctrines to show that, contrary to his assertion that they came from the plain Gospel, they were an innovation peculiar to Luther.

Luther received his copy of Henry's treatise while he was working on a German translation of the New Testament, a project he had begun in the seclusion of Wartburg, relying on the scholarly help of Philip Melanchthon and Erasmus's Greek edition of the New Testament. This was the famous September Testament, as it came out near the end of that month in 1522. Luther's would not be the only German New Testament. The Catholic polemicist Hieronymus Emser (1478–1527), secretary of Luther's great enemy, Duke George, would put out his own German translation, "based upon Luther's yet armed with anti-Lutheran annotations."[243]

Notable in Luther's first edition—and well worth quoting at length—is his declaration of what has been called the gospel within the Gospel, or one might suggest more accurately, the canon within the canon. As we have seen above, this naturally flowed from Luther's assumption that the New Testament text represented a kind of decline from the original preaching of the Word. Luther's narrowing of the Gospel to its original point entailed the opening of the biblical canon, if only to narrow it accordingly. In his preface to the first edition he set forth a ranking of the books of Scripture in such a way that cannot help but remind us of Marcion's restricting of the canon of Scripture to St. Paul and part of the Gospel of Luke.[244] "You are in a position now rightly to dis-

---

242 Quoted in Marius, *Martin Luther: The Christian between God and Death*, pp. 342–343.

243 Dickens, *The German Nation and Martin Luther*, pp. 122–123, and Kenneth Strand, *Reformation Bibles in the Crossfire: The Story of Jerome Emser, His Anti-Lutheran Critique and His Catholic Bible Version* (Ann Arbor, MI: Ann Arbor, Publishers, 1961).

244 Marcion was the single most influential heretic of the second century, a man who *through scriptural exegesis* eliminated the entire Old Testament and offered the first canon of the New Testament, consisting *only* of edited versions of the Gospel of Luke and edited versions of the Pauline epistles. The core of Marcion's doctrine was quite simple and quite heterodox. He argued that the God of the Old Testament and the God of the New Testament are two different deities, a system he worked out based upon his exegesis of St. Paul's epistles (particularly the sharp Pauline contrast between Law and Gospel), but which was surely based on his adherence to a modified form of Gnosticism. The Old Testament God was the creator Demiurge, the God of Law who said to Isaiah: "I form light and create darkness, I make weal and create woe, I am the LORD, who do all these things" (Isaiah 45:7). In contrast, the Father of Jesus Christ

criminate between all the books, and decide which are the best," states Luther, after introducing the doctrine of justification by faith alone to the reader.

> The *true kernel and marrow of all the books*, those which should rightly be ranked first, are the gospel of John and St. Paul's epistles, especially that to the Romans, together with St. Peter's first epistle. Every Christian would do well to read them first and most often, and, by daily perusal, make them as familiar as his daily bread. You will not find in these books much said about the works and miracles of Christ, but you will find a masterly account of how faith in Christ conquers sin, death, and hell; and gives life, righteousness, and salvation. This is the *true essence of the gospel*, as you have learned.
>
> If I were ever compelled to make a choice, and had to dispense with either the works or the preaching of Christ, *I would rather do without the works than the preaching*; for the works are of no avail to me, whereas His words give life, as He himself declared. John records but few of the works of Christ, but a great deal of His preaching, whereas the other three evangelists record many of His works, but few of His words. It follows that the gospel of John is unique in loveliness, and of a truth the principal gospel, far, far superior to the other three, and much to be preferred. And in the same way, the epistles of St. Paul and St. Peter are far in advance of the three gospels of Matthew, Mark, and Luke.
>
> In sum, the gospel and the first epistle of St. John, St. Paul's epistles, especially those to the Romans, Galatians, and Ephesians, and St. Peter's first epistle, are the books which show Christ to you. They teach everything you need to know for your salvation, even if you were never to see or hear any other book or hear any other teaching. In comparison with these, the epistle of St. James is an epistle full of straw, because it contains nothing evangelical.[245]

It is interesting to note that Luther's denial of the apostolic authorship of the Epistle of James, which he had stated previously in 1519, was challenged by none other than Karlstadt in 1520, who warned Luther, "If it is permissible to make something great or little as one pleases, it will happen at last that the dignity and authority of [biblical] books depends on our power. And then, by whatever right any Christian is allowed to reject my ideas, I have the same right . . . to esteem my own highly and trample down those of others. . . . Brother, I beg you, am I not able to say the same about all scripture if I follow you?"[246]

Significantly, Luther did not offer separate prefaces for any of the four gospels, even John's, but he did provide a lengthy preface to St. Paul's Letter to the Romans, which he called "the most important document in the New Testament, the gospel in

---

is not the God who revealed himself to the Jews, but an entirely different God, a God of love and mercy, whom Marcion identified with the unknown God spoken of by St. Paul in Acts 17:23. A concise analysis of Marcion can be found in W.H.C. Frend, *The Rise of Christianity* (Philadelphia, PA: Fortress Press, 1984), pp. 212–218.

245 In Dillenberger, ed., *Martin Luther: Selections from His Writings*, pp. 18–19. Emphasis added.

246 Quoted in Sider, *Andreas Bodenstein von Karlstadt: The Development of His Thought, 1517–1525*, p. 97.

its purest expression."[247] Clearly, Luther meant the entire New and Old Testament to be read through Romans, his hermeneutical lens being the doctrine of justification by faith alone. Again, there is a definite parallel to Marcion insofar as Paul is used by both as a foil against the Judaizers, in Luther's case the Judaizers being Romanizers who bring works righteousness through the sacramental ministrations of a priestly class into their understanding of the New Testament. Luther ends the preface to Romans, "this epistle gives the richest possible account of what a Christian ought to know, namely, the meaning of law, gospel, sin, punishment, grace, faith, righteousness, Christ, God, good works, love, hope, and the cross. . . . Therefore, it seems as if St. Paul had intended this epistle to set out, once for all, the whole of Christian doctrine in brief, and to be an introduction preparatory to the whole of the Old Testament." [248]

It should surprise us, perhaps, that Luther had to provide his readers with a hermeneutical lens in handing them the Bible. With his constant stress on the return to the plain words of Scripture, it would seem that given the plain text, especially in their native tongue, readers could not help but to arrive at Luther's conclusion. Luther himself stated in his preface that "It would only be right and proper if this volume were published without any preface . . . to speak for itself," but averred that this cannot be done because "many unscholarly expositions and introductions have perverted the understanding of Christian people till they have not an inkling of the meaning of the gospel as distinct from the law, the New Testament as distinct from the Old Testament." Therefore, the reader "must be shown what to expect in this volume, lest he search it for commandments and laws, when he should be looking for gospel and promises."[249] Luther had in mind not only papists, but those seemingly on his own side against Rome, like Karlstadt and the Zwickau prophets.

Absent this lens, other books of Scripture could mislead us. Some books are so misleading that their authenticity and canonicity must be questioned. Luther (following Erasmus) downgrades the epistle of James, saying, "I do not hold it to be of apostolic authorship," and giving the following reasons. First and foremost, "because, in direct opposition to St. Paul and all the rest of the Bible, it ascribes justification to works, and declares that Abraham was justified by his works when he offered up his son." But also "not once does it give Christians any instruction or reminder of the passion, Resurrection, or spirit of Christ," adding ominously that "All genuinely sacred books are unanimous here, and all preach Christ emphatically. . . . The true touchstone for testing every book is to discover whether it emphasizes the prominence of Christ or not." But what Luther actually meant is seen by negation, for the "epistle of James . . . only drives you to the law and its works," and "I therefore refuse him a place among the writers of the true canon of my Bible; but I would not prevent anyone placing him or raising him where he likes, for the epistle contains many excellent passages."[250]

247 This preface is also contained in Dillenberger, ed., *Martin Luther: Selections from His Writings*, with the quote on p. 19.

248 Ibid., p. 34.

249 Ibid., p. 14.

250 Ibid., pp. 35–36.

Luther also, in separate prefaces, rejected the Pauline authorship of Hebrews (calling it a mixed bag of jewels and straw), the difficulty evidently being its emphasis on the continuity of Old and New Testament priesthood and sacrifice, a continuity that called into question his dialectical approach. In addition, he asserted that the book of Revelation was neither apostolic nor prophetic.[251]

We cannot overestimate the effect Luther's public judgment of the canon had upon future scriptural scholarship. Ranking the books of the Bible according to a "true kernel," thereby creating the "true touchstone for testing every book," will take many forms over the next centuries, often in imitation of Luther's emphasis on St. Paul, but sometimes in direct opposition, where St. Paul is the great distorter rather than illuminator of the "true canon." Because it will become increasingly obvious—as it did for Luther's own critics, both Protestant and Catholic—that individual books do not provide unanimous affirmation of the chosen kernel, exegetes will increasingly turn to sorting through individual texts, layering them according to authentic and spurious, early and late, pure and tainted passages, a tendency that will reaffirm the above-mentioned attempt to recover the original Gospel proclamation from the Scriptural text witnessing the decline.

In contrast to Luther, this mode of approach, this method, need have no essential relationship to sincere religious inquiry of a seeking Christian, but could be used just as well according to a schema defined by a general, detached history of religion, or a particular current of modern philosophy, or even the context-driven political needs of the particular exegete. And while it is true to say that all of this is quite aside from, and antagonistic to, Luther's intentions, it is also fair to say that the introduction of this approach from within Christianity in the sixteenth century made it all the easier to co-opt it from the outside for quite different purposes.

Two Kingdoms Come

The publication of Luther's translation of the New Testament in 1522 had another unintended and yet entirely predictable result: the attempt to suppress it by hostile German princes, in particular, his most fervent enemy, Duke George of the nonelectoral part of Saxony. Luther's response was *Secular Authority: To What Extent It Should Be Obeyed* (1523), of which he said, "I might boast . . . that, since the time of the Apostles, the temporal sword and temporal government have never been so clearly described or so highly praised as by me."[252]

As W.D.J. Cargill Thompson notes, this was not merely a boast. In seeming conformity to Machiavelli, Luther was consciously rejecting the entire tradition of medieval political philosophy, and over and above this, the classical political philosophy of

251 Marius, *Martin Luther: The Christian between God and Death*, pp. 355–357.

252 This assessment comes from his later tract, *Whether Soldiers, Too, Can Be Saved* (1526), in Martin Luther, *Works of Martin Luther* (Philadelphia, PA: Muhlenberg Press, 1931), Vol. V, p. 35.

Aristotle and Plato.[253] He was not concerned as were Plato and Aristotle with the question of what is the best regime nor with distinctions between good and bad regimes.[254] In part this was due to Luther's belief that the secular authority was ordained by God, and hence, one cannot question its validity by comparing it to something better. The state we have is the one God wishes us to have. But in greater part, this was due to his severing the connection between the order of the soul and the order of the city (if we may use the terms of classical political philosophy). As we have already seen, Luther divided the good of the soul and its righteousness from the works, the activities, of the body, resulting in a pronounced dualism of soul and body, and hence, of spiritual and temporal things. God was directly in control of both, nonintersecting realms. As Luther would define it later, "The spiritual government or authority should direct the people vertically toward God that they may do right and be saved; just so the secular government should direct the people horizontally toward one another, seeing to it that body, property, honor, wife, child, house, home, and all manner of goods remain in peace and security and are blessed on earth."[255]

An important consequence of this was the support provided through Scripture to whatever regime happened to exist, without discriminating between different kinds of regimes or better and worse regimes. But there were other effects, as Thompson elaborates. Just as Luther's nominalism entailed a rejection of the analogical relationship of creation to God, so also his approach to politics entailed the rejection of the analogical relationship between the natural and supernatural realm that had been a staple of medieval political theory prior to Ockham. In Thompson's words:

> An inevitable consequence of Luther's rejection of good works as a necessary factor to salvation was that he no longer saw this world as being preparatory to the next, in the sense that what one does in this world contributes directly to one's fate in the next. Instead of the hierarchical worldview of Aquinas, which treated the natural order as a necessary preliminary stage to the order of supernature, Luther thinks in terms of two separate but parallel realms, the temporal and the spiritual, in which the Christian exists simultaneously in this life. The Christian on earth stands in a dual relationship with God—old man and new man, flesh and spirit, "*simul justus, simul peccator,*" temporal person and spiritual person.[256]

This dualism, as Thompson points out, was akin to the sharp divide we find in both Ockham and even more Marsilius of Padua,[257] so that in yet another important way, Luther carries forth—unwittingly—the broad contours of Marsilius's Averroism.

253 W.D.J. Cargill Thompson, *The Political Thought of Martin Luther* (Totowa, NJ: Barnes & Noble Books, 1984), pp. 3–5.

254 Ibid., pp. 5, 68–69. Luther did assert that monarchy was superior to mob rule, but this was not a principled, detailed argument. See Duncan Forrester, "Martin Luther and John Calvin," pp. 311–312.

255 Martin Luther, *Commentary on Psalm 101,* in Pelikan, ed., *Luther's Works,* Vol.13, *Selected Psalms II,* p. 197.

256 Thompson, *The Political Thought of Martin Luther,* pp. 24–25.

257 See also Forrester, "Martin Luther and John Calvin," pp. 296, 302, 313.

The result was that in Luther's teaching, the ideas of Marsilius and Ockham "re-entered the mainstream of European political thought, becoming for a time the staple of protestant political theory."[258] The effect goes further still. In so sharply separating these realms, Luther contributed to the creation of an entirely secular political order, and it was this order that ultimately defined how Scripture would be politicized.

Witness the arguments of *Secular Authority*. Luther begins by chastising rulers who "think they have the power to do and command their subjects to do, whatever they please. And the subjects are led astray and believe they are bound to obey them in everything. It has gone so far that the rulers have ordered the people to put away books, and to believe and keep what they [i.e., the rulers] prescribe."[259]

Against his earlier affirmation of the prince's authority over the pastorate, Luther was now compelled to retreat and modify. In an effort to spell out his position as a kind of midway point between complete control of religion by the secular power and a Münzter-like theocratic revolution from below, Luther put forth a two kingdoms doctrine—not two swords, two keys, or two lights, but two distinct kingdoms with fundamentally different aims, the spiritual and the secular, the "kingdom of God" and the "kingdom of the world."[260] Never the twain should mix, except to the detriment of each, as he would later make vivid in his *Commentary on Psalm 101* (1534):

> The devil never stops cooking and brewing these two kingdoms into each other. In the devil's name the secular leaders always want to be Christ's masters and teach Him how He should run His Church and spiritual government. Similarly, the false clerics and schismatic spirits always want to be the masters, though not in God's name, and to teach people how to organize the secular government. Thus the devil is indeed very busy on both sides, and has much to do.[261]

It is fair to point out that Luther's two kingdoms doctrine arises out of the exigencies of the situation; that is, having originally declared for complete submission to secular authority, he now had to backpedal, given that one such prince was now confiscating German New Testaments along with Luther's works. But we must also understand that Luther's two kingdoms doctrine follows directly upon his doctrine of justification, and its attendant dualism. There are Christians—although "among thousands there is scarcely one true Christian"—who have faith and are therefore justified, and "these people need no secular sword or law. And if all the world were composed of real Christians, that is, true believers, no prince, king, lord, sword, or law would be needed." By contrast, "All who are not Christians belong to the kingdom of the world and are under the law. Since few believe and still fewer live a Christian life . . . God has provided for non-Christians a different government outside the Christian estate

258 Thompson, *The Political Thought of Martin Luther*, p. 8.

259 Martin Luther, *Secular Authority: To What Extent It Should Be Obeyed*, in Dillenberger, ed., *Martin Luther: Selections from His Writings*; quote, p. 365.

260 Ibid., pp. 368, 370. See also Luther, *Whether Soldiers, Too, Can Be Saved*, p. 39.

261 Luther, *Commentary on Psalm 101*, pp. 194–195.

and God's kingdom, and has subjected them to the sword. . . ."[262] It is, therefore, "out of the question that there should be a common Christian government over the whole world, nay even over one land or company of people, since the wicked always outnumber the good."[263] Politics cannot be Christianized; or, to take it from the other direction, politics must be thoroughly secularized, having no other aim, it would seem, than earthly life.[264]

Luther thereby provided a theological justification for the transformation of the meaning of the term "secular." Previously, the term "secular" order could even refer to priests (such as Wycliffe), who did not belong to a specific religious order, or more broadly, to the temporal as distinguished from the ecclesiastical. But even here, the temporal power worked *sub specie aeternitatis*. With Luther, the secular order was being redefined by an entirely this-worldly aim.

Luther's goal was not to create the modern secular state, but to remove religious authority from the governing powers. While faith is to be grounded *sola scriptura*, the secular power does not use the Bible to govern.[265] The secular power governs by reason and the natural law, which do not pertain to the realm of the spirit, but do pertain to the realm of the flesh. Yet, as Cargill points out, this demotion of reason to merely secular concerns, and the elevation of faith completely above reason with no analogical connection between the two, bring about a kind of Averroism, however unintended.[266] Faith is irrational rather than supernatural, and reason is entirely independent and thoroughly natural.

There are other important implications as well. One cannot help but be reminded of Marsilius, and even Machiavelli, insofar as "imagined republics" do not play any role in Luther's political reasoning. Further, since Luther viewed political power as an ordained external force to keep sinners under control (rather than, as with Aristotle and St. Thomas, a positive order that helps perfect natural potentialities), his tendency (with Thomas Hobbes after him) was to view political order, no matter how harsh, as vindicated solely because any political order was better than the complete anarchy (the chaos of Satan) that would inevitably break loose without it.[267] Luther's division of the sacred from the purely secular also prepared the way for acceptance of the modern assumption that the state is entirely a-religious and concerned only with the well-being of the body, and that religion is purely an inner, spiritual, and private concern (which we will see played out in John Locke). Luther thereby contributed to the West's reception of a purely secular, materialistic notion of politics adumbrated by Marsilius and Machiavelli, and later enunciated by Hobbes and Locke, where government is defined solely by external coercion, bodily preservation, and physical comfort.[268]

---

262 Luther, *Secular Authority*, pp. 369–370.

263 Ibid., p. 371.

264 Thompson, *The Political Thought of Martin Luther*, p. 70.

265 Ibid., pp. 80–81, and Forrester, "Martin Luther and John Calvin," p. 306.

266 Thompson, *The Political Thought of Martin Luther*, pp. 80–81.

267 Ibid., pp. 52–53, 65–66.

268 Especially given Luther's adamant rejection of Aristotle, this casting of politics in terms of the efficient

Whatever the implications, we must be careful to keep in mind Luther's original intentions. Luther rooted the sacred-secular distinction in the soul-body distinction precisely because it allowed him to limit the reach of government—an understandable goal, given the desire of German princes to suppress both his New Testament and his theological writings. "Worldly government has laws which extend no farther than to life and property and what is external upon earth. For over the soul God can and will let no one rule but Himself. Therefore, where temporal power presumes to prescribe laws for the soul, it encroaches upon God's government and only misleads and destroys the souls." So that, "When a man-made law is imposed upon the soul, in order to make it believe this or that . . . there is certainly no word of God for it."[269] Therefore, "it is useless and impossible to command or compel any one by force to believe one thing or another," for "every man is responsible for his own faith, and he must see to it for himself that he believes rightly. . . . Since, then, belief or unbelief is a matter of every one's conscience, and since this is no lessening of the secular power, the latter should be content and attend to its own affairs and permit men to believe one thing or another, as they are able and willing, and constrain no one by force."[270] As we shall see, this is precisely the position set out by Benedict Spinoza, one of the great fathers of modern scriptural scholarship and modern political liberalism.

Ambiguities or difficulties immediately arose in Luther's own time. As R. W. Scribner points out, "Luther was perfectly willing to encourage a ruler to impose reform on his subjects when it would lead to his introducing 'right belief'. Thus, in 1525 he advised the Grand Master of the Teutonic Knights to secularise his territories, declare himself a secular prince, and introduce religious reform, by which means many souls would be 'won for the Gospel.'"[271] In his *Commentary on Psalm 82* (1530), more specifically on 82:4 ("Rescue the small and the poor, deliver them out of the hand of the godless"), Luther argued that the secular power could punish those who deny doctrines "clearly grounded in Scripture and believed throughout the world by all Christendom."[272] Such an admonition immediately entangled secular authorities in political exegesis. He also suggested that in conflicts between "papists and Lutherans," wherein "both parties claim that the Scriptures are on their side" and "neither party is willing to yield or be silent," then "let the rulers take a hand. Let them hear the case and command that party to keep silence which does not agree with the Scriptures. This the great emperor Constantine did when he caused Athanasius and Arius to be heard and their case judged by his procurator, Probus."[273] Hence another entanglement of

---

cause or force controlling matter/body will also help to lay the groundwork for the acceptance of the new materialist physics. See Thompson on Luther's government as merely external force, *The Political Thought of Martin Luther*, pp. 47–48.

269 Luther, *Secular Authority*, pp. 382–383.

270 Ibid., pp. 384–385.

271 Scribner and Dixon, *The German Reformation*, pp. 36–37.

272 Martin Luther, *Commentary on Psalm 82*, in Pelikan, ed., *Luther's Works*, Vol. 13, *Selected Psalms II* (Saint Louis, MO: Concordia Publishing House, 1956), p. 61. Forrester, "Martin Luther and John Calvin," p. 317. Forrester misidentifies this as Psalm 86.

273 Luther, *Commentary on Psalm 82*, pp. 62–63. Forrester, "Martin Luther and John Calvin," p. 317.

politics and exegesis. Luther was also quite willing to renege on his assertion of absolute political obedience when the opportunity arose, as, for example, when "he ended up urging the princes to resist the emperor as the servant of the pope and therefore of Anti-Christ."[274]

A related difficulty arose from Luther's notion that "every man is responsible for his own faith, and he must see to it for himself that he believes rightly." The principle could be invoked by the likes of Karlstadt, Müntzer, Bucer, and Zwingli for theological positions, rooted in Scripture, but radically at odds with Luther's. Whatever Luther's inclinations to let the Word do its work, and keep secular princes out of it, the disturbances of public order caused by rival scriptural interpretations must be attended to by the secular power.

It is hard to resist the conclusion of Duncan Forrester in regard to Luther's two kingdoms theory that, in these matters, Luther "bristles with contradictions and it is impossible to interpret the majority of his statements on the issue as more than impulsive and often thoughtless responses to particular situations," so that "it would be more than difficult to argue that in this matter he does not create an 'infernal confusion' between the two kingdoms he so clearly differentiated elsewhere."[275]

Müntzer and the Peasant Rebellion

In order to understand these difficulties more vividly we need only return to a consideration of Thomas Müntzer and the Peasant Rebellion. As with Wycliffe, Luther's theological efforts seemed to ignite political rebellion among the lower orders. Luther well understood how politically combustible his theological position was. As he himself said, "Had I desired to foment trouble, I could have brought great bloodshed upon Germany. Yea, I could have started such a little game at Worms that even the emperor would not have been safe."[276]

Unlike Luther, Müntzer had no compunction about tying theological to social revolution; indeed, he thought it absolutely necessary. After being ousted from Zwickau, Müntzer tried his mode of Reformation elsewhere (including at Prague, among the Hussites), but with little success, finally settling in the city of Allstedt as preacher at St. John's Church. Gathering the peasants in a *Bund* for political-theological rebellion, Müntzer believed himself to be the biblically prophesied leader of the fifth epoch (Daniel 3:44–45), and appealed to the German princes to join him in a divinely-mandated revolution that would unseat them from power, and usher in a new age of a purified democracy of the elect.

Behind Müntzer's revolutionary programs was the ecclesiological belief that outside his church, the church of the elect, there was no salvation, and the elect had an obligation to put the nonelect to the sword (a scripturally-based cleansing that found ample support in the Old Testament admonitions not merely to destroy idols but

274 Thompson, *The Political Thought of Martin Luther*, p. 14.

275 Forrester, "Martin Luther and John Calvin," pp. 317–318.

276 From one of Luther's sermons, quoted in Oyer, *Lutheran Reformers against Anabaptists*, p. 33.

idolaters as well).[277] Since the New Testament provided evidence that the kingdom of God belonged to the poor, Müntzer easily found support for the elect being simply equivalent to the commoners oppressed by the Church, the princes, and the nobles. The bottom-up revolution was, again, not merely theological. Sounding eerily like the later revolutionary Karl Marx, Müntzer declared, "Everybody should properly receive according to his need. Any prince, count, or lord who refuses to do this even when seriously warned should be hanged or have his head chopped off."[278] Leaving Allstedt, and after some wondering, Müntzer settled upon Mühlhausen in 1525, where he set a kind of revolutionary base, training the peasants for open theological-political revolt. In May, Müntzer and his forces were soundly defeated at the battle of Frankenhausen, and Müntzer himself executed.

Not surprisingly, Luther declared Müntzer to be satanically inspired. As with the other "fanatics," Müntzer focused on a core spiritual experience that used the biblical text as the occasion for that experience. Since the regenerative experience itself was primary, Müntzer believed the text that provided the occasion was secondary. For Luther's "true kernel" of Scripture, Müntzer substituted the experience itself, and asserted that this kernel has always existed in human nature, even prior to the Bible, awaiting its awakening by the Holy Spirit. In fact, the Bible itself, because of its inevitable distorting, interpretive overlay, could even hinder the awakening of the true kernel of faith. This led Müntzer to make the kind of claim about the politicization of the Bible that should sound rather familiar to twenty-first-century academic ears. In John Oyer's words:

> Müntzer was cynical and scornful of Luther's justification by faith, for it was absolutely contingent on an understanding of the Bible. And the Bible could be properly interpreted only by the theologians, who were in turn hand in glove with the civil authorities. A racket if there ever was one! The civil authorities were determined to so influence the interpretation of the Scripture that the masses of the people would not be enabled themselves to understand its social implications. Müntzer believed in a radical amelioration of the misery of the lower classes, and he believed Christianity, rightly interpreted, meant a complete equality of all men.[279]

To Müntzer, and the many he influenced, the politicization of Scripture from the top demanded a counterpoliticization from the bottom. As a good reformer, he obviously believed that he was interpreting Scripture as it was meant to be understood. Take the following example as indicative of the problem. As noted above, Luther used Romans 13:1–4 to argue that the church was properly subordinated to the state. Müntzer focused on Romans 13:3–4, arguing that Paul was really saying that civil gov-

277 Ibid., pp. 17–18, 20, and Marius, *Martin Luther: The Christian between God and Death*, p. 400.

278 Quoted in Marius, *Martin Luther: The Christian between God and Death*, p. 420.

279 Oyer, *Lutheran Reformers against Anabaptists*, p. 19.

ernments bear the sword legitimately only if they are godly. If they are not, rebellion is justified, and the elect must pick up the sword instead.[280]

And so, in the appeal to Scripture alone, two completely different arguments arose, both of which have immense implications for the political realm, and therefore the adjudication of which would be of the utmost concern for the German princes. The problem, as Richard Marius points out, is that Müntzer's

> justification for violence would seem to have been as great as Luther's justification for resignation in the face of oppression. The Bible itself is divided on that score. The book of Revelation—regarded suspiciously by Luther . . . but part of the New Testament canon—portrays a great holy war at the end of time in which blood shall run up to the horses' bridles and the defeated battalions of the Antichrist shall be not only slaughtered on earth but condemned to everlasting torments in a burning hell.[281]

Making things even more confusing, although Luther may have had misgivings about the Book of Revelation, his entire viewpoint was suffused by apocalypticism, as Heiko Oberman has made quite clear.[282] In fact, Luther believed that he was a prophet in the last days of the Antichrist before the return of Christ, and therefore, despite his intentions, he stoked the fires of Müntzer's revolutionary-apocalyptic fires. That fire broke out in the Peasant Revolt in the spring of 1525, with Müntzer at its head.

The peasants issued a manifesto, the so-called *Twelve Articles*, which in good German fashion set forth their grievances, not against Rome, but against the princes and nobles of Germany. The *Twelve Articles* did not threaten direct revolution but simply listed items for redress, notably that they be allowed to choose their own pastors (the first article) and that "if any one or more of these articles should not be in agreement with the word of God, which we do not think, we will willingly recede from such article when it is proved to be against the word of God by a clear explanation of the Scripture" (the twelfth article).[283] While the other articles seem to contain little directly related to Scripture at all—covering everything from tithing, serfdom, to hunting and wood rights, rents, and so on—since in imitation of Luther the peasants asserted that their political demands would be withdrawn only if "proved to be against the word of God by a clear explanation of the Scripture," Scripture could not help but be drawn into the most urgent political questions. Luther himself would be drawn in since he was named by the peasants as a source of authority who could adjudicate the demands.

Luther's response, quickly written while Müntzer was gathering forces, was his *Friendly Admonition to Peace concerning the Twelve Articles of the Swabian Peasants.*

---

280 Ibid., pp. 20–21.

281 Marius, *Martin Luther: The Christian between God and Death*, p. 421.

282 Oberman, *Luther: Man between God and the Devil*, pp. 8–12, 46–49, 67–74, 79–81.

283 The *Twelve Articles* can be found in Hans Hillerbrand, ed., *The Protestant Reformation* (New York: Harper & Row, 1968); quote on p. 66.

Luther begins by chastising the princes and lords for this "mischievous rebellion," for they "do nothing but flay and rob" their subjects so that they can "lead a life of splendor and pride, until the poor common people can bear it no longer." He bluntly warned them: "The Sword is at your throats. . . ."[284]

Luther was well aware that (recalling Wycliff's situation) some of the princes were "beginning to blame this affair on the gospel and say it is the fruit of my teaching." But he maintained his innocence precisely because it was he who had "striven earnestly against rebellion," and, moreover, only he resisted the "murder-prophets" like Müntzer and the Zwickau prophets who "stir up the people against you. . . ."[285] In short, the rulers should mend their ways. On behalf of the peasants—and against his treatment of Karlstadt—Luther now asserted that the peasants' desire "to hear the gospel and choose their pastors" cannot be rejected. Luther went even further, stating that "no ruler ought to prevent anyone from teaching or believing what he pleases, whether gospel or lies. It is enough if he prevents the teaching of sedition and rebellion."[286]

To the peasants, Luther declared that even if they were to win against the higher powers, they would lose their souls because as Christians they may not "appeal to law," nor may they "fight," but rather, they must "suffer wrong and endure evil; and there is no other way (I Corinthians 6)."[287] They must not avenge themselves (Romans 12), they must suffer injustice gladly (2 Corinthians 11), they must not go "to law about property" (I Corinthians 6), and they must, as Christ admonished, "wish good to those who wrong us" (Matthew 7). If the peasants truly want to bear the name of Christians, "it is Christian law not to strive against wrongs, not to grasp after the sword, not to protect oneself, but to give up life and property, and let who takes it take it; we have enough in our Lord, who will not leave us, as He has promised. Suffering, suffering; cross, cross! This and nothing else, is the Christian law!"[288]

Luther was well aware of the peasants' appeal to Scripture: "The man who framed your articles is no pious and honest man, for he has indicated on the margin many chapters of Scripture, on which the articles are supposed to rest . . . and leaves out the passages by which he would show his own wickedness and that [wickedness] of your own enterprise." Such selective exegetical support proved that "not one of the articles . . . teaches a single point of the gospel, but everything is directed to one purpose; namely, that your bodies and your properties may be free. In a word, they all deal with worldly and temporal matters."[289] That is, Luther charged them with politicizing the Gospel.

Needless to say, the restless and oppressed peasants were by and large not impressed with Luther's friendly advice. It appeared to them that he was merely the mouthpiece for "conservative" Lutherans in the upper classes, as well as princes

284 Martin Luther, *Friendly Admonition to Peace concerning the Twelve Articles of the Swabian Peasants* in Hillerbrand, ed., *The Protestant Reformation*; quotes from pp. 68–69.

285 Ibid., pp. 69–70.

286 Ibid., p. 71.

287 Ibid., p. 78.

288 Ibid., p. 76.

289 Ibid., pp. 79–80.

and nobles of whatever religious stripe; that he was preaching a kind of dualism of theological revolution and political resignation; and that he was therefore politicizing his exegesis on behalf of those in power. As we have seen, other equally fervent and learned exegetes found both theological and political revolution in the Bible. But for Luther, the danger of peasant rebellion was too horrifying to countenance. As he would say a year later in his *Whether Soldiers, Too, Can be Saved*:

> We cannot pipe much to the mob. It goes mad too quickly . . . and it is better that the tyrants do wrong a hundred times than that they once do wrong to the tyrants. If wrong is to be suffered, then it is better to suffer it from the rulers than that the rulers suffer it from their subjects. For the mob has no moderation and knows none, and in every individual in it there stick more than five tyrants. Now it is better to suffer wrong from one tyrant, that is, from the ruler, than from unnumbered tyrants, that is, the mob.[290]

Luther's protector Frederick the Wise died on May 5, 1525, as revolution bubbled ever closer to the surface. Luther did his part by trying to calm disgruntled peasants through preaching. He was not well received. One congregation rang the bell during his entire sermon to drown him out. Had they known that, at the very same time, he was giving advice to rulers that if the peasants rebelled it was their Christian duty to crush them without mercy, they would have done far worse.[291]

Soon reports trickled in of new demands and castles being plundered. Luther wrote *Against the Robbing and Murdering Gangs of Peasants*, a short tract that can endear him to no one, and caused many of his admirers to shudder, even while "pleasing many of the more ruthless rulers."[292] Of course, it did not enhance his standing among the peasants when he called for "anyone who can" to "smash, strangle, and stab, secretly or openly"[293] rebellious peasants as a matter of Christian duty.

On May 15 at Frankenhausen, peasant forces met those of the princes (one of them being Philip of Hesse, very soon to be converted to Lutheranism). The peasant forces were encouraged by Müntzer to fight against impossible odds: a rainbow appeared in the sky, matching the one decorating his standard, a sign of seeming victory. Well over half the peasant forces were slaughtered, and Müntzer was captured, tortured, and beheaded. More slaughter followed, both in pitched battles, but also in revenge after the revolt was effectively suppressed. Lutheran leaders drove home the message that to rebel is a sin. Catholic leaders took the opportunity to hunt down Lutherans as dangerous insurrectionists. Amidst the savagery, Luther answered his critics with *An Epistle on the Hard Little Book against the Peasants*, in which he made clear that he would not take back one word, and as long as the rebellion continued the princes should kill both the innocent and guilty. During that same month, Luther took a wife, the ex-nun Katherine von Bora. Seven years later, Luther, looking back on the Peasant Revolt,

290 Luther, *Whether Soldiers, Too, Can Be Saved*, p. 45.

291 Marius, *Martin Luther: The Christian between God and Death*, p. 428.

292 Edwards, *Luther and the False Brethren*, p. 65.

293 Quoted in Marius, *Martin Luther: The Christian between God and Death*, p. 431.

would say, "In the rebellion, I struck all the peasants." Moreover, "All their blood is on my neck. But I know it from our Lord God that he commanded me to speak."[294]

The Victory of the Prince and Preaching the Law

Within a month after the Peasant Revolt had been effectively suppressed, the Catholic and Protestant divisions that would soak the soil of Germany in blood for over a century began to solidify. Catholic princes in the north, such as Luther's inveterate enemy Duke George and Albrecht of Mainz, united themselves in a vow to destroy Lutheranism. In the south, Philip of Hesse and John of Saxony vowed with equal fervency to defend it. Despite Luther's intention, his doctrines won princely converts for precisely the wrong reason. As Richard Marius argues:

> Princes found advantages to going over to the Lutheran side, and for once they read Luther aright when they pondered his demand for obedience among the people. Luther's stress on obedience became a monotonous theme in his preaching ever afterward. It is far too simple to explain these conversions [of princes] by any one influence. But at least it could be said that these transformations [i.e., the political adoption of Lutheranism by princes] would not have happened had the princes not had proof that Luther supported their right to authority no matter how cruel their authority might be. He could rage against the sins of the nobles; they were content to ignore him since he had proven that his way was finally resignation rather than rebellion.[295]

Perhaps Marius is being too cynical here in attempting to read the true motives of the various princes.[296] We can say that, abstracting from the private motives of princes that we cannot know, Luther's doctrines did provide a way for German princes to break from Rome, and remain entirely in charge of the religion within their own peaceful realm, equally protected from the dangers of the likes of Karlstadt, Müntzers, and the Zwickau prophets.

Affirming Lutheranism was not only a political affair of princes, but individual cities as well, especially those under more distant imperial control. In respect to the imperial cities, which owed allegiance only to the Catholic emperor, of the sixty-five, a little more than half became completely Protestant, with most of the others tolerating both Catholics and Protestants and only fourteen remaining entirely intolerant of Protestantism.[297] Many cities were controlled by their councils, especially imperial cities. In acting as a political body, their actions were representative of the entire citizenry in varying degrees. As R. W. Scribner warns, "Even when an entire town

294 Ibid., pp. 432–433.

295 Ibid., pp. 434–435.

296 Marius adds that, because of this stress on obedience, "Lutheranism ceased to be a large popular movement and became an affair of the princes." Ibid., p. 435.

297 Dickens, *The German Nation and Martin Luther*, p. 180.

committed itself to institutionalized reform, it would be a mistake to assume that all its inhabitants did so with the same enthusiasm or motives."[298] In cities such as Erfurt and Ulm, insofar as reform made headway, it was often brought about by a single individual gaining political control of the council (in the mentioned cases, Adolarius Huttener and Bernhard Besserer, respectively).[299]

The city of Nuremberg, for instance, decided upon Lutheranism through its city council around 1525, and hence the civil magistrates became the overseers of the new religious orthodoxy, expelling Catholics, outlawing the Roman Catholic Mass, and substituting an appropriate Lutheran or Evangelical service, assuming complete control of the appointment and training of ministers, eliminating saint days and reducing holy days, and so on, so that (in A. G. Dickens's words), "a body of patrician laymen thus erected nothing less than a territorial Church."[300] Of the utmost importance for our purposes, these reforms were not done on the basis of being "Lutheran," but on the basis of their being scriptural. A similar example is found in the more liberal German city of Strassburg (Strasbourg), in which the city council likewise affirmed civil control over religious matters, more along the lines of Reformed rather than Lutheran theology, and more out of a desire for peace than inherent evangelical zeal of their own. Yet, as with many other such cities, they soon found themselves beset by more radical reformers, the Anabaptists, who also claimed scriptural support. For the sake of peace and doctrinal unanimity, the council had (like Luther himself) to reject the influx of Anabaptism based upon Scripture.[301] In a very real sense, the city council replaced the Church Council, an interesting case in point being the city of Kempten, which, in 1533, voted 800 to 174 in favor of the abolition of images, thereby (unwittingly, perhaps) overriding the seventh General Council of Nicaea (787).[302] But again, such voting was representative of only a small number of the inhabitants.[303]

Even though reformers made headway in cities, in many cases, they were unable to enforce rejection of the opposition. Erfurt was compelled to accept a compromise, allowing both Catholic and Lutheran worship because, for quite complex reasons, neither was able to oust the other.[304] The case of Münster is, of course, a well-known example of a complete takeover by the most radical Anabaptists, which filled both Catholics and Lutherans with horror. In addition to all of this, important "shades" of doctrinal difference (as vindicated by Scripture) arose in individual cities, depending on which evangelical reformer predominated. Wherever the effect of Zwingli or Bucer

298 Scribner and Dixon, *The German Reformation*, p. 26.

299 Ibid., p. 29.

300 Dickens, *The German Nation and Martin Luther*, pp. 135–146.

301 Ibid., pp. 146–153.

302 Ibid., p. 188.

303 To illustrate, in another reform referendum in Ulm three years earlier, 1600 voted, but out of a population of 14,000. Even for those who voted, the "results may tell us little about who went along with the decision out of ignorance, indifference or fear. . . ." Scribner and Dixon, *The German Reformation*, pp. 29–30.

304 Dickens, *The German Nation and Martin Luther*, pp. 169–176.

took hold, such as for example in Ulm,[305] Strassburg, and Augsburg, there the predominant Eucharistic theology of evangelical worship was anti-sacramental. In general, the cities of the southwest and extreme south became Reformed, that is, held to something like Karlstadt's position on the sacraments, as elaborated by Zwingli and Bucer.[306]

Such is an overview of the early divisions, but things did not, of course, remain static. Near the end of the 1630s the princes began to assert their power more strongly, and as noted above, it was to their distinct advantage to affirm Lutheranism, so that "a second Reformation, stabilizing yet sterilizing, followed upon the popular and enthusiastic Reformation of the cities. Across most of northern Germany ecclesiastical laws were applied and reforms enforced by the legal authority of the princes."[307] By this time popular support for the Reformation had begun to wane. As R. W. Scribner argues:

> After a brief period of mass enthusiasm, it retreated to being a minority phenomenon. At a crude estimate, during the first generation of the Reformation, up to mid-century, and perhaps even during the second, probably no more than 10 per cent of the German population ever showed an active and lasting enthusiasm for reformed ideas. Where massive numbers were "won" after 1526, to what became the new church, it occurred involuntarily, through a prince deciding that his territory should adopt the new faith. When we speak of the extensive hold "Protestantism" had on Germany by the second half of the sixteenth century . . . this was because there were large numbers of "involuntary Protestants" created by the princes' confessional choices.[308]

Even in Luther's Wittenberg, we should remind ourselves, "reform had to secure the approval of the Elector of Saxony," so that while "the town council directed reform of the church . . . it kept the Elector of Saxony carefully informed at each step, and virtually acted as an executor of the sovereign prince."[309] This happened with Luther's approval, especially after the death of Frederick and the accession of his brother John, an enthusiastic, open proponent of Lutheranism who was more zealous to implement reforms with greater speed.

It was at this point that Luther initiated visitations to assess the quality of the reforms, and assessment soon led to *civil* implementation and oversight.[310] While Luther claimed that such visitors had no authority to enforce reform, he:

305 As an important note, there was significant opposition to evangelical reform in Ulm by women who "continued to lead devotion to images after the introduction of reform in 1531. Some Ulm women even claimed to have had a miraculous vision in 1528, an event hushed up by the authorities because it was an embarrassment to their advocacy of reform." Scribner and Dixon, *The German Reformation*, p. 27.

306 Dickens, *The German Nation and Martin Luther*, pp. 186–187, 190.

307 Ibid., p. 196.

308 Scribner and Dixon, *The German Reformation*, p. 34.

309 Ibid., p. 36.

310 Thompson, *The Political Thought of Martin Luther*, pp. 144–147.

> then proceeds to deprive his argument of much of its moral force by bringing in the authority of the magistrate by the back door. For he concludes by saying that although visitors have no power of their own to enforce the visitation, since their authority is purely spiritual, the magistrate has a duty to maintain peace and unity among his subjects and to prevent discord from arising. Hence if anyone refuses to observe the injunctions of the visitors, the prince has the right and, indeed, the duty to banish them from his territories in order to prevent discord and rebellion from breaking out.[311]

And so, "under John and his son and successor, John Frederick, the Elector gradually acquired increasing responsibility for the direction of the church. The same pattern was followed outside Saxony in most of the north German princely states which embraced the Reformation in the 1530s and 1540s."[312]

We must conclude, then, that just as we cannot treasure an ideal notion of the papacy in the Middle Ages, free from political entanglements, neither can we so view the Reformation in Germany as it developed very early on. "From the very beginning . . . *the institutionalization of reform was an erastian phenomenon*: that is, the church was subjected to the control of secular authority."[313] It is essential to understand that the drive for secular control did not arise *ex nihilo* with the Reformation. "A major goal of German politics at all levels well before the Reformation was to submit the church and its agencies to secular control."[314] It is not surprising, then, that Luther's two kingdoms doctrine "had little real practical meaning," and that the state soon took control over the proper interpretation of Scripture wherever Lutheranism took hold.

> The various acts of legislation establishing the formal framework of church reform throughout Germany and Switzerland . . . attest the effective control of the church by the secular power. Almost everywhere this was achieved by means of Ecclesiastical Statutes (*Kirchenordnungen*), issued by secular authorities to regulate religion. . . . The institution of ecclesiastical reform was the conclusion of a long struggle between church and state over who should control ecclesiastical life, and the state clearly emerged as the victor.[315]

Another complicating factor that bears directly on the politicization of scripture was Luther's recommendation to secular authorities that they maintain schools for the proper education of clergy, which he took to be indispensable precisely because knowledge of the original languages was necessary for proper exegesis.[316] The formal education of the pastors meant that a priesthood of all believers gave way to the dis-

311 Ibid., p. 146.

312 Ibid., p. 148.

313 Scribner and Dixon, *The German Reformation*, p. 36. Emphasis in original. This is also the conclusion of Thompson, *The Political Thought of Martin Luther*, p. 154.

314 Scribner, Porter, and Teich, *The Reformation in National Context*, p. 9.

315 Scribner and Dixon, *The German Reformation*, p. 37.

316 Ibid., pp. 49–50.

tinction between ordained (a kind of "clerical elite") and lay, and the clerical elite was controlled by the secular power.

Much the same situation arose in regard to Luther's desire to educate children. The original plan to have all heads of household responsible failed quite early. The burden of such education then fell to the state, so that "reformers willingly collaborated with political authorities in drafting school ordinances setting up educational systems in cities and territories wherever Lutheranism had become the established religion." The inevitable result: "The state being in nearly all instances the moving force behind the establishment of new schools and the reform of old ones, political ends came inevitably to be fused with religious objectives."[317] This is no small point, since it goes without saying that Lutheranism demanded a scriptural basis for its religious objectives, and therefore the fusion of Scripture with political ends could not help but to politicize the text.

A further complicating factor must be added. Even in Luther's own Wittenberg, that is, under what would seem to be the best conditions, the congregation's response soon cooled to tepid at best. In a sermon of November 8, 1528, Luther railed against the parishioners, "What shall I do with you, people of Wittenberg! I shall not preach to you the kingdom of Christ, because you don't take it up. You are thieves, robbers, merciless. To you I must preach the law!"[318] Luther's vitriol was aimed not only at their moral condition but at their lack of financial support. As moral conditions declined, rather than improved, with time, "Luther preached more and more to emphasize the law."[319]

As we recall, for Luther, the law was for the unregenerate, and since he believed that there were very few true Christians (and not merely as a theoretical point, but in his practical experience), then preaching and teaching in support of the law came more and more to be linked with the desire for moral control from the state. Or to put it another way, ironically Lutheranism emphasized more and more the demands of the law in the Bible, precisely because the people proved themselves less and less capable of receiving the Gospel (and, on being pounded by the law and threatened with hell, became more estranged from and hostile to their pastors[320]).

This unhappy situation is well documented in the exhaustive visitation records to parishes performed by the church-state nexuses during the rest of the sixteenth century, which despite some islands of success, reported appalling ignorance of both clergy and laity of evangelical doctrines (or even the most fundamental Christian doctrines), religious indifference (churches were nearly empty, and there was a general hostility to catechesis), and moral laxity (with the tedious repetitions of problems with drunkenness,

---

317 Gerald Strauss, "Success and Failure in the German Reformation," *Past and Present* (May 1975): 30–63; quote from p. 36. See also Strauss, "Protestant Dogma and the City Government: The Case of Nuremberg," *Past and Present* (April 1967): 38–58.

318 Quoted in Marius, *Martin Luther: The Christian between God and Death*, p. 475.

319 Ibid., p. 476.

320 On this estrangement and hostility, see Hans-Christoph Rublack, "Success and Failure of the Reformation: Popular 'Apologies' from the Seventeenth and Eighteenth Centuries," in Fix and Karant-Nunn, *Germania Illustrata*, pp. 141–165.

fornication, adultery, blasphemy, and gambling).[321] Thus, the politicization of Scripture entailed an emphasis on the law for the sake of moral-political order that was seen to be crumbling, even though the primary intention of the preacher might be to bring his congregation to a crisis of remorse and helplessness that would make way for a Luther-like acceptance of entirely free justification. In this mixture of motives, Lutheranism helped prepare the way for the later belief, so important for exegesis in the second half of the seventeenth century, that the real core of Scripture, the "true kernel" if we may borrow from Luther, was actually to provide moral shoring for the political realm.

The Schmalkaldic War tore Germany apart in 1546–1547, and with a victory by the Catholic emperor, some cities were forcibly re-catholicized, a situation that only added to the volatility of Germany. Luther was by this time inactive, dying in Eisleben on February 18, 1546. Before he died, he suffered bouts of serious illness (1526, 1537) and severe depression (1527), the death of a daughter (1528), the final break among reformers at Marburg in regard to the proper scriptural interpretation of the Eucharist (1529), then the death of his father (1530) and his mother (1531). During this time he also produced a complete translation of the Bible into German (1534), but also, to his shame, one of the worst anti-Semitic diatribes ever penned, *Of the Jews and Their Lies* (1543). Indeed, the last sermon he ever preached, four days before his death, was an excoriation of the Jews.

A decade after Luther's death came the Peace of Augsburg (1555), in which the famous principle *cuius regio, eius religio* was enunciated. Exhaustion forced at least a temporary compromise, but we must remember that it specifically excluded the non-Lutheran Protestants, both the less radical Reformed and the more radical Anabaptist, and that it "benefited the princes more than any other estate," so that, "the dominant power in south-west Germany was now an erastian Protestant prince. . . ."[322] An interesting effect of this, we note in passing, was the exile of Martin Bucer to Cambridge, where he carried his Reformed ideas into the midst of a very different kind of Reformation in England.

Conclusion

During Luther's life—actually, during the crucial years from 1517 to 1525—all the basic tenets and tendencies of Reformation theology were set down, either by Luther

---

321 Strauss, "Success and Failure in the German Reformation," pp. 43–63, and again, Rublack, "Success and Failure of the Reformation," pp. 153–154, who makes clear that in some cases, the vices were now given a new foundation in Luther, albeit against his intention. One Jakob Andreae "saw no improvement of life in the Protestant part of Germany, where the Word of God had been spread. 'People say, "We understand that we can gain eternal life by faith in Jesus alone. . . . As we cannot pay for it with fasting, almsgiving, prayers, or any other good work, [so] let's not be bothered with this kind of work."' Andreae complained that excessive eating and drinking replaced fasting and that modesty was replaced by pride. Luxury of dress and disregard of the poor were held to be symbols of rejecting Catholicism. Protestantism was characterized by failure to attend Sunday service and by drunkenness, which made it no longer possible to determine 'whether [one] is Lutheran or Papist.'"

322 Scribner and Dixon, *The German Reformation*, p. 43.

or his opponents among the reformers. As we have stressed, the focus on Scripture alone as the authority did not bring uniformity but almost immediate and intractable diversity, such that exegetical differences ushered in political solutions, which were exacerbated considerably by the peculiar political situation in Germany, but which were duplicated elsewhere in Europe.[323] Despite Luther's intentions, playing the authority of the princes against the papacy meant inadvertently giving the authority over interpretation to the secular powers, and as we have seen, the erastian solution necessarily entailed politicization of the Bible.

But the situation is even more complex. It does not take much historical imagination to understand how the Schmalkaldic War was a premonition of the even more bloody Thirty Years' War that ended a century later. In noting this, we should not fall prey to the simplistic and popular notion that these were solely and simply wars of religion. In truth, they were just as deeply political as religious, religion more often than not acting as a pretext for political ends and a means of rallying support of the ruled for the sake of the rulers. That having been said, the notion that religious differences caused political conflict must be given its due, both in the obvious sense that differences in religion so often defined political conflicts, and in the rhetorical sense insofar as later Enlightenment propaganda seared into the Western mind the notion that differences in religion, nay, religion itself, was the cause of all human misery (as the religious wars seemed to prove). Both senses led to a growing desire to remove the source of conflict, and this desire defined the context of the first fathers of modern biblical scholarship: Thomas Hobbes, Benedict Spinoza, John Locke, and John Toland. To put it in a more incendiary way, modern scriptural scholarship arose in no small part as a solution to a problem: how to ameliorate political conflict caused by rival interpretations of the biblical text.

But that is not the whole story. As we have glimpsed in Machiavelli, a new secular spirit, coeval with Luther, was gaining a hold on key intellectuals during the sixteenth and seventeenth century. According to this spirit, Christianity was one more religion among many that rational men, philosophers, have had to deal with in all times. The difficulty is that Christianity had inverted the proper relationship of the philosopher to religion, so that the Church now stands over the state, and irrational revelation stands over philosophy. To bring sanity again to the political and intellectual order for too long dominated by Christianity, a revolution must take place. Since an open revolution by philosophy is impossible, a covert one is necessary, one that will leave decisive marks upon the modern scriptural scholarship, for it is carried out by the very same fathers mentioned above: Hobbes, Spinoza, Locke, and Toland.

This revolution brings with it a transformation of the very notion of "secular," from meaning the political order (the order of those in the world) as distinguished from the ecclesiastical order, to meaning what it does for us today, a this-worldly orientation set in antithesis to religion. Luther was an essential step in preparation for this revolution: in radicalizing the distinction between secular and sacred, body and soul,

323 For an analysis of the problems caused by this focus on Scripture alone, see Travis L. Frampton, *Spinoza and the Rise of Historical Criticism of the Bible* (London: T. & T. Clark, 2006), Chs. 2–3.

law and Gospel, philosophy and revelation, he helped to drive a distinction into a dialectical antithesis, one that would help to make this-worldly aims autonomous. Much like Ockham, Luther's attempt at reform helped to carry forth Marsilian ends, and in doing so, enabled the West to slide easily into the quintessentially modern notion of secularism.

In this regard, the part played by nationalism and the erastianism engendered (albeit indirectly) by Luther were of no small import. It should be clear why many historians see the political context and the rise of nationalism as essential causes for Luther's success. Without the desire for a national church, without national resentment between Italy and Germany, without German envy of the "national" church of the French and the justified feeling that many Catholics were self-interested Romanists, without the protection of Romantic-messianic nationalists like Hutten, without the shield of the German princes, it is difficult to see how Lutheranism could have taken hold. But such nationalism brings with it, as we have seen with the German humanists, princes, and bureaucrats, some rather unsubtle attempts to yoke Scripture to national destiny and civil machinery.

Turning from these broader concerns back to Scripture itself, quite obviously the principle of *sola scriptura* decisively focused theological debate on Scripture with a new intensity, whether the debate occurred among Protestants or between Protestants and Catholics. Rival political stances had to be settled exegetically, but this could not remain merely a matter of pummeling each other with rival scriptural passages. Debates about proper interpretation necessarily led to debates concerning the difference between the accepted Vulgate and the original Greek; debates about the original Greek led to a fervent search among the various available manuscripts, which not only uncovered manuscript differences but fueled the desire to settle such differences by a more fervent search for more manuscripts. In this way, interpretive differences created a kind of industry of textual scholarship, producing more and more questions that only scholars had any hope of resolving. This had the interesting but entirely unintended effect of removing biblical interpretation from the hands of the common man to whom it had just been given, and handing it to academic experts, thereby creating an exegetical elite that duplicated the function of the Catholic *traditio* in defining interpretation authoritatively.

In regard to particular exegetical controversies, the intra-Protestant debates (and Protestant-Catholic debates as well) about the nature of the Eucharist reveal how quickly exegesis and politics became entwined. On a more subtle level, desacramentalization made possible the removal of any priestly authority that could stand opposed to the state. Luther went part of the way in removing most of the sacraments, and reducing the status of the others by focusing on the promise of justification as primary. In viewing Christ as united to the individual soul rather than to the Church, he went further still. But if the removal of priestly status—begun but not completed by Luther—was to be accomplished, it would call for a further radicalization of Luther's dialectical antithesis of the New to the Old Testament, and this would be carried through in the next generations of exegetes, some working faithfully to take Luther's premises to what they considered their logical conclusion, some working from the secular side to remove impediments to secular control of the Church. We shall meet both as history unfolds.

It should be clear by now how Luther's political-theological arguments connect to later political liberalism. In wanting to protect the individual believer from encroachments by the state, Luther limited the state to the care of the body only (again, duplicating Marsilius's emphasis on politics defined solely in terms of care of the body). Thus limiting the state, Luther affirmed something like the later liberal doctrine of individual belief in which each is allowed to make his own path to heaven as long as he disturbs no one else in the here and now. Again, it is Benedict Spinoza who will spell out the full doctrine as co-opted by liberal political philosophy, a doctrine that will be grounded in a view of the biblical text and exegesis that is (unlike Luther's) easily discernible in its paternity of the modern historical-critical method.

We now turn to England, and pick up again those Marsilian and Machiavellian strands of thought as they come to define the English Reformation of Henry VIII.

CHAPTER 6

ENGLAND AND HENRY VIII

We have already seen in some detail how politics and exegesis became entwined among Wycliffe and his followers. It remains now to trace how their influence dovetailed with Marsilian and Machiavellian ideas to produce the Reformation of Henry VIII. Why spend significant effort on England of the sixteenth century when so many scholars place the beginning of modern scriptural scholarship in Germany in the nineteenth century? Because such placement is actually misplacement. In James Barr's apt words:

> People often suppose that biblical criticism is a German innovation or invention, and those in the English-speaking world who are hostile to it have often cited its supposed German origin in order to frighten people away from it. It is more true, however, to say that the cradle of biblical criticism lay in the English-speaking world: only from near the end of the eighteenth century onward did Germany become the main centre for its development.[1]

Barr's comments occur in the Preface of Henning Reventlow's thorough study of the roots of modern scriptural scholarship, *The Authority of the Bible and the Rise of the Modern World*. According to Reventlow himself, the "main course of development . . . goes from the Continent to England and then at a later stage back to the Continent again." It is in England, "with its characteristic theological and philosophical history, not to mention its distinctive ecclesiastical politics, that typical views of the world developed which were to have lasting influence in forming even the hidden presuppositions in the interpretation of the Old Testament and in biblical exegesis in general." For these reasons, "England can claim a prominent place in the history of the interpretation of the Bible."[2]

In this movement from the continent to England, and from England back to the continent, we find that the theological and philosophical ores imported from the Continent are purified and remolded into the peculiarly modern assumptions that are so familiar to modern scriptural scholarship in particular and are so characteristic of the modern worldview in general. This refining in England occurred at two particularly important junctures in English history, the Reformation of England under Henry VIII (considered here) and the English Revolution of the mid-seventeenth century and its aftermath (to be covered in detail later). In each case, England becomes the filter

1 From the forword by James Barr to Henning Graf Reventlow, *The Authority of the Bible and the Rise of the Modern World*, translated by John Bowden (Philadelphia, PA: Fortress Press, 1985), p. xii.

2 Ibid., p. 4.

through which earlier developments are handed on to the Enlightenment. The political Averroism of Marsilius is mediated through political Averroism formulated during the reign of Henry VIII. The raw embrace of a particular kind of paganism against Christianity that appears in Machiavelli is transformed into a much gentler and subtler creature—the English Deism that enacts the Enlightenment's humiliation of Scripture on behalf of reason.

The raw materials for this alloy were imported from the continent to England in the sixteenth and seventeenth centuries, and the finished intellectual products were exported from England during the latter half of the seventeenth. These became the finished presuppositions defining the Enlightenment on the continent in the eighteenth and nineteenth centuries, reaching Germany last of all. To prove this grand claim, we must begin by an investigation of the situation in England during the reign of Henry VIII, when the decisive shift to the political interpretation of Scripture took place.

Historical Conditions: Wycliffe and the Lollards

It might be tempting, given the way that Henry VIII exercised power, to see the creation of the Anglican Church, the national church that governed the interpretation of Scripture, as merely a creation of Henry's own sexual foibles and endless ambitions. But in the story of Wycliffe, one can see that groundwork for the subordination of the Church to the state was already well advanced by the beginning of Henry's reign.

On the theoretical level, there were the erastian doctrines of Wycliffe that so well matched the arguments of Marsilius—whose ideas were well known in the intellectual circles supporting Henry's seizure of power over the Church. Where Marsilius's ideas had first prepared for Wycliffe's, now the situation was, in important respects, reversed. The long-standing influence of Wycliffe in England, especially in the more popular form of Lollardy, prepared the way for the reintroduction of Marsilius's *Defensor Pacis* at the upper levels of power.

Of course, one can hardly overestimate the importance of Wycliffian and Lollard doctrines themselves. Pious calls for disendowment and popular anticlericalism were easily translatable into a very practical and political policy of stripping shrines and monastic houses. The call for secular control over ecclesiastical affairs for the sake of reform prepared for Henry's declaration of the king as head of the Church. As we have seen, the notion of an *Anglicana Ecclesia* and a mystical notion of divinely ordained monarchy were already running full steam during the reign of Edward III, and it was Edward who issued the *Ordinance and Statute of Praemunire* in 1353, forbidding appeals to Rome over English courts. Along with all of this, the English bishops had for quite some time been accustomed to focus on secular business, trained in civil rather than canon law, and regularly acted as civil servants in the service of the crown. "This civilian emphasis harmonised admirably with the bureaucratic and diplomatic employment of the bishops; more important, it helps to explain why, almost to a man, they followed King Henry when he severed relations with the Papacy."[3] Erastianism was in the English air long before Henry's declaration of royal supremacy. Thus, it might be better to say that the infamous divorce from Henry's first wife was not the cause but the occasion for the creation of the official Church of England.

The King's Great Matter

Henry VIII was born in London on June 28, 1491, the second son of King Henry VII, the first ruler of the house of Tudor. Henry VII, a Lancastrian, had married Elizabeth of the house of York in 1486, thereby uniting the two houses that had spilled so much blood in the War of the Roses (1455–1485), close upon the end of the Hundred Years' War with France. Henry VIII's elder brother, Arthur, died when Henry was just eleven, making young Henry heir to the throne. Henry VII died on April 21, 1509. And so it happened that in the very year of Machiavelli's zenith of power in Florence (and three years before, driven from power, he would pen *The Prince)*, two years after Martin Luther was ordained a priest (and eight years before the Augustinian monk would nail his ninety-five theses to the door of the castle church at Wittenberg), Henry VIII became king of England.

Henry mounted the throne just prior to turning eighteen, but even before his birthday arrived, he would marry Catherine, the daughter of Ferdinand and Isabella of Spain. Catherine, who was six years Henry's elder, had been the wife of Henry's brother Arthur, but Arthur had died less than half a year after his marriage. Henry's marriage to Catherine was arranged after Arthur's death, and Henry received a papal dispensation from Pope Julius II. Later, even as Catherine was two months pregnant with their first child, Henry was involved with a mistress, Anne Hastings. While Anne may have been the first, she was by no means the last. The boy born to Catherine on New Year's Day of 1511, also named Henry, would quickly die.

After Anne Hastings, King Henry would have affairs with Elizabeth Blount (who was married at the time to Gilbert Tailboys and who in 1519 bore Henry a son, Henry Fitzroy) and then Jane Popyngcort. It was during this time period that Catherine bore Henry a stillborn son (1513), a premature son (1514), then a living daughter, Mary, on February 18, 1516, and another stillborn child in 1518.

As noted in Chapter 5, Henry took up his pen in response to Luther's Theses published in 1517, defending the Catholic faith against Luther with a treatise entitled *Assertio Septem Sacramentorum* (*Defence of the Seven Sacraments*). It came out in 1521, and proved an immediate bestseller. In writing it, he received theological help from Thomas More and John Fisher, both of whom he would later execute. Henry had a specially bound copy sent to Pope Leo X, to whom his treatise was dedicated, and

3 A. G. Dickens, *The English Reformation*, second edition (University Park, PA: Pennsylvania State University Press, 1991), p. 67.

from whom he would receive in turn the honorary title *Fidei Defensor* (Defender of the Faith) in a papal bull of October 11, 1521. As Henry had ambitions to become the Holy Roman Emperor, the honorific title was of no small consequence.

Chapter XI of Henry's *Assertio Septem Sacramentorum* was entitled *De Sacramento Matrimonii*, directed against Luther's argument that marriage was not a sacrament. For Henry, this was heresy, and it was (so he argued) precisely the rejection of divorce that distinguished Christian from pagan marriage, marking Christian marriage as sacramental and restoring marriage to its original purity:

> [T]he Gentiles, because it was acted as a human Thing amongst them, were wont, by Compacts and human Laws, to take Wives, and after to reject them again. *Divorcement* was not lawful in former Times amongst the People of God: For though God, by *Moses*, permitted the Bill of Divorcement among the *Hebrews*; yet *Christ* confesses that it was indulged them for the Hardness of the People's Hearts: *For, from the Beginning* (saith our Saviour,) *it was not so* [Mark10:2–12; Matthew 19:3–12]. But *Christ* hath restored Christians to pristine Sanctity, consecrating Marriage with an indesolvable Bond of Society; unless in Case of Fornication between those, whom no human Error, but God himself, has joined together.[4]

Even more interesting, Henry proved his position by quoting the entirety of St. Paul's admonitions to husband and wife in Ephesians 5:22–32, which ends (in his Latin) "*Sacramentum hoc magnum est, ego autem dico in Christo et Ecclesia*." This same passage bids "Husbands love your Wives, even as Christ loved the Church, and delivered himself for it. . . . So also Men ought to love their Wives as their own Bodies; he that loveth his Wife, loveth himself." From this, Henry concluded that "the Marriage of Man and Wife is a Sacrament, which represents the Conjunction of Christ with his Church: For he [the apostle Paul] teacheth, that God consecrated Matrimony, that it might be the Mystery [*sacramentum*] of Christ joined with his Church."[5] Henry adduced many other proofs, both from Scripture and from the Church Fathers. "But why search we so many Proofs in so clear a Thing?" he then asked, "especially, when that only Text is sufficient for all, where Christ says, *Whom God has joined together, let no Man put asunder* [Matthew 19:6]. O the admirable Word! Which none could have spoken, but the Word that was made Flesh!"[6] Henry ended by reminding Luther that the whole of Church history is against him—the Scriptures, the Fathers, the manifest "public Faith of the Church, for so many Ages before us. . . ." All, chided Henry, "have esteemed Marriage as a Sacrament, (which makes Wedlock honourable, and does by Grace, not only conserve the Bed unspotted from Adultery; but also washes away the Stains of Lust, turns Water into Wine, and procures a holy Pleasure of abstaining, even

4 This is the English translation from Rev. Louis O'Donovan, Henry VIII, King of England, *Assertio Septem Sacramentorum or Defence of the Seven Sacraments* (New York: Benziger Brothers, 1908), p. 368.

5 Ibid., pp. 368–371.

6 Ibid, p. 388.

from lawful Pleasures.)"[7] A great feast of words Henry would soon enough have to eat because of his desire to divorce Catherine, a desire that would lead him to cut and retie "the Conjunction of Christ with his Church."

Neither before the publication of his *Defence* nor after did Henry "conserve the Bed unspotted from Adultery." He took as mistress in the early 1520s Mary Boleyn (married at the time to William Carey), and it was some time in early 1526 that Henry transferred his amour to Mary's sister, Anne Boleyn. At first Henry tried to convince Anne to be his mistress, offering to forego, in a fit of gallant love, all other mistresses.[8] Anne had no inclination whatsoever to join in Henry's long line of courtesans, but instead gave the king a very simple choice, the queen's crown or nothing. So arose "the King's Great Matter."

Another Great Matter: Tyndale and the English Bible

William Tyndale created another great matter for Henry, an English translation of the Bible, the second after the Wycliffe Bible (which still existed in manuscript among Lollard circles), and the first done from Greek and Hebrew. Tyndale's almost single-handed creation is the true foundation of the more famous King James Version, rather than the one completed by Wycliffe's circle.

In the spring of 1524, about two and a half years after Henry VIII was declared Defender of the Faith by Pope Leo X, the ordained priest William Tyndale sailed from England, never to return. Tyndale, not yet thirty at the time of his departure, was an expert linguist. Animated by Protestant doctrines he had learned on the sly as a student at Oxford and Cambridge, his great passion was to translate Scripture into the English tongue from the original languages.

Tyndale's first destination was Germany, and he was soon to be found in the company of Luther and Melanchthon in Wittenberg. Finishing his translation of the New Testament by 1525, Tyndale looked for a printer. This was three years after the appearance of Luther's German translation of the New Testament, and the very year of Germany's Peasant Rebellion. The rebellion, we recall, was immediately associated by both German princes and other European monarchs—including Henry VIII—as linked to Luther's doctrines and his translation of the Bible into the vernacular (as a

7 Ibid., 392–394.

8 In a letter to Anne, he wrote: "I beseech you now, with the greatest earnestness, to let me know your whole intention, as to the love between us two. For I must of necessity obtain this answer of you, having been above a whole year struck with the dart of love, and not yet sure whether I shall fail, or find a place in your heart and affection. This uncertainty has hindered me of late from naming you my mistress, since you only love me with an ordinary affection; but if you please to do the duty of a true and loyal mistress, and to give up yourself, body and heart, to me, who will be, as I have been your most loyal servant . . . I promise you that not only the name shall be given you, but also that I will take you for my mistress, casting off all others that are in competition with you, out of my thoughts and affection, and serving you only." Ladbroke Black, *The Love Letters of Henry the Eighth* (London: Blandford Press, Ltd., 1933), p. 29.

kind of treatise for revolutionaries, so they thought). Since Tyndale's translation came with marginalia that made clear his Lutheran (even Zwinglian, or more accurately proto-Puritan) theology, his translation seemed linked to political rebellion. For Henry, the connection was doubly reinforced on his own soil by the association of Wycliffe and the Bible produced by his followers and the Peasant Revolt of 1381, and the consequent related political turmoil caused by Hus in Bohemia. Small wonder that the English government was on the lookout to destroy all copies of Tyndale's translation headed for England.

At least eighteen thousand copies of Tyndale's New Testament translation were printed between 1526 and 1528, and despite the English government's efforts, a good number were smuggled into England. He followed with a translation of the Pentateuch in 1530. But all during this time Tyndale, still in Europe, was a hunted man, a political exile, for whom English agents on the continent were avidly searching.

But the Bible is not the whole of the story. In 1528 Tyndale published (in Antwerp) *The Obedience of a Christian Man*, a book first read by Anne Boleyn, and then brought to Henry who, after reading it, exclaimed, "This is a book for me and for all kings to read."[9] Whatever Henry thought of the dangers of translating the New Testament into his mother tongue at the time, he was certainly enthusiastic about Tyndale's theological-political treatise (or what he hastily read of it). *Obedience* has been commonly called "the first, and the most important, book in the earliest phase of the English Reformation."[10] Its importance lies, in great part, in being "the first thorough-going [English] apologia of Caesaropapism."[11]

Echoing Wycliffe, Tyndale declared that translation into English was licit, for the apostles themselves "no doubt preached in the mother tongue," and further, that "Saint Jerome also translated the Bible into his mother tongue," so "Why may not we also?" Furthermore, "the Greek tongue agreeth more with the English than with the Latin. And the properties of the Hebrew tongue agreeth a thousand times more with the English than with the Latin."[12]

Tyndale's main point in *Obedience* was not linguistic, but to answer the very charge that hovered over other vernacular translations: that to translate into the mother tongue "causeth insurrection and teacheth the people to disobey their heads and governors, and moveth them to rise against their princes and to make all common and to make havoc of other men's goods."[13] To this charge, Tyndale argued that, "Christ himself taught all obedience," so that the real source of insurrection is not the Bible in the vernacular, but "the bloody doctrine of the Pope which causeth disobedience, rebellion and insurrection." For "he teacheth to fight and to defend his traditions and whatsoever he dreameth with fire, water and sword and to disobey

9 Quoted in J. J. Scarisbrick, *Henry VIII* (Berkeley and Los Angeles: University of California Press, 1968), p. 247.

10 David Daniell, ed., William Tyndale, *The Obedience of a Christian Man* (London: Penguin Books, 2000), Introduction, p. viii.

11 Scarisbrick, *Henry VIII*, p. 247.

12 Tyndale, *The Obedience of a Christian Man*, "William Tyndale . . . unto the reader," p. 19.

13 Ibid., Prologue, p. 26.

father, mother, master, lord, king and emperor: yea and to invade whatsoever land or nation that will not receive and admit his godhead."[14]

In contrast to the pope, the Bible teaches obedience to temporal authority (leaning on the thirteenth chapter of St. Paul's Romans): "Let every soul submit himself unto the authority of the highest powers. There is no power but of God. The powers that be are ordained by God. Whosoever therefore resisteth that power resisteth the ordinance of God."[15] This assertion is set by Tyndale as the summit within a structure of ascending ordained powers, parents over children, husbands over wives, masters over servants, and kings over subjects.[16] God is the one who puts the kings on top, for "God . . . hath given laws unto all nations and in all lands hath put kings, governors and rulers in his own stead, to rule the world through them," and (in accordance with Exodus) they rule as judges in "all causes . . . of injury or wrong."

Tyndale even sets out a quasi-deification of secular authorities. Under Moses, the causes of disputants were to "be brought unto the gods: whom the gods condemn the same shall pay double unto his neighbour. Mark, the judges are called gods in the scriptures because they are in God's room and execute the commandments of God . . . Whosoever therefore resisteth them resisteth God . . . and they that resist shall receive their damnation."

This identity of secular judges with gods did indeed find its way into Tyndale's later rendering of the Pentateuch. He translated Exodus 21:6 (dealing with Hebrew slaves who chose to stay with their masters): "Then let his master bring him unto the gods and set him to the door or the doorpost, and bore his ear through with an awl, and let him be his servant for ever" (with Tyndale's marginal comment, "Gods are the judges which are in God's stead"). Exodus 22:27 was rendered "Thou shalt not rail upon the gods [i.e., judges], neither curse the ruler of thy people."[17] The appellation of divinity is appropriate, Tyndale argues:

> For God hath made the king in every realm judge over all, and over him is there no judge. He that judgeth the king judgeth God, and he that resisteth the king resisteth God and damneth God's law and ordinance. If the subjects sin they must be brought to the king's judgment. If the king sin he must be reserved unto the judgment, wrath and vengeance of God. And as it is to resist the king, so is it to resist his officer which is set or sent to execute the king's commandment.[18]

Obedience is due the ruler "though he be the greatest tyrant in the world," for (sounding just like Thomas Hobbes over a century later) "yet is he unto thee a great benefit of God and a thing wherefore thou oughtest to thank God highly. For it is

---

14 Ibid., p. 30.

15 Ibid., "The obedience of all degrees . . ." p. 36.

16 Ibid., pp. 31–36.

17 David Daniell, ed., William Tyndale, *Tyndale's Old Testament, Being the Pentateuch of 1530, Joshua to 2 Chronicles of 1537, and Jonah,* modern spelling edition (New Haven: Yale University Press, 1992).

18 Tyndale, *The Obedience of a Christian Man,* "The obedience of all degrees . . ." pp. 39–40.

better to have somewhat [i.e., something] than to be clean stripped out of all together . . . it is better to suffer one tyrant than many and to suffer wrong of one than of every man."[19] While Tyndale reminds kings of their duties,[20] the command of obedience to tyrants remains uncompromising.

No greater affirmation of royal supremacy could have been handed to Henry VIII, and it is no wonder that he heartily affirmed Tyndale's *The Obedience of a Christian Man*. In it, Tyndale goes far beyond Luther's two kingdoms doctrine, giving undivided scriptural support for one kingdom headed by one king.

Tyndale's aim was to eliminate the temporal power of the papacy, as he makes clear: "Neither can the profession of monks and friars or anything that the Pope or bishops can lay for themselves, except them from the sword of the Emperor or kings, if they break the laws. For it is written, let every soul submit himself unto the authority of the higher powers [Romans 13:1]."[21] Futhermore, "the King ought to rid his realm from the wily tyranny of the hypocrites and to bring the hypocrites under his laws. . . ."[22]

Since the pope was, for Tyndale, the Antichrist,[23] he had no claim even to spiritual power, so that biblical support could only have come from illicit modes of scriptural interpretation. Important for our purposes, Tyndale repeated the complaints of Ockham and Luther about the use of allegory in scriptural exegesis, claiming that "our miserable captivity and persecution under Antichrist the Pope" in great part "sprang first of allegories."[24] Allegorical readings (and Tyndale classes tropological and anagogical under allegorical) are used by the pope to buttress his power, and consequently, for the papacy, the literal meaning is "nothing at all." Even more, the "Pope hath taken it clean away and hath made it his possession. He hath partly locked it up with the false and counterfeited keys of his traditions, ceremonies and feigned lies. And partly driveth men from it with the violence of sword."[25] Emphasis on the literal meaning, especially as presented in a vernacular translation (with instructive marginalia), would bypass such traditions, ceremonies, and lies, and remove the scripturally-based source of the pope's pretended political power, which means for Tyndale putting that power back into the hands of the king (with appropriate scriptural support). Certain modes of exegesis have immense political implications.

But there was more of England's future packed into Tyndale. As noted above, Tyndale's theology was actually more radical than Luther's, and it is with justice that he is often credited with being the founder of English Puritanism.[26] One aspect of his theology demands attention: the inversion of the Lutheran view of law.

19 Ibid., p. 41.
20 Ibid., pp. 63–68.
21 Ibid., p. 40.
22 Ibid., p. 184.
23 Ibid., pp. 88–108.
24 Ibid., pp. 159–160.
25 Ibid.," p. 156.
26 See the bibliography in Reventlow, *The Authority of the Bible and the Rise of the Modern World*, p. 105, fn. 131.

In his Prologue to the Pentateuch of 1530, Tyndale offered a seemingly very Lutheran overview of the law-promise dialectic. The reader should "Seek therefore in the scripture as thou readest it first the law, what God commandeth us to do. And secondarily the promises, which God promiseth us again, namely in Christ Jesu our Lord."[27] But in the 1534 edition Tyndale amended the passage, creating a complete inversion of Lutheran theology even amidst many other seemingly Lutheran affirmations:

> Seek therefore in the scripture as thou readest it, chiefly and above all, the covenants made between God and us. That is to say: the law and commandments which God commandeth us to do. And then the mercy promised unto all them that submit themselves unto the law. For all the promises throughout the whole scripture do include a covenant. That is: God bindeth himself to fulfil that mercy unto thee only, if thou wilt endeavour thyself to keep his laws: so that no man hath his part in the mercy of God, save he only that loveth his law and consenteth that it is righteous and good and fain would do it, and ever mourneth because he now and then breaketh it through infirmity, or doth it not so perfectly as his heart would.[28]

Obviously, Tyndale's affirmation of the centrality of law and morality was double assurance that translating Scripture into the vernacular would not lead to antinomianism and political revolution. Tyndale's Prologue to the 1534 edition of the New Testament made the same assertions about covenant even more strongly. Against others who corrupt Scripture, Tyndale offered "the key to open it withal," so that the "right way: yea and the only way to understand the scripture unto our salvation, is, that we earnestly and above all thing, search for the profession of our baptism or covenants made between God and us." So far, so Lutheran. But here again Tyndale's understanding of covenant is an inversion of Luther's. Using the example of one of the beatitudes, "Happy are the merciful, for they shall obtain mercy" (Matthew 5:7), Tyndale declared, "Lo, here God hath made a covenant with us, to be merciful unto us, if we will be merciful one to another. . . ." So that the "general covenant wherein all other are comprehended and included, is this: If we meek ourselves to God, to keep all his laws, after the example of Christ: then God hath bound himself unto us to keep and make good all the mercies promised in Christ, throughout all the scripture."[29] (Tyndale also apparently saw this notion of covenant theology applying on the national level as well, as indicated by his Prologue to the Book of Jonah, so that he provided an early example of what is called "national covenant theology."[30])

---

27 Tyndale, *Tyndale's Old Testament*, Prologue, pp. 7-8.

28 Ibid., p. 10. Daniell, the editor, has split the earlier Prologue from the later revisions.

29 David Daniell, ed., William Tyndale, *Tyndale's New Testament (1534)*, modern spelling edition (New Haven: Yale University Press, 1989), Prologue, p. 4.

30 On this point see Reventlow, *The Authority of the Bible and the Rise of the Modern World*, p. 108, and Tyndale, *Tyndale's Old Testament*, "The Prologue to the Prophet Jonas," pp. 634–635.

In these words of Tyndale, we find no Lutheran dialectical antithesis of law and Gospel; rather, here Tyndale would seem to affirm an almost Pelagian understanding of the ability to fulfill the law (which looks quite similar to the quasi-Pelagian notion among nominalists that so enraged Luther). *If* we fulfill the moral commandments, which are almost fully present in the Old Testament, *then* God has bound himself by a covenant to grant us his mercy. Of course, this affirmation of Old Testament law goes hand in hand with a bitter denunciation of all Old Testament ceremony as incipient papalism, the result being that, with Tyndale, the Old and New Testaments are not related through typological fulfillment (Catholicism) or by dialectical antithesis (Luther), but as two closely related books of morality. The important historical implication in regard to the politicization of Scripture is that Tyndale's view tends inadvertently to affirm the Marsilian argument that the sole purpose of religion is limited to providing moral (and hence peaceable) citizens, and to lay the foundation for the later Deist notion that Jesus Christ was a moral exemplar whom we should imitate. Moreover, since Tyndale jettisons any papal-sacramental intrusions into the political realm by eliminating the ceremonial aspects of the Old Testament that would allow a Roman foot in the national door, his approach would make Scripture all the more amenable to nationalist purposes.

Henry actually had Tyndale sought out on the continent in 1531 to offer him a job of translating the Bible into English, but the king soon changed his mind most vehemently. Even with Tyndale's hearty and almost unqualified affirmation of kingly power and his stress on morality, both of which were meant to assure Henry that neither Tyndale himself nor a vernacular translation would cause revolution, Henry had not yet split from Rome, and because Tyndale was so openly Lutheran in his theology, Henry feared a repetition of rebellion from below.[31] On top of that, Tyndale had denounced Henry's divorce in no uncertain terms in his *Practice of Prelates* (published in 1530, but not read by Henry until later).[32] On May 21, 1535, Tyndale was finally captured by English agents on the continent, and handed over to imperial authorities, and on October 6, 1536, executed, crying out, "Lord, open the King of England's eyes."[33] By then, Henry had declared his supremacy over the English state and church.

Ironically, Tyndale's arguments helped to legitimate both Henry's supremacy and the divorce itself, as well as Tyndale's own execution. As queen, Anne Boleyn would keep a gilded copy of Tyndale's New Testament, the revised edition of 1534, with her coat of arms on the title page and *Anna Regina Angliae* on the spine. But she could no

31 On Henry's reaction to Tyndale as a Lutheran rebel see Derek Wilson, *In the Lion's Court: Power, Ambition, and Sudden Death in the Reign of Henry VIII* (New York: St. Martin's Press, 2001), pp. 337–338. Given that Henry's reaction occurred after reading Tyndale's replies to St. Thomas More, he must not have read very far in *Obedience of a Christian Man*, or he would have known immediately Tyndale's Lutheranism.

32 See David Katz, *God's Last Words: Reading the English Bible from the Reformation to Fundamentalism* (New Haven: Yale University Press, 2004), pp. 33–34.

33 For an account of Tyndale's capture and death see Benson Bobrick, *Wide as the Waters: The Story of the English Bible and the Revolution It Inspired* (New York: Simon & Schuster, 2001), pp. 133–135.

longer act as his patroness and protectress behind the scenes—meeting her own execution five months before Tyndale. In his marginalia for Romans 13:1–7 of that very edition, Tyndale gave witness to the Caesaropapism that would claim both his life and Anne's: "Though thou were of power to resist the power, yet were thou damned in thy conscience if thou didest it, because it is against God's commandment."[34]

On October 4, 1535, almost exactly one year *before* Tyndale's execution, Miles Coverdale (a one-time associate of Tyndale) took the first complete English Bible to the press, which consisted largely of Tyndale's translation. The so-called Matthew Bible, the first full English version officially sanctioned by the king, was published a year after Tyndale's execution. It, too, was largely co-opted from Tyndale's translation (this was hidden from Henry behind the pseudonym "Thomas Matthew," listed as the translator). But such were not the only tangles in regard to Scripture and the king's expression of supremacy. Many more appear in the course of events and arguments that led up to this momentous step.

The Path to Royal Supremacy

By spring of 1527 Henry had convinced himself that he had scriptural support for an annulment in two texts in Leviticus: "You shall not uncover the nakedness of your brother's wife; she is your brother's nakedness" (18:16) and "If a man takes his brother's wife, it is impurity; he has uncovered his brother's nakedness, they shall be childless" (20:21).[35] Against these scriptural mandates, no pope could offer a dispensation, thus Julius's document was null and void. A sign that God was on his side, so Henry thought, was that he had endured the Levitical curse of childlessness.

Of course, Henry did not lack a child. There was Mary and also his illegitimate son, Henry. Further, in his exegesis, Henry apparently did not consider as an important counterargument Deuteronomy 25:5–10, where it is taken as mandatory that if a brother *dies*, a remaining brother "shall take her [the widow] as his wife." But Henry was not as much interested in accurate and thorough exegesis as he was in the charms of Anne Boleyn and his own political desires, and he seemed completely convinced that God was punishing him for violating Leviticus by giving him no male heir.

To get an annulment from Rome therefore became Henry's great passion, and he relied on his most influential political advisor, Cardinal Wolsey, for its achievement. Thomas Wolsey was a butcher's son, and ambitious almost without parallel, grasping political and ecclesiastical honors and appointments at an unprecedented pace. He had received the cardinal's hat in 1515, the only cardinal in England, and became Lord High Chancellor at the same year. In 1518 he was named papal legate, and hence ranked above the Archbishop of Canterbury. In historian Neville Williams's words, "Never before had one man amassed so many important offices in church and

34 Tyndale, *Tyndale's New Testament (1534)*.

35 Against rumors, it seems to have been Henry himself, rather than Wolsey, who seized upon the passages in Leviticus. Scarisbrick, *Henry VIII*, pp. 152–154.

state, and his wealth, like his power, was regal in scale."[36] That low-born Wolsey had amassed so much power and money brought him many enemies; that he did so under the cloak of being papal legate shifted some of that animosity toward Rome.

Cardinal Wolsey was not at all interested in a break from Rome; quite the contrary, since Rome was the very source of his power—and his boundless ambitions included the papal throne itself (this is why he had prodded Henry to write his *Assertio Septem Sacramentorum*). When Pope Leo X died in 1521, Wolsey offered to pay Spanish troops to "overpower the conclave in Rome," but Emperor Charles V emerged victorious in the struggle, and had his old tutor elected as Adrian VI.[37]

So Wolsey set to work. On May 17 an extraordinary tribunal, a secret court, was called by the cardinal for the purpose of calling Henry to account for living unlawfully with Catherine for eighteen years, explicitly against God's law. At this time, Wolsey did not know of Henry's desire to marry Anne.

The contrivance of the court is all too evident, establishing the desired "guilt" by the very charge and trial. Wolsey undertook this proceeding by virtue of being a papal legate, an attempt at dry-run legitimation by Rome. But events on the continent threw things into a spin. In early May 1527, Rome was sacked by the troops of Emperor Charles V, the nephew of England's Queen Catherine, and Pope Clement was under imperial power. On the first of June, England learned of Rome's sack and the pope's captivity. Worries began to overshadow Wolsey's designs. How could he hope to get an annulment from a pope under the thumb of Queen Catherine's nephew?

Wolsey was soon off to France with a plan "audacious almost beyond belief and with few rivals, if any, in English history."[38] He would go to Avignon during the pope's imprisonment, call together the cardinals, and himself take up rule of the Church in the emergency interim. From this temporary position of power he could negotiate European peace, and, of course, grant Henry's annulment (without the captured pope's knowledge, but having temporarily signed away his powers, with his implicit consent). With that aim in view, Wolsey crossed the channel with a fully drawn-up commission for Clement to sign, ceding all power of the papacy temporarily to him.

---

36 Neville Williams, *Henry VIII and His Court* (New York: Macmillan Company, 1971), p. 58. Williams's description of Wolsey's accustomed pomp serves as an accurate character description. "There had never been a subject wielding so much power and living in such magnificence as the Cardinal. Two great crosses of silver were carried before him in procession, the first, a double cross, like the cross of Lorraine, as Legate, the other as Archbishop and the crucifers were the tallest priests in the realm, and also before him were borne two silver pillars and two gilt poleaxes; a handsome page walked bareheaded behind his master bearing the great seal in a silk purse. Out of doors Wolsey wore the cardinal's red-tasselled hat, but in church it was carried in procession and placed on the high altar. He rode on a mule, symbolising humility, yet the beast was decked out with costly red and gold trappings. Nearly a thousand persons were entered on his household roll, gentlemen and yeomen, chosen for their height and features no less than for their competence and devotion to Wolsey's service. . . . This army of servants wore his distinctive crimson velvet livery, embroidered with a cardinal's hat—the device that even decorated his gilded bed posts." Ibid., pp. 92–93.

37 Ibid., p. 93.

38 Scarisbrick, *Henry VIII*, p. 146.

Meanwhile, the secret court had folded, but the news of Henry's intentions was no longer secret, even to Catherine. Henry disclosed to her late in June 1527 the stunning news that they had been living together almost twenty years, sinning against divine law. Henry evidently hoped she would be suitably aghast at infringing upon the strictures of Leviticus, but instead "Catherine burst into tears at this terrible sentence and temporarily unsteadied Henry. . . ."[39] She soon informed the emperor, and Charles immediately notified all parties, including the pope and Henry, that the divorce should not go through. At the same time, Wolsey's grand plans began to unwind. Neither pope nor cardinals had any intention of following Wolsey's designs, and even worse, Henry had decided to go around Wolsey and appeal directly to Clement, arguing that he receive papal dispensation for bigamy so that he could marry Anne even without divorcing Catherine.[40]

Wolsey found out about the "secret bull" and immediately stopped its delivery, but Henry did another end run around him with a second secret bull written for the pope's approval, which exceeded the first in audacity. In it, Henry asked that *if* he were granted an annulment of his marriage to Catherine then he should be allowed to marry Anne. He needed papal approval to marry Anne because, having had Anne's sister, Mary, as his courtesan, Henry was now related "in the first degree of affinity" to Anne through illicit intercourse with Mary, thereby making it necessary for Henry to be cleared of the charge of violating the very two Leviticus passages that he wanted to use to annul his marriage to Catherine! Henry argued that such was not the case, and provided a stunning example of appeal to the literal sense of Scripture: the two texts in Leviticus refer to a man's brother, not sister. "The distinction was not, perhaps, an impressive one, but it would have been enough to settle Henry's malleable conscience."[41] By invoking the Scriptures to settle the King's Great Matter, Henry initiated what amounted to international exegetical warfare over the next few years, using the most up-to-date weapons forged and honed by the humanists. In Scarisbrick's description:

> A galaxy of Greek and Hebrew scholars, Christian and Jew, of theologians and canonists, of religious houses and universities, first in England and then on the Continent, were to be called upon to provide evidence for the king. Soon English agents were abroad, in France and Italy especially, quizzing and cajoling, ransacking libraries, interrogating university faculties, drawing of lists of signatories in this or that friary, urging canonists and Scripture scholars to take up the pen. . . . Meanwhile, of course, the other side had been no less energetic. Men great and small rallied to defend Queen Catherine, meeting tract with tract, opinion with opinion. By 1529–30 the king's divorce had occasioned an international debate as violent and swift-moving, though

39 Ibid., p. 156.

40 Ibid., p. 159.

41 Ibid., pp. 160–161.

on a much smaller scale, as the contemporary conflict between Catholic and Protestant polemicists.[42]

Henry's proponents were both industrious and exegetically imaginative, and it would be hard to find another historical instance of politicizing a text with such intensity. The passage in Deuteronomy pertained to the old Law, merely ceremonial and now superceded by Christ, they argued. Or the Levirate law was a particular not a general command, and the particulars of Henry's Great Matter did not therefore fit. Or the text was taken to be merely allegorical rather than literal. Or, the word *frater*, brother, could mean either sibling or, more generally, merely a relative, and it meant sibling in the Leviticus passages that counted for Henry, and relative in the Deuteronomy passage that counted against him.[43]

But the problem with all these efforts was twofold: the passages had already been well worked over by Fathers and scholars for centuries (given the nature of hereditary monarchies, the complexities of consanguinity was an issue well plowed), and the overwhelming interpretation was against Henry; and second, opposing Henry were some of the best and most learned minds of the day, including his own bishop John Fisher and the formidable Cardinal Cajetan. On top of all this, Pope Julius's dispensation that allowed Henry to marry Catherine in the first place was not novel at all, but had many precedents.[44] In fact, a bull by Pope Innocent III (*Deus qui Ecclesiam*), which had passed into canon law, made the case against Henry definitive.[45]

But all of this did not stop Henry from sending out his first volley in the government propaganda campaign in late fall of 1531, "a laborious pamphlet of 154 folios which at length rehearsed the scriptural, patristic, early conciliar and medieval authorities on the King's side."[46] It was put forward as a purely academic argument using all the scholarly ammunition gained on the Continent, and does not even mention Henry or Catherine or the particularities of their marriage dispute. Even when translated from Latin to English, it was an unlikely candidate for sweeping opinion to the king's side, but the tendentious and political use of Scripture is undeniable. Realizing their mistake, royal apologists (now led by Thomas Cromwell) soon put forward a popular version, *The Glass of Truth* (1532).[47]

Even before the time of Cromwell, the indefatigable Henry and the ever-inventive Wolsey tried many other means, from writing out other proposals for Clement to sign (including a proposal in 1528 to allow Henry bigamy), to entreating Catherine to enter a nunnery (she steadfastly refused), threatening the papacy that England would break

42 Ibid., p. 164.

43 Ibid., pp. 164–165.

44 Ibid., pp. 177–178.

45 Ibid., p. 179.

46 The wonderfully cumbersome English title was *The Determination of the most famous and excellent Universities of Italy and France, that it is unlawful for a man to marry his brother's wife and that the pope hath no power to dispense therewith*. G. R. Elton, *Policy and Police: The Enforcement of the Reformation in the Age of Thomas Cromwell* (Cambridge: Cambridge University Press, 1972), p. 174–175.

47 Ibid., pp. 176–179.

its allegiance to Rome and side with the Lutherans, and tricking the pope into signing a document without perusing its contents. Nothing worked. Catherine appealed to Rome to hear her case, and Rome agreed, thereby removing the decision from English soil and also ensuring a ruling against England's king.

As Henry's chances became ever dimmer, Wolsey fell from the king's favor, by the end of the 1520s falling so far and fast (as pushed by discontented nobles and Anne Boleyn), that he would be arrested near the end of 1530, dying on the way to London to answer charges of treason. He had been asked to step down as Lord Chancellor in 1529, and, fatefully, Thomas More was chosen in his place, but it was really Thomas Cromwell who, by this time or not much after, had insinuated himself as the great architect behind Henry's new order, which rose in part on the politicization of Scripture.

The new order had to be built from within. Henry summoned Parliament in October 1529, and the Reformation Parliament (as it came to be called) commenced on November 3. By the end of the next summer, Henry had laid aside the old strategy of pleading with Rome and took up a new one. "Hitherto he had questioned the theology upon which a papal dispensation rested; now he enunciated a new theory of English monarchy."[48] In short, Henry overcame papal claims by proclaiming a doctrine of Caesaropapism, and thus, in regard to scriptural affirmation, Henry turned from worrying about Leviticus to affirmations of Davidic kingship in the Old Testament.[49]

Nothing was absolutely new here. Henry's strategy was the extension of the notion of an English national church with a Davidic king already existing in the fourteenth century, manifested in Edward III and given flesh by royal apologists at the time, chief of which was Wycliffe. It contained an appeal to history as well as Scripture, since Henry found instantly attractive the notion that the early Church had been one without a papacy, and one in which loosely organized bishops owed obedience not to Rome, but to Caesar.[50] And subjects owed all obedience to their king, as Tyndale had argued.

In the early morning of July 11, 1531, Henry rode from Windsor Castle on a hunting expedition. Riding at his side was Anne Boleyn. Left behind, never to be seen again by Henry, was Queen Catherine. By the end of 1532, Anne and Henry were living together, and by mid-January 1533 she was pregnant. The King's Great Matter was getting greater with each passing day, for he could not have a legitimate male heir born out of wedlock (and he was sure Anne was carrying a boy). He and Anne were married in secret on January 25. In late March, Thomas Cranmer was quickly appointed Archbishop of Canterbury, and within two weeks penned a request to King Henry to hear his case—an obvious sign of where Cranmer's loyalties lay. Bypassing Rome, on May 23, 1533, Cranmer, servant of the crown, would give his judgment in England's ecclesiastical court that Henry's marriage to Catherine was null and void from the very beginning, and therefore his marriage to Anne was licit.

48 Scarisbrick, *Henry VIII*, p. 261.

49 Ibid., p. 273.

50 Ibid., p. 290.

Anne was, of course, not to be the last of Henry's wives, nor of his even longer string of mistresses. But her brief reign as queen changed everything: the state (rather than papal) annulment of Henry's marriage marks the turning point at which the Church *in* England becomes the Church *of* England. The creation of a purely national church was made all the more necessary because, upon hearing of Cranmer's annulment and Henry's marriage, Pope Clement condemned both and excommunicated Henry in July 1533.

Denying the papacy's right to hear the case was no longer enough. About a year and a half after Archbishop Cranmer had Henry's marriage to Catherine annulled, Parliament passed the Act of Supremacy (November 1534):

> Albeit the King's Majesty justly and rightfully is and oweth to be the Supreme Head of the Church of England, and so is recognized by the clergy of this realm in their Convocations, yet nevertheless for corroboration and confirmation thereof, and for increase of virtue in Christ's religion within this realm of England, and to repress and extirp all errors, heresies, and other enormities and abuses heretofore used in the same; be it enacted by authority of this present Parliament, that the King our Sovereign Lord, his heirs and successors, kings of this realm, shall be taken, accepted, and reputed the only Supreme Head on earth of the Church of England, called *Anglicana Ecclesia*. . . .[51]

By this act, the spiritual and political powers were fused in the king (or would be soon enough), and it became simultaneously a treason to commit heresy—and even more ominously, a kind of heresy to commit treason by denouncing his Supreme Headship (as the martyrs John Fisher and Thomas More were soon to find out). Further, the act contained all the ambiguity that would give rise to a decisively political interpretation of Scripture, which must be made to speak unambiguously on its behalf.

Whatever their private motivations, Henry and Parliament intended the king's supremacy to appear as a return to the situation of the great emperors, especially Constantine and Justinian, but also to mythical English kings—all of whom were in turn modeled upon Old Testament kings. But since Henry was the king of England, not the emperor of Christendom, the universality of the *Ecclesia* had to be restricted and re-formed by the *Anglicana*; that is, the universality of the Church had to be qualified, in the deepest sense, by the English political situation (a situation that, like all such things political, would undergo many changes). The King's Great Matter put Henry in place to take the advice of Marsilius and Machiavelli, as mediated to him by his ministers.

Machiavelli, Marsilius, and the Henrician Apologists

Much scholarly debate has centered upon whether or how much Henry VIII (through Cromwell) was influenced by Machiavelli's arguments. Machiavelli had written *The*

51 Gerald Bray, ed., *Documents of the English Reformation* (Minneapolis, MN: Fortress Press, 1994), pp. 113–114.

Prince in 1513, less than five years after Henry VIII became king, and probably finished the *Discourses* in 1517, the year Luther initiated the Reformation. In the year of Machiavelli's death, 1527, a new group of scholars were gathered under the patronage of Wolsey for his new college, men who after Wolsey's fall would become the political apologists for Henry's new order. These young men were likely picked under the guidance of Edward Foxe, who would become (in 1530) the continental agent of Henry's divorce and who would write one of the great apologies for royal supremacy, *De Vera Differentia Regiae Potestatis et Ecclesiasticae* (in 1534), a treatise that appeals at length to Scripture (as well as to the Fathers and certain medievals) to demonstrate that the king is the rightful head of the Church.[52] Among these scholars were Richard Morison, who would freely use Machiavelli in helping to form and justify Henry's policies, and Thomas Starkey, who would use Marsilius's *Defensor Pacis* as the political template for Henrician reform.

Morison and Starkey belonged to a larger group of scholars who spent a significant time in the household of Reginald Pole. In 1519 (and again in 1521) Pole had been sent to study in Italy under the patronage of Henry VIII, settling in Padua. With the fall of Wolsey, his flock of scholars scattered from England, and "by one means or another, they began to appear in Italy during the years after Wolsey's fall, either in the household of Thomas Winter, Wolsey's natural son who gravitated discontentedly between London, Paris, and Padua, or in that of Reginald Pole, whose house in Padua had already become a center for English students in Italy."[53]

Padua was a great center of learning, and was strongly Averroist, even more so in the sixteenth century than it had been in the fourteenth. In Padua, scholars had easy access, not only to ancient classics, but to the works of Padua's famous son Marsilius and also to Machiavelli's books as they came off the presses.[54] Pole was quite generous in his support of young (and often quite poor) scholars, and his own international reputation as a scholar and patron of learning approached that of Thomas More. With the downfall of Wolsey, it became politically important for Henry to get Pole to declare himself in regard to the King's Great Matter. Publicly, Pole was able to evade explicit declaration for several years, but privately, his mind was set against Henry by a now-famous meeting in 1528 with the new definer of policy, Thomas Cromwell. In it, he made "the discovery that henceforth the guide for English policy would not be Plato [as Pole might have hoped] but Machiavelli."[55]

This famous meeting has been thoroughly worked over by scholars, some going so far as to assert that it was merely a fiction later contrived by Pole's overheated mind, and also that Cromwell would have had no access to Machiavelli's works at that early

52 Elton, *Policy and Police*, p. 182.

53 W. Gordon Zeeveld, *Foundations of Tudor Policy* (London: Methuen & Co., Ltd., 1969), pp. 37–38. For a lively account of Pole's household as the breeding place for Tudor policy under Henry, see the entirety of Zeeveld's Ch. 3.

54 Ibid., p. 46.

55 Ibid., p. 76.

date, since the official first publication date was 1532.[56] However, handwritten copies of Machiavelli's works circulated long before they were officially published (at least three Italian booksellers were busily pirating editions of Machiavelli's *Prince* in the 1520s). There was also a well-traveled route between England and Italy along which the English humanists moved back and forth. Whether Cromwell himself obtained a copy that early, it was available to the English scholars at Padua, including Richard Morison—who was well acquainted with Machiavelli and would make use of his arguments in helping define policy under Cromwell from 1536 onward.

The accusation that Cromwell was well acquainted with Machiavelli prior to this was made by Pole in a later account of a meeting with Cromwell in his *Apologia ad Carolum Quintum*, written in 1539, eleven years after the meeting. In it, Pole asserted that Cromwell offered him a copy of Machiavelli's *Prince*. As a consequence of this meeting and after several years reflection, Pole became quite convinced that Cromwell had corrupted the king with Machiavelli's counsels, and that events as they unfolded after 1528—from the annulment, the declaration of supremacy, the official break with Rome, the violent and greedy suppression and despoiling of the monasteries, and the murder of political opponents of the caliber of Thomas More and John Fisher (as well as members of Pole's own family)—were all the result of Machiavelli's satanic influence (via Cromwell) on King Henry. Pole had certainly read Machiavelli's *Prince* thoroughly. As Felix Raab points out, "there is nothing surprising in the fact that Pole should condemn the author as an enemy of mankind," and "still less surprising that Pole should associate Machiavelli with Satan, and Thomas Cromwell with both."[57]

In a letter to the Privy Council by 1540, John Leigh informed them that Pole had warned him that Machiavelli "had already poisoned England and would poison all Christendom."[58] We also have at least some corroborating evidence of this poison near the crown. In 1537 Henry Lord Morley sent Thomas Cromwell an Italian copy of Machiavelli's *Florentine Histories*, recommending especially the example of Florentine rebellion against Rome. "As the King's cause is somewhat like, note how little the Florentines reputed the Romish bishop's [Clement VII] cursings. Show the very words to the King; his Majesty will be pleased to see them."[59] But even more illuminating, as Morley wrote to Cromwell, "This book of Machiavelli *De Principe* is surely a very special good thing for your Lordship which are so nigh about our sovereign lord in counsel to look upon for many causes, as I suppose your self shall judge when ye have seen the same."[60]

Had Cromwell already seen a copy of *The Prince*? We know only that Morley, who knew Cromwell, supposed Machiavelli's advice would accord well with Henry's desires

56 For an account of the vagaries and current state of scholarship on this issue see Peter Donaldson, *Machiavelli and Mystery of State* (Cambridge: Cambridge University Press, 1988), Ch. 1.

57 Felix Raab, *The English Face of Machiavelli* (London: Routledge & Kegan Paul, 1964), p. 31.

58 Quoted in Zeeveld, *Foundations of Tudor Policy*, p. 14.

59 Victoria Kahn, *Machiavellian Rhetoric from the Counter-Reformation to Milton* (Princeton: Princeton University Press, 1994), p. 136.

60 Quoted in Donaldson, *Machiavelli and Mystery of State*, p. 32.

and Cromwell's policies, and that neither Henry nor Cromwell would be insulted by the suggestions. Pole can hardly be blamed for seeing parallels between Henry VIII's actions and policies and the blunt political advice of Machiavelli. "Whether Cromwell had read *Il Principe* [*The Prince*] when he spoke to Pole in 1528, whether he read it later, whether he ever read it all—to Pole, Cromwell was the practical manifestation of Machiavellian doctrine, the result of a conscious divorce between spiritual values and political conduct."[61]

All in all, then, it might be historically safer to consider Machiavelli in terms of *justification* of those actions and policies, rather than their initial cause. As Zeeveld states, "Essentially, Henry's problem was to discover theoretic warrant for a *fait accompli* without the sacrifice of catholicity or conformity." [62] Such would be in the spirit of Machiavelli himself, whose theory is molded according to what successful princes *actually do* to obtain and maintain power. In believing Machiavelli to be the cause, Pole was perhaps seeing him as the best "theoretical" justification after the fact, and it can hardly be denied that the policies pursued by Henry and his closest advisors conforms to the dicta of "reason of state." Ironically, it was the young scholars of Pole's own circle in Padua who offered their services to Henry and Cromwell, and "it was because of their efforts that expediency found justification in theory."[63] Morison, Starkey, and the other royal apologists "accepted the royal supremacy as an established fact and turned their efforts to providing it with a logical and historical *raison d'être*."[64]

From 1536 on, Machiavelli did indeed exert influence through Morison.[65] Richard Morison was born in extreme poverty and rose to wealth and prominence. His rise as spokesman for royal supremacy came about during the "conservative" religious rebellion (called the Pilgrimage of Grace) against the king's policies in October 1536. Morison's government propaganda from this point and thereafter references Machiavelli's works, and his "most 'Machiavellian' work," *A Remedy for Sedition*, was written as a response to the Pilgrimage.[66] Given that both Henry and Cromwell exerted direct and continual editorial influence on whatever was published from the government presses, clearly both of them approved. Zeeveld concludes that, "the quality of Morison's mind is best represented by his familiarity with the works of . . . Niccolò Machiavelli. Of the impact of that powerful mind on Morison, and through him on the political policy of Cromwell, there is no longer room for doubt."[67] This influence would continue well beyond 1536, as Morison would rise in the ranks to become Cromwell's secretary, a member of Parliament, and finally, a member of the inmost political circle,

61 Raab, *The English Face of Machiavelli*, p. 32.

62 Zeeveld, *Foundations of Tudor Policy*, p. 113.

63 Ibid.

64 Ibid., p. 121.

65 1536 being the very year that Pole officially broke with Henry, sending him in May his scathing criticism of the king's policies, the *Pro Ecclesiasticae Unitatis Defensione*: *On the Defense of Unity of the Church*.

66 Raab, *The English Face of Machiavelli*, p. 38. As we will note below, Raab backs away from affirming the Machiavellian influence upon Morison as strongly as Zeeveld does.

67 Zeeveld, *Foundations of Tudor Policy*, p. 184.

the Privy Chamber, all the while "writing propaganda under the surveillance of both Cromwell and the King and publishing from the King's press," and in these official capacities, Morison "knew and made habitual use of his knowledge of Machiavelli's political works in the practical business of politics."[68] Raab, however, observes that Morison betrayed an odd mix of Machiavellianism and fairly conventional piety (with "Protestant leanings").[69] One of the chief aims of Henry's propaganda was to convince the restless population, in part through appeals to Scripture, that disobedience to the king was disobedience to God.[70] The title of a later tract written by Morison against Pole illustrates the general tenor of his approach: *An Invective agenste the great and detestable vice, treason* (1539), wherein he defended the royal supremacy, in part on scriptural grounds of absolute obedience to the king.

However much Machiavelli came to matter, Marsilius of Padua's influence was even more direct and pervasive.[71] "In articulating the arguments for a national church directed by Henry, there was a wide search by Henrician polemicists for earlier works that developed a theory of national sovereignty. Chief among these was the *Defensor Pacis* of Marsilius." The case for royal supremacy over a national church demanded both a denial of the papacy and a complete subordination of church to state within the realm. Cromwell found the arguments of Marsilius of Padua to be most beneficial, and a number of disciples of Marsilius were employed in Henry's defense, notably Thomas Starkey, Edward Foxe, Richard Sampson, William Marshall, and Stephen Gardiner, as well as a "score of lesser known or anonymous pamphleteers."[72] As historian Paul O'Grady notes, whether all these apologists were "directly inspired by the *Defensor Pacis* or not," their various arguments share the commonality of being "cast in the

68 Ibid., p. 189.

69 Raab, *The English Face of Machiavelli*, pp. 36–40.

70 On the propaganda campaign see Elton, *Policy and Police*, Ch. 4.

71 Dickens even claims that Marsilius was more the author of Henrician erastianism than Wycliffe. Dickens, *The English Reformation*, pp. 106–108,118–123, 131, 195–199. Some scholars have come to doubt this connection, for example, Thomas Mayer, *Thomas Starkey and the Commonweal: Humanist Politics and Religion in the Reign of Henry VIII* (Cambridge: Cambridge University Press, 1989), Ch. 5. For an analysis of the debate (as seen through the eyes of a doubter) and bibliography, see Francis Oakley, "Conciliarism in England: St. German, Starkey, and the Marsiglian Myth," in Thomas M. Izbicki and Christopher M. Bellitto, *Reform and Renewal in the Middle Ages and the Renaissance* (Leiden: Brill, 2000), pp. 224–239. Oakley's case is based on two considerations: the first, that evidence for influence is often based upon similarities between the arguments of particular Henrician reformers and the arguments of Marsilius, rather than direct, acknowledged textual dependence; and the second, that the kinds of arguments purported to come from Marsilius could just as well have come from conciliarist thinkers like Jean Gerson, whom some reformers specifically name. In response, we note that appeal to councils over the pope was found both in Ockham and in Marsilius, so pointing out conciliarist tendencies as an alternative source would hardly count against at least indirect influence by Marsilius. But since we do have direct evidence of the presence of Marsilius's works in England, and Wycliffe's position seems to duplicate that of Marsilius in many respects, then it is fair to assume both a direct and indirect influence of Marsilius.

72 Paul O'Grady, *Henry VIII and the Conforming Catholics* (Collegeville, MN: The Liturgical Press, 1990), p. 42. O'Grady's analysis in Chapter 3 of the Marsilian roots of the apologists of Henry's reform is essential reading.

Marsiglian mold."[73] Those who relied on Marsilius directly, such as Starkey, "no doubt read him in the original Latin, then transcribed the essence of this thought in terms appropriate to Henrician reality."[74]

However early Cromwell himself had read Marsilius, by the mid 1530s he found his arguments compelling enough to ensure the publication of an English translation of the *Defensor Pacis* (done by William Marshall, who had also translated the very useful attack on the *Donation of Constantine* by Lorenzo Valla in 1534,[75] some fifteen years after Hutten presented Luther with his German edition). Only "four days after the first English edition of the *Defensor Pacis* was completed under Cromwell's subsidy [on July 27, 1535], Starkey, acting as Cromwell's agent, sent a copy to Reginald Pole in Padua in an effort to elicit a favorable opinion on the divorce." In a letter to Pole accompanying the copy, Starkey wrote in typical Marsilian mode that Christ did not found a kingdom of this world, and hence left worldly governance to kings, and that the policy of royal supremacy "schalbe somewhat in your mynd confermyd by the redyng of Marsilius, whome I take, though he were in style rude, yet to be of a grete jugement, & wel & gud reysonsys groundyd in phylosophy."[76] Unbeknownst to Henry and his partisans, Reginald Pole had long ago already made up his mind against Henry and the new order.

In contrast to Pole, Thomas Starkey happily embraced both Marsilius and the role of apologist for Henry's new order. As with Morison, he wrote his apologetic works with the "closest possible cooperation with both Cromwell and Henry."[77] An interesting and illuminating vignette, Starkey's apologetic tract, *An exhortation to the people, instructynge theym to unitie and obedience* (published in 1536), was returned for a rewrite by Cromwell because (in Starkey's words) Henry "dyd not gretely approve hyt [it], saying hyt was not drawen out of scrypture."[78] The appeal to Scripture was especially important because Starkey's arguments represent the first presentation of "the Anglican *via media*," wherein many things previously thought to be essential are termed "things indifferent," or *adiaphora*—one of the designated items of indifference being Petrine supremacy. Starkey argues that the authority to remove things to indifference is scriptural: "things indifferent I call all such things which by God's word are neither prohibited or commanded . . . but left to worldly policy whereof they take their full authority. . . ."[79] Thus Scripture, for Starkey, seemed to support a Marsilian prince.

Beyond all these direct connections, the general parallels between Marsilius's arguments and Cromwell's policies are striking, to say the least.[80] While Starkey and

73 Ibid., p. 61.

74 Ibid., p. 43.

75 Elton, *Policy and Police*, p. 186.

76 Zeeveld, *Foundations of Tudor Policy*, pp. 133–135.

77 Ibid., p. 142.

78 Quoted in Zeeveld, *Foundations of Tudor Policy*, p. 147.

79 Quoted in Elton, *Policy and Police*, p. 193.

80 See especially Harry S. Stout, "Marsilius of Padua and the Henrician Reformation," *Church History* (1974), 43, pp. 308–318.

others supplied supportive arguments, Cromwell was the true architect of Henry's declaration of supremacy, and the steps by which it came to be formally expressed, and then implemented, bear more than surface resemblance to Marsilian ideas. As with the *Defensor Pacis*, Cromwell asserted that royal supremacy was absolutely necessary for civil peace, so that "the King our Sovereign Lord . . . shall be taken accepted and reputed the only Supreme Head in Earth of the Church in England . . . for the conservation of the Peace Unity and Tranquility of this Realm."[81] Recall, moreover, that Cromwell himself was not an ecclesiastic, and in his capacity as appointed vicar-general "denied all clerical coercive authority and himself personified temporal sovereignty in ecclesiastical areas" as "the church's court of last appeal. Cromwell's policy was aimed at both the institution and doctrines of the English church in an attempt to effect the total subordination of church to state."[82]

Not surprisingly, this total subordination included the authority to judge cases of matrimony, and Cromwell relied on Marsilius's arguments on behalf of Ludwig of Bavaria, contained in the *Defensor Minor*, that only the human legislator is empowered to judge concerning the validity and dissolution of marriages, and all ecclesiastical expressions of power to the contrary are groundless.[83] Of course, the arguments of the *Defensor Minor* were based on those of the *Defensor Pacis*. Perhaps no advice of Marsilius was so readily received as that found in the *Defensor Minor,* which gave theoretical justification for the dissolution of Henry's marriage to Catherine.

81 Quoted in ibid., p. 310.

82 Ibid., pp. 311–312.

83 In the *Defensor Minor* Marsilius argued (in true Averroistic form) that divine law and human law had entirely different ends, "the best end or condition in the future world" and "the best end or condition . . . in this world." As with the *Defensor Pacis*, ecclesiastics have no secular, coercive power at all (including power over marriages), and he cited Scripture in his defense (II Timothy 2:4; I Corinthians 3:3, 6:4; II Corinthians 1:24). After some roundabout reasoning, Marsilius declared that the validity of marriage should be judged by "the human legislator" who, having coercive power, also has the power of "pronouncing judgement regarding whether the dissolution of the marriage is to occur or not"—adding that, "there must be conformity in this with divine law." But since ultimately the secular arm calls the councils and sends its members, and the council determines the meaning of Scripture, it is not difficult to see the deck stacked for the secular arm. If that were not enough, Marsilius argued that marriage "is not primarily a spiritual matter," that is, a sacrament, "but it can be called spiritual because it is a *sign or representation* of a spiritual matter. . . ." Marsiglio of Padua, *Defensor Minor* in Cary Nederman, ed., *Writings on the Empire:* Defensor minor *and* De Translatione Imperii (Cambridge: Cambridge University Press, 1993), 1.2–4 (pp. 1–2), 2.6 (pp. 5–6), 12.2 (p. 40), 15.9–10 (pp. 58–59, emphasis added). See also Stout, "Marsilius of Padua and the Henrician Reformation," p. 314. The context for Marsilius's reasoning in regard to marriage are illuminating. Pope John XXII died in 1334, to be replaced by Benedict XII. Sometime during 1339–1341, Marsilius was working on several other writings, collected in his *Defensor Minor*, a treatise that would also prove to be of much importance in the coming centuries. Sometime around 1339, Ludwig asked Marsilius his opinion in regard to a particular quandary. Ludwig desired that his son, also named Ludwig, marry Margaret Maultasch, the Countess of Tyrol (wishing to have Tyrol, the southern part of the Duchy of Bavaria, under his political control). Two obstacles blocked this marriage: first of all, Margaret was already married to Prince John Henry of Bohemia, although since they were married (in 1330) at the ages of twelve and ten respectively, the marital union was reported to be unconsummated. Secondly, there was a problem of consanguinity, since Margaret's grandmother and Ludwig's grandfather were sister and brother. Finally, given that Ludwig had been excommunicated and placed under interdict, there was no hope of papal cooperation in a dispensation.

There is also a distinctly Marsilian tone in the famous *Act in Restraint of Appeals* (1533) crafted by Cromwell, which distinguished historian A. G. Dickens considers to be a document that summarized the doctrine of Marsilius's *Defensor Pacis* "in a few masterly phrases."[84] In the *Act* Cromwell declared that "this realm of England is an empire, and so hath been accepted in the world," and is "governed by one supreme head and king," and henceforth "all causes testamentary, causes of matrimony and divorces, rights of tithes, oblations and obventions . . . shall be from henceforth heard, examined, discussed, clearly, finally, and definitively adjudged and determined within the king's jurisdiction and authority and not elsewhere, in such courts spiritual and temporal of the same. . . ." Consequently, "any foreign inhibitions, appeals, sentences, summons, citations, suspensions, interdictions, excommunications, restraints, judgments, or any other process or impediments, of what natures, names, qualities, or conditions soever they be, from the see of Rome, or any other foreign courts or potentates of the world, or from and out of this realm, or any other the king's dominions, or marches of the same, to the see of Rome, or to any other foreign courts or potentates, to the let or impediment thereof in any wise notwithstanding" are null and void.

There are other parallels. Starkey, following Marsilius, defined law primarily in terms of its coercive power. Insofar as they have the proper form of law, issued by a coercive power, they are legitimate.[85] Of course, in accord with Marsilius and Cromwell, only the secular power could be an agent of coercion. In an important respect, the royal supremacy went beyond Marsilius because, unlike Marsilius, Henry conceived power as united in him, not emanating from the people, and carried out by a Parliament under his complete control. For this reason, "Cromwell could not go as far as Marsilius on the issue of checking the king's authority, and instructed Marshall to dilute the translation of the *Defensor Pacis* by omitting the section on punishing the unjust ruler." To get around Marsilius's frequent references to the people as ultimately authoritative, "Marshall consistently translated Marsilius' term the 'people' to mean 'not of the rascall multitude, but of the parlyament.'"[86] But it was Henry's Parliament.

Even for Henry's infamous dissolution of the monasteries, closing of shrines, and the seizure of their wealth for the crown, there is ample Marsilian precedent. While disendowment was a constant cause for Wycliffe and the Lollards, before them, Marsilius had argued (in the context of the poverty controversies) that, for its own good, the Church should be stripped of its wealth. Undoubtedly, then, Cromwell was the great engineer of the entire program of subordination of the Church, and a significant part of the theoretical justification came from Marsilius.[87]

For his own part, Henry was quite deft, even Machiavellian, in justifying his actions as religiously motivated. Because of the various theological factions, he was able to defend disendowment and seizure as religious reform. He could play on the

84 Dickens, *The English Reformation*, p. 131.

85 Stout, "Marsilius of Padua and the Henrician Reformation," p. 311.

86 Ibid., p. 312.

87 Ibid., p. 131.

iconoclasm of the reformers and their cries against idolatry, as well as their animosity toward religious orders, in justifying his shutting down of shrines. Henry certainly profited from this undertaking; the shrines were great pickings, as is made clear in the despoiling of the shrine of England's most famous saint, Thomas Becket. "Twenty-six wagon-loads of wealth were plundered from Becket's shrine and taken to the Mint and the bones of the saint who had opposed Henry Plantaganet were scattered by order of Henry Tudor," notes historian Neville Williams. Henry used it to build a great monument to his monarchy, Nonsuch Palace, which rose not just on the wealth of the monasteries but on their very stones, which were used to build it. In the inner court of Nonsuch, there was a massive statue of Henry on the throne.[88]

Machiavelli and Marsilius, then, exerted significant influence on Henrician policy, at bare minimum providing justification after the fact for Henry's Caesaropapism. But more importantly, both thinkers' arguments and fundamentally secular world-view entered the English mind. Perhaps this is more the case for Machiavelli than for Marsilius in the long run, given the enormous influence Machiavelli's "republican" arguments, mainly from his *Discourses*, would have upon English republicans such as Marchamont Nedham, James Harrington, Henry Neville, and Algernon Sidney during the English Revolution of the mid-seventeenth century.[89] Essential to this influence (as we shall examine it, gathered up and radicalized even further in the arguments of John Toland after the Revolution) is the Machiavellian treatment of religion as not true but useful in keeping the masses under control. This will entail an even more radical approach to the politicization of Scripture than that found among the Henricians, one that decisively formed the first recognizably modern scriptural exegetical assumptions and methods.

The declaration of royal supremacy put the English Church entirely under the jurisdiction of the English state. Henry wanted his control to come directly from God, so that he was the lord over both parliament and the church—and as lord over the latter, he was lord over Scripture as well. This is made stunningly clear in the frontispiece for the 1539 Great Bible that featured King Henry, secure on his throne, handing down a copy of the Bible to both Archbishops Cranmer and Cromwell, the Church and state. God himself floats approvingly over the scene, speaking the words of Acts 13:22, "I have found a man after my own heart, who shall perform all my desire." In later editions, since Cromwell himself was erased by Henry, the printer had to follow suit.[90]

In asserting such complete supremacy, Henry manifested powers of the Machiavellian prince. Because of his peculiar historical situation and his particular

88 Williams, *Henry VIII and His Court*, pp. 165–166.

89 There is a significant body of literature dealing with the influence of Machiavelli during this period. See, for example, not only the above–cited Raab, *The English Face of Machiavelli*, and Kahn, *Machiavellian Rhetoric From the Counter–Reformation to Milton*, but also J.G.A. Pocock, *The Machiavellian Moment: Florentine Political Thought and the Atlantic Republican Tradition* (Princeton: Princeton University Press, 1975); Vickie Sullivan, *Machiavelli, Hobbes, and the Formation of a Liberal Republicanism in England* (Cambridge: Cambridge University Press, 2004); and Paul Rahe, ed., *Machiavelli's Liberal Republican Legacy* (Cambridge: Cambridge University Press, 2006).

90 Bobrick, *Wide as the Waters*, pp. 150–157.

aims, he found himself faced with the necessity of founding (in Machiavelli's words) "new modes and orders." Precisely because it was not just a political issue but theological as well, to obtain the divorce it was necessary that Henry become like one of Machiavelli's great founders (Moses, Cyrus, Theseus, and Romulus), with the power of both prince and prophet, who sanctions his new mode and order by direct appeal to divine origin and sanction (in Henry's case, by divine right of kings as supported through selective appeal to the Old Testament kings as priests and to the New Testament call for subordination to Caesar). In contrast to Machiavelli's assertion that, in the use of religion to sanction one's founding, "it is easy to persuade them of something, but difficult to keep them in that persuasion," Henry found both undertakings difficult. For this reason, Machiavelli's consequent advice ("And thus things must be ordered in such a mode that when they no longer believe, one can make them believe by force") became all the more necessary to follow.

The Marsilian elements became marked as well, more in relationship to Cromwell and his circle, rather than Henry himself. The declaration of royal supremacy was an act of parliament, which Cromwell understood to be acting as the great secular legislator over the Church. Contrary to the king himself, Cromwell tended to portray Henry's supremacy as something conferred upon him by Parliament—in conformity with Marsilian principles of secular sovereignty as well as English traditions of ascendant parliamentary power (that is, from the people, to Parliament, to the king).[91] Whatever Cromwell's private difference with Henry, both were in agreement that the state was to exercise complete control over the Church, and from the mid-1530s until his fall, Cromwell himself "held unlimited ecclesiastical jurisdiction in England, subject only to the King's pleasure."[92]

Playing Out of Royal Supremacy

The very same year that Parliament passed the Act of Supremacy and Henry's marriage to Anne was made secure (1534), Henry had already shifted his desires to Jane Seymour. Catherine of Aragon died in early January 1536, and in mid-May of that same year Anne Boleyn was beheaded on charges of adultery (which, by convoluted reasoning, was an act of treason). Cromwell had been the agent of this queen's removal as well. Two days before her execution, Archbishop Cranmer was able to rule in court that Henry's intercourse with Anne's sister had rendered null his marriage to Anne after all (in accordance with a compliant interpretation of Leviticus), and on the day she was beheaded Cranmer offered a dispensation from consanguinity for Henry so that he could marry Jane Seymour (which he did eleven days later). Now that Henry was supreme head of the church, things could move quite quickly. Jane Seymour would die in October of the following year, giving Henry his male heir, Edward VI.

91 Scarisbrick, *Henry VIII*, pp. 393–397.

92 Dickens, *The English Reformation*, p. 143.

Anne of the German Duchy of Cleves, a Lutheran, would be Henry's next wife, a suitable political-theological alliance, as the Protestant-leaning Thomas Cromwell thought, given that her older sister was married to Elector John Frederick of Saxony, a great champion of the reformers. Upon seeing her in person, Henry took an immediate dislike to Anne (which initiated Cromwell's decline), but not wanting to offend the Germans, he married her on January 6, 1540, and had the marriage annulled six months later. Henry married Catherine Howard less than a month after the annulment—in fact, the very day that Thomas Cromwell was beheaded. In February 1542, Catherine was executed on grounds of adultery, hence treason, and buried near the chapel where Anne Boleyn lay.

Henry now had time to turn at least some of his attention to matters of the church, one result being the *King's Book*, published at the end of May 1543 (less than two months before Henry would marry his final wife, Catherine Parr). Its actual title was the more cumbersome *A Necessary Doctrine and Erudition for Any Christian Man; Set Forth by the King's Majesty of England, &c*. The *King's Book* replaced the *Bishops' Book* of 1537 (the actual title of the latter being *The Institution of a Christian Man*), and received its name because Henry himself provided the introduction. Somewhat echoing Luther's troubles, Henry complained that, now that Rome had been ousted and "God's truth" had been opened by "setting forth and publishing of the scriptures," the cleansed house was being reinvaded by new demons citing Scripture to their various causes: "hypocrisy and superstition being excluded and put away, we find entered into some of our people's hearts an inclination to sinister understanding of scripture, presumption, arrogancy, carnal liberty and contention . . ."[93] In short, publication of the Scriptures in English caused an immediate upswell of rival interpretations that were upsetting peace and contradicting the official interpretation, and so:

> [W]e be therefore constrained, for the reformation of them in time, and for avoiding of such diversity in opinions as by the said evil spirits might be engendered, to set forth, with the advice of our clergy, such a doctrine and declaration of the true knowledge of God and his word, with the principal articles of our religion, as whereby all men may uniformly be led and taught the true understanding of that which is necessary for every Christian man to know, for the ordering of himself in this life, agreeably to the will and pleasure of Almighty God.[94]

To make sure the house stayed clean, the *King's Book* was to be the official lens through which the English version of the Scripture was to be read. In Henry's words, "this book containeth a perfect and sufficient doctrine, grounded and established in holy scripture,"[95] the implication, of course, being that it was now impermissible to believe that "holy scripture" would establish doctrine in any other way. To enforce

93 T. A. Lacy, ed., *The King's Book, or A Necessary Doctrine and Erudition for Any Christian Man, 1543* (London: Society for Promoting Christian Knowledge, 1932), Preface, p. 3.

94 Ibid., p. 4.

95 Ibid., p. 5.

this, Henry put the Bible into the hands of the official clergy, ministers of the king, but bid the laity to take from Scripture what the clergy fed them. The clergy, the teachers, were to have full access to

> both the Old and New Testament . . . but for the other part of the church, ordained to be taught, it ought to be deemed certainly, that the reading of the Old and New Testament is not so necessary for all those folks, that of duty they ought to be bound to read it, but as the prince and the policy of the realm shall think convenient, so to be tolerated or taken from it. Consonant whereunto the politic law of our realm hath now restrained it from a great many, esteeming it sufficient for those so restrained to hear and truly bear away the doctrine of scripture taught by the preachers. . . .[96]

As one can imagine, in the treatment of the Creed, the ninth article dealing with "The holy catholic church" is rather lengthy, given what it must both assert and deny. The explanation envisions a system of national churches "in divers countries" which

> for their most necessary government, as they be distinct in places, so they have distinct ministers and divers heads in earth, governors and rulers, yet be all these holy churches but one holy church catholic, invited and called by one God the Father to enjoy the benefit of redemption wrought by our only Lord and Saviour Jesu Christ, and governed by one Holy Spirit, which teacheth to this foresaid holy church one truth of God's holy word in one faith and baptism.[97]

Their unity "standeth not by knowledging of one governor in earth over all churches," therefore, "the unity . . . of the church is not conserved by the bishop of Rome's authority or doctrine" but "by the help and assistance of the Holy Spirit of God, in retaining and maintaining of such doctrine and profession of Christian faith, and true observance of the same, as is taught by the scripture and the doctrine apostolic." Each national church that does "inviolably . . . observe the same may be worthily called (as it is indeed) an apostolic church. . . ."[98] Therefore the church of Rome is, at best, like the "church of France, Spain, England, or Portugal," one more national church.[99] The pope, however, unjustly claims to rule all the other national churches, "and doth wrest scripture for that purpose, contrary both to the true meaning of the same, and the interpretation of ancient doctors of the church; so that by that challenge he would not do wrong only to this church of England, but also to all other churches, in claiming this superiority without any authority by God so to him given. . . ."[100] Of course, the affirmation of a system of national churches opens up a difficulty, since they obviously have a "diversity

96 Ibid., p. 6.
97 Ibid., p. 33.
98 Ibid., p. 34.
99 Ibid., p. 35.
100 Ibid., pp. 35–36.

of traditions . . . alteration in rites, ceremonies, and ordinances."[101] Since this diversity is merely national, what depth of allegiance does one owe to the national church? The *King's Book* asserts that

> every Christian man ought to honour, give credence, and to follow the particular church of that region . . . wherein he is born or inhabiteth. And as all Christian people, as well spiritual as temporal, be bound to believe, honour and obey, next unto himself, Christian kings and princes, which be the head governors under him in the particular churches, to whose office it appertaineth not only to provide for the tranquility and wealth of their subjects in temporal and worldly things, to the conservation of their bodies, but also to foresee that within their dominions such ministers be ordained and appointed in their churches as can and will truly and purely set out the true doctrine of Christ. . . .[102]

One can hardly imagine a more Marsilian account of the lordship of the ruler over the church, except that for Marsilius this was the emperor while for Henry it was the national king. The difficulty with the formula was twofold. The actual diversity among the different national churches seemed to strike at the purported unity. If one happened to be born in Luther's Wittenberg, matrimony would not be a sacrament, but if one were born in Henry's realm, it would (at least in 1543, as declared in the *King's Book*). Yet both claimed scriptural and apostolic support. A second difficulty would become obvious soon after the death of Henry in January 1547, when those of a more radical religious bent would surface and push the new, more feeble King Edward VI, and hence the Church of England, to a more Zwinglian theology.

As the subsequent history of England makes amply clear, transfer of doctrinal control to the king could not help but end in doctrine suffering political definition by whatever kings and queens succeeded Henry. Since scriptural interpretation was one of the primary modes of authorizing the course of each successive monarch as "Supreme Head of the Church of England," we should not be surprised to find that, given the subsequent history of England, exegesis in service to the monarchy will display a startling, even humorous malleability.

Part of the humor is caught in that famous and mischievous song, "The Vicar of Bray," which celebrates in broader terms the theological flexibility of an all-too-typical English clergyman bent on keeping his post no matter which way the political (and hence, religious) winds blow.

> In good King Charles's golden days,
> When loyalty had no harm in't,
> A zealous High Churchman I was,
> And so I gained preferment.
> To teach my flock I never missed:
> Kings were by God appointed;

---

101 Ibid., p. 35.

102 Ibid., pp. 36–37.

And they are damned who dare resist
Or touch the Lord's anointed.

And this is law I will maintain
Until my dying day, sir,
That whatsoever King shall reign,
I'll be Vicar of Bray, sir.

When Royal James obtained the Throne,
And Popery grew in fashion,
The Penal Law I hooted down,
And read the Declaration;
The Church of Rome I found would fit
Full well my constitution;
And I had been a Jesuit
But for the Revolution.

And this is law I will maintain
Until my dying day, sir,
That whatsoever King shall reign,
I'll be Vicar of Bray, sir.

When William, our deliverer, came
To heal the nation's grievance,
Then I turned cat-in-pan again,
And swore to him allegiance
Old principles I did revoke,
Set conscience at a distance,
Passive obedience was a joke,
A jest was non-resistance.

And this is law I will maintain
Until my dying day, sir,
That whatsoever King shall reign,
I'll be Vicar of Bray, sir.

When glorious Anne became our Queen,
The Church of England's glory,
Another face of things was seen,
And I became a Tory.
Occasional Conformist Face!
I damned such moderation;
And thought the Church in danger was
By such prevarication.

And this is law I will maintain
Until my dying day, sir,
That whatsoever King shall reign,
I'll be Vicar of Bray, sir.

When George in pudding-time came o'er
And moderate men looked big, sir,
My principles I changed once more,
And so became a Whig, sir;
And thus preferment I procured
From our Faith's great Defender;
And almost every day abjured
The Pope and the Pretender.

And this is law I will maintain
Until my dying day, sir,
That whatsoever King shall reign,
I'll be Vicar of Bray, sir.

The illustrious House of Hanover,
And Protestant Succession,
By these I lustily will swear
While they can keep possession
For in my faith and loyalty
I never once will falter,
But George my King shall ever be,
Except the times do alter.

And this is law I will maintain
Until my dying day, sir,
That whatsoever King shall reign,
I'll be Vicar of Bray, sir.

It is noteworthy that the time period covered in this song begins with the reign of Charles II (1660–1685), and ends with the reign of George I (1714–1727). Almost two centuries after Henry's death, the vagaries of politics in England were still determining the verities of doctrine. Needless to say, rival parties used rival scriptural texts and arguments. But the result of such continual doctrinal revolutions was not amusing, as theological opponents became political enemies, and those on the outside were often viciously persecuted and violently killed.

A way out of the dilemma had to be found, and in fact, soon enough, two ways were attempted: one that more radically affirmed the political control of doctrine by the sovereign so that peace would be achieved by force, and another that trivialized doctrinal differences so that peace could be achieved by indifference. In both cases, peace was the highest goal. Both ways would have their respective, profound effects on the history of scriptural interpretation. Both ways would be fashioned substantially in England, the first way by Thomas Hobbes, the second by John Locke, John Toland, and the Deists.

Henry's Reformation

The reformers sought to base theological authority in Scripture alone, not only because they rejected the authority of the pope and (to a lesser extent) councils, but because of the evident and authoritative power of the Scriptures themselves. Henry, on the other hand, needed to undermine both the authority of pope *and* general Church councils, for both would undoubtedly rule against him.[103] It might appear that Henry genuinely advocated conciliarism at times, but this was for the most part a bluff against papal power, and furthermore, when appealing to a general council, Henry always meant a Marsilian council, called and directed by secular rulers.[104] His appeal to the authority of Scripture gave him a theological source of authority to use against both the papacy and any general council, and appeal to Scripture worked as a vindication of his position as long as he was the declared Supreme Head of the Church of England and hence both the ultimate interpreter of Holy Writ and the ultimate enforcer of doctrine. And so, when in 1536 Henry told the assembled clergy to "determine all things by Scripture and not by custom or unwritten verities," this meant, as O'Grady points out, that "[i]nsofar as the King posited any spiritual arbiter in matters of faith, this was scripture, as interpreted by the Supreme Head himself."[105]

It is for this pragmatic and no theological reason that Henry would embrace a kind of *sola scriptura*. He needed scriptural sanction for his vast re-formation of English political and theological framework. Whatever Henry's ultimate theological convictions, he lived before the secular age, and that meant religious sanction was politically necessary. It is not outside the realm of possibility that, with Polybius, Marsilius, and Machiavelli, he considered ruling the masses without the terrors of religion to be impossible. Even if Henry himself did not reason thusly, the combined influence of the changes he initiated and the introduction of Machiavelli and Marsilius into the halls of power would soon enough bring this purely utilitarian view of religion to the surface. This view would appear three centuries hence as the oft-caricatured tendency of the upper classes in England, secretly agnostic, to go through the religious motions for the sake of keeping the lower classes in check. In so doing, they would be playing

103 This seems to be another decisive point against Oakley's skepticism about Marsilius's influence. Conciliar thought was focused on reform of the Church, while the Marsilian appeal to council was grounded in a desire to have the secular power in charge of religion.

104 Scarisbrick, *Henry VIII*, pp. 390–391.

105 O'Grady, *Henry VIII and the Conforming Catholics*, p. 10.

out perfectly the Machiavellian-Marsilian political use of Christianity for the sake of civil peace.

That is not at all to deny that, in England, there were many sincere Protestants like Tyndale and Cranmer who longed for a regime in which Scripture ruled the hearts of all, including the king. But it seems all too clear that, for Henry himself, the appeal to Scripture was defined by the goal of civil peace and the retention of power, and the same must at least be suspected of Cromwell, Starkey, Morison, and the other Henrician apologists. Certainly the circle of Paduan apologists around Cromwell used all the same passages as Marsilius to justify their position. The pattern of exegesis is anything but accidental, the only difference being that, while Marsilius downplayed the Old Testament (since it was used by popes who appealed to Moses, Melchisedech, and Samuel as priests lording it over kings), the Henrician apologists used the Old Testament to affirm the complete power of kings over priests (relying instead on David, Jehoshaphat, Hezekiah, and Josiah). In regard to the New Testament, appeals to obedience to Caesar amply salted all apologies, and even though Tyndale himself would fall victim to the scripturally-based Caesaropapism that he helped to create, his arguments would live on without him.

Henry VIII's *via media*, then, was not defined by a theological aim of hitting the mean between two extremes, the Radical Reformation and Roman Catholicism. It was not, as has often been maintained, essentially conservative, but radical in its shift of authority from the pope to the king. In historian J. J. Scarisbrick's words:

> That Henricianism was merely 'Catholicism without the pope' will not do. . . . During Henry's reign, the English church shifted a good way from the old orthodoxy. It moved erratically, now lurching towards Wittenberg [i.e., Lutheranism], now pulling back—as diplomacy, the varying fortunes of jostling factions among the hierarchy, the king's own instincts and doubtless several other factors dictated. And over this strange evolution Henry himself presided. He was never a Lutheran; indeed, in some matters he was intransigently conservative. But that febrile, wayward mechanism, Henry's mind, was in ferment—exploring, questioning, seizing on novelties, often pushing far away from its theological past, juxtaposing new and old in a curious medley. The picture sometimes presented of Henry having halted after lifting the yoke of Rome off his realm and himself, of him either not feeling or resisting the demand for further theological advance, is inadequate.[106]

What truly defined Henry's reform was not adherence to a beheaded and re-headed Catholicism, but adherence to himself and the exigencies of his reign. "The Royal Supremacy made Henry the spiritual father of his people and master of that new institution, the national Church of England. . . . Henry consistently maintained . . . that the spiritual men were ministers of the crown, *his* clergy, exercising an authority delegated by him."[107] That Henry, as supreme head, was not essentially conservative (i.e.,

106 Scarisbrick, *Henry VIII*, pp. 399–400.

107 Ibid., p. 384.

merely the new pope over the old Church) is clear from his ongoing efforts—stretching from 1531 nearly up until the time of his death—to negotiate with Lutheran German states as potential allies against the emperor and the pope. These political negotiations entailed doctrinal concessions on Henry's part, which he was quite willing to make. They broke down continually not primarily for doctrinal but political reasons, and because the reformers disapproved of Henry's lengthening string of divorces and executions.

The more accurate picture of Henry, then, is of an astute politician who understood that in order to maintain his rule in especially religiously tumultuous times (he had created much of the tumult), *he* would have to control and direct theology. He was not, as he is sometimes portrayed, a victim, pushed and pulled this way and that into strange compromises by theological factions. "Surely a more viable picture emerges of Henry the Lion-tamer, possessed in full measure of his second daughter's [Elizabeth's] genius for keeping potentially disruptive factions in dynamic equilibrium," argues O'Grady. "That Henry himself presided over the contending parties, favoring first one side, then the other, and again, taking his own very personal course; this must be grasped if we are to put Henrician Catholicism [i.e., his alleged theological conservatism] in its proper perspective."[108]

The conservative aspects of Henry's reign were not essentially theological, but were largely defined by the desire to conserve political power, and so "radical" or Reformation aspects would appear and intermix when politically useful. In his early years, before his attempted divorce, when he had hopes of becoming the emperor through the blessings of the pope, he could write a *Defense of the Seven Sacraments* (even while he was busily violating the sacrament of marriage). When it later become clear that his divorce made such ambition impossible to achieve, and that political exigencies made theological compromise desirable, he would help craft and royally approve the *Ten Articles* (1536), where, following Luther, four of the seven sacraments mysteriously disappeared (including matrimony).

Henry also turned against his original defense of the sacrament of holy orders, and his attack on monasticism no doubt pleased Lutherans and more radical reformers. But again, we gain a clue to his later animosity to religious orders in his political situation. He found it politically and financially beneficial to close the monasteries and shut down pilgrimage sites; soon enough in his reign his extravagant spending required a new influx of wealth and the closing of religious houses and shrines was an economic and political boon, both in filling his emptying coffers and in securing political allegiance to new nobles who received the vacated lands at his generous behest. Furthermore, the religious orders stood as counterevidence to his assumption of spiritual supremacy.

Henry might appear to be theologically conservative in his intransigent affirmation of priestly celibacy (which gave hope to conservatives). His affirmation was not, however, theologically motivated. "In a particularly vigorous outburst against the clergy, which he made in April 1541 to two foreign ambassadors, he argued that,

108 O'Grady, *Henry VIII and the Conforming Catholics*, p. 13.

unless celibacy were enforced, clerics would build up menacing strength through family clientage, make benefices hereditary and thereby become an even greater threat to the authority of princes."[109]

Other signs of theological conservatism vanish under close inspection as well. The Supreme Head of the Church was indeed a lifelong attendant at daily Mass, yet in 1546, "at a famous scene at Hampton Court, Henry would discuss with the French ambassador a plan for abolishing the Mass in both England and France . . . the suggestion could scarcely have been made by a man for whom the Mass was sacrosanct."[110] As Scarisbrick notes in regard to this illuminating episode, "It was not so much that Henry kept 'religious conscience and diplomatic necessity' apart as that the first was subservient to the second. Henry's religion could be moulded to any shape, as prestige, profit and power required."[111]

If we attend to the difference between public proclamations (which could appear conservative) and Henry's activities and words behind the scenes, it is evident that there was a wide gap, and so "it is clear that his mind was on the move, that he was toying with violent novelty, questioning and doubting much more of the Faith of his forefathers than merely the Roman primacy. The result was a highly personal admixture of new and old. Henry was his own theologian."[112] It was political expediency that defined Henry's theology, and consequently defined the use to which Scripture was put by apologists of his policies.

Henry's version of the Anglican *via media* was, therefore, a theological patchwork, scripturally sanctioned but politically defined. As noted above, the original mode of the *via media* was the declaration by Starkey, "things indifferent . . . which by God's word are neither prohibited or commanded . . . but left to worldly policy whereof they take their full authority." Supposedly, this was a middle way between radical reformers who believed that the entire Bible must be instantiated without remainder and the papacy that built up theocratic power from thin biblical evidence thickened by tradition and papal proclamation. But it is not difficult to see that Starkey drew the line between indifferent and essential in order to benefit the implementation of Henry's new order, so that "worldly policy" defined what "by God's word are neither prohibited or commanded."

We have then, in Henry, both in theory and fact, a Marsilian ruler, not an emperor but a national king, a man in both person and policy that brought the pages of the *Defensor Pacis* to life in England. Given the mode by which he did it, it is hard to deny Pole his suspicions that Machiavelli played his part as well, at least indirectly. In any case, Henry provided an example of Machiavellianism as vivid as Pope Alexander VI. The arguments of Machiavelli and Marsilius gained a beachhead on England's shores

109 Scarisbrick, *Henry VIII*, pp. 418–419.

110 For an account of this famous episode, and the controversy surrounding it, see ibid., pp. 419–420, 472–478.

111 Ibid., p. 477.

112 Ibid., p. 417.

during the reign of Henry, and their inherent secularism would slowly seep into the English soil as well. Such will become evident in later chapters.

Another segment of Henry's theological patchwork merits attention. In retaining some elements from Catholicism and mixing them with Lutheran and more radical theology, Henry provided hope to all parties that England could go in any direction if (given the declaration of royal supremacy), the crown could be secured by any one of the disparate theological factions nurtured by Henry's eclecticism. Precisely because Henry's new modes and orders placed full political and religious power in the sovereign, the changing of sovereigns brought often quite radical changes in doctrine and scriptural exegesis. The peace that royal supremacy was to protect and achieve, and the power that it was to nurture and sustain, were both continually undermined by the changing fortunes of the political realm. In order to stabilize politics, peace and power had to be even more firmly rooted, and this would require a far more radical approach, both to the nature of sovereignty and to the method of scriptural exegesis. Thomas Hobbes, the father of modern scriptural exegesis, would provide it, but only after a revolution of a different order, one on a cosmological scale, could provide it with an all-embracing theoretical structure. Before turning to Hobbes, we will need to examine this great cosmological revolution.

CHAPTER 7

DESCARTES AND THE SECULAR COSMOS

We have considered several crucial but fairly straightforward interactions of politics and scriptural interpretation in which the former co-opted the latter. But there are deeper roots that ground what is distinctively modern about the historical-critical method. It is a truism that the modern worldview is a secularized one, entirely stripped of the supernatural. Since it was in such intellectual soil that the modern approach to Scripture grew up, it is essential to delve into its causes—namely, the new understandings of nature, science, and philosophy that laid down the presuppositions on which Scripture scholarship came to rest. As David Dungan rightly states, "Nothing is rightly understood about the rise of modern biblical criticism if close attention is not paid to the shifting meanings given to the term 'nature' throughout the period."[1] Little, too, can be understood about the politicization of Scripture as it determines the origins of modern biblical criticism if close attention is not paid to the great cosmological shift that occurs in the seventeenth century. What it yielded was both a secular understanding of rationality and scientific method, *and* a secular understanding of politics. The two occur as part of one revolution because the shift in the meaning of nature includes human nature as well. First to the shifting definitions of rationality and scientific method.

This would seem an entirely tendentious assertion to many, especially those in the contemporary academic discipline of scriptural scholarship. It amounts to maintaining that scriptural scholars, in order to comprehend the assumptions and methods of their own craft, would have to understand the history of philosophy and science as well.

So they should. As a small but significant down payment on the reader's patience during this chapter, in which we present a synopsis of the monumental philosophical and scientific shift, we offer the following from the great and influential nineteenth century scriptural scholar David Friedrich Strauss, almost invariably the first of the modern critiques studied in the typical survey course taken by students of Scripture in graduate school. The key introductory chapter of Strauss's *Life of Jesus Critically Examined* is entitled "Development of the Mythical Point of View." In it, Strauss declares matter-of-factly that an "account is not historical," and hence "the matter related could not have taken place in the manner described," wherein "the narration is irreconcilable with the known and universal laws which govern the course of events.

1 David Dungan, *A History of the Synoptic Problem: The Canon, the Text, the Composition, and the Interpretation of the Gospels* (New York: Doubleday, 1999), p. 149.

Now according to these laws, agreeing with all just philosophical conceptions and all credible experience, the absolute cause never disturbs the chain of secondary causes by single arbitrary actions of interposition."[2] In short, miracles cannot happen. For Strauss, the exegetical assumption that miracles are fictions is based on a philosophical-scientific fact that "the absolute cause never disturbs the chain of secondary causes by single arbitrary actions of interposition." We hope to make clear the assumptions behind what Strauss took to be a philosophical-scientific fact: that we live in a disenchanted, or more accurately, entirely secular, machine-like cosmos.

To do the task properly, we would have to enter thoroughly into the history of philosophy and science stretching from the fourteenth to the seventeenth century, and cover a multitude of figures and concepts both well known and obscure. We cannot beg that much of the reader's patience. We propose instead to capture the essence of the great cosmological shift that occurred during this epoch through an analysis of one of its central figures, René Descartes, who unites in himself all the essential aspects of the "shifting meanings given to the term 'nature' throughout the period" that mark the transition to modernity.

Even more, in Descartes, we shall see, very clearly and distinctly, the formulation of all four aspects of the modern historical-critical method. He is taken to be, rightly, the father of *modern* philosophy, but also the father of the "mania" for *method*.[3] The approach famously exemplified in his method becomes the hallmark of the *critical* analysis, and his attitude toward *history* becomes the characteristically modern outlook.

The modern cosmological shift and the focus on method are intimately related. As we shall see, the modern passion for method *follows upon*, and is *defined by*, the new understanding of nature. If this new understanding of nature can rightly be viewed as essentially secularizing, either in intent or effect, then it would follow that the method built upon it would have an inevitably secularizing effect as well. Hence the new, secular political focus set forth by Marsilius and Machiavelli in the fourteenth and sixteenth centuries would finally have received a cosmological foundation in the seventeenth century. Or to put it another way, their politicizing of Scripture could now receive support from a new science of nature.

But Descartes was more than a mere bearer of historical trends begun by others. His peculiar union of skepticism and critical method rather quickly produced in many of his admirers an entirely skeptical and critical approach to Scripture. As the eminent historian of skepticism Richard Popkin argues, there were two major intellectual developments in the seventeenth century: "the launching of 'the new philosophy' with Descartes's presentation of his method for overcoming skepticism

---

2 Peter Hodgson, ed., David Friedrich Strauss, *The Life of Jesus Critically Examined*, fourth edition, (Philadelphia, PA: Fortress, 1972), Section 16, introduction, pp. 87–88.

3 "It was Descartes . . . whose *Discourse on Method*, published in 1637, raised to fever-pitch the mania for method characteristic of the late sixteenth and early seventeenth centuries. (As his contemporary Pascal wrote: 'The whole world is in search of a method of reasoning that does not go astray.')." David Lachterman, *The Ethics of Geometry: A Genealogy of Modernity* (New York: Routledge, 1989), p. 141.

and his construction of the new metaphysical basis for science," and "the unfolding of the theological consequences of a historical and critical approach to the Bible." These developments give modernity its characteristic stamp. "Modern philosophy issuing from Cartesianism and modern irreligion issuing from Bible criticism became two of the central ingredients in the making of the modern mind, the 'enlightened' scientific and rational outlook." These are usually seen as two separate developments, but Popkin correctly maintains they must be understood "as parts of a common intellectual drama," wherein "the development of modern irreligion" is the result of "the application of the Cartesian methodology and the Cartesian standard of true philosophical and scientific knowledge, to the evaluation of religious knowledge."[4] This application was made most assiduously by Benedict Spinoza, whose status as one of the great fathers of the modern historical-critical method is acknowledged by all. In short, Spinoza's critical analysis of Scripture is impossible to understand without a thorough knowledge of Descartes. (This will be quite evident when Spinoza takes center stage later on.) We may begin unfolding this drama with an account of Descartes's arguments in the context of his life and times.

Nativity and Life

Descartes's status as the father of modern philosophy is almost unquestioned, and in Descartes's case, the approbation of fatherhood is particularly apt. As Roger Lundin, David Lachterman, Gerald Bruns, and others have pointed out, Descartes initiates an entirely new notion in philosophy, that of "self-fathering."[5] In Lachterman's words, "Descartes gave birth to himself,"[6] a strange but, as we shall see, entirely appropriate image. Before witnessing this philosophical self-birthing, we should acquaint ourselves with Descartes's natural birth and the general outlines of his life in the context of his time.

René Descartes was born in La Haye, Touraine, on March 31, 1596, two years before the end of the French Wars of Religion between Catholics and Protestants (1562–1598). He would be baptized four days later, on the third of April, in Saint-Georges church. The family's parish church had previously been handed over to the Protestants, so the honor fell to Saint-Georges, a bit farther away.[7] His mother would

4 Richard Popkin, "Cartesianism and Biblical Criticism," in Thomas Lennon, John Nicholas, and John Davis, eds., *Problems of Cartesianism* (Kingston and Montreal: McGill-Queen's University Press, 1982), pp. 61–81; quotes from p. 61.

5 Roger Lundin, Clarence Walhout, and Anthony Thiselton, *The Promise of Hermeneutics* (Grand Rapids, MI: Eerdmans Publishing Company, 1999), p. 3; Gerald Bruns, *Hermeneutics Ancient and Modern* (New Haven: Yale University Press, 1992), p. 199; and especially Lachterman, *The Ethics of Geometry: A Genealogy of Modernity*, pp. 129–130.

6 Lachterman, *The Ethics of Geometry: A Genealogy of Modernity*, p. 130.

7 Geneviève Rodis-Lewis, *Descartes: His Life and Thought*, translated by Jane Marie Todd (Ithaca and London: Cornell University Press, 1995,1998), p. 3.

die a little over a year later, giving birth to another son. She bequeathed her fragile health to René.

Descartes was twenty-one in 1618, the first year of the Thirty Years' War (1618–1648). Prior to that, he had completed his years of study at the Jesuit College of La Flèche in Anjou (1606–1614), and received his baccalaureate and his licentiate in canon and civil law at the University of Poitiers in November 1616. The year 1618 found him in Holland, a volunteer in the army of Prince Maurice of Nassau, defending Protestantism against the Spanish-Austrian monarchy. A year later, he was in Germany, having joined up with the army of the Duke of Bavaria, Maximilian I, on the opposite side. It was in Germany in 1619, while resting in winter quarters outside of Ulm, that Descartes allegedly had his unifying intellectual vision that would culminate in his revolutionary method.

According to Descartes, this vision took place during his meditations in a *poêle*, a heated room he had rented to allow him freedom to think away from the drudgery and crudity of barracks life. It was in this *poêle*, so the self-made legend has it, that Descartes conceived of a new foundation for human knowledge based upon a new mode of philosophizing, and through this conception became the father of modern philosophy. We shall offer an account of his revolutionary philosophy below, but first we must broaden our vision to take in the political and religious context of his meditations, for this broader vision will allow us to see more clearly how Descartes's revolution in philosophy affected the modern approach to scriptural scholarship.

Descartes was born into political and religious turmoil that ended in the stalemate of the Edict of Nantes (1598), which acknowledged Catholicism as the official religion of France but guaranteed Protestants ("Huguenots") the right to worship and hold public office.

From our contemporary perspective of religious toleration, this edict might seem to be an advance toward sanity, but that is to ignore that our contemporary perspective had yet to be advanced, and further, to obscure the part later played by Descartes in fashioning it. From the perspective of the time, such "toleration" signaled fatigue, and hence a temporary rest from conflict rather than a permanent solution.

We will also misunderstand the religious wars, either before or after Descartes, if (with so many historians) we insist on characterizing them as exclusively religious.[8] What was true of Luther's time is all the clearer in the wars stretching from the mid-sixteenth to the mid-seventeenth century: doctrinal differences, especially as rooted in rival interpretations of Scripture, could not by themselves flame into religious wars if political ambitions did not use them as shield and standard.[9]

In Descartes's France, for example, the Valois kings Francis I (1515–1547) and Henry II (1547–1559) were as staunchly Catholic as they were staunchly monarchist. Strong, centralized control of both their realm and of the Church was inseparably united for them.

8 In respect to the more famous Thirty Years' War, see the concise arguments in S. H. Steinberg, *The Thirty Years' War and the Conflict for European Hegemony, 1600–1660* (New York: W. W. Norton, 1966).

9 William Cavanaugh, "A Fire Strong Enough to Consume the House:" The Wars of Religion and the Rise of the State," *Modern Theology* 11.4 (1995): 397–420.

Many of the nobles who chaffed at the monarchy became Huguenots, along with a great number of artisans, shopkeepers, merchants, and lawyers who were equally unhappy to be taxed yet excluded from power. As a result, political rivalries came to be associated with, and supported by, the rival interpretations of Scripture as expressed by Catholic and Calvinist theology. When Henry II was accidentally killed in a tournament in 1559, the lack of strong Valois successors made Huguenot rebellion inviting, and civil war broke out in 1562. Biblical interpretation thereby became ineluctably political, and the political motives were often in command.

The hostilities of the Thirty Years' War had only been raging for about a year and a half when the young Descartes had his "vision" on the tenth of November, St. Martin's Eve, 1619, exactly three years since he had received his licentiate in canon and civil law. One might be somewhat skeptical of the historical accuracy of pinpointing a day with such precision, and further, of attributing to Descartes a comprehensive flash of insight that would contain an entire intellectual revolution.[10] But it is beyond dispute that very soon Descartes would indeed initiate a philosophical revolution. During the period (while in France) from 1625 to 1628, Descartes composed his *Rules for the Direction of the Mind* (or perhaps better, *of Genius*[11]) in which he set forth his grand universal science, the *mathesis universalis,*[12] which would (so he promised) rid humanity of all error by placing the entirety of knowledge on a single firm foundation. He abandoned the *Rules* before completion, however, only to begin work in 1629 on an even more ambitious work, *The World,* an entirely mechanistic account of creation and nature that accorded with his *mathesis universalis.*

By this time, Descartes was in Holland, a haven for liberal thinking, and would stay there until 1649, a total of over twenty years. He praised Holland in his autobiographical *Discourse on Method* as "a country where the long duration of the [Thirty Years'] war has established such well-ordered discipline that the armies quartered there seem to be there solely for the purpose of guaranteeing the enjoyment of the fruits of peace with even greater security," and even more important, it was a country "where among the crowds of a great and very busy people" who are "more concerned with their own affairs than curious about the affairs of others, I have been able to live as solitary and as retired a life

10 Readers interested in sorting through the details of Descartes's day vision, and even more the succession of dreams that night, may wish to consult John R. Cole, *The Olympian Dreams and Youthful Rebellion of René Descartes* (Urbana and Chicago: University of Illinois Press, 1992).

11 To attempt to translate Descartes's title, *Regulae ad directionem ingenii,* is an exercise in frustration because there is no English equivalent to *ingenium*, which means, variously, nature, natural constitution, disposition, cleverness, talent, mental power, and genius. Perhaps the most exact would be "inborn talent," which is both literal and reflects Descartes's notion of training one's intellectual capacities by his method.

12 The one and only use by Descartes of the term *mathesis universalis* occurs in Rule IV of his *Rules*, where it is defined as "a certain general science which explains everything which can be asked about order and measure, and which is concerned with no particular subject matter. . . ." Translation from Descartes, *Philosophical Essays: Discourse on Method; Meditations; Rules for the Direction of the Mind*, translated by Laurence Lafleur (New York: Macmillan Publishing Company, 1964).

as I could in the remotest deserts—but without lacking any of the amenities that are to be found in the most populous cities."[13]

Hearing of Galileo's condemnation in 1633, and sensing danger to himself, Descartes suppressed publication of *The World*. During his stay in Amsterdam—on October 15, 1634, as Descartes himself records!—he conceived a daughter (with a servant woman, Hélène Jans) who would be born at Deventer on June 19, 1635, and baptized in the Reformed Church as Francine. Descartes would pass her off as his niece to avoid scandal, and she died in September of 1640 of scarlet fever.

In 1637, Descartes published his famous *Discourse on Method*, a somewhat cryptic autobiographical account of his philosophical approach (to which we shall return below) that presented Descartes's mature reflections, albeit in guarded form. It was written at Utrecht, and published at Leiden. In 1641, he published his equally famous *Meditations on First Philosophy*. In that same year, the first public controversy surrounding Descartes's philosophy broke out at the University of Utrecht, where a disciple of Descartes, Regius (a professor of medicine since 1638), proclaimed unabashedly the full implications of Descartes's mechanism while rejecting the spiritual half of Cartesian dualism—declaring that he taught Descartes's true thought, and charging Descartes himself with dissimulating about his purely materialistic view. Although Descartes immediately tried to distance himself from Regius, those defending Aristotelianism and reformed orthodoxy against Cartesianism, led by Utrecht professor Gijsbertus Voetius, asserted that Regius did indeed express the hidden implications of Descartes's philosophy. Soon after, the liberal theological wing of the Reformed Church came to the defense of a moderate Cartesianism, a position advanced by Johannes Cocceius, who became a professor at the University of Leiden in 1650.[14] In 1644, Descartes published his *Principles of Philosophy*. As soon as the late 1640s, "all the Dutch universities, especially Utrecht and Leiden, lapsed into a philosophical struggle unprecedented in European history since ancient times for acrimony, duration, and divisiveness."[15] Both the reach of Cartesian thought and acrimony of dispute only increased over the next decades, spreading from the Netherlands all over Europe.[16]

In 1649, the year following the end of the Thirty Years' War, Descartes would leave for Sweden at the request of Queen Christina, and would publish his last philo-

---

13 Descartes, *Discourse on Method*, III.31. We use Donald Cress's translation from the original French edition, contained in René Descartes, *Discourse on Method* and *Meditations on First Philosophy* (Indianapolis, IN: Hackett Publishing Company, 1980). Cress's translation includes the standard pagination from Charles Adam and Paul Tannery, *Oeuvres de Descartes*, 13 vols., which is followed here.

14 For greater detail see Theo Verbeek, *Descartes and the Dutch: Early Reactions to Cartesian Philosophy* (Carbondale, IL: Southern Illinois University Press, 1992); Rosalie Colie, *Light and Enlightenment: A Study of the Cambridge Platonists and the Dutch Arminians* (Cambridge: Cambridge University Press, 1957), pp. 49–65; Ernestine van der Wall, "Orthodoxy and Scepticism in the Early Dutch Enlightenment," in Richard Popkin and Arjo Vanderjagt, eds., *Scepticism and Irreligion in the Seventeenth and Eighteenth Centuries* (Leiden: Brill, 1993), pp. 121–141.

15 Jonathan I. Israel, *Radical Enlightenment: Philosophy and the Making of Modernity 1650–1750* (Oxford: Oxford University Press, 2001), pp. 24–25.

16 See ibid., pp. 29–58.

sophical work, *The Passions of the Soul*. He died in Stockholm on February 11, 1650, after having caught a cold on the way to the Queen's 5:00 A.M. philosophy lesson.

Descartes's philosophic career spanned the bloodiest and most infamous of the religious wars. What relationship, if any, does the religious and political context have to the substance and form of Descartes's philosophy? To answer that question, we turn to Descartes's *Discourse on Method*.

Conflict as Context of Descartes's Method

The full title of Descartes's *Discourse* is *Discourse on the Method of Rightly Conducting the Reason and Seeking Truth in the Field of Science*. The original, intended title was *The Project of a Universal Science which Can Elevate Our Nature to its Highest Degree of Perfection*. These grandiose titles seem at odds with his more subdued, even humble self-assessment in the first part of the *Discourse* that "my purpose here is not to teach the method that everyone ought to follow in order to conduct his reason correctly, but merely to show how I have tried to conduct mine."[17] Indeed, he remarks that he is "putting forward this essay as merely a history—or, if you prefer, a fable. . . ."[18] The history, or fable, turns out to be a kind of autobiography, an appropriate literary form for someone engaged in refounding all knowledge on his own insights.[19]

The *Discourse* begins with an arrestingly paradoxical statement: "Good sense [*bon sens*] is the most evenly distributed commodity in the world, for each of us considers himself to be so well endowed therewith that even those who are the most difficult to please in all other matters are not wont to desire more of it than they have."[20] Descartes begins with a wry smile, in the form of an old French proverb, pointing to the very difficulty that his method is designed to dissolve: human beings are satisfied with their opinions, whatever their actual caliber; such self-satisfaction with one's own good sense, or reason, leads to a chaos of opinions, and hence inevitable conflicts, not only philosophical but also political and, we assume, religious.

How can we assume this? Descartes brings attention to two sorts of conflict in regard to religion, or to be more exact, in regard to Christianity. Part II of the *Discourse* begins, "I was in Germany then, where the wars—which are still continuing there—called me; and . . . the onset of winter held me up in quarters where . . . I remained for a whole day by myself in a small stove-heated room. . . ." Significantly, his revolutionary philosophy is birthed in the *poêle* amidst the ravages of religious war. It is precisely in this circumstance that Descartes asserts that the project of radical reconstruction of human knowledge must be undertaken by *one man* because "there is less perfection in works made of several pieces and in works made by the hands of several masters

17 Descartes, *Discourse on Method*, I.4.

18 Ibid.

19 For interesting reflections on Descartes's use of autobiography as the mode of philosophy see Richard Kennington's interpretive essay in René Descartes, *Discourse on Method*, translated with an interpretive essay by Richard Kennington (Newburyport, MA: R. Pullins Company, 2007), pp. 59–77.

20 Descartes, *Discourse on Method*, I.1–2.

than in those works on which but one master has worked."[21] As an example, he notes that societies that gradually grow from barbarism to civilization under the leadership of many masters are not as well ordered as those that, "From the very beginning . . . have followed the fundamental precepts of some prudent legislator." Immediately following this, he remarks that, "it is quite certain that the state of the true religion [*la vraie religion*], whose ordinances were fixed by God alone, ought to be incomparably better governed than all the others."[22] That "ought" presents us with another paradox, another wry smile from Descartes, for it is uttered in the midst of the Thirty Years' War, in which Christians are killing Christians, each making rival theological claims, each satisfied with his "good sense," the *bon sens* of his interpretation of Scripture. Perhaps Descartes's method, "the true method [*la vraie méthode*] of arriving at the knowledge of everything my mind was capable of attaining,"[23] is in some way meant to remedy this malady as well.

There is another conflict in regard to religion that Descartes mentions twice, at the beginning of Part V and of Part VI.[24] The conflict is quite personal. As we mentioned above, Descartes's *World* was not published because, having learned of Galileo's condemnation, Descartes feared he would be similarly persecuted. As we learn in Part V of the *Discourse*, in which Descartes provides a summary of *The World*, the difficulty is not just Descartes's adherence to Copernicanism, but even more, his entirely mechanistic account of nature, an account that accords with his *mathesis universalis*, and which all but reduces human beings to mechanical animals. Since this grand synthesis forms the essence of Descartes's method, then we are made aware by the author himself of a most serious conflict with his method and "the true religion, whose ordinances were fixed by God alone." If that conflict is to be resolved—and not just avoided out of the fear of persecution—we rightly wonder whether it is not the "true religion" that must conform to Descartes's method, which would seem to require a radical transformation.

But unlike later modern philosophers, who will have a direct impact on the development of modern scriptural scholarship, such as Thomas Hobbes and Benedict Spinoza, Descartes does not delve into the analysis and exegesis of Scripture.[25] Instead, he lays revelation aside, and attempts his famous proofs of the immortality of the soul and the existence of God. That is, Descartes turns to a consideration of natural theology, or more exactly, a particular kind of natural theology, one that implicitly harmonizes with his new mechanistic philosophy of nature rather than the view of nature found in revelation (at least, as understood by the Catholic Church, the religion

21 Ibid., II.11.

22 Ibid., II.12.

23 Ibid., II.17.

24 Ibid., V.40–41 and VI.60.

25 On Descartes's sparing treatment of Scripture see H.J.M. Nellen, "Growing Tension between Church Doctrines and Critical Exegesis of the Old Testament," in Magne Sæbø, ed., *Hebrew Bible/Old Testament: The History of Its Interpretation*, Vol. II, *From the Renaissance to the Enlightenment* (Göttingen: Vandenhoeck & Ruprecht, 2008), Ch. 32, pp. 823–826, and V. Carraud, "*Les références scripturaires du corpus cartésien*," *Bulletin Cartésien* XVIII, *Liminaire* II, *Archives de Philosophie* 53.1 (1990): 11–21.

he claims as his own). It is well worth considering whether Descartes's famous proofs somehow place religion on a new, firmer foundation made by one master, a foundation that would avoid the kinds of religious conflicts that fueled the Thirty Years' War. In order to consider this possibility, we must examine how and why Descartes lays revelation aside, the nature of his method, and the proofs themselves.

Laying Faith Aside: Averroism Rechauffé

Although there does not seem to be any direct influence of the arguments of Averroes, or even Marsilius, upon Descartes, there are certain illuminating similarities that should not go unnoticed.[26] Again, the *Discourse* is autobiographical, and the first part covers, among other things, Descartes's early education, including his education in theology. He reveals that he studied at "one of the most celebrated schools in all of Europe," La Flèche, under the tutelage of Jesuits. In retrospect, he explains (in a way both condescending and surprisingly curt) that "theology teaches one how to go to heaven," and further on he adds that he "revered our theology, and I desired as much as the next man to go to heaven; but having learned as something very certain that the road is no less open to the most ignorant than to the most learned, and that the revealed truths [*vérités révélées*] leading to it are beyond our understanding, I would not have dared to subject them to my feeble reasonings." To subject revealed truths to reason, "it was necessary to have some extraordinary assistance from heaven and to be more than a man."[27] We are not far from Marsilius's Averroistic assertion that "we can say nothing [about revelation] through demonstration, but we hold it by simple belief apart from reason," and that the truths of faith, completely unknowable by reason, "must be piously held." In both cases, it is hard to take such patronizing praise as sincere.

Further hints of a Marsilian approach also occur in the dedicatory letter of the *Meditations*. We recall Marsilius's presentation of scriptural authority as circular: "the holy Scriptures must be firmly believed and acknowledged to be true is assumed as self-evident to all Christians; but . . . it could be proved only by the authorities of these Scriptures themselves. . . ." Addressing the "Dean and Doctors of the Faculty of Sacred Theology of Paris," Descartes points to the same circularity: "God's existence is to be believed in because it is taught in the Holy Scriptures, and, on the other hand . . . the Holy Scriptures are to be believed because they have God as their source. . . ." The reason for this circularity, he argues, is that "faith is a gift of God." Of course, that only opens him to the charge of a larger circularity. Rather than defend the faith against this charge, Descartes merely

---

26 We are not the first to note this connection between Averroism, Descartes, and modern historical-critical scholarship. See Klaus Scholder, *The Birth of Modern Critical Theology: Origins and Problems of Biblical Criticism*, translated by John Bowden (London: SCM Press, 1990), Ch. 5.

27 Descartes, *Discourse on Method*, I.6–8.

notes that, "this cannot be proposed to unbelievers because they would judge it to be a circle."[28] In short, he emphasizes the circularity, rather than attempting any resolution.

To return to the *Discourse*, Descartes decides that in order to reach truth, he must "reject as absolutely false everything in which I could imagine the least doubt, so as to see whether, after this process, anything in my set of beliefs remains that is entirely indubitable."[29] Prior to this, however, he informs the reader that he will "put aside . . . the truths of the faith [*vérités de la foi*], which have always been the first ones [*les premières*] in my beliefs," thereby exempting them from doubt.[30] He does not tell us, after laying them aside, *how* the truths of the faith are true, but we can safely infer that they do not meet the test of truth set forth by Descartes himself, that "the things we conceive very clearly and distinctly are all true."[31] If the truths of faith *were* able to be conceived by reason very clearly and distinctly in the same way that we can conceive of (say) geometrical proofs, then they would not be "beyond our understanding." Furthermore, we may infer that if Scripture itself revealed truths clearly and distinctly, then religious differences could not arise from rival interpretations and fuel religious wars.

Whether Descartes made these inferences is debatable since he remains silent during the rest of the *Discourse* about the status of the truths of the faith. But he certainly seems to be presenting something like a double truth—the truths of faith that are beyond understanding and the natural truths obtained by his method. Since only the latter are taken to be indubitable, he would appear (in Klaus Scholder's assessment) to be deciding "the question of double truth . . . in favour of the universal rule of reason."[32] Of course, in order to judge whether and what kind of double truth he presents, and from this to draw the consequences for the modern preoccupation with method, we must carefully examine his "true method," beginning with its autobiographical nature.

Descartes's Method

The linking of autobiography with promises of a universal science that defines the conduct of reason and delivers us from imperfection is essential to Descartes's project. The autobiographical nature of the *Discourse* reveals Descartes's own assessment of his demiurgic, originative power. He is consciously self-fathering, we might say, and it is he and he alone who can deliver humanity from a past of endless error. Hence, we see the literary importance of Descartes's rejection of all previous human intellectual endeavors and traditions and his presentation of himself giving birth to an entirely new philosophy alone in the *poêle* that would once and for all set both philosophy

28 Descartes, *Meditations on First Philosophy*, Dedication, 2.

29 Descartes, *Discourse on Method*, IV.31–32.

30 Ibid., III.28. Our translation.

31 Ibid., IV.33.

32 Scholder, *The Birth of Modern Critical Theology*, p. 113.

and humanity on a firm foundation. As we shall see, the method is the *strategy* for achieving his aims.

To recognize his method as strategy, we must first see how Descartes unites in his thinking the three aspects of the shifting meaning of, and approach to, nature that come to be characteristic of modernity: the *mathematization*, the *mechanization*, and the *mastery* of nature. In regard to the first, Descartes is of course famous for his discovery of analytic geometry—or more accurately, Cartesian geometry[33]—a discovery he made public in 1637 in his *Geometry*, a treatise published with two others, *Optics* and *Meteorology*. The *Discourse* was published as the introduction to these treatises, and the treatises were meant to illustrate the power and promise of Descartes's method as adumbrated in the *Discourse*.

To understand the heart of Descartes's geometry we must see it as constructive rather than abstractive, as active rather than passive.[34] This insight is essential for our grasp of Descartes's famous "rule" of his method that "the things we conceive very clearly and distinctly are all true,"[35] and conversely, that all things that fail to satisfy these twin epistemological criteria, should be considered entirely dubious.[36] Louis Dupré has aptly captured the central connection between construction and the criteria of clarity and distinctness: "Descartes's epistemic conditions can be met only by the mind's own constructions, such as [in] mathematics and logic."[37] More accurately, they are to be met only in Descartes's *own* mathematical constructions, the products of his singular genius.

We can now begin to see the appropriateness of understanding Descartes as self-fathering. Descartes *conceives* of an entirely new way of understanding mathematics and gives birth to it himself, out of himself. What, then, is unique about his analytic geometry? To be all too brief, Descartes presents a way to unite algebra and geometry so that—if we follow the mode of his procedure—geometric shapes and relationships can be translated into algebraic formulae, and then an even larger, more comprehensive class of algebraic formulae can be translated back into a *symbolic* geometry capable

33 We call it Cartesian not only because it bears the marks of being formed for larger goals of Descartes's own making, but also because our contemporary analytic geometry is significantly developed, or at least different from, Descartes's *Geometry*. It is an offspring that resembles its parent, but is not identical. For a short discussion of the surface differences, see Carl Boyer, *A History of Mathematics*, second ed. (New York: John Wiley & Sons, Inc., 1991), pp. 333–346. For the most profound differences, see Lachterman, *The Ethics of Geometry: A Genealogy of Modernity*, pp. 141–187, as well as Jacob Klein, *Greek Mathematical Thought and the Origin of Algebra* (New York: Dover Publications, 1992), pp. 197–211.

34 This might seem to go against his statement in the *Meditations* that when he imagines a triangle, "its nature, essence, or form is completely determined, unchangeable, and eternal. I did not produce it and it does not depend on my mind" (V.64). As will become clear in the paragraphs below, while this may be true of geometrical figures before being taken up into Descartes's geometry, their re-presentation in Cartesian geometry is entirely of Descartes's own making.

35 Descartes, *Discourse on Method*, IV.33.

36 See Rule II of Descartes's *Rules for the Direction of the Mind*.

37 Louis Dupré, *Passage to Modernity: An Essay in the Hermeneutics of Nature and Culture* (New Haven: Yale University Press, 1993), p. 84.

of representing all relationships of magnitudes, numerical or geometric, as ratios and proportions of lines, thereby creating a *mathesis universalis*.[38] In this way, there is a striking simplicity in symbolic presentation, but the simplicity represents, at one glance, a multitude of "condensed" mathematical truths, truths that will lead (promises Descartes) to further discoveries.

This, in itself, was a significant intellectual feat, but as such, a purely theoretical one. Descartes's brilliance consists in *imposing the theoretical conception upon nature*, that is, in mathematizing it. As Jacob Klein notes, Descartes's true genius "consists of identifying . . . the 'general' object of this *mathesis universalis*—which can be represented and conceived only *symbolically*—with the 'substance' of the world, with corporeality as 'extensio.'"[39] That is, Descartes self-consciously fashioned a mathematical ontology, stripping everything from nature but homogeneous extension, so that there could be a simple identity between his *mathesis universalis* and nature.[40]

It is important to stress that the path to mathematization was prepared by Ockham's nominalism. In championing nominalism, Ockham removed the reality of universals that inhered in similar-looking substances, so that nouns like sheep, cow, dog, pig, and so on do not have real referents in nature. There is no common form or species that all sheep as sheep share. Despite our common-sense view that nouns really refer to something both real and common, there are only particulars. Universal forms have reality only in the abstracting intelligence, which bases itself, for convenience, on the similar appearances of the particular things we happen to call sheep, cows, dogs, pigs, etc. Ockham thereby created an intellectual vacuum, removing species-name universals but not supplying anything in their place. Nominalism leaves us with a mass of particulars. Since (at least) human nature abhors such a vacuum, the substitution of mathematical universals for species-name universals was all the easier and more welcome. Descartes's revolution consisted in the substitution of mathematical forms for Aristotelian forms as the universals governing particulars. Contrary to all too many histories of science, forms were not done away with; there was merely a substitution of mathematical forms for common-sense forms. In this substitution, we have a com-

---

38 Descartes, *Discourse on Method*, II.19–20. For a masterful analysis of Descartes's *mathesis universalis*, see Lachterman, *The Ethics of Geometry: A Genealogy of Modernity*, pp. 141–187 and Klein, *Greek Mathematical Thought and the Origin of Algebra*, pp. 197–211.

39 Klein, *Greek Mathematical Thought and the Origin of Algebra*, p. 197.

40 Descartes, *Rules for the Direction of the Mind*, Rule XII. The stripping away of all that is not homogeneous extension is precisely what allows Descartes to advance a universal science of proportion, where all beings, no matter how different they appear, *can* be treated proportionately. For the ancients, things that were different in kind could not be considered in ratio, and hence could not be considered in proportion. Descartes gets around this problem precisely by translating geometric figures into algebraic formulae that are purely formal, abstracting both from geometric figures *and* numbers (A:B::C:D) so that he has a "pure" science of proportion, which can in turn be represented by his symbolic geometry. This "pure" science of proportion is only applicable to nature *if* things in nature are rendered fundamentally homogeneous, i.e., fundamentally of the same kind. In addition to Lachterman and Klein, see the insightful essay by Stephen Gaukroger, "The Nature of Abstract Reasoning: Philosophical Aspects of Descartes's Work in Algebra," in John Cottingham, ed., *The Cambridge Companion to Descartes* (Cambridge: Cambridge University Press, 1992), pp. 91–114.

ing together of the *via moderna* of Ockham with a *via moderna* peculiar to Descartes (although not unassociated with that of Machiavelli, as we shall see) that warrants him being called a father of *modern* philosophy.

We are so Cartesian in outlook that it is difficult for us to see what is revolutionary in his identification of the abstract world of mathematics with the real world of nature. We tend to take the identity for granted. Sufficient insight may be gained by recalling the view of mathematics against which he was revolting, the Aristotelian as exemplified in the Thomistic. According to this view there are three speculative or theoretical sciences: physics (i.e., natural philosophy), mathematics, and metaphysics (or natural theology).[41] To be all too brief again, both Aristotle and St. Thomas argued that mathematics was the most certain science *to us* because it is entirely abstract; that is, it does not, like natural philosophy, deal with real, ontologically complex, and diverse things in nature, but abstracts from them certain properties for consideration. Precisely because mathematical "objects" are abstract, they are far more easily dealt with and have far more exact properties than the real objects in nature. We can abstract the notion of a sphere from an orange or the moon, and a mathematician can deal with the precise properties of homogeneous geometrical spheres without having to understand the far greater complexity of heterogeneous and ontologically diverse objects in the real world like oranges or the moon. Because they are entirely abstract and therefore quite simple, numbers and geometrical shapes are very clear, distinct, and certain for us. But since nature is not primarily mathematical, but only accidentally so, physics or natural philosophy is far less certain a science than mathematics.

Given this background, we can more readily grasp Descartes's revolutionary move. He declared that the most certain science to the human mind, mathematics, can indeed define *all* of science if we reconceive nature as entirely mathematical. In this reconception, nature (or being) conforms to what is most clear and distinct *for* the human intellect (simple geometric extension) and simultaneously conforms to what is completely amenable to analysis via Descartes's symbolic *mathesis universalis*. Descartes thereby compels the order of being, the *ordo essendi*, to conform to the order of human mathematical knowing, the most certain mode of order of the human *ordo cognoscendi*, and hence the easiest for us to learn. What does not conform to mathematics is either unreal, or mere epiphenomena of mathematically-defined matter.

Furthermore, mathematically-defined matter is mechanical, and this in two senses. First, like numbers, it is passive and inert; while mathematicals are quite exact, they are also "dead." For matter understood as mathematically-defined—the easiest and most obvious mode being the conception of matter as a geometrical point, an atom—motion does not come from some internal principle of growth, but like a machine, matter is subject to motion only through force from the outside that moves the material parts. Second, mathematically-defined nature is machine-like as part of the overall

41 Aristotle, *Metaphysics*, 1025b19–1026a32 and 1063b36–1064b14; and St. Thomas's commentary on Boethius's *De Trinitate*, questions 5 and 6, which are conveniently gathered by Armand Maurer in Thomas Aquinas, *The Division and Methods of the Sciences* (Toronto, Ontario: Pontifical Institute of Mediaeval Studies, 1986), fourth revised edition.

identification of the human-made and the natural: just as nature is reduced to the artificial abstractions of mathematics, so also nature is reduced to the artificial technical functioning of a machine. In neither case is nature considered the product of a wisdom above the merely human.

This identity of geometry and nature in Descartes differs from Galileo's before and Newton's afterward precisely in this: Descartes understands that the mathematical order comes *from him*, whereas Galileo and Newton treat it as something independent of them in nature that they are discovering. That difference accounts for Descartes's characteristic dismissal of intellectual achievements prior to him, his insistently solipsistic mode of procedure, and his adamancy that only *he* can carry his project through.[42]

In such Promethean assertions, Descartes was more deeply aware, so it seems, than either Galileo or Newton that the self-conscious union of mathematics and mechanism entails a great shift, *the* great shift, from the locus of certainty and truth residing in nature (and hence, ultimately in the Creator of nature), to the locus of certainty and truth residing in human beings (and most prominently, in Descartes). That is why Descartes maintains in his *Rules for the Direction of the Mind* that if one follows his method, "he will surely discover through the rules given that nothing can be known prior to the intellect itself, since the knowledge of all other things depends upon this, and not conversely."[43]

Again, this is not merely an "intellectual" shift. Nature itself had to be reconceived so as to conform to what is most easily known, distinct, and certain for the human intellect, mathematics. The active nature of intellection involved in the reconception of nature must lead to the actual remaking of nature, to its complete mastery (a focus Descartes inherited from Francis Bacon, whom we will examine in some detail in our chapter on Locke).[44] To achieve this, Descartes conceives of homogeneous extension as essentially malleable—such is, it seems, the real lesson of Descartes's famous wax illustration in the *Meditations*[45]—and consequently that nature is capable of being entirely

42 Descartes, *Discourse on Method*, I.11–II.12, VI.69.

43 Rule VIII. Descartes, *Philosophical Essays: Discourse on Method; Meditations; Rules for the Direction of the Mind*, translated by Lafleur, p. 175.

44 There can be little doubt of Descartes's indebtedness to Francis Bacon on this point, and, in turn, Bacon's indebtedness to Machiavelli's notion of "mastering" Fortune. That Bacon had read Machiavelli with care is obvious, since he quite openly quoted a number of times from both *The Prince* and *Discourses on Livy*, and did so with no hint of disapproval. See, e.g., Bacon's *The Advancement of Learning* in Brian Vickers, ed., Francis Bacon, *The Major Works* (Oxford: University of Oxford Press, 1996), II, pp. 270–271, 279, 282, 284. On Bacon's notion of the mastery of nature see his entire *The Great Instauration* in Fulton Anderson, ed., *The New Organon and Related Writings* (New York: Macmillan Publishing Company, 1988); *The New Organon*, I, lxxxi, xcviii, cxxix; and Bacon's "*Historia Mechanica*," in *The Advancement of Learning*, II, esp. pp. 177–178 in Bacon, *The Major Works*.

45 Descartes, *Meditations on First Philosophy*, AT, II.30–31. In order to show that the senses cannot be trusted, or more exactly, that bodily things cannot be distinctly known through the senses, Descartes brings wax near a fire, melts it, and argues that, since the previous sensible qualities of the wax's original taste, smell, temperature, color, shape, size, and even sound (when knocked) have disappeared, then what the wax really is must be perceived only through the mind, not through sensible qualities. However true this debatable point may be, this exercise functions to support his reductionist view that matter is only malleable extension: "what remains after we have removed everything [by heat] which does not belong to the wax: only that it is something extended, flexible, and subject to change."

re-formed by human art. The creative power of the human intellect can thereby pass into matter, and nature may be demiurgically remade, reshaped, according to human will. By human art, *technē*, we may then become the fathers of a new creation. This project of remaking nature becomes the framework of a complete revolution in understanding history: it allows the substitution of secular for sacred history by demarcating history according to the successive technological mastery of nature.

Such re-creation is, as he makes both clear and certain in his *Discourse*, the ultimate goal of his method. At the beginning of the *Discourse*, Descartes offers the reader a short synopsis of each of the six parts, Part VI setting forth "what reasons moved him to write."[46] That is, Part VI gives us the final cause, as it were, the goal of the work, and hence the end of the method.[47] What then is the end at which the method aims?

Again, Part VI begins by informing the reader that a treatise Descartes had written, entitled *The World*, was not published because, having learned of Galileo's condemnation, Descartes feared he would be similarly persecuted. After noting why he withdrew *The World*, Descartes reveals what his new view of physics would achieve *if* it were allowed to proceed unhindered by persecution or other obstacles.

> For these general notions [of my physics] show me that it is possible to arrive at knowledge that is very useful in life and that in place of the speculative philosophy taught in the Schools, one can find a practical one, by which, knowing the force and the actions of fire, water, air, stars, the heavens, and all the other bodies that surround us . . . we could . . . make ourselves, as it were, masters and possessors of nature. This is desirable not only for the invention of an infinity of devices that would enable us to enjoy without pain the fruits of the earth and all the goods one finds in it, but also principally for the maintenance of health, which unquestionably is the first good and the foundation of all the other goods in this life; for even the mind depends so greatly upon the temperament and on the disposition of the organs of the body that, were it possible to find some means to make men generally more wise and competent than they have been up until now, I believe that one should look to medicine to find this means . . . [so that] we might rid ourselves of an infinity of maladies, both of body and mind, and even perhaps also the enfeeblement brought on by old age. . . .[48]

It is impossible to miss the entirely secular focus of Descartes's aims. The goal of his physics, and indeed his method itself, is to make us "masters and possessors of nature," meaning that we can enjoy the fruits and wealth of the earth "without pain,"

46 Ibid., AT, 1.

47 Method comes from the Greek *hodos*, being a way, path, road, a journey, and by extension, *meta* + *hodos*, a way or manner of doing a thing. As such, it is not a neutral instrument, but is defined by the intended goal, hence the importance of discerning the goal of his method. On this point see Richard Kennington, *On Modern Origins: Essays in Early Modern Philosophy* (Lanham, MD: Lexington Books, 2004), Ch. 6.

48 Descartes, *Discourse on Method*, VI.61–62.

but even more, that we can conserve health, "the first good and the foundation of all the other goods in this life," overcoming even old age. Just how far he imagines health as the principal good is revealed in his assertion that *because* the mind "depends so greatly upon the temperament and on the disposition of the organs of the body," that *medicine*—not philosophy or theology—will make men wiser than they have ever been.[49] This amounts to an implicit rejection of both classical and Christian emphasis on the primacy of the soul, one that reaffirms Marsilius's completely bodily understanding of politics and Machiavelli's frank this-worldly turn.

If we might go deeper into the latter, the goal of his physics seems to be to undo the curse of Genesis and take us to a new Eden—not a heavenly paradise, but a very earthly Eden. To recall Machiavelli's rejection of imagined for real and this-worldly republics and kingdoms, Descartes similarly rejects a "speculative" physics for a very practical one, one that focuses on the mastery of nature, rather than the contemplation of nature. This mastery, so he promises or prophesies, will lead to the elimination of the curse of the ground, and hence of "toil," "thorns and thistles," "sweat," and perhaps even the curse that man should return "to dust" in death (Genesis 3:17–19). In short, Descartes promises a secularized version of salvation that finds its fulfillment, not in Christ, but in a kingdom of this world.

The new primacy of human art over nature is seen clearly in Descartes's account of nature that, because the mechanism was so thorough, invited condemnation by religious authorities. In the *Discourse*, he offers a softened account, and does so *as if* it were merely hypothetical.[50] As opposed to the creation account in Genesis, Descartes presents a protodeistic account wherein God "create[d] enough matter . . . somewhere in imaginary space" and put it in motion "so that he concocted as confused a chaos as the poets could ever imagine and that later he did no more than apply his ordinary conserving activity to nature, letting nature act in accordance with the laws he established."[51] And "by such activity alone all the things that are purely material could have been able, as time went on, to make themselves just as we now see them."[52]

49 In this, Descartes seems in complete agreement with Lucretius, who, in arguing that we have no immortal, immaterial soul, used as a proof that "the mind, like a sick body, can be healed and directed by medicine. This too is a premonition that its life is mortal." Lucretius, *De Rerum Natura* 3.510–511.

50 Descartes, *Discourse on Method*, V.41–42.

51 Ibid., V.42.

52 Ibid., V.45. While the initial "chaos" might remind us of the void in Genesis 1:2, his exact description—a "chaos as confused as the *poets* could imagine" (emphasis added)—bears greater resemblance to the chaos inherent in the creation account of the Epicurean poet Lucretius, whose *De Rerum Natura* was one of the major sources of ancient Epicurean materialism circulating around early modern Europe (and undoubtedly known to Descartes, if by no other source, than through his early mathematical and atomist mentor, Isaac Beeckman). The near duplication of Lucretius's creation account (whether intentional or not) is of the utmost significance. Given that Lucretius's aim was to undermine religion, he presented a purely materialist account of creation in which all is brought about through the chaotic, random jostling of atoms acting according to the laws of nature. For Lucretius, the laws of nature replace the need for an intelligent cause, and the laws themselves merely arise from the very nature of brute, atomic matter moving in the void. See Lucretius, *De Rerum Natura*, 1.1021–51; 2.167–81; 2.1058–1104; 4.823–57; 5.419–31.

Cosmic creation by mechanism entails a mechanistic account of human beings as automata run by heat from the heart.[53] According to Descartes, the movement of the heart "follows just as necessarily from the mere disposition of the organs . . . as do the motions of a clock from the force, placement, and shape of its counterweights and its wheels."[54]

Descartes's mechanism thereby collapses art and nature, a collapse that is licit because "the laws of mechanics . . . are the same as the laws of nature," so that there is no essential difference between a machine and a living thing. The mechanical properties of heat displace the animating properties of spirit: in fact, heat *is* life, acting as what Descartes calls "animal spirits."[55]

But just how much does heat, or animal "spirits," explain? Descartes lists the changes in the brain that cause wakefulness, sleep, dreams; our perception of light, sounds, odors, tastes, heat, and other qualities that "imprint various ideas through the medium of the senses"; how hunger, thirst, and other internal passions "can also send their ideas"; the common sense that receives ideas, retains them in memory, and through imagination manipulates the ideas; and the movement of all the muscles in response to objects.[56]

The assumption of thoroughgoing mechanism is, we stress, essential to his method. That is, the famous criteria of clarity and certainty, epitomized in geometric reasoning, demands that nature be constituted according to what is very clear and certain to us *as artisans*, the machines we make. For Descartes, then, life must be reduced to mechanism for the same reason that nature must be reduced to geometrically defined, homogeneous substance. Mastery also entails that nature be machinelike, for if natural things were fundamentally different from manmade things, then we could not remake nature according to the principles of human technical "creation."

We have now seen that Descartes's method cannot be considered apart from his mathematization and mechanization of nature and his goal of mastering nature. Rather, the method is the union, as conceived by Descartes, of the three. What effect will this method have upon the development of the modern historical-critical method?

First, the new mathematical-mechanical account of nature entirely removes mystery from nature. That is, nature is considered to be something entirely intelligible to

53 Descartes was unwilling to assert, even hypothetically, that the laws of nature working on matter could create either animal or human life; that is, he remains silent about the possibility. Instead he supposes, in his alternative creation account, that "God formed the body of a man entirely similar to one of ours . . . without making it out of any material other than the type I had described, and without putting in it, at the start, any rational soul, or anything else to serve as a vegetative or sensitive soul, but merely exciting in the man's heart one of those fires without light . . . which, having no other nature but that which heats up hay when it has been bundled up before drying, or which boils new wines while they are left to ferment on the stalk." Descartes, *Discourse on Method*, V.45–46.

54 Ibid., V.50.

55 "And finally, what is most remarkable in all this is the generation of animals spirits that are like a very subtle wind, or better, like a very pure and lively flame that, rising continually in great abundance from the heart to the brain, and from there [the "flame"] goes through the nerves into the muscles, and gives movement to all the members, without the need for imagining any other reason . . . [than] the laws of mechanics, which are the same as the laws of nature. . . ." Ibid., V.54.

56 Ibid., V.55.

the human intellect so that it reveals nothing of a superior intellect in its construction. The wisdom of God becomes identical to the wisdom of man. There is not, then, an analogy of being that exists between nature and God, in which the mysterious wisdom and power of God are only glimpsed in the profundities of His creation. Rather, there is either no analogy at all (and God is, following Ockham, utterly obscure), or an implied identity (which we shall see blossom in Spinoza's pantheism).

Second, mystery is removed from nature by making it entirely law-mechanism driven. As a consequence, miracles become more and more problematic, or to bring it to the future of biblical scholarship, the miracles in Scripture become more and more dubious as science advances, submitting ever more of nature under its mathematical-mechanical paradigm. Soon enough, the method of exegesis becomes inseparable from the doubt of the miraculous, defining in large part what it means to be critical. A critical approach to history, then, is united to a doubt of supernatural intervention as reported in Scripture, so that the task of the exegete will be redefined in terms of finding alternative explanations of the supernatural that accord with, or at least do not violate, the new secular order of nature. The order is secular precisely because supernatural irruptions are considered impossible.

Third, as mentioned above, the ever-more complete technical mastery of nature displaces salvation history as that which defines history. History begins with the first successful attempts to define nature mathematically and control it technically. Prior to this, humanity's history was at best cyclical, and it was cyclical precisely because it was "precritical." As a result, the fundamentally critical and decidedly modern stance toward those who lived prior to this "scientific revolution" is that of the skeptic, one who methodically doubts their claims to wisdom about nature, God, and humanity.

Dubious Means

This dubious stance deserves a closer look, since it is intimately a part of Descartes's program. It may seem odd to leave a deeper consideration of the most distinctive feature of Descartes's method until now. We have refrained from the ordinary course of treating doubt first and foremost for a very important reason: Descartes's methodical doubt is actually part of his *strategy*. It serves to clear the ground for the presentation of his already-formed philosophy.

Descartes makes it seem as if the naive assumption of doubt is the proper beginning point of philosophy, and hence strikes a skeptical and innocent pose before he reveals his positive philosophical account *as if* doubt leads, simply and straightforwardly, to his philosophy. A little reflection will show us that this skeptical pose is as much a ruse as his putting forth his mechanistic account of creation merely hypothetically.

For Descartes, mathematics determines the criteria of clarity and certainty from the very beginning, hence all that is merely probable, all that is not mathematical, can be set aside as inconsequential, or dubitable. In short, mathematics first, doubt second. This is all the clearer in Descartes's *Rules*, in which he wrote far more candidly. There, the "universal wisdom" he promises in Rule I entails in Rule II that the mind be concerned *only* with what we find to be "certain and indubitable," and "only arithmetic and geometry are free from the taint of any falsity or uncertainty." Thus, "we reject all knowledge which is merely probable, and judge that only those things should be believed which are perfectly known, and about which we can have no doubts."

The pose of doubt allows him to reject all that fails to conform to the preestablished criteria defined by mathematics. All previous philosophy is merely groundless squabbling because no one prior to Descartes had achieved the intellectual union of mathematical construction and mathematized nature. For the same reason, all previous opinions and traditions can be tossed aside as irrelevant, and theology itself set aside (with all due expressions of piety) because it is irrational. The senses can be doubted because they take nature as it is, as it presents itself, rather than reducing it to a nonsensible, subvisible homogeneous extension capable of mathematical treatment according to his new physics. Thus, the posture of doubt is inseparable from the method *because* it serves to remove the obstacles to Descartes's unique union of mathematization, mechanization, and mastery.

This is an extraordinarily important point precisely because of the acid role played by the assumption of skepticism in modernity as it relates to religion, and in particular, to the Bible itself. Considering first the historical context of Descartes, it becomes clear how useful methodical doubt would be in dissolving the religious conflicts of the Thirty Years' War. If we follow Descartes's method, all the sources of religious conflict are left behind because none of them can satisfy his newly defined criteria of truth. Revealed truths are set aside because they are nonrational. Neither the Bible itself nor its traditional interpreters can claim true knowledge; at best, they can express a kind of nonrational fideism. It is science (as narrowly defined by Descartes) that provides the true revelation, and in contrast to the promises of biblical enthusiasts, it provides very real, this-worldly release from suffering in an earthly paradise through mastery of nature.

Looking beyond Descartes's immediate historical context, we shall find that the habitual posture of doubt ingrained by following Descartes's method will become the unquestioned beginning point of many of the most prominent scriptural scholars toward the biblical text. But the skeptical stance toward the Bible is one side of a two-sided coin, the other being mathematically defined rationality, a mechanical view of nature, and the new goal of the technical mastery of nature that provides a secular substitute for the kingdom of God.

Descartes's doubt is not some methodically neutral position that yields indubitable and objective truth, but a means for establishing the goals of the "I" that doubts. For this reason no treatment of Descartes and his characteristic stance of doubt would be complete without a more explicit analysis of the "I," the pure thinking soul of the Cartesian *cogito*, especially as Descartes's account relates to theology.

The Cogito *and Descartes's God*

Many treatments of Descartes leap straight into Descartes's proofs of the soul and God without noticing, first of all, the important *context* of these proofs. An essential part of that context is Descartes's mechanism. In the last paragraph of Part V, after immersing readers in his mechanistic account, he remarks that

> the subject of the soul . . . is of the greatest importance; for, after the error of those who deny the existence of God . . . there is nothing that puts weak minds at a greater distance from the straight road of virtue than imagining that the soul of animals is of the same nature as ours and that, as a consequence, we have no more to fear nor to hope for after this life than have flies or ants. . . .[57]

This is an arresting remark for someone who has just offered a relentlessly mechanistic account of human beings that all but reduces them to animal automata. Given the obvious danger, it was certainly prudent of Descartes to have offered his famous proofs of the existence of the immortal soul and of God in Part IV, the previous part, so that they would be fresh in readers' minds as they read Part V, thereby helping to guard them from "imagining that the soul of animals is of the same nature as ours." His mechanism *by itself* would seem to lead to the conclusion that "we have no more to fear nor to hope for after this life than have flies or ants. . . ." Without the soul and God, morality would lose all hold on "weak minds." Whatever else Descartes intended in regard to his famous proofs, they very clearly serve a political-moral function (one that bears at least some resemblance to the use of religion for similar purposes in Marsilius and Machiavelli).

As for the caliber of the proofs themselves, however much sincerity and effort Descartes may have invested in these proofs in Part IV (and the more lengthy proofs in the *Meditations*), they remain highly dubious. In regard to the twin criteria of clarity and certainty, they pale by comparison in regard to his vivid mechanistic analysis of the still-warm animal heart in Part V of the *Discourse*. In regard to their reception by readers, his proofs have remained to this day objects of endless controversy (whereas various modifications of his mechanism have succeeded handsomely). We will not enter either into the interminable controversies surrounding Descartes's proof of the soul and God except to note that they are interminable. Insead, let us examine the *mode* of proof used in Part IV, which reveals the consequences of his project for modern theology.

The famous methodical Cartesian doubt has, as its goal, severing the dependence of the intellect on nature as it presents itself, on tradition, and on all previous philosophy ("orphaning" it, we might say[58]), and focusing the mind on its own naked, independent power, the "I" of the "*cogito ergo sum*." This "ego" is, however, not really

---

57 Ibid.

58 We borrow the phrase from Roger Lundin's insightful analysis, "Interpreting Orphans: Hermeneutics in the Cartesian Tradition," in the above-mentioned Lundin, Walhout, and Thiselton, *The Promise of Hermeneutics*, Ch. 1.

naked. Descartes's argument is set up in such a way that the allegedly naked intellect is formed, or clothed, by *his* method, a clothing made possible by that very stripping away of any external authority through doubt. The "I" truly refers ultimately to Descartes, for it is he, through his new *mathesis*, who ultimately creates and therefore defines what thinking is by defining the order of knowing, the *ordo cognoscendi*.

Thus, the *cogito* itself contains Descartes's entire philosophic revolution. Descartes proclaims that, while all else is subject to some doubt, "this truth—*I think, therefore I am*—was so firm and certain that the most extravagant suppositions of the skeptics were unable to shake it." But he draws the entirely illicit conclusion that "I could accept it without scruple as the first principle of the philosophy I was seeking."[59] It is illicit for the straightforward reason that Descartes's argument amounts to claiming that *while I am doing X, I cannot doubt I exist because I could not being doing X if I did not exist*. X could be any activity, from sneezing to scratching. What is important for our purposes is why Descartes would assume the primacy of thinking as the activity that affirms existence.

To say "I think, therefore I am" could mean (1) my thinking causes me to exist or (2) only while I am thinking, I know I exist. The first is manifestly absurd *unless* Descartes simply meant to define himself, scholastically, *as God*, whose essence it is to exist as a purely spiritual, thinking being, and whose thoughts cause being. Some obvious warrant for this is found in Descartes's subsequent conclusion that "I was a substance the whole essence or nature of which was merely to think, and which, in order to exist, needed no place and depended on no material thing. Thus this 'I,' that is, the soul through which I am what I am, is entirely distinct from the body."[60] Descartes would seem to be declaring himself to be "I am who am," a Father in the most fundamental sense, a self-caused being (Exodus 3:14). This sense would also be fully in accord with his declaring, "I think, therefore I am" to be the "first principle of the philosophy I was seeking," since the first principle of metaphysics (as Descartes knew from his scholastic training at the college of La Flèche) is God. Given that Descartes reconceives nature according to what is certain and clear to us, and constructs its deepest intelligibility according to his own *mathesis universalis*, self-deification would be an understandable temptation.

If we take the *cogito* in the more benign sense—while I am thinking, I know that I exist—then again, one may as well substitute sneezing and scratching for thinking. Laying this difficulty aside, we may focus on the revolutionary mode of his argument for the existence of God.

Descartes moves from his indubitable first principle (himself as a thinking thing) to a demonstration of the existence of God, an interesting move precisely because,

59 Descartes, *Discourse on Method*, IV.32.

60 Ibid., IV.32–33. The last conclusion about the self-subsistence of the soul is not only unwarranted, but directly contradicts his assertion in Part VI (which we have already viewed above), that "the mind depends so greatly upon the temperament and on the disposition of the organs of the body that, were it possible to find some means to make men generally more wise and competent than they have been up until now, I believe that one should look to medicine to find this means."

despite Descartes's protestations to the contrary, the certainty of God's existence thereby rests upon Descartes *as first principle*. It makes sense that Descartes did not take the normal, scholastic route of proving God's existence from the effects of God in nature (a demonstration *quia*, through the effects, rather than *propter quid*, through the cause itself). In his mechanistic view, no such proof from effect to cause is possible since nature is a self-running, self-contained mechanism. As Richard Kennington has noted, in Descartes:

> There is no ascent from nature to God because Cartesian nature shows no evidence of being made by God. Cartesian nature is mechanism. "The laws of nature," says Descartes, "are the same as the laws of mechanics." Since mechanism is devoid of purposes, nature shows no evidence of the purposes of God. Thus Cartesian physics, in its mechanistic character, determines in this negative way the character of the proofs of God's existence: they cannot begin in nature. The sequence of the *Discourse*, first metaphysics, then physics, is the reverse of the true sequence. But if nature shows no evidence of a divine author, then this theocentric metaphysics [as presented by Descartes] is in profound discord with the Bible.[61]

The contradiction could not be more striking. Instead of the usual demonstration through creation or nature as it manifests the deity's power and wisdom, Descartes attempts a proof through himself, through his essence defined as a thinking thing. He asserts that he can think of a being "truly more perfect than I was, and even that it had all the perfections of which I could have any idea. . . ." This idea must exist *as* God because "existence was contained in it. . . ."[62]

Of course, Descartes's argument is fallacious. For example, thinking of a perfect horse doesn't cause that perfect idea of a horse to exist because we insist that the perfect horse, to be perfect, includes existence in its definition. While Descartes admits that there will be those who are not persuaded by his argument,[63] he then asserts (oddly enough) that

> even what I have already taken for a rule—namely that all the things we very clearly and very distinctly conceive are true—is certain only because God is or exists, and is a perfect being, and because all that is in us comes from him. Thus

61 Kennington, *On Modern Origins: Essays in Early Modern Philosophy*, pp. 117–118.

62 Descartes, *Discourse on Method*, IV.36. Descartes interestingly enough continues "in the same way as the fact that its three angles are equal to two right angles is contained in the idea of a triangle . . . consequently, it is, at the very least, just as certain that God, who is a perfect being, is or exists, as any demonstration in geometry could be." This is a suspicious equation of the certainty of geometry with the certainty of God, especially since Descartes considered his geometry to be primarily constructive or creative. Such an equation would lend support to the possibility that Descartes might have understood himself to be offering a philosophic account of the deity in accord with the Marsilian observations about philosophers creating the gods to reinforce the moral order needed for political peace.

63 Descartes, *Discourse on Method*, IV.37–38.

> it follows that our ideas or our notions, being real things and coming from God, insofar as they are clear and distinct, cannot to this extent fail to be true.[64]

Descartes offers as the reason for this strange assertion that if we don't know that "all that is real and true in us comes from a perfect and infinite being," then "however clear and distinct our ideas may be, we would have no reason that assured us that they had the perfection of being true."[65] That is, even though someone may demonstrate that the interior angles of every triangle are equal to two right angles, he cannot know that the demonstration is true unless he is assured that a perfect and infinite being adds to the demonstration the perfection of being true.

The problem with this assertion, of course, is that we cannot separate "the perfection of being true" from the demonstration of geometrical truth that gives us the clear and distinct idea. Adding "a perfect and infinite being" seems to be perfectly redundant. Whatever Descartes's ultimate intentions, the problem is circularity: the idea of God is not itself clear and distinct otherwise it would not need a demonstration, but yet it is somehow needed to ground his mathematical method (even though geometers seem to function quite well without continual divine affirmation).

Coming at the difficulties in another way, although it may seem quite humble to assert that we need God as a guarantor of certainty, in Descartes's argument God is really functioning as a redundant guarantor of Descartes's mathematically-based criteria of truth, and hence his entire project of shifting certainty *to us*. We cannot help but wonder if, consciously or unconsciously, this God is not fashioned by Descartes precisely for this very purpose: to serve as the guarantor of *his* project, and maintain virtue in weak minds.

Ultimately, we cannot judge Descartes's intentions and sincerity in putting forth his arguments for the proof of the soul and God's existence, although many other prominent philosophers did, such as Henry More, Julien de la Mettrie, Pierre Gassendi, Gottfried Leibniz, John Locke, Baron d'Holbach, and Jean Le Rond d'Alembert.[66] But we may assess them in regard to our larger analysis, and note some of the most important and enduring effects.

Especially in the *cogito*, Descartes presents a model, in himself, of what he takes to be the one and only proper mode of thinking. In so successfully attracting disciples, he became (in the words of Roger Lundin), "the authority for all who would live without authority, the founder of the tradition of spurning tradition, and the father of all who would live without the aid or imposition of their parents."[67] In this tradition, which surely affected the modern historical-critical method, doubt of all else is yoked to the

---

64 Ibid., IV.38.

65 Ibid., IV.39.

66 On this question see Hiram Caton's insightful analysis, "The Problem of Descartes's Sincerity," *The Philosophical Forum* (Spring 1971), Department of Philosophy, Boston University, II.3, pp. 355–370. See also Louis Loeb, "Is There Radical Dissimulation in Descartes's *Meditations*?" in Amélie Oksenberg Rorty, ed., *Essays on Descartes's Meditations* (Berkeley, CA: University of California Press, 1986), pp. 243–270.

67 Lundin, Walhout, and Thiselton, *The Promise of Hermeneutics*, p. 12.

supremely self-confident "I," creating the so-called "hermeneutic of suspicion." The suspicious "I" is critical of all else, but tends (with Descartes) to be entirely uncritical of itself, its own assumptions, and its own projects. The loss of awe and humility before the Book of Nature soon colors the "I's" attitude toward the biblical text and the *traditio* that gave it birth and carried it forth through history.

Further, just as Descartes designates himself as metaphysical first principle, and from himself proves the existence of a God as defined by, and functioning for, the sake of his philosophical project, so also the exegete will begin with the canons of certainty as defined by himself, and then determine what God can be in terms of these canons. On closer inspection, these canons of certainty are almost invariably defined by what the exegete considers "scientific," which just as invariably means something like Descartes's mathematical-mechanical philosophy.

The effect of accepting that philosophy, or one of its many modern permutations, is that it compels the exegete to take the opposite beginning point to the biblical text. The exegete must accept a self-contained universe from which God has absented Himself. At best God can be glimpsed as the distant cause of the laws of nature, but the laws themselves are as self-contained as the universe. God as Father, whose wisdom surpasses mere human wisdom as the heavens do the earth, a Father continually present to His beloved creation, continually active in His redemptive pursuit of humanity, manifesting His power and love both through nature and miracle, must be set aside as appropriate to previous ages of immaturity.

Such "setting aside" had its root in the assumption that nature is defined by what is most certain to us (mathematics and mechanics), and consequently that there is nothing mysterious about it. Nature, creation, does not manifest a higher, more comprehensive wisdom against which our merely human intellects pale. Our response to nature is not one of awe, and then worshipful thanksgiving, but a kind of pride in identity with the Creator's mind, and then, since we are continually improving nature as a raw material, simple pride in ourselves as demiurgic creators who surpass God. Given that science therefore reveals all, revelation is superfluous, or more accurately, since the writers and actors of the Bible were prescientific, revelation is a kind of embarrassment of the childhood of man. If it is to have any use at all, it must be for those who remain prescientific, whose weak minds can digest only salutary moral stories, and who need such stories to keep them on the path to virtue. Thus Descartes's arguments point, in the end, to the place where Machiavelli and Marsilius began, that is, with a purely politicized view of religion.

Conclusion

No one is in doubt that by the nineteenth century an entirely secularized cosmos was in place, or that an almost if not entirely secularized mode of biblical scholarship reached full flower in that same century. The two are intimately connected. Biblical scholars of the nineteenth century like D. F. Strauss proclaimed that they were basing their mode of exegesis on science, which is to say, on the secularized view of science that conformed to the secularized cosmos, one purged of angels and demons, heaven and hell, immaterial souls, miracles and sacraments, and all but the faintest whiff of theism. That fully secularized cosmos had its most evident origins in Descartes's union of the mathematization, mechanization, and mastery of nature. Whatever was Descartes's intention, this was the far-reaching effect.

The mathematization of nature led inevitably to the notion that things in nature must obey mathematically defined laws, whose strict necessity must also pertain in nature. Consequently, miracles cannot happen in reality for the same reason that they do not happen in geometry. This compete mathematical-ontological determinism meant that there could be no extra-natural irruptions from the Divine, a belief oddly enough reinforced theologically by the later Deist identification of God's wisdom with the mathematical-geometrical laws themselves. With this identification, for God to act against the laws would be to act against His wisdom, even His own nature.

An exegete armed with such assumptions—as was D. F. Strauss in the nineteenth century, but more importantly Benedict Spinoza in the seventeenth—must treat reports of miracles not as real events, but *misunderstood* events, events that only *appeared* to violate the laws of nature. Having accepted these assumptions, the exegete must either reject the entire Bible as hopelessly deluded since it is drenched in the miraculous, or systematically shear away the miraculous from the nonmiraculous, to get at what really *could* have happened, and this includes digging out the *real* causes of why the biblical authors and actors wrongly and naively believed miracles could occur (e.g., from psychic illusion brought on by stress, from confusing dreams with reality, from ignorance or misunderstanding of natural phenomena, from the desire to manipulate the ignorant, etc.).

But there is another important effect of the mathematization. Descartes introduced radical doubt of the senses not just because the senses sometimes err, but even more deeply, because the mathematical ontology, rooted in the subvisible world of atomic homogeneous material extension, displaces the reality of our everyday experience of the world as primary. The effect is to place us in a state of permanent doubt in regard to the world of sense, and so to render the everyday world—the world we assume to be real, and which forms the basis of our ordinary thinking and language, symbols, and metaphors—an unreliable source of truth. To understand this important point more clearly, recall the famous words of Galileo, undoubtedly one of Descartes's mentors in the desire to mathematize nature:

> Philosophy is written in the great book which is ever before our eyes—I mean the universe—but we cannot understand it if we do not first learn the language and grasp the symbols in which it is written. This book is written in the mathematical language, and the symbols are triangles, circles, and other geometrical figures, without whose help it is impossible to comprehend a single word of it; without which one wanders in vain through a dark labyrinth.[68]

68 Galileo Galilei, *Opere Complete di Galileo Galilei* (Firenze: 1842), vol. IV, p. 171. Quoted in E. A. Burtt, *The Metaphysical Foundations of Modern Physical Science* (New York: Doubleday, 1932), p. 75.

To say (with Galileo) that nature is written in the language of Euclidean geometry, and that *without* understanding this language it is "impossible to comprehend a single word of it," so that *without* mathematics "one wanders in vain through a dark labyrinth," is simultaneously to imply that most human beings are consigned, by their ignorance of Euclidean geometry and its application, to complete ignorance of nature. This is even more the case with Descartes, for not only does he also assert that nature is essentially, ontologically mathematical, but that the only way to understand it is through his own geometric method.

The acceptance of this kind of mathematization, as it permeated Western intellectual culture, set up an ever greater antagonism to the biblical presentation of revealed truth. Since the ancient Hebrews or Christians had at best very crude and practical knowledge of geometry, then it would become quite difficult to see them as the sole vehicle for revelation. (One would do better to go for enlightenment to the Greeks themselves, or even to the Egyptians or Babylonians; at least they had more advanced mathematics.) Their error lay in their reliance on nonmathematical (that is, prescientific) modes of knowing, which amounted to knowing little if anything at all.

Since those in the Bible took the natural world to be intelligibly ordered by God, and they believed that its intelligibility was made manifest in quite ordinary things through quite ordinary eyes, they treated—indeed, celebrated—the everyday world as revealing God's wisdom. Thus, the language of revelation, as they understood it, was quite earthy, based on the experiences of mothers and fathers, farmers and soldiers, shepherds and tentmakers. Further, the cultic practices not only used everyday objects but took natural things to be conveyers of God's highest, most mysterious revelations. They failed to realize that "we cannot understand it [nature] if we do not first learn the language and grasp the symbols in which it is written." But there is no correlation between the book of nature understood solely through mathematics and the Bible. Mathematization removes any real relationship between our everyday experience of nature and the true knowledge of nature through mathematics.

Once a mathematical philosophy of nature is accepted as divining the nature of the cosmos, there is little left for biblical revelation to offer, except to function as a kind of moral book for those incapable of understanding the requisite mathematics for natural philosophy. That the world is conceived as mechanical, as an entirely self-contained machine that needs at most only a winding-up by an otherwise entirely detached deity, only reinforces the trends of mathematization. The result is, to repeat, the creation of a new kind of Averroism, in which a mathematical-mechanical philosophy of nature replaces Aristotelianism as the completely self-contained, secular explanation of the universe.

As with the original Averroism, the new Averroism introduced by Descartes coupled the self-contained secular account with a fideism directed entirely at morality in this world (and any otherworldly pursuits that do not interfere with the self-contained cosmos as defined by the aims of the secular philosophy of nature). There should be little doubt that Descartes's condescendingly pious treatment of the truths of revelation betrayed an underlying, purely philosophic theism that contradicted biblical revelation at many points (even though Descartes would prudently remain silent about them).

Here, then, is the source of the modern "double truth" that will take successive forms, setting up distinct tensions. Soon after Descartes, a purely rational Deism grounded in the new mathematical-mechanical science of nature would stand in tension with a biblically-based, nonscientific theology. This Deism forms the intellectual matrix from which the historical-critical method was refined in late eighteenth- and nineteenth-century Germany.

However, there is more to Descartes's influence than is found in his treatment of nature. No one can doubt Descartes's position as the father of modern philosophy, nor how pervasively Cartesianism has influenced the formation of the modern mind. This is as true for biblical scholars as it is for philosophers, and nowhere more evident than in the passion for method. The "mania for method" so characteristic of modernity, and especially evident among modern scholars of the Bible, partakes of the same revolutionary shift seen in Descartes that tends to place the locus of truth and certainty in human beings, and endows them with the status of creators and judges, omniscient by virtue of their knowledge of mathematical-physical laws, omnipotent by virtue of their technical mastery of nature.

We may go so far as to say that the shift from nature to method *is* the revolution, for method becomes that by which all else is judged and re-formed according to human will. The exact parallel in biblical studies will be the shift from the *text* itself as authoritative to the *method* of the exegete, in which the method becomes that by which revelation is judged and re-formed according to the will of the interpreter. In parallel to Descartes's rejection of tradition, the method displays the ingenuity of the exegete *over against* the tradition of interpretation, so that the exegetical monographs and dissertations unfold like the autobiographical drama of the *Discourse*: a survey of all previous opinions, whether traditional or offered by other, rival exegetes; an account of their dubious nature; and the offering of a new method that supercedes all previous exegesis and displays the genius of the writer. Not surprisingly, the Cartesian habit of considering oneself rationally self-sufficient, in a position of unquestionable authority over the biblical text and the interpretive tradition, leads to continual attempts at "self-fathering" in biblical studies just as it does in the history of modern philosophy.

Following upon this, it should be clear why hermeneutics becomes the especial passion and focus of modern biblical studies insofar as, in following modern philosophy, it has been formed in the Cartesian image. The shift from text to hermeneutics is merely a variant, or better, a subspecies of the modern shift in focus from nature to epistemology, from the things known to the human knower, from the *ordo essendi* to the *ordo cognoscendi*, from being to the *cogito*, the Cartesian "thinking thing." In Descartes, the shift is made possible by the denial of the reality of the everyday world of the senses, along with the rejection of all opinions, philosophic or otherwise, that have been based upon an "uncritical" acceptance of this world. Since the principle of order cannot come from "out there," then we must look for it in ourselves. The cost of this shift is well summarized by Frederick Wilhelmsen.

> If a man accepts Descartes's initial principle, he is forced immediately to ask the following question: If I am philosophically—that is, critically—certain of only one thing at the outset of my philosophizing, and if this one thing is the existence of myself as a thinking principle, then how am I able (if I am able at all) to move from this primitive certitude to a knowledge of the existence of the extra-mental world, of things existing independently of my own understanding? This is the famous "critical problem" that has plagued thinkers since the time of Descartes.[69]

This same critical problem exists in biblical studies, only it is framed in terms of hermeneutics and the gap that separates the interpreter from the text: How is the hermeneut—cut off from the tradition of interpretation, from the liturgical context of the living, believing Church, and freed from the authority of the text by the independence of his judgment—to move to the extracritical reality of the Scriptures?

While many attempts to establish extracritical reality will be attempted over the next centuries, in the end, the Scriptures seem to be treated like Cartesian wax. Since the authority of the Scriptures and their inherent unity are the very things that the critical method rejects, then the text itself becomes completely malleable in the hand of the exegete, who re-forms it according to purposes and projects of his own making. The text is analyzed only to be resynthesized, deconstructed only to be reconstructed. In so doing, the exegete becomes like Descartes, the demiurgic authority himself. He or she then becomes the new principle of unity that defines content, canon, and interpretation, the self-sufficient "I" that judges from outside the law of prayer and law of belief. In parallel to Descartes, interpretive authority shifts from the *lex orandi* and the *lex credendi* to the *ordo cognoscendi* of the exegete (often defined by the philosophy of the day). Since there is inherent in modernity a secular bent, a built-in rejection of transcendence, the new philosophical goals imposed upon the text as reordering principles by exegetes tend to be political. As we shall see, this politicizing of Scripture can take various forms, from overt winnowing of the text to remove all supernatural chaff, leaving only the moral grain that supports political order, to much subtler methods of layering the text historically to demonstrate that spiritual, otherworldly elements are later accretions upon an earlier, original, nonspiritual, earthly core. One of the earliest examples of such politicizing is also one of the earliest and most thorough, that of Thomas Hobbes.

---

69 Frederick Wilhelmsen, *Man's Knowledge of Reality: An Introduction to Thomistic Epistemology* (Englewood Cliffs, NJ: Prentice-Hall, 1956), p. 14.

CHAPTER 8

THOMAS HOBBES

Thomas Hobbes: An Overview

In his own use of scripture, Thomas Hobbes accomplished an impressive synthesis of the various strands of thought examined here so far: he unified the purely secular aim of Marsilian and Machiavellian political thought with a secular cosmology needed to support it, and did so through an explicitly nominalist (mathematical-mechanistic) philosophy that focuses on the complete mastery of nature, especially human nature—all of which he put forth in the context of the particularities of the English political scene. His work is rightly seen as central (for better or worse) to the growth of modern thought.

In regard to the secular cosmology, Hobbes carried forth the assumption that the basis of all reasoning is mathematical and that nature itself is completely mechanical. Having reduced both reason and nature, Hobbes was able to supply a completely mechanical conception of human nature, wherein human thought and action are reduced to epiphenomena of the Galilean law of inertial motion. Whereas Descartes had provided a quite similar mechanistic account, he still allowed for an immaterial soul, thereby creating a dualism of matter and spirit. Hobbes simply clipped off the immaterial aspect and offered a thoroughly materialist account of human nature and human thought. As with Descartes, Hobbes placed the locus of all truth in human thought (albeit through nominalism), and, further, argued that all reasoning is ultimately reducible to each individual's desire for power. Accordingly, Hobbes offered a version of philosophical nominalism wherein universals are purely conventional, agreed-upon signs or tokens by which human beings satisfy their desires.

Although Hobbes (like Bacon and Descartes) stressed the mastery of nature, his real target was human nature. Hobbes believed that if we followed his account of human nature (which reduced all human thought and action to the pursuit of power and pleasure and the avoidance of pain and death), human nature itself could be mastered by a new materialist political science, and civil peace would be its lasting achievement. Again, as with Marsilius, the goal was political peace.

In conformity with the pattern of the Averroism of Marsilius, and following a path similar to Descartes, Hobbes's secular cosmology is entirely self-contained. In accord with Marsilius and Machiavelli, Hobbes also provided a "natural" account of religion as rooted in fear and ignorance that demonstrated both its pernicious influence and its political utility. But in contrast to Marsilius and Descartes (and perhaps in continuity with Machiavelli), Hobbes allowed no Averroistic dualism, or double truth. For Hobbes, there was only political truth, and to this truth revelation itself must entirely submit. One could hardly ask for a more perfect integration of the different manifestations of the *viae modernae*.

Hobbes's *summa* would have major implications for modern scriptural scholarship. His materialist cosmology and reductionist political science were antithetical to religion in general and Christianity in particular. Yet Hobbes believed that religion, born in fear and ignorance, was ineradicable. Given his own particular historical context—the Thirty Years' War and the English Civil Wars—religion had moreover become a violently disruptive political force. Rather than avoid a direct confrontation with Christianity (as had Descartes), Hobbes attempted to reconstitute Christianity itself through an entirely novel exegesis of Scripture that would support the complete subordination of Christianity to the state, and therefore end the religious controversies that seemed to be destroying civil peace. In doing so, he provided the general principles, albeit retrospectively, for Henry VIII's claim of royal supremacy as well as the entire Machiavellian tradition of "reason of state." It was through this politicized exegesis that Hobbes became the true father of modern scriptural scholarship. This point must sink in: Hobbes's *secular-political aim defined and determined his exegetical methods*, so that his methods carry forth the secular-political aim whether later exegetes wielding those methods realize it or not.

The central text in which Hobbes's extensive treatment of Scripture occurs is his famous *Leviathan*, also one of the founding texts of modern political philosophy (or to be more exact, of modern political liberalism). At the very beginning, we receive a warning sign right away that Hobbes will introduce a new approach to Scripture and that it will be politicized. Hobbes informed the reader in his Epistle Dedicatory to the *Leviathan*, "That which perhaps may most offend, are certain Texts of Holy Scripture, alledged by me to other purpose than ordinarily they use to be by others. But I have done it with due submission, and also (in order to my Subject) necessarily; for they [i.e., certain passages of Scripture] are the Outworks of the Enemy, from whence they impugne the Civill Power."[1] This candid admission—or warning—by Hobbes captures well both his novelty in the use of Scripture and the political goal that defined it.

For his efforts, Hobbes was immediately branded an atheist and purposeful subverter of Christianity by his contemporaries. Yet this same Hobbes, as we have noted above, has rightly been called by our contemporary scholars the father of modern

1 Thomas Hobbes, *Hobbes's Leviathan*, reprint of the 1651 edition of *Leviathan, or The Matter, Forme, & Power of a Common-wealth Ecclesiasticall and Civill* (Oxford: Clarendon Press, 1965), Epistle Dedicatory. The dedication is to "Mr Francis Godophin."

scriptural scholarship[2] (and by some, even commended for his orthodoxy[3]). This juxtaposition should lead us to the most obvious question, a question of pedigree if nothing else: How could a man all but universally reviled as an atheist in his day become a revered father of scriptural scholarship in our own? That is a question well worth asking, and the answer will emerge in our analysis.

T. Hobbesii Malmesburiensis Vita[4]

Thomas Hobbes was born in 1588 in England, a bit over a half century after Parliament passed Henry VIII's Act of Supremacy. Although Hobbes's *Leviathan* would not be published until 1651, Henry VIII's demand that the English sovereign be "reputed the only Supreme Head on earth of the Church of England, called *Anglicana Ecclesia,*" could not have had a more willing and thorough advocate.

Since Henry VIII's death in 1547, England had been yanked from all sides by contending religious factions, in great part because Henry's precedent of the sovereign-take-all in religious matters meant that both political and religious controversies were concentrated in the crown. Henry's successor, the sickly Edward VI (ruling from 1547 to 1553), whom Henry had sired with Jane Seymour, was a pawn for those who wanted to push the *Anglicana Ecclesia* toward a more radical Protestantism. But with Mary (ruling from 1553 to 1558), the daughter of Henry and Catherine, England

---

2 For attributions of Hobbes's importance to the history of biblical scholarship, see Jon D. Levenson, *The Hebrew Bible, the Old Testament, and Historical Criticism: Jews and Christians in Biblical Studies* (Louisville: Westminster/John Knox Press, 1993), pp. 95 and 117; John H. Hayes, "The History of the Study of Israelite and Judaean History," in John H. Hayes and J. Maxwell Miller, eds., *Israelite and Judaean History* (London: SCM Press, 1977), p. 45; J. Samuel Preus, "The Bible and Religion in the Century of Genius: Part II: The Rise and Fall of the Bible," *Religion*, 28 (1998), p. 22; Joseph Blenkinsopp, *The Pentateuch: An Introduction to the First Five Books of the Bible* (New York: Doubleday, 1992), p. 2; James Barr, "Interpretation, History of Modern Biblical Criticism," in Bruce M. Metzger and Michael D. Coogan, eds., *The Oxford Companion to the Bible* (Oxford: Oxford University Press, 1993), p. 322; Richard Popkin, "Bible Criticism and Social Science," in Robert S. Cohen and Marx W. Wartofsky, eds.) *Methodological and Historical Essays in the Natural and Social Sciences* (Dordrecht: D. Reidel Publishing, 1974), p. 339; Samuel Sandmel, *The Hebrew Scriptures: An Introduction to Their Literature and Religious Ideas* (New York: Alfred A. Knopf, 1963), p. 328; R. K. Harrison, *Introduction to the Old Testament* (Grand Rapids: Eerdmans, 1969), pp. 9–10; James K. Hoffmeier, *Israel in Egypt: The Evidence for the Authenticity of the Exodus Tradition* (Oxford: Oxford University Press, 1996), p. 155, n. 2; Edwin Curley, "Notes on a Neglected Masterpiece: Spinoza and the Science of Hermeneutics," in Graeme Hunter, ed., *Spinoza: The Enduring Questions* (Toronto: University of Toronto Press, 1994), p. 70; and Henning Graf Reventlow, *The Authority of the Bible and the Rise of the Modern World*, translated by John Bowden (Philadelphia, PA: Fortress Press, 1985), Part II, Chapter 3. Our thanks to Jeffrey Morrow for his extensive research on this attribution.

3 See A. P. Martinich, *The Two Gods of Leviathan* (Cambridge: Cambridge University Press, 1992), Howard Warrender, *The Political Philosophy of Hobbes* (Oxford: Clarendon Press, 1957), and even more, Paul Cooke's analysis of both in *Hobbes and Christianity: Reassessing the Bible in Leviathan* (Lanham, MD: Rowan & Littlefield, 1996). For a list of others vouching for Hobbes's orthodoxy, see Cooke, Ch. 2.

4 *T. Hobbesii Malmesburiensis Vita* or *The Life of Thomas Hobbes of Malmesbury* is the title Hobbes gave to his autobiographical poem written in Latin.

was immediately pulled back to Catholicism through the power of the monarchy and Parliament. Queen Mary married Philip II (future King of Spain, 1556–1598), the son of the deeply Catholic and very powerful Charles V (1519–1556). As a result, the attempt to restore England to Catholicism was hopelessly entwined with English political fears of subordination to Spain and absorption by the Habsburg dynasty.

After the death of Queen Mary in 1558, the daughter of Henry and Anne Boleyn ascended the throne. Queen Elizabeth would give the *Anglicana Ecclesia* its most decisive stamp, that of moderate Protestantism—and even this she pursued with characteristically English moderation. Elizabeth would reign until 1603, making her politically expedient approach to religious matters a kind of national habit.

Although Queen Mary had died in 1558, her husband, Most Catholic King of Spain since 1556, lived to rule for nearly a half century, making his rule contemporaneous with that of Queen Elizabeth, and nearly as long lasting. Philip II was zealous both to consolidate the vast European holdings his father, Charles V, had bequeathed to him, and even more, to reverse the Reformation. He soon brought Spain to its height as an international power, and it was he who sent the seemingly invincible Spanish Armada to England in 1588, both to bring England back to the faith and to punish Queen Elizabeth for interfering in Philip's attempts to bring the Netherlands under his full control.

News of the approach of the Armada so vexed a woman with child in the parish of Westport in Malmesbury, North Wiltshire, England, that she gave birth prematurely. The date was April 5, Good Friday morning, and the child born of fear was Thomas Hobbes, the son of Thomas Hobbes, senior, a barely literate vicar of the poor nearby parish of Brokenborough.[5] Hobbes's autobiographical poem, written in Latin when he was eighty-four and rendered into English by an anonymous contemporary translator, marked well the central underlying theme of Hobbes's life and philosophy, present at his nativity:

> My Native place I'm not asham'd to own;
> Th'ill Times, and Ills born with me, I bemoan:
> For Fame had rumour'd, that a Fleet at Sea,
> Wou'd cause our Nations Catastrophe;
> And hereupon it was my Mother Dear
> Did bring forth Twins at once, both Me, and Fear.[6]

---

5 Not Westport itself, as John Aubrey claims in his famous *Aubrey's Brief Lives*, edited by Oliver Lawson Dick (Ann Arbor, MI: University of Michigan Press, 1957). On this, see Noel Malcolm, "A Summary Biography of Hobbes," in Tom Sorell, ed., *The Cambridge Companion to Hobbes* (Cambridge: Cambridge University Press, 1996), p. 14.

6 Quoted in Thomas Hobbes, *The Elements of Law Natural and Politic*, edited and translated by J.C.A. Gaskin (Oxford and New York: Oxford University Press, 1994), p. 254. The original Latin is as follows:

> *Non est ut patriae pudeat; sed tempus iniquum*
> *Conqueror, et mecum tot quoque nata mala.*
> *Fama ferebat enim diffusa per oppida nostra,*
> *Extremum genti classe venire diem.*
> *Atque metum tantum concepit tunc mea mater,*
> *Ut pareret geminos, meque metumque simul.*

Hobbes received a solid education, especially in Latin and Greek, and was sent to Magdalen College at Oxford when he was fourteen (1603). Apparently, he was already there when his father fell out in his duties as vicar. Upon slandering a fellow cleric, Thomas senior shirked the fine and was threatened with excommunication later that same year. So incensed was the elder Hobbes at the situation that he later attacked the slanderee upon meeting him in the churchyard at Malmesbury, an offense punishable by excommunication. The father fled, dying in obscurity in London, most likely never to be seen again by his soon-to-be-illustrious offspring.[7]

On the larger scene, Queen Elizabeth died in 1603, and with her, the Tudor monarchy. The Stuart line came to the throne through Elizabeth's cousin, King James VI of Scotland, who became James I (1603–1625), a strong advocate of divine-right monarchy who immediately raised the hackles of Parliament. In addition, James was a theologically mixed bag, the son of the devout Catholic, Mary Queen of Scots, and the former king of Scotland, a Calvinist stronghold. Oppressed Catholics, disappointed that he did not suspend their persecution, planned to blow up Parliament (or so it is alleged) in the Gunpowder Plot (1605), the discovery of which led to a wave of anti-Catholic sentiment matching that of 1588, the year of the Armada's attack. Puritans, likewise hoping for sympathy, soon realized that James I was not about to give up his Henrician privileges as head of the Anglican Church to the more democratically inclined Puritans. The latter would not be so easily brushed aside, as their power had been steadily rising in English society, especially in the lower house of Parliament, the House of Commons. Over the next decades, discontent bubbled ever closer to civil war.

In 1608, having completed his education with a bachelor of arts, twenty-year-old Hobbes entered the service of William Cavendish, the future Earl of Devonshire, as a tutor to Cavendish's son, also named William. During his time as tutor, while he and his charge were traveling on the continent, one of the student's tasks was to translate Francis Bacon's *Essayes* into Italian, and back in England, Hobbes came to know Bacon quite intimately (perhaps beginning somewhere around 1618) and acted as his secretary.[8]

By 1628, both the first and the second Earl of Devonshire had died, so Hobbes left the Cavendishes and became a tutor to the son of Sir Gervase Clifton. It was during this service that, while in Europe—in Geneva, Switzerland, in 1630, to be exact, where Hobbes had gone because it was removed from the ongoing battles

---

7 Malcolm, "A Summary Biography of Hobbes," p. 15. See also the account in Aubrey, *Aubrey's Brief Lives*, p. 148.

8 Aubrey, Hobbes's biographer and friend, offers the following account. "Mr. Thomas Hobbes was beloved by his Lordship [i.e., Francis Bacon], who was wont to have him walke with him in his delicate groves where he did meditate: and when a notion darted into his mind, Mr. Hobbs [sic] was presently to write it downe, and his Lordship was wont to say that he did it better than any one els about him . . ." "His Lordship would often say that he better liked Mr. Hobbes's taking his thoughts, then any of the other [secretaries] because he understood what he wrote, which the others not understanding, my Lord would many times have a harde taske to make sense of what they writt." Aubrey, *Aubrey's Brief Lives*, "Francis Bacon," p. 9, and "Thomas Hobbes," p. 150.

of the Thirty Years' War—he was suddenly struck with the glories of Euclid, a moment famously captured by the inimitable biographer Aubrey.[9]

In parallel to Descartes's efforts, Hobbes would conceive of his own deductive form of geometrical-mechanical philosophy based upon the atomism of Galileo. Unlike Descartes—who was at this very time working on his mechanistic *The World*—Hobbes would leave no room for immaterial reality, and he later chided Descartes for trying to maintain an impossible dualism of spirit and matter, when the monism of matter was fully sufficient.[10] In regard to Descartes's mechanism, Hobbes (upon reading Descartes's *Discourse* and *Optics* soon after publication) was rather piqued that the Frenchman had beat him into print, and in 1640–1641 carried on a bitter dispute about who deserved the honor of introducing a purely mechanistic account of physics and human perception.[11]

Returning from Europe in 1631, Hobbes came again to the service of the Cavendish family, this time as tutor of the third Earl of Devonshire. He returned to the Continent in 1634 with the young earl, where he was introduced into the new philosophical circle around Marin Mersenne, and met Galileo in the spring of 1636. He remained until October 1636, only to flee from England to Paris again in late 1640 for fear of reprisal for his *Elements of Law*, which contained all the essentials of his later, more famous work, *Leviathan*. While abroad, he began *Leviathan*, which was published shortly after his return to England again in 1651. During that same time, he became tutor to the Prince of Wales (1646), who would later become England's Charles II. King Charles I (1625–1649), a defender of divine-right monarchy, would be beheaded by those defending the rights of Parliament against the king.

Charles I did not lose his head solely because he attempted to rule without Parliament. He had married the Catholic sister of King Louis XIII of France, Henrietta Maria, a move that aroused the already inflamed anti-Catholic animosity of almost all Anglicans and all the Puritans. His attempt, through Archbishop of Canterbury William Laud, to impose a high Anglicanism noticeably more Catholic than the

9 Ibid., "Thomas Hobbes," p. 150. "He was 40 yeares old before he looked on Geometry; which happened accidentally. Being in a Gentleman's Library, Euclid's Elements lay open, and 'twas the 47 *El. Libri* I. He read the Proposition. *By G*—, sayd he (he would now and then sweare an emphatical Oath by way of emphasis) *this is impossible*! So he reads the Demonstration of it, which referred him back to such a [previous] Proposition; which proposition he read. That referred him back to another, which he also read. *Et sic deinceps* [and thus, one after another] that at last he was demonstratively convinced of that trueth. This made him in love with Geometry.

"I have heard Mr. Hobbes say that he was wont to draw lines on his thigh and on the sheetes, abed, and also multiply and divide."

10 See the Third Set of Objections to Descartes's *Meditations* written by Hobbes, along with Descartes's replies: ". . . that which thinks is something corporeal," maintained Hobbes against Descartes's *cogito*, "for, as it appears, that the subjects of all activities can be conceived only after a corporeal fashion . . . [and since] we cannot separate thought from a matter that thinks, the proper inference seems to be that that which thinks is material rather than immaterial." Translation from Elizabeth Haldane and G.R.T. Ross, *The Philosophical Works of Descartes* (New York: Dover, 1955), Vol. II, Objection III.ii, pp. 61–62.

11 Malcolm, "A Summary Biography of Hobbes," pp. 25–26.

Elizabethan middling political-theological compromise only drove the flames of discontent higher, bringing the Calvinist Scots to rebellion.

Charles I had attempted to rule alone from 1629 to 1640, but the Scottish rebellion made calling Parliament into session for sufficient funds a necessity. The members of Parliament were more concerned with taking the opportunity to advance their own power and limit the king's. Hobbes's pro-royalist *Elements of Law*—in which, as in the later *Leviathan*, absolute sovereignty was based not on divine right but on his mechanistic psychology—made him an enemy of Parliament. In November 1640, anti-royalists in the Long Parliament, led by John Pym, attacked royalist absolutism with sufficient animosity that Hobbes sensed he was in danger. It was then that he fled to Paris. That same John Pym, with his fellow Puritans, would lead their party and hence England into civil war in 1642.

During Hobbes's stay abroad, England was immersed in civil war, which, while it began as largely a political question concerning the respective rights and powers of king and Parliament, soon was driven instead by the theological differences between Puritans and Anglicans. In Oliver Cromwell's words, "Religion was not the thing at first contested for, but God brought it to that issue at last . . . and at last it proved that which was most dear to us."[12] Cromwell, the brilliant military leader of the Parliamentary party, filled his New Model Army for the most part with radical Protestants, who fought well not only against the Anglican royalists (or Cavaliers, as they were known), but after capturing Charles I in 1646, against the more moderate Presbyterians in Parliament, who wanted to restore Charles but with a Presbyterian state church. The king escaped, only to be recaptured and then beheaded on January 30, 1649, by order of the Rump Parliament (all that was left of Parliament after the radicals had purged the Protestant moderates).

Between 1649 and 1653, England was ruled by the Rump Parliament, which had, according to its democratic-theological sectarian beliefs, abolished both the monarchy and the House of Lords, and proclaimed that England would be a Commonwealth, with Cromwell at its ever more powerful head. It was during this period that Hobbes arranged for the publication of his *Leviathan* in the spring 1651, and himself returned to his home country at the very end of the year (the strong anti-Catholic statements in *Leviathan* having stirred the French monarchy against him). Hobbes had given Charles II a copy of the *Leviathan* while both expatriates were in Paris in September of that year.

As time passed, dissent by various factions among Protestants (as well as the anger of rebellious royalist Anglicans and Catholics), brought Cromwell to rule ever more absolutely, entering the stage of full military dictatorship between 1655 and his death in 1658. In 1660, the monarchy was restored in Hobbes's "pupil," Charles II (1660–1685), albeit in a much subdued form. Hobbes would die during Charles II's reign, on December 4, 1679. He had chiseled on his tombstone, *Vir probus, et fama eruditionis Domi forisque bene cognitus*,[13] although it is delightfully rumored that he

12 Quoted in Maurice Ashley, *The Greatness of Oliver Cromwell* (New York: Collier Books, 1962), p. 65.

13 "He was an honorable man, and the fame of [his] learning, was well known, at home and abroad."

considered "Here is the true philosopher's stone" instead. An anonymous broadside of the time offered another:

> Here lies *Tom Hobbes*, the Bug-bear of the Nation,
> Whose *Death* hath frighted *Atheism* out of *Fashion*.[14]

As one can see, the first part of Hobbes's life leading up to the publication of the *Leviathan* spanned the period of the Thirty Years' War (1618–1648), a war of which Hobbes could not help to be vividly aware given that much of this time he was actually on the Continent and moved about to avoid the heat of the conflict. But even more vivid were the English Civil Wars—pitting king against Parliament, factions in Parliament against each other, and entangling the full spectrum of religious differences existing at that time: Catholic, state-Church Anglican, Calvinist-Puritan, and radical Anabaptist. These great religio-political conflicts convinced Hobbes that civil peace could be achieved only by the most radical kind of revolution, one that would change the very foundation of politics, by transforming the very nature of reality. Such a revolution entailed an entirely new approach to religion—and this, Hobbes understood quite clearly, meant an entirely new approach to biblical exegesis.

The Reaction to the Leviathan

We begin with a short account of the reaction to Hobbes's *Leviathan*, precisely because it differs so strikingly from the assessment offered by a significant number of scholars today. Perhaps the most famous of Hobbes's foes was the eminent Bishop John Bramhall. It was an age when titles were themselves extended summaries of the book, and Bramhall's attack on Hobbes was no exception, the first half of it being: *The Catching of Leviathan, or the Great Whale. Demonstrating, out of Mr. Hobs his own Works, That no man who is thoroughly an Hobbist, can be a good Christian, or a good Common-wealths man, or reconcile himself to himself.*[15] But Bramhall's was only one of a myriad of counterattacks launched against Hobbes.[16]

---

14 From a broadside, *The Last Sayings or Dying Legacy of Mr Thomas Hobbes of Malmesbury* (London, 1679), quoted in Samuel Mintz, *The Hunting of Leviathan: Seventeenth-Century Reactions to the Materialism and Moral Philosophy of Thomas Hobbes* (Cambridge: Cambridge University Press, 1962), p. 20. Along with Mintz, one should consult John Bowle, *Hobbes and His Critics: A Study in Seventeenth Century Constitutionalism* (New York: Barnes & Noble, 1969).

15 And continues, *Because his Principles are not only destructive to all Religion, but to all Societies; extinguishing the Relation between Prince and Subject, Parent and Child, Master and Servant, Husband and Wife: and abound with palpable contradictions.* See the reproduction of the title page in John Bramhall, *Castigations of Mr. Hobbes* (New York & London: Garland Publishing, 1977), p. 449. *The Catching of Leviathan* was offered as an appendix by Bramhall to *Castigations of Mr. Hobbes, His Last Animadversions, in the case concerning Liberty, and Universal Necessity.*

16 Other notable contemporary books are, e.g., Thomas Tenison, *The Creed of Mr Hobbes Examined* (1670); Edward Hyde, Earl of Clarendon, *A Brief View and Survey of the Dangerous and Pernicious Errors to*

Hobbes already had a reputation as an atheist (whether deserved or not) that aroused fears when he was appointed tutor of the exiled Prince of Wales five years before the *Leviathan* even appeared.[17] It's no surprise then, that fifteen years after its appearance, on the ominous date of 1666 (after the awful plague of 1665 and the Great Fire of 1666 that burned four fifths of London), a committee within the House of Commons was given the task to "receive Informacion toucheing such bookes as tend to Atheisme Blasphemy or Prophanenesse or against the Essence or Attributes of God. And in particular . . . the booke of M[r] Hobbs called the Leuiathan."[18] Obviously, Hobbes's philosophy was popularly taken to be impious enough to have occasioned the wrath of God, and it was castigated not only for its alleged atheism, but also because its materialist philosophy led to libertinism. Hobbes was therefore blamed, quite pointedly, for the "sudden" decadence of society. Sir Charles Wolseley, in his *Reasonableness of Scripture-Belief* (1672), claimed that, "most of the bad Principles of this Age are of no earlier date then [sic] one very ill Book, are indeed but the spawn of the Leviathan."[19] Others of the time maintained that libertinism was already prominent before the *Leviathan*, but Hobbes's work provided them with the principles for their unprincipled pursuit of pleasure[20] (as seems to be the case of the notorious libertine, John Wilmot, Earl of Rochester, whose deathbed conversion from and denunciation of Hobbesianism in 1670 provided a famous lesson of where Hobbes's thought was leading the age[21]).

Interestingly enough, although many scientists among the newly established Royal Society (1660) shared with Hobbes a passionate attachment to mechanism, Hobbes's name carried such an odor of atheism among the public that whatever the merits of his scientific writings, he was not offered an invitation. Part of the problem, as both Noel Malcolm and Robert Kargon point out, is that the new mechanistic atom-

---

Church and State, In Mr. Hobbes's Book, Entitled Leviathan (1676); John Dowel, *The Leviathan Heretical* (1683); Sir Charles Wolseley, *The Unreasonablenesse of Atheism made manifest* (1669, second edition), which is clearly aimed in great part at Hobbes, and contains an insightful "Atheists' Catechism" that makes clear the Epicurean associations of Hobbes's atomism with ancient Epicureanism; Henry More, *An Antidote Against Atheism* (1653), likewise directed at Hobbes; Alexander Ross, *Leviathan drawn out with a Hook* (1653); William Lucy, *Observations, Censures and Confutations of Notorious Errors in Mr Hobbes His Leviathan* (1663); Rev. John Eachard, *Mr Hobbs's State of Nature Considered in a dialogue between Philautus and Timothy* (1672); John Whitehall, *The Leviathan Found Out; or the Answer to Mr. Hobbes's Leviathan, In that which my Lord Clarendon hath past over* (1679); an anonymous work, *True Effigies of the Monster of Malmesbury: or, Thomas Hobbes in His Proper Colours* (1680).

17 Contemporary Robert Baillie wrote that "the placeing of Hopes [Hobbes] (a professed Atheist, as they speak) about the Prince as his teacher, is ill taken. . . . Let such wicked men be put from about him." Quoted in Mintz, *The Hunting of Leviathan: Seventeenth-Century Reactions to the Materialism and Moral Philosophy of Thomas Hobbes*, p. 12; the original being from Baillie's *Letters and Journals of Robert Baillie*, edited by David Laing (Edinburgh: A. Lawrie, 1841–42), Vol. II, pp. 388, 395.

18 Quoted in Malcolm, "A Summary Biography of Hobbes," pp. 35–36.

19 Quoted in Mintz, *The Hunting of Leviathan: Seventeenth-Century Reactions to the Materialism and Moral Philosophy of Thomas Hobbes* pp. 134–135.

20 The view of Eachard in his *Mr Hobbs's State of Nature Considered* (1672).

21 See Robert Parsons, *A Sermon Preached at the Funeral of the Rt Honorable John Earl of Rochester* (1680).

ism was already associated in the public mind with its unsavory ancient advocates, Epicurus and Lucretius, as well as with bubbling undercurrents of atheism in the mid-sixteenth century, making members of the Royal Society wary of feeding flames of suspicion already high enough.[22] Adding to their fear of external censure, Hobbes embodied their own secret fears that atheism could not be detached from their beloved mechanical philosophy.[23] The eminent atomist Robert Boyle himself attempted to set Hobbes straight in his *An Examen of Mr T. Hobbes* (1662), having been aroused by "the dangerous Opinions about some important, if not fundamental Articles of Religion I had met with in his *Leviathan*. . . ."[24]

Hobbes's arguments aroused animus in the universities as well, not only because he had attacked them directly for teaching politically seditious philosophies, but even more, because his writings seemed to threaten the entire theological, political, and moral order. In 1669, a Fellow of Corpus Christi College, Daniel Scargill, was compelled to make a public declaration of his Hobbesian guilt.[25] One may well doubt the sincerity of Scargill's confession, given that he could only recover his fellowship upon reciting it, but there can be no doubt about Cambridge University's general attitude towards Hobbes. The University of Oxford publicly burned both the *Leviathan* and Hobbes's *De Cive* in 1683.

Divines were similarly incensed, as we have seen most notably with Bishop Bramhall. Bishop Vesey stated in 1677 that "this great *Leviathan* takes pleasure in that deluge of *Atheism* he has spued out of his mouth," and that Hobbes's "doctrines have had so great a share in the debauchery of his generation, that a good Christian can hardly hear his name without saying of his prayers."[26] Thomas Tenison, later archbishop of Canterbury, penned the critical *Creed of Mr Hobbes Examined* (1670) while still a parish priest.

---

22 See Malcolm, "A Summary Biography of Hobbes," p. 35, and his more detailed "Hobbes and the Royal Society," in G.A.J. Rogers and Alan Ryan, eds., *Perspectives on Thomas Hobbes* (Oxford: Clarendon Press, 1988), pp. 43–66. As Robert Kargon points out, "Hobbes's notoriety deeply affected the fortunes of atomism in England. He made the paganism of the ancient atomic philosophy a living, burning issue in mid-seventeenth-century England. The task of purifying atomism from its ancient stigma of atheism was difficult enough; Hobbes added the bulk of his unorthodoxy to it. His friends were forced to dissociate themselves from his position in order to gain a respectable place for atomism in natural philosophy. The battle for atomism was begun in the shadow of Hobbes." See Robert Kargon, *Atomism in England from Hariot to Newton* (Oxford: Clarendon Press, 1966), p. 62. See also A. P. Martinich, *Hobbes: A Biography* (Cambridge: Cambridge University Press, 1999), pp. 296–310. Another problem was that Hobbes himself was critical of methods embraced by the Royal Society, especially Robert Boyle, as is evident in his *Dialogus Physicus* (1661).

23 See Richard Westfall, *Science and Religion in Seventeenth-Century England* (Ann Arbor, MI: The University of Michigan Press, 1973), pp. 108–110.

24 Quoted in Mintz, *The Hunting of Leviathan: Seventeenth-Century Reactions to the Materialism and Moral Philosophy of Thomas Hobbes*, p. 87.

25 That he "gloried to be an *Hobbist* and an *Atheist* . . . Agreeably unto which principles and positions, I have lived in great licentiousness, swearing rashly, drinking intemperately, boasting myself insolently, corrupting others by my pernicious principles and examples, to the Dishonour of God, the Reproach of the University, the Scandal of Christianity, and the just offence of mankind." Quoted in ibid., pp. 50–51.

26 Quoted in ibid., pp. 56–57.

The name of Hobbes, along with his reputation, was dispersed across the Continent as well, and the publication of Benedict Spinoza's *Tractatus Theologico-Politicus* only confirmed in many minds the irreligious outcome of accepting Hobbes, for Spinoza seemed to carry the exegetical principles fashioned by Hobbes to their logical and corrosive conclusion.[27] And, indeed, he did, as the analysis here will show.

In short, whatever may ultimately be said upon a fair examination of Hobbes's arguments, no one can deny that both during his lifetime and long after he had a reputation not much different than Machiavelli's. As we have seen from the broadside quoted above, Hobbes's positions were well enough known that they became a subject even for popular parody during his life, and he played the part of a stock atheist just before and then after his death in popular dramas of the Restoration period.[28] An anonymous work published twenty-five years after Hobbes expired, *Visits from the Shades*, portrayed him as an unrepentant sinner from hell, proud to declare his subversive principles of exegesis:

> I invalidated the Miracles of *Moses*, and all the *Major* and *Minor* prophets of the Old Testament: I made their Inspiration no more than common Dreams, and ordinary Visions: I lessened the stupendous Actions of our blessed Saviour; I leveled the cures of the Dumb, the Leperous and the Blind, as things incident to an ordinary Physician; nor stopp'ed I at any thing, but perverted one Text by another, till I shook the Belief of them all.[29]

All this is, of course, not to condemn Hobbes out of the mouths of others, but it does bring to light in rather vivid detail what would seem to be a significant problem of pedigree in regard to the approbation of Hobbes as the father of modern scriptural scholarship.

A further significant complication noted above is that scholarship over the last century has swayed so far to the opposite side of declaring Hobbes's orthodoxy, that one well wonders if it could be the same Hobbes under consideration. John Hunt declared in 1870, "not only is Hobbes a professed believer in Christianity, but in the most orthodox form of it."[30] In a famous essay of 1938, A. E. Taylor saw Hobbes as something of a Kantian, "a fundamentally honest man . . . with an almost overwhelming sense of duty," which was accompanied by a "sense of their [i.e., duties'] transcendent obligatoriness." Speaking personally, Taylor remarked that, "his religion does impress me as a genuine thing, and it is not very different from that of many worthy persons of to-day who would be sincerely shocked if they were to be accused of 'atheism.'"[31] Similar reassessments were made by, among others, F. C. Hood (*The*

27 See ibid., pp. 57–60.

28 See ibid., pp. 137–140.

29 Quoted in ibid., p. 22.

30 John Hunt, *Religious Thought in England* (London: Strahan & Co, 1870; reprint AMS Press, 1973), Vol. I, p. 383.

31 A. E. Taylor, "The Ethical Doctrine of Hobbes," in K. C. Brown, *Hobbes Studies* (Cambridge: Harvard University Press, 1965), pp. 35–55, quote on p. 53.

Divine Politics of Thomas Hobbes, 1964), Howard Warrender (*The Political Philosophy of Hobbes: His Theory of Obligation*, 1957), and A. P. Martinich (*The Two Gods of Leviathan: Thomas Hobbes on Religion and Politics*, 1992).

If Hobbes was nearly universally excoriated as the "Monster of Malmesbury" by his contemporaries, what could account for his rehabilitation during the last century? Either his own contemporaries pegged Hobbes unfairly, or what is meant by theism or Christianity amongst our contemporaries has undergone significant revision since the seventeenth century.

We suggest that the latter is the case, the revision having been initiated in no small degree by the gradual acceptance of Hobbes's thought, not just in regard to religion, but as formative of modern political liberalism. The reason Hobbes's religion seems so congenial today is due, in no small part, to his being the father of modern biblical scholarship as well as one of the founding fathers of modern political philosophy, and hence modern liberalism. We have accepted the form of religion that fit his state because we live within Hobbes's fulfilled vision of politics. Recall Levenson's assertion that "historical criticism is the form of biblical studies that corresponds to the classical liberal political ideal. It is the realization of the Enlightenment project in the realm of biblical scholarship."[32] It is not accidental, then, that Hobbes is called both the father of modern political philosophy *and* the father of modern biblical scholarship; the latter paternity follows upon the former. Hobbes's politicization of Scripture served his larger radical reconstruction of politics, and this reconstruction served the designs of the modern liberal state. The results of modern biblical scholarship, as indebted to Hobbes, have so formed our understanding of Christianity that Hobbes's originally shocking assertions appear eminently agreeable, and hence his original persecution exceedingly unjust. We do well to recover some of the original shock that attended his revolution.

The Revolution in the Leviathan

Hobbes's context was the cosmological revolution already launched by the two great mechanists on the continent, René Descartes and the French philosopher and priest Pierre Gassendi (1592–1655). Hobbes knew both well, and was an especially close friend of Father Gassendi, whom he met during his tour of the Continent between 1634 and 1636. Gassendi was the most adamant contemporary champion of Epicurus (albeit, so he thought, cleansed of atheism).[33] A short account of Epicurus's arguments is necessary to understand the tremendous implications of his revival, especially in regard to the materialism of Hobbes.

32 Levenson, *The Hebrew Bible, the Old Testament, and Historical Criticism*, p. 118.

33 Gassendi's defense and rehabilitation of Epicurean atomism written before Hobbes published the *Leviathan* were contained in his *De Vita et Moribus Epicuri* (1647), *Animadversiones in Decimum Libri Diogenis Laertii, qui est de Vita, Moribus Placitisque Epicuri* 1649), and *Syntagma Philosophiae Epicuri, cum Refutationibus Dogmatum, Quae Contra Fidem Christianum ab eo Asserta Sunt* (1649).

Ancient materialist atomism was rediscovered in the Renaissance and once again became influential, especially as it was presented in the philosophy of the Greek Epicurus (341–270 BC) and his Roman disciple, Lucretius (c. 94–55 BC).[34] Recall that Epicurean atomism was explicitly defined *against* theology, and indeed may be rightly considered the first fully secular philosophy, for its defined goal was to achieve tranquility in *this world* by eliminating religion.

Epicurus's end was freedom from disturbance—*ataraxia* in Greek; peace of mind, we might say. This desire for peace of mind adumbrates the kind of peace sought many centuries later by Marsilius of Padua for the political realm. What disturbs our this-worldly tranquility? For Epicurus, *the* problem is religion. Our lives could be tranquil but for two related problems: first, humanity is beset with the notion that natural phenomena, like floods, disease, and thunderstorms are instruments used by the gods to punish us, and second, that if the gods fail to harm us in this world, then they will get us in the afterlife and our misery will have no end. In order to enjoy this world in peace, Epicurus argued, we need to rid ourselves of religion.

Epicurus realized that it would take a cosmic revolution, a redefinition of reality, to render religion powerless, even pointless. To effect this, he took over the atomistic arguments of Democritus and argued thusly: The foundation of all reality is the atom, an inert, homogeneous, nonliving, featureless material entity that is eternal and indestructible. From the random association of atoms as they move through the void of infinite space over infinite time, banging and jostling, hooking and unhooking, all visible things are built up all by mere chance—countless stars, countless planets, countless life forms inhabiting each of them, including countless intelligent beings.

The need for the gods is thereby annihilated twice over. Since atoms are eternal, they have no beginning, and hence they need no Creator. Since everything we see around us, no matter how magnificent, including ourselves, was created by random association of atoms, then chance and matter replace the need for a divine, creating and ordering, wisdom.

Since everything is caused by the motion of atoms, then all natural events—from disease and plague to thunder, lightening, and flood—are the results of purely physical causes. They are not omens or punishments sent from the gods to trouble us in this life. But since *we* are also soulless material beings, made only of a particular arrangement of atoms, when we die there is no part of us that can exist in an afterlife and suffer eternal punishment or eternal bliss. *This* is our only life, and hence peace in this world is our only peace.

The Christians of the first centuries, realizing the obvious implications of Epicurus's arguments, rejected his atomistic account of nature as essentially atheistic. They buried Epicurus under scorn, and for about ten centuries he stayed buried. But in the fifteenth century, the writings of both Epicurus and his Roman disciple, Lucretius,

34 For an in-depth analysis of both Epicurus and Lucretius see Benjamin Wiker, *Moral Darwinism: How We Became Hedonists* (Downers Grove, IL: InterVarsity Press, 2002), especially Chs. 1–3, and also Leo Strauss, *Spinoza's Critique of Religion*, translated by E. M. Sinclair (Chicago: University of Chicago Press, 1997), especially Ch. I.

were unearthed, and soon circulated all over Europe, raising many secret and some not-so-secret admirers.

A half century before Hobbes traveled to the Continent, the doctrines of the ancient atomists had already gained a foothold in England near the end of the sixteenth century in a group gathered around the "Wizard Earl," Henry Percy, ninth Earl of Northumberland (and these may have been influenced in turn by the Epicureanism of Giordano Bruno, who stayed at Oxford from 1583 to 1585). Members of the Northumberland Circle were suspect, two of the more famous, Sir Walter Raleigh [Ralegh] and Thomas Harriot [Hariot], being publicly denounced as Epicurean atheists in the 1590s.[35] Of the former, Robert Parsons charged that in "Sir Walter Ralegh's school of atheism . . . both Moses and our Savior, the old and the New Testament are justed at. . . ."[36] and Aubrey says of Hariot that "He did not like (or valued not) the old storie of the Creation of the World. He could not believe the old position; he would say *ex nihilo nihil fit*. . . . He made a Philosophical Theologie, wherin he cast-off the Old Testament, and then the New-one would (consequently) have no Foundation. He was a Deist. . . . The Divines of those times look't on his manner of death [by cancer in 1621] as a Judgement upon him for nullifying the Scripture."[37]

Harriot had many disciples, both directly and through the dispersion of his papers after his death, Sir Charles Cavendish (1591–1654) being a prominent member of the last group. Sir Charles Cavendish was the brother of William Cavendish, the Earl of Newcastle, with whom Hobbes served as tutor. Along with Thomas Hobbes and others, this group of avid atomists came to be called the Newcastle Circle.

Even before his tour of the Continent between 1634 and 1636, then, Hobbes was a mechanist tinged with the doctrines of Epicurus,[38] but the tour solidified his thinking. He was both attracted to and repulsed by Descartes's system, and took care to distinguish his mechanism carefully from the Frenchman's precisely because of their resemblance. Hobbes worked on *De Corpore*, an account of his mechanical philosophy, all through the 1640s—that is, all through his exile on the continent during the Thirty Years' War and the English Civil Wars—but would not publish it until 1655.[39] It was during this time that Hobbes became an ever closer friend of Pierre Gassendi, and through this friendship, the writings of Gassendi praising Epicurus were mediated to England.

As noted above, Hobbes would have no part of the spirit-matter dualism of Descartes, but held to the original fully materialist position of Epicurus and Lucretius,[40]

35 See Jean Jacquot, "Thomas Harriot's Reputation for Impiety," *Notes and Records of the Royal Society of London*, IX (1952), pp. 164–187.

36 Quoted in Kargon, *Atomism in England from Hariot to Newton*, p. 28.

37 Aubrey, *Aubrey's Brief Lives*, p. 123.

38 As evidenced in his so-called "Little Treatise" (1630).

39 Hobbes would end up closer to Descartes, asserting that all space is filled with atoms and fluid aether, rather than atoms and the void, as Epicurus maintained (and Hobbes had held in his earlier drafts of *De Corpore*). Hobbes undoubtedly was swayed toward Descartes by the difficulties of pure Epicureanism explaining action at a distance without a physical medium.

40 Again, with some modification, accepting the void earlier, but later rejecting it for the fluid aether.

so that the human soul was itself both material and mortal, and all actions and all the complexities of living organisms, including human beings, were reducible to brute matter in motion. Obviously, such a position immediately smacked of the atheism of Epicurus, and it was this highly suspect mechanistic physics that Hobbes put boldly and clearly at the very foundation of his greatest work, the *Leviathan*.

The Structure of the Leviathan

The structure itself of the *Leviathan* is instructive of its aims. The overall pattern is Averroistic, or better, Marsilian, since it follows the pattern laid down in the *Defensor Pacis*.[41] The first half is devoted to a thoroughgoing reductionist account of political life based upon Hobbes's entirely self-contained mechanistic-materialist physics, and the second part is designed "to 'confirm' by revelation the rationally established conclusions of the first."[42]

As with Marsilius, Hobbes presented a truncated view of politics, one without any upward thrust, designating civil peace as the highest and defining good of human life. But whereas Marsilius rooted his politics in our animal needs (as defined by Aristotle), Hobbes aimed even lower, reducing all our actions, ultimately, to the material reactions of invisible atoms in terms of their purely material and efficient causes. Hobbes therefore radicalized Marsilius's focus on the efficient causes of this-worldly peace in the context of a view of politics confined to material needs and desires, and did so by eliminating all notions of formal and final causes from physics, and hence from politics.

In this first half of the *Leviathan* (Parts I and II), Hobbes presented his entirely natural account of human beings and politics. For the most part, theological explanations are not just entirely superfluous, but directly contrary to Hobbes's philosophy. Going far beyond Aristotelian Averroism, Hobbes's mechanism is unambiguously, even brutally deterministic, explicitly denying the immortality of the soul. In its indebtedness to Epicureanism, Hobbes's system implied the eternality of the universe as well, and further, in true Epicurean fashion, even asserted that God is a bodily rather than spiritual being.[43] Finally, as with Epicureanism, both nature and human nature are fundamentally amoral and nonteleological. As did Marsilius, Hobbes offered a natural account of religion that would ultimately determine his explicit treatment of Christianity in the second half.

The second half of the *Leviathan* (Parts III and IV) is devoted to theology, but instead of merely consigning it to a separate fideistic realm (as in Latin Averroism

---

41 By "following the pattern," we do not mean to assert that there is an historical connection between Marsilius and Hobbes, but that the pattern is the same. Still, it is an interesting question, given that Marsilius's work was such an important treatise for the Henrician circle, whether Hobbes might have read it.

42 Gewirth's (Chapter 2, p 25) very words quoted above, in relation to Marsilius's *Defensor Pacis*.

43 While Hobbes avoided this in the first printing of the Leviathan, in his later Latin edition (in the Appendix) he was quite clear. Speaking in the third person, he states that "*Affirmat quidem Deum esse corpus*."

and in Descartes), Hobbes radicalized Marsilius's aims, and completely redefined Christian theology according to political utility, reducing belief to a fideism that cleaved to the sovereign's definition of religion—a power that includes the absolute political right to define how Scripture will be interpreted. Nor did Hobbes leave the sovereign power without exegetical resources. He provided the politicized principles of interpretation that earned him the honor of being the father of modern scriptural scholarship. The goal of his politicized exegesis is this-worldly peace. As he makes clear in the Conclusion, "my Discourse of Civill and Ecclesiasticall Government" was "occasioned by the disorders of the present time. . . ."[44] These philosophical and exegetical principles, so Hobbes hoped, would bring an end to such bloody conflicts as he had just experienced in the Thirty Years' War and the English Civil Wars of religion.

The First Half of Leviathan: *The Mechanical Man*

In accordance with his materialism, Hobbes reduced everything to brute atomic matter in motion.[45] Hobbes's materialist assertions are couched in the popular anti-Aristotelianism of the day, not only as it existed among the new breed of mechanists, but also among Protestants, who saw Aristotelianism as a pagan corruption that had deformed Christianity (as evidenced in Catholicism).[46] In the context of removing this corruption—or, perhaps, using this context as a shield—Hobbes reduced human beings and their actions to the necessary motions of inert atomic matter. This reductionism will prove essential to his later exegesis of Scripture.

Hobbes began with the Galilean law of inertia,[47] thereby providing a scientific foundation for his Epicurean account of human nature in terms of atomic motion. For Hobbes, sensation is caused by an "Externall Body, or Object, which presseth

44 Hobbes, *Hobbes's Leviathan*, "A Review, and Conclusion," p. 556 [395]. Pagination is from the Clarendon Press reprint of 1965, but the page numbers of the original edition appear in brackets.

45 The materialism could not be more thorough, as he makes clear later in the work, IV.34 and 46.

46 Thus, Hobbes was able to use a common Protestant position as a shield to put forward his materialist philosophy, and in a way that will become an established tenet of modern historical-critical scholarship. Hobbes will argue that all notions of immateriality in the Bible—whether in regard to the human soul or the existence of angels and demons—are the result of the contaminations of Greek philosophy, so that exegesis properly expunges them, leaving only the "original" materialist-friendly substrate. The "critical" aspect of the method is therefore supplied by Hobbes's materialism; the "historical" aspect of the method follows upon the materialist premises, layering the biblical text from early to late in accordance with Hobbes's purposes. Of course, this layering would also appeal to a Protestant assumption that the original and pure church must be recovered from the layers of historical accretions, an assumption that would bring them to embrace the same historical-critical methods (thereby, ironically, serving the cause of Hobbes).

47 In Hobbes formulation: "THAT when a thing lies still, unlesse somewhat els stirre it, it will lye still for ever . . . [and] when a thing is in motion, it will eternally be in motion. . . . When a Body is once in motion, it moveth (unless something els hinder it) eternally; . . . so also it happeneth in that motion, which is made in the internall parts of man, then, when he Sees, dreams, &c." Hobbes, *Hobbes's Leviathan*, I.2, p. 13 [4].

the organ proper to each Sense," which sets off a chain reaction "by the mediation of Nerves, and other strings, and membranes of the body" that continues "inwards to the Brain, and Heart." The internal rebounding of this reaction, makes it *seem* as if we sense the object outside of us even though all we actually experience is our own internal "*seeming*, or *fancy*," and that is what "men call *Sense*."[48] This material chain reaction explains imagination as well, "For after the object is removed, or the eye shut, wee still retain an image of the thing seen," and this is called "*Imagination*" by Latins, and "*Fancy*" by Greeks, but in either case, "IMAGINATION therefore is nothing but *decaying sense*; and is found in men, and many other living Creatures, as well sleeping, as waking."[49] Thoughts, both sleeping and waking, are simply old images retained in the memory.[50] And so Hobbes provided an entirely mechanical view of human nature, including human thought.

Exorcising Spirits with Nominalism

This mechanical presentation of sensation, imagination, and thought is immediately put to use in confirming nominalism. Since sensation is always particular, and we do not actually perceive the object outside of us, but only our internal "fancy" (our own internal perception of our sensation), there is no room for any Aristotelian notion of "*intelligible species*," or universals (i.e., forms) in nature. Rather, such universals are only names. By this, Hobbes not only showed his continuity with the nominalist position, but even more important, provided a materialist explanation for why people believe in spiritual beings—since, for classical thought, the immaterial soul was the form of the body. The philosophical error of believing in self-existent universals brings with it the philosophical error of believing in self-existent immaterial souls, i.e., in spirits. This explanation serves a very political purpose.

> From . . . ignorance of how to distinguish Dreams, and other strong Fancies, from Vision and Sense, did arise the greatest part of the Religion of the Gentiles in time past . . . and now adayes the opinion that rude people have of Fayries, Ghosts, and Goblins; and of the power of Witches . . . And for Fayries, and walking Ghosts, the opinion of them has I think been on purpose, either taught, or not confuted, to keep in credit the use of Exorcisme, of Crosses, of holy Water, and other such inventions of Ghostly men.[51]

Although Hobbes allows that "God can make unnaturall Apparitions: But that he does it so often, as men need to feare such things . . . is not [the] point of Christian faith." More to the political point, "If this superstitious fear of Spirits were taken away, and with it, Prognostiques from Dreams, false Prophecies, and many other things

48 Ibid., I.1, p. 11.
49 Ibid., I.2, p. 13 [5].
50 Ibid., I.2, pp. 15–16 [6], I.3, pp.18–19 [8].
51 Ibid., I.2, p. 17 [7].

depending thereon, by which, crafty ambitious persons abuse the simple people, men would be much more fitted than they are for civill Obedience."[52] Much of Hobbes's later exegesis of the Bible will be dedicated to taking away this "superstitious fear of Spirits" by eliminating them from the text as so many "Fancies."

Reason as Will to Power

Hobbes then set about reducing reason to a mere instrument of the passions, so that the goal of reason is not contemplation, but, "*regulated* by some desire," to calculate the means of attaining it.[53] For Hobbes, we are all born equal as creatures of sense and desire. Reason is brought into being by passion—"the Thoughts, are to the Desires, as Scouts, and Spies, to range abroad, and find the way to the things Desired. . . ."[54] Therefore, the causes of the "difference of Witts [i.e., the ability to reason], are in the Passions," and the "Passions that most of all cause the differences of Wit, are principally, the more or lesse Desire of Power, of Riches, of Knowledge, and of Honour. All which may be reduced to the first, that is Desire of Power."[55] In continuity with Marsilius's and Machiavelli's lowering of the goal of politics by the removal of contemplation, Hobbes's redefinition of reason ensures that reason is merely an instrument of animal passion, and in continuity with Machiavelli, that the defining passion is the desire for power. Thus, to anticipate Nietzsche's later formulation, all reason is disguised will to power.

A New Route to Sola Scriptura

Materializing reason had immediate theological implications. Reducing reason itself to corporeal imagination entailed that "there is no Idea, or conception of any thing we call *Infinite*" for we can only form an image of finite things. An important consequence is that "When we say any thing is infinite, we signifie onely, that we are not able to conceive the ends, and bounds of the thing named. . . . And therefore the Name of *God* is used, not to make us conceive him; (for he is *Incomprehensible*; and his greatnesse, and power are unconceivable;) but that we may honour him."[56] Hobbes's materialist doctrine of imagination and thought therefore disallows any natural knowledge of God, the result being that God can only be known through Scripture. Since only the sovereign can interpret Scripture (as we find out later), that is no small political benefit.

The same effect was achieved, or better, reinforced by duplication, through the assertion of mechanism itself. Consulting for the sake of clarity Hobbes's *De Corpore*,

52 Ibid., I.2, pp. 17–18 [7–8].
53 Ibid., I.3, p. 20 [9–10].
54 Ibid., I.8, p. 57 [35].
55 Ibid., I.8, p. 56 [35].
56 Ibid., I.3, p. 23 [11].

one sees Hobbes assert that *because* philosophy (hence science) is defined *only* by material and efficient causes, "Therefore it excludes *Theology*, I mean the doctrine of God, eternal, ingenerable, incomprehensible. . . ." Hobbes's argument, examined carefully, contains two reasons for theology's exclusion. The attributes of God mentioned have no rational significance since reason has been defined materially: reason only grasps matter in motion (and hence focuses on change or flux), the generation of bodies, and body itself, which is finite and hence comprehensible. But further, theology is excluded because Hobbes defined nature *so that* it is self-contained; that is, nature is understood solely in terms of material and efficient causality, with no need for any additional cause outside itself.

Thus, belief in God is not rational because God is utterly incomprehensible in a materialist account of reason, and, moreover, God is entirely unnecessary for our complete understanding of nature. The result, of course, is the complete independence of the secular world from the intrusions of the sacred. The elimination of theology is made complete by asserting that philosophy "excludes all such knowledge as is acquired by Divine inspiration, or revelation, as not derived to us by reason, but by Divine grace in an instant, and, as it were, by some sense supernatural."[57] While this might seem to be pious deference to revealed theology, it allowed Hobbes to adopt a doctrine of *sola scriptura* that would entirely subordinate the Bible to the will of the political sovereign.

The first explicit treatment of Scripture in *Leviathan* occurs in Chapter 4, "Of Speech," Hobbes's main goal being to assert his nominalism, his point being that whatever might be said about the importance of Adam's naming things in the Garden, "all this language gotten, and augmented by *Adam* and his posterity, was again lost at the tower of *Babel*, when by the hand of God, every man was stricken for his rebellion, with an oblivion of his former language."[58] By the hand of God, language devolves into chaos from its divine origin, only to arise again with a purely human origin; that is, Hobbes used the Babel story as a way to assert his nominalism, "there being nothing in the world Universall but Names; for the things named, are every one of them Individuall and Singular."[59]

Mathematization, Mastery of Nature, and the Redefinition of Reason

Hobbes's nominalism was necessitated by his atomism and mechanistic account of sensation. Universals are not real because each thing we sense is a quite particular agglomeration of atoms, a seeming whole that is really only the sum of its particular invisible atomic parts. We apply names to things by convention as a matter of convenience,

57 Thomas Hobbes, *De Corpore*, translation from the English version, *Elements of Philosophy Concerning Body*, in Mary Whiton Calkins, ed., Thomas Hobbes, *Metaphysical Writings* (La Salle, IL: Open Court, 1905), I.8,

58 Hobbes, *Hobbes's Leviathan*, I.4, p. 24 [12].

59 Ibid., I.4, p. 26 [13].

given that such universals have no foundation in reality. Thus, "*truth* consisteth in the right ordering of names in our affirmations. . . . So that in the right Definition of Names, lyes the first use of Speech; which is the Acquisition of Science. . . ."[60] Following the trend of mathematization in Galileo and Descartes, Hobbes declared that true science must be a nominalism modeled on Euclidean geometry, geometry being "the onely Science that it hath pleased God hitherto to bestow on mankind,"[61] where "men begin at settling the significations of their words; which settling of significations, they call *Definitions*; and place them in the beginning of their reckoning."[62] Hobbes's embrace of Euclidean geometry as the model for reasoning was so thorough that he later on defined reason entirely according to mathematics as a mode of adding and subtracting.[63]

Thus, Hobbes offered a variation of mathematical ontology, more explicitly atomistic than Descartes's, where nature is redefined as a kind of geometry of atomic points in motion acting according to the law of inertia. As with Galileo and Descartes, without knowledge of this mathematical ontology, there is no knowledge of nature at all, for "Nature worketh by Motion; the Wayes, and Degrees whereof cannot be known, without the knowledge of the Proportions and Properties of Lines, and Figures."[64] And so "they that study natural philosophy, study in vain, except they begin at geometry. . . ."[65]

By redefining reason as subservient to the will, Hobbes also incorporated the Baconian-Cartesian project of mastering nature as well, as Hobbes's definition of philosophy makes clear: "BY PHILOSOPHY, is understood *the Knowledge acquired by Reasoning, from the Manner of the Generation of any thing, to the Properties; or from the Properties, to some possible Way of Generation of the same; to the end to bee able to produce, as far as matter, and humane force permit, such Effects, as humane life requireth.*"[66] In short, philosophy is merely the more systematic presentation of reason's fundamen-

60 Ibid., I.4, p. 28 [15].

61 Ibid. One wonders whether Hobbes was stating this ironically, since he just denied that Adam was taught mathematics, and also gives an account of geometry gotten purely by human endeavor (I.4, pp. 26–27 [14]).

62 Ibid., I.4, p. 28 [15].

63 "WHEN a man *Reasoneth*, hee does nothing else but conceive a summe totall, from *Addition* of parcels; or conceive a Remainder, from *Subtraction* of one summe from another: which (if it be done by Words,) is conceiving of the consequence of the names of all the parts, to the name of the whole; or from the names of the whole of one part, to the name of the other part. . . . In summe, in what matter soever there is place for *addition* and *subtraction*, there also is place for *Reason*; and where these have no place, there *Reason* had nothing to do." Ibid., I.5, pp. 32–33 [18].

64 Ibid., IV.46, p. 522 [369].

65 Hobbes, *De Corpore*, VI.6.

66 Hobbes, *Hobbes's Leviathan*, IV.46, p. 518. In *De Corpore*, in more explicitly Baconian language, Hobbes stated that, "The *end* or *scope* of philosophy is, that we may be able to make use of effects formerly seen for the sake of our convenience [*ad commoda nostra*]; or that, by application of bodies to one another, we may produce the like effects of those we conceive in our mind, as far forth as matter, strength, and industry, will permit, for the utility of human life [*ad vitae humanae usus*]." *De Corpore*, I.6. Translation from the English version as modified by the original Latin. This goal of the utilitarian mastery of nature is quite evident in Hobbes's assertion that, "The end of knowledge is power," and his focus on the "utility of philosophy [*philosophiae utilitas*]" rather than the ancient goal of knowing for its own sake. *De Corpore*, I.6–7.

tal subordination to desire, and this understanding of philosophy is the foundation of his method.[67] We thus have Hobbes's own union of mathematics, mechanism, and mastery in his method.

The Denial of Good and Evil

But redefining reason as subservient to will also entails an entirely amoral and nonteleological account of the origins and ends of human action (thereby giving Machiavellianism a foundation in his Epicurean account of nature). As Hobbes already made evident in his account of sensation, our action (or "endeavor," as he calls it) is really a re-action, the result of objects from without pressing on the senses, and our consequent reaction. This internal mechanical reaction is the source of all human action, the "small beginnings of motion . . . called ENDEAVOR." As with all mechanical motion conceived according to Hobbes's atomism, endeavour can be either attractive or repulsive, and from this mechanical "truth," Hobbes provided startling conclusions for human psychology.

> This Endeavour, when it is toward something which causes it, is called APPETITE, or DESIRE . . . And when the Endeavour is fromward something, it is generally called AVERSION. . . . That which men Desire, they are also sayd to LOVE: and to HATE those things, for which they have Aversion. . . . But whatsoever is the object of any mans Appetite or Desire; that is it, which he for his part calleth *Good*: And the object of his Hate, and Aversions, *Evill*; And of his Contempt, *Vile* and *Inconsiderable*. For these words of Good, Evill, and Contemptible, are ever used with relation to the person that useth them: There being nothing simply and absolutely so; nor any common Rule of Good and Evill, to be taken from the nature of the objects themselves; but from the Person of the man (where there is no common-wealth;) or, (in a Common-wealth,) from the Person that representeth it. . . .[68]

In sum, the origins of human action are inscrutable (since they begin with invisible atomic motions) and merely mechanical—and hence amoral. Because they are merely mechanical they are neither good nor evil in themselves, but (in line with Hobbes's nominalism) each of us imposes the universal names "good" and "evill" to the particular sensations that happen to cause physical pleasure or pain. This purely mechanical explanation is meant to displace all other more high-flown notions of good and evil, love and hate, and to describe the ignoble origin of all human action, no matter how nobly we might present it. Even in regard to the individual, there is no standard of good and evil "because the constitution of a mans Body, is in continuall mutation" so that "it is impossible that all the same things should always cause in him

67 This is quite evident in Hobbes's explicit treatment of "Method" in *De Corpore*, VI.1, where philosophy is again characterized solely in terms of producing desired effects in terms of purely material causes.

68 Hobbes, *Hobbes's Leviathan*, I.6, pp. 39–41 [23–24]. See also I.15, p. 122–123 [79–80].

the same Appetites, and Aversions: much less can all men consent, in the Desire of almost any one and the same Object."[69]

The Elimination of Beatitude

The difficulty of reconciling this account with Scripture should be evident, and interestingly, it is in this chapter that Hobbes explicitly but curtly treats religion as a species of fear, that is, as a mechanical aversion: "*Feare* of power invisible, feigned by the mind, or imagined from tales publiquely allowed, RELIGION; not allowed, SUPERSTITION. And when the power imagined, is truly such as we imagine, TRUE RELIGION."[70] It might seem that Hobbes is merely being facetious here—and indeed, it is hard not to note a barely hidden smirk—but defining religion in terms of fear is essential to his entire political project, as we shall see.

Having given us the origin of all human "motion," Hobbes made clear that the end was no different than the beginning. He defined human happiness, or felicity, in purely this-worldly, nonteleological terms, as "*Continuall successe* in obtaining those things which a man from time to time desireth. . . ." So that there is "no such thing as perpetuall Tranquillity of mind, while we live here; because Life it selfe is but Motion. . . ."[71] Thus, as he states later, "there is no such *finis ultimus,* (utmost ayme,) nor *Summum bonum,* (greatest Good,) as is spoken of in the Books of the old Morall Philosophers." Consequently, "I put for a generall inclination of all mankind, a perpetuall and restlesse desire of Power after power, that ceaseth onely in Death."[72] For Hobbes, this rather bleak redefinition of happiness was scientific—that is, it is based on his belief that the Galilean law of inertia is the cause of all motion, even human motion—and therefore could serve as a sure foundation of a new political science based on the new materialist physics.

This materialist notion of felicity is sharply distinguished and separable from otherworldly felicity that "God hath ordained to them that devoutly honour him," which "a man shall no sooner know, than enjoy; being joyes, that now are incomprehensible, as the word of Schoole-men *Beatificall Vision* is unintelligible."[73] As with Marsilius and Descartes, it is difficult to detect any sincerity in such faint and obscure praise.

We have, in Hobbes, a kind of Averroistic "double truth" in regard to happiness, where this-worldly happiness is purely physical and nonteleological, and otherworldly happiness promised by religion is simply unintelligible. Of course, that keeps otherworldly notions of happiness from interfering with a politics based entirely on a this-worldly felicity physics of self-preservation and pleasure.

69 Ibid., I.6, p. 40 [24].
70 Ibid., I.6, p. 44 [26].
71 Ibid., I.6, p. 48 [29].
72 Ibid., I.11, p. 75 [47].
73 Ibid., I.6, p. 48 [30].

Indeed, this hedonistic physics provides the key to establishing civil peace through the use of desire and aversion, for "Desire of Ease, and sensuall Delight, disposeth men to obey a common Power," and "Fear of Death, and Wounds, disposeth to the same. . . ."[74]

In setting forth these passions as the twin pillars of his new science of politics, Hobbes both agreed with and transformed Machiavelli and Marsilius. Obviously, given his definition of earthly felicity, he was likewise lowering the aim of politics (and hence lowering all the more the subordinated form of religion). But Hobbes also lowered the kind of citizen, the kind of human being, that the sovereign powers should seek to mold and maintain, and that brought him to praise the inversions of the two lowest cardinal virtues[75] as politically desirable: the most peaceable citizen is intemperate and cowardly, habituated to physical pleasures and horrified by pain and hardship.[76]

But these twin pillars are yet insufficient to bring civil peace, for there is another great disturber of political order: religion. Hobbes therefore offered a philosophical, natural account of the cause of religion itself, one that sounds strikingly reminiscent of both Machiavelli and Marsilius.

The Natural Cause of Religion

There are two natural causes of religion—curiosity and fear. Curiosity, "a Lust of the mind,"[77] is found only in human beings, and is ultimately rooted in our peculiar desire for power. The passionate desire to know the natural causes of things, as a species of the desire for power, is found only in some human beings. In these few, it brings them to a notion of "one God Eternall, Infinite, and Omnipotent . . . one First Mover; that is, a First, and an Eternall cause of all things; which is that which men mean by the name of God."[78] Although this appears to be a philosophic proof of the existence of God (sounding almost exactly like St. Thomas's), Hobbes already established that God "is Incomprehensible, and above their understanding," so that we truly know nothing of the "Divine Nature," but use such high-flown names "*Piously*, to honour him with attributes, or significations, as remote as they can [be] from the grossenesse of Bodies Visible."[79] (Given that Hobbes was later to assert that God was corporeal, one can only wonder at the caliber of such piety.) In any case, Hobbes thereby gave readers a mechanistic account of how philosophers have fallen into the error of believing that reason can establish a natural theology.

---

74 Ibid., I.II, p. 76 [48].

75 The traditional order of the cardinal virtues, highest to lowest, are prudence, justice, courage, and temperance.

76 Hobbes made this clear by noting that "needy men, and hardy, not contented with their present condition; as also all men that are ambitious of Military command, are enclined to continue the causes of warre. . . ." Ibid.

77 As he earlier defined it, Ibid., I.6, p. 44 [26].

78 Ibid., I.12, p. 83 [53].

79 Ibid., I.12, pp. 83–84 [53–54].

Ignorance and the consequent fear are the other causes of religion, and such ignorance is both the cause and the cure of civil unrest. Here, we are treated to an account of the origin of religion and its political use that augments that of Machiavelli and Marsilius (perhaps worthy of earning Hobbes another honorary epithet, the father of modern sociology of religion[80]).

> Ignorance of naturall causes disposeth a man to Credulity, so as to believe many times impossibilities . . . yet from the feare that proceeds from the ignorance it selfe . . . are enclined to suppose, and feign unto themselves, severall kinds of Powers Invisible; and to stand in awe of their own imaginations; and in time of distresse to invoke them; as also in the time of an expected good successe, to give them thanks; making the creatures of their own fancy, their Gods. By which means it hath come to passe, that from the innumerable variety of Fancy, men have created in the world innumerable sorts of Gods. And this Feare of things invisible, is the naturall Seed of that, which every one in himself calleth Religion; and in them that worship, or fear that Power otherwise than they do, Superstition.
>
> And this seed of Religion, having been observed by many; some of those that have observed it, have been enclined thereby to nourish, dresse, and forme it into Lawes; and to adde to it of their own invention, any opinion of the causes of future events, by which they thought they should best be able to govern others, and make unto themselves the greatest use of their Powers.[81]

So important is religion for the maintenance of political power that Hobbes cannot leave it at that, but dedicates another entire chapter to it (Chapter 12, one of the two longest in Part I), all but duplicating the Epicurean account found in Book 5 of Lucretius's *De Rerum Natura*. Because of our desire to secure felicity (as defined above), we are continually troubled by "Anxiety," so that "man . . . in the care of future time, hath his heart all the day long, gnawed on by feare of death, poverty, or other calamity. . . ." Such "perpetuall feare, always accompanying mankind in the ignorance of causes, as it were in the Dark, must needs have for object something. And therefore when there is nothing to be seen, there is nothing to accuse, either of their good, or evill fortune, but some *Power*, or Agent *Invisible*. . . ." So it is that the "old Poets" were right, that "the Gods were at first created by humane Feare. . . ."[82]

The belief in invisible powers originally came from dreams, fancies of the imagination produced during sleep, which "men not knowing that such apparitions are nothing else but creatures of the Fancy, think [them] to be reall, and externall Substances;

---

80 See, for example, the treatment of religion by American sociologists in the late nineteenth and early twentieth century, which merely duplicates Hobbes's assertions, in Christian Smith, *The Secular Revolution: Power, Interests, and Conflict in the Secularization of American Public Life* (Berkeley, CA: University of California Press, 2003), Ch. 2.

81 Hobbes, *Hobbes's Leviathan*, I.11, pp. 80–81 [51].

82 Ibid., I.12, pp. 82–83 [52–53].

and therefore call them Ghosts" because in their dreams, the fancies "appear, and vanish when they please. . . ." This belief in powers invisible explains both the false belief in the immaterial "Soule of man" and in external "Invisible Agents."[83]

The belief in invisible powers, coupled with ignorance of the true causes of "good and evill fortune," result in worship. For out of ignorance, we plead with, thank, and take oaths by these imagined invisible powers. Lucky guesses as to what will happen lead people to believe in "Prognostiques" of future good or evil fortune. "And in these foure things, Opinion of Ghosts, Ignorance of second causes, Devotion towards what men fear, and Taking of things Casuall for Prognostiques, consisteth the Naturall seed of *Religion*. . . ." And since such things occur in particular circumstances and in relationship to the passions and fears of particular men, Hobbes could thereby account for "ceremonies so different, that those which are used by one man, are for the most part ridiculous to another."[84]

Hobbes was therefore able to give an historical, sociological, materialist account of the origin of religion and religious plurality, one that did not distinguish between true and false, but merely searched into the particular origins of peculiar rites and beliefs. In so doing, he furthered Machiavelli's deflation of the particular claims of Judaism and Christianity by treating both alongside other pagan religions according to the new materialistic physics. In doing so, it becomes increasingly difficult to see how Judaism and Christianity are distinct from pagan religions, especially since he regards the "seeds" of religion to be natural, and hence presumably the root of all religion.

These "seeds" of religion, Hobbes maintained, "have received culture from two sorts of men." One sort is immediately recognizable from Machiavelli and Marsilius, those who "have nourished, and ordered them [the seeds], according to their own invention." The other is those who "have done it, by Gods commandement, and direction. . . ." Hobbes thereby divided the culturing of the seeds of religion between the Gentiles on the one hand, and Jews and Christians on the other. The division matters little for his purposes, because the political aim is identical: "both sorts have done it, with a purpose to make those men that relyed on them, the more apt to Obedience, Lawes, Peace, Charity, and civill Society."[85] By constraining the end of both toward politics, Hobbes essentially nullified any real difference, a fact all the more clear in the second half of the *Leviathan*.

Having offered a purely natural account of religion, Hobbes interestingly enough dropped it, and returned to his famous, purely natural explanation of human nature and the origins of human society. In this explanation, God is simply absent, an omission made all the bolder since this alleged original state stands in such stark and obvious contrast to the account of human origins in Genesis.

83 Ibid., I.12, p. 83 [53].

84 Ibid., I.12, p. 85 [54].

85 Ibid.

The State of War, the Invention of Rights, and the Mortal God

Following upon Hobbes's mechanistic, hedonistic psychology, in the state of nature all are equal and equally desirous. Since, as we have already learned, there is no natural good and evil, all seek to satisfy their endless desires in a moral void, and hence the natural state is one of "Warre; and such a warre, as is of every man, against every man. . . . And the life of man, solitary, poore, nasty, brutish, and short."[86]

In this state, as opposed to Eden, there is no possibility of sin, for the "Desires, and other Passions of man, are in themselves no Sin. No more are the Actions, that proceed from those Passions, till they know a Law that forbids them. . . ."[87] As shocking as this sounds, Hobbes made quite clear that he meant what he said. "To this warre of every man against every man, this also is consequent; that nothing can be Unjust. The notions of Right and Wrong, Justice and Injustice have there no place. Where there is no common Power, there is no Law: where no Law, no Injustice. Force, and Fraud, are in warre the two Cardinall virtues."[88] Although this may sound brutal and stark—and certainly, completely irreconcilable with the scriptural account of our natural state—it was for Hobbes simply a scientific correlation of two levels of mechanical motion, both amoral: the level of human motion and the level of atomic motion.

In one of the most significant reformulations of moral discourse in the history of the West, Hobbes gave moral-political names to these mechanical motions. He defined the atomic preservation of inertial motion as the absolute *right* of self preservation: "THE RIGHT OF NATURE . . . is the Liberty each man hath, to use his own power, as he will himselfe, for the preservation of his own Nature: that is to say, of his own Life; and consequently, of doing any thing, which in his own Judgement, and Reason, hee shall conceive to be the aptest means thereunto."[89] Since atomic inertial motion is nonteleological and constrained only by obstruction, Hobbes defined "LIBERTY" as "the absence of externall Impediments. . . ."[90] Reason's subservience to passion, especially the passion for self-preservation of motion, became the "LAW OF NATURE" that is "found out by Reason, by which a man is forbidden to do, that, which is destructive of his life, or taketh away the means of preserving the same. . . ."[91] This "law" simply followed from the origin of our motion as a material reaction issuing in desire and aversion, and reason's entirely subordinate function in maximizing pleasure and minimizing pain. Reason cannot help but to serve the passions, and hence it must serve our appetites and aversions, including our aversion to pain and death.

Again, since the preservation of motion is as amoral on the human level as it is on the atomic level, then the natural "condition of Man . . . is a condition of Warre of every one against every one; in which case every one is governed by his own Reason;

---

86 Ibid., I.13, pp. 94–97 [60–62].
87 Ibid., I.13, p. 97 [62].
88 Ibid., I.13, p. 98 [63].
89 Ibid., I.14, p. 99 [64].
90 Ibid.
91 Ibid.

and there is nothing he can make use of, that may not be a help unto him, in preserving his life against his enemyes; It followeth, that in such a condition, every man has a Right to every thing; even to one anothers body."[92]

To extricate us from this natural, amoral chaos, Hobbes used motion against motion, endeavor against endeavor, passion against passion, the fear of violent death against the endless desire for power. Thus, a second law of nature arose, which was really a restatement of the first, for its ultimate focus was the preservation of motion: "*That a man be willing, when others are so too, as farre-forth, as for Peace, and defence of himselfe he shall think it necessary, to lay down this right to all things; and be contented with so much liberty against other men, as he would allow other men against himself.*"[93] This "mutuall transferring of Right, is that which men call CONTRACT."[94] When parties to the contract perform their respective parts "at some determinate time after, and in the mean time be trusted . . . the Contract . . . is called PACT, or COVENANT. . . ."[95] This entirely mechanist and secular account grounds Hobbes's account of government, and will underlie his treatment of the Covenants as they occur in the Old and New Testament (thereby making amply evident that his treatment of Scripture is governed by a design alien to the text itself).

Since such contracts, or covenants, "without the Sword, are but Words, and of no strength to secure a man at all . . . if there be no Power erected, or not great enough for our security,"[96] there must be a common power over all, to which each gives up his right. "This done, the Multitude so united in one Person, is called a COMMON-WEALTH, in latine CIVITAS. This is the Generation of that great LEVIATHAN, or rather (to speake more reverently) of that *Mortall God*, to which wee owe under the *Immortall God*, our peace and defence." This one "person" uniting the multitude is "called SOVERAIGNE."[97]

The sovereign receives the absolute right of nature, in his person, that each of his subjects has given up. The sovereign's power is therefore absolute and indivisible. Consequently, there can be no covenant alongside the civil contract, "for there is no Covenant with God, but by mediation of some body that representeth Gods person; which none doth but Gods Lieutenant, who hath the Soveraignty under God."[98] Hobbes verified this from Scripture, citing Exodus 20:19, in which the Israelites say to Moses: "*Speak thou to us, and we will heare thee, but let not God speak to us, lest we dye.*" This, Hobbes remarks, showed "absolute obedience to *Moses*."[99]

92 Ibid.
93 Ibid., I.14, p. 100 [64–65].
94 Ibid., I.14, p. 102 [66].
95 Ibid.
96 Ibid., II.17, p. 128 [85].
97 Ibid., II.17, p. 132 [87–88].
98 Ibid., II.17, p. 134 [89].
99 Ibid., II.20, pp. 157–158 [105].

The Political Subordination of Ghostly Power

As we will see, Moses played an essential part for Hobbes, providing him scriptural sanction for an elevation of Henry VIII's Act of Supremacy to a universal law applicable to all political sovereigns. Entailed in this elevation of the Act of Supremacy to a universal principle was the declaration that political sovereignty is indivisible in regard to religion because "*a Kingdome divided in it selfe cannot stand*." Therefore, the sovereign cannot "give away the government of Doctrines," for if he does, "men will be frighted into rebellion with the feare of Spirits."[100] As with Henry VIII, so with all political sovereigns; they must each have full control over their respective state churches, and "all Subjects are bound to obey that for divine Law, which is declared to be so, by the Lawes of the common-wealth." [101]

Obviously, for Hobbes, there cannot be two swords or two kingdoms, both a "*Temporall*" and a "*Ghostly*," for "When . . . these two Powers oppose one another," as they surely will, "the Common-wealth cannot but be in great danger of Civill warre, and Dissolution."[102] For "seeing the *Ghostly* Power challengeth the Right to declare what is Sinne it challengeth by consequence to declare what is Law, (Sinne being nothing but the transgression of the Law;) and again, the Civill Power challenging to declare what is Law, every Subject must obey two Masters, who both will have their Commands be observed as Law; which is impossible."[103]

In this clash of powers, the civil power has the advantage of being visible, but yet the Spiritual power, "because the fear of Darknesse, and Ghosts, is greater than other fears," will always stir up trouble against the civil power.[104] Thus, the civil sovereign cannot countenance any other religion than that sanctioned by his will, for "a Common-wealth is but one Person, it ought also to exhibite to God but one Worship," and this "Publique Worship" must be "*Uniforme*." The politically enforced uniformity goes so far, that only those "Attributes [of God] that the Soveraign ordaineth" are to be allowed.[105] Having entirely subordinated religion to the state, Hobbes brings the first half of the *Leviathan* to a close.

The Second Half of Leviathan: *The* Leviathan *Swallows the Bible*

Hobbes himself noted that Part III (the beginning of the second half of the *Leviathan*) presented a kind of break in the argument. In the previous thirty-one chapters he had

100 Ibid., II.18, p. 139 [92–93].

101 Ibid., II.26, p. 221 [149]. Hobbes offers here the proviso, as long as it doesn't go against the Law of Nature. But Hobbes' Law of Nature simply describes an individual's necessary desire for self preservation at all costs as directed by reason to recognize what actually contributes to self-preservation. Since, for Hobbes, the only alternative to absolute sovereignty is civil war, therefore the Law of Nature dictates absolute obedience to the sovereign. Ibid., II.20, p. 160 [106–107].

102 Ibid., II.29, p. 253 [171].

103 Ibid., II.29, p. 253 [171].

104 Ibid., II.29, pp. 253–254 [172].

105 Ibid., II.31, p. 283 [193].

argued "from the Principles of Nature onley; such as Experience has found true, or Consent . . . has made so. . . ." He would now turn to a consideration of "the Nature and Rights of a CHRISTIAN COMMON-WEALTH," that depended upon "Supernaturall Revelations of the Will of God," and therefore on the nature and status of prophecy.[106]

With some understatement, Hobbes remarked in the book's "Review and Conclusion" that "there are some new Doctrines," where "New Wine . . . bee put into New Cask. . . ."[107] The new cask is Hobbes's materialist philosophy; the new wine is Hobbes's exegetically reconstructed state religion.

Hobbes's first move, reminiscent of Marsilius theoretically and Henry VIII practically, was to establish a doctrine of *sola scriptura*. Placing all authority of revelation in the text allowed him, by a several-stage argument, to root its interpretation and authority in the political sovereign alone. How does God speak to man, asked Hobbes: "it must be either immediately; or by mediation of another man. . . ." God does not speak immediately to the reader in Scripture, "but by mediation of the Prophets, or of the Apostles, or of the Church. . . ."[108] The problem of exegesis, then, shifts from the text to the character of the writers and editors of the text, and so to a discussion of true and false prophets.

The Two Marks of True Prophecy

Since many men pretend to be inspired, then how can we tell a true from a false prophet? There are "two marks," stated Hobbes. "One is the doing of miracles; the other is the not teaching any other Religion than that which is already established."[109] As we shall see, the first mark is wholly determined by the second mark.

To begin with Hobbes's treatment of the first mark, miracles were another cause of sedition found both in the biblical text and in his own society. Being strictly and completely deterministic, Hobbes's materialism would not allow miraculous interventions.

---

106 Ibid., III.32, p. 286 [195]. To say the least, Hobbes has already sown significant doubt about the veracity of prophecy before he explicitly takes up his consideration of the "Word of God . . . Propheticall" in Part III, defining it in Part I as a species of madness brought on by a desire for power. See Ibid., I.8, pp. 56–63 [35–40].

107 Ibid., "A *REVIEW*, and *CONCLUSION*," p. 557 [396].

108 Ibid., III.32, p. 287 [196]. It is, in fact, this very mediation that distinguished reason (or science) from faith, for as Hobbes argued in the first half, science begins with definitions (as long as they accord with Hobbes's mechanism). When we do not reason from such definitions, then we do so from mere opinion; and when we accept the opinions of another, it is belief and faith, "*Faith, in* the man; *Beleefe*, both *of* the man, and *of* the truth of what he sayes." As compared to reason, faith is taken "not from the thing it self, or from the principles of naturall Reason, but from the Authority, and good opinion wee have, of him that hath sayd it. . . ." The results for Scripture could not be more profound, and reverberate for the next centuries as the central problem of the new exegesis. "And consequently, when wee Believe that the Scriptures are the word of God, having no immediate revelation from God himselfe, our Beleefe, Faith, and Trust is in the Church; whose word we take, and acquiesce therein. . . . So that it is evident, that whatsoever we believe, upon no other reason, then what is drawn from authority of men onely, and their writings; whether they be sent from God or not, is Faith in men onely." Ibid., I.7, pp. 51–52 [31–32].

109 Ibid., III.32, p. 288 [196–197].

But unlike later advocates of the new materialism, Hobbes did not simply deny miracles; rather, he tamed them through exegesis. Using the Bible for support, he defined miracles politically. God uses them *"for the making manifest to his elect, the mission of an extraordinary Minister for their salvation."*[110] All the miracles of the Old and New Testaments were wrought "to beget, or confirm beleefe, that they [the mediators, such as Moses, the true prophets, Jesus and the Apostles] came not of their own motion, but were sent by God,"[111] and therefore render "men . . . the better inclined to obey them."[112] Hobbes therefore shifted the purpose of miracles from a direct revelation of God's glory and power, to a much more politically salutary goal, the confirmation of the mediator, who, for Hobbes, was always the political sovereign.

Furthermore, Hobbes injected enough skepticism about miracles that the sovereign power must decide which alleged miracles are to be believed. This was necessary for two reasons. First of all, those who are ignorant of natural causes will take something to be miraculous, "which other men, knowing to proceed from Nature . . . admire not at all."[113] Further, as the Egyptian magicians in Exodus demonstrated, it is quite possible through "Imposture, and delusion, wrought by ordinary means" to duplicate miracles, as when the magicians also changed a rod into a serpent and water into blood, and filled the land with frogs.[114] Hobbes then offered other examples of "innumerable and easie tricks" used to dupe the ignorant, some of which come scandalously close to calling into question miracles of the Old and New Testament. The artistry of the ventriloquist can make "his voice seem to proceed . . . from distance of place," and hence "is able to make very many men beleeve it is a voice from Heaven, whatsoever he please to tell them." Moses the ventriloquist? St. John the Baptist? Christ himself? Then there are "the Impostures wrought by Confederacy. . . . For two men conspiring, one to seem lame, the other to cure him with a charme, will deceive many: but many conspiring, one to seem lame, another so to cure him, and all the rest to bear witnesse; will deceive many more."[115] The Apostles in confederacy with Christ? After Christ?

While Hobbes himself did not raise these questions, it is difficult to imagine that they did not arise spontaneously in the minds of his readers, whatever his ultimate intentions may have been. In any case, raising this much skepticism about miracles allowed Hobbes to inject "Gods Supreme Lieutenant," the "Soveraign power," as the judge of all miracles. This political judging of the miraculous extended to one of the most powerful and politically disruptive instruments of the papacy, the sacramental power (which entailed the politically disruptive power to excommunicate):

> [I]f a man pretend, that after certain words spoken over a peece of bread, that presently God hath made it not bread, but a God, or a man, or both, and neverthelesse it looketh still as like bread as ever it did; there is no reason for

110 Ibid., III.37, p. 341 [235].
111 Ibid., III.37, p. 340 [234–235].
112 Ibid., III.37, p. 339 [234].
113 Ibid.
114 Ibid., III.37, p. 342 [235–236].
115 Ibid., III.37, p. 343 [236–237].

> any man to think it really done; nor consequently to fear him, till he enquire of God, by his Vicar, or Lieutenant [i.e., the political sovereign], whether it be done or not.[116]

It must be remembered that Hobbes wrote these lines during the English Civil Wars, in particular, when the anti-sacramental party under Cromwell and the Rump Parliament was in power. Of course, when the Church of England was restored with Charles II, the sacrament was restored with it, thereby affirming Hobbes's argument, that the sovereign power determines "whether it be done or not." As long as the Eucharist was in the service of the state church, and not beholden to the foreign power of the papacy, it mattered little. Either way, the sovereign would have to mandate whatever exegesis of John 6:35–66 suited his purposes.

To conclude in regard to the miraculous, no miracle can count against the sovereign power, for "how great soever the miracle be, yet if it tend to stir up revolt against the King, or him that governeth by the Kings authority, he that doth such miracle, is not to be considered otherwise than as sent to make triall of their allegiance. For these words, *revolt from the Lord your God*, are in this place [i.e., in regard to Moses' authority, and hence all sovereign authority] equivalent to *revolt from your King*."[117]

Just to be sure, Hobbes simply declared that the time of miracles is over: "Miracles now cease," a declaration that accords nicely with the materialist notion that they never could have happened anyway—and so we are left to deal with *only* the biblical account of miracles wrought in the distant past. Consequently, the two marks of true prophecy are reduced to (1) the miracles and prophecies as reported in the Bible, and (2) not teaching against the established religion.[118] Thus, Hobbes was able to focus his entire argument on the biblical text, first upon the question of who has authority over the text (therefore on the political question of the establishment of religion), and second, on the content of Scripture itself.

Authority over Scripture

Before descending to an analysis of any particular book, Hobbes asserted that the "*Canon*" of Scripture must be defined politically, for "Soveraigns in their own Dominions are the sole Legislators; [so that] those Books only are Canonicall . . . which are established for such by the Soveraign Authority."[119] This was not just a handy way to deal with Reformation disputes about the biblical canon, but was rooted in the entire argument of the *Leviathan* so far. Settling the canon politically brings us out of the chaos of civil, religious war, the brutality of which reminds us how easily we may slip back into the ultimate chaos of the Hobbesian state of nature.

116 Ibid., III.37, p. 344 [237].

117 Ibid., III.32, p. 289 [197].

118 Ibid., III.32, pp. 290–292 [197–198].

119 Ibid., III.33, p. 291 [199].

Hobbes was not content with a natural explanation of each political sovereign's right to define the biblical canon; he offered scriptural support as well. The question in regard to canon was not one of content (what books should be included) but "of the Power to make the Scriptures . . . Laws."[120] Before the Ten Commandments, there was no written law, and hence no question of canon. The question then becomes, "Who it was that gave to these written Tables the obligatory force of Lawes"? While they "were made Laws by God himself," they were given directly to Moses on Mount Sinai, not to the people of Israel. The people of Israel were, in fact, "forbidden to approach the Mountain to hear what God said to Moses," and further, obliged themselves to absolute obedience to whatever Moses, as mediator, commanded.[121] Since "Moses, and Aaron, and the succeeding High Priests were Civill Soveraigns," therefore "the Canonizing, or making of the Scripture Law, belonged to the Civill Soveraigne."[122] The same was true of the "Judiciall Law," "Leviticall Law," and Deuteronomy. Whether they were written or unwritten at the time of Moses, laws were "made Canonicall by Moses the Civill Soveraign."[123] Later, the entire Old Testament including the Prophets was "lost in the [Babylonian] Captivity and sack of the City of Jerusalem," but found and recanonized under Ezra after captivity, Ezra being "High Priest" and therefore "their Civill Soveraigne," so that "it is manifest, that the Scriptures were never made Laws, but by the Soveraign Civill Power."[124]

What of the New Testament? Before these writings were "received, and authorized by Constantine the Emperour," there was no canon because, absent a civil sovereign, there was no power of law, backed by the sword, to declare the canon. In the early Church, "it was not the Apostles that made their own Writings Canonicall, but every Convert made them so to himself." Prior to Constantine, then, there was a kind of textual state of nature, and the New Testament texts "were not obligatory Canons, that is, Laws, but onely good, and safe advice, for the direction of sinners in the way of salvation, which every man might take, and refuse at his owne peril, without injustice."[125] Neither the Apostles, nor later bishops or Church councils, had the right to declare the New Testament canon, for their kingdom, as Christ commanded, was not of this world, and "they that have no Kingdome" in this world, "can make no Laws" in this world. "And consequently, the Books of the New Testament, though most perfect Rules of Christian Doctrine, could not be made Laws by any other authority then that of Kings, or Soveraign Assemblies."[126]

An obvious problem with Hobbes's solution is that it would potentially lead to the existence of as many legitimate versions of the Bible as there are political sovereigns.

120 Ibid., III.42, p. 402 [281].

121 Hobbes again offers the entirely unwarranted exegetical proof that the people of Israel, in saying to Moses, "*Speak thou to us, and we will hear thee; but let not God speak to us, lest we dye*" (Exodus 20:19), were sealing a contract with Moses as their absolute sovereign. Ibid., III.42, p. 403 [282].

122 Ibid., III.42, pp. 403–404 [282].

123 Ibid., III.42, p. 404 [283].

124 Ibid., III.42, p. 405 [283–284].

125 Ibid., III.42, pp. 406–407 [284–285].

126 Ibid., III.42, p. 410 [287].

On behalf of Hobbes, we might say that, given the already reigning belief in *sola scriptura*, the existing disagreements about the canon between Catholics and Protestants and among Protestants themselves, and the politically entrenched reality of *cuius regio, eius religio*, such was already an accomplished fact awaiting philosophical and (ironically) scriptural support. This fact supported Hobbes's underlying assumption that all such questions were really reducible to the desire for power.

Hobbes was only too willing to follow his own lead. Entirely consistent with his theory and the ghost of Henry VIII, Hobbes proudly declared, "I can acknowledge no other Books of the Old Testament, to be Holy Scripture, but those which have been commanded to be acknowledged for such, by the Authority of the Church of *England*."[127] It mattered little if, with different monarchs, that canon might change—for the mutability and diversity of canon is not a problem as long as each sovereign has absolute power over his state church.

The State Church and Its Chief Pastor

The word "church" in Scripture, Hobbes noted, signified "divers things." The Greek *ecclesia* sometimes refers to the house where Christians assemble, sometime to "the Congregations there assembled." But the original meaning was a "Congregation, or an Assembly of Citizens," and so "I define a CHURCH to be, *A company of men professing Christian Religion, united in the person of one Soveraign; at whose command they ought to assemble, and without whose authority they ought not to assemble*." A bluntly political end to his short exegesis.[128]

This, of course, rules out any nonpolitical, or transpolitical, universal church, for "there is on Earth, no such universall Church, as all Christians are bound to obey; because there is no power on Earth, to which all other Common-wealths are subject. . . ." This assertion we have already seen in Henry VIII's *King's Book*. The very distinction of temporal and spiritual government, Hobbes added, is a sham, "brought into the world, to make men see double, and mistake their *Lawfull Soveraign*." Simply and politically put, there is "no other Government in this life, neither of State, nor Religion, but Termporall," otherwise "there must needs follow Faction, and Civil war in the Common-wealth, between the *Church* and *State*. . . ." There is only one sovereign, and "one chief Pastor," and "that one chief Pastor is, according to the law of Nature . . . the Civill Soveraign. . . ."[129] All other pastors are political servants of the sovereign, and they teach and preach only what the "chief Pastor" allows.[130]

Hobbes then presented a supportive exegetical history of Israel, one that also demonstrated that his contract theory was biblically affirmed. He began with the "Contract of God with Abraham," where Abraham's covenant with God binds all his

127 Ibid., III.33, pp. 291–292 [199].

128 Ibid., III.39, pp.361–362 [247–248].

129 Ibid., III.39, pp. 362–363 [248].

130 Ibid., III.42, pp. 421–427 [295–299].

ancestors as well, the lesson being that "in every Common-wealth" subjects "ought to obey the laws of their own Soveraign, in the externall acts of profession of Religion."[131] Since the patriarch could forbid "his Subjects" from holding "any doctrine which Abraham should forbid," so also, "it is lawfull now for the Soveraign to punish any man that shall oppose his Private Spirit against the Laws. . . ."[132] And finally, "they that have the place of Abraham in a Common-wealth, are the onely Interpreters of what God hath spoken," because "as none but Abraham in his family, so none but the Soveraign in a Christian Common-wealth, can take notice what is, or what is not the Word of God."[133]

The covenant passed from Abraham, to Isaac, to Jacob, but "afterwards no more, till the Israelites were freed from the Egyptians, and arrived at the Foot of Mount Sinai: and then it was renewed with Moses. . . ."[134] Here, Hobbes derived an exact reproduction of his contract theory through a rather strained exegesis. Whereas the subjects of the patriarchs were bound by Abraham's covenant independently of their wills, in regard to Moses, the Israelites gave up their rights to Moses at the foot of Sinai, freely making him their sovereign. For, in fear of the thunder, lightening, smoke, and trumpet on the mountain, "*they said unto Moses, speak thou with us, and we will hear, but let not God speak with us lest we die*. Here was their promise of obedience; and by this it was they obliged themselves to obey whatsoever he [Moses] should deliver unto them for the Commandement of God."[135]

Moses therefore became the scriptural archetype of the Hobbesian sovereign, and Hobbes wasted no time drawing the catechetical lesson in regard to scriptural interpretation.

> [W]e may conclude, that whosoever in a Christian Common-wealth holdeth the place of Moses, is the sole Messenger of God, and Interpreter of his Commandments. And according hereunto, no man ought in the interpretation of the Scripture to proceed further then the bounds which are set by their severall Soveraigns. For the Scriptures since God now speaketh in them, are the Mount Sinai. . . . To look upon them, and therein to behold the wondrous works of God, and learn to fear him is allowed; but to interpret them; that is, to pry into what God saith to him whom he appointeth to govern under him, and make themselves Judges whether he govern as God commandeth him, or not, is to transgresse the bounds God hath set us, and to gaze upon God irreverently.[136]

Important for Hobbes's argument is that Scripture supported unambiguously the unifying of political and theological power in one person. But this presented a prob-

---

131 Ibid., III.40, p. 364 [249]. Hobbes adds, parenthetically, "they who have no supernaturall Revelation to the contrary," but since he had already disallowed private revelations as a source for political disobedience, it is of no effect.

132 Ibid., III.40, pp. 364–365 [250].

133 Ibid., III.40, p. 365 [250].

134 Ibid.

135 Ibid., III.40, p. 366 [250–251].

136 Ibid., III.40, p. 368 [252].

lem, for papal arguments often took this to be a sign of the supremacy of spiritual over temporal-political power. Hobbes dealt with this problem cleverly, admitting in his biblical history that after Moses the theological-political power was indeed vested in "the High Priest" who had authority until the time of Saul. But at the time of Saul, Israel had been reduced to a kind of state of nature during the period of the judges, where *"every man did that which was right in his own eyes."*[137] But after the judges came the kings, and this brought about Hobbes's desired result, for "whereas before, all authority, both in Religion, and [political] Policy, was in the High Priest; so now it was all in the King." This transition comes about because the people rebelled, casting off the High Priest, "with the consent of God himself," and asked for a king to govern them. In "deposing the High Priest of Royall authority, they deposed that peculiar Government of God. . . . Having therefore rejected God, in whose Right the Priests governed, there was no authority left to the Priests, but such as the King was pleased to allow them. . . ." Scripture affirmed the kings' "supremacy in Religion," such as when Solomon *"thrust out Abiathar from being Priest before the Lord"* (1 Kings 2:27)—"a great mark of Supremacy in Religion," Hobbes added—and when Solomon dedicated the Temple and "blessed the People . . . which is another great mark of Supremacy in Religion."[138] A more apt exegesis supporting Henry VIII and his Act of Supremacy could hardly be imagined.

It is difficult to deny that Hobbes molded the Old Testament history to support his political theory. What of the New? In regard to Christ himself, Hobbes drilled in two important points for his political ends: the "Kingdome of Christ is not to begin till the generall Resurrection," and that in the meantime, we are to remember that Christ always counseled obedience to temporal authority, both in regard to obedience to the "Scribes and Pharisees [who] sit in Moses seat" (Matthew 23:2) and in regard to Caesar.[139] But given the terrible dangers of civil war, being chief pastor is not enough; the sovereign must be a prophet as well.

The Sovereign as Supreme Prophet

Since prophecy is both the mode of revelation and a great disturber of civil order, Hobbes contrived to make the "Christian Soveraign" the "Soveraign Prophet" as well, thereby making him the judge of all prophecy. The reason, again, was frankly political, and purely negative: if the sovereign is not also the supreme prophet, then civil chaos will ensue.

> For when Christian men, take not their Christian Soveraign, for Gods Prophet; they must either take their owne Dreames, for the Prophecy they mean to bee governed by, and the tumour of their own hearts for the Spirit of God; or they

137 Ibid., III.40, p. 369 [253].

138 Ibid., III.40, pp. 370–371 [254].

139 Ibid., III.41, pp. 375–379 [262–264].

> must suffer themselves to bee lead by some strange Prince; or by some of their fellow subjects, that can bewitch them, by slaunder of the government, into rebellion . . . and by this means destroying all laws, both divine, and humane, reduce all Order, Government, and Society, to the first Chaos of Violence, and Civill warre.[140]

Enthroning the sovereign as chief prophet was accomplished through a rather clever exegesis. Hobbes had already severely deflated the status of prophecy through his materialist psychology, reducing alleged inspirations to excesses of the desire for power, a form of madness ending in pride, or to ignorance or their own powers of reasoning (or a combination of both, we presume). What, then, was the status of the Old Testament prophets?

As mediators between God and human beings, all the prophets of the Old Testament received their communication from God either directly in some mysterious way or in the form of visions and dreams, "that is to say, from the imaginations which they had in their sleep, or in an Extasie: which imaginations in every true Prophet were supernatural; but in false Prophets were either naturall, or feigned."[141] Such a declaration—which Hobbes supported with a long but selective exegesis of various Old Testament books[142]—merely accentuated the difficulty: how, or better *who* should distinguish true from false prophets?

Part of the answer was had by distinguishing between "*supreme*" and "*subordinate*" prophets. Moses was the first Supreme prophet, then after him, the High Priests "as long as the Priesthood was Royall"; and after the Jews "rejected God," and embraced kingship, the "Kings . . . were also his chief Prophets. . . ." Hobbes placed especial emphasis on kings who either acted as priests or who commanded priests, such as Saul, David, and Solomon (citing as authority I Samuel 13:9, 14:18–19, 23:2; I Kings 2:27). "In the time of the New Testament," however, "there was no Soveraign Prophet, but our Saviour."[143] The sovereign prophet was, then, always someone in whom both king and prophet are united.

All other prophets are subordinate to a sovereign prophet, a point Hobbes proved exegetically by appeal to Numbers 11:24–29, in which God took some of Moses' spirit and placed it upon the seventy elders, "By which it is manifest, first, that their Prophecying to the people, was subservient, and subordinate to the Prophecying of Moses."[144] And furthermore, this "spirit" they received was not the "substantiall Spirit of God," for then they would be equals to Christ, but instead was metaphorical, and hence "signifieth nothing but the Mind and Disposition to obey, and assist Moses in the administration of the Government."[145]

---

140 Ibid., III.36, p. 337 [232].
141 Ibid., III.36, p. 331 [227].
142 Ibid., III.36, pp. 326–331 [224–228].
143 Ibid., III.36, pp. 331–332 [228–229].
144 Ibid., III.36, p. 333 [229].
145 Ibid.

To ensure that subordinate prophets remain in their place, Hobbes created a further distinction. While the way God spoke to the sovereign prophet was both direct and completely mysterious, the subordinate prophets receive their messages only indirectly, through dreams and visions.[146] That, according to Hobbes's materialist psychology, makes them suspect, and "consequently men had need to be very circumspect, and wary, in obeying the voice of man, that pretending himself to be a Prophet," and who "requires us to obey God in that way, which he in Gods name telleth us to be the way to happinesse."[147]

> For he that pretends to teach men the way of so great felicity, pretends to govern them; that is to say, to rule, and reign over them; which is a thing, that all men naturally desire, and is therefore worthy to be suspected of Ambition and Imposture; and consequently, ought to be examined, and tried by every man, before hee yeeld them obedience; unlesse he have yielded it them already, in the institution of a Common-wealth; as when the Prophet is the Civill Soveraign, or by the Civil Soveraign Authorized.[148]

And so, the sovereign is an heir to Moses, and prophecy an office of the state in the service of the sovereign. Subjects are to be skeptical of all other claims of prophecy, for all such claims mask the prophet's hidden desire for power. Prophets who speak against the sovereign cannot be true prophets, for in acting against the sovereign they reduce society to "the first Chaos of Violence, and Civill warre."[149] Of course, in counseling suspicion of the alleged prophets of his own day, who under pretence of divine inspiration were tearing England in contradictory religious and political directions thereby leading them into civil war, Hobbes prepared the way for hermeneutics wherein all prophets would be "suspected of Ambition and Imposture."

Seeing Hobbes's complete subordination of both the canon and content of Scripture to the civil sovereign, it is clear he had no qualms about the political manipulation of the text to suit his ends. One is not surprised, then, that this treatment continued as Hobbes descended to more particular questions of the content of Scripture.

The Sovereign Exegesis and Mosaic Authorship

In Chapter Thirty-three of Part III Hobbes undertook an analysis of the antiquity and authorship of particular books of the Bible, asserting famously that Moses could not have written the entire Pentateuch (based on retrospective statements in the text that only make sense if written after his death, e.g., Deuteronomy 34:5–12,

---

146 Ibid., III.36, p. 332 [228–229].

147 Ibid., III.36, p. 335 [230].

148 Ibid.

149 Ibid., III.36, p. 337 [232].

which speaks of Moses' death). So that, "It is therefore sufficiently evident, that the five Books of *Moses* were written after his time, though how long after it be not so manifest."[150]

In all too many references to Hobbes as father of modern scriptural scholarship, that is all we hear of his contribution—an attribution entirely too thin to capture the nature and extent of his patrimony, as should be evident. Even more illuminating, the denial that Moses authored the entire Pentateuch, based on the reference to his own death, did not begin with Hobbes, but is found as far back as the medieval Spanish rabbi, Aben (Ibn) Ezra (1092–1167), a very influential biblical commentator among both Christian and Jews, as well as by Karlstadt and Luther (1483–1546), and the great biblical and rabbinic scholar, John Lightfoot (1602–1675), among others. The denial of Mosaic authorship, with specifically unorthodox implications, was also carried out by the radical Protestant sects, the Levellers and Ranters, in the mid-seventeenth century, and by Isaac La Peyrère (1596–1676), who almost certainly knew Hobbes and whose biblical criticism circulated in the 1640s in manuscript.[151]

Thus, Hobbes's importance does not reside in denying Mosaic authorship, a charge that is often misrepresented or misinterpreted anyway. As Hobbes immediately made clear in the above passage, he was not *completely* denying Mosaic authorship, for "though *Moses* did not compile those Books entirely, and in the form we have them; yet he wrote all that which hee is there said to have written. . . ."[152] Hobbes treated the other books of the Old Testament in like fashion,[153] and the New Testament as well, in every case seeking out exegetical clues that divided the alleged author from the entirety of the text as received, but generally not denying the traditional authorship entirely. What, then, was Hobbes really doing?

Hobbes's real goal was not to undermine completely the authority of Scripture and traditional authorship, but to shift the question of authority from the *text and authorship* to the *authority* of interpretation (and hence to the authority of the interpreter, the political sovereign). Hobbes's short analysis of the authorship of texts does indeed drive exegetical wedges between the biblical characters (e.g., Moses) and the later compilers and editors, but it does so *for the sake of* the political sovereign's right to declare both canon and interpretation. If the biblical text itself shows evidence of human will defining and mediating what shall be considered as inspired revelation, it will be all the easier to acquiesce to the sovereign's political mediation of revelation.

150 Ibid., III.33, p. 293 [200].

151 Richard Popkin, "Spinoza and Bible Scholarship," in James Force and Richard Popkin, eds., *The Books of Nature and Scripture: Recent Essays on Natural Philosophy, Theology, and Biblical Criticism in the Netherlands of Spinoza's Time and the British Isles of Newton's Time* (Dordrecht: Kluwer Academic Publishers, 1994), pp. 1–7. We shall return to La Peyrère in the following chapter on Spinoza.

152 Hobbes, *Hobbes's Leviathan*, III.33, p. 293 [200].

153 To be exact, Joshua, Judges, Ruth, Samuel, Chronicles, Esdras, Nehemiah, Esther, Job, Psalms, Proverbs, Ecclesiastes, Song of Songs, and the Prophets.

The Politicized Scope of Scripture

Unsurprisingly, then, Hobbes's main concern was not as such the question of authorship, but the subordination of Scripture to politics. "In summe, the Histories and the Prophecies of the old Testament, and the Gospels and Epistles of the New Testament, have had one and the same scope, to convert men to the obedience of God," or more exactly, to those who "did represent the person of God. . . ."[154]

This notion of "scope" is extremely important, for it allowed Hobbes to appeal to an overarching interpretive principle—an alleged whole—in relation to which the individual passages of Scripture may be scrutinized and sorted. Of course, Hobbes's understanding of the "whole" was entirely political. As he informs the reader:

> And in the allegation of Scripture, I have endeavoured to avoid such texts as are of obscure, or controverted Interpretation; and to alledge none, but in such sense as is most plain, and agreeable to the harmony and scope of the whole Bible; which was written for the reestablishment of the Kingdome of God in Christ. For it is not the bare Words, but the Scope of the writer that giveth the true light, by which any writing is to bee interpreted; and they that insist upon single Texts, without considering the main Designe, can derive no thing from them cleerly; but rather by casting atomes [i.e., atoms] of Scripture, as dust before mens eyes, make every thing more obscure than it is; an ordinary artifice of those that seek not the truth, but their own advantage.[155]

King Versus Pope

Given that the "scope" Hobbes chose was entirely political, it is not surprising that the question of exegesis is not *what* the Scriptures say, but *who* has the authority to define both canon and content. Recalling the particular history of England, it is equally unsurprising that Hobbes put the question in either-or terms, in the familiar context of the struggles of Henry VIII against the papacy: "*Whether Christian Kings, and the Soveraigne Assemblies in Christian Common-wealths, be absolute in their own Territories, immediately under God; or subject to one Vicar of Christ, constituted over the Universall Church; to bee judged, condemned, deposed, and put to death, as hee shall think expedient, or necessary for the common good.*"[156]

Hobbes's new mode of exegesis was therefore recast in the form of the medieval debate between emperor and pope, but with three all-important differences. First and most obvious, Hobbes replaced the one emperor with the many kings, which not only reflects the much different situation in the seventeenth century, where a multitude of national kings had all but erased any notion of a return to a united empire, but even

154 Hobbes, *Hobbes's Leviathan*, III.33, p. 299 [204].

155 Ibid., III.43, p. 471 [331]. See also his "Review and Conclusion," p. 554 [394].

156 Ibid., III.33, p. 301 [206].

more, the fractured condition of Christianity itself since the Reformation, whereby *cuius regio, eius religio* became an established fact in search of a principle.

The second great difference is that this battle between kings and pope will now be fought with a materialist cosmology that completely undermines the spiritual authority of the papacy and therefore supports the multiplicity of state churches, howsoever many there be. It was in providing this service that Hobbes truly became the father of modern scriptural scholarship.

Following upon this, Hobbes's philosophical arsenal was be aimed, for the most part (but not entirely), at the Catholic Church, and hence his exegesis was designed to strip from the biblical text, once and for all, anything that might be of use to Rome. Hobbes therefore relied upon the anti-Catholic sentiments as the current that would carry his principles forward (a ploy that worked all the better, given that Protestants tended to be, in their animosity to Aristotle, more likely to embrace the atomistic physics of matter in motion that undergirded Hobbesian materialism).

Exorcising Spirits from the Text

Hobbes's first exegetical step was to divest Scripture of all notions of immateriality, which he presented as a pagan contamination of Aristotle. Belief in immaterial substances is not biblical, Hobbes declared, but rather was "built on the Vain Philosophy of Aristotle. . . ." His real complaint, as we recall from above, was that the belief in immaterial substances frightens men "from Obeying the Laws of their Countrey with empty names . . . For it is upon this ground, that when a Man is dead and buried, they say his Soule (that is his Life) can walk separated from his Body, and is seen by night amongst the graves." And "who, that is in fear of Ghosts, will not bear great respect to those that can make the Holy Water, that drives them from him?"[157] Ghosts empower priests, a victory ultimately for the papacy against the king, the spiritual power over the temporal.

Hobbes attacked such ghosts with his complete materialist cosmology: "For the *Universe*, being the Aggregate of all Bodies, there is no reall part thereof that is not also *Body*," so that, "*Substance* and *Body*, signifie the same thing; and therefore *Substance incorporeall* are words when they are joined together, destroy one another, as if a man should say, an *Incorporeal Body*."[158]

157 Ibid., IV.46, pp. 526–527 [372–373].

158 Ibid., III.34, pp. 302–303 [207]. Also, a bit later: "The World, (I mean not the Earth onely, that denominates the lovers of it *Worldly men*, but the *Universe*, that is, the whole masse of all things that are) is Corporeall, that is to say, Body; and hath the dimensions of Magnitude, namely, Length, Bredth, and Depth: also every part of Body, is likewise Body, and hath the like dimensions; and consequently every part of the Universe is Body; and that which is not Body, is no part of the Universe: And because the Universe is All, that which is no part of it, is *Nothing*; and consequently *no where*." Ibid., IV.46, p. 524.

This, of course, presented a problem for Scripture, since Hobbes already asserted, and repeats here,[159] that notions of ghosts arise ultimately not from Aristotelianism, but from ignorance of the material, psychological causes of what appears to be immaterial, as well as the inability to distinguish dreams from reality. But that would seem to condemn Scripture, replete with language of the spirit, to a book of ignorance and nonsense. It would then be of no political use.

To avoid this, Hobbes maintained that almost every reference to spirits in Scripture is merely "metaphoricall," with the exception of a few places "whereby God is said to be a *Spirit*; or where by the *Spirit of God*, is meant God himself." Yet rather than allowing there to be even one immaterial substance—for if there is one, then why not more?—Hobbes asserted that speaking of God this way is not descriptive, but merely honorific, for (again) "the nature of God is incomprehensible"[160] (a move that, again, enhances the Averroist assertion that belief in God is utterly irrational since He is utterly incomprehensible). As we have already noted, Hobbes would later declare that God is also a body.[161]

Yet, as it turned out, very few places in Scripture, even in regard to God, would be left unscathed by Hobbes's attempt to render all seeming immateriality as mere metaphor. In doing so, Hobbes cleared a path for all later attempts to show that the original or primitive religion of the Jews was earthy and material, and was only later contaminated by Greek influence. For example, we find out that the Spirit of God moving upon the waters in Genesis 1:2 is to be understood as "Wind," and is referred to God only "because it was Gods' work."[162] In Genesis 41:38, Spirit of God means the wisdom in Joseph, and more particularly a certain kind of "wisdome," or skill, displayed in a particular kind of work, as in Exodus 28:3, where God instructs Moses "to speak to the wise of heart, whom I have filled with a spirit of wisdom" to make Aaron's garments.[163] Moreover, wherever we read of the spirit of wisdom, understanding, counsel, fortitude, or fear, we can be assured that what is "manifestly . . . meant, [is] not so many Ghosts, but so many eminent *graces* that God would give him [i.e., the recipient]."[164] Or spirit could mean "extraordinary Zeal, and Courage," as in Judges

159 Ibid., III.34, p. 303 [207–208].

160 Ibid., III.34, p. 304 [208].

161 In the 1651 English version of the *Leviathan*, he does not yet assert that God himself is corporeal, but rather argues that the attribution of "Incorporeall . . . to God himselfe" may be done out of piety as long as we understand that "wee consider not what Attribute expresseth best his Nature, which is Incomprehensible; but what best expresseth our desire to honour Him." Ibid., IV.46, pp. 524–525 [371].

162 Ibid., III.34, p. 304 [208].

163 Ibid., I.8, p. 60 [38] and III.34, pp. 304–305 [209]. Contemporary readers may already find that Hobbesianism has done its work well in regard to their translations of this passage. The RSV renders it "to all who have ability, whom I have endowed with an able mind . . . " and the New American "to the various expert workmen whom I have endowed with skill. . . ." Hobbes could not read Hebrew (at least not very well), but his Latin and Greek were quite good, thus his biblical consultations were with the Vulgate and Septuagint, the Vulgate being "*loqueris cunctis sapientibus corde quos replevi spiritu prudentiae*," and the Greek being "*lalēson pasi tois sophois tē dianoia ous eneplēsa pneumatos aisthēseōs*."

164 Ibid., III.34, p. 305 [209]. Hobbes cites Exodus 31:3–6, 35:31 and Isaiah 11:2–3.

and Samuel.[165] In Genesis 2:7, where it states that God breathed into man the breath of life, it means only that "God gave him life," so that like instances where the Spirit of God seems to refer to life breathed into someone, it means only that the person is alive, "not that any Ghost, or incorporeall substance entred into; and possessed his body."[166]

Spirit may also mean authority, as in Numbers 11:17, where God takes some of the spirit that was on Moses, and puts it upon the seventy elders, so that they prophesied, which means no more than that they had received authority to prophecy "according to the mind of Moses, that is to say, by a *Spirit*, or *Authority* subordinate to his own."[167] In the same way, St. Paul in Romans 8:9 uses the term "*Spirit of Christ* . . . not meaning thereby the *Ghost* of Christ, but a *submission* to his doctrine."[168] And when the text refers to Jesus himself as full of the Holy Ghost or Holy Spirit, these "may be understood, for *Zeal* to doe the work for which hee was sent by God the Father. . . ."[169] The sum and substance of all this exegesis was this:

> How we came to translate *Spirits*, by the word *Ghosts*, which signifieth nothing, neither in heaven, nor earth, but the Imaginary inhabitants of mans brain, I examine not: but this I say, the word *Spirit* in the text signifieth no such thing; but [is] either properly a reall *substance*, or Metaphorically, some extraordinary *ability* or *affection* of the Mind, or of the Body.[170]

Although his materialism would seem to bring him to deny spirits altogether (hence, on his own admission, making him guilty of "Atheisme"[171]), Hobbes did not deny spirits, but in true Epicurean fashion,[172] makes them corporeal, that is, "really *Bodies*."[173] The reason Hobbes opted for corporeal spirits was not just one of consistency with his materialism, but because of the ineradicable omnipresence of angels in the Bible. As Hobbes himself noted, "I was enclined to this opinion [that there were no spirits at all] . . . But the many places of the New Testament, and our Saviours own words, and in such texts, wherein is no suspicion of corruption of the Scripture, have extorted from my feeble Reason, an acknowledgment, and beleef, that there be also Angels substantiall, and permanent," although that they are "Incorporeall, cannot by Scripture bee evinced."[174]

---

165 Ibid. Hobbes cites Judges 3:10, 6:34, 11:29, 13:25, 14:16–19; and I Samuel 11:6 and 19:20.

166 Ibid., III.34, p. 306 [209]. Hobbes cites Job 27:3 and Ezekiel 2:30.

167 Ibid., III.34, p. 306 [209–210].

168 Ibid., III.34, p. 306 [210].

169 Ibid.

170 Ibid., III.34, p. 307 [210].

171 Ibid., I.8, p. 61 [38].

172 By this we mean that Epicurus, and later Lucretius, did not argue that gods didn't exist, but that they were (along with everything else) made of material atoms. See Diogenes Laertius, *Lives*, "Epicurus," 10.123. See also Cicero's account of the Epicurean materialist deities, in *De Natura Deorum*, I.43–56. Hobbes extended the notion of Epicurean bodily deities to angels, a move made necessary by their appearance in Scripture.

173 Hobbes, *Hobbes's Leviathan*, IV.46, p. 525 [371]; IV.34, pp. 307–312 [210–214].

174 Ibid., III.34, p. 312 [214].

Hobbes therefore argued that God could make "apparitions" that are "reall, and substantiall; that is to say, subtile Bodies" that he then used as "Ministers, and Messengers . . . to declare his will," yet these "are not Ghosts *incorporeall*" but "Corporeall."[175] However, most instances of such apparitions in both the Old and New Testaments are not real beings, but "some image raised (supernaturally) in the fancy" by God.[176] This is an important emphasis, for if we recall Hobbes's mechanist psychology, while God can raise such images in the fancy, such fanciful images are vividly marked out as the ignoble cause of "false" religion, ancient and modern, and end in political sedition: "From . . . ignorance of how to distinguish Dreams, and other strong Fancies, from Vision and Sense, did arise the greatest part of the Religion of the Gentiles in time past," and now "keep[s] in credit the use of Exorcisme, of Crosses, of holy Water, and other such inventions of Ghostly men." In short, this "credit" lends credence to "the *Ghostly* Power" of Rome against the "*Temporall*."

Casting Out Demons from the Text

As Hobbes acknowledged in the first half of the *Leviathan*,[177] one of the intractable problems is the appearance of demons and demoniacs in the New Testament. But if demonic possession is real, then the power of the priest, especially the Roman Catholic priest, trumps the power of the king. To combat this, Hobbes put the appearance of demonic possession down to the ignorance of the Jews of Jesus' time. How could the Jews have come to this belief, since the Old Testament (on Hobbes's reading) does not support the notion of immaterial, evil spirits who can inhabit bodies?

There are two reasons: pagan contamination and Jewish ignorance. As to the first, Hobbes argued that, while belief in immaterial beings is originally the result of ignorance, "Governours of the Heathen common-wealths" cleverly used this ignorance—with the aid of "the Poets, as Principall Priests of the Heathen Religion"—for the sake of "Publique Peace, and to the Obedience of Subjects necessary thereunto," using good and evil "*Dæmons*, the "one as a Spurre to the observance, the other, as Reines to withhold them from Violation of the Laws." The political use of good and evil spirits, or demons, spread with the heathen powers, in particular, with the power of Greece through the conquests of Alexander the Great. "And by that meanes, the contagion was derived also to the Jewes, both of *Judæa*, and *Alexandria*, and otherparts, whereinto they were dispersed."[178]

Along with this historical source of contamination, Hobbes added the Jews' own alleged ignorance, even intellectual sloth, "the want of curiosity to search naturall causes. . . ." Since they have no such desire, whenever they "see any strange, and unusuall ability, or defect in a mans mind," they "must needs thinke it supernaturall;

175 Ibid., III.34, p. 307 [211].

176 Ibid., III.34, pp. 309–311 [211–213].

177 Ibid., I.8, p. 61 [38].

178 Ibid., IV.45, pp. 499–500 [353].

and then what can it be, but that either God, or the Divell is in him?" Thus, out of ignorance, "they called *Dæmoniaques*, that is, *possessed by the Devill*, such as we call Madmen or Lunatiques; or such as had the Falling Sicknesse; or that spoke anything, which they for want of understanding thought absurd. . . ."[179] For this very reason, the "Scribes" of Jesus' time "said he had *Belzebub*" (Mark 3:21) and that Jesus "*hath a Divell, and is mad. . . .*" (John 10:20).[180]

Yet the problem has not been entirely solved. For, if such belief comes from ignorance, "why then does our Saviour proceed in the curing of them [demoniacs], as if they were possest; and not as if they were mad?"[181] Hobbes offered two answers, one oblique and one more direct. Both his answers to this quandary will reverberate throughout modern scholarship.

First, Hobbes's oblique answer. To those who point to Christ's obvious dealing with demons, Hobbes gave the same answer as he would "to those that urge the Scripture in like manner against the opinion of the motion of the Earth. The Scripture was written to shew unto men the kingdome of God, and to prepare their mindes to become obedient subjects; leaving the world, and the Philosophy thereof, to the disputation of men, for the exercising of their naturall Reason."[182]

A veritable treasure trove of exegetical assumptions and presumptions flow from Hobbes here: (1) Belief in demonic possession is by implication equivalent to belief in geocentrism; (2) Scripture's sole purpose is moral anyway, or more directly political, and obsession with demons diverts us from the true, core message of the text; and (3) theology may not question philosophy, even when the type of philosophy at issue, materialism, is fundamentally antithetical to theology. (Nor was Hobbes an unqualified champion of the freedom of scientific inquiry—asserting that even if the Earth moves, as heliocentrism claims, the civil sovereign has the right to silence such claims if "they be contrary to the Religion established" or if "they tend to disorder in Government, as countenancing Rebellion, or Sedition."[183])

More directly, Hobbes dealt with demons by driving an exegetical wedge between Jesus and his hearers. Jesus' rebuke of devils must be interpreted in the same way as his rebuking of the wind (Matthew 8:26), and rebuking a fever (Luke 4:39). As for "those Divels . . . said to confesse Christ; it is not necessary to interpret those places otherwise, than that those mad-men confessed him." That is, the real cause of possession (a seeming spiritual malady) is physical. And so, concluded Hobbes, "I see nothing at all in the Scripture, that requireth a beliefe, that Dæmoniacks were any other thing but Mad-men."[184]

179 Ibid., IV.45, p. 500 [353].
180 Ibid., I.8, p. 61 [38].
181 Ibid. See also IV.45, p. 500 [353–354].
182 Ibid., I.8, pp. 61–62 [38–39].
183 Ibid., IV.46, p. 536 [380].
184 Ibid., I.8, p. 62 [39].

The Political Problem of Heaven and Hell

From devils we may move on to their previous and current abodes. One of the more interesting reconstructions of Scripture for political purposes occurred in regard to heaven and hell, for it is precisely here, where the stakes are highest, that the great battle waged between the "Temporall" and "Ghostly" kingdoms is most fervent. If the ultimate hinges of all human action are desire and aversion, pleasure and pain, heaven and hell create a most serious obstacle to the political subordination of religion. No one could state the problem more clearly and bluntly than Hobbes himself.

> The maintenance of Civill Society, depending on Justice; and Justice on the power of Life and Death, and other lesse Rewards and Punishments, residing in them that have the Soveraignty of the Common-wealth; It is impossible a Common-wealth should stand, where any other than the Soveraign, hath a power of giving greater rewards than Life; and of inflicting greater punishments, than Death. Now seeing *Eternall life* is a greater reward, than the *life present*; and *Eternall torment* a greater punishment than the *death of Nature*; It is a thing worthy to be well considered, of all men that desire (by obeying Authority) to avoid the calamities of Confusion, and Civill war, what is meant in holy Scripture, by *Life Eternall*, and *Torment Eternall*; and for what offences, and against whom committed, men are to be *Eternally tormented*; and for what actions, they are to obtain *Eternall life*.[185]

The political goal could not be more transparent, and as a result the politicized exegesis of Scripture more glaringly manipulative. If any could doubt up to this point that the father of modern historical-critical scholarship had radically different designs than the faithful in his treatment of Scripture, then this chapter of the *Leviathan* alone should settle the question.

A New Heaven on Earth

As if to lead by example, Hobbes began by acknowledging his ultimate political "submission . . . to the interpretation of the Bible authorized by the Common-wealth, whose Subject I am"[186] and then launched into an exegesis on behalf of the sovereign. Hobbes's strategy was first to materialize the kingdom of God exegetically, and then, building upon this, to treat "the place . . . [of] Eternall Life" similarly.

He first cast doubt on an otherworldly afterlife: "the place wherein men are to live Eternally, after the Resurrection, is the Heavens . . . as where the stars are, or above the stars, in another Higher Heaven . . . is not easily to be drawn from any text that I can find."[187] In fact, it has already been "proved out of divers evident places of Scripture . . .

185 Ibid., III.38, p. 345 [238].

186 Ibid., III.38, pp. 346, 350–351 [238, 241].

187 Ibid., III.38, p. 348 [240].

that the Kingdom of God is a Civil Common-wealth . . . wherein he [God] reigneth by his Vicar, or Lieutenant," so that "after the comming again of our Saviour . . . the Kingdom of God is to be on Earth."[188] Most important of all, this kingdom will not arrive until the "comming again of our Saviour," for the "greatest, and main abuse of Scripture," Hobbes warned, was the belief "that the Kingdome of God . . . is the present Church," for that does away with the civil sovereign as mediator of all divine things.[189]

Hobbes proved that the Kingdom of God was intended to be an earthly kingdom by a deft appeal to the literal meaning of the text, declaring that the "Kingdome . . . of God, is a reall, not a metaphoricall Kingdom; and so taken, not onely in the Old Testament, but the New . . ."; that is, it is "a Kingdome upon Earth," a "Civill Kingdome."[190] To prove this exegetically, Hobbes began in the Old Testament on solid ground, where the various texts do, of course, refer to an earthly kingdom. The "originall" kingdom was established by the covenant between God and Abraham, and referred directly to the very earthly promised land of Canaan.[191] The same was true with the Mosaic covenant, thereby making it "manifest . . . that by the *Kingdome of God*, is properly meant a Common-wealth, instituted (by the consent of those which were to be subject thereto) for their Civill Government. . . ."[192] The Old Testament covenant, we recall, duplicated Hobbes's civil contract theory.

But even in the New Testament, Hobbes assured the reader, the Kingdom of God is "a Kingdome upon Earth." For the Angel Gabriel promised an earthly reign in Luke 1:32–33. And Christ was put to death "as an enemy of Cæsar," and the "title of his crosse" itself attests to his political aspirations, "*Jesus of Nazareth, King of the Jews*." Even the Lord's Prayer, proclaiming "*thine is the Kingdome*" and "*Thy Kindgome come*" means only a political "Restauration of the Kingdome of God" in continuity with the Old Testament. Christ could not be referring to God's own nonearthly kingdom, "for such a Kingdome God always hath," so he must be referring to a terrestrial kingdom,[193] the "Restauration" of which will not occur until after Christ's second coming.

"There be so many other places that confirm this interpretation, that it were a wonder there is no greater notice taken of it . . ." mused Hobbes. The reason for overlooking this "literall interpretation of the *Kingdome of God*," charged Hobbes, was the underlying desire for political power by ecclesiastics, who avoid the literal interpretation because "it gives too much light to Christian Kings to see their right of Ecclesiasticall Government."[194]

Hobbes admitted that "this doctrine (though proved out of places of Scripture not few nor obscure) will appear to most men a novelty. . . ." Why does he then "propound it"? The answer is frankly political, and in fact, pertains directly to the civil war in England surrounding the time of *Leviathan*'s publication. He was "attending the end of

188 Ibid., III.38, p. 350 [241].
189 Ibid., IV.44, p. 474 [334–335].
190 Ibid., III.35, pp. 318–319 [219].
191 Ibid., III.35, p. 315 [216–217].
192 Ibid., III.35, p. 317 [218].
193 Ibid., III.35, p. 319 [219].
194 Ibid., III.35, pp. 319–320 [219–220].

that dispute of the sword, concerning the Authority, (not yet amongst my Countreymen decided,) by which all sorts of doctrine are to bee approved, or rejected. . . ."[195] Because civil war is a lapse into the state of nature where there exists no settled authority, it remains unsettled what doctrines are to be held, even doctrines about heaven and hell. However novel Hobbes's interpretation, doubtless it would serve to support the sovereign power.

Hobbes offered the sovereign plenty of exercise in political exegesis. In regard to heaven, when the Psalmist declared (133:3) that "*Upon Zion God commanded the blessing, even Life for evermore*," we can see that "Zion, is in Jerusalem, upon Earth. . . ." And in Revelation 21:2, where St. John declares, "*I John saw the Holy City, New Jerusalem, coming down from God out of heaven*," it clearly meant that "the new Jerusalem, the Paradise of God, at the coming again of Christ, should come down to Gods people from Heaven, and not they goe up to it from Earth."[196] Wherever we find "Kingdome of Heaven, is meant the Kingdom of the king that dwelleth in Heaven . . . because our King shall then be God, whose *throne* is Heaven; without any necessity evident in the Scripture, that man shall ascend to his happinesse any higher than Gods *footstool*, the Earth."[197]

What of those sticky passages—say, Luke 20:37–38—in which Christ quite evidently seems to be denying the Sadducees' rejection of the Resurrection *and* the immortality of the soul? Here, Christ seemed clearly to be arguing that God, in speaking to Moses from the burning bush, was declaring himself to be the God of Abraham, Isaac, and Jacob, thereby demonstrating that "*he is not a God of the Dead, but of the Living*. . . ." Do not such passages prove, against Hobbes, that "though their bodies were not to ascend till the generall day of Judgement, yet their souls [i.e., of Abraham, Isaac, and Jacob] were in Heaven as soon as they were departed from their bodies"?

No, asserted Hobbes. In this passage Christ was referring only to the "resurrection of the Body," for as Hobbes already made clear, immaterial substances cannot exist. So, "our Saviour meaneth, that those Patriarchs [Abraham, Isaac, and Jacob] were Immortall . . . by the will of God,"[198] that is, even though they ceased to exist at death, it was God's will to entirely re-create them at the time of the general resurrection. Likewise, eternal life for the "faithful Christian" meant that "he [will] die a natural death, and remaine dead for a time; namely, till the Resurrection," so that "Immortall Life (and Soule and Life in the Scripture, do usually signifie the same thing) beginneth not in man, till the Resurrection, and day of Judgement. . . ."[199]

Thus, to support his political goals, Hobbes put forth a version of Annihilationism (also called Mortalism), the heretical belief that we are completely annihilated at death, only to be recreated *ex nihilo* by God at the Day of Judgment.[200] Annihilationism

195 Ibid., III.38, pp. 350–351 [241].

196 Ibid., III.38, p. 347 [239].

197 Ibid., III.38, p. 348 [240].

198 Ibid., III.38, p. 349 [240–241].

199 Ibid., III.38, pp. 348–350 [240–241]. See also IV.44, pp. 486–490 [343–346].

200 Hobbes was not the only one to put forth a doctrine of Mortalism, either during this period or before. See George L. Mosse, "Puritan Radicalism and the Enlightenment," *Church History*, Vol. 29 (1960),

was quite a useful doctrine for Hobbes's entire philosophical system of modified Epicureanism. First, it accorded nicely with his materialism, which, prior to and independently of any considerations of Scripture, denied the existence of the immortal soul, and fit even more nicely with Epicurus's insistence that such materialism provided the cure for the worst sources of disturbance plaguing human beings, the desires and fears related to the afterlife.[201]

A Kinder, Gentler Hell

In making the kingdom of God a mere earthly kingdom, Hobbes let some of the air out of heaven: Hobbesian eternal bliss was strikingly like earthly bliss, and hence it did not promise much beyond what the sovereign could offer in the here and now. What then of hell? Hobbes's response was ingenious and (one cannot help but think) entirely disingenuous, even though quite influential.

Following Machiavelli's characteristic mode of deflation, Hobbes first placed biblical beside pagan beliefs about hell.[202] Having aroused suspicion by proxy, he then maintained that in Scripture, the place and nature of punishment was defined in various passages by a kind of metaphorical or poetic slide, a move that allowed for a good deal of demythologizing. Since the giants of the earth were wiped out by the great flood, "the place of the Damned, is therefore also sometimes marked out, by the company of those deceased Giants" in water (as in Proverbs 21:16; Job 26:5–6; and Isaiah 14.9), so that the place of "the Damned, (if the sense be literall,) is to be under water." Likewise, because Sodom and Gomorrah were consumed for their wickedness by fire, "the place of the Damned is sometimes expressed by Fire, and a Fiery Lake," as in Revelation 21:8, so that "Hell Fire, which is here expressed by Metaphor, from the reall Fire of Sodome, signifieth not any certain kind, or place of Torment; but is to be taken indefinitely, for Destruction. . . ."[203] From the "Plague of Darknesse" in Exodus, came the metaphorical placing of the damned in like darkness.[204] And finally, from the Jewish repugnance to the "Valley of . . . Hinnon," where worshippers of Molech sacrificed children, and later Jews made a burning garbage pit called Gehenna, came the "notion of *Everlasting*, and *Unquenchable Fire*."[205] Hobbes reached the conclusion: "that which is thus said concerning Hell Fire, is spoken metaphorically," the original, real ground of each metaphor itself having nothing to do with life after death.[206] Much of the sting of hell was therefore taken out by philology.

pp. 424–439, and Norman Burns, *Christian Mortalism from Tyndale to Milton* (Cambridge: Harvard University Press, 1972).

201 See Laertius, *Lives*, "Epicurus," 10.63–67, 124–125.

202 Hobbes, *Hobbes's Leviathan*, III.38, p. 351 [242].

203 Ibid., III.38, p. 352 [242–243].

204 Ibid., III.38, pp. 352–353 [243].

205 Ibid., III.38, p. 353 [243].

206 Ibid.

And demons? If demons exist, and they truly vex humanity, both in this and in the next life, then the power of the priest trumped the power of the king, a thing that Hobbes would not allow. He therefore performed a philological exorcism. Because the names Satan, Diabolus, and Abaddon "have been left untranslated, as they are, in the Latine, and Modern Bibles . . . they seem to be the proper names of *Dæmons*," whereas they really only name "an office, or quality"—the enemy, the accuser, and the destroyer respectively. Mistaking them for proper names, made "men . . . more easily seduced to believe the doctrine of Devills; which at that time was the Religion of the Gentiles, and contrary to that of Moses, and of Christ."[207] In fact, Hobbes observed, "by the *Enemy*, the *Accuser*, and *Destroyer*, is meant, the Enemy of them that shall be in the Kingdome of God," and since that shall be on earth, "by *Satan*, is meant any Earthly Enemy of the Church." An interesting result, to say the least, but certainly one useful to the sovereign as supreme head of the church.

The torments of hell? In regard to intensity, they will be such as those who "live under evill and cruell Governours" now experience. In regard to duration, the temporal sovereign wins out, for while the "fire prepared for the wicked, is an Everlasting Fire . . . it cannot be inferred, that hee who shall be cast into that fire, or be tormented with those torments, shall endure, and resist them so, as to be eternally burnt, and tortured, and yet never be destroyed, nor die."[208] The damned are snuffed out, never to suffer again. Any earthly sovereign, with the tools of slow torture, could easily top that.

Disenchanting the Sacraments

Next to ghostly interpretations of the kingdom of God, Hobbes named the "second generall abuse of Scripture" to be "the turning of Consecration into Conjuration, or Enchantment."[209] As we have already seen, Hobbes's political goal brought him to undermine the sacraments, principally the Eucharist. Properly, the "Lords Supper" merely "put men in mind of their Redemption," but crafty priests "by saying of the words of our Saviour, *This is my Body*, and *This is my Blood* . . . turning the holy words into the manner of a Charme" pretended that "his very Body" was there, even though the words "produceth nothing new to the Sense. . . ." If we deny it, "they face us down, that it [the charm] hath turned the Bread into a Man; nay more, into a God; and [they] require men to worship it, as if it were our Saviour himself present God and Man, and thereby to commit most grosse Idolatry." The words of consecration are therefore to be taken as "*This signifies, or represents my Body*; and it is an ordinary figure of Speech: but to take it literally, is an abuse. . . ."[210] Here, literalism would not serve politics.

207 Ibid., III.38, p. 354 [244].

208 Ibid., III.38, p. 355 [244–245].

209 Ibid., IV.44, p. 477 [337].

210 Ibid., IV.44, pp. 478–479 [337–338].

A second pernicious form of "Enchantment" was "the Sacrament of Baptisme," wherein demons were allegedly driven away by Holy Water, Salt, and Holy Oil.[211] By now, the political problem such sacraments present should be evident to readers. If the devil was driven away, the Holy Spirit actually entered into the baptized, and sacramental baptism was necessary for salvation, it followed that the priesthood was more important than the secular power. For this reason, Hobbes rendered baptism nonsacramental, as a kind of contract, a "renewing of their [i.e., believers'] Pact with God," one that made believers "obliged to obey him [Christ] for King" when Christ's kingdom begins after the resurrection. But since Christ demanded that we obey Caesar, baptism cannot grant license for rebellion against the king in the name of God. To deflate baptism even more, Hobbes conjectured that "the cause of the rite of Baptisme . . . may be probably thought to be an imitation of the law of Moses, concerning Leprousie," where those declared clean of leprosy were "admitted into the campe after a solemne Washing. And this may therefore bee a type of the Washing in Baptisme; wherein such men as are cleansed of the Leprousie of Sin by Faith, are received into the Church with the solemnity of Baptisme."[212]

The Inversion of Typology

Hobbes's treatment of "type" here illuminates his entire approach, and hence the approach of those to follow, and therefore demands our attention. For Hobbes, it is important that baptism not be a "type" in the original sense of scriptural typology. According to this sense of typology, developed by the Church Fathers, types in the Old Testament culminate in the New, so that what began in the Old Testament on the earthly level, and is partially fulfilled there, is fulfilled definitively in the New, in a way that transforms the type spiritually and supernaturally.[213] Thus, Adam is a type of Christ; the old, earthly covenant is a type of the new, heavenly covenant; the animal sacrifices at the Temple were a type of Christ's sacrifice on the cross; the Passover meal was a type of the Eucharist, and so on.

The flow of typology, properly understood, is *forward* in the Divine economy, *toward* the culmination in Christ. So that, while types of baptism occur in the Old Testament—from the effects of the Noachian flood upon a sinful world to the washing of lepers—baptism is a transformation of the types into a new reality, the cleansing of the soul by the Holy Spirit Himself, which begins, by grace, a new creation in the believer. Hobbes's typology inverted the order, flowing not toward culmination and spiritual transformation, but backward, toward the reduction to some earthly, original meaning. This inversion has already been seen in his treatment of the kingdom of God.

---

211 Ibid., IV.44, p. 479 [338].

212 Ibid., III.41, p. 380 [265].

213 On typology and its place in the Divine economy of salvation see Scott Hahn, *Letter and Spirit: From Written Text to Living Word in the Liturgy* (New York: Doubleday, 2005), Ch. 2.

Hobbes's reversal of typology was meant especially to undermine the Catholic Church's interpretation of Scripture through a reductive historical analysis that purported to recover the original, real meaning from amidst the detritus of spiritual overlay. After Hobbes, this inverted exegesis will be taken up again and again to unwind the claims of the Church's typology, which is based upon a forward-moving Divine economy, the overarching plan in creation and salvation history by which humanity is brought ever more deeply, through the Church, into the mystery of the Holy Trinity. But given Hobbes's aim to subordinate religion to the state, typology must be inverted by tracing backward historical types to the most politically useful, nonspiritual origins (real or exegetically imagined).

An additional weapon in this typological reversal is the tracing of types back to pagan sources, a refining of Machiavelli's method of the deflation of Christianity. Hence Hobbes mused that the rite of baptism might have been drawn from certain "Ceremonies of the Gentiles," wherein a man thought dead who recovered was treated as if having undergone a second birth, and so in need of being "washed from the uncleannesse of their nativity. . . ." This allowed Hobbes to claim that "this ceremony of the Greeks . . . crept into the Religion of the Jews" during the time Judea was under the dominion of Alexander."[214] Having sown the suspicion of pagan contamination, Hobbes immediately averred that baptism "most likely" proceeded from "the Legall Ceremony of Washing after Leprosie," since "it is not likely our Saviour would countenance a Heathen rite. . . ."[215] Of course, that still reduced baptism to a purely symbolic ritual, an historical holdover, not a fulfillment and transformation of an older rite. In so doing, Hobbes used the Anabaptist rejection of sacraments, and its suspicion of sacramentalism as creeping paganism, for a purely secular purpose.

Hobbes swept away other sacraments, doctrines, and traditions, especially Catholic, in much the same way.[216] The gist of the sweep is that whatever counts against the power of the civil sovereign in religion must be a contagion from "the Religious Rites of the Greeks and Romanes . . ."; that is, "old empty Bottles of Gentilisme, which the Doctors of the Romane Church, either by Negligence, or Ambition, have filled up again with the new Wine of Christianity. . . ."[217] Although the Roman Catholic Church is not the sole enemy of his political goals—Hobbes also mentioned Presbyterians, since they replaced civil government with ecclesiastical[218]—it is certainly the chief object of his attack, and hence the chief target in his mode of exegesis.

Hobbes's Least Common Denomination

Given that Hobbes placed all power in the civil sovereign to determine every aspect of religion, did he offer any advice concerning the form it should take? Hobbes

214 Hobbes, *Hobbes's Leviathan*, III.41, p. 380 [265].

215 Ibid.

216 Ibid., Part IV, which contains the entirety of what Hobbes considers pernicious.

217 Ibid., IV.45, p. 518 [366].

218 Ibid., IV.44, p. 475 [335] and more directly, IV.47, p. 539 [382].

presented the thinnest form of Christianity possible, what we might call the Least Common Denomination, for it has only one article, "that *Jesus is the Christ*."[219] This is the only "Beleef" preached by Jesus himself, John the Baptist, and the Apostles.[220] In fact, claimed Hobbes, the passage in Matthew (16:18–19) that popes urge for Petrine authority did not mean that Peter himself was the rock on which the Church was built, but that his profession that Jesus was the Christ is the "onely Article" of faith necessary for salvation.[221] This article makes "the Faith required to Salvation" to be "Easie."[222]

The thin form had immediate political advantages. First, it was so thin that excommunication becomes impossible, because almost no one could be *"an Hæretique."*[223] Therefore, no one need fear hell because they do not hold some allegedly essential doctrine over and above the stated minimum. And further, since most of the religious disagreements in Hobbes's day concerned doctrines beyond that truncated core, then Hobbes's declaration of the "Easie" way to salvation provided an easy way to nullify all political conflicts based on such disagreements. Of course, the sovereign is free to impose any further doctrine, as he likes.[224]

The Long Shadow of Leviathan

Given our thorough examination of the *Leviathan,* we can now discern that, contrary to most attributions of paternity to Hobbes in regard to modern scriptural scholarship, Hobbes offered far, far more than a mere skeptical vignette on Mosaic authorship of the Pentateuch (or, for that matter, the oft-cited bizarre, heretical notion that the Trinity of persons actually refers to Moses, Jesus, and the Apostles).[225]

It is also clear that Hobbes's exegesis was, first to last, entirely politicized, offering a nearly endless arsenal of support for the subordination of every aspect of Scripture, from canon to interpretation, to the arbitrary authority of the civil sovereign. The ghost of Henry VIII could not be more adequately served. Hobbes entirely justified the Machiavellian notion of "reason of state," giving the fullest justification of Caesaropapism by building divine right monarchy (ironically) on an entirely materialist foundation. He did so by the ruthless subordination or exorcism of all supernaturalism, so that no kingdom could stand against the civil sovereign's.

But the fact that Hobbes politicized his exegesis is not as important as his various *assumptions* and *aims,* and the *way* he went about confirming these assumptions in Scripture and bending the text to his aims, for the *way,* the *via,* provided

219 Ibid., III.42, p. 389 [272].
220 Ibid., III.42, p. 401 [281], p. 430 [301–302].
221 Ibid., III.42, p. 430 [301–302].
222 Ibid., III.43, p. 463 [325–326].
223 Ibid., III.42, p. 396–398 [277–279].
224 Ibid., III.3, p. 421 [295].
225 Ibid., III.42, pp. 382–383 [267–268].

the methods of the *via moderna* of later exegetes. (And here, calling it the *via moderna* seems highly appropriate, given that Hobbes combined the two *viae modernae*, the one running from Ockham through the nominalists and the other from Machiavelli into Descartes.)

As with Descartes, so also with Hobbes: The methods that arise from Hobbes are neither neutral nor scientific; they arise from his assumptions and aims. In taking up these same methods, later exegetes will, wittingly or not, be carrying forward Hobbes's project of politicizing the text, and making of Christianity a secular servant rather than a spiritual master.

To illustrate, Hobbes's crude mechanist psychology provided a way to undermine the authority of prophets and priests who challenged the political sovereign by reducing inspiration to madness and the belief in spirits to nonsense. Later exegetes will offer slightly more refined versions of mechanistic psychology, but the results will be much the same. Since the power of miracles diverted authority to the priest, Hobbes's mechanism allowed him to eliminate the contemporary possibility of miracles and to purge almost all miracles from the text. Later exegetes will simply declare miracles impossible contradictions to the laws of nature, and read them out of Scripture. Hobbes's attempts to demonstrate that the Kingdom of God was earthly and political were all spent in buttressing the power of the civil sovereign. Later exegetes will likewise find that Jesus, rather than preaching an otherworldly kingdom, was actually preaching a merely moral Gospel that fits us to be good and peaceful citizens. Hobbes used the reigning anti-Aristotelianism as a shield to smuggle in his materialism, maintaining that all spiritual interpretations of Scripture were caused by Greek contamination. Later exegetes, following Hobbes's lead, will divide Scripture into layers, the original and pure being earthy and earthly, and the later spiritualizing elements being alien corruptions from the Greeks. In order to break the power of the papacy, Hobbes asserted that Roman Catholicism was largely warmed-over paganism, an historical overgrowth, grown from the natural seed of religion and grafted with the superstitions of the Greeks and Romans. Later exegetes will treat Christianity itself as just one more *species* of religion, thereby treating it as one more bush from the natural seed. For the sake of peace in an era of religious war, Hobbes declared that there is only one essential doctrine of Christianity, and all else is superfluous (and hence unworthy of the shedding of blood). Of course, for Hobbes, that Jesus is the Christ ultimately means (via tortured exegesis) that the sum of Christianity is obedience to the civil sovereign. Later exegetes will take over this notion of the fundamental moral core of Christianity, a notion that, since it couldn't be gotten from the text itself, had to be derived by stripping everything away from Scripture but the alleged core. The heart (for core is derived from *cor*, Latin for heart), while still weakly beating, will be used to pump moral blood, however thin, into the increasingly secular state.

Perhaps the greatest irony of Hobbes's project—born as it was amidst the ravages of the English Civil War and the Thirty Years' War—is how thoroughly it failed. This does not mean that Hobbes failed to have an historical impact; indeed, he became the father of modern political liberalism. Insofar as we find the modern state, in any of its permutations, to be a subspecies of the great and original Leviathan, we see that

Hobbes was a great success. But his ruthless subordination of the church to the state did not lead, as Hobbes hoped and promised, to enduring civil peace, but rather to ever more ruthless political wars as the states became ever more secular. If the Thirty Years' War was the last great religious war, it was neither the last nor the most devastating war. The state itself, in receiving all the devotion formerly bestowed upon Christianity, became all the more passionately aggressive, as the era of religious wars gave way to the age of national wars that became increasingly bloody as they became more purely secular. And so, the savagery of the Thirty Years' War was more than matched by the savagery of the French Revolution. In comparison to the two World Wars of the twentieth century, both entirely nationalistic and secular, the religious wars of the sixteenth and seventeenth century fade into insignificance. When we add the tens of millions slaughtered by Marxist states, explicitly defined against Christianity and bent on its extermination (not mere subordination), there is no comparison left.

Yet even in Hobbes's day, the contribution of religion to wars was not as simple as it seemed. Scholars have more carefully traced the true causes of the great conflicts that formed the context of Hobbes's project, and it is now clear that nationalism and dynastic conflicts were more influential than religious differences.[226] That is not to exonerate Christians from what blame they deserve, but it makes plain that the political subordination or elimination of Christianity does not bring peace.

In the seventeenth century, however, the dream of lasting political peace free from religious turmoil was vivid, and the hope for a cure inspired others with equal passion and audacity, those who had imbibed Descartes and Hobbes and presented an even more radically secularized project. We now turn our attention from England back to the Continent, and focus on the Netherlands, the home of Benedict Spinoza and his circle of radical friends.

226 See especially Geoffrey Parker, *The Thirty Years' War* (London and New York: Routledge & Kegan Paul, 1984); Richard Bonney, *The Thirty Years' War 1618–1648* (Oxford: Osprey Publishing, 2002); S. H. Steinberg, *The Thirty Years' War and the Conflict for European Hegemony, 1600–1660* (New York: W. W. Norton, 1966); Richard Dunn, *The Age of Religious Wars: 1559–1689* (New York: W. W. Norton, 1970); William Cavanaugh, "A Fire Strong Enough to Consume the House": The Wars of Religion and the Rise of the State," *Modern Theology* 11.4 (1995): 397–420.

CHAPTER 9

SPINOZA AND THE BEGINNING OF THE RADICAL ENLIGHTENMENT

> Spinoza, Benedictus de, a Jew by birth, and afterwards a deserter from Judaism, and lastly an atheist, was from Amsterdam. He was a systematic atheist who employed a totally new method. . . . [H]is *Tractatus theologico-politicus*, published in Amsterdam in 1670, [is] a pernicious and detestable book in which he slips in all the seeds of atheism that were [later on] plainly revealed in his *Opera posthuma*[1] [1677]. . . . All those who have refuted the *Tractatus theologico-politicus* have found in it the seeds of atheism. . . . It is not as easy to deal with all the difficulties contained in that work as to demolish completely the system that appeared in his *Opera posthuma*; for this is the most monstrous hypothesis that could be imagined, the most absurd, and the most diametrically opposed to the most evident notions of our mind.[2]

These harsh words are not those of an orthodox reactionary, but came from the pen of Pierre Bayle, from his article on Spinoza in Bayle's infamous *Dictionnaire historique et critique* (1695–1697).[3] Bayle was the most important skeptic of the late seventeenth century—a self-proclaimed fideist in religion, even while continually charged with atheism—and his skeptical attacks on Christianity and the Scriptures in the *Dictionnaire* acted as a treasure house for the eighteenth century deist and atheist cynical assaults upon revealed religion.

Whether Bayle's assessment is accurate, it is worthy of note not only because it was made by someone of Bayle's highly questionable orthodoxy (and fairly soon after the publication of Spinoza's *Tractatus*[4]), but also because it marks very clearly the

1 The *Opera posthuma* contained (in Latin) Spinoza's *Ethics, Letters, Political Treatise* (unfinished), *Treatise on the Emendation of the Intellect*, and a *Compendium of Hebrew Grammar*. A Dutch translation came out in the same year (without the Hebrew Grammar).

2 Pierre Bayle, *Historical and Critical Dictionary, Selections*, translated by Richard Popkin (Indianapolis, IN: Hackett Publishing, 1991), pp. 288–297.

3 Bayle's article on Spinoza and Spinozism is the single longest article in the *Dictionnaire*. Extensive entries on Spinoza and Spinozism also occurred in Johann Heindrich Zedler's dauntingly large 64-volume *Grosses vollständiges Universal-Lexicon aller Wissenschaften und Künste* (1731–1750), and in the famous *Encyclopédie* (1751–1766) of Denis Diderot and Jean Le Rond d'Alembert—in both cases, more extensive than offered for John Locke.

4 Bayle received his copy of Spinoza's *Tractatus* in May 1679. Jonathan I. Israel, *Radical Enlightenment: Philosophy and the Making of Modernity 1650–1750* (Oxford: Oxford University Press, 2001), p. 285. Given the popularity of Bayle's *Dictionnaire* over the next century, Bayle's assessment of Spinoza was more likely to be read than Spinoza's *Tractatus* or the posthumously published *Ethics*.

two major charges against Spinoza that arose immediately. The first is that the book in which we find Spinoza's famous biblical exegesis, the *Tractatus*, contains the seeds of atheism, seeds intentionally planted by the author. Second, is that Spinoza's underlying philosophical system, published only after his death, asserted something so profoundly disturbing, a "most monstrous hypothesis," that it went far beyond even the most radical thought of the period. As Bayle intimates in the above, there an essential relationship between Spinoza's "monstrous hypothesis" and the alleged "seeds of atheism" planted in the *Tractatus*.

We find a like assessment by none other than David Hume, one of the most acerbic critics of religion in the century following Spinoza. In Hume's *Treatise of Human Nature*, he refers to Spinoza as "that famous atheist," asserting that the "fundamental principle of the atheism of *Spinoza* is the doctrine of the simplicity of the universe, and the unity of that substance, in which he supposes both thought and matter to inhere"; that is, the fundamental principle is Spinoza's doctrine of the identity of God and nature as one substance, a doctrine that Hume, for his own reasons, refers to as a "hideous hypothesis."[5]

If the notably unorthodox assessed Spinoza in such a way, it is not difficult to imagine the effect of his writings on the orthodox of the time. In Jonathan Israel's words, Benedict Spinoza was "the supreme philosophical bogeyman of Early Enlightenment Europe. . . . In fact, no one else during the century 1650–1750 remotely rivaled Spinoza's notoriety as the chief challenger of the fundamentals of revealed religion, received ideas, tradition, morality, and . . . divinely constituted political authority."[6]

Here is an irony familiar from the story of Hobbes. This same Spinoza, who shocked his contemporaries on every level, is just as commonly regarded (in hindsight) as another father of modern scriptural scholarship.[7] In fact, since Spinoza is all

---

5 L. A. Selby-Bigge, ed., David Hume, *A Treatise of Human Nature*, second edition (Oxford: Clarendon Press, 1978), I.iv.5, pp. 240–241.

6 Israel, *Radical Enlightenment*, p. 159. Israel points out (ibid and pp. 12–13) that there is an interesting historiographical obscuring of Spinoza's notoriety, which began in the nineteenth century, which claimed that Spinoza was "rarely understood and had very little influence" during the early Enlightenment. This claim, which runs completely against the evidence from the time period, is quite curious, but understandable *if* we take into account that the nineteenth century witnessed the bursting into full flower of Spinozism as orthodoxy in philosophical systems such as Hegel's. By the nineteenth century, Spinozism had so imbued the intellectual backdrop that the charge of atheism and radicalism was no longer intelligible. Thus, the initial charges of atheism could only be credited to a misunderstanding that would be cleared up in time.

7 The attribution of patrimony to Spinoza is vast, but not always deep. For a bibliography, see Travis Frampton, *Spinoza and the Rise of Historical Criticism of the Bible* (London: T. & T. Clark, 2006), Introduction. For short accounts of Spinoza within the context of scriptural interpretation, see Henning Graf Reventlow, *Epochen der Bibelauslegung,* Band IV: *Von der Aufklärung bis zum 20. Jahrhundert* (München: Verlag C. H. Beck, 2001), IV.2, pp. 92–113; Steven Nadler, "The Bible Hermeneutics of Baruch de Spinoza," in Magne Sæbø, *Hebrew Bible/Old Testament: The History of Its Interpretation*: Vol. II, *From the Renaissance to the Enlightenment* (Göttingen: Vandenhoeck & Ruprecht, 2008), C.33, pp. 827–836; Roy Harrisville and Walter Sundberg, *The Bible in Modern Culture: Baruch Spinoza to Brevard Childs*, second edition (Grand Rapids, MI: Eerdmans, 2002), Ch. 2; John H. Hayes, "The History of the Study of Israelite and Judaean History," in John H. Hayes and J. Maxwell Miller, eds., *Israelite and Judaean History* (London: SCM Press, 1977), pp. 45–46.

the more systematic in his exegesis, he generally receives more credit than Hobbes. As with Hobbes, to understand this strange fact we shall have to analyze Spinoza's own thought in detail in the context of his own time.

Spinoza's Early Life

Baruch de Espinoza was born on November 24, 1632, the son of Miguel (Michael) de Espinoza and his second wife, Hanna Debora Despinosa. Michael's first wife, Rachel de Spinoza, died in 1627, leaving behind two children, Isaac and Rebecca; Hanna died in 1638, having had three children, Baruch, Mirjam, and Gabriel. Michael's third wife, Ester d'Espinosa, died in 1653, the year before Michael died. Baruch was called Bento by his family (the Portuguese form), and so is known to us more famously by the Latin form of Baruch, Benedictus (all three meaning "the blessed one").

As with many in Amsterdam, Spinoza's family were *marranos*, that is, the descendants of Jews from Spain and Portugal who had been forced to convert to Christianity, but who secretly practiced Judaism (albeit in attenuated forms). Many had emigrated to the Netherlands, fleeing the Inquisition and taking haven in the reputedly most tolerant country in Europe so that they could live openly as Jews again. Baruch's father had been born in Portugal, the son of a prosperous merchant, Isaac. Baruch himself was born a New Jew in Amsterdam. In order to regain their centuries-long suppressed heritage, the New Jews were attempting to revive Judaism, and essential to that effort was an immersion in Hebrew, the Law, and the Talmud. Such was Baruch's earliest education at the Talmud Torah school of Amsterdam, in which he continued until he was about fourteen years old.

Baruch's father was a merchant and community pillar in Amsterdam, a *parnas* (governor) of the synagogue, then the Jewish school, and finally (1649–1650) a member of the *mahamad* (or, *ma'amad*), the council that could discipline rabbis. Just six years after his own father served as one of the council, on July 27, 1656, twenty-four-year-old Baruch would receive a sentence of excommunication from the *mahamad*, which stated that the ruling council members, "having for some time known the evil opinions and works of Baruch de Espinoza . . . [and] have endeavored by various ways and promises to draw him back from his evil ways; and not being able to remedy him, but on the contrary, receiving every day more news about the horrible heresies he practices and taught [to others], and the awful deeds he performed . . . [have] resolved . . . that the said Espinoza be put to the *herem* [ban] and banished from the nation of Israel. . . ."[8]

It is worth noting two things: first, the ban came two years after Baruch's father's death, and second, the council affirmed that it has "for some time known the evil opinions and works of Baruch de Espinoza." As recent scholars have argued, it appears

8 Quoted in Yirmiyahu Yovel, *Spinoza and Other Heretics: The Marrano of Reason* (Princeton: Princeton University Press, 1989), p. 3. For a more in-depth analysis see Asa Kasher and Shlomo Biderman, "Why Was Baruch De Spinoza Excommunicated," in David Katz and Jonathan I. Israel, *Sceptics, Millenarians and Jews* (Leiden: E. J. Brill, 1990), pp. 98–141.

certain that Baruch began to have doubts about his Judaism rather early and that he embraced the radical philosophy that would lead to his expulsion from the synagogue even while his father was still alive, but out of deference to him, kept it to himself.[9] After his father's death, Baruch made his opinions sufficiently known that the *mahamad* took public action.

Influence of Cartesianism and the Seeds of Doubt

How long before his expulsion Spinoza had doubts may never be settled with any exactitude, but there can be no doubt that one of the main influences that came to bear strongly on him was Cartesianism (although others will become apparent). As noted in Chapter Seven, Descartes lived in the Netherlands for over twenty years, and it was in the Netherlands where Cartesianism first thoroughly soaked the intellectual culture and the implications of Cartesianism first began to be disputed.[10]

In particular, we know that Spinoza learned Latin from Franciscus van den Enden (1602–1674), an ex-Jesuit born in Antwerp who was not only a classical scholar but studied both law and medicine.[11] Even more, he was a self-proclaimed Cartesian and was "steeped in Machiavelli, whose *Discorsi* influenced him profoundly,"[12] and it was van den Enden who likely introduced Machiavelli to Spinoza.[13] This connection would be of no small significance if Spinoza is, in Edwin Curley's assessment, "arguably the

9 Yovel, *Spinoza and Other Heretics: The Marrano of Reason,* Ch. 3; Margaret Gullan-Whur, *Within Reason: A Life of Spinoza* (New York: St. Martin's Press, 1998), pp. 43–71; and especially Israel, *Radical Enlightenment: Philosophy and the Making of Modernity 1650–1750,* pp. 164–174.

10 See Theo Verbeek, *Descartes and the Dutch: Early Reactions to Cartesian Philosophy* (Carbondale, IL: Southern Illinois University Press, 1992); Klaus Scholder, *The Birth of Modern Critical Theology: Origins and Problems of Biblical Criticism,* translated by John Bowden (London: SCM Press, 1990), Ch. 6; H. Siebrand, "On the Early Reception of Spinoza's Tractatus Theologico-Politicus in the Context of Cartesianism," in C. De Deugd, ed., *Spinoza's Political and Theological Thought* (Amsterdam: North-Holland Publishing, 1984), pp. 214–225; and Tammy Nyden-Bullock, *Spinoza's Radical Cartesian Mind* (London: Continuum, 2007), Chs. 1–3.

11 On van den Enden, see Israel, *Radical Enlightenment: Philosophy and the Making of Modernity 1650–1750,* ch. 9; Frampton, *Spinoza and the Rise of Historical Criticism of the Bible,* pp. 176–182; Wim Klever, "A New Source of Spinozism: Franciscus van den Enden," *Journal of the History of Philosophy,* Vol. 29 (October 1991), pp. 613–631; Nyden-Bullock, *Spinoza's Radical Cartesian Mind,* pp. 34–40.

12 Israel, *Radical Enlightenment: Philosophy and the Making of Modernity 1650–1750,* p. 176. Machiavelli, as well as Hobbes, influenced other Dutch radical Cartesians, important examples being Lambertus van Velthuysen (1622–1685) and Johan de la Court (1622–1660). See Nyden-Bullock, *Spinoza's Radical Cartesian Mind,* Ch. 2.

13 Steven Nadler, *Spinoza: A Life* (Cambridge: Cambridge University Press, 1999), pp. 111, 270. On the use by Spinoza of Machiavellian premises and arguments see Steven Smith, *Spinoza, Liberalism, and the Question of Jewish Identity* (New Haven: Yale University Press, 1997), pp. 34–38; Eco Mulier, *The Myth of Venice and Dutch Republican Thought in the Seventeenth Century* (Assen, Netherlands: Van Gorcum, 1980), pp. 170–181; Edwin Curley, "Kissinger, Spinoza, and Genghis Kahn," in Don Garrett, ed., *The Cambridge Companion to Spinoza* (Cambridge: Cambridge University Press, 1996), pp. 315–342, reprinted in Genevieve Lloyd, ed., *Spinoza: Critical Assessments. Volume III: The Political Writings* (London and New York: Routledge, 2001), pp. 143–166.

most Machiavellian of the great modern political philosophers"[14]; Spinoza himself praised Machiavelli as "that most farseeing man."[15]

Significantly, van den Enden owned a bookshop that catered to freethinkers, and himself had a reputation as an atheist. After 1652, he opened a school for the instruction of Latin and Greek, and Spinoza not long after became one of his pupils. Although it is likely that Spinoza had heard of Descartes prior to this, and was "caught up in the general intellectual turbulence in Holland precipitated by Cartesianism . . . it was specifically van den Enden who first pointed him in a radical direction, either at the beginning of the 1650s or, as seems far more likely, in the late 1640s, when Spinoza was in his late teens."[16] Spinoza's longtime friend, Jarig Jelles, reported in his Preface to Spinoza's *Opera posthuma*, that long before Spinoza was expelled from the synagogue, his study of Descartes brought him to rebel inwardly against his education in Judaism.[17] It is also likely that Spinoza was enrolled at the University of Leiden in the late 1650s, where Cartesianism first flourished in the Netherlands. In fact, Spinoza's first published book (1663) was *Principles of Cartesian Philosophy*.

But Descartes was not the only influence. Sometime after finishing at the Talmud Torah school, Spinoza took up the reading of a number of medieval Jewish, Christian, and Arabic authors, among which were Maimonides and Averroes (the latter, for the most part, in the form of commentaries on Aristotle).[18] There is also direct evidence that Spinoza read the Jewish Averroist Gersonides (Levi ben Gershon, 1288–1344).[19]

All signs, then, point to the wide reading and intellectual precocity of Spinoza. In fact, while the *Principles* was Spinoza's first published work, it was not his first *written* work. Already in 1658, when he was about twenty-six, he had begun his *Treatise on the Emendation of the Intellect*, and in 1660 he began an esoteric presentation of his philosophy meant only for a small circle of like-minded individuals, called *Short Treatise on God, Man, and His Well-being*. In 1662, he had completed the first part of his *Ethics*, the clearest and most radical presentation of his philosophy. As noted above, his *Tractatus theologico-politicus* was published anonymously in 1670, a treatise that proved so appalling to his fellow citizens that the States of Holland issued a formal condemnation of it on July 19, 1673 (a condemnation that also included "other

14 Curley, "Kissinger, Spinoza, and Genghis Kahn," p. 143. In part, Curley bases this assessment upon the startling similarity between the opening two paragraphs of Spinoza's *Political Treatise* and Chapter XV of Machiavelli's *Prince*, wherein both authors rejected the notion that politics should be based upon how men actually act rather than any notion of how they ought to act. Ibid., pp. 154–155.

15 Benedict Spinoza, *A Political Treatise*, V.7, included in Benedict de Spinoza, *A Theologico-Political Treatise* and *A Political Treatise*, translated by R.H.M. Elwes (New York: Dover, 1951).

16 Israel, *Radical Enlightenment: Philosophy and the Making of Modernity 1650–1750*, p. 169.

17 Ibid., p. 164.

18 See Harry Wolfson, *The Philosophy of Spinoza* (New York: Meridian Books, 1934), I, i, pp. 8–11; Shlomo Pines, "Spinoza's 'Tractatus Theologico-Politicus,' Maimonides, and Kant," *Scripta Hierosolymitana* 20 (1968), pp. 3–54; Warren Harvey, "A Portrait of Spinoza as a Maimonidean," *Journal of the History of Philosophy* 19 (1981), pp. 151–172.

19 Wolfson, *The Philosophy of Spinoza*, I, iv, pp. 108–111.

atheistical and heretical writings," one of these being Hobbes's *Leviathan*, the Dutch translation of which was published in Amsterdam in 1667).[20]

It is important to note that Spinoza's philosophy was generally condemned as an offshoot of Cartesianism, demonstrating quite clearly (so it was urged) the latent tendency of Descartes's dualism to lead to complete materialism. Thus, in the last quarter of the 1600s and first half of the 1700s, Spinoza came to be seen as the logical and pernicious outcome of Cartesianism, whatever Cartesians urged to the contrary. Much of the condemnation of Descartes, carried on not only by universities and the various church bodies, but even more importantly, by political bodies, was really a condemnation of Spinoza, and much of the bitterness arose from Spinoza's treatment of Scripture.[21]

A typical assessment, notable because it occurs so early (1661), is found in the travel diary of one Olaus Borch, who wrote that "at Rijnsburg [where Spinoza recently moved from Amsterdam] there is . . . an apostate Jew, in fact practically an atheist who does not respect the Old Testament and considers the New Testament to be of no more weight than the *Koran* and Aesop's *Fables*. . . ."[22]

Other Radicals: Da Costa, De Prado, and La Peyrère

Spinoza was not the only radical philosopher in the Netherlands, nor was he the only one to offer a thoroughly secular critique of Christianity and Scripture. Uriel da Costa (c. 1584–1640), Juan de Prado (c. 1612–c. 1670), and Isaac La Peyrère (1596–1676) each in his own way added to the climate of radical criticism in the Netherlands and influenced Spinoza.

Da Costa committed suicide when Spinoza was only eight years old.[23] He was originally a New Christian born in Portugal (c. 1583–84), one of the many Jews whose

20 Israel argues convincingly that the standard view, that Spinoza's *Tractatus* circulated widely for four years after publication without any attempt to suppress it, is incorrect. See Jonathan I. Israel, "The Banning of Spinoza's Works in the Dutch Republic (1670–1678)," in Wiep Van Bunge and Wim Klever, *Disguised and Overt Spinozism Around 1700* (Leiden: E. J. Brill, 1996), pp. 3–14.

21 See Israel, *Radical Enlightenment: Philosophy and the Making of Modernity 1650–1750*, pp. 26, 32, 34, 36, 42, 47, 51–53, 210–217.

22 Ibid., p. 163.

23 For a short account of da Costa's work and life, and his connection to Spinoza, see Yovel, *Spinoza and Other Heretics: The Marrano of Reason*, pp. 42–54; José Faur, *In the Shadow of History: Jews and* Conversos *at the Dawn of Modernity* (Albany, NY: SUNY Press, 1992), pp. 110–141; and Leszek Kolakowski, "The Tragic Career of Uriel da Costa" in Zbigniew Janowski , ed., Leszek Kolakowski, *The Two Eyes of Spinoza & Other Essays on Philosophers* (South Bend, IN: St. Augustine's Press, 2004), pp. 95–102; F. Niewöhner, "Die Religion Noahs bei Uriel da Costa und Baruch de Spinoza. Eine historische Miniature zur Genese des Deismus," in C. De Deugd, ed., *Spinoza's Political and Theological Thought* (Amsterdam, Oxford: North-Holland, 1984), pp. 143–149. For a profound analysis of da Costa in relationship to modern biblical criticism see Leo Strauss, *Spinoza's Critique of Religion*, translated by E. M. Sinclair (Chicago: The University of Chicago Press, 1997), Ch. 2.

ancestors had been forced to convert to Catholicism. Wanting to return to Judaism, he left for Amsterdam, but (so he reported) found there only disappointment among the New Jews, and so became a deist, having rejected both revealed religion and the immortality of the soul (as evidenced in his unpublished *Da mortalidade da Alma*[24]). Banned by the Jews, he eventually (and insincerely) recanted, but again rebelled against the Judaism of Amsterdam, only to be cast out of the synagogue for the second time. Publicly humiliated, unable to live either in isolation from the Jewish community or among it, he wrote his famous autobiographical *Exemplar humanae vitae*,[25] and soon after committed suicide (1640). The *Exemplar* would later be published by the liberal Dutch theologian Philip van Limborch.[26] Significantly, da Costa's rejection of revealed religion was heavily influenced by Epicureanism.[27]

Juan de Prado did not arrive in Amsterdam until 1655. Originally a *marrano* from Spain, de Prado was at first a secret Judaizer among a hostile Christian culture, who studied philosophy and medicine. But by the early 1640s, his fervent Judaism had already become unsettled by doubts (these, apparently, having been planted by the skeptic *converso*, Juan Piñero). Upon his arrival in Amsterdam and experience of life among the New Jews, the seeds of doubt bloomed. De Prado met Spinoza in the year he arrived in Amsterdam from Spain, and "although Spinoza did not find a mentor or a 'corruptor' in de Prado, the contact between the two men certainly helped them to boost and articulate their dissenting ideas."[28] De Prado's case was brought before the *mahamad* the same year as Spinoza's, and a few days after Spinoza's ban, de Prado publicly repented; his insincerity soon enough became clear, and so he was officially banned six months later. As with da Costa, de Prado held a deism formed in part by essential Epicurean beliefs: that the world was eternal rather than created, that there is no afterlife, and that the revealed religions are merely human-made, and inferior to reason. Spinoza met regularly with de Prado.[29]

Isaac La Peyrère merits a closer look, given his independent status as a precursor to modern biblical criticism. La Peyrère was born into a rich and powerful Calvinist family, and may even have had *marrano* blood.[30] He is famous for his *Prae-Adamitae*,

24 Faur, *In the Shadow of History*, p. 129. The contents of *Da mortalidade da Alma* are not known directly, but indirectly through quotations in Semuel da Silva, *Tratado da Immortalidade da Alma*.

25 See Faur, *In the Shadow of History*, for a detailed analysis of da Costa's life as compared with his autobiographical account in the *Exemplar*.

26 Ibid., p. 113.

27 Strauss, *Spinoza's Critique of Religion*, pp. 58–63 and Faur, *In the Shadow of History*, p. 132.

28 Yovel, *Spinoza and Other Heretics: The Marrano of Reason*, p. 68.

29 On de Prado, see Yovel, *Spinoza and Other Heretics: The Marrano of Reason*, pp. 57–80; Frampton, *Spinoza and the Rise of Historical Criticism of the Bible*, pp. 150–156; and Faur, *In the Shadow of History*, pp. 146–155.

30 On La Peyrère see especially Richard Popkin, *Isaac La Peyrère (1596–1676): His Life, Work and Influence* (Leiden: E. J. Brill, 1987). In addition see Richard Popkin, "Spinoza and Bible Scholarship," in James Force and Richard Popkin, eds., *The Books of Nature and Scripture: Recent Essays on Natural Philosophy, Theology, and Biblical Criticism in the Netherlands of Spinoza's Time and the British Isles of Newton's Time* (Dordrecht: Kluwer Academic Publishers, 1994), pp. 6–7; Yovel, *Spinoza and Other*

a book that was published in the Netherlands in 1655, the same year he arrived in Amsterdam, but as we mentioned previously, circulated for over a decade before publication (and after publication, continued to be one of the most frequently refuted authors between 1655 and 1800[31]). La Peyrère was formally accused of atheism and impiety rather early in his life (1626), but exonerated by the support of sixty pastors (a sign, perhaps, more of his family's prestige than the caliber of his Reformed orthodoxy).[32]

In 1640, La Peyrère was sent to Paris to be a secretary to the Prince of Condé, and was thereby introduced into a circle of eminent philosophers including Father Mersenne, the champion of Epicureanism, Father Pierre Gassendi, Hugo Grotius, and Thomas Hobbes, who was on the Continent during this period. During this period, La Peyrère was already working on the argument that would be presented in the *Prae-Adamitae*.[33] In addition to his notion of the pre-Adamites, La Peyrère was also possessed by the millenarian expectation that, with the conversion of the Jews, a new age would be ushered in when the Jews, recalled to France, would be led triumphantly to Palestine by Louis XIV (the thesis being published anonymously as his *Du Rappel des Juifs*, 1643).[34]

Interestingly enough, it was the deposed Queen Christina of Sweden, Descartes's last patroness, who persuaded La Peyrère to publish his *Prae-Adamitae* anonymously in Holland, and likely provided the money. The book circulated widely over Europe in several translations, was just as quickly burned and banned, and La Peyrère was arrested in Brussels in February 1656 by order of the archbishop of Malines. La Peyrère felt abandoned by Protestants, and was gently persuaded that if he made a per-

---

Heretics: The Marrano of Reason, pp. 80–84; Scholder, *The Birth of Modern Critical Theology: Origins and Problems of Biblical Criticism*, pp. 82–87; H.J.M. Nellen, "Growing Tension between Church Doctrines and Critical Exegesis of the Old Testament," in in Sæbø, ed., *Hebrew Bible/Old Testament, The History of Its Interpretation*: Vol. II, *From the Renaissance to the Enlightenment*, Ch. 32, pp. 817–823; and John Sandys-Wunsch, *What Have They Done to the Bible? A History of Modern Biblical Interpretation* (Collegeville, MN: Liturgical Press, 2005), pp. 101–107. On a deeper level, see Leo Strauss's analysis of La Peyrère in *Spinoza's Critique of Religion*, Ch. 3. La Peyrère was born in Bordeaux, "where many of the Protestants were suspected of being secret Jews, or Marranos of Portuguese origin." Popkin, *Isaac La Peyrère*, p. 5.

31 Ibid., p. 3.

32 Ibid., p. 5.

33 Mersenne showed a copy to Grotius, the result being a scathing prepublication condemnation of La Peyrère's thesis by Grotius, *Dissertatio altera de origine Gentium Americanarum adversus obtrectatorem* (1643). Both La Peyrère and Grotius were attempting to explain the American Indians, who seemed to fall outside salvation history. Ibid., p. 6.

34 Although this claim may seem rather wild, it fits into a pattern of similar claims made by others not only about France, but also Spain, Portugal, and England. In regard to France, the claim went all the way back to followers of Joachim of Fiore (c. 1132–1202), and forward to Jean de Roquetaillade in the mid-fourteenth century, Guillaume Postel (1510–1581), and even the Italian Tommaso Campanella (1568–1639). See ibid., ch. 5. In England, millenarianism flourished in the latter half of the seventeenth century, not only among radicals of the Interregnum, but among the Newtonians as late as the first quarter of the eighteenth century. See Margaret Jacob, *The Newtonians and the English Revolution, 1689–1720* (Hassocks, Sussex: The Harvester Press, 1976), Ch. 3.

sonal apology to the pope (Alexander VII) and converted to Catholicism, he would be forgiven and protected. He followed the advice, and once in Rome, set about writing a recantation—"a most hypocritical apology," in Popkin's words[35]—that did not require him to say that his theories were false. He further hoped to sweeten his treatment by substituting Pope Alexander VII for Louis XIV in his messianic scheme. His strategy was to put forth his arguments of the *Prae-Adamitae* as hypotheses in accord with reason and Scripture, leave it to his detractors to prove otherwise, and submit to the pope's decision upon the matter. His abjuration was officially accepted on March 11, 1657. After travel, La Peyrère settled down as a lay member of the Oratorians outside of Paris, to the day of his death holding out privately that his pre-Adamite theory was rational and salutary to Christianity, but in accord with his agreement with the pope, refraining (for the most part, anyway) from publishing any direct defense.[36]

In his *Prae-Adamitae*, La Peyrère denied that Adam was the first man, denied that Moses wrote the entire Pentateuch as it has come down to us, and sharply questioned the accuracy of the biblical text as received. The source of La Peyrère's assertion that there were *Men before Adam* (the English title, as published in 1656) was fourfold. First, classical and pagan sources affirmed a nonbiblical history much more ancient than the six-thousand-year-old Earth as inferred from Genesis (he offered accounts from the Chaldeans [i.e., Babylonians], Egyptians, Scythians, Chinese, and Mexicans, being especially impressed by the astronomical discoveries and calculations of the Babylonians and Egyptians[37]). Second, was the discovery of people entirely unconnected with biblical salvation history, most notably the American Indians but also the Eskimos. Third, the Genesis account of Cain (4:14–17) seemed to infer the presence of other human beings not begotten from Adam and Eve. In addition, La Peyrère interpreted St. Paul's statement in Romans 5:12–14 to mean that sin was in the world before Adam, and hence there were men before Adam. Fourth, his messianic theory demanded a prehistory because Adam and Eve were the first Jews (rather than the first human beings).[38] In regard to this last point, the Gentiles were the pre-Adamites who, before Adam, lived in a quasi-Hobbesian, lawless state of nature in complete brutality

35 Richard Popkin, "Spinoza and La Peyrère," in Robert Shahan and J. I. Biro, eds., *Spinoza: New Perspectives* (Norman, OK: University of Oklahoma Press, 1978), pp. 177–195. Citation from p. 186.

36 On the above, see the entirety of Chapter 2 on the life of La Peyrère in Popkin, *Isaac La Peyrère*. La Peyrère's promise did not keep him from attempting to publish an indirect defense in the footnotes of a French translation of the Bible, where he presented his pre-Adamite thesis as condemned by the Church but yet as reasonably explaining alleged discrepancies in the Old Testament. It was suppressed by the time he got to Leviticus. He also continued to rewrite his *Rappel des Juifs*, even though he was assured by his friend Richard Simon (whom we will meet in the next chapter) that it would be censored. Along with Popkin's treatment in *Isaac La Peyrère*, see his "Bible Criticism and Social Science," in Robert Cohen and Marx Wartofsky, eds., *Methodological and Historical Essays in the Natural and Social Sciences* (Dordrecht, Holland: D. Reidel, 1974), pp. 339–360, especially pp. 342–343.

37 La Peyrère was heavily indebted to Claude Saumaise's historical account of ancient astronomy and astrology, *De Annis Climactericus* (1648), from which he inferred that the time period necessary to gather such information was immense, stretching back far beyond the biblical six thousand-year history. Popkin, *Isaac La Peyrère*, p. 48.

38 Ibid., pp. 42–44.

but without sin.[39] The Gentiles were made of corruptible matter, as opposed to the Jews, beginning with Adam, who were made for immortality; and even more scandalous (given its association with Epicureanism), the world itself was eternal.[40]

La Peyrère's denial of Mosaic authorship was not original, but it was more forceful than others because he, like Spinoza after him, multiplied the number of alleged textual imperfections to make his case that the Pentateuch as we have it was the work of many hands.[41] In his *A Theological Systeme upon That Presupposition That Men Were Before Adam*, a work published the same year and on the same theme as the *Prae-Adamitae*, La Peyrère remarked that the present Pentateuch is obviously a "heap of Copie confusedly taken," for "Whoever but slightly revises [i.e., reads] those Bookes, shall observe more things of this kind [textual imperfections], and many things everywhere in them confus'd and obscure, yea contradictory to one another, as cold to hot, day to night. . . . [and so we must] Believe that these things were diversly written, being taken out of several authors."[42] Accordingly, the task of the exegete is to sift through the biblical text as received, and separate the original text from the confusion of the later copyists. This separation leaves nothing of importance behind because the elements of Scripture necessary for salvation are retained, while what is unnecessary is identified with what is confused or obscure.[43]

As Hobbes had his own agenda in denying Mosaic authorship, so did La Peyrère: If doubt could be cast on the authenticity of much of the biblical text—especially those parts that conflicted with his pre-Adamite thesis—then it would not need to be considered a complete history of the world, but only a partial one, merely a history of the Jews from their creation (in Adam and Eve) onward. La Peyrère therefore set about particularizing the Bible's historical account. To take a famous example, the flood of Noah was not universal, but affected only the areas known to the Jews of the time. Since it was not universal, that explains why some older civilizations make no mention of it.[44]

But even though the Bible was not a universal history, it contained the key to all history since all will be saved through the Jews. Christians were themselves grafted onto the Jews, and even though the Jews had rejected Christianity, their imminent conversion to Christianity would be the event that finally redeems all the Gentiles descended from the pre-Adamites, an event that would culminate in the Jews being recalled to France and then led to the Holy Land by Louis XIV, whereupon Jerusalem

39 The connection to Hobbes is unmistakable but one need not assume that it was Hobbes who influenced La Peyrère. The influence may well have been mutual.

40 Ibid., pp. 45–46, 52, and Frampton, *Spinoza and the Rise of Historical Criticism of the Bible*, pp. 207–217.

41 On this, see Strauss, *Spinoza's Critique of Religion*, pp. 75–77.

42 Quoted in Frampton, *Spinoza and the Rise of Historical Criticism of the Bible*, p. 215. See also Popkin, *Isaac La Peyrère*, pp. 48–49, 53, and Popkin, "Spinoza and Bible Scholarship," p. 6.

43 Strauss, *Spinoza's Critique of Religion*, p. 75.

44 Popkin, *Isaac La Peyrère*, pp. 50–51.

will be rebuilt as the center of the universe.[45] It is impossible to deny the very political, this-worldly implications of his version of messianism, especially insofar as they seem to duplicate (albeit for different reasons) the Hobbesian assumption that the Kingdom of God will be in this world.[46]

It seems likely that Spinoza met La Peyrère while the latter was in Amsterdam, but it is quite certain that Spinoza had a copy of the *Prae-Adamitae* in his library and that the immediate notoriety of the book that was so scandalous would have attracted Spinoza's attention and even sympathy. Spinoza's one-time teacher Menasseh ben Israel had a prepublication copy of the *Prae-Adamitae*, writing his own refutation within a year after its publication.[47] Certainly, La Peyrère's book was absorbed by de Prado, and hence would become part of the Spinozan circle's ongoing discussions, and much of La Peyrère's criticisms of the biblical text would make it into Spinoza's *Tractatus*, albeit with the messianism left behind.[48]

A most potent combination this was. "The combination of La Peyrère's Biblical criticism and Spinoza's naturalistic metaphysics," notes Richard Popkin, "eliminated the supernatural dimension and transformed religious history into an effect of human fear and superstition."[49] Spinoza would provide an important inversion of La Peyrère, one that depended in no small part on what it inverted. As Popkin succinctly puts it, "La Peyrère's Messianic view led him to secularize all human history except Jewish history. Spinoza's philosophical God led him to secularize all human history, *especially* Jewish history."[50] Of course, La Peyrère's influence stretched beyond Spinoza, important examples being the radical Quaker biblical critic Samuel Fisher (1605–1665) and the French Oratorian priest Richard Simon (1638–1712). As we shall see in later chapters, both will radicalize La Peyrère's arguments (and Simon himself was influenced by Spinoza as well). Given the daring nature of his arguments, the web of La Peyrère's influence stretched in ever larger circles.

---

45 Ibid., pp. 53–54.

46 La Peyrère distinguished between Jewish and Christian messianism, the Christian occurring first with Christ, and the Jewish, the political, providing the messianic culmination of history. Popkin, ibid., pp. 56–57. There is no reason to exclude the possibility that La Peyrère was being somewhat Machiavellian about his real views, so that, as Leo Strauss maintained, "his concern [to harmonize with the Gospel, and the Church's teaching and authority] is no more than the masking of his unbelief by formulations soothingly couched in the terminology used in orthodox dogmatics. It is not hard to hit on the reason for La Peyrère's procedure: he was not born for martyrdom." Strauss, *Spinoza's Critique of Religion*, p. 78. Although some evidence suggests this, a more thorough analysis of La Peyrère's work would be necessary either to support or refute this possibility. Strauss seems to underplay La Peyrère's messianism considerably.

47 Popkin "Spinoza and La Peyrère," p. 188.

48 Popkin, *Isaac La Peyrère*, pp. 84–85, and Popkin, "Spinoza and La Peyrère," p. 189; Nellen, "Growing Tension between Church Doctrines and Critical Exegesis of the Old Testament," pp. 822–823; and Strauss's list in *Spinoza's Critique of Religion*, pp. 264–268, 327.

49 Popkin, "Spinoza and La Peyrère," p. 190.

50 Ibid., p. 191.

The Radical Circle of Collegiants: Koerbagh and Meyer

In addition to the direct and indirect influence of van den Enden, da Costa, de Prado, and La Peyrère, Spinoza was part of a larger circle of Collegiants, which included Remonstrants, Mennonites, Socinians, deists, and religious skeptics, many of whom were taken popularly to be atheists and who championed the new "rational" science against revelation. In this circle appeared, among others, Johannes and Adriaen [or Adriaan] Koerbagh, Lodewijk Meyer, Jarig Jelles, Pieter Balling, Simon Joosten de Vries, Pieter Serrarius, Abraham van Berckel, Johannes Bouwmeester, and Jan Rieuwertsz [or Rieuwertszoon].[51]

From the lives of some of these men, the nature of that Amsterdam circle will become apparent. Abraham van Berckel, a doctor of medicine, was the translator of Hobbes's *Leviathan* into Dutch (1667) and Jan Rieuwertsz was a dedicated publisher of the most radical literature, especially Spinoza's.

The brothers Koerbagh deserve a bit more extensive treatment. Both of them ran afoul of the Dutch Calvinist hierarchy in the mid-1660s, Adriaen for living unmarried with a woman and fathering a child out of wedlock and Johannes for spreading atheism (denying the Trinity, the divinity of Christ, the inspired unity of the Bible, miracles, the Resurrection, the afterlife, and, significantly in regard to Spinoza's influence, asserting the identity of God and nature).[52] In 1668, the brothers (or perhaps just Adriaen) published *A Garden of All Kinds of Loveliness without Sorrow*, which amounted to a dictionary that even more acerbically denied the basic tenets of Christianity, and charged that Christian doctrines were merely *political* obfuscations used to control the masses. Adriaen followed the *Garden* with *A Light Shining in Dark Places*, which remained unpublished. In it, we find more of the same, not only a specific rejection of Christianity, but a demonstration that the Bible is a book of obfuscation and contradiction. While his *Garden* was influential in spreading his radical critique, *A Light* probably had little influence beyond the Amsterdam circle. But for that very reason, it sheds more light on the kind of thinking going on among Spinoza's friends, and hence on the radical underground.

Essential to Koerbagh's critique was the Spinozist notion we will explore in more detail below, that God is *identical* to nature—God is nature; nature is God—so that the only true religion is the rational reflection on nature through the new mathematical-mechanical science. This identity of human mathematical reason and being meant that reason is indeed the Word of God, rather than Scripture or Christ Himself. In agreement with Spinoza's pantheism, for Adriaen Koerbagh all things were finite modifications of God's infinite being, the Word/reason made mathematical-mechan-

---

51 On the constitution of this circle see Frampton, *Spinoza and the Rise of Historical Criticism of the Bible*, Ch. 6; Leszek Kolakowski, "Dutch Seventeenth-Century Non-Denominationalism and *Religio Rationalis*: Mennonites, Collegiants and the Spinoza Connection," in Kolakowski, *The Two Eyes of Spinoza & Other Essays on Philosophers*, pp. 43–83; Andrew Fix, *Prophecy and Reason: The Dutch Collegiants in the Early Enlightenment* (Princeton: Princeton University Press, 1991); and Nyden-Bullock, *Spinoza's Radical Cartesian Mind*, Ch. 3.

52 Israel, *Radical Enlightenment: Philosophy and the Making of Modernity 1650–1750*, pp. 187–189.

ical flesh, as it were.[53] In such redefinition of terms, we see an important mode of argument, one used even more effectively by Spinoza and that became part of the rhetorical *modus operandi* of the radical Enlightenment of the eighteenth century. In Michiel Wielema's words:

> Instead of confronting his audience directly with an abstract philosophical framework opposed to their belief system, he uses their conventional religious notions as a vehicle for introducing his own naturalistic views, thereby undermining these same notions. For Koerbagh the "Word of God" is no longer a religious concept but a philosophical one and the way he uses it is intended to confuse his readers in order to prepare them for enlightenment.[54]

The omnipresence of this rhetorical mode in the coming centuries, both in philosophy and especially in the biblical studies, cannot be overstressed. Common or traditional terms are purposely put to new uses, definitions are blurred, ultimate intentions are hidden: Reason does not mean reason in its commonly taken, full-bodied sense but as restricted to its mathematical-mechanical mode; nature is not living nature met with on the everyday level, and known intimately by ordinary folk, but nature as a reductionist, colorless, mechanical system; God is not the personal God revealed to the Hebrews but a code equivalent for nature or an aloof impersonal mechanical technician; Christ is not God Incarnate but a moral exemplar (with the implicit implication that belief in the Incarnation is idolatry[55]).

In Koerbagh, the disparity between orthodoxy and heterodoxy is still evident enough, and radical enough, to be picked up both in his time and even in ours. But as this rhetorical mode permeates the eighteenth- and nineteenth-century mind, the discrepancies disappear, even to the exegete, as the radical is normalized through centuries-long intellectual domestication, making it all the more difficult to recognize. That is one of the great benefits of viewing the disparity in its new and raw form in Koerbagh.

Unsurprisingly, Koerbagh rejected the Trinity, declaring it to be an irrational concept violating the canons of simple mathematics. But this was not mere Socinianism, which indeed had a strong presence in the theologically tolerant Netherlands. For Koerbagh, the problem was not (as with the Socinians) that the Trinity was unbiblical, but that, as with Spinoza, the spiritual Trinity violated the materialist understanding of God. There is only *one* substance, God, and that substance is material, the substrate or substance of nature (Koerbagh coining the term "ipstance," from the Latin *ipse* to signify its independence[56]). The distinction of three Divine Persons was unacceptable

53 Koerbagh has been unfairly passed over by scholars, and this means that there is a dearth of material on his important work. In our analysis we rely on Jonathan Israel and the excellent essay by Michiel Wielema, "Adriaan Koerbagh: Biblical Criticism and Enlightenment" in Wiep Van Bunge, ed., *The Early Enlightenment in the Dutch Republic, 1650–1750* (Leiden: Brill, 2003), pp. 61–80.

54 Ibid., p. 66.

55 Ibid.

56 Ibid., p. 67.

to Koerbagh, not only because it falsely claimed to be purely spiritual and above reason, but also because, in his "monistic metaphysics," all distinctions in regard to this substance were equally modifications of this one substance and they are infinite in number rather than triune.[57]

In regard to Scripture, we have some very important differences between Koerbagh and Spinoza. Whereas Spinoza simply declared Scripture to be irrational, and theology and philosophy to be utterly distinct, Koerbagh treated Scripture with a combination of disdain and respect. He believed it contained many contradictions, absurdities, and obscurities, but that at least *some* of the obscurity was intentional, a purposeful hiding of philosophic truth of the enlightened from the ignorant masses or at least an accommodation by these "proto-philosophers" to the unphilosophic. Part of Koerbagh's analysis consists in digging out the esoteric philosophic ore,[58] again, a pattern that will be repeated in the next centuries.

As with Hobbes, Koerbagh treated Roman Catholicism as the most bitter enemy of reason, which is to say, the presentation of Christian faith most glaringly at odds with the reductionist, mathematical-mechanical cosmos. Catholicism represented for him the most comprehensive and purposeful obscuring of rational religion with an overlay of irrational, unfounded spiritualism—all for the sake of maintaining the power of the priests over the people. Koerbagh thereby revived Machiavelli's assessment of the priesthood, but without Machiavelli's characteristic nudge-and-wink at the cleverness of its members.

What is the source of Koerbagh's disagreement with Machiavelli? Since Koerbagh was on the side of the people and not the prince, demystification or disenchantment of the biblical text became a theological-political mission precisely because the belief in spirits, demons, immaterial souls, heaven and hell, all serve, through the authority of the Bible, to keep the masses in unenlightened servitude to ecclesiastics.[59] In a truly enlightened government, the Church would be kept firmly under the control of the democratic government, and civil servants would be initiated into the new philosophy so that they could be proper guardians of the new religion of reason. As Wielema remarks, this really meant, "All civil sovereigns should become monistic philosophers—or Koerbaghians!"[60]

In Koerbagh's revolution, then, a purely rational exegesis of the Bible was necessary to empower the people, and this exegesis was sanctioned and controlled by the civil authorities. Yet even with this early Enlightenment optimism, Koerbagh thought that the Bible might even be beyond exegetical repair. In *A Light* he offered himself to the government as one who could write *another* Bible, one that would eliminate the obscurities, contradictions, scientific errors, and other sources of theological confusions that formed the multiple interpretations grounding the multiple warring Christian sects.[61]

57 Ibid., p. 68.
58 Ibid., pp. 69–71.
59 Ibid., pp. 72–76.
60 Ibid., p. 78.
61 Ibid., p. 79.

The government found Koerbagh's radicalism neither enlightened nor amusing. In 1668, Adriaen was arrested, tried in ecclesiastical court, and sentenced to have his right thumb cut off, have his tongue bored with a hot iron, pay an enormous fine, and serve a prison term of thirty years. He died in prison a year later, a sign to others of his circle that the enlightened would have to be more circumspect. If such persecution could happen in the Netherlands, then like-minded radicals elsewhere must be even more delicate in fomenting intellectual revolution.

In 1666, the same year the English House of Commons was instructed to examine Hobbes's *Leviathan*, there appeared one of the most important books of Amsterdam's radical circle, *Philosophia S. Scripturae Interpres*, published anonymously, but actually penned by Lodewijk Meyer and printed by Jan Rieuwertsz.[62] The *Philosophia*, along with Spinoza's *Tractatus theologico-politicus* and Hobbes's *Leviathan*, were consistently named during the latter part of the 1600s—not just in the Netherlands, but all over Europe[63]—as the most dangerous and abominable books. Moreover, the *Philosophia* was often bound together with the *Tractatus*, sold as a set to those eager to absorb or refute them.

Meyer's *Philosophia* was both influential in its own right, and also served as a stepping-stone to the publication of Spinoza's *Tractatus* four years later, demonstrating to those it shocked that the step from Cartesianism to Spinozism was short indeed. As we have seen, Descartes steered clear of any entanglement with Scripture, but set it aside as divine truth inscrutable to human reason. Meyer had no such scruples, the main argument of his *Philosophia* being that "true philosophy . . . is the certain and infallible norm both for explicating the Holy Books and for investigating their explications. It is in this sense that we would wish the title of our treatise to be understood. . . ."[64]

True philosophy meant Cartesian philosophy, as Meyer made clear by his zealous praise of Descartes, "the first who, after so many ages, brought hidden truth to light out of the hideous gloom of dense darkness," "that new star, brightest and most splendid, that arose for the world of philosophy in this our age, the most noble René Descartes," "this incomparable man," the "chief founder and propagator" of true philosophy, who "first lit a torch for the world of letters and showed the way by his example. . . ."[65] Quite clearly, it was not, for Meyer, just any philosophy that was to be the "certain and infallible norm" of Scriptural interpretation. It was philosophy as

62 The full title of the first edition gives us the gist of Meyer's position: *Philosophia S. Scripturae Interpres: Exercitatio Paradoxa, In qua, veram Philosophiam infallibilem S. Literas interpretandi Normam esse, apodictice demonstratur, & discrepantes ab hac Sententiae expenduntur, ac refelluntur*. On Meyer, see Nyden–Bullock, *Spinoza's Radical Cartesian Mind*, pp. 44–47.

63 Israel, *Radical Enlightenment: Philosophy and the Making of Modernity 1650–1750*, pp. 203–217. See also Scholder, *The Birth of Modern Critical Theology: Origins and Problems of Biblical Criticism*, pp. 132–136.

64 Lodewijk Meyer, *Philosophy as the Interpreter of Holy Scripture*, translated by Samuel Shirley (Marquette, WI: Marquette University Press, 2005), I.5, p.105.

65 Ibid., Prologue, p. 25; I.5, pp. 108–109; Epilogue, p. 240.

conceived by Descartes, where both reason and truth were defined by mathematical-mechanical physics.[66]

Meyer's method as applied to Scripture, "following in Descartes' footsteps," began with doubt, "rejecting in theology whatever can be rejected as doubtful and uncertain."[67] As with Descartes, the stance of doubt allowed the exegete to stand outside history and tradition, making it "not . . . necessary to consult theologians and interpreters of the Divine Word and commentators of all ages and countries and of every sect, and carefully weigh their opinions."[68] All that was needed is the "inner light" of reason.

But again, this inner light of reason was reason as defined by Descartes, elevated to such heights that it was identified with the Holy Spirit (which may explain Meyer's extravagant praise of Descartes). For Meyer, "no one can be completely certain of the meaning of the Holy Writings . . . unless he perceives its truth clearly and distinctly by the natural light of his intellect and is intimately conscious of that perception within himself. . . ." Speaking of his opponents, Meyer asserted that "if this clear and distinct perception together with its consciousness is what they [the Reformed, or Calvinist, theologians] call the internal persuasion and the internal testimony of the Holy Spirit, then they hold the same opinion as we do. . . ."[69] "But if what they have in mind is some supernatural illumination," Meyer added bluntly, "we deny there is any such thing. . . ."[70]

Collapsing the Holy Spirit into Cartesian reason was part of a more comprehensive collapse of the supernatural into the natural. Meyer remarked, "how worthless is the opinion of those who hold that, in respect of certainty, nature is subordinate to grace, science to revelation, truth ordinarily revealed to truth extraordinarily revealed; and not merely subordinate, but opposed. Each of these should be regarded as on an equal footing." The reason Meyer gave for this equality was that "truth cannot be contrary to itself or surpass itself, although it may be got and acquired in diverse ways."[71]

But the equality of reason and revelation really meant the subordination of revelation to Cartesian mathematical-mechanical philosophy, as Meyer made evident in his treatment of the Eucharist and the Most Holy Trinity. As we have seen, as a result of the Reformation the meaning of Christ's words, "This is my Body," was hotly contested. What did Christ really have in mind?

---

66 Ibid., I.5, p. 108, Epilogue, p. 240. Even more clearly, see Meyer's Preface to Spinoza's *Principles of Cartesian Philosophy*, in which Meyer praises Descartes as "that brightest star of our age" who "laid the unshakable foundations of philosophy," leaving to posterity all "parts of Philosophy," and not just mathematics, "demonstrated with mathematical method and with mathematical certainty." Meyer's Preface is included in Benedict Spinoza, *Principles of Cartesian Philosophy*, translated by Samuel Shirley (Indianapolis, IN: Hackett Publishing Company, Inc., 1998), p. 2. In his Preface, Meyer makes clear that Spinoza had already gone beyond Cartesianism.

67 Ibid., Prologue, p. 28.

68 Ibid., Epilogue, p. 230.

69 Ibid., III.14. pp. 195–196, 199–201.

70 Ibid., III.15, p.203.

71 Ibid., I.5, pp. 111–112.

> It is philosophy that tells us; by its assistance the Reformed have confirmed their opinion and have shown that the views taken by the Catholics and Lutherans are absurd. From the science of physics they have demonstrated that bread, with its accidental qualities remaining intact, cannot be transformed substantially into another body, nor can one and the same body be in more than one place at a time, nor can two bodies occupy one and the same place.[72]

The science of physics, of course, was the mechanistic physics of Descartes that, with all modern materialist doctrines, was incompatible with any doctrine of the Eucharist, except the purely symbolic (and, in fact, Descartes as a Catholic tried to provide his own materialist account of the Eucharist to replace transubstantiation). As for the Trinity, Meyer sided with the Socinians, but for philosophical rather than biblical reasons: the Trinity is irrational and impossible; reason can have no clear and distinct idea of it; hence the doctrine of the Trinity must be rejected.[73]

Oddly, Meyer's *Philosophia* contained very little actual exegesis of Scripture, and even less on what the outcome of the application of his method to Holy Writ might be. Most of Meyer's efforts are spent negatively, piling up difficulties that face any exegete in getting at the true meaning of Scripture, thereby demonstrating that all theological contenders (whether Catholic, Lutheran, Reformed, etc.) are unable to secure true and uncontested interpretations of Scripture, thus proving that natural reason is the only light that can illumine Scripture's true meaning.

Meyer does, however, make clear the political context of his application of Cartesian method to Scriptural exegesis. Christians are divided by diverse interpretations of Scripture, and these divisions have most serious political ramifications. "So much passion and fervour have they [theologians] displayed that the Christian world is torn and rent into pieces as if into separate Churches, and its inhabitants are not merely at variance in mind and morals but in some cases have become mortal enemies."[74] The main advantage of adopting his method was consequently political: so that "the weapons of disputes and contentions which are so ardently and fiercely brandished would be taken away, and peace restored and established for ever throughout the Christian world."[75]

As noted above, Meyer's *Philosophia* and Spinoza's *Tractatus* often traveled together as one book, a marriage that made perfect sense. Meyer provided the framework as a prolegomenon, and Spinoza (as we shall soon see) spelled out the full consequences, consequences all the more radical precisely because of Spinoza's radicalizing of Descartes.[76]

Interestingly enough, a bit over a century (1776) after the publication of Meyer's *Philosophia*, a Latin copy was published with extensive notes and Preface, by none

---

72 Ibid., I.6, pp. 117–118.

73 Ibid., III.16, pp. 206–208.

74 Ibid., Prologue, pp. 24–25.

75 Ibid., Epilogue, p. 230.

76 Again, Meyer was fully aware of how far Spinoza was going beyond Descartes, as he makes known in his Preface to Spinoza's *Principles of Cartesian Philosophy*, pp. 5–6.

other than one of the most important (but obviously later) "founders" of biblical criticism, Johannes Salomo Semler.[77] As J. C. O'Neill states, in regard to New Testament scholarship, "There is hardly a theory or a hypothesis in New Testament studies from his day to ours that does not depend on Semler's teaching." Significantly, Semler was the teacher of Johann Jakob Griesbach and Johann Gottfried Eichhorn, and influenced Gotthold Lessing as well.[78] Such is the reach of Spinoza and his circle. The radicalism was there at the beginning, and passed along with and to the later giants of the historical-critical method.

Clearly, Spinoza's philosophy and hence his treatment of Scripture were part of a larger, more general philosophical movement rooted in the new mechanist-materialist worldview as interpreted according to a mathematical-mechanical approach, and which had direct implications for a radically new approach to Scripture. Spinoza would go on to provide one.

Liber Pestilentissimus

In regard to the Amsterdam circle, Spinoza may have originally been a follower of van den Enden, but soon enough, Spinoza emerged as the leader. Yet it was not until 1670 that he dared publish his own contribution, the *Tractatus theologico-politicus*, and even then, only anonymously. Almost immediately, local governments took it into their hands to confiscate the *Tractatus* from bookshops, and the various religious synods proclaimed horror and condemnation. The book was described in the liberal Netherlands variously as "godless," "*liber pestilentissimus*," "appalling," "vile and blasphemous as any that are known of, or that the world has ever seen," and declared illegal under the Netherland's existing anti-Socinian legislation, therefore making it subject to immediate confiscation by all local authorities. The Dutch government, including its liberal pensionary Jan de Witt, considered Spinoza to be the most dangerous of the Dutch atheists.[79]

Although the *Tractatus* was immediately suppressed, as Israel notes, "during the mid-1670s," only five years after its original publication in the Netherlands, "the book was selling right across Europe, penetrating far more extensively than would normally be possible under such circumstances," i.e., the circumstances of immediate official attempts at suppression.[80] The reason: Spinoza's inner circle had already prepared "a complex operation designed to mask the launching of successive new editions and facilitate international distribution," thanks largely to Spinoza's friend and publisher, Jan Rieuwertsz.[81] Wherever it went—Germany, France, England—it

---

77 Israel, *Radical Enlightenment: Philosophy and the Making of Modernity 1650–1750*, p. 200.

78 J. C. O'Neill, *The Bible's Authority: A Portrait Gallery of Thinkers from Lessing to Bultmann* (Edinburgh: T. & T. Clark, 1991), pp. 40–41.

79 On the reception of the *Tractatus*, see Israel *Radical Enlightenment: Philosophy and the Making of Modernity 1650–1750*, ch. 16.

80 Ibid., p. 279.

81 Ibid., p. 281.

was almost as immediately condemned, even as its influence spread like fire in dry tinder. With amazing rapidity, Spinoza changed from being an isolated and obscure philosopher to the much-scorned leader of an international movement. In the words of Jonathan Israel:

> By the mid-1670s Spinoza stood at the head of an underground radical philosophical movement rooted in the Netherlands but decidedly European in scope. His books were illegal but yet, paradoxically, excepting only Descartes, no other contemporary thinker enjoyed, over the previous quarter century so wide a European reception, even if in his case that reception was overwhelmingly (even if far from exclusively) hostile.[82]

Although Spinoza wanted to follow up with the publication of his *Ethics*, which contained the philosophy underlying the *Tractatus*, the hostility aroused by the latter convinced him that publication was too dangerous during his lifetime. Those remaining after Spinoza died in 1677 gathered the *Ethics* with other of Spinoza's works and published them that same year.

Clearly, Spinoza's contemporaries found the *Tractatus* to be quite shocking, a kind of direct attack on biblical revelation. Insofar as Spinoza became one of the founding fathers of the modern historical-critical method, what was once shocking is now merely academic and commonplace. Before examining the *Tractatus*, one must take account of Spinoza's philosophy, his radical worldview, since it contains the seismic shift that surfaced as the shock in his *Tractatus*. As with Hobbes, Spinoza's mathematical-mechanical philosophy determined his exegetical principles. In David Lachterman's more pointed terms, a proper analysis of Spinoza reveals "how intimately reciprocal the relationship between commitment to the explanatory intentions of modern physics and the dismantling of scriptural theology turn out to be."[83]

Spinoza's Pantheism

As mentioned above, Spinoza was working on the *Ethics*, his foundational philosophical work, through the entire decade previous to publishing the *Tractatus theologico-politicus*. Since his underlying philosophy determined his treatment of Scripture in the *Tractatus*, we must have at least a general account of what Bayle called his "monstrous hypothesis."

Perhaps the easiest way to grasp the rudiments of Spinoza's complex and difficult philosophy would be to understand it as it was understood by those in his own time, as a radicalization of Cartesianism that exchanged Descartes's famous spirit-matter dual-

82 Ibid., p. 285.

83 David Lachterman, "Laying Down the Law: The Theological-Political Matrix of Spinoza's Physics," in Alan Udoff, ed., *Leo Strauss's Thought: Toward a Critical Engagement* (Boulder & London: Lynne Rienner Publishers, 1991), p. 126. See also his "The Physics of Spinoza's *Ethics*," in Robert Shahan and J. I. Biro, eds., *Spinoza: New Perspectives*, pp. 71–111.

ism for a materialist monism. To his contemporaries, the shocking element in Spinoza was his refusal to absent God from his mechanistic account of nature (as did Descartes and most mechanists), or even to ascribe a material nature to God as a separate being (as did Epicurus, Lucretius, and eventually Hobbes). Instead, Spinoza simply collapsed God and nature, divinizing nature and naturalizing God.

Of course, Spinoza himself did not characterize his philosophy in terms of "collapse," but as the result of a strictly philosophical deduction based on the geometrical model of Euclid's *Elements*, as the full Latin title to his *Ethics* attests: *Ethica ordine geometrica demonstrata*.[84] Spinoza even appended the Euclidean Q.E.D. (*Quod Erat Demonstrandum*) to each "Proof" provided for a proposition—an imitation not only of Euclid himself but also of Averroes and the Spanish Jewish philosopher Hasdai Crescas (1340–1410/11).[85]

To begin, Spinoza asserted that God by definition is "an absolutely infinite being; that is, substance consisting of infinite attributes, each of which expresses eternal and infinite essence."[86] While this may have an orthodox ring considered by itself, Spinoza soon demonstrated what he really intended: that there is *only* one substance, God. For Spinoza, "Existence belongs to the nature of substance" precisely because "God, or substance. . . . necessarily exists" and "There can be, or be conceived, no other substance but God."[87] In short, God is not distinct from created nature, created substances; rather, all things are modifications of His substance, "infinite attributes, each of which expresses eternal and infinite essence." Therefore, "God is the immanent, not the transitive, cause of all things."[88] Since God is not distinct from nature, His divine necessity completely determines nature: "Nothing in nature is contingent, but all things are from the necessity of the divine nature determined to exist and act in a definite way,"[89] so that "Things could not have been produced by God in any other way or in any other order than is the case."[90] To recall a distinction reaching all the way back to Ockham, Spinoza identified God's *potentia absoluta* and His *potentia ordinata*, that is, His absolute power and His power as expressed in the particular order of creation, by the identifying of God with creation.[91]

This immanentism allowed Spinoza to avoid Cartesian dualism even while retaining its categories, not as distinct names for distinct things, but as two names for the same thing. To offer an especially important example, Spinoza asserted both that,

---

84 Spinoza's faith in and passion for geometric order is seen as well in his re-presentation of Descartes's philosophical arguments in quasi-Euclidean deductive steps.

85 See Wolfson, *The Philosophy of Spinoza*, I, ii, pp. 41–42.

86 Baruch Spinoza, *Ethics*, I, Def. 6. We use the translation by Samuel Shirley included in Baruch Spinoza, *Ethics; Treatise on the Emendation of the Intellect; and Selected Letters* (Indianapolis, IN: Hackett Publishing, 1992).

87 Ibid., I, Props. 7, 11, 14.

88 Ibid., I, Prop. 18.

89 Ibid., I, Prop. 29.

90 Ibid., I, Prop. 33.

91 On this, see Lachterman, "Laying Down the Law: The Theological-Political Matrix of Spinoza's Physics," p. 136.

"Thought is an attribute of God; i.e., God is a thinking thing" and that "Extension is an attribute of God; i.e., God is an extended thing."[92] He can maintain both at once precisely because of the Cartesian identity of mathematical thinking and mechanical being: both thought *and* things are essentially geometrical, therefore they are not really distinct *if* one accepts a mechanistic account of intellection. In regard to the whole universe, the intelligibility of its geometrical-mechanical order *is* its geometrical-mechanical order, the laws that govern nature *are* nature, or in Spinoza's words, "The order and connection of ideas is the same as the order and connection of things."[93] In this, Spinoza went even beyond Descartes, and offered the most complete identity of the *ordo cognoscendi* and the *ordo essendi*.[94]

It followed from this that individual things in nature are not real substances (as they appear to us), but merely modifications of one substance in accordance with the laws of nature. Thus, Spinoza made the principle distinction, not between Creator and creature, but between *natura naturans* (literally, nature naturing, using the active participle) and *natura naturata* (nature natured, using the passive participle).[95] In both, God is identical to the noun, the substance, *natura*. The active powers of God (i.e., material extension acting necessarily according to its nature) determined matter in particular configurations, thereby constituting the particular but transitory things of nature, *natura naturata*. Yet the particular things of nature are not truly distinct from God-substance-nature; they are simply modifications or modes of it.

Nor did Spinoza shrink from applying this to human beings as well: "The being of substance does not pertain to the essence of man; i.e., substance does not constitute the form of man," or more clearly, "the essence of man is constituted by definite modifications of the attributes of God."[96] Human beings (like all things in nature) are "an affection or mode [of substance] which expresses the nature of God in a definite and determinate way."[97] As an affection or mode of the one substance, each human being is a transitory and particular union of lesser bodies,[98] and (as Epicurus and Lucretius argued) this union dissipates at death. In Spinoza's words, "The force [*vis*] whereby a man persists in existing is limited, and infinitely surpassed by the power of external causes."[99]

However, there are two ways in which at least the human mind can be considered to be eternal. Insofar as a particular human being, as a material entity, perceives the order of nature, he has transitory participation in the eternal order of the divine mind,[100] a kind of panentheistic parallel to Averroes's notion of personal immortality

---

92 Spinoza, *Ethics*, II, Props. 1 and 2.

93 Ibid., II, Prop. 7.

94 On this complete identity, see Lachterman, "Laying Down the Law: The Theological-Political Matrix of Spinoza's Physics," pp. 130–131.

95 Spinoza, *Ethics*, I, Prop. 29, Scholium.

96 Ibid., II, Prop. 10 and Corollary.

97 Ibid., II, Prop. 10, Proof.

98 Ibid., For the physics of human mortality, see the entirety of II, Proposition 13.

99 Ibid., IV, Prop. 3.

100 Ibid., II, Prop. 11.

through a temporary union with the Agent Intellect. For Spinoza, intellectual participation occurred in understanding particular, transitory things (*natura naturata*) as completely defined and determined by the one substance (*natura naturans*, or God). This kind of knowledge Spinoza called "intuition," or the "third kind of knowledge." "This kind of knowledge proceeds from an adequate idea of the formal essence of certain attributes of God to an adequate knowledge of the essence of things."[101] That is, the highest kind of knowledge is the simultaneous understanding of the universal laws of nature *and* their determinations in particular things, so that the particular things are completely comprehended as manifestations of the universal laws intrinsic to substance-nature-God.

This intuition can be applied to the particular human being himself, thus allowing him to realize a *certain kind* of immortality in relationship to himself, not a personal immortality, but the intuition of oneself as an *existing* manifestation of God-substance-nature that, while actually transitory, is eternal *insofar* as this manifestation always was and always remains an eternal possibility of God-substance-nature (as an *essence* even though it does not always exist). In Spinoza's veiled theological words, "there is necessarily in God an idea which expresses the essence of this or that human body under a form of eternity [*sub specie aeternitatis*]."[102] Spinoza can then maintain, although somewhat paradoxically, that "The human mind [*Mens humana*] cannot be absolutely destroyed along with the body, but something of it remains, which is eternal."[103] By this, Spinoza did not mean that an individual soul is immortal: "we do not assign duration to the mind except while the body endures. . . . However, since that which is conceived by a certain eternal necessity through God's essence is nevertheless a something . . . this something, which pertains to the essence of mind, will necessarily be eternal."[104]

Spinoza's Averroism and Its Effect on Scripture

The possibility of such participation allowed Spinoza to "rank" human beings according to the knowledge of which they are capable and that they actually pursue and achieve (again, in parallel to Averroes, although the most proximate source seems to have been van den Enden's *Free Political Propositions*, 1665[105]), and this ranking has important ramifications both for the theological and political aspects of the *Tractatus*

101 Ibid., II, Prop. 40, Scholium 2.

102 Ibid., V, Prop. 22.

103 Ibid., V, Prop. 23.

104 Ibid., V, Prop. 23, Proof.

105 See Nyden-Bullock, *Spinoza's Radical Cartesian Mind*, pp. 55–56. On the connections between Averroes and Spinoza see Stephen Chak Tornay, "Averroes' Doctrine of the Mind," *The Philosophical Review*, Vol. 52, No. 3 (May 1943), pp. 270–288; Irving L. Horowitz, "Averroism and the Politics of Philosophy," *The Journal of Politics*, Vol. 22, No. 4 (November 1960), pp. 698–727; Craig Martin, "Rethinking Renaissance Averroism," *Intellectual History Review*, Volume 17, Issue 1, March 2007, pp. 3–28.

theologico-politicus, creating an even stronger version of the new Averroism than we found in Descartes.

Spinoza conceived of three levels of knowledge. The first was "knowledge from casual experience," also referred to as "knowledge of the first kind, opinion, or imagination," wherein we perceive "individual objects presented to us through the senses in a fragmentary and confused manner without any intellectual order." This kind of knowledge included the perception of symbols. The second was called "reason," wherein we "have common notions and adequate ideas of the properties of things. . . ." Here, we must be particularly clear that Spinoza's view of reason was restricted to the mathematical-mechanical mode of reason. And finally, we have the third and highest kind of knowledge, intuition.[106] Significantly, "Knowledge of the first kind is the only cause of falsity; knowledge of the second and third kind is necessarily true."[107] For Spinoza, most people have knowledge only of the first kind. Even more important, the Bible presents us with knowledge only of this first kind, a "fact" that for Spinoza was of the utmost political and theological importance. Mathematical-mechanical science, or natural philosophy, offers us the second and third kind.

Clearly, Spinoza's account of nature was entirely opposed to the traditional Judeo-Christian account of the true distinction between the Creator God and His creation. It is not surprising that the *Ethics* (which again, Spinoza refused to publish while alive) shocked his contemporaries when it appeared shortly after his death. In retrospect, although he may have shocked his contemporaries, Spinoza's radical move makes perfect sense. Whereas others had held back, Spinoza simply took the mathematization and mechanization of nature to its logical conclusion.[108]

The emphasis here is on *logical*. Cartesianism presented an impossible dualism of spirit and full-blown mechanism, a contradictory hybrid of a non-mechanical and mechanical cosmology, or more accurately, of the furious opposites of Judeo-Christian and Epicurean cosmology, with no real interaction. From this starting point, one could try to live in a kind of schizophrenia, where the supernatural and natural realms are entirely unrelated, a condition that would seem to duplicate the dualism of Averroism, or, one could jettison the supernatural realm completely, as atheists of the nineteenth century would do. But one may try a third alternative, as Spinoza seemingly did, and infuse one opposite into the other, so that God is nature and nature is God.

Two important points must be made about Spinoza's alternative. First, the collapse of God into nature actually "solved" a problem that beset all attempts to maintain Cartesian dualism: Since the mechanistic account of nature was self-contained, then God seemed to be redundant. Why should we invoke God as the cause of nature and nature's order, when nature itself is its own cause and is governed by its own laws?

---

106 Spinoza, *Ethics*, II, Prop. 40, Scholium 2.

107 Ibid., II, Prop. 41.

108 Again, to quote David Lachterman, "Spinoza's central legacy to modern science is his sustained reflection on the most general conditions that must be satisfied if the new mathematical physics is to be both true of the world in its totality *and* adequately intelligible to human minds." Lachterman, "Laying Down the Law: The Theological-Political Matrix of Spinoza's Physics," p. 126.

By identifying God with nature, Spinoza "saved" divine causality by making God's causality, indeed God Himself, intrinsic to nature. Thus was born an even harsher determinism than was originally found in the Aristotelianism of Averroes and the Latin Averroists.

But second, and relating directly to his effect on scriptural scholarship, by identifying God with nature and assuming that the order of nature was identical to the clearest, most certain science of mathematics, Spinoza completely and purposely eliminated supernatural revelation as a possibility. God's essence is *entirely* revealed in nature; He *is* nature; therefore the highest science, the one that truly grasps God's essence, is mathematical-mechanical natural science, which, since God is identified with nature, is identical to natural theology.

Biblical revelation thereby becomes both a theological and political problem, one that duplicated the problem faced by Averroes, and occasioned Spinoza's Averroistic response. In regard to theology, since the biblical authors were obviously pre-Cartesian and hence prescientific (in the sense that they did not either know or embrace a mathematical-mechanistic account of nature), then they could not be the vehicle of the highest truth about God (in Spinoza's hierarchy of knowledge, the second and third kinds of knowledge), but rather could only present "knowledge of the first kind, opinion, or imagination." Here is an almost exact duplication of Averroes's hierarchy of knowledge, with the substitution of a mathematical-mechanical philosophy of nature for Aristotelianism.

In this schema, the biblical actors and authors must be understood to have perceived knowledge only according to the lowest rung, where knowledge is of "individual objects presented . . . through the senses in a fragmentary and confused manner without any intellectual order." In regard to politics, however, Christianity seemed to be on the highest rung, an inversion of the proper order. Therefore, Judaism and Christianity, which were based on the Bible, were philosophical and political antagonists and obstacles to the natural religion espoused by Spinoza.

The Theological-Political Question and Spinoza's Politicized Answer

Spinoza was thereby faced with a task that was as much political as it was theological—a truth ensconced in the very title *Tractatus theologico-politicus*. The question for Spinoza, the very question that defined the *Tractatus theologico-politicus*, was this: *How can a man of reason live among men governed solely by their imaginations?* This presentation of the question accords perfectly with Spinoza's privately given reasons for writing the *Tractatus*, as evidenced in a letter to Henry Oldenburg, in which Spinoza claims he is being "driven" to write "a Treatise about my interpretation of Scripture" because (1) the prejudices of the theologians are "among the chief obstacles which prevent men from directing their minds to philosophy"; (2) he must fend off the opinion of the "common people" who "accuse me falsely of atheism"; and (3) the "freedom of philosophizing, and of saying what we think; this I desire to vindicate in every way" against suppression "through the excessive authority and impudence of the preachers."[109]

Nota bene: Spinoza's overriding concern in writing what is rightly considered to be one of the seminal texts defining the historical-critical method is to protect philosophy from biblically based theologians, especially those with political power. The aim defines the method.

Obviously the question of how a man of reason can live among those governed by their imaginations was not merely theoretical for Spinoza. He regarded all the conflicts and miseries associated with the Thirty Years' War, the persecution of his ancestors by Spanish and Portuguese Catholics, his own persecution by the Jews of the Netherlands, and the persecution of his freethinker friends and himself by Dutch Calvinists, as ultimately the result of men governed by imagination, and hence irrationality. The irrationality cannot be brushed aside, Spinoza thought, for the multitude will always be more powerful and prevalent than the enlightened few, and Christianity itself had immense power over the imagination of men at the time of Spinoza. What then is the man of reason to do? In Yirmiyahu Yovel's words, "This question defines the philosophical program of Spinoza's *Theological-Political Treatise* and informs it throughout."

> The overall aim of this work is to establish mental and institutional mechanisms that will transform the imagination [of the multitude] into an external imitation of reason, using state power and a purified popular religion as vehicles of a semirational civilizing process. . . . Purified religion and the rationalized state are thus designed to engender in the multitude the same conduct that the rational model requires.[110]

The tension at the center of the *Tractatus theologico-politicus* is defined by the attempt both to keep the authority of the Bible—as a powerful instrument of control over those who can be governed only by their imagination—and simultaneously to reconstruct the Bible as an image of Spinoza's religion of reason. As Yovel argues, the hermeneutics used by Spinoza entail that:

> The content of the Bible be reinterpreted to suit the message of the new universal religion [of reason]. Although Spinoza insists that biblical hermeneutics must become an objective science, he also expects it to serve as a means for reforming historical religion by reducing the true meaning of the prophets, and what is held to be the word of God, to a concise set of general and rather secular principles, such as justice, solidarity, and mutual help.[111]

---

109 Letter XXX, A. Wolf, *The Correspondence of Spinoza* (New York: Russell & Russell, Inc., 1966).

110 Yovel, *Spinoza and Other Heretics: The Marrano of Reason,* p. 130.

111 Ibid., pp. 132–133.

In Steven Smith's words, "The aim of the *Treatise* as a whole is nothing less than the replacement of the prophet-priest of the past with the historian-philologist of the present as the authoritative interpreter of Scripture."[112] But the method of the historian-philologist, as conceived by Spinoza, is defined by this political goal, which recalls Levenson's insight that "historical criticism is the form of biblical studies that corresponds to the classical liberal political ideal. It is the realization of the Enlightenment project in the realm of biblical scholarship."[113] Uniting the insights of Yovel, Smith, and Levenson, one might say that the historical-critical method as originally designed by Spinoza is neither neutral nor scientific, but is rather the form of biblical studies that purposely transforms the Bible to act as a political support to keep order in a secular state, so that, as Smith argues, Spinoza's *Tractatus* ought to be considered a "classic of modern liberal democratic theory."[114] Insofar as he "purposely transforms" the text, Spinoza himself becomes one of the founding fathers of the method. For the followers, who far outnumber the founders, one may substitute "implicitly" for "purposely," because the followers seem largely unaware of the original design of the tools. To understand the original design, it's necessary to analyze the most obvious intersection of Spinoza's cosmology with that of the Bible.

The Laws of God-Nature and the Elimination of the Miraculous

We begin with Spinoza's treatment of miracles in the *Tractatus* (Chapter 6) because in it we see most clearly how Spinoza's philosophy determined his exegesis. We can do no better than to quote Spinoza himself:

> If something were to come about in nature which did not follow on the basis of its laws . . . it would necessarily conflict with the order that God has set in nature for eternity through the universal laws of nature; and so it would be contrary to nature and its laws; and, consequently, faith in it [a miracle] would make us doubt everything and lead us to Atheism . . . [therefore] a miracle, whether [it is considered to be] contrary to nature or above nature, is a mere absurdity.[115]

Considered by itself, this statement is insufficient to reduce miracles to "absurdity." If God is the Creator of nature and its laws, He would certainly be powerful enough to manipulate nature and break or bend the laws at will. It is *only* if God is completely identified with nature that miracles—alleged violations of the order of

112 Smith, *Spinoza, Liberalism, and the Question of Jewish Identity*, p. 77.

113 Jon D. Levenson, *The Hebrew Bible, the Old Testament, and Historical Criticism* (Louisville, KY: Westminster/John Knox Press, 1993), p. 118.

114 Smith, *Spinoza, Liberalism, and the Question of Jewish Identity*, p. 25.

115 All quotations from Benedict Spinoza, *Theologico-Political Treatise*, translated by Martin Yaffe (Newburyport, MA: R. Pullins & Company, 2004), 6.1.33–34. The numbers refer to the chapter, paragraph, and sentence number rather than the page number of the translation.

nature—would be impossible, for then God's nature would contradict itself. Of course, that is exactly the identity assumed in the *Ethics*, and so it makes perfect sense for Spinoza to declare in the *Tractatus* that "Nothing comes about in nature . . . which conflicts with its universal laws. . . . Nature . . . always observes laws and rules which involve eternal necessity and truth. . . . For . . . the virtue and power of nature are the very virtue and power of God, and the laws and rules of nature are the very decrees of God. . . ."[116]

To those who have not read Spinoza's *Ethics* (the very situation of the first readers of the *Tractatus*), the actual and only possible foundation of the assertion that miracles are impossible—that God *is* nature—was obviously not apparent. But it was from this hidden foundation, expressed in quasi-orthodox terms, that Spinoza argued that "it very clearly follows that the noun 'miracle' cannot be understood except with respect to the opinions of human beings, and signifies nothing else but a work whose natural cause we cannot explain on the mode of some other, usual thing; or, at least, that the one who writes or narrates the miracle cannot so explain it."[117]

Here, Spinoza revealed the key to his method of interpreting Scripture, even while concealing the ultimate reasons (that is, the "monstrous hypothesis"). *Since* miracles are impossible, *therefore* the scientific exegete must look for another explanation of their common occurrence in Scripture. Or more simply, since the cause of the biblical presentation of miracles cannot be God-nature, then the cause must be in human beings. The focus of exegesis thus shifts from the text as it presents itself as a source of knowledge about the Divine, to the task of ferreting out the various causes of the belief in miracles in "the opinions of human beings." In terms of the *Ethics*, this meant an examination of "knowledge of the first kind, opinion, or imagination" by those who have knowledge of the second and third kind. Since knowledge of the first kind, "knowledge from casual experience," is based on perception "through the senses in a fragmentary and confused manner without any intellectual order," the text itself must reflect that fragmentation and confusion, and it is the job of the exegete to sort out and reorder it according to his superior knowledge of God-nature. This is the pattern informing Spinoza's entire exegetical method.

Mirabile dictu, Spinoza found scriptural support for the denigration and elimination of the miraculous. In Deuteronomy 13:1–5, Spinoza informed readers, Moses condemns a false prophet "even if he were to make miracles." And worse, even having seen "so many miracles," the Israelites following Moses out of Egypt made a golden calf anyway, a sign that they "could not form any sound concept of God" even with the belief in miracles (Exodus 32:8). Furthermore, even though prophets believed in miracles, they remained confused about the relationship between "the order of nature" and "the concept they had formed of God's providence," a confusion rooted in their ignorance of the simple and absolute *identity* of the order of nature and God's providence. Spinoza concluded that, "it is . . . established on the basis of Scripture itself

116 Ibid., 6.1.16.

117 Ibid., 6.1.17.

that miracles do not give true knowledge of God; nor do they teach God's providence clearly." [118]

The obverse of this statement is that philosophers, not prophets, *do* teach about God's providence clearly. Accordingly, Spinoza praised Solomon, whom he called "the Philosopher,"[119] and "whose Prophecy and piety are not commended in the sacred books so much as his prudence and wisdom are."[120] Solomon the philosopher taught exactly what Spinoza teaches, that divine law and the laws of nature are identical. In support of this, Spinoza cited Ecclesiastes 1:10–12, wherein Solomon "very clearly teaches that nothing new happens in nature," a doctrine perfectly in accord with Spinoza's complete determinism.[121]

Although prophets are confused, "Philosophers, who endeavor to understand things not on the basis of miracles but on the basis of clear concepts . . . know for certain that God directs nature as his universal laws require . . . and thus that God has a plan not for the human race alone but for the whole of nature."[122] Therefore, God's providence is *not* manifested through the special history of the Jews, but through a mathematical-mechanical account of the history of nature of which human beings are merely a part.[123] Spinoza's rejection of miracles consequently brought him to an inversion of salvation history, wherein salvation history is subsumed under natural history, the supernatural under the natural, the Creator under the created, and all reexplained accordingly. Seen through the eyes of orthodoxy, his views represented the greatest mode of idolatry possible.

Yet this very mode became Spinoza's method of interpretation. The starting assumption was that "when Scripture says that this or that was done by God or God's will, it understands nothing else but that it was done in accordance with the laws and order of nature, and not, as the vulgar opine, that nature meanwhile stopped acting or that its order was temporarily interrupted."[124] Oddly enough, Scripture really did not teach this directly, "since it is not part of it [Scripture] to teach matters through natural causes," therefore, the true teaching must be "elicited by implication on the basis of some of the Histories in Scripture which are by chance narrated at more length and with more details."[125]

A curious assertion. What did Spinoza intend? By this, Spinoza meant that in many passages of the Bible that would seem to be reporting something supernatural, the real natural cause can be surmised by the illumed exegete. For example, in I Samuel 9:15–16, when God tells Samuel that he will send Saul to him, what really

118 Ibid., 6.1.36–44.

119 Ibid., 6.1.94. On the connection to Solomon see Jonathan I. Israel, "Spinoza, King Solomon, and Frederik van Leenhof's Spinozistic Republicanism," in H. De Dijn, F. Mignini, and P. van Rooden, "Spinoza's Philosophy of Religion," *Studia Spinozana,* vol. 11 (1995): pp. 303–317.

120 Benedict Spinoza, *Theologico-Political Treatise*, 4.4.34.

121 Ibid., 6.1.94–96.

122 Ibid., 6.1.43.

123 Ibid., 6.1.46.

124 Ibid., 6.1.47.

125 Ibid., 6.1.48.

happened can be surmised from the description: Saul happened to be looking for his lost asses; he resolved to go back home without finding them; on the way he was told by a servant that Samuel might be able to tell him where they were; and so he went to Saul—everything happening according to the "very order of nature."[126] Likewise, in Genesis 9:13, when God puts a rainbow in the heavens for Noah as a sign of His everlasting covenant, "this action of God's is also none other than the refraction and reflection of the sun's rays which the same rays undergo in drops of water."[127] Spinoza's hidden premise in this treatment of the rainbow had immense implications: it represents the rejection of special, revelatory providence as manifested in covenant. Again, providence or salvation history is subsumed under natural history.

This identity of God and nature sets up not so much a hermeneutic of suspicion, as one of *condescension*. For Spinoza, "there is no doubt that everything that is narrated in Scripture happens naturally," yet this may not be immediately apparent to the reader. The reason, Spinoza asserted, was again that "it is not part of Scripture to teach matters through natural causes, but only to narrate those matters that broadly occupy the imagination," a "Method and style which better serve . . . for impressing devotion in the psyches of the vulgar."[128] The Bible is not a philosophy text, "but only narrates matters in the order and phrases by which it can move human beings—and mainly the plebs—to devotion in the greatest degree; and because of this, it speaks of God and of matters quite improperly, no doubt since it is not eager to convince reason, but to affect and occupy human beings' fancy and imagination."[129] One could ask for no better restatement of Polybius's notion of religion that so influenced Marsilius and Machiavelli.

Spinoza's method therefore assumed that some natural cause always underlies the rhetorical or imaginative language of the supernatural. Sometimes the real cause is evident in Scripture (as in Exodus 10:12–13, when a strong wind blowing for a day and a night carries in the plague of locusts against the Egyptians[130]). Sometimes the man of science, as exegete, must discern the true cause (as when "Elisha to rouse a boy who was believed dead . . . had to lie on the boy several times until he first warmed up and at last opened his eyes" or when Christ used spittle and dust to "heal the blind" in John 9:6[131]). Sometimes the cause is the indiscriminate and childlike mixing up of false opinions with narrative fact (as with those of Joshua's time who believed that the sun moved around the earth *and* who experienced during a victorious battle that the "day was longer than usual," and therefore asserted that during the battle that God made the sun stand still[132]). Sometimes what appears as miraculous or extraordinary

126 Ibid., 6.1.49.

127 Ibid., 6.1.51.

128 Ibid., 6.1.54.

129 Ibid., 6.1.64.

130 Ibid., 6.1.56.

131 Ibid., 6.1.58–59. Spinoza evidently believed that Elisha merely warmed up a child not really dead, and that spittle and dust made a kind of natural cure for visual impairment.

132 Ibid., 6.1.73. Spinoza offers as a scientific cause that "from the excessive chill that was in the atmosphere at that time (see Joshua 10:11), a greater refraction than usual could have occurred, or some other such thing . . ." 2.8.5.

is really only a metaphorical or symbolic representation (as when God is reported as descending upon Mount Sinai or Elijah ascending to heaven on a chariot of fire[133]). And sometimes the fault is in the reader who may not "know the phrases and tropes of the Hebrews. For he who does not pay sufficient attention to them will attach many miracles to Scripture which its writers were never thinking to narrate. . . ." Examples include the Jewish hyperbole of Isaiah 13:10 and 13, depicting the sack of Babylon as accompanied by a darkening of the heavens, and a trembling of earth and heaven; or the Jewish propensity of speaking of good fortune as directly caused by God, as is seen in Isaiah 48:21, where Isaiah speaks of God directly providing water for the exiles returning from Babylonia to Jerusalem, when "he means to signify nothing else but that the Jews, as it happened, discovered fountains in the desert by which they eased their thirst."[134] "Yet," admitted Spinoza candidly, "there will be times when the text cannot be salvaged by finesse."

> For since everything that is narrated in Scripture as having happened in reality . . . necessarily happened in accordance with the laws of nature . . . if something is found which can be demonstrated apodictically to conflict with the laws of nature or to have been unable to follow on the basis of them, it is plainly to be believed that it was inserted in Sacred Writ by sacrilegious human beings. For whatever is contrary to nature is contrary to reason; and what is contrary to reason is absurd, and therefore refutable as well.[135]

The hermeneutic of condescension allows this alternative precisely because the source of this condescension to the vulgar is not Divine but human. That is, the ultimate cause of the condescension is that the Bible has its origin in and among the vulgar, or more kindly, it was written *by* those who were prescientific *for* those who were prescientific. In other words, the Bible is entirely a work of the *first* kind of knowledge. Since this first kind of knowledge is not really knowledge—but is rooted in sense perception, imagination, opinion, and ignorance of natural causes—the Bible cannot teach truth. What then does it teach—or more exactly, what then *can* it teach? The answer lies in the rest of the *Tractatus*.

Spinoza's Moral Vulgate

Spinoza sets forth a clear distinction, a version of the double truth familiar to modern ears: "reason is the realm of truth and wisdom, whereas Theology is that of piety and obedience,"[136] and "obedience toward God consists only in love of neighbor. . . ."[137] So that, "on the basis of Scripture itself, without any difficulty or ambiguity, we have

133 Ibid., 6.1.76.
134 Ibid., 6.1.80–85.
135 Ibid., 6.1.67.
136 Ibid., 15.1.36.
137 Ibid., 13.1.9–10.

perceived the sum of it to be to love God above all and one's neighbor as oneself. . . ."[138] For Spinoza, the *entire* aim of Scripture is to teach morality, a position that will become commonplace among the Deists, but which had already appeared in ancient pagan thinkers like Polybius and in the *via moderna* stemming from Machiavelli. Scripture must be confined to teaching morality *and nothing else* (that is, limited to a political-moral function) for a specific reason—one that is not very flattering to Scripture or to believers.

Scientists and philosophers—that is, those capable of the second and third kinds of knowledge—are capable of reasoning about morality. The problem is that "for deducing things on the basis of intellectual notions alone, a long chain of perceptions is very often required—and, besides, the utmost caution, clarity of intellect, and the utmost continence as well, all of which are rarely found in human beings . . . "[139] But "since Scripture as such was first revealed for the use of a full nation [i.e., the Israelites], and ultimately for that of the human race as such, what is contained in it necessarily has to have been mostly accommodated to suit the grasp of the plebs," otherwise it would be written "only for the learned"[140] and hence could not be used to inculcate morality effectively. Consequently:

> Scripture treats and teaches matters in the mode in which they can be most easily perceived . . . It does not deduce and chain matters together from axioms and definitions, but only says them simply and . . . narrated in the style and phrases by which the spirit of the plebs can be stirred the most. . . . From all this it follows that the teaching of Scripture does not contain grand theories or philosophical matters, but only very simple matters, which can be perceived even by the slowest.[141]

Of course, since philosophers and scientists are, unlike the vulgar, capable of reason, they have no need of Scripture. Reason gives them clearly what Scripture offers only obscurely. "One who is ignorant of them [i.e., the Sacred Books] and nevertheless recognizes by the natural light that there is a God . . . and furthermore has the true plan of living, is altogether blessèd; indeed, his [plan of living] is more blessèd than the vulgar, since besides true opinions he has in addition a clear and distinct concept."[142] Going even further, Spinoza asserted that such a one "is absolutely blessèd and really has Christ's spirit in him."[143] In making the highest revelation of Scripture moral, and defining morality in purely secular terms (as we shall see), Spinoza made revelation superfluous, at least for the "enlightened."

But such is not the case for the many. Again, the vulgar, the great majority of humanity, are not capable of reason, and so they are incapable of following the moral

138 Ibid., 12.2.45.
139 Ibid., 5.4.2.
140 Ibid.
141 Ibid., 13.1.2–4.
142 Ibid., 5.4.9.
143 Ibid., 5.4.18.

law *as* law. This has immediate political implications, which recall Marsilius's and Machiavelli's political use of religion:

> [S]ince the true aim of the laws is usually obvious only to a few, and most human beings are more or less incapable of perceiving it and [therefore] live on the basis of anything but reason, therefore to restrict everyone equally, lawgivers have wisely established another aim, quite different from the one that follows necessarily from the nature of the laws [in themselves, as known by reason]: namely, by promising upholders of the laws what the vulgar love most [i.e., the pleasures of heaven], and on the other hand threatening those who violate them with what the vulgar fear most [i.e., eternal punishments]. And so they have endeavored to curb the vulgar as a horse by the rein, so far as it can be done.[144]

Obedience through Scripture for the vulgar is politically essential: "everyone absolutely can obey," while there "are only a very few, compared with the whole human race, who acquire the habit of virtue from the guidance of reason alone. . . ."[145] For this reason—and here Spinoza will differ markedly from later Enlightenment figures—Scripture is *politically indispensable*: the many can never be enlightened.[146] Echoing Hobbes, Spinoza declared in his Preface, "I have recognized that it is equally impossible to take away superstition from the vulgar as to take away dread," dread being that which preserves and fosters superstition.[147] It would therefore be foolish to reject Scripture for the sake of reason because Scripture provides "great solace . . . for those who are not so strong in reason," and furthermore, since it teaches moral obedience to those who cannot be taught otherwise, "no mediocre utility follows for the Republic. . . ."[148]

Precisely because Scripture is indispensable for the vulgar, the majority, the philosophic few must have a way of handling Scripture that allows it to have the proper moral effect, even while denying any theoretical or philosophical status to revelation. Note that Spinoza explicitly maintained that his *Tractatus* was written for the "Philosopher reader," and not for the "vulgar, and all who struggle with the same emotions as the vulgar. . . ."[149] The method of exegesis espoused by Spinoza, then, must be understood in light of his aim and the audience. In this exact spirit one must understand Spinoza's claim that "I painstakingly set about to examine Scripture anew in a full and free spirit and to affirm nothing about it and admit nothing as its teach-

144 Ibid., 4.2.2.

145 Ibid., 15.1.67.

146 On this notion of "enlightened" exegesis of Scripture see Paul Bagley, "Spinoza, Biblical Criticism, and the Enlightenment," in John McCarthy, ed., *Modern Enlightenment and the Rule of Reason, Studies in Philosophy and the History of Philosophy*, Vol. 32 (Washington, DC: Catholic University of America Press, 1998), pp. 124–149.

147 Benedict Spinoza, *Theologico-Political Treatise*, Preface, 1.7. To be exact, dread is the fear of bad fortune, a fear that brings human beings to try to influence the future by religious practices and supplications. See Preface, 1.1–3.

148 Ibid., 15.1.56–57.

149 Ibid., Preface, 6.1–2.

ing which I was not taught by it very clearly," and "With this caution, I therefore contrived a Method of interpreting the Sacred scrolls. . . ."[150] As with Descartes, the method was entirely determined by his philosophic system, and further, defined by his political aim.

Clearing the Ground of Prophets

The bulk of Spinoza's method is concerned with clearing the ground, i.e., removing from Scripture any content or authority other than what can loosely be understood as moral. This was achieved in several ways, beginning with his treatment of prophecy and prophets.

By identifying God with nature, Spinoza eliminated the orthodox belief that God is both *other than* and *above* nature, so that knowledge of His essence is impossible through knowledge of nature or creation. According to the orthodox position, we can know *that* God exists through His effects, but His effects do not reveal His surpassing nature, His essence. If we are to know God's essence, He must reveal it in some way beyond nature. On the orthodox view, then, revelation by God of His essence gives us *super*natural knowledge. Such knowledge is given by God to the prophets.

Spinoza's underlying assumption from the *Ethics* was that God is *identical* to nature. It was on the basis of this identity that Spinoza asserted in the *Tractatus* that "everything . . . in nature involves and expresses the concept of God by reason of its essence and perfection," so that "the more we know natural things, the greater and more perfect is the knowledge of God which we acquire." Consequently, "the more we know natural things, the more perfectly we know God's essence. . . ."[151] Since the divine nature and divine law are the same thing, it follows that divine law is nothing other than the laws of nature, and that to know the divine law is the same as to know the laws of nature. For this reason, the achievement of our highest good—the perfection of our intellect in knowledge of God-nature—"does not require a faith in histories. . . . Nor can a faith in histories, however certain, give us knowledge of God, or consequently love of God as well."[152] Science, not biblical revelation in the form of stories, gives us the highest knowledge of God, hence scientists, not prophets, truly reveal who or what God is.[153] We are brought to the brink of Lessing's ditch.

Because God *is* nature for Spinoza, the ancient prophets—who were evidently not scientists—could not possibly be revealing truths about God's nature. Prophets could only be speaking in terms of the first kind of knowledge, that is, of opinion and imagination and "in a fragmentary and confused manner without any intellectual order." "Prophets were not endowed with a more perfect mind," Spinoza informed

150 Ibid., Preface, 5.1–2.

151 Ibid., 4.3.3.

152 Ibid., 4.3.1–4.2; 4.4.6–7.

153 Ibid., See especially Spinoza's hubristic assertions at 1.4.1.

readers, "but with a more vivid power of imagining. . . ."[154] Indeed, it was the very vividness of their imagination that counteracted their rationality, "For those who are very powerful in imagination are less capable of purely understanding things. . . ."[155] Since they could not understand things, they can at best function only as vehicles of moral certitude, for "Prophetic certainty was not mathematical, but only moral."[156]

This prophetic "certainty" was further relativized. Because the prophets were governed by imagination, and hence were incapable of having rational certainty, they needed some kind of a sign that would "go along with the imagination" to vouchsafe the revelation.[157] Since the prophets were ruled each by his *own* opinions and imagination, it followed that the sign taken by each prophet that rendered him "certain of his Prophecy" differed with "respect to the opinions and capacity of the Prophet," the result being that "the revelation itself varied with each Prophet with respect to the disposition of the temperament of the body, with respect to that of the imagination, and with respect to the pattern of the opinions he had embraced beforehand." Therefore, "if the Prophet was cheerful, to him were revealed victories, peace, and whatever moves human beings to joy besides. . . . If, on the other hand, he was sad, to him were revealed wars, comeuppances, and every evil." And so, when Elisha was made happy by music, he prophesied good tidings to the king of Israel (II Kings 3:13–20). But when Ezekiel was angry and Jeremiah sad, they "prophesied calamities of the Jews." Or, "if the Prophet was elegant, he perceived God's mind in an elegant style too; and if he was confused, he did so confusedly." And so, Isaiah and Nahum are elegantly written, while the prophecies of Ezekiel and Amos "were written in a cruder style." The same pattern occurred in regard to the images the prophets used, for "if the Prophet was rustic, there were cows and sheep, etc. If, however, he was a soldier, there were generals and armies. If, finally, he was a courtier, a royal throne and the like were represented to him." And so we have the "courtly Isaiah" (1:11–20) and the "rustic Amos" (5:21–24).[158]

The sum of Spinoza's analysis—clear from just scratching the surface of his many-page treatment—is that biblical prophecy revealed only the character of the prophet himself, rather than anything about God and His actions: "Prophecy never rendered Prophets more learnèd, but left them in their preconceived opinions; and on that account, we are hardly bound to believe them concerning merely theoretical matters."[159] The result: "we are not bound to believe the Prophets in anything else besides what is the aim and substance of revelation."[160] The aim and substance was merely moral, as Spinoza defined it.

This treatment of prophecy covered the entire Old Testament, and not just the prophetic books. In his analysis, Spinoza treated Isaiah, Jeremiah, and Ezekiel, but

154 Ibid., 2.1.1.

155 Ibid., 2.1.4.

156 Ibid., 2.3.8, and 2.5.1.

157 Ibid., 2.3.1.

158 Ibid., 2.5.1–2.6.8.

159 Ibid., 2.7.12.

160 Ibid., 2.10.3.

also, among others, Adam, Abraham, Noah, Moses, Elijah, Joshua, Samuel, David, and Solomon. The treatment of Moses is of particular interest, since he is *the* lawgiver of the Old Testament. Since both Moses and the Hebrews were ignorant of the laws of nature, they could not know, or have revealed to them, divine law. Therefore, the extensive set of laws revealed in the Pentateuch that came to define the Jewish nation turn out to be merely particular, political laws concerned with the preservation of that people alone.[161] The laws reveal not God, but merely the nature of Hebrew society, just as prophecies reveal only the character of the prophet.

Spinoza extended this type of analysis to the New Testament as well: "Nor is it to be stated otherwise about Christ's reasons by which he convinced the Pharisees of their stubbornness and ignorance, and exhorts the disciples to true life: namely, he accommodated his reasons to the opinions and principles of each one." And so, when the Pharisees accuse Jesus of being possessed, and He replies, "if Satan casts out Satan, he is divided against himself; how then will his kingdom stand?" (Matthew 12:26), He "meant nothing except to convince the Pharisees on the basis of their own principles, and not to teach that there are Demons or some kingdom of Demons." Likewise, when Christ speaks of not despising children, "for I tell you that in heaven their angels always behold the face of my Father who is in heaven" (Matthew 18:10), "He means to teach nothing else but that they [i.e., the disciples] not be proud or despise anyone; and he does not, in truth, mean to teach the rest of what is contained in his reasons [about angels]: these he brings in to persuade the disciples better of the matter."[162] That is, Christ came "solely to teach the universal law," and so He did not intend "anything more than teaching moral lessons. . . ."[163] Spinoza was thereby able to drive a wedge between what Christ *said* (wherein "he accommodated himself to the mental cast of the populace," that is, "to the mental cast of the plebs"[164]) and what He really, secretly believed (Spinoza's philosophy, since it is not possible to believe—or, at least at this time to *say*—that Christ himself would be unenlightened).

Spinoza was not satisfied merely to assert that Scripture is only useful for the sake of moral exhortation, but felt compelled to remove *everything but* morality from serious consideration. He did this in two ways: by turning exegetical attention from truth to meaning, and by maximizing the contradictions and confusions of Scripture in all areas but the moral. Both ways were set forth (although not completed) in his chapter explicitly dedicated to "The Interpretation of Scripture."

From Truth to Meaning

The context of this chapter, as Spinoza made clear, was the same as that set by him in the Preface to the entire work: religious discord. Of course, it was not mere theological

161 Ibid., See the entirety of Ch. 3.

162 Ibid., 2.10.6–8.

163 Ibid., 5.1.14.

164 Ibid., 4.4.28–30.

disagreement that concerned Spinoza, but theological discord as it was expressed in political discord. Returning to the Preface, there Spinoza revealed that what had "driven me to write" the *Tractatus* was that those who "profess the Christian religion—that is, love, gladness, peace, continence, and faith toward all—should clash in a more than inequitable spirit and exercise the bitterest hatred toward one another daily. . . ."[165] Chapter Seven renewed the complaint that "religion is not confined to charity [i.e., morality], but to disseminating discords among human beings and propagating a most antagonistic hatred, which they [adherents] cover with the false name of divine zeal and ardent enthusiasm."[166] The root cause of such disagreements was the exegetical focus on what is obscure in Scripture to the neglect of what is clear; that is, exegetes focused on the opinions and imaginings in Scripture based on the first kind of knowledge *as if* they were actually a guide to some higher truth, when in reality they were merely an indication of the ignorance, imagination, opinions, confusions, and personal characters and ambitions of the writers. Theological speculation based on such a shoddy foundation could only yield a multitude of conflicting interpretations, all of which were enflamed with religious zeal and hence caused intractable political conflicts.

Against this, Spinoza argued in Cartesian fashion that what is clear—the universal moral doctrines, so he claims—should be the foundation and aim of exegesis. There is no truth in Scripture but moral truth, and if the warring sects would realize that, then religious conflict would no longer disturb civil peace. Consequently, Spinoza presented "the true method of interpreting Scripture" so "That we might be extricated from these turmoils, free the mind from theological prejudices, and not rashly embrace human fantasies as divine lessons. . . ."[167]

Such, in a nutshell, was Spinoza's aim, the aim that defined his method of interpretation. Hence his method is fundamentally a secular political one, a point of no small importance given his place at the beginning of the developments of the modern historical-critical method. In Steven Smith's words, Spinoza's *Tractatus* "stands at the beginning of what would later become known as the 'higher criticism' of the Bible. This higher criticism aims at nothing less than the historical understanding and reconstruction of the Bible. Spinoza's biblical criticism is, then, historical criticism; its goal is the historicization or secularization of the biblical text."[168]

Surprisingly, Spinoza's overriding interpretive principle was a variation on *sola scriptura*, that "knowledge of Scripture be sought solely from Scripture."[169] He deduced this principle from the fact that true knowledge, knowledge of the second and third kind, does not appear in the Bible. That is, exegesis of Scripture is largely an analysis of the first kind of knowledge, an analysis of the opinions, imaginings,

165 Ibid., Preface, 3.4–4.1.

166 Ibid., 7.1.5.

167 Ibid., 7.1.8.

168 Smith, *Spinoza, Liberalism, and the Question of Jewish Identity*, p. 56.

169 Spinoza, *Theologico-Political Treatise*, 7.5.30 and 7.1.12.

and ignorance of the biblical actors and writers, so that, in Spinoza's method, "we are laboring solely from the sense of the speeches, and not from their truth."[170]

Exegesis must focus its efforts on *meaning* rather than truth, on the language and intentions of the biblical actors and writers. For example, we can learn from an analysis of Scripture that "Moses clearly teaches that God is jealous . . . hence it is plainly to be concluded that Moses believed—or at least wanted to teach—this same thing, however much we might believe that this tenet conflicts with reason."[171] The question for the exegete is not whether God really is jealous, but whether Moses believed (or at least, taught) that He is jealous and why.

This shift from truth to meaning helped to transform scriptural exegesis into an historical rather than a doctrinal discipline, a shift that significantly contributed to the nascent *historical*-critical method. The "foundations and principles of knowledge of the Scriptures," Spinoza declared quite frankly, are "*nothing else* but the straightforward history of them."[172] This approach—focusing on the coming-to-be of Scripture—was in strict parallel to Spinoza's understanding of science, as Spinoza himself proclaimed in the *Tractatus,*[173] where individual things do not have essences, but are temporal manifestations of homogeneous matter built up and torn down over time.[174]

Maximizing the Contradictions and Confusions: The Endless Tasks of the New Exegete

But getting to the meaning would not be easy, as Spinoza soon enough made clear. There arise a seemingly endless list of historical questions that must be answered before the exegete can discover the meaning of the text. Before we can grasp the meaning of Scripture, we must understand "the nature and properties of the language in which the books of Scripture were written," and this requires "a History of the Hebrew language. . . ."[175] But then Spinoza pointed out a host of semantic difficulties and obscurities in Hebrew,[176] demonstrating that "so many ambiguities . . . arise that no method can be given by which they are all able to be determined."[177] On top of that, exegetes would also have to sort out, in each book, all things that "are ambiguous or obscure, or seem to conflict," and then attempt to find out what each author really meant (as in the above exercise with Moses).[178] This would involve an historical analysis of "the life, mores and studies of the author of each book, who he was, on what occasion, at what time, for whom and, finally, in what language he wrote," as well as the "fortune of each

170 Ibid., 7.3.3.

171 Ibid., 7.3.12.

172 Ibid., 8.1.1. Emphasis added.

173 Ibid., 7.1.9–10.

174 See Yovel's insightful analysis, *Spinoza and Other Heretics: The Marrano of Reason,* pp. 161–164.

175 Spinoza, *Theologico-Political Treatise,* 7.2.1–3.

176 Ibid., 7.5.32–8.11

177 Ibid., 7.9.1.

178 Ibid., 7.3.1–13.

book: namely, how it was first received and whose hand it fell into; furthermore, how many variant readings it had, and by which council it was accepted among the sacred ones [books]; and, finally, how all the books that everyone now confess to be sacred coalesced into one corpus."[179] This history of the fortune of each book is necessary to discern "whether it could have been tampered with by adulterous hands or not, whether errors crept in, whether they were corrected by men sufficiently experienced and worthy of faith."[180] Piling difficulty upon difficulty, Spinoza concluded that the exegetical obstacles were "so great that I would not hesitate to affirm that either we are ignorant of the true sense of Scripture in very many passages, or else we guess at it without certainty."[181]

Those who feel pressed down by the weight of Spinoza's list of obstacles might remember that piling them up was part of a strategy to show that the Bible can *only* function as a source of moral authority for the masses, and not of truth. The shift to exegesis as fundamentally historical allowed Spinoza to maximize the contradictions and confusions of Scripture in all areas *but* the moral.

As an extension of this strategy, Spinoza undertook a several chapter analysis of the question of the authorship of the books of the Old and New Testament, duplicating material already found in Hobbes and elsewhere, and adding his own.[182] One very important addition—an expansion of Hobbes's assertion that it was Ezra who determined the Old Testament canon—was Spinoza's argument that the Old Testament was "all written by one and the same Historian, who wanted to write the antiquities of the Jews from the first origin [i.e., Creation] down to the City's first sacking [i.e., the sack of Jerusalem in 587 BC by the Babylonians]," and that *historian* was Ezra.[183] Ezra obviously wrote long after the events, and since he "set a certain goal for himself," which included explaining "the law of God to the human beings of his time," he therefore chose from among his sources what suited his purposes.[184] In short, "All these books . . . conspire as one . . . in teaching the sayings and edicts of Moses and demonstrating them through the outcome of events," so that, presumably, history from Creation to Sinai, and from the death of Moses to the fall of Jerusalem in the early sixth century BC, all demonstrate Ezra's belief that adherence to the Law brings prosperity and rejection brings destruction.

Spinoza's overarching point, then, was that the Old Testament did not have its unity from God or from a providential salvation history, but from a very particular historian with very particular goals. It did not teach the truth about God; it did not even teach very clearly about Moses or the Law; rather, the Old Testament revealed

179 Ibid., 7.4.1–2.

180 Ibid., 7.4.6.

181 Ibid., 7.11.6.

182 Ibid., Chs. 8–12. Spinoza was influenced both by reading Hobbes directly, and perhaps even more, indirectly, through the works of such ardent Hobbesian proponents in the Netherlands as John and Peter van den Hove. See M. J. Petry, "Hobbes and the Early Dutch Spinozists," in C. De Deugd, ed., *Spinoza's Political and Theological Thought*, pp. 150–170, especially pp. 152–156.

183 Spinoza, *Theologico-Political Treatise*, 8.1.73–87.

184 Ibid., 8.1.79 and 1.97.

first of all merely the particular opinions, desires, and prejudices of Ezra and, to some extent, his own time.

In this regard, the exegete's primary concern becomes a type of *redaction* criticism, an examination of the editing work of Ezra. As it turns out, Ezra did a sloppy, hasty job of it; he did nothing "but gather histories from different writers and . . . simply write them down; and he left them to posterity not yet examined and ordered."[185] Yet, since Ezra did rely on previous texts, it would be possible to recover at least some scraps of the originals, separating out the sources from the redaction, and then turning to a kind of *source* criticism, a task that Spinoza demonstrated to drill into the reader the difficulties and confusions involved here as well.[186]

Spinoza implied that illustrating the enormity of the task might "provoke him [the reader] into a hopeless undertaking," the reduction to hopelessness, it seems, being part of Spinoza's overall design. That is, Spinoza defined this exegetical exercise by the nearly hopeless task of recovering the historical origin of the Bible's original, preedited sources. A unified interpretation ever recedes because the flow of exegesis is toward maximum *disunity* of the text, and it therefore produces an endless multiplication of ever larger technical commentaries focused on ever-shrinking textual shards. The predictable (and hence prophetic) result would seem obvious. Since historical sources are scanty and contestable, and endless conjectures about editors and subeditors can be made, very little if anything can be said with certainty about the text—certainly nothing with *doctrinal* certainty. Furthermore, the multiplication of technical exegetical texts would create an ever-growing "scientific" propaedeutic obstacle to any doctrinal argument about the text by the learnèd, one that would effectively seal off the vulgar from Scripture as effectively as the difficulty of calculus keeps them from saying anything serious about nature.

The Residual Morality

Given Spinoza's expressly political aims, it is not surprising what Spinoza claimed could be salvaged from the Bible. If we follow the method of natural science, we shall find "on the basis of the history of Scripture . . . what is most universal" in the Bible, that is, what "Scripture everywhere teaches so clearly and so expressly that there would never be anyone who would waver about its sense . . ." is a thinly theistic morality: "a unique and all-powerful God exists who cares for everyone and cherishes above all those who adore him and love their neighbor as themselves, etc."[187] Of course the tenets of this morality are properly understood by philosophers, and not the vulgar, as a deduction from human nature.

This "universal teaching of Scripture," the moral core, then acted as an interpretive grid for the rest of Scripture so that "whatever is found . . . in Sacred Writ which

185 Ibid., 9.1.3.

186 Ibid., 9.1.5–57.

187 Ibid., 7.5.3–5.

is obscure or ambiguous is to be explained and determined by Scripture's universal teaching."[188] Spinoza's "universal teaching of Scripture" is another version of Hobbes's interpretive scope (the goal of which was "to convert men to the obedience of God," or more exactly, to those who "represent the person of God . . ."). But while Hobbes and Spinoza shared the same notion of a politically useful interpretive grid, they diverged on the implications. Whereas Hobbes was the founder of what one might call purely secular divine right (or better, liberal absolute monarchy) lodged in a sovereign who has complete control over every aspect of religious doctrine and practice, Spinoza was the founder of the purely secular notion of religious toleration as defined by the modern quasi-democratic liberal state. Thus, toleration takes the place of absolutism.

The Birth of Toleration

Since the moral core of Scripture was alone certain and beyond dispute, "there is no reason why we should be so worried about the remaining things. For, since for the most part we cannot embrace the remaining things by reason and understanding, they are matters more of curiosity than of utility."[189] The "remaining things" that are not certain are the very causes of theological controversy. By relegating them to *adiaphora*, Spinoza hoped to render them politically impotent, mere matters of opinion (which they really *are*, according to his philosophy).

Spinoza's terse reasoning was as follows. Since "the whole law consists in this alone: in love towards one's neighbor,"[190] then "we are bound to believe nothing else on the basis of the bidding of Scripture but what is absolutely necessary for executing this commandment,"[191] and "this very commandment is the sole norm of the whole catholic faith; and all the dogmas of the faith . . . are to be determined through it alone."[192] As a modest expansion of this one great commandment, Spinoza provided his famous enumeration of "the dogmas of the universal faith"—just seven, to be exact—which included the obvious (the first being, that "God exists"), but also a moral circumscription of worship (as consisting *only* in "love toward one's neighbor") and a Polybian assertion of the need for belief in individual salvation based on works (for "If human beings were not to believe this firmly, there would not be any cause why they would prefer to comply with God rather than with the pleasures").[193]

In a complete inversion of Luther, Spinoza therefore declared that it "follows that we can judge no one to be faithful or faithless except on the basis of works. Namely, if the works are good, however he may dissent in his dogmas from the other faithful, he is still faithful. And on the contrary, if the works are evil, however he may agree

188 Ibid., 7.5.7.
189 Ibid., 7.11.10.
190 Ibid., 14.1.13.
191 Ibid., 14.1.14.
192 Ibid., 14.1.15.
193 Ibid., 14.1.38–46.

in words, he is still faithless."[194] If someone is externally moral and hence law abiding, then whatever else he may happen to believe—*and this includes Spinoza himself*—is entirely inconsequential.

Spinoza even provided a positive affirmation of the diversity of beliefs, one that should sound strikingly familiar to us today, as we are his heirs. Since "faith does not require true dogmas so much as pious ones, that is, such as move the spirit toward obedience," then faith must be privatized and defined by the particularities of what happens to "move" each person. But "the common mental cast of human beings is quite varied and . . . opinions regulate human beings in a different mode, inasmuch as those that move this one to devotion move another to laughter and contempt . . . it follows that no dogmas over which there can exist controversy among honorable men pertain to the catholic or universal faith."

In short, to each his own, for "since each recognizes himself best, he has to think as he sees best for confirming himself in the love of Justice."[195] Fundamental religious disagreements, which used to be cause for bloodshed, can now be considered merely descriptions of "what moves" the individual, and no one can be wrong about what happens to move him

> so long as he concludes nothing with the aim of taking a greater license to sin, or of becoming less obedient to God. Indeed . . . each is bound to accommodate these dogmas of faith to suit his own grasp, and to interpret them to himself in the mode in which it seems easier to him to be able to embrace them without any hesitation, but with the spirit's complete consent. For . . . just as long ago faith was revealed and written down in accordance with the grasp and opinion of the Prophets and the vulgar of the time, so too each is now bound to accommodate it to his own opinions. . . . For we have shown that faith does not require truth so much as piety. . . .[196]

And then Spinoza adds, "How salutary and how necessary this Teaching is in a republic, so that human beings might live peacefully and harmoniously—and I say, how many and how great the causes of disturbances and wicked deeds which it might prevent—I leave for everyone to judge."[197] Such is the glory and utility of complete doctrinal toleration. In conformity to his account of the origins of the Bible, Spinoza's toleration is built upon the defects of the vulgar, accommodating theological dogma to their various opinions so as to make them more readily obedient—a duplication, or continuation, of the vulgar accommodation manifested in Scripture itself.

Such toleration covers and hence protects the fool *as well as* the philosopher. This leads to Spinoza's oft-declared "aim" of the entire *Tractatus*, the complete separation of philosophy and theology.[198] This radical split, which also divides reason and reli-

---

194 Ibid., 14.1.25.

195 Ibid., 14.1.34–37.

196 Ibid., 14.1.49.

197 Ibid., 14.1.51.

198 Ibid., Preface, 5.7–12; 2.10.10; 14.1.5; 14.12.1–4; 16.1.1.

gion, science and faith, would soon enough became a welcome dogma and has by now become a near truism. It is therefore well worth investigating its inauguration more carefully.

The Great Divorce of Reason and Faith

The foundation of Spinoza's divorce of philosophy from theology is the inseparable divide that exists between the first kind of knowledge (the unphilosophic or prephilosophic knowledge of the vulgar, the many, and hence of the biblical text), and the second and third kinds (that of scientists and philosophers). While Spinoza's reasons for declaring the separation are more in the spirit of Averroes, it is certainly fair to say that the separation received some affirmation from Luther's attempt to distance revelation from reason. Having noted this, however, it is clear that Spinoza's presentation of the radical disjunction between reason and faith is more in the spirit of modernity. Spinoza declared that

> there is no commerce and no affinity between Theology and Philosophy. . . . For the goal of Philosophy is nothing but truth, while that of Faith, as we have abundantly shown, is nothing but obedience and piety. . . . Furthermore, the foundations of Philosophy are common notions; and these have to be sought on the basis of nature alone. As for those of Faith, however they are histories and language, and they are to be sought on the basis of Scripture and revelation alone. . . .[199]

The power of reason is limited, Spinoza admitted, but *only* in that it "does not extend so far as to be able to determine that human beings could be blessèd by obedience alone, without any understanding of things."[200] Such is hardly a compliment; it means only that, since philosophy does understand that true blessedness consists in the knowledge of nature-God (knowledge that the unphilosophic lack), reason cannot discern how the many, without understanding, could be blessèd through mere obedience to moral precepts.

In contrast to philosophy, theology (i.e., biblical revelation) "wants—and can want—nothing contrary to reason. For it [theology] determines the dogmas of the Faith . . . *only* to the extent that obedience is sufficient. Precisely how they are to be understood by reason of their truth, however, it leaves for reason to determine—which is really the light of the mind, without which it sees nothing but dreams and fantasies."[201] Simply put, theology must stick to moral exhortation and let reason establish the exact meaning and parameters of theological claims; meanwhile, theology completely abandons reason to philosophy. This abandonment allows the meaning of moral obedience to be determined by philosophy for the sake of civil peace, so that the above-mentioned free-

199 Ibid., 14.2.1–3.

200 Ibid., 15.1.36.

201 Ibid., 15.1.36.

dom of the vulgar to accommodate dogma to their own prejudices is always overseen by philosophy. To understand this and its implications more fully requires an analysis of Spinoza's explicit treatment of politics, which brings the *Tractatus* to conclusion.

The politicus *of the* Tractatus theologico-politicus

It may surprise readers of the *Tractatus theologico-politicus* that after Spinoza's extensive treatment of the *theologico* in the first fifteen chapters, his account of the *politicus* was not biblical but largely Hobbesian (with some important differences).[202] One would expect that, after declaring that morality was simply and clearly revealed in Scripture—and indeed, is *all* that Scripture reveals—at least the content and political context of morality for Spinoza would bear an obvious resemblance to that found in the Bible. Such is not the case, however.

In regard to the similarities and differences of the Hobbesian and Spinozan scheme, what Hobbes achieved by *excluding* God from his amoral mathematical-mechanical account of nature, Spinoza obtained by *identifying* God with his amoral mathematical-mechanical account of nature.[203] To outline the steps in Spinoza's reasoning, since (1) "the power of nature is the very power of God," (2) God has "the highest right to everything," and further, since God is everything and everything is God, then (3) the "universal power of the whole of nature is nothing besides the power of all individuals together," it therefore follows that (4) "each individual has the highest right to everything it can do" and (5) "the highest law of nature is that each thing endeavor . . . to persevere in its state—and do so by taking no account of another but only of itself. . . ."[204] Thus, the "natural right of each human is . . . determined not by sound reason, but by longing and power."[205]

As with Hobbes, in this state of nature—the presocial state—there was neither good nor evil (which accords perfectly with what Spinoza asserted in the *Ethics*[206]). Thus, each "is permitted to consider as an enemy one who wants to impede him from fulfilling his spirit."[207] One might wonder—as Spinoza himself noted[208]—how this amoral state of nature could be reconciled with revelation, which Spinoza repeatedly affirmed taught nothing but charity from first to last. His surprising answer was that the natural state "is prior to religion both by nature and in time," and so in the state

202 See Smith, *Spinoza, Liberalism, and the Question of Jewish Identity*, pp. 122–130; Edwin Curley, "The State of Nature and Its Law in Hobbes and Spinoza," *Philosophical Topics* 19 (1991): 97–117, reprinted in Lloyd, ed., *Spinoza: Critical Assessments, Volume III*, pp. 122–142; Curley, "Kissinger, Spinoza, and Genghis Kahn"; Robert McShea, *The Political Philosophy of Spinoza* (New York: Columbia University Press, 1968), Ch. IX; M. J. Petry, "Hobbes and the Early Dutch Spinozists," pp. 150–170.

203 See Wolfgang Bartuschat, "The Ontological Basis of Spinoza's Theory of Politics," in C. De Deugd, ed., *Spinoza's Political and Theological Thought*, pp. 30–36.

204 Spinoza, *Theologico-Political Treatise*, 16.1.3.

205 Ibid., 16.3.1.

206 Spinoza, *Ethics*, Part IV, Prop. 8 and Proof.

207 Spinoza, *Theologico-Political Treatise*, 16.3.3.

208 Ibid., 16.8.1.

of nature prior to revelation, no one can be "bound by any obedience toward God," which comes "only on the basis of a revelation confirmed by signs. . . ." Therefore, the "natural state is . . . without religion and law, and consequently without sin and wrong," a truth, Spinoza assured the reader, that is "confirmed by the authority of Paul."[209] Spinoza's proof text came from Romans 5:13, in which St. Paul maintained that "there is no sin before there is law."[210]

Again following Hobbes, Spinoza asserted that the only way out of the dangers of a state of nature—the only way for each to preserve himself—was for all to give up their rights to a common, higher power, a sovereign "bound by no law."[211] Following our right to self-preservation, "we are bound to execute absolutely all the commands of the highest power, even if it commands the most absurd things," since it is this power that in fact does preserve our lives.[212] Each subject's right to self-preservation is defined by the highest sovereign power; that is, "he is now bound to live solely on the basis of the latter's [i.e., the highest power's] plan and defend himself solely by his protection."[213]

This included religion as defined by the highest power; that is, Spinoza's sovereign retained the same political rights to define religion as Hobbes's. Spinoza supported this claim by a *reductio ad licentiam*:

> [S]ince human beings usually err in the greatest degree about religion and in view of the diversity of their mental casts fantasize many things with great contentiousness, as experience testifies more than enough, it is certain that if no one is bound to comply with the highest power in those things that he deems to pertain to religion, then . . . no one who judged a statute to be contrary to his own faith and superstition would then be bound by it; and so, under this pretext, each could assume a license for everything. . . . [Therefore,] the highest right to make statutes concerning religion, however it might judge this, belongs to the highest power . . . and all are bound to comply with its decrees and commands concerning religion on the basis of the faith given to it, which God bids be altogether kept.[214]

The highest power itself retains the right either to follow or ignore religious moral commands: "if the highest power did not want to obey God in his revealed right, it is permitted at its own peril and harm. . . ."[215] Therefore, nothing constrains the sovereign's use or misuse of religion other than its own self-preservation as the sovereign, and hence nothing constrains its purely political use of Scripture.

209 Ibid., 16.8.2–5.

210 Ibid., 16.2.8.

211 Ibid., 16.6.3 and 16.6.20.

212 Ibid., 16.6.4.

213 Ibid., 16.7.2–3.

214 Ibid., 16.8.18–19.

215 Ibid., 16.8.15. If the sovereign power is heathen, Spinoza asserts that either no contract should be made with him, or if one is made, one should be obedient unless "a certain special revelation has promised help against a Tyrant . . . " Ibid., 16.8.20.

This returns to Henry VIII and Hobbes, but with this important difference: Spinoza championed the democratic manifestation of sovereignty, wherein each gives up his "natural right," transferring "all the power he has to society, which will thus retain the highest right of nature over everything, that is, the highest imperium," and the "right of such a society is called, in truth, Democracy, which is thereby defined as an assembly . . . of human beings which, collectively, has the highest right to everything it can do," being "bound by no law. . . ."[216] Consequently, the political majority have the absolute power over religion, including over the interpretation of Scripture.

In this regard, it is important to note that Spinoza's praise of democracy was made in terms of its being most like the natural state,[217] that is, the political condition that most closely approximates the natural condition "without religion and law, and consequently without sin and wrong." Ironically, the attempt to approximate this original condition without religion and law is the context for the political interpretation of Scripture in a Spinozan democratic regime. The desired result would seem to be a minimizing of dogma (so as to appeal to a majority of the citizens), and a consequent maximizing of intellectual and political freedom—the very goals, as we have seen, that Spinoza incorporates into the method of his exegesis.

Spinoza therefore politicizes the Bible in a very particular way, using its interpretation to undergird his notion of a liberalized democracy. A sterling example of such exegesis occurs in his account of Moses. As with Machiavelli and Hobbes, Spinoza declared that this absolute right of the sovereign was manifested in Moses himself as the political founder of Israel, affirming by his mode of argument that Moses' actions were properly interpreted according to pagan wisdom. This complete politicization of Moses reveals the heart of Spinoza's use of Scripture.

Spinoza's discussion of Moses as a theologico-political founder was set in the context of his larger argument about the practicality of sovereign power. The absolute right that the sovereign *should* have will "in many ways" remain "merely theoretical" if a way is not found for the sovereign power to control *everything*.[218] Control over others' bodies by fear of physical punishment would not be enough for full sovereignty because subjects still retain the inner desire, and hence the right, to do as they will.[219] True obedience demanded inner conformity: "obedience does not have to do so much with outward action, as with the inward action of the psyche. And so, he is most under another's imperium who chooses with a full spirit to comply with another in all his commands; and it follows that *one who rules over his subjects' minds holds the greatest imperium*."[220]

Precisely here, religion becomes necessary for rule, or more exactly, philosophy must use religion to rule, for the vulgar multitude (as Spinoza never tired of repeating) is incapable of following rational commands. Consequently, the plebs must be

216 Ibid., 16.6.1–3.

217 Ibid., 16.6.1, 16.615, 20.6.3.

218 Ibid., 17.1.1.

219 Ibid., 17.1.2–5.

220 Ibid., 17.1.8. Emphasis added.

completely controlled by the kind of knowledge of which they are capable, the first kind, the kind associated with revealed religion, imagination, opinion, and ignorance. Spinoza then turned to Moses, to revealed religion, to illustrate the kind of power religion provides. "I will note the things that divine revelation long ago taught Moses toward this end," the end being the most secure preservation of the imperium, an end that requires that "everyone, whatever his mental cast, would put the public right ahead of private advantages. . . ."[221]

However, Spinoza veered away from an immediate consideration of Moses, and turned instead to the pagan Alexander the Great as set forth in the writings of Quintus Curtius Rufus, a first-century Roman politician, rhetorician, and historian. Curtius's *History of Alexander* is cited prominently in Spinoza's Preface as teaching that fear or dread is the origin of superstition, and further that, "*Nothing regulates a multitude more effectively than superstition*."[222] The very curse of the vulgar, so to speak, is their cure. In Chapter 17, the lesson concerning the regulation of the vulgar is made more explicit.

Curtius's *Alexander* teaches that "to keep themselves secure . . . Kings who had usurped the imperium . . . endeavored to persuade [their subjects] that they drew their descent from the immortal Gods," for "if everyone else did not look on them as equals but believed them to be Gods, they would readily suffer being ruled by them. . . ." This entailed, as Spinoza made clear (hearkening back to Machiavelli), purposeful acts of dissembling "to persuade the ignorant. . . ."[223] Noting that "Monarchs have devised many such things for the security of their imperium," Spinoza immediately took up the question of Moses—in particular "what divine revelation long ago taught Moses to this end."[224]

According to Spinoza, when the Israelites escaped from Egypt, they were free of all obligations, returning to a kind of state of nature in the desert, and hence they regained their full natural rights.[225] In this "natural state" "they resolved on the basis of the counsel of Moses—in whom they had the greatest faith—to transfer their right to no mortal but only to God. . . ." They thereby constituted a kind of original democracy, insofar as no human being was above any other, and this democracy was directly under God as sovereign, so that "God alone . . . held the imperium of the Hebrews."[226] (Although Spinoza added later that "in reality . . . they [the Israelite people] retained the right of the imperium until they transferred it to Moses. . . ."[227]) Furthermore, in

221 Ibid., 17.2.2–4.

222 Ibid., Preface, 1.7 and 2.3.

223 Ibid., 17.3.9–13.

224 Ibid., 17.3.17. Spinoza says only that he dismisses all the pagan accounts and turns to Moses, not because the pagan accounts are false or reprehensible, but because the Mosaic account allows him "to arrive at what I mean . . ." Ibid., 17.3.17.

225 Ibid., 17.4.1.

226 Ibid., 17.4.3–8 and 17.5.1.

227 Ibid., 19.1.10.

this imperium, this "Kingdom of God," there was a complete identity of religion and politics so that "civil right and Religion . . . were one and the same."[228]

But at Mount Sinai, having witnessed the thunder and lightening, "on hearing God speak," the Israelites were literally "thunderstruck," so that they were "Full of dread"—the very condition, one notes, that gives birth to superstition, a birth that is possible because the vulgar, having no knowledge of natural causes, attribute such phenomena to invisible divinities. In fear of their lives, the Israelites immediately approached Moses and said: "*You . . . go and hear everything said by our God, and you*— not God—*will speak to us. Everything that God speaks to you, we will obey, and we will execute it*." "By these words," Spinoza (duplicating Hobbes) maintained, "they clearly abolished the first compact and transferred their right to consult God and interpret his edicts to Moses absolutely." That is, Moses received absolute imperium over all things, through and over religion, precisely in "the right to consult God alone in his tent."[229] Moses' absolute imperium consisted in him being both prophet and prince.

For the rest of Chapter 17, Spinoza treated the history of Israel, as known through the Old Testament, in the same way that an ancient pagan historian (e.g., Curtius or Tacitus) would read it if he were to come upon it. The triumphs and failures of Israel are then interpreted, not as salvation history, but as profane, political history. The ups and downs of the Jews are understood not in relationship to adherence to or apostasy from a holy covenant, but in terms of the prudent and imprudent use of religion as a moral-political force for the control of the vulgar. In this respect, Spinoza's treatment of the Levites is of particular importance because it reveals what he believed to be the cause of political decline.[230]

In an interesting spin on Luther's notion that the point of the Law is to condemn and that Scripture mandates a priesthood of all believers, Spinoza marked the decline of Israel as occurring from the very first giving of the Law and the establishment of the Levitical priesthood. Basing his argument on Ezekiel 20:25 (in Spinoza's text, "*I have also given them statutes that were not good and rights they did not live by, so that I have defiled them through their gifts, by sending back every opening of the womb*—that is, the firstborn—*that I might destroy them, that they might know that I am Jehovah*"[231]), Spinoza asserted that both the Law and the establishment of the Levites as the priestly class were punishments for the Israelites' apostasy committed in worshipping the golden calf. For "it is to be noted that the first intent was to hand over the whole sacred service to the firstborn, not to the Levites (see Numbers 8:17); but after everyone except the Levites prayed to the calf, the firstborn were repudiated and defiled, and the Levites chosen in their place (Deuteronomy 10:8); this change, the more I consider it, compels me to break out in the words of Tacitus: God's cares at that time were not

228 Ibid., 17.4.9.

229 Ibid., 17.5.2–6.

230 On the importance of Spinoza's treatment of the Levites see Smith, *Spinoza, Liberalism, and the Question of Jewish Identity*, pp. 149–151.

231 Spinoza, *Theologico-Political Treatise*, 17.12.32.

for their security, but for vengeance."[232] If there had not been this separate priestly class, but priestly functions had been given to the firstborn of all in every tribe, "right and honor would have been equal for all the tribes, and everything would have gone on very securely. For who would have wanted to violate the sacred right of his blood-relatives? Who would prefer anything else but to feed his blood-relatives—brothers and parents—on the basis of religious piety? Than to be taught by them the interpretation of the laws? And, finally, than to await from them the divine answers?"[233]

This version of the priesthood of all believers was not to be, however. Instead, the priesthood was held by an hereditary tribal class that retained its power through the alleged power of prophecy, even in the times of the kings, as evidenced by the ability of the prophet Samuel to "transfer the right to rule [from Saul] to David because of one offense." Therefore the kings "had an imperium within the imperium, and ruled precariously."[234] The same situation occurred in the early Church, since Christianity grew up as an entity independent of the Roman Empire, "with the disapproval of those who held the imperium and whose subjects they were." As a result, churchmen were accustomed to carrying on their "sacred duties, and ordering and decreeing everything on their own, without taking any account of the imperium."[235] This allowed for continued conflict between Church and state, and after the Reformation, between Church and church.

The lesson that Spinoza drew from these considerations was threefold: the political power, the imperium, must control religion completely (hence, no separate priestly class can be allowed); religion itself must be defined entirely by the morality that serves political order (so that spiritual intrusions by alleged prophets cannot disturb the political order); and finally, that the best or original political condition is the one in which political and religious power are united in the many as sovereign.[236] In Spinoza's words, "Religion receives the force of right solely from the decree of those who have the right to command," and "Religious worship and the exercise of piety has to be accommodated to the peace and utility of the Republic and, consequently, be determined solely by the highest powers—who thus have to be its interpreters as well."[237] Of course, the entirety of Spinoza's exegesis was bent on providing the sovereign power with an accommodating method of scriptural interpretation.

What keeps the sovereign—even and especially the sovereign power of the many in a democracy—from becoming tyrannical? Or further, since there are obviously a multiplicity of kings in Spinoza's Europe, what keeps the warring religious factions *within* states from simply becoming the warring religious factions *among* states?

---

232 Ibid., 17.12.33.

233 Ibid., 17.12.39.

234 Ibid., 17.12.54.

235 Ibid., 19.3.3.

236 This was a lesson that Spinoza wished to be heeded not only in general, but in the Netherlands in particular. See Michael Rosenthal, "Why Spinoza Chose the Hebrews: The Exemplary Function of Prophecy in the *Theological-Political Treatise*," *History of Political Thought* 18 (1997): 207–241, reprinted in Lloyd, ed., *Spinoza: Critical Assessments, Volume III*, pp. 245–279, especially pp. 262–268.

237 Spinoza, *Theologico-Political Treatise*, 19.1.1–2.

Spinoza found the answer to both in the fundamental limitation of political sovereignty, the practical inability to control the minds of its subjects. In the state of nature, each has the absolute right to think and act as he pleases. The right to think as one pleases is rooted in the particular "mental cast" of each individual, his particular desires, imagination, and opinions, and (following Descartes) "each deems that he alone knows everything. . . ." The right to think as one pleases, of course, leads to the right to act as one pleases. But of course, this right leads to anarchy, and hence would soon bring violent death in the state of nature. Therefore, each individual gives up the right to *act* as he pleases when entering civil society, but not the right to *think* as he pleases—and this, only because there is no practical way to control completely the thought of others, either by political power or by reason.

This focus on acting, or works, exactly duplicated Spinoza's earlier assertion that the result of exegesis of the Bible shows that Scripture teaches no doctrine but obedience, that all else must be considered *adiaphora* and hence merely a private affair. Serious theological differences are reduced to mere reflections of what moves each individual, very personally and particularly, to be moral. As theological differences become mere personal preferences, they will cease upsetting international peace just as they ceased upsetting national peace.

Even more deeply and personally, Spinoza's theological-political solution also provided philosophy itself with peace and protection, for "the best republic grants the same freedom of philosophizing to each which we have shown faith grants to each."[238] It does so—interestingly enough—by granting that all are equally philosophers regardless of the caliber of their opinions, a grant made in accordance with the ineradicable human belief (again, noted by Descartes) that "each deems that he alone knows everything. . . ."

The prudent state duplicates the state of nature in regard to thought, for "in the natural state, reason has no more right than appetite,"[239] even while it denies the state of nature in regard to actions. Both the good state and the good religion (and since the state entirely defines religion, there is no difference) allow the greatest latitude in thought and speech, and judge individuals *only* insofar as they are peaceable, that is, insofar as they act in accordance with the state's moral-legal mandates. Again, for Spinoza, the best regime is democratic, where the many are sovereign, but as it must be clear by now, this precedence does not issue from any esteem for the majority of mankind, whom Spinoza considers ineradicably vulgar and unphilosophic.

Spinoza's affirmation of democracy is rooted in a kind of flattery of the many, for given that "each deems that he alone knows everything," liberal democracy flatters "each" with the right to think about the highest things—philosophy and theology—just as he pleases, provided he allows the same right to all others. The flattery thereby leads to the protection of the truly philosophic, like Spinoza; or to put it in other terms, democracy eliminates persecution by eliminating the distinction between orthodoxy and heterodoxy, wisdom and foolishness. Those who are highest on the

238 Ibid., 20.4.15.

239 Ibid., 19.1.7.

Averroistic hierarchy, the philosophers, are protected from those who are lowest, the vulgar, by the public pretence that both philosophy and theology have been democratized. Yet, ironically, Spinoza takes away with one hand what he offers with the other, by making the analysis of Scripture possible only to the highly educated, the elite exegetes who are well versed in the original languages, history, literary forms, etc. To keep the elite from turning against the philosophers, Spinoza fashions an exegetical method that produces the conclusions that reduce Scripture to a merely moral prop for civil order, one that allows the greatest freedom for philosophy. In fact, since Spinoza's philosophy ultimately defines the method, then the applied method serves to reaffirm Spinoza's philosophy even without the exegete's own knowledge or consent. Exegetes thereby confirm Spinoza's rational religion, and disseminate it to the multitude. To recall Yovel's important insight, the goal of Spinoza's work was "to establish mental and institutional mechanisms that will transform the imagination [of the multitude] into an external imitation of reason, using state power and a purified popular religion as vehicles of a semirational civilizing process. . . . Purified religion and the rationalized state are thus designed to engender in the multitude the same conduct that the rational model requires.[240]

Spinoza thereby bequeathed to the West and the modern liberal democratic state its founding charter, complete with the appropriate religion, one that allows for, and even encourages, the greatest diversity of opinions about God and the soul, even while it narrows the public focus on religion to moral rectitude. As we have seen in great detail, the founding charter was itself an achievement of Spinoza's exegetical method. Or, as Martin Yaffe succinctly states, the central lesson of Spinoza's *Tractatus* could be summed up as an apology for "liberal religion (including modern-scientific biblical criticism) and liberal democracy,"[241] the former being the handmaid of the latter.

Summary and Conclusion

As we have seen, Spinoza continued the Marsilian-Machiavellian assessment of religion as being born from fear and ignorance, but nourished by political figures or founders who realized its wonderful utility for controlling the masses. He also, with Descartes and Hobbes, affirmed a new, purely secular cosmos, one that stood in direct contradiction to the biblical cosmos, and with Hobbes, used this secular cosmology as the foundation of his biblical criticism.

Although both Hobbes and Spinoza politicized Scripture, Hobbes's aim was to affirm a kind of divine right monarchy marked by political absolutism, while Spinoza's aim was seemingly the opposite, to ground something like liberal democracy and complete religious toleration. One might say that Hobbes devised the exegesis that would retroactively support Henry VIII and the Act of Supremacy, while Spinoza offered an exegesis that would proactively support and radicalize the famously liberal govern-

240 Yovel, *Spinoza and Other Heretics: The Marrano of Reason*, p. 130.

241 Spinoza, *Theologico-Political Treatise*, "Glossary," p. 254.

ment of the Netherlands.[242] But while this assessment is true, dwelling on the obvious surface differences would prevent one from seeing more deeply into both their similarities and their differences.

What Hobbes achieved by exclusion of the Divine, Spinoza got by inclusion. In making God inaccessible to reason because he is utterly incomprehensible, Hobbes put forth no natural theology. Therefore, he made the domain of theology revelation alone, and so was able to use a doctrine of *sola scriptura* to ensure that the sovereign was *the* interpreter of Scripture. Since the sovereign was the interpreter, he could use any doctrines derived from Scripture, no matter how speculative or practical, that would support his regime. Although Hobbes suggested a thin, moral theism (the Least Common Denomination), the thrust of his argument supported *cuius regio, eius religio*, whatever that *religio* might happen to be. Consequently, he made theological room for all denominations (even while remaining implacably hostile to Catholicism since it could never be brought under political rein).

As a result, Hobbes permitted a modified heaven and hell; allowed prophecy even while constraining it to the sovereign as chief prophet; used, rather than eliminated, miracles; rooted the determination of the canon in the sovereign, rather than calling the canon entirely into question; and gave the sovereign absolute power to condemn not only any theological doctrine but also any philosophical *and* scientific arguments that could disturb the peace or call his sovereignty into question. Hobbes's argument, and hence his exegesis of Scripture, was *entirely* political, and its implied motto was "peace at *any* cost."

Rather than exclude God, Spinoza identified Him with nature. Since nature was thoroughly understood by human reason—in principle, if not yet in detail—then there was no revelation higher than that provided by mathematical-mechanical science. For Spinoza, a kind of divinization comes through science, or more exactly, from the third kind of knowledge, and he was therefore unwilling to permit Scripture to encroach upon this highest, divinelike knowledge, even for the sake of civil peace.

As a result, Spinoza's exegetical aim was not simply to subordinate revelation to the political sovereign (leaving revelation more or less intact), but to subordinate revelation to reason as he understood it. The difference manifests itself throughout Spinoza's exegesis. Spinoza did not merely suggest a thin moral theism to a political sovereign as one possible option; he demanded it of the biblical text itself, and hence drove out all miracles, all prophecy, all notions of heaven and hell, all doctrinal theology through his exegetical method. Consequently, Spinoza produced a great shift, perhaps *the* great shift in the modern politicization of Scripture, from a politicized exegesis in support of *cuius regio, eius religio*, to a politicized exegesis in support of liberal democracy.

In support of this aim, Spinoza was quite adamant in introducing a systematic skepticism of the claims, and hence of the text, of revelation. Whereas Hobbes called the authorship and authority of books into question only insofar as it would allow him to place the power of putting the determination of the canon and interpretation

242 See Smith, *Spinoza, Liberalism, and the Question of Jewish Identity*, Ch. 2.

of the text in the hands of the sovereign, Spinoza attacked the very notions of authorship, authority, and canon. Hobbes wanted to use the Bible as a political tool; Spinoza wanted to ensure that it could never become a political tool again *except* insofar as it provided imaginative moral stories for the weak-minded, the vulgar, the unenlightened. This exception is no small thing, because it meant that exegesis was to become an exercise of the enlightened, the scientific elite, who (following Spinoza) simultaneously gutted Scripture of all claims to revelatory truth *and* exaggerated and redefined the alleged moral core. In general, that redefinition duplicated Spinoza's political liberalism—emphasizing salvation by peaceableness (works) and doctrinal tolerance (either through indifference or complete privatization, both the handiwork of Spinoza).

As even a casual look at the next centuries of scriptural scholarship attests, the philosophic core driving the exegetical project will change, from Spinozan, to Lockean, Hegelian, Marxist, Heideggerian, and so on. (The bewildering variety of modern philosophies after Spinoza raises an obvious but often overlooked difficulty for the peculiarly modern view, which has its source in Spinoza, that religion is marked by intractable diversity precisely because it is irrational; as it turns out, human philosophic rationality is marked by the same intractable diversity.) Whatever the philosophical variety, the authority of exegesis will reside, not in the political sovereign, but in the enlightened philosophy that informs exegesis. Each in turn will provide yet another variation of Spinoza's hermeneutic of condescension. But this is also a hermeneutic of self-divinization. Therefore, each will invest his philosophy with all the religious certainty and zeal originally invested by Spinoza in his particular philosophy, and each will exhibit the same unshakable faith and enthusiasm in the spread of its gospel and the progressive divinization of humanity. This divinization soon enough focuses on the process rather than the goal. History itself becomes a kind of god, and hence secular political history becomes salvation history.

In one way it is misleading to tag Spinoza as the father of modern scriptural scholarship, as if he were the singular source. Not only was he obviously dependent upon Hobbes, but even more, he was part of a much larger, quite productive radical circle in the Netherlands, many of whom had completely rejected the authority of the Bible, or even more telling, were engaged in ideological reconstruction of it. If the ideas of Uriel da Costa, Juan de Prado, Isaac La Peyrère, Johannes and Adriaen Koerbagh, and Lodewijk Meyer in regard to Scripture sound like they came out of eighteenth-century France or nineteenth-century Germany, it is because of the influence of the radical Enlightenment that had its birth in seventeenth-century Netherlands. Therefore, Spinoza must share his honorific paternity with this larger circle.

A second obvious but often overlooked point. If the origins of the modern critical methods can be traced to a significant extent to the radical Enlightenment in the Netherlands, then one must admit that religious persecution was the context for the deconstruction and reconstruction of the biblical text by Spinoza and his circle. To put it in its most poignant form, just as gross hypocrisy in the papacy and ecclesiastical hierarchy was the context for Machiavelli's treatment of religion as essentially a mask for political power, so also the persecution of the Jews was the context for Spinoza's systematic reduction of the biblical text to feckless moral cheerleader. If orthodox

Christians would today lament the ill effects of the modern critical scriptural scholarship, let them lament the causes as well.

That having been said, it is fair to demand that Spinoza's arguments must stand or fall on their own merits, after one has examined his critical methods in light of his assumptions and aims. It should by now be clear that his exegetical methods were determined by his adherence to a pantheistic form of mathematical-mechanical determinism *and* Spinoza's political goals. The elimination of the miraculous in the text was determined by the elimination of contingency from the universe and the identification of God with nature (itself acting according to mathematical-mechanical laws). The turn from the truth of revelation to the character of the prophets was justified because any mode of knowledge less than the mathematical-mechanical philosophy must be merely the imaginative, subjective projections of the subrational. The claim that Scripture may safely be reduced to a merely moral core was rooted in Spinoza's dour assessment of intellectual capacities of the passion-filled, irrational mob, which could not possibly grasp the mathematical-mechanical philosophy. The setting up of endless tasks that face the exegete before anything of doctrinal certainty can be affirmed from Scripture, was a clever way to discharge the energy of those who would previously go to battle over different doctrinal interpretations. Ingeniously, it allowed Spinoza simultaneously to affirm *sola scriptura* and render it harmless.

Pointing all this out does not condemn any and every method routinely used among modern scriptural scholars if it bears any resemblance to those used by Spinoza. For example, although Spinoza's redaction criticism in regard to Ezra functioned as a way to place endless obstacles in front of exegetes and hence dissipate religious passions that could flame into war, that does not mean that the separation of editorial layers is always suspect and politically motivated. But it might warn us that when such criticism becomes an end in itself, endless academic debates about editorial layers and editorial identity have exactly the effect Spinoza desired. Thus, while we should avoid an uncritical rejection of modern historical-critical methods, given this analysis of Spinoza's assumptions and motivations, we should be equally wary of uncritical acceptance. Because Spinoza's assumptions so thoroughly determine his method of approaching Scripture, it is best to conclude with a critical inquiry into the assumptions concerning reason and science.

It is essential to remember that Spinoza held a severely restricted view of reason, that is, a view of reason restricted to one of its modes, mathematical reason. This restricted account of reason (and hence science) stands or falls on the reductionist mathematical-mechanical account of nature upon which it was built, and this restricted view of nature may itself be unreasonable.

If nature cannot be simply identified with mathematical concepts, but instead the order of nature is ultimately supramathematical, then the inherent intelligibility of nature exceeds the mathematical mode of human reason (even while it condescends to it). Indeed, if the order of nature *both* exceeds human reason *and* condescends to it (so that even while mathematical concepts do not constitute reality, such concepts are instrumentally and strangely enough effective and illuminating of reality), then one could hardly imagine a stronger case for divine design by a God whose wisdom far exceeds ours. If such is the case, we cannot follow Descartes and Spinoza in defining nature essentially according to those mathematical concepts that happen to be most clear and certain to us; the *ordo essendi* would not essentially conform to the most certain mode of the human *ordo cognoscendi*. In saying this, one need not deny that mathematics is an effective intellectual tool for inquiring into nature, nor deny that mechanism has served as an effective model for science. One must, however, question the identity of the tool and the model with nature itself.[243]

To put it in more biblical terms, if the order and complexity of nature are not *essentially* mathematical and mechanical, but the mathematical and mechanical modes of reason are merely effective *models* of scientific investigation, then Spinoza's system would manifest the most absurd and self-blinding type of pride and idolatry that deforms nature to fit what is most easily understood by human reason, and then gives it divine sanction by divinizing nature accordingly. Such idolatry would obscure the fundamental truth that the Creator of nature exceeds the creature, not just in power but in wisdom.

To put it in quasi-biblical terms, if the *logos* of nature is not reducible to the *logos* of the human mathematical mode of reasoning, then Spinoza's simple identity of the mathematical-mechanical model of science and God's *Logos* would be fundamentally flawed. Moreover, if God's *Logos* as revealed in nature exceeds what is most clear and certain to the *logos* of the human mathematical mode of reasoning, then nothing prevents the obvious possibility that God's *Logos* itself exceeds what it condescends to reveal of itself in creation. Nothing else is needed to open the human *logos* to the possibility of the revelation of supernatural truth about and by the Divine *Logos*.

This leads to a rather startling conclusion. As strange as it may sound to professional biblical scholars in academia, the fundamental issue deciding the caliber of Spinoza's biblical hermeneutics (and hence what he has bequeathed to his progeny as one of the fathers of modern biblical criticism) is the accuracy and adequacy of Spinoza's account of reason and nature. To state it another way, from above rather than from below, a single confirmed miracle would call into question a significant part of the entire historical-critical project *if* its recognition could break the tight circle of the "positivist" mind initiated by Descartes and perfected by Spinoza. The positivist mind rejects both the miraculous and the possibility that the order of nature both condescends to and exceeds the grasp of human reasoning power. This rejection is based not on a successful, complete understanding and technical mastery of nature, but on its reflections upon its partial successes, the promise of endless future successes, and finally and most importantly, Cartesian self-reflection on its own powers.

Such positivism creates a miracle-proof mindset that has direct bearing on the effect of Spinozism on scriptural scholarship. As Leo Strauss noted, "The authority of Scripture was shaken prior to all historical and philological criticism, but also prior to all metaphysics, through the establishment of the positive mind, through the disen-

243 For an extended analysis of these points see Benjamin Wiker and Jonathan Witt, *A Meaningful World: How the Arts and Sciences Reveal the Genius of Nature* (Downers Grove, IL: InterVarsity Press, 2006).

chantment of the world and through the self-awareness of the disenchanting mind." Spinoza's "critique is built on denial of the possibility of miracles on the conviction that he can demonstrate the impossibility of miracles." But that demonstration would entail that complete intellectual and technical mastery of nature was not only possible but actual. This Spinoza could not do, except by way of an argument that presented the promise of its completion as metaphysical certainty. That confusion of promise with certain completion is what constitutes the positivist mind. The rejection of the possibility of the miraculous is the result of a kind of Cartesian self-absorption through continual reflection on its own powers. In Strauss's words, "it is not the advancing positive method, proceeding from point to point, but only the reflection of the positive mind on itself, the recognition by the positive mind that it represents a progress beyond the previously prevailing form of consciousness (a finding that first takes the form of the crude antithesis between superstition, prejudice, ignorance, barbarism, benightedness on the one hand, and reason, freedom, culture, enlightenment on the other) which creates a position impregnable to proof by miracles."[244] This reflection of the positivist mind upon itself is perfectly ensconced in the historical-critical demarcation by modern scriptural scholars of the history of scriptural scholarship into precritical and critical. To see why, one must follow the unfolding of the positivist mind, whose effect on the history of scriptural scholarship will be decisive.

244 Strauss, *Spinoza's Critique of Religion*, p. 136.

CHAPTER 10

THE AMBIGUOUS RICHARD SIMON

The Ambiguous Richard Simon

To understand the shape and direction of biblical studies in the eighteenth century, insofar as they lead to more determinate formulations of the historical-critical method, is largely to follow the fallout of Hobbes and Spinoza. As one wades through the literature, one finds either radicalizations of these thinkers or vehement attacks upon them (especially the latter).

That does not mean that the vast literature is easily sorted out between the two sides, conservatives and radicals. The difficulty is that those attacking Hobbes and Spinoza fall into four fairly distinct species. The first are the conservatives, those who vilify them from the standpoint of defending orthodoxy and the sanctity of Holy Writ, and who make no concessions to the criticisms and new methods of Hobbes and Spinoza. The second are those who take the criticisms and new methods seriously, incorporate what they deem worthy, and launch a counteroffensive that is a mixture of old and new. This second group could justly be called the liberal wing, and they were animated, at least to all appearances, by a sincere desire to defend the faith and the Bible. They were equally animated by a friendliness, if not zeal, for the new mathematical-mechanical philosophy. Third, and most difficult to catch, are those who, under threat of persecution (which could be quite severe at this point, even in the Netherlands), spread Hobbesianism and Spinozism *under the guise* of an assault on the very doctrines they wished to spread. And finally, we have the openly radical, who make no concessions to orthodoxy except their own anonymity, publishing their attacks through clandestine channels.

In this chapter, we examine Richard Simon as representative of the second group—or possibly the third. In the enthusiastic Jean Steinmann's words, Simon was "the greatest biblical critic of ancient France. His importance equals that of Erasmus of Rotterdam or Baruch Spinoza. . . . From the Renaissance to the end of the nineteenth century his genius dominates biblical exegesis."[1] Yet he was, as Francis Nichols rightly

1 Jean Steinmann, *Richard Simon et les origins de l'exégèse biblique* (Paris: Desclée de Brouwer, 1960), p. 7. Translated and quoted in Nichols, "Richard Simon, Faith and Modernity," in Francis Nichols, ed., *Christianity and the Stranger* (Atlanta, GA: Scholars Press, 1995), pp. 115–168, quote on p. 117.

states, "a virtual pariah in his own age and remains in many ways a conundrum to this very day."[2]

Using Spinoza Against Sola Scriptura

Richard Simon (1638–1712) is yet another figure often called a father of modern biblical scholarship, or more accurately, the father of modern Old Testament study,[3] a man who "definitively marked a point of no-return in biblical criticism."[4] The honor is based upon his *Histoire critique du Vieux Testament* (hereafter *Histoire*), published in 1678, less than a decade after the publication of Spinoza's *Tractatus*.[5] As Simon made clear in his Preface, Spinoza was the occasion for his writing the *Histoire*. Simon claimed that he would "easily answer all the false and pernicious consequences drawn by Spinosa," who "has shewn his ignorance, or rather malice in crying down the Authority of the Pentateuch."[6]

But it is an open question whether Simon actually conceded more than he overthrew, and hence inadvertently did more to advance Spinoza than many an outright defender of Spinozism. Noted deist Anthony Collins later captured this paradox, calling Simon the scholar "who has labour'd so much to prove the uncertainty of Scripture."[7] Much of this labor was spent in incorporating, even strengthening, the Spinozan criticisms that Simon considered of merit but for a quite un-Spinozan purpose: Simon (a French Catholic priest of the Congregation of the Oratory) thought he could undermine the Protestant position of *sola scriptura* by demonstrating that these

2 Nichols, "Richard Simon, Faith and Modernity," p. 117.

3 Although the attribution is nearly universal, one suspects, given the paucity of studies of Simon, that (in the words of Justin Champion) "Simon is perhaps more commonly referred to than actually read. Except for a few important works, there have been few major studies of Simon's life and works." Justin Champion, "Pere Richard Simon and English Biblical Criticism, 1680–1700," in James Force and David Katz, *Everything Connects: In Conference with Richard Popkin* (Leiden: E. J. Brill, 1999), pp. 39–61, citation from p. 41.

4 Pierre Gibert, "The Catholic Counterpart to the Protestant Orthodoxy," in Magne Sæbø, ed., *Hebrew Bible/Old Testament: The History of Its Interpretation*: Vol. II, *From the Renaissance to the Enlightenment* (Göttingen: Vandenhoeck & Ruprecht, 2008), Ch. 21, pp. 758–773, quote on p. 773. See also in the same volume John Rogerson, "Early Old Testament Critics in the Roman Catholic Church—Focusing on the Pentateuch," pp. 837–850 (on Simon, pp. 838–843).

5 We will use the 1682 English translation of *A Critical History of the Old Testament* done by "a Person of Quality," printed by Walter Davis, and reprinted by Classic Reprints No. 61 (Pensacola, FL: Vance Publications, 2002). This and other English editions had been preceded by the French edition's arrival on English shores. Champion, "Pere Richard Simon and English Biblical Criticism, 1680–1700," pp. 43, 47–48.

6 Simon, *A Critical History of the Old Testament,* Author's Preface, p. iii. Preface pages are unnumbered in text. To avoid confusion, we have used lower case Roman numerals, beginning from the first page of the Preface.

7 Quoted in Jonathan Israel, *Radical Enlightenment: Philosophy and the Making of Modernity 1650–1750* (Oxford: Oxford University Press, 2001), p. 451.

uncertainties demanded recourse to an interpreting magisterium, thereby affirming the Catholic position of the necessity of both Tradition and Scripture.[8]

As Simon states in the Preface to his *Histoire*, the "great alterations . . . to the Copies of the Bible since the first Originals have been lost, utterly destroy the Protestant and Socinians[9] Principle, who consult onely these same Copies of the Bible as we at present have them." Simon happily admitted that there are "so many alterations" over the years, and that these "depended upon the pleasure of Transcribers" who "took the liberty of adding and leaving out certain letters according as they thought fit," even though "the sense of the Text often depends upon these letters," and to all this must be added "the uncertainty of the Hebrew Grammar." All this and more makes it clear that "it is almost impossible to translate the Holy Scripture," thereby making nonsense of "Those Protestants . . . who affirm that the Scripture is plain of it self," and who were "obliged to suppose it plain and sufficient for the establishing the truth of Faith without any Tradition." And so, "If the truth of Religion remain'd not in the Church, it would be unsafe to search for it at present in Books [i.e., the various books of the Bible]," consequently, "if we join not Tradition with the Scripture, we can hardly affirm any thing for certain in Religion."[10]

Simon thereby duplicated the argument by La Peyrère (although put to quite different use) that the Scriptures as received are not the original, but multilayered copies put together by later scribes. The duplication was not accidental, given that Simon was a friend of La Peyrère (getting to know him quite well when the latter joined the Oratorians as a lay member) and knew his work quite thoroughly. While picking up on the critical elements (including the denial of Mosaic authorship), Simon left behind La Peyrère's pre-Adamite and messianic arguments. By all accounts, even though Simon borrowed from La Peyrère, Simon was a far better scholar, and that made what he borrowed all the more powerful.[11]

Simon's overall plan was, in a sense, ingenious. While he bent his labors to attacking the threat of Spinozism, Simon also used Spinoza's multiplication of textual problems and even his exegetical methods to fight Protestantism by undermining *sola scriptura*. Simon thus staked out a middle position in the first fallout of Spinoza's *Tractatus*, but one that presented an ominous either/or. Although one must "take heed of multiplying these [textual] additions or corrections, as Spinosa and some others have very injudiciously done," yet "we ought not absolutely to deny them, or too subtilly or nonsensically explain them, for these additions [residing in the Church's *traditio*] are of the same Authority as the rest of the Scripture. . . ." If this delicate balance

8 Ibid., p. 450. See also Douglas Knight, *Rediscovering the Traditions of Israel: The Development of the Traditio-Historical Research of the Old Testament, with Special Consideration of Scandinavian Contributions*, revised ed. (Missoula, MT: Scholars Press, 1975), pp. 39–51.

9 While Socinians rejected the Trinity, they did so on the basis of *sola scriptura*.

10 Simon, *A Critical History of the Old Testament*, Author's Preface, pp. viii–ix.

11 See Richard Popkin, *Isaac La Peyrère (1596–1676): His Life, Work and Influence* (Leiden: E. J. Brill, 1987), pp. 87–88.

was not maintained, "we must confess the whole [Bible] not to be equally Divine and Canonical. . . ."[12]

Whatever Simon's intentions, his position represented a fundamental break with the Catholic orthodoxy he wished to defend. It was not simply the denial of Mosaic authorship, but his rejection of the *traditio*'s attempt to explain the alleged textual imperfections by other means. As it developed, the Catholic position in regard to Scripture's seeming imperfections was that what seemed disunited and imperfect, proved upon humble, faithful, and prayerful reading—guided by the Holy Spirit and Tradition—to be whole and harmonious, containing hidden perfections under seeming imperfections.[13] Various ways arose to explain apparent imperfections: exegetes had recourse to a complex account of divine accommodation, to literal and spiritual senses, and even to the notion of purposely-placed divine stumbling blocks in the text to trip up the prideful and draw the humble to closer examination. Against this, Simon accepted the surface incongruities at face value—even rejoiced in them—so that the need for *traditio* became absolute.

In some respects, Simon's tactic worked. The angst engendered in Protestants by Simon's work was well expressed by John Evelyn in a March 19, 1682, letter to the bishop of Oxford, John Fell.[14] Simon's *Histoire* posed "great danger and fatal consequences" precisely because it "exposes not only the Protestants and the whole Reformed Churches abroad, but . . . the Church of England at home, which with them acknowledges the Holy Scriptures alone to be the canon and rule of faith."[15] For Evelyn, Simon was such a danger precisely because the *Histoire* was both excruciatingly thorough and exceedingly scholarly, and its very thoroughness made it almost unanswerable.[16] In Richard Popkin's apt words, "Simon, with a deft touch and with incredible erudition, drowned his opponents in learning and in a sea of problems."[17] Since textual and historical criticism only proved ever more thoroughly to undermine Scripture, criticism by itself, independent of *traditio*, could not substantiate *sola scriptura*. As a sign of his effectiveness, most of the forty or so works written against Simon during the late seventeenth and eighteenth centuries were by Protestants.[18]

12 Simon, *A Critical History of the Old Testament,* Author's Preface, p. iv.

13 See David Dungan, *A History of the Synoptic Problem: The Canon, the Text, the Composition, and the Interpretation of the Gospels* (New York: Doubleday, 1999), especially Chs. 7–10, and Stephen Benin, *The Footprints of God: Divine Accommodation in Jewish and Christian Thought* (Albany, NY: SUNY Press, 1993).

14 John Evelyn (1620–1706) was a prominent Anglican figure, a royalist, and with Robert Boyle and others one of the founding lights of the Royal Society. John Fell (1625–1686) was another royalist, a scholar of St. Cyprian, a Tory who imposed Anglican orthodoxy at Oxford University after 1660, and expelled John Locke from study at Christ Church.

15 Quoted in Champion, "Pere Richard Simon and English Biblical Criticism, 1680–1700," p. 43.

16 On this point, see Gerald Reedy, S.J., *The Bible and Reason: Anglicans and Scripture in Late Seventeenth-Century England* (Philadelphia, PA: University of Pennsylvania Press, 1985), pp. 108–113.

17 Richard Popkin, "Bible Criticism and Social Science," in Robert Cohen and Marx Wartofsky, eds., *Methodological and Historical Essays in the Natural and Social Sciences* (Dordrecht, Holland: D. Reidel, 1974), p. 349.

18 Nichols, "Richard Simon, Faith and Modernity," p. 136.

Backfiring Against Traditio

But Simon's mode of affirming the *traditio* was equally problematic. Although he affirmed *traditio* loud and long, Simon offered very little to substantiate his view of it, so that *traditio* acted more like an arbitrary Hobbesian authority settling intractable disputes than a divinely guided shepherd leading its flock into the deeper mysteries of God's Word. Even more obviously problematic, drowning his opponents "in a sea of problems" helped to drag his own party under the waters as well, since in undermining the certainty of Scripture, Simon was also destroying *traditio*'s support of its authority and mission as affirmed from Scripture.

Given all this, it is not altogether surprising that the reward for Simon's labors was, more often than not, to be classed *with* Spinoza as a pernicious subversive, all the more dangerous than Spinoza for hiding his secret Spinozism under a veil of Catholic orthodoxy. This was indeed the charge, for example, made by Jean Le Clerc in his *Sentiments de quelques théologiens de Hollande* (1685), a doubly ironic charge, given that Le Clerc was suspected by some of the same type of subterfuge.[19] Even more dangerous for Simon was the charge of Bishop Bossuet (Jacques Bénigne Bossuet, 1627–1704), notable enemy of Protestants, who upon reading prepublication excerpts, pronounced the *Histoire* "a mass of impieties and a rampart of freethinking." Bossuet would later attack Simon's views in his *Défense de la Tradition et des Saints Pères*. In it, he put his finger on a most serious problem: Simon claimed to undermine *sola scriptura* in the name of Tradition, but he also turned against the Church Fathers, especially St. Augustine, in his exegetical positions. Was he not therefore undermining both Scripture and *traditio*? If so, was not Simon therefore a wolf in shepherd's clothing? "We must not abandon the teaching of the Church Fathers and the tradition of the Church to the new critics any longer," warned Bossuet.

> If it were only heretics who rose up against such a holy authority, we would fear the seduction less, since we know their error. But when Catholics and priests, priests, I say, and I say it with sadness, enter into their sentiment and raise up in the Church the same standard of rebellion against the Church Fathers; when they take the part of innovators against the Church under innocent appearance, then we must fear that the faithful, having been deceived, might say like the Jews of old when the false Alcimus insinuated himself among them: 'A priest of the line of Aaron . . . has come . . . and will not do us any wrong' (1 Maccabees 7:14). . . .'"[20]

Bossuet, not about to let this happen, sounded the alarm, engaging in a life-long struggle against Simon. As a result of this quickly kindled animosity, nearly the entire

19 Israel, *Radical Enlightenment: Philosophy and the Making of Modernity 1650–1750*, pp. 452–453.

20 Quoted in Nichols, "Richard Simon, Faith and Modernity," p. 155.

first print run in Paris was "pulped" by the churchmen of the Church that Simon was so curiously trying to defend. Simon himself was expelled from the Oratory.[21]

Simon, John Locke, and Liberalism in England

A few copies of the *Histoire* escaped to England and Amsterdam (and eventually, evading the censors, various editions found their way back to France).[22] The man responsible for bringing it into England was Henri Justel (1620–1693). Given the effect of Simon in England, some attention to Justel is warranted. Justel believed that Simon's work—if it were recast by a Protestant—would actually help the Protestant cause. He wrote to the great philosopher and mathematician Leibniz in July of 1677 (about a year before publication in French) that:

> Soon we will have a historical critique of the books of the Bible where there will be many bold assertions. The author maintains that the Canon of Scripture was not settled until after the Exile, and that the Sanhedrin was able to add and remove whatever it wanted from Scripture, which he believes to have been maltreated just like any other book. There are many things of that nature which seem dreadful to me. However, this work will be good and useful.[23]

Justel knew of Simon's work prior to publication and had an ongoing correspondence with him between 1672 and 1686. Justel was connected to John Locke as well, meeting frequently with Locke while the latter was in France between 1675 and 1679. This connection between Simon and Locke would prove critical in the development of modern scriptural scholarship, so it is necessary to illuminate their relationship.

Locke himself was intensely interested in getting a copy of the *Histoire*, and rather impatiently implored Justel to secure him one. Whether it was through Justel or another, Locke had a copy by 1681 and obtained other editions of the *Histoire* as well, reading Simon's work carefully, as evidenced by his notes on the text.[24]

It is both intriguing and illuminating to glance at the wider context of this Simon-Justel-Locke connection. Since the end of the Thirty Years' War (1648) France had risen to be Europe's most powerful nation, first under the guidance of Cardinal

---

21 On the suppression of Simon in France see especially Patrick Lambe, "Biblical Criticism and Censorship in *Ancien Régime* France: The Case of Richard Simon," *Harvard Theological Review* 78:1–2 (1985): 149–177. In Bossuet's later words, "I have never opened one of his [Simon's] books without presently discerning a hidden design to undermine the foundations of religion." From Bossuet's correspondence, quoted in Lambe, pp. 167–168.

22 It seems that fifteen or twenty copies survived, one of which found its way to England; one of the copies that appeared in Amsterdam was a manuscript copy full of errors and omissions, but a copy corrected by a Paris edition was printed four years later in 1685. "Once in the hands of the Dutch printers, the book was unstoppable and ran into many editions." Ibid., p. 158.

23 Ibid., p. 156.

24 See Champion, "Pere Richard Simon and English Biblical Criticism, 1680–1700," on Justel and Locke, pp. 44–47.

Richelieu (1624–1642), then Cardinal Mazarin (1642–1661), and finally, under the rule of the magnificent Louis XIV (1661–1715). To the rest of Europe, Louis XIV represented a union of powerful absolute monarchy and Roman Catholicism, although it is more accurate to say Gallican Catholicism, since the Church was effectively under control of the French state.

That same Bishop Bossuet who was so horrified by Simon's *Histoire* was also the great apologist for divine right, absolute (but not arbitrary) monarchy, using Scripture as the foundation of his argument in his *Politics Drawn from the Very Words of Holy Scripture*. Bossuet was also the author of the famous Four Gallican Articles (1682) that denied the pope had dominion over temporal affairs, affirmed the authority of general councils over the pope, declared the ancient liberties of the Gallican Church inviolable, and asserted that the judgments of popes are reformable by councils. Marsilius could not have asked for more. In the great, long-standing Church and state controversies stretching back to the Middle Ages, Bossuet and seventeenth-century France came down firmly on the side of the national monarch. This same Bossuet did all he could to destroy the French Protestants, the so-called Huguenots, and happily approved the 1685 Revocation of the Edict of Nantes, the edict that had been adopted by Henry IV in 1598 to end the French civil-religious wars by granting rights to the Huguenots.

Henri Justel was a Huguenot, but one who leaned more toward the new scientific circles than toward Calvinism.[25] Following his father, who had also been a royal secretary, Henri became a secretary to Louis XIV while the future king waited to come of age. When he did in 1661, Justel's "career blossomed at the heart of Louis XIV's cabinet."[26] Further, Justel was a French agent of the newly established Royal Society in England, and his Paris home was frequently visited by English travelers, including John Locke. Being privy to France's political affairs, he caught wind of the coming Revocation of the Edict of Nantes, and decided to take up an invitation by England's own King Charles II, the recently restored Stuart monarch. Justel sold his library, arriving in England in 1681 to be appointed as royal librarian at St. James's Palace and to be unanimously elected to the Royal Society. Ironically, one of the most hospitable friends of this Huguenot refugee was none other than John Evelyn, who was so incensed by Simon's work.

It is fair to say, given Justel's connection to Locke, his agency and election to the Royal Society, and his advocacy of Simon, that he fit in well with the liberal theological tendencies of his Anglican connections, which would come to dominate England during the late seventeenth and early eighteenth centuries. "Liberal" in this context

25 Geoffrey Treasure asserts that he was far more skeptical than would behoove a true Huguenot. See his "'That great and knowing virtuoso': the French background and English refuge of Henri Justel," in Randolph Vigne and Charles Littleton, *From Strangers to Citizens: The Integration of Immigrant Communities in Britain, Ireland and Colonial America, 1550–1750* (Brighton: Sussex Academic Press, 2001), pp. 205–213.

26 Stephen W. Massil, "Immigrant Librarians in Britain: Huguenots and Some Others," p. 6. Available online at http://www.ifla.org/IV/ifla69/papers/058e-Massil.pdf. The information on Justel taken from this article is found on pp. 6–8.

suggests a moderate Whig, as opposed to radical Whig on the far left and Tory on the far right. The importance of these English political factions will become clear later, in the careers of Locke and John Toland, especially given the hidden radical strains of such moderates as Locke. At this point, it is enough to understand that Justel's piety was most likely not that of his devout Huguenot ancestors, and further, that in the larger political arena, exiled Huguenots would find common cause with England against the France of Louis XIV. How these two points are related remains to be explored, especially in regard to his advocacy of Simon in England.

If we return again to a consideration of Simon's text, more ambiguity is added when we examine the peculiar history of the English translation, *A Critical History of the Old Testament* (hereafter *Critical History*). Not one, but two imprints appear in 1682, one by Jacob Tonson and the other by Walter Davis (the latter being the translation used here). The translation of both was apparently done by Henry Dickinson, a young lawyer, and the duplication was caused by Dickinson's back and forth wrangling in regard to Tonson, who was initially quite displeased to discover the heterodox nature of the work, but did finally agree to publish it, with the addition of some laudatory poems to entice and calm the reader.[27] In one, the reader is assured that "the sacred oracles may well endure/th'exaltest search, of their own truth secure/Though at this press some noisy zealots bawl"; in another, Simon is compared to Esdras, reviving the Law: "To vindicate the Sacred Books, A new/But onely Certain Method, you persue,/And shewing Th'are corrupted, prove 'em true."[28] Not great poetry, but it does express the optimism, shared with Justel but not with John Evelyn, that Simon was addressing pressing critical problems vexing serious students of Scripture.

Yet another twist: in 1684, two translations of Simon's *Histoire* appeared, one in English (*Critical Enquiries into the Various editions of the Bible*) and one in Latin (*Disquisitiones criticae de variis per diversa loca et tempora Bibliorum editionibus*), both the work of radical Whig printers, Thomas Bradyll and Richard Chisell respectively.[29] The typical concern of radical Whigs (as opposed to moderate Whigs), was to tear down both Christianity and the crown, replacing the former with a religion of nature and the latter with a republican government. Obviously, they saw a quite different use for Simon than did Justel and Dickinson.

27 Dickinson apparently did not think it heterodox, but as he states at the beginning of the Davis edition (anonymously), he regards it as a source "from when we may draw convincing Arguments for the confuting of all the atheistical Opinions of our Age"—presumably those of Spinoza. He adds that he wished "this Criticism had been made by some of our own Communion; who might have alter'd nothing of the substance of it, but have left out onely some small reflexions upon the Protestants. . . ." Given the reaction by Tonson, as well as the initial reaction on the Continent, Dickinson added that there may be some who "at first sight, shall be scandaliz'd with this Author's free way of handling the Holy Scriptures," to whom Dickinson gives the advice, either let it alone or read it all the way through. On Dickinson, see Champion, "Pere Richard Simon and English Biblical Criticism, 1680–1700," pp. 48–49.

28 Quoted in ibid., pp. 49–50.

29 The original printer of the English translation, Robert Hughes, a Roman Catholic, was replaced by Bradyll. See ibid., p. 51.

The *Critical Enquiries* and the *Disquisitiones* both claim to come from Simon's original manuscript, but are actually identical abridgments of Simon's *Histoire* that proclaim to the reader that offensive passages have been omitted, but in reality (to quote historian Justin Champion) contain "a vulgarization of all the most provocative elements."[30] In true Machiavellian duplicity, the vulgarization actually emphasizes the purely destructive aspects of Simon's work.

The author of both translations seems to have been John Hampden (1653–1696), a radical Whig politician and a friend of John Locke. Harden was an ardent republican who during the 1680s plotted behind the scenes the overthrow of England's fragile Stuart monarchy, his house providing the meeting place for conspirators in 1683.

Traveling on the Continent between 1680 and 1682, Hampden had met and worked with Richard Simon, and continued to correspond with him between 1682 and 1685. In 1688, Hampden wrote a confession in which he admitted having been corrupted by Simon, being "so unhappy as to engage myself in the sentiments and the principles of the author of the Critical History of the Old Testament," which "did tend to overthrow all the belief which Christians have of the truth and authority of the Holy Scriptures, under pretence of giving great authority to Tradition." Even more, Hampden maintained that a future project of Simon's, a "critical polyglot Bible," for which Hampden provided initial funding, in "design . . . tended to destroy the certainty of the books of the New Testament as well as the Old." In sum, he presented Simon as offering mere critical destruction, rather than a peculiar defense of orthodoxy, a methodical design that aided the radical Whig cause in its struggles to undermine Christianity and the monarchical state that was supported by it.[31] How much stock to place in the sincerity of Hampden's repudiation of his "heinous sins" in his confession is unclear, but it is certain that he both knew Simon well and reworked the *Histoire* to his own more radical purposes, proving how easy and tempting it was to co-opt Simon's work for impious aims, and even more, the overriding political goal that often defined the co-option.

Simon in Germany

Simon's reception in Germany is equally illuminating for the history of modern biblical criticism.[32] German scholars obviously read both French and Latin, and so had access to Simon's original work and to the Latin edition that began circulating in 1681. As Leibniz was a member of Henri Justel's circle of friends, he was introduced to Simon and his arguments in the 1670s, and Leibniz's assessment was that Simon's argument in the *Histoire* was a two-edged sword.[33] By the next decade, both critical

30 Ibid., p. 53.

31 Ibid., pp. 56–57.

32 On the reception of Simon in Germany we rely upon John Woodbridge, "German Reponses to the Biblical Critic Richard Simon: from Leibniz to J. S. Semler," in Henning Graf Reventlow, Walter Sparn, and John Woodbridge, eds., *Historische Kritik und biblischer Kanon in der deutschen Aufklärung* (Wiesbaden: Otto Harrassowitz, 1988), *Wolfenbütteler Forschungen* (41), 65–87.

33 Ibid., pp. 68–69.

reviews and denunciations of Simon appeared on the German academic scene. The denunciations came from orthodox Lutherans, such as Johann Benedict Carpzov, who lumped Simon in with La Peyrère, Hobbes, and Spinoza (1684); Herman Witsius (1695, second edition), who treated Simon as companionable with the likes of Hobbes, Spinoza, and Le Clerc; Matthias Honcamp (1688) and Johannes Henricus Maius (1690), who criticized both Simon and Le Clerc as equally pernicious; and Johann Henrici Heidegger (1700), who saw Simon and Spinoza as a common threat.[34] The early trend to demonize Simon would continue in the 1700s.

But this early and almost invariably negative reaction was soon ameliorated by more positive presentations. In 1713, Leonhard Christoph Ruhl translated *Richard Simonii Historia Critica Commentatorum praecipuorum Veteris et Novi Testamenti*, with an appreciative Preface by Jacob Reimmann, a friend of Leibniz, who recommended that readers sift the good from bad in Simon, noting (ironically) that Simon could be used to undermine papal claims.[35] Others followed with more positive, if cautious, affirmations, including Johann Christian Edelmann, Johann David Michaelis, Siegmund Jacob Baumgarten, Johann Salamo Semler, and Johann Gottfried Herder, the latter four praising Simon as heralding a new age in biblical criticism, and both Michaelis and Herder hailing him as "*Vater der neuern Critik*" and "*Vater der Kritik A. und N. T. in den neuern Zeiten*" respectively.[36] Semler published German translations of Simon's works in 1776–1777,[37] the very same time, we recall, that Semler came out with a dual bound copy of Meyer's *Philosophia* and Spinoza's *Tractatus* in Latin. Anyone familiar with the history of biblical scholarship will know the importance of these figures.

A more detailed examination of Simon's treatment of the Old and New Testaments will help clarify the various reactions, from orthodox horror and unorthodox co-option, to being heralded as the "Vater" of modern biblical criticism. Through this, the ways that Simon contributed to the assumptions and aims of modern biblical scholarship will become clear.

Simon and the Old Testament

Simon shifted the focus of biblical studies from the substance of the text to the history of the text, asserting that, "It is impossible to understand thoroughly the Holy Scriptures unless we first know the different states of the Text of these Books according to the different times and places, and be instructed of all the several changes that have happened to it."[38] That, of course, explains the title of his work, *A Critical History of the Old Testament*, a title that immediately bespeaks

34 Ibid., pp. 71–73.
35 Ibid., pp. 76–77.
36 Quoted in ibid., p. 81.
37 Ibid., pp. 82–83.
38 Simon, *A Critical History of the Old Testament*, Author's Preface, p. i.

its patrimony in the historical-critical method.[39] In words that seem strikingly like a twentieth-century exegete, Simon maintained, "I am persuaded one cannot reade the Bible with profit, if one be not first of all instructed in that which regards the Criticisme of the Text. . . ."[40] Wedging the "criticisme" between the text and the reader seemed a good way to create critical distance, allowing a gap that could only be filled by *traditio*; the unintended result, however, was that exegetes, using methods that were extensions of Spinoza's through Simon, became the new interpretive magisterium.

But that, again, was an unintended effect. Simon meant to buttress *traditio*, even in his explanation of the transmission of the text. For Simon, study of the history of the text revealed that, for example, although Moses did not write all of the Pentateuch, we may still consider it wholly inspired because its compilation (including any additions made) was overseen by "the Prophets or publick Writers, who took care of collecting faithfully the acts of what pass'd of most importance in the State [i.e., the Hebrew Commonwealth]. . . ." Although we may not know who these many, nameless editors and writers were, "we need not too curiously enquire, as usually men do, who were the Authours of each particular Book of the Bible, because it is certain that they were all writ by Prophets, which the Hebrew Commonwealth never wanted as long as it lasted."[41] In fact, all the difficulties brought up in regard to Mosaic authorship of the Pentateuch could be simultaneously accepted and swept away as unimportant, for the Pentateuch was written by Moses *and* the "publick Writers."[42] Simon therefore quite happily provided a detailed textual demonstration of why "Moses cannot be [the] Author of the Books which are attributed to him."[43]

The presence of these various writers explained why the Old Testament text had a layered editorial history, for

> these same Prophets, which may be call'd publick Writers . . . had the liberty of collecting out of the ancient Acts which were kept in the Registers of the Republick, and of giving a new form to these same Acts by adding or diminishing what they thought fit; we may hereby give a very good reason for the additions and alterations in the Holy Scriptures without lessening of their Authority, since the Authours of these additions or alterations were real Prophets directed by the Spirit of God. Wherefore their alterations in the ancient Acts are of as great Authority as the rest of the Text of the Bible.[44]

39 As Nichols points out, the use of "critique" in the title "shocked people because the word '*critique*' had then, as it does today, a pejorative sense as well." Nichols, "Richard Simon, Faith and Modernity," pp. 159–160.

40 Simon, *A Critical History of the Old Testament,* I.1, pp. 2–3.

41 Ibid., Author's Preface, p. ii. These "Prophets, Scribes, as they are termed the Bible or publick Writers . . . did faithfully collect the transactions that passed in the whole [Hebrew] state and kept them in Registries ordain'd for that purpose." Ibid., I.1, p. 3.

42 Ibid.

43 Ibid., I.5–7, pp. 36–59. Simon deals with the rest of the books in the Bible in the same way. Ibid., I.8.

44 Ibid., Author's Preface, pp. ii–iii.

By this stratagem Simon believed he could "easily answer all the false and pernicious consequences drawn by Spinosa from these alterations or additions for the running down the Authority of the Holy Scripture, as if these corrections had been purely of humane Authority. . . ."[45] Simon therefore expressed no concern about highlighting the alleged alterations Spinoza used to undermine Scriptural authenticity, precisely because, in Simon's scheme, they too were inspired. Furthermore, that such alterations and corrections took place over time under the inspiration of the Holy Spirit foreshadows something like the Catholic understanding of Tradition as the inspired caretaker and interpreter of Holy Writ.

The problem with Simon's solution was that some of the actions of the "publick Writers" do not seem to fit well with any notion of a Providential oversight guiding the whole process and giving meaning to the various incongruities beyond their merely being incongruous. For example, Simon maintained that some of the disorder of the biblical text was the result of the ancient "way of writing of Books . . . upon little leaves, which were usually onely roll'd one upon another, without being sown together upon a little Roller." As is the case with all human things, "the order of these ancient Leaves or Scrolls has not been carefully enough kept," the result being that "the order of things has been sometimes chang'd." And so, declared Simon, "we ought not to blame the Authours of the Holy Scripture for the disorder in some places of the Holy Scripture; but we ought to complain of a misfortune which has happened to all ancient books."[46] But as critics of Simon realized, the occurrence of the same misfortune as occurs in all ancient books meant that the Bible displayed all the same imperfections.

Simon also offered another important reason for imperfections in Scripture, one that hearkened back to Spinoza. If the writers "have not always observed the [historical] order of the times" in the biblical narrative, the reason is that they were "abridging . . . Scripture to give it to the People" in a way "which they thought . . . most proper for the instructing of the People."[47] The biblical text we have, then, is "onely an abridgment of the Acts which were preserv'd intire in the Registery of the [Hebrew] Republick. . . ."[48]

Simon's notion of abridgment introduced two gaps between the original events and the Bible as we have it. First and most obvious is the gap that existed between the more plentiful original sources and the abridgment. The result is that the lost original sources become the Bible, or better, the Ur-Bible behind the Bible, the real object of attention of the historically minded exegete. Only the Ur-Bible can resolve many of the textual difficulties with which faith had previously struggled blindly.

> If we had the Annals of the Kings of *Judah* and *Israel*, whence *Esdras* has taken the best part of his Chronological History, we might without doubt find a great

45 Ibid., Author's Preface, p. iii.

46 Ibid., Author's Preface, p. vi. Simon uses the example of Sarah being ninety years old in Genesis 17:17 and then later, at 17:20, being described as beautiful and hence desirable enough to be taken as a wife by Abimelech.

47 Ibid., Author's Preface, p. vii.

48 Ibid., Author's Preface, p. v.

> deal to resolve the difficulties which we meet with upon this Subject, but we want these ancient Histories which had been collected by the Prophets; nay moreover we have but abridgments of what is come down to our hands.[49]

But here another gap opened up with the judgment of the last editor. Simon, following Hobbes, Spinoza, and others, believed Ezra responsible for much of the final editing, although how much is ultimately uncertain.[50] In speaking of such an editor, Simon laid the stress not on the inspiration of the Holy Spirit, but on the "liberty . . . taken by those who made the Collection of the Records, and composed a body of Scripture for the publick use, *fitting them to their own times and design*; which is usual with those who abridge the Books of others. . . ."[51] As a result, "it is hard to explain why those who have made a collection of every Book of the Bible in particular, have spoke but of certain Acts, without touching upon others more remarkable . . ."[52] Indeed, it is not just hard, but impossible, for "what we have at present is but an abridgment of the ancient Records, which were much larger, and . . . those who made the abridgments had particular reasons which we cannot understand."[53] Thus, the text, even though clear in many places, was ultimately shrouded in darkness (not mystery), and only a historical-critical recovery of the original sources, an historical analysis of the needs and beliefs of the editor's own time, and finally, a psychological reconstruction of each editor could shed any light. We are not far from Spinoza's assertion that the goal of exegesis is the recovery of meaning but not truth.

The process of abridgment not only opened up gaps, but also resulted in textual faults, "repetitions and transpositions in the Scripture," infelicities made even worse because the "Hebrews were not very polite Writers, [so] that they usually transpos'd, or repeated the same thing, and that sometimes they onely begin one matter, and then on a sudden go to another, and afterwards reassume their former discourse."[54] One cannot expect too much of them, for "at that time they did not observe with such exactness as we do at present those little niceties of Grammar, the use of which has been but of late ages."[55]

Beyond all this, the abridgment itself has been prey to the ravages of time. Not only have the "first Originals . . . been lost," but the copies have been victims of "the carelesness of Transcribers."[56] And since the copies from which translators must make copies are multiple, each with its own history, thus all the above difficulties are multiplied accordingly.[57] Many, if not all, of the Hebrew copies of the Old Testament extant contained a double difficulty in their final form: the Hebrew language itself changed

49 Ibid., I.3, p. 26.

50 Ibid., I.4, pp. 29–33 and I.8, pp. 62–63.

51 Ibid., I.3, p. 27. Emphasis added.

52 Ibid., I.3, p. 27.

53 Ibid.

54 Ibid., Author's Preface, p. viii.

55 Ibid., I.3, p. 24.

56 Ibid., I.1, p. 2.

57 See Simon's discussion of the various extant copies, ibid., I.10–13.

over time, and the text bore within it the history of the language itself, which resulted in more confusions for the translator. Furthermore, these texts were copied by Jews after the Babylonian captivity who didn't speak Hebrew, a fact that only compounded the confusions in the text.[58] If all that were not enough, between the time of the return from Babylon, philosophical speculation entered the transmission of the texts, so that "Allegories past [sic] very freely among the *Jews* at their return from *Babylon*, and the Doctours took pleasure in inventing new senses of the Scripture, to render themselves of more esteem by their subtilties," so that "We ought not therefore to wonder that the Hebrew Copies of the Scriptures have received many alterations made by Doctours who chiefly applied themselves to vain subtilties."[59] The Septuagint has all the same problems and more, given that it is once removed from the Hebrew, and so it could not be used to correct defects.[60] The problem of textual fidelity only became worse with time, for "The Jews [especially the Pharisees] at the time of our Saviour apply'd themselves almost to nothing but their Traditions, Allegories and Parables. The literal sense of the Scripture was wholly neglected, and by consequence there was little care taken in getting correct Copies."[61]

This context provided, for Simon, an explanation for the way the New Testament is written. While Christ blamed the Pharisees for following their own traditions, oddly enough "he has not wholly rejected them, on the contrary, he has follow'd their method in the explanation of the Scripture. . . ." And not just Jesus. "S. *Paul* had been of the Sect of the *Pharisees*, has likewise interpreted Scripture according to the prejudices of Tradition, and the Church in the beginning seem'd to prefer this manner of explaining the Bible. . . ." That is why both Christ and the Apostles quote the Old Testament inexactly: "they have had more regard to the sense than to the letter of the Text," a regard "according to the method of the *Pharisees*, who related not the words of the Text when they quoted it, being persuaded that Religion depended more on the authority of the Tradition than from the bare words of Scripture, which were subject to various interpretations." In doing this, we cannot blame them, "since they follow'd the method approv'd by the chief Doctours of that time."[62] By implication, Jesus and the Apostles followed a textually loose, and hence corrupting tradition—an odd way for the Holy Spirit to work.

Neither were the early Church Fathers, in their relationship to the Jews, standing on very solid textual ground, given that they tended to rely on the Septuagint, believing that "the Septuagint Translation onely is authentick and Divine, and that what is not conformable to it, has been corrupted. But as this Principle is not true, we ought to conclude that the consequences the Fathers have drawn from thence are likewise false."[63] Simon gives a very important example. Christians read Isaiah's prophecy that

58 Ibid., I.15–16.
59 Ibid., I.16, pp. 108–109.
60 Ibid., I.16, pp. 110–113.
61 Ibid., I.17, p. 113.
62 Ibid., I.17, p. 114.
63 Ibid., I.18, p. 122.

a virgin shall bring forth a child (Isaiah 7:14), but that translation is based upon the Septuagint—that is, upon translating a Hebrew word into Greek. Since such translation may be done variously, the Jews cannot be chided because they "have translated a Hebrew word otherwise than the Septuagint. It is ordinary for persons in disputing to translate according to the sense they think most favours their opinion, the [Hebrew word in the] Text nevertheless remains the same, and the change is onely in the Translation."[64] Thus, it becomes harder, if not impossible, for Christians to argue, based on the biblical text, that Christianity is a fulfillment of Judaism (especially since the Jews, when faced with Christian apologists, actually became more faithful to the original Hebrew in their translations).[65]

So many translations; so many opinions. Since the fever for accurate translation arose again with the Reformation, and hence amongst theological controversy, translations only multiplied, and Simon spent the entirety of Book II of his *Critical History* examining in detail the differences among the many translations, stretching from ancient to modern times. In this Book, he made it quite clear, by extensively treating the first five centuries of Christianity, that the problem of multiple translations and editorial judgments has always plagued the Church.

Of course, this implied that the official translation of Roman Catholicism, the Vulgate, shared in all these uncertainties. To this, Simon answered, "I dare . . . boldly say, there are few persons who have understood the intention of the Council of *Trent*, when it pronounc'd this ancient Latin Translation authentick." That, of course, occasioned an explanation of the "proper signification of the word *Authentick*, according to the intention of the Council. . . ."[66]

The word "authentic," Simon maintained, cannot be understood according to its "most ancient and proper signification," the "true Original of a thing." Since the entirety of his argument has shown no such originals exist—either of the Old or New Testament texts—such a sense of authenticity was impossible.[67] Happily, there is "another way of explaining this word *Authentick*," one that supported *traditio*. Historically, when theological disagreements arose even prior to the Reformation, and rival translations were brought forth, the matter was settled by the Church Councils. In regard to the Vulgate, "It was absolutely necessary for the Western Church to have a Translation of the Bible, to be guided by as well in Disputes, as in Sermons and other publick actions," so "the Fathers of the Council of *Trent* wisely declar'd for the ancient Latin Interpretation, and that of all other Latin ones, that only should be call'd authentick, because the others which had been made during the Schism, were to be suspected. . . ." Beyond this, the Vulgate "had for several Centuries been authoriz'd in the Latin Church; which however makes it not infallible and free from all faults, since the same Council commanded it to be corrected, and those who did correct it were neither Prophets, nor inspir'd by God."[68]

64 Ibid., I.18, p. 120.

65 Ibid., I.19, pp. 128–129.

66 Ibid., II.14, pp. 91–92.

67 Ibid., II.14, p. 92.

68 Ibid., II.14, pp. 92–93.

So "authentick" did not mean faultless. It did not even mean the best or only translation. "Although the other Translations have not been declar'd authentick, they nevertheless are so, if the Authors of them dealt ingenuously [as opposed to disingenuously], and had no other design but to explain the Original as well as they could." What then *is* the difference between authentic and inauthentic? "There is only this difference betwixt the Vulgar [i.e., the Vulgate] and the other Translations, that we are oblig'd to acknowledge the Vulgar for authentick, *because it has been so declar'd. . . .*"[69] *Traditio* trumped, but again, seemingly more like an arbitrary sovereign, declaring order, any order, in the midst of chaos. For Simon, the Church had to choose *some* translation since the Bible must be "publickly us'd" in worship, and in regard to use, custom is nine tenths of the law, so to speak.[70] In other words, Simon offered a reason that paralleled his explanation given in regard to the ancient Hebrew "publick Writers" abridgment of documents, the need for "fitting them to their own times and design" for "the instructing of the People."

Authenticity boiled down to *use* as defined by time and place, and confirmed by the official organ of *traditio* and so defined, seemed determined more by political exigencies than an overarching unity brought about by the Holy Spirit. Such authenticity by no means excluded consulting other translations: "We have then the liberty of going to the Hebrew Text, the Septuagint, and even to all the modern Translations of the Bible, for attaining of a greater knowledge of the holy Scripture."[71] But such freedom created a kind of two-tiered treatment of Scripture by scholars: private recognition of the faults of the Vulgate (or for that matter, any and every translation), coupled with public reverence for the officially sanctioned translation. "We ought . . . for quietness sake to use in publick no other Translation, than what the Church presents to us. . . ." The scholars know that whatever translation is in use is sanctioned only *by* use, while the worshippers and ecclesiastics naively treat it as wholly inspired and unique, for they are "prejudic'd by the commonly receiv'd opinion, that the . . . Translation then read in the Church had been inspir'd by God."[72] The scholars know better, even though they act for the sake of peace, for "quietness sake," to treat it *as if* it were inspired, a pose that smacks of a patronizing duplicity.

Perhaps the importance of *traditio* for Simon is seen most clearly in his treatment of the translations done by Luther and other Protestant reformers. With the rejection of *traditio* for *sola scriptura*, argued Simon, the Protestants not only generated hasty and hence inferior translations, but unable to agree on the translations as they appeared, kept creating new ones.[73] Yet, in reading Simon's analysis, one begins to wonder if the problem was not so much bad translation, but multiple authentic

69 Ibid., II.14, p. 93.

70 Ibid., II.14, p. 91.

71 Ibid., II.14, p. 96.

72 Ibid., II.14, p. 97. In this passage, in order to make his point, Simon is actually referring to the time of St. Augustine, remarking that Augustine would not allow the new translation of St. Jerome to be read in church, because the "Septuagint Translation" was hallowed by use.

73 Ibid., II.23–25.

translations, each done according to the interest of the particular Protestant denomination. Each had faults, but then again, so did the Vulgate.

From all this, Simon issued a rather startling conclusion, at least for the time: "The Criticism we have already made, as well of the *Hebrew* Text, as of the different Translations, plainly shews, that we have at present no exact Translation of the Holy Scripture," and even more doleful, "If we consider the difficulties which have already been observ'd, it seems impossible for us to succeed."[74] Yet what seemed impossible must be done. "Notwithstanding all these difficulties, we ought first of all to establish a *Hebrew* Text, and observe the various Readings according to the Rules of Criticism, as we use to do in other Books. In the Translation these same Variations may be translated, and put in the Margin, and the best reading may be kept for the Body of the Translation. . . ."[75] Although the presence of so many alternate readings, as a "Method," posed a problem for Protestants who "alledge the Scripture to be the only Rule of their Religion," the multiplicity was no threat to "the Romish Church, who besides the Scripture acknowledges true Tradition as a Principle of its Religion." Catholics, then, should "not [be] asham'd to confess that the Hebrew Text of the Bible may be interpreted several ways by reason of the Equivocation of the Hebrew."[76] One is tempted to say that, given Simon's spin, it is difficult to avoid the conclusion that Tradition acts, not in concord with Scripture, but in spite of it. Or to put it the other way around, a way perhaps closer to Simon's aim, *if* Scripture were indeed without such faults, *traditio* would no longer have a positive function since Simon imagined *traditio* as a kind of Hobbesian king bringing order by mere fiat to a textual state of war.

As the reader soon finds out, Simon was not ashamed of magnifying and multiplying textual difficulties to the very end of the work, providing no resolution but the fiat of *traditio.* He declared the need above all for a new translation, but this provided the occasion for enumerating even more difficulties,[77] and then instead of offering a "method" of resolving the difficulties, Simon launched into an extended historical analysis of the many ways previous exegetes have tried to sort them out, a history of "Method"[78] running from Jewish commentators and the early Church Fathers down to Simon's own day. But there the *Histoire critique du Vieux Testament* ends. No resolution is offered, only an unlimited horizon stretching in all directions upon which future exegetes may travel before reaching the Promised Land.

The overall effect upon the reader of Simon's *Histoire,* it is fair to suggest, would have been much the same as it was after reading Spinoza's extended treatment of the textual difficulties facing exegetes: despair at the suggested project. Indeed, despite his warning about the excesses of Spinoza and his followers, Simon piled up the difficulties standing between the reader and the text of the Old Testament far higher than

74 Ibid., III.1, p. 1.

75 Ibid., III.1, p. 3.

76 Ibid., III.2, p. 7.

77 Ibid., III.3–4.

78 Ibid., III.5–24

Spinoza had. Recall that Simon had asserted, very vaguely, at the beginning that while it is true that the Hebrew Bible is the result of layer upon layer of writing, editing, and rewriting, the belief in the inspired and Providential nature of the Bible was not undermined "since the Authours of these additions or alterations were real Prophets directed by the Spirit of God." But nowhere after that do we receive an account of this Spirit, and what unifying plan He may have had. Whatever that unifying plan, it does not find expression in any identifiable unity of the biblical text itself (which, if there were one, might provide a substitute for *traditio*). Instead, Simon purposely maximized the problems in the text and translation so as to place the entire weight of authority on the Church. He then neglected to give an account of the authority of *traditio* as anything more than an answer to the practical needs of the faithful, so if that same Spirit were still at work in the Church, it must be the rather less awesome spirit of political utility. Small wonder that Simon's efforts were met by even Catholic readers with a cry of alarm, rather than a cry of relief at having been delivered from Spinoza.

Simon's Treatment of the New Testament

Even though Simon is considered more the father of modern Old Testament scholarship, he wrote *A Critical History of the Text of the New Testament* (*Histoire Critique du text du Nouveau Testament*, 1689) as well.[79] Perhaps the reason he is given patriarchal status to Old rather than New Testament scholarship is that Simon's treatment of the New Testament is *comparatively* more benign.

Simon began his critique of the New Testament by asserting that textual criticism was as old as the Church, pointing to both Origen and even more important Jerome as the two chief ancient representatives of "This kind of Labour," which "is termed Critical; in as much as it Judges and Determines the most Authentick Readings, which ought to be inserted into the Text."[80] This was a reminder that the now venerable Vulgate was once young, and was itself the result of Jerome's textual criticism. Yet, innocent and accurate as this sounds, the reader of his *Critical History of the Old Testament* is immediately reminded of the rather peculiar meaning of "Authentick" used by Simon as politically and ecclesiologically useful, and rightly wonders where he might be headed.

"My principal aim," remarked Simon, "is to write a Supplement to the Defects of those who compile the different Readings out of the [New Testament] Manuscripts, without distinguishing the Good from the Bad," [81] although much later he asserted that, "I have no other design in this Work than to treat of the Text of the New

79 The original French came out in 1689, as did the English translation.

80 Ibid., Author's Preface, p. i. As with the previous work, there is no pagination in the text. We begin numbering, using Roman numerals, with the first page of the Preface.

81 Ibid., Author's Preface, p. ii.

Testament, and to establish as much as is possible the Writings of the Apostles. . . ."[82] This effort was a necessary preparation for the task of judging authenticity.

Without such critical work, theology for Simon was more or less stunted, and indeed *has been* stunted up until fairly recently. Those ages "when Barbarism reigned over all Europe," running from sometime after St. Augustine until the Renaissance, there was a "neglect [of] Critical Studies" because they lacked "those helps, which they [scholars] now enjoy to pursue those Studies, which are absolutely necessary to a perfect Knowledg of Divinity." Indeed, in Simon's own age, "we cannot but see the manifest Errors of some Divines . . . who know not the true Laws of Criticism."[83]

This last is a telling remark, upon which hang all kinds of implications. Whatever his intentions, Simon appeared to replace personal sanctity with impersonal scholarly "Laws of Criticism" (obvious counterparts to the "Laws of Nature"). As a result, the depth of one's personal sanctity no longer qualified one to see the deeper mysteries hidden in the Bible from the profane eyes of the unbeliever or the undisciplined eyes of the novice. Only a scholar could plumb the depths of the text, and that occurred not through personal faith or holiness but impersonal, critical laws that did not seem to demand either faith or holiness at all to function. It also followed that insofar as the Church has functioned with less than perfect knowledge of the Laws of Criticism, it has been as ignorant of Scripture as it was ignorant of nature without knowledge of the Laws of Nature. The very *traditio* upon which he so heavily relied was therefore set in a rather awkward light as being almost entirely ill equipped to judge scriptural matters.

Be that as it may, Simon next marked a significant difference between the situation of the Hebrews and that of the first Christians in regard to manuscripts and their preservation. Christ himself wrote nothing, and demanded nothing of His Apostles but to preach. Unlike the Hebrews, Christ founded no state. As a result, "the Christians not having at that time any State separate from that of the Jews . . . they had no Persons appointed to record any thing of importance which pass'd among them. And this is the reason that we find not here, as in the Old Testament, any publick Writers who had the Charge of collecting the Acts of their State." Rather than being officially sanctioned, the Gospels were written "at the request of those People who were willing to preserve the memory of that which the Apostles had preached to them." St. Paul's epistles were written for "the Instruction of Churches which were already erected." And the Acts of the Apostles were "published to no other end but to shew to the Faithful the Progress of the Christian Religion upon its first advance into the World."[84]

Precisely because there was no Christian state, and hence were no official state scribes, there arose all too many writings: not just those of the Apostles and St. Paul

82 Ibid., I.16, p. 142.

83 Ibid., Author's Preface, p. iii. Simon later states that "some Learned Persons in all Ages have taken care to render them [the Holy Books] correct." Even "The Most barbarous Ages have produced Books, which they call, *Correctoria Bibliae*, or Corrections of the Bible," Author's Preface, p. v.

84 Ibid., I.1, p. 2.

but a morass of others as well.[85] It therefore became difficult to determine the false from the true, the heretical from the orthodox. As in the Old Testament, *traditio* delivered believers from this confusion of texts. For, while the heretical works even disagreed among themselves, "the Doctrine of the Apostles was perfectly uniform in the Churches that they had planted," and "the Fathers made use of this Uniformity of Doctrine to confirm and establish the truth of the Apostolical Writings." Thus, the deposit of writings kept at apostolic churches functioned as public archives, just as the Hebrews kept their records in "Registers of the Republick."[86]

Just as *traditio* delivered the early Church from heretics, so also it must now deliver it from Protestantism. "We cannot imagine any thing more opposite to good reason," argued Simon, than the Reformed notion that acknowledgment of the biblical canon is "not so much by the common agreement and consent of the Church, as by the testimony and inward persuasion of the Holy Ghost," a testimony that did not keep the Remonstrants from breaking away from the strict Calvinist Reformed.[87] For Simon, this "inner persuasion" was no different than the inner conviction of ancient heretics, the Gnostics, Marcionites, and so on, that their writings and canon were authentic. Therefore, feelings of inner persuasion can and do only lead to a chaos of canons, translations, and interpretations that only "constant Tradition" can cure. "This Spirit . . . ought without doubt to be preferred to a private Spirit that can only serve to make a division therein."[88]

Simon applied this principle to several of the textual questions that had arisen in his day, questions that would continue to intrigue and divide biblical scholars thereafter. For example, in regard to the question of who wrote the Gospels, Simon maintained that "the constant Tradition of the Church is the mark by which we distinguish the Divine and Canonical Books from those that are not so; and it is this same Church that hath added, or at least approved of the Titles of the four Gospels, to denote to us, that these Gospels were written by Apostles, or by their Disciples; which does not in the least agree with this private Spirit of some Protestants."[89]

---

85 This seems to be the cause, at least in part, of the number of copies of the canonical New Testament writings with their many textual variations, the other cause being the rapidity of Christianity's spread to all the nations. See ibid., II.29, p. 112.

86 Ibid., Author's Preface, I.1, p. 3.

87 Ibid., I.1, p. 10.

88 Ibid., I.1, p. 10. Simon brought this comparison between the private Spirit and the Spirit of Tradition up again in a discussion of the ancient heretic, the Manichean Faustus, and his treatment of the letters of St. Paul. "But let us leave these Hereticks who had no certain Principles, and were therefore obliged sometimes to have recourse to their *Paraclet*, which was their great Engine. We see almost the same thing at present in some illuminated and enthusiastick Persons, who for want of good reasons are forced to fly to I know not what private Spirit that discovers to them the most hidden Mysteries of the Christian Religion. I would entreat these People to reflect a little on the Conduct of the ancient Ecclesiastical Writers in their Disputes against Hereticks, and on their manner of arguing; they will find therein neither *Paraclet*, nor private Spirit, but solid Arguments, that are very far from the Fanaticism which is predominant in our Age." Ibid., I.15, p. 141.

89 Ibid., I.2, p. 15.

In regard to the question about the age of New Testament manuscripts, Simon argued that in its battle against heretics, "the most ancient Fathers of the Church" did not have "recourse to any Originals that had been kept in the Apostolical Churches, but only to true and exact Copies of them, which being found the same in all these Churches, were in the place of the Originals themselves."[90] And so, it was not original manuscripts that refuted heretics, but the *traditio* using copies, thereby doubly reaffirming the need for *traditio*. It was because the ancient Christians "had not a regular Body of a State," that the originals were lost.[91]

The focus of the ancients was on apostolic tradition, argued Simon, but again, the focus was on *use*, for "any Copy whatsoever, provided it were used in the Orthodox Churches, might be relied on, as if it had been the first Original written with the hand of the Apostles."[92] The fidelity with which these texts had been handed on since—inasmuch as "there is no Book the Copies whereof are more authentick than those of the New Testament"—ought to bring us to "acknowledge the peculiar Providence of God in the preservation of these Books. . . ."[93] Again we remind ourselves (as Simon reminded the reader) that "authentick" does not mean "original" or most accurate.

In regard to the question of which writings were canonical or heretical, *traditio* defined which were authentic. The implication of Simon's argument, which he meant to be a decisive point against Protestantism, was that those who reject *traditio* would ultimately be forced to vindicate *sola scriptura* by recovering the actual original New Testament documents, a task that the ravages of time (and Simon's tireless elucidation of problems) make self-defeating.

As to the question of which Gospel was written first, Simon asserted that we know by *traditio* that it was Matthew, and that Matthew was originally written in Hebrew.[94] The same is true for the traditional order and authors of the other Gospels, Mark, Luke, and John.[95] In speaking of the Gospels, Simon distinguished between the original copy and translations, affirming the primacy of *traditio* in discerning which are authentic. For example, even though Matthew was originally written in Hebrew, it was the "constant Tradition of the Church alone that gives authority to this Version," i.e., the accepted Greek translation. Such translations are not themselves directly inspired, but determined as authentic (in Simon's sense) by the prudence of the Church. Yet, in regard to inspiration, "It is much more reasonable only to admit this Inspiration for the Originals on the Holy Scriptures, which have been translated into different Languages according to the necessities and occasions of the Churches. . . . She [the Church] speaks

90 Ibid., I.4, p. 30.

91 Ibid., I.4, p. 31.

92 Ibid., I.4, p. 32.

93 Ibid.

94 Ibid., I.5, p. 39. During his own time, "some Authors" offered the argument that St. Luke's Gospel must be first, given that Luke accuses those who have written before him of inaccuracy, a charge that couldn't be leveled at Matthew, Mark, and John. Ibid.

95 Ibid., I.10, pp. 12, 13.

in general of the Gospel of S. *Matthew*, which is Divine and Canonical in whatsoever Language it be written."[96]

Much the same principle was used by Simon to explain why the New Testament writers quoted the Septuagint rather than the original Hebrew. It was not that the Septuagint ought to be preferred to the original Hebrew in accuracy or inspiration. The Apostles used the Greek "for no other end, but to accommodate themselves to the capacity of the People, whom they instructed, and who read the Bible in *Greek*," yet "there can be no consequence drawn from thence, to give more Authority to the Version of the Septuagint than to the *Hebrew* Text. . . ."[97]

Further, "the Evangelists and the Apostles did not confine themselves in their quotations to the rigor of the Letter, because that was in no wise needful for carrying on their Work. They did content themselves sometimes, with delivering the sense of the Words, which they adapted to their Discourse."[98] Hearkening back to his treatment of the Old Testament, Simon also maintained that the many copyists of the New Testament documents, who lived after the Apostles, acted within *traditio*, when they "revised those ancient Copies, intending nothing but to make them clear, without being at pains to confine themselves to the true Reading of the Evangelists and the Apostles," giving paraphrases, abridging places where the words seemed superfluous, and transposing passages, "yet it will not be found that the sense has suffered any alteration."[99] Therefore, the extant manuscripts bear the layers of editors who transmitted them.

In regard to the use of allegorical or mystical senses of Scripture, as opposed to the literal, Simon maintained again that such was the mode of explanation used by many of the Jews at the time of Jesus (principally, the Pharisees[100]), and that Jesus and His disciples followed suit. Here it is important that Simon affirmed the proper allegorical interpretation only through *traditio*. Against critics of allegory, Simon asserted, "'Tis true, that that which is meerly Allegorical cannot suffice as a positive Proof for the Confirmation of a Religion: But when those Allegories are Founded on Tradition, they may be used and applyed to Matters of Fact, which are already agreed upon by Tradition."[101] Although this assertion was directed immediately against Jews who rejected allegorical interpretations of the Old Testament that lent support to Christianity as Judaism's fulfillment, it applied equally as well to Protestants who objected to allegorical readings of Scripture that supported the papacy. Note, however, that Simon was not offering a reasoned account of allegory, nor a scriptural vindication of it; rather, allegory was permissible solely by Tradition's fiat.

For the same reason, the interpretive tradition of the Jews at the time of Jesus (mainly that of the Pharisees), which had no direct basis in the Old Testament, was

96 Ibid., I.9, pp. 79–80.
97 Ibid., II.20, pp. 28–29.
98 Ibid., II.20, p. 29.
99 Ibid., II.30, pp. 142–143.
100 Ibid., II.21, pp. 40–41.
101 Ibid., II.21, p. 37. See also II.22, pp. 56–57.

a legitimate foundation for New Testament exegesis, and hence for Church Tradition, since the Jews "believed many things [e.g., in hell and the resurrection of the dead], whereof they had no Literal proofs in all the Old Testament, being only founded on their Traditions." In fine, the Jews did not function according to some doctrine of *sola scriptura* in regard to the books of the Old Testament. Jesus and the Apostles accepted both Scripture and Jewish Tradition, and so "the Writings of the Evangelists and the Apostles, ought to be Expounded with a relation to this *Idea* of the *Jewish* Faith, and not to that which may be conceived of their belief, with a reference to the Books of the Old Testament only; because those Books contain but one part of their Religion, the other part being comprehended in their Traditions."[102] Simon put forth this argument in the context of showing how ancient heretics, failing to take this into account, rejected many of the canonical writings as not grounded in the Old Testament, but it was clear that the real aim of the argument was again to undermine contemporary Protestantism's use of *sola scriptura* against Catholic Tradition, especially in its winnowing down the number of canonical books.

Simon's treatment of such questions is always thorough, often insightful, but again, relies on *traditio* in such a way that the reader is never clear about the deeper justification of its authority. That recalls, once again, the central problem of Simon's critical histories: the functioning of the Holy Spirit. Parallel to the problem of how the Holy Spirit is related to *traditio*, arises the problem of how the Holy Spirit is related to the writings of the New Testament. Simon admitted that objections had been raised against his presentation of "the Inspiration of the Sacred Writings" in regard to his "Critical History of the Old Testament," so that "I shall here Handle it more particularly, with respect to the Writings of the Evangelists and the Apostles."[103]

By way of an answer, Simon brought up the views of Hugo Grotius (1583–1645) and Spinoza. According to Simon, Grotius argued that only the prophetic writings were inspired in the traditional sense, whereas the histories were merely faithful reports, and the historians "were not Prophets, but Grave and Prudent Men, who would neither deceive others, nor be deceived themselves." Thus, even the Gospel of Luke was canonical, not because it was inspired, "but because the Primitive Church did Judge that they were written by godly Men, with great faithfulness and Treat of things that are of very great importance to our Salvation." "Spinosa did exactly follow the Opinion of *Grotius*," claimed Simon, asserting that the Apostles wrote not as prophets but "as particular Doctors . . . because they have nothing that is Prophetical."[104]

Against both, Simon maintained that "those Men do deceive themselves" who do not accept "any Inspiration, but that of the Prophecies," for "'Tis not necessary, for a

102 Ibid., II.22, p. 56.

103 Ibid., II.23, p. 59.

104 Ibid., II.23, pp. 60–61. Simon reports taking this from Grotius's *Votum pro Pace Ecclesiastica* (1642), a book devoted to the cause of Christian reunion. Grotius's *Annotationes in Vetus et Novum Testamentum* (1644–1650) is more explicitly devoted to an explication of exegesis under this new view of inspiration. Grotius was a humanist scholar, passionately devoted to the wisdom of antiquity, and just as passionately determined to bring about religious reconciliation for the sake of civil peace.

Book's being inspired, that it should be indited by God, word for word," a notion that Simon called a "false Idea."

> Jesus Christ, who promised to his Apostles that the Spirit of God should guide them in all the functions of their Ministry, did not therefore, deprive them of their Reason and Memory: Although they were inspired, they continued to be Men still, and managed their Affairs as other Men. *I freely own, that there was not need of Inspiration, to put in record such matters of Fact, whereof they themselves were Witnesses.* But this does not hinder, but that they were directed by the Spirit of God in all that they put in Writing, so as not to fall into error.[105]

How, then, was Simon's position different from that of Grotius and Spinoza? The difference, Simon informed readers, was that "the Ancient Ecclesiastical Writers did acknowledge this Inspiration of the Evangelists and Apostles." That is, there seems to be no difference, except the acknowledgment by *traditio*. The ecclesiastical writers spoke of the Apostle's mode of writing "in the same manner, as they speak of other Writers, who are not inspired"; yet, despite that, the Apostles' writings must be considered inspired *because* "those very Doctors have clearly maintained it."[106] The implication, which Simon himself drew out, was that Grotius and Spinoza would be correct, "if they [the ecclesiastical writers] had not expresly maintained it [that *all* the writings were inspired] in other places of their Works." In this sense, Simon can assert against Grotius and Spinoza, that (echoing the words of St. Paul, Timothy 3:16), "*all Scripture is given by Divine Inspiration.*" [107] This is a curious solution indeed, but one that accords with Simon's curious view of *traditio*. It would seem to imply that the Holy Spirit does not guide *traditio*, but *traditio* guides the Holy Spirit.

Simon further elaborated his position on inspiration in the context of a dispute that arose between "the Divines" of the "University of *Douay*" and the "Jesuits of *Louvain*," concerning the way God's grace and foreknowledge are related to the human free will.[108] This controversy had an exegetical aspect. Estius (Willem Hessels van Est, 1542–1613) at Douay, taking side against the Jesuits, argued that "all the Holy Scripture was indited by the Spirit of God, not only as to the matter, or things therein contained, but also in respect of the words and all their circumstances; so as

105 Ibid., II.23, p. 61. Emphasis added.

106 Ibid.

107 Ibid., p. 62.

108 Ibid., p. 64. The controversy centers upon what came to be called "Molinism," after Luis de Molina (1535–1600). Without going into the details of the controversy, one can glean the basic outlines in the decree (September 5, 1607) of the exasperated Pope Paul V (1605–1621), who declared that the Dominicans could not justly be accused of Calvinism nor the Jesuits of Pelagianism, and neither side was forthwith permitted to accuse the other of heresy. Dominicans focused on God's absolute omniscience (seemingly at the expense of free will, so that they could be considered to be aligning themselves with Calvin's strong doctrine of predestination), and the Jesuits focused on the freedom of the human will (seemingly at the expense of God's grace and omniscience, and hence were accused of holding to the Pelagian primacy of human action for salvation).

there is no word in Scripture, nor any ranging of words, but what comes from God." Simon regarded this position as "very little agreeable to the Doctrine of the Ancient Ecclesiastical Writers,"[109] and sided with the Jesuits, offering their three propositions (which had been censured) for approval of the reader. These propositions, declared Simon, are "really agreeable to good sense, neither do they much vary from the Theology of the Ancient Fathers. . . ."[110] The propositions are as follows:

> First, "That a thing should be Holy Scripture, it is not necessary that all the words thereof should be inspired by God."
>
> Second, "It is not necessary for all Truths and Sentences, to be immediately indited by Inspiration to the Writer."
>
> Three, "A Book, as for example, the second of the *Maccabees*, which was written by Men only without the assistance of the Holy Ghost, does afterwards become Holy Scripture, if the Holy Spirit doth testifie that there is nothing that is false, in that Book."[111]

In light of subsequent developments in historical-critical scholarship, the prophecies uttered by the Divines at Douay against the Jesuits at Louvain are quite interesting. As reported by Simon, in regard to the second proposition, the Divines asserted that

> if it be once granted [as the Jesuits argue], that it is not necessary, that every Truth and Sentence should be immediatly indited by the Spirit of God; there will be endless disputes, not only about that which is particularly delivered in Scripture by immediate Inspiration, but also about entire Gospels, the History of which may be known in a humane manner: It will be also question'd, in general, if all the Books of the Scripture that are not Prophetical, have been immediately suggested by the Holy Ghost, to those who were the Writers thereof.[112]

Against the third proposition, the Divines warn that the Jesuits' proposition "could not be maintained, without acknowledging, that the Histories of *Thucydides*, and of *Livie*, might for the same reason be reckoned amongst the Books of the Scripture; if the Holy Ghost should testifie to us, that there is nothing of falshood in those Histories." They concluded that "a thing is not therefore given by Divine Inspiration; because it so falls out, that it is approved of afterwards; but that, on the contrary, it is approved, because it was Inspired"—a position that directly contradicted Simon's notion of *traditio*.[113]

---

109 Ibid., II.23, p. 64.

110 Ibid., II.23, p. 65 and see his affirmation at II.24, p. 77.

111 Ibid., II.23, p. 65.

112 Ibid., II.23, p. 67.

113 Simon does insist that the "testimony of the Holy Ghost" comes first (Ibid., II.24, p. 77) but gives no other doctrine of how such inspiration takes place other than through the affirmation by *traditio*.

Simon made his agreement with the Jesuits quite clear, praising their efforts and the intellectual freedom given them by the order, and moreover commending them for not blindly following "Opinions of St. *Thomas*, and St. *Augustine*," nor the "Opinions that were most received in the Schools in their time, concerning the Inspiration of the Sacred Writings," the shedding of scholasticism providing them the "occasion of making new discoveries in this Science. . . ."[114] In particular, Simon picked out the efforts of Jesuit Cornelius à Lapide (Cornelis Cornelissen van den Steen, 1567–1637) for praise. Lapide (reported Simon) maintained quite sensibly that "the Holy Ghost did not indite all the Sacred Writings after the same manner." While the law and the prophets were indeed directly inspired, it was not necessary that the "Histories, and the Exhortations to Piety, which the Holy Pen-Men had learned, by seeing, hearing, reading, or meditation . . . be Inspired or Indited by the Spirit of God; because those Writers knew such things very well."[115]

As Simon quickly admitted, this affirmation might seem to present a problem, "seeing it may be objected that this Opinion [of Lapide and affirmed by Simon] is the same with that of *Grotius* and *Spinoza*, who acknowledged no other Inspiration but that of the Prophetical Writings. . . ."[116] Yet, averred Simon, there was this important difference: The "Historical and Moral" parts of Scripture (in the words of Lapide) were "also indited by the Holy Ghost, first, because he did assist the Writers; that they could never be deceived; and again, because he suggested to them, that one thing should be rather written than another." Although the Holy Spirit "did not suggest to them either their conceptions, or the remembrance of those things which they did know," the Spirit did "Inspire them in this respect only, that they might put one conception rather than another." This view of inspiration Simon regarded as "good Sense."[117]

Speaking for himself, Simon elucidated this position. Although the ancient heretics (somewhat akin to Spinoza?) rejected some parts of the New Testament as uninspired, their mistake was not so much in their judgment that something was uninspired, but in their rejection of what they considered uninspired. So that, "if it should be granted to those Hereticks, that St. *Paul*, and the rest of the Apostles were not Inspired in all that they write, it does not therefore follow, that we ought to reject a part of their Writings. It is sufficient, that we own with the Jesuits, that there is nothing but Truth in those very places which were not Inspired, and that the Holy Ghost had committed them to us as such."[118] To give a concrete example used by Simon, St. Paul says, "When you come, bring the cloak that I left with Carpus at Troas, also the books, and above all the parchments" (2 Timothy 4:13). St. Paul seems not in need of inspiration here, but that does not mean we reject this statement because it is uninspired. "It is sufficient that they [seemingly, those responsible in the early Church]

114 Ibid., II.23, pp. 68–69.

115 Ibid., II.23, p. 70.

116 Ibid., and see also II.24, p. 76.

117 Ibid., II.23, p. 70.

118 Ibid., II.23, p. 72

were persuaded that the Holy Writers were guided by the Spirit of God in every part of their Writings, so as not to fall into any error."[119] Paul had a coat; he left it with Carpus at Troas, and there were indeed books and parchments he wanted as well. Not inspired or inspiring, but free from error.

But where to draw the line? Again, citing Lapide approvingly, Simon argued that "in Histories of things which were seen and heard, and in the Exhortations that concern Morality, there is no need for any immediate Inspiration, because there is nothing that is Prophetical therein."[120] Despite his protestations, the line Simon drew was little different than the one drawn by Spinoza, for it would be all too easy to class the Gospels as histories, and hence to maintain that they were not directly inspired by the Holy Spirit—and indeed, that is precisely what Simon (following Lapide) did: "an immediate Inspiration was not necessary for Writing of Histories. The Evangelists writ that which they had seen, or that which they learned upon certain grounds."[121] This provided a way to reconcile apparent contradictions among the Gospels. Since they are not directly inspired—Simon spoke of their "bare direction of the Spirit of God"[122]—they may differ in style but not substance, so to speak. "For it is to be supposed, that the manner wherein the Evangelists express the same thing, does wholly proceed from themselves. It is sufficient that they agree in the substance of things, whilst it is not necessary that they should joyn in the Expressions. Every one of them might choose his own Words according to his pleasure."[123]

Given that Simon's account of the Holy Spirit's indirect inspiration was so thin—and his position consequently so easily mistaken for Spinoza's—the difference between secular history and biblical history would become hard to discern, except for the obvious fact (as Simon pointed out) that Thucydides and Livy "have not written of things that concern our Salvation."[124] But since inspiration is not needed to discern historical truth, then nonbiblical historical texts rise to equivalency with what is redundantly affirmed as true by the Holy Spirit via *traditio*. Furthermore, since the historical aspects of the Bible are then taken as merely historical and uninspired, rather than as an essential part of salvation history, then (if truth is truth) nonbiblical historical texts, if they are more thorough, constitute a corrective. We are not far from Machiavelli.

Further wrestling by Simon with Spinoza yielded the same ambiguous results. Spinoza was correct in marking the difference in inspiration between the prophetic and the nonprophetic writings. But "the ground of *Spinoza*'s error was, that a Man could not use his Reason, and be also guided by the Spirit of God, at the same

119 Ibid., II.24, p. 73.

120 Ibid., II.24, p. 75.

121 Ibid. Likewise, later Simon states that "Jesus Christ commanded his Disciples to go and Preach the Gospel, to all Nations of the Earth: but their Histories, which we call Gospels, are nothing else but Collections of their Sermons, which were animated by the Spirit of God, whom their Master had promised to them." Ibid., II.25, p. 80.

122 Ibid.

123 Ibid., II.24, p. 76.

124 Ibid., II.24, pp. 76–77.

time; as if by becoming God's Interpreter, he must cease to be a Man, and be only a Passive Instrument. . . ."[125] That is, Spinoza "does always confound Prophecy with Enthusiasm."[126] The Spirit and reason may both act, with "a Subordination betwixt the two," wherein "one does not destroy the other." Spinoza's fundamental error, Simon argued, was to consider prophecy and reason as mutually exclusive.[127] Yet, in looking at the case of Moses, Simon admitted that there was a mixture of reasoning under direct guidance of the Holy Spirit and unguided or indirectly guided reasoning: "It was not necessary that God should indite all his Reasonings and all his [moral] Exhortations. It is enough that he guided him by his Spirit, and that he prevented his falling into error. This being supposed, we will freely agree with *Spinosa*, that *Moses* said many things, that were not revealed to him. . . ."[128] But which is which? Simon was not clear, and the lack of clarity invited the kind of aggressive exegetical treatment Spinoza envisioned wherein the text divided was the text conquered.

The same problem plagued Simon's treatment of morality. In regard to the moral exhortations, the guidance of the Holy Spirit seemed indistinguishable from the light of reason, so that the light of reason, without revelation, would seem wholly sufficient: "it was not necessary, for their purpose [the Apostles] that God should indite to St. *Paul* and the other Apostles, all their Discourses on Morality. It was permitted them to make use of their natural Lights, and to use all the means with which their Reason could furnish them, for persuading the People."[129] Again, if nonbiblical sources had better, clearer, more thorough accounts of morality, they would stand as a corrective to the biblical account.

As a final irony, given Simon's all-important stress on *traditio*, the Protestant translator of his work into English added in a postscript (after duly praising Simon's efforts) that, "'Tis not to be wondered that he has committed Mistakes, having had the Misfortune to be brought up in the *Church of* Rome, which uses the Holy Scriptures chiefly in order to corrupt them; equaling if not preferring Traditions to them, founding its Infallibility on its self, being supported by the intricate Juggles of the *Canonists*, and the Gibberish of the *Schoolmen*." Against this corrupt tradition, the translator offers instead "the Scriptures and uncorrupted Antiquity," presumably the early Church to which Simon had deferred to make his case for *traditio*.[130] Herein exists the irony and the manifest and inviting weak point of his entire argument: All that was needed to tumble Simon's argument into Spinoza's was a sustained historical and exegetical attack on *traditio*, one that Protestants were all too happy and willing to provide.

---

125 Ibid., II.25, p. 81.
126 Ibid., II.25, p. 83.
127 Ibid., II.25, p. 82.
128 Ibid.
129 Ibid., p. 83.
130 Ibid., Translator's Postscript to the Reader, unnumbered.

Conclusion

One need not belabor what is by now quite obvious. Simon's attempt to vanquish Protestantism's claim of *sola scriptura* by amplifying Spinoza's approach to exegesis only served to provide a much firmer scholarly foundation for Spinozism. Thus, to acknowledge the immense influence of Richard Simon on the future of modern biblical scholarship is simultaneously to recognize the greater paternity of Spinoza. But that admission contains a lesson important for the present thesis. Whatever Simon's intentions in taking Spinoza's methods to the extreme, the methods themselves bore Spinoza's original intentions. Given that Simon's case for *traditio* was so weak, it had little effect on shoring up the Catholic cause against Protestantism; given that his extension of Spinoza was so strong, it provided a great rich storehouse for deists and the anti-Christian radical Enlightenment against the authority of the Bible.

More harm, then, was done by Simon's good intentions than by the devious intentions of, for example, the brothers Koerbagh or Lodewijk Meyer, and part of this was the fact that, despite his troubles, Simon was always a priest in good standing, personally sober and morally upright, untainted by any scandal except his writings, and passionately convinced that he was helping the cause of Mother Church against the hidebound unreasoning traditionalists who closed their eyes to the latest scholarly research. Simon thought that he could be more modern than the most modern of his day, and therefore secure the Church against the intellectual assaults gathering with ever greater strength outside her walls. As will appear, Simon inadvertently provided an enormous arsenal of ammunition for the very forces against which he hoped to guard.

CHAPTER 11

THE ENGLISH CIVIL WARS, MODERATE RADICALS, AND JOHN LOCKE

The Place of John Locke

As history makes clear, the twenty years of turmoil from 1640 to 1660, the period of the English Civil Wars, were decisive in the transformation of English political, social, and religious life. Their effect on the development of modern biblical scholarship is far less appreciated, but is no less decisive. During this period, both the moderate and the radical aspects of the new approach to Scripture were nourished and grew tremendously, especially as united with the parallel (and often overlapping) developments occurring in the Netherlands during the same general period.

The radical English pedigree can be traced from the Levellers, the Quaker Samuel Fisher, the republicans, and up through John Toland, who unites the English with Dutch radicalism. This line of descent begins at the outskirts of Christianity and ends up with a reaffirmation of a kind of paganism. Although it may seem to have "lost out" to the more moderate elements during this period, it survived and in fact became even more radical and influential, disseminated largely in clandestine form during the eighteenth century but rising to power again during the nineteenth century in every aspect of intellectual life, especially scriptural scholarship. This will become clear in the career and legacy of Toland.

The moderate English pedigree of modern scriptural scholarship (most often associated with Protestant Liberalism or mild deism) may be traced from the new propertied, Presbyterian class as it comes into power during this period, especially as it consciously incorporated the new mechanistic worldview as its grounding cosmology. This line of descent begins with the transfer of power from the king and nobility to the Parliament and propertied during the Civil Wars, but includes the successful struggle for theological domination by the Latitudinarians—most importantly, Robert Boyle, the Royal Society, the Newtonians, and especially John Locke, whose life provides a useful autobiographical framework for these developments.

Locke is universally recognized as one of the most influential philosophers of the Enlightenment, so much so that the eighteenth century might well be considered Lockean. Locke's influence reaches far beyond the normally accredited areas of epistemology and political philosophy, however, as will become clear in his use and treatment of Scripture.

John Locke, a Moderate Borne among Radicals

John Locke was born in a humble thatched cottage during the reign of Charles I on August 29, 1632, the son of John Locke senior, a lawyer and member of the minor gentry of Somerset, and Agnes Keene, the beautiful daughter of a tanner (and nearly ten years older than her husband).[1] He was baptized the same day by the ardent Puritan Dr. Samuel Crook of the Wrington parish in Somerset County, a dissenter under the wings of the Anglican Church. Although Locke's immediate ancestors were all of the merchant class, Sir William Locke, his great great-grandfather, was mercer to Henry VIII and also the sheriff of London. Soon after his birth, the Lockes would move on to Belluton, living in a small Tudor farmhouse. Two other children would be born, Peter and Thomas. Only one, Thomas, would live.

Both parents were Puritans, seemingly of a more liberal sort. At the time of Locke's birth, King Charles I had been ruling without Parliament for about three years, and would continue his personal rule until 1640, when he was forced to call Parliament into session to deal with the crisis with Scotland. The conflict between the crown and Parliament would not be resolved, and the First Civil War broke out in 1642. Locke's father was a captain of cavalry in the Parliamentary army.

It would not be too off the mark to see the English Civil Wars of the mid-seventeenth century as a rebellion against Henry VIII's Act of Supremacy, especially insofar as he had tried to support it through an appeal to the Protestant principle of *sola scriptura*. Of course, he meant this principle as the means by which the power to interpret Scripture would be rooted in the person of the sovereign, not (as Puritans and other dissenters would later assert) as a principle by which the sovereign himself could be judged.

Henry had securely lodged all power in the sovereign, both of church and state, and Parliament simply did his bidding in religion and politics. Elizabeth, during her long reign, had done much the same. But the first Stuart kings, James I and Charles I, ran into more difficulties. Though they did not rule differently in principle than Henry and Elizabeth, the situation in England was changing in the first half of the seventeenth century. The Anglican Church's power was increasingly rubbing against the ever more potent Puritan faction, and the royal court proved less and less able to tax and control the new propertied class that had been gaining social and economic momentum for some time. The nexus of Puritan dissatisfaction and the new propertied class was Parliament, and it was the propertied class through Parliament that finally rebelled against the crown (with the help of the common people, without whom the rebellion would have been crushed).

1 In what follows, we use (unless otherwise noted), the biography of Locke by Maurice Cranston, *John Locke: A Biography* (Oxford: Oxford University Press, 1985).

It was neither simply an economic rebellion, nor a political rebellion, nor a religious rebellion, for all three were inextricably bound together, as inseparable in the minds and hearts of all parties as it was in their lives. For this very reason, the political interpretation of Scripture was assumed by all as the proper mode of justification of their beliefs and actions, which meant that the principle of *sola scriptura* became unhinged from the Act of Supremacy. So powerful was the appeal to the individual spirit of interpretation, however, that among the radical, it became unhinged even from the authority of Scripture itself, resulting in something akin to the Cartesian *ego*, an inner divine light, indistinguishable from natural reason, that judged the Bible itself and found it wanting.

A rough but fair generalization to illustrate this tight knot of political interests, aims, and aspirations that formed the context of the English Civil Wars, might say that the conservation of ancient privilege and estates was bound to monarchy and sacerdotal, Episcopal rule. In James I's famous words, "No bishop, no king, no nobility." The protection of new wealth and industry was bound to a kind of Presbyterian rule in both Parliament and church. This was the faction that finally won out. But there was a third party, wherein economic and social powerlessness and desperation were bound to more radical religious, economic, and political ideas.

Although the latter two groups were united in fighting against the crown, they had differences among themselves, most prominently represented in the division between the Presbyterians and Independents (the latter containing many different radical sects, most notably the Levellers). To generalize once more, the Presbyterian faction would accept compromise with the king, if only he would yield to Parliament; the Independents, representing the more radical elements, wanted an all-out war, and as commonwealthmen or republicans, pushed both for an army and a society free (or at least much more free) of inherited rank associated with property, either old or new. The Presbyterian faction believed that the king should be subordinated to Parliament, which itself would represent the new propertied class; the Independent faction believed that there should be no king at all, and that Parliament got its powers, as a republican representative body, from the people. The Presbyterian faction would gladly take a state church, as long as it was Presbyterian; the Independent faction would rather rid England of a state church altogether.

Locke's family sided with Parliament. Through the patronage of his father's commander, Colonel Alexander Popham, Locke was able to attend one of the best schools in England, the Westminster School, beginning in 1647. The rather famous headmaster there was, ironically, a staunch royalist and Anglican, Richard Busby. There, Locke studied the Latin and Greek classics, as well as Hebrew. By this time, the New Model Army had decisively won the First Civil War (1642–1646), only to be thrown back into the Second Civil War (1647–1649) when Charles I escaped from captivity on November 11, 1647, thereby galvanizing royalist forces to fight once again.

The period of the Second Civil War was a time of political, philosophical, and theological radicalism bubbling to the surface that would culminate in regicide—with the beheading of Charles I on January 30, 1649, and the declaration that henceforth England would be a commonwealth or republic, rather than a monarchy. Charles's beheading took place during Locke's second year at Westminster, and headmaster Busby kept his boys in to pray for the king during this fateful event. Locke was elected a King's Scholar the following year, allowing him to live gratis at Westminster. Locke continued his studies amidst this social and theological upheaval. From Westminster, he moved on to Christ Church College, Oxford (where he had received a scholarship), arriving in 1652, at twenty years old, receiving his bachelor of arts in 1656, and his master of arts in 1658.

Locke's time at Oxford, then, coincided with the greatest political unrest. These were the years of the Third Civil War (1649–1651), overlapping with the Commonwealth (1649–1653), and with the breakdown of order and consequent military dictatorship of Oliver Cromwell's Protectorate (1654–1658). Hobbes, whose *Leviathan* had been published in 1651, seemed to be vindicated: our natural state was a state of war, and the only release, to be put into the hands of an absolute sovereign (providing he was not a Catholic). Locke felt himself in "great Bedlam England," a country gone mad.[2]

Oxford had been solidly royalist, serving from 1642 to 1646 as the king's headquarters during the First Civil War, but was then taken over by the Parliamentary army. All were required to take an oath of loyalty to Parliament or be purged (and in the summer of 1653, Parliamentary visitors demanded that non-Puritan students be purged). Cromwell's chaplain, John Owen, became dean, and students were required to hear two sermons a day. The chancellor of Oxford was none other than Oliver Cromwell, and when he stepped down, his son Richard. Owen himself was something of an advocate of religious toleration, and hence deflected the Parliamentary visitors' attempt to purge his students under Oliver Cromwell. Under Richard, Owen himself would be demoted and then purged in 1659, replaced by an avid Presbyterian, Edward Reynolds, and (much to Locke's displeasure) Puritan rule at the college became more rigid. He complained in a letter, "We are all Quakers here and there is not a man but thinks he alone hath this light within and all besides [him] stumble in the dark."[3]

As even this short comment makes clear, Locke was quite uncomfortable with rigid Puritans, and even more so with the radical offshoots such as the Quakers, in whom *sola scriptura* had been replaced by the "inner light" that judges all things. To get some sense of this radicalism is essential, especially insofar as it relates to the use and treatment of Scripture, as a necessary background to understand Locke's "moderate" treatment of the Bible in his later works.

Radical Revolutions and Scripture

During the Civil Wars (especially the Second), state censorship broke down, and radical political, biblical, and philosophical approaches burst out in the chaos, wild

2 From a letter written on November 8, 1656. Quoted in Cranston, *John Locke*, p. 42.

3 From a letter written on October 20, 1659. Quoted in ibid., p. 43.

and suppressed hopes and ideas leaping into flame.[4] More crucially, Parliament's New Model Army was forced to recruit and advance soldiers from the commoners among whom the most radical ideas and hopes were to be found.

As the army became more successful, the radical Protestants became more powerful, the most notable being the so-called Levellers. Among the Levellers, there were the even more radical Diggers (or True Levellers) and the Ranters. The Levellers were common folk whose situation had become even more difficult during this period. The late 1640s were a time of terrible social and political crises. Civil war combined with failed crops made the circumstances of the poor desperate, and to them, all distinction or privilege, property, or rank was suspect, whether it be a king, a nobleman, an Anglican bishop, a parson, a hedge that kept the poor off the nobleman's lands, or even the Bible itself.

To illustrate, on a Sunday in the spring of 1649, the very year that England officially became a commonwealth and Locke was in his second year at Westminster, six soldiers entered the parish church of Walton-on-Thames and declared the abolition of the Sabbath, of church tithes, ministers, church magistrates, and the Bible itself. Such was the origin of the Diggers, so called because the soldiers then went outside, and in defiance of both the Sabbath and the aristocratic-oligarchic monopoly on the ownership of land, began to dig up the ground on St. George's Hill just outside of London, declaring it their own for common use.[5]

One Gerrard Winstanley would soon join them, and claim to have a vision "telling him to publish it abroad that 'the earth should be made a common treasury of livelihood to whole mankind, without respect of persons.'"[6] Hence the Diggers came to be called the "True Levellers," for they meant to level all class- and property-based distinctions. This was vindicated through a particular reading of Scripture. According to Winstanley, "In the beginning of time the great creator, Reason, made the earth to be a common treasury," so "The poorest man hath as true a title and just right to the land as the richest man," consequently "All laws that are not grounded upon equity and reason, not giving a universal freedom to all . . . ought . . . to be cut off with the King's head."[7] This was not a merely theoretical cry, but at heart a truly practical one. Winstanley wanted the lands held by the nobility in waste (lands that had been used as "commons" by the poor before the new propertied class enclosed them for their own production) to be given to the poor to cultivate. "True religion and undefiled is

---

4 As Christopher Hill notes, the breakdown of censorship helped to bring about an "explosion" of printing. "This aspect of the printing explosion of the 1640s is not always sufficiently emphasized. For the first time in English history anyone could get into print who could persuade a printer that there was money in his or her idea. Significant numbers of persons (including women) who had had no university education, often no grammar school education even, found no obstacles to publication." Christopher Hill, *The English Bible and the Seventeenth-Century Revolution* (New York: Penguin Books, 1994), p. 198.

5 See Christopher Hill, *The World Turned Upside Down: Radical Ideas During the English Revolution* (London: Penguin Books, reprint 1991), p. 110.

6 Ibid., p. 112.

7 Quoted in ibid., pp. 132–133.

to let every one quietly have earth to manure."[8] An earthy but exact slogan—and also quite revolutionary, given that most people had no property.

As Winstanley soon made clear, the leveling of society demanded a cosmic leveling, wherein even God is brought to the level of nature, thereby offering a kind of proto-Spinozan pantheism that would prepare the ground for the introduction of Spinoza to England: "The whole creation . . . is the clothing of God," so that "The Father is the universal power that hath spread himself in the whole globe. . . ." Christ was reduced to a spirit living within each person, who recognizes the Divine in nature, so that one looks to the "objects of the creation," not the Bible, priest, or minister for divine revelation. "To know the secrets of nature is to know the works of God."[9] Accordingly, Winstanley treated the Bible as, at best, an allegory of truths known by reason, thereby rejecting any actual Garden of Eden, Virgin Birth, the Resurrection, and, indeed, rejecting its claim of inspiration completely.[10]

Winstanley was not the only one to unite pantheism with radical politics. Ranter Jacob Bauthumley declared that God was in everything: "man and beast, fish and fowl, and every green thing, from the highest cedar to the ivy on the wall." He "does not exist outside his creatures," so that God is in "this dog, this tobacco pipe, he is me and I am him," he is "dog, cat, chair, [and] stool."[11] For some Ranters this affirmation of their own divinity led them to assert that sin did not exist, and that actions previously described as sin ("swearing, drunkenness, adultery and theft, etc.") were no sin at all.[12] In regard to Scripture, since each was God, there was no need of revelation, and in fact the Bible was not only superfluous but pernicious. According to some Ranters, the Bible "hath been the cause of all our misery and divisions . . . of all the blood that hath been shed in the world," and consequently, there would never be peace until all Bibles were burned.[13] Here one sees an exemplary and early instance of the Scripture politicized from below, the assumption being that the Bible could *only* be a political tool of oppressors.

Very often this rejection of the Bible was, oddly enough, biblically based, and on its own terms, religious rather than irreligious, spiritually akin to the *Schwärmer* against whom Luther railed. It was a logical extension of the priesthood of all believers who, once they had the spirit within, had no more use for the "dead letter" of the Bible, as John Everard declared in his *The Gospel Treasure Opened* (second edition, 1659).[14] In the anonymous *Tyranipocrit Discovered* (1649), the author declared that it was not the Bible, but the "Knowledge of God within ourselves and in his other

8 Quoted in ibid., p. 130.

9 Quoted in ibid., pp. 139–142.

10 Ibid., pp. 144–145.

11 Ibid., see Chapter 9 on the Seekers and the Ranters. Quotes on p. 206.

12 Ibid., pp. 207–208.

13 Ibid., pp. 262–263. On the whole issue of radicalism during this period, see also Christopher Hill, "Freethinking and Libertinism: the Legacy of the English Revolution," in Roger Lund, ed., *The Margins of Orthodoxy: Heterodox Writing and Cultural Response, 1660–1750* (Cambridge: Cambridge University Press, 1995), pp. 54–70.

14 Quoted in Christopher Hill, *The English Bible and the Seventeenth–Century Revolution*, pp. 182–183.

creatures, that is all in all to us."[15] The Bible became the occasion for spiritual awakening, but once the spirit within was awakened, it had no need of a mere text, and what the spirit counseled was, quite often, complete political, social, moral, and religious revolution, far beyond what the much more solid and staid Puritans would countenance. Such was the path by which Puritan principles were transformed into those of the Quakers (at this time, "Quaker" was a more general term of abuse thrown against all radicals, than the name of a well-defined sect).

The inner light that displaced the authority of Scripture brought a critical examination of the text itself in terms reminiscent of later biblical scholars. As a consequence, rejection of Scripture as authoritative was also based upon a close analysis of the text itself. By this time, the search by believing divines to establish the best Greek manuscript reading—such as Brian Walton's six-volume *Biblia Sacra Polyglotta* (published, 1654–1657)—had produced, through the display of textual variations, a fertile field of doubt for the skepticism of religious radicals. William Walwyn was reported as saying that "'the Scripture is so plainly and directly contradictory to itself' that he did not believe it to be the Word of God," and Lawrence Clarkson declared that there was "so much contradiction" in it that "'I had no faith in it at all, no more than a history."[16] Clement Writer, in his *Fides Divina* (1657), asserted that since the Bible contained so many errors of transcription and translation, and further, there were so many disagreements about which books were indeed inspired, it could not "be a divine testimony."[17] And finally, and most important, the Quaker Samuel Fisher—who knew and worked with Spinoza[18]—claimed that it is foolish to call the Bible the Word of God, given the unreliability of the text. Fisher then spent extended exegetical effort to show that unreliability, and concluded that not the Bible but the inner light is the true Word of God. The Quakers, asserted Fisher in his *Rustick's Alarm to the Rabbis*, "own not the said alterable and much altered outward text and letter, or Scripture, but the holy truth and inward light and spirit, which the Scripture it self testifies to . . . the word of God, which is living, the only firm, infallible foundation of all saving faith, and invariable right rule of holy life."[19] The Bible, rather than being an inspired unity, was for Fisher "a bulk of heterogeneous writings, compiled together by men taking what they could find of the several sorts of writings that are therein, and . . . crowding them into a canon. . . ."[20] What made Fisher's works so influential, as Christopher Hill remarks, is that it was "popular Biblical

---

15 Ibid., p. 196.

16 Quoted in Hill, *The World Turned Upside Down*, p. 262–263.

17 Quoted in ibid., p. 265.

18 On this connection between Fisher and Spinoza see Richard Popkin, "Spinoza's Relations with the Quakers," *Quaker History* 73 (1984), pp. 14–28, and also Popkin, "The Hebrew Translation of Margaret Fell's 'Loving Salutation.' The first publication of Spinoza?" 21 *Studia Rosenthalia* (1987).

19 Quoted in Travis Frampton, *Spinoza and the Rise of Historical Criticism of the Bible* (London: T. & T. Clark, 2006), p. 219.

20 Quoted in Hill, *The World Turned Upside Down*, pp. 266–267.

criticism, based on real scholarship," Fisher having been educated at Trinity College of Oxford University.[21]

Locke could not help but be aware of this unsettling political, philosophical, and theological radicalism churning up his country during this period. As one important instance makes clear, he was quite sick of such unbridled religious "enthusiasm," as it was called. Locke was present at the Westminster Hall trial of the Quaker James Nayler in 1656. In this decade, James Nayler (rather than George Fox) was considered the leader of those called Quakers, who at this time were indistinguishable from Levellers and Ranters. Quakers were the radicals of this period, and Nayler was arrested as their leader by a Parliament increasingly impatient with disorder. Retired cavalryman Nayler believed that the Christ within had indeed made *him* Christ, and he came from Exeter into Bristol in 1656 riding on a donkey, women throwing palms before him and shouting "Holy! Holy! Holy!" and crying their hosannas. He was arrested and sent to London. After the trial, Locke wrote with evident distaste, "I am weary of the Quakers."[22]

A Hobbesian Key to Locke

The experience of civil war, nearly anarchic radicalism, and military dictatorship brought the moderates to invite Charles II to take the throne in 1660, a move that Locke happily welcomed. "I find that a general freedom is but a general bondage, that the popular asserters of public liberty are the greatest ingrossers of it too," wrote Locke. "All the freedom I can wish my country or myself is to enjoy the protection of those laws which the prudence and providence of our ancestors established and the happy return of his Majesty has restored."[23]

The monarchy and state church were restored under the control of Parliament, but this imposition of order did not at once stamp out all fires of discontent. During late 1660, Locke (now a tutor at the college) wrote a defense of the power of the civil magistrate to determine every aspect of religious worship, and during 1661–1662 he penned two further works, one reaffirming the imposition of a state church, the other affirming *sola scriptura* against Catholicism.[24] The Hobbesian tone of his arguments is quite striking, leaving no doubt that Locke (despite his

21 Ibid. On Fisher, see also Justin Champion, "Apocrypha, Canon and Criticism from Samuel Fisher to John Toland, 1650–1718," in Allison Coudert, et al, eds., *Judaeo-Christian Intellectual Culture in the Seventeenth Century* (Dordrecht: Kluwer Academic Publishers, 1999), pp. 91–117; and Frampton, *Spinoza and the Rise of Historical Criticism of the Bible*, pp. 217–223.

22 From a letter of November 15, 1656. Quoted in Cranston, *John Locke*, p. 42. For an account of Nayler, especially as he represents the radicalism of the Quakers of the time, see Hill, *The World Turned Upside Down*, pp. 248–252.

23 Quoted in Cranston, *John Locke*, p. 59.

24 See Philip Abrams, ed., John Locke, *Two Tracts on Government* (Cambridge: Cambridge University Press, 1967). On the context, see Abrams's extended introduction, and also J. R. Milton, "Locke's Life and Times," in Vere Chappell, ed., *The Cambridge Companion to Locke* (Cambridge: Cambridge University Press, 1994), p. 7.

later attempts to distance himself) was deeply influenced by the *Leviathan*.[25] Sidestepping the question of the source of the monarch's authority—"whether the magistrate's crown drops down on his head immediately from heaven or be placed there by the hands of his subjects"—Locke asserted that "the supreme magistrate of every nation, what way so ever created, must necessarily have an absolute and arbitrary power over all the indifferent actions of his people."[26] Very early on, then, Locke had read the great mechanist Hobbes, and affirmed, for the sake of political order, his secular grounding of authority. One might say, then, that at the time of the Restoration Locke was, like Hobbes, both essentially radical and accidentally conservative: radical in accepting something like Hobbesianism as the foundation of order and conservative in his desire to maintain the particular status quo of political order in England.[27]

Locke, Robert Boyle, and a Moderate Cosmos

It was in the very year of the Restoration that Locke met Robert Boyle (1627–1691). Locke had become interested in the new mechanical approach to nature not only from Hobbes, but also from his reading of Descartes and Daniel Sennert (1572–1657), the latter a German physician and atomist.[28] Locke's relationship with Boyle, the foremost English proponent of mechanism other than Hobbes, did everything to deepen Locke's budding attachment to the new corpuscular philosophy. This connection with Boyle is significant because it was in England largely through Boyle and Hobbes (with the aid of cross-fertilization of Gassendi on the Continent) that the atomism associated with the pagan Epicurus received its Christian baptism, and modern materialism was thereby

25 Witness Locke's cribbing (to use the apt phrase of Cranston) of Hobbes's infamous description of the state of nature, wherein (Locke warned) there is "no peace, no security, no enjoyment, enmity with all men and safe possession of nothing, and those stinging swarms of misery which attend anarchy and rebellion." Quoted in Cranston, *John Locke*, p. 62.

26 Quoted in ibid., p. 60. By "indifferent," Locke was explicitly referring to the notion of *adiaphora* first put forth under Henry VIII, wherein the king could impose laws governing the details of worship even though such things have no explicit scriptural sanction.

27 One important sign of Locke's seemingly contradictory position is that in 1659 he was corresponding with radical republican and pantheist Henry Stubbe, who believed that, since God is immanent in nature, miracles were natural events. Hence he denied supernatural revelation, and with it, special inspiration of the Bible. Locke warmly affirmed Stubbe's plea for toleration, but regarded it as *impractical* (at least, for the time being). For Locke's correspondence with Stubbe in regard to the latter's *An Essay in Defence of the Good Old Cause; or a Discourse Concerning the Rise and Extent of the Power of the Civil Magistrate in Reference to Spiritual Affairs*, see ibid., pp. 44–45. On Stubbe, see James Jacob, "Boyle's Atomism and the Restoration Assault on Pagan Naturalism," *Social Studies of Science* 8 (1978), pp. 211–223 (discussion of Stubbe, pp. 218–222), and Jacob, *Henry Stubbe, Radical Protestantism and the Early Enlightenment* (Cambridge: Cambridge University Press, 2002).

28 For an account of Sennert see Andrew G. Van Melsen, *From Atomos to Atom: The History of the Concept Atom* (New York: Harper & Brothers, 1960), pp. 81–89. It may have been that Locke only got his Descartes secondhand at this point, but he was certainly reading him in earnest by 1667. Cranston, *John Locke*, p. 100.

given its peculiar (albeit transient) theist formulation as taken up into Newtonianism. But just as important, Boyle also combined this Christianized materialism with Francis Bacon's utilitarian view of science as technical mastery of nature for this-worldly benefit, a union that provided a justification for the powerful Presbyterian commercial class against the nobility. This formulation—an attempted union of a utilitarian materialism with a Latitudinarian version of Christianity—produced a kind of liberal Protestantism or moderate deism that so decisively stamped the eighteenth and nineteenth centuries. It was this moderate radicalism that would help to define Locke's mature thought, and some attention to Boyle is therefore necessary for grasping Locke.[29]

To summarize Boyle's position in its larger theological and political context (or more accurately, the position of the Royal Society that Boyle largely defined), we must take into account its formulation in light of the Civil Wars and the Restoration. Boyle's aim was to advance a moderate (i.e., Latitudinarian) Protestantism against radical Protestantism and Catholicism, one that avoided both the theological and philosophical radicalism and enthusiasm that proved so disruptive during the Civil War years, and on the other hand avoided not only Catholicism itself but also the politically and theologically conservative pull backward toward the alliance of Stuart kings, Anglo-Catholicism, and rule by the nobility.

Against Catholicism, which found support in Aristotelian metaphysics, Boyle put forth mechanist atomism. Against theological and philosophical radicals, Boyle set out a version of atomism that he thought disallowed atheist materialism, pantheism, or any kind of Averroism based on the world being a self-governing entity.[30] Against religious conservatives who wished to reinstate the Laudian Anglican Church conservatism of the Stuarts and crush all dissenters, Boyle argued for a religious compromise that contained enough latitude that most dissenters could fit comfortably (i.e., be "comprehended") under the umbrella of the Anglican state church, very broadly defined. Finally, to unite all moderate parties in a common project, and not just by a common enemy, Boyle focused the energies of the new commercial class on Bacon's project of mastering nature for the sake of this-worldly comfort and prosperity. Some attention to Bacon's project formulated about two decades before the outbreak of England's Civil Wars will help clarify the foundation and aims of the Royal Society.

"I entreat men to believe," Bacon declared of his new science, "that it is not an opinion to be held, but a work to be done; and to be well assured that I am laboring

---

29 On Boyle's motivations, both theological and political, see James Jacob, "Robert Boyle and Subversive Religion in the Early Restoration," *Albion* 6 (1974), pp. 275–293; "Restoration, Reformation and the Origins of the Royal Society," *History of Science* 13 (1975), pp. 155–176; the above-cited "Boyle's Atomism and the Restoration Assault on Pagan Naturalism"; "The Anglican Origins of Modern Science: The Metaphysical Foundations of the Whig Constitution," *Isis* 71 (1980), pp. 251–267; and finally, his book *Robert Boyle and the English Revolution: A Study in Social and Intellectual Change* (New York: Burt Franklin & Co., Inc., 1977).

30 On this see P. M. Rattansi, "The Social Interpretation of Science in the Seventeenth Century, " in Peter Mathias, ed., *Science and Society 1600–1900* (Cambridge: Cambridge University Press, 1972), pp. 1–32.

to lay the foundation, not of any sect or doctrine, but of human utility and power,"[31] for the "true and lawful goal of the sciences is none other than this: that human life be endowed with new discoveries and powers,"[32] so that "man [may] endeavor to establish and extend the power and dominion of the human race itself over the universe" in an "empire of man over things."[33]

Bacon presented the establishment of this empire as an essentially Christian undertaking, one that fit into a new theology of history. His religious beliefs seem to have been a mix of public Anglicanism and more secretive Calvinist leanings, as is revealed in his private "Confession of Faith." [34] Such a combination was by no means extraordinary, but the "Confession," written on the model of a credal statement, does contain an interesting deviation or addition from all known creeds at the time: that God "by his eternal Word created all things," and that God "created heaven and earth . . . and gave unto them constant and everlasting laws, which we call Nature, which is nothing but the laws of creation. . . ." These laws were in full "force" when God rested on the seventh day, but as a result of the fall, they "received a revocation in part by the curse, since which time they change not."[35]

How did this tie into his emphasis on the mastery of nature? It appears that Bacon believed that our mastery was a reimposition of our original dominion, in which, by dissecting nature and rediscovering the hidden "everlasting laws" of creation, we are able to effect (and even surpass) our original, full dominion over nature.[36] This theology of dominion was vividly presented in Bacon's enormously influential *New Atlantis*, a short, modern utopian masterpiece that provided the blueprint for England's famed scientific Royal Society.

In the fable, Englanders shipwreck on an unknown island, Bensalem (Arabic for "Son of Peace," an emphasis that cannot help but recall Marsilius), the inhabitants of which are Christian. Amazingly, in contrast to England and Europe of Bacon's own time, there is no religious controversy, even though they have the Bible as the foundation of their faith. Bensalem was miraculously delivered a copy of the Bible (a larger version, with all the canonical books plus a few others) that had been put in an ark and cast into the sea by the Apostle Bartholomew, arriving in a pillar of light off the coast of Bensalem about 50 AD. The islanders' faith has been preserved, intact and without dissent, for 1600 years, built on a *sola scriptura* foundation and aided by a priesthood at the service of the state. Bensalemite Christianity looks suspiciously like the state Anglicanism of Bacon's day, but without any turbulent undercurrent of religious and political dissent that would soon wrack England with civil war.

---

31 Francis Bacon, *The Great Instauration* in Fulton Anderson, ed., *The New Organon and Related Writings* (New York: Macmillan Publishing Company, 1988), p. 16, also p. 29.

32 Ibid., I, aphorism lxxxi.

33 Ibid., I, aphorism cxxix.

34 See Bacon's "Confession" in Brian Vickers, ed., Francis Bacon, *The Major Works* (Oxford: University of Oxford Press, 1996), pp. 107–112, and Vickers's illuminating notes.

35 Ibid., p. 108.

36 Bacon, *The Great Instauration*, "Proem," p. 3.

The reason for Bensalem's peace is that the focus of this utopian island is not the church, but "Salomon's House; which house or college . . . is the very eye of this kingdom. . . ."[37] Salomon's House is a scientific research college, the goal of which is the mastery of nature for the sake of the amelioration of human misery and the expression of full, demiurgic dominion over nature.

The house would seem to be named after its founder, King Solamona, the "lawgiver" of Bensalem, who reigned three hundred years before the arrival of the Bible, a king "wholly bent to make his kingdom and people happy."[38] It was he who erected and instituted "an Order or Society" that came to be called Salomon's House, a society "dedicated to the study of the Works and Creatures of God."[39] The house was actually named, not after the king but out of deference to the Biblical King Salomon[40] (Calvin's spelling of Solomon), renowned for his wisdom—a wisdom that, in Bacon's hands, receives an interesting twist. It turns out that the islanders "have some parts of his works which with you [i.e., the shipwrecked Englanders] are lost; namely, that Natural History which he wrote" about plants and animals.[41]

This elevation of Solomon to eminent natural scientist was central to Bacon's project of providing biblical justification for the mastery of nature. Bacon anchored his justification especially to Solomon, understood as a king engrossed in and dedicated to "the glory of inquisition of truth; for so he saith expressly, 'The glory of God is to conceal a thing, but the glory of the king is to find it out'" (Proverbs 25:2). The twist provided by Bacon is not only that Solomon becomes the paradigmatic natural philosopher, but that natural philosophy is dedicated to the re-creation of fallen nature for the sake of this-worldly comfort, peace, and prosperity. In the *New Atlantis*, Salomon's House—also called the College of the Six Days' Works[42]—is aimed at more than the study of nature; rather, "The End of our Foundation," as an eminent Bensalemite explains, "is the knowledge of Causes, and secret motions of things; and the enlarging of the bounds of Human Empire, to the effecting of all things possible."[43]

---

37 Francis Bacon, *New Atlantis*, in *Major Works*, pp. 457–489, quote on p. 464.

38 Ibid., p. 469.

39 Ibid., p. 471.

40 According to the story, before the great flood there was great concourse among all nations, and many Jews came to Bensalem, and made known the wisdom of Solomon, thus explaining how the island could be aware of a biblical figure before miraculously receiving the Bible.

41 This conjecture may not be entirely fanciful in Bacon's eyes, since outside the fable, in his *Advancement of Learning*, he praises "Salomon the king" for compiling a natural history of plants and animals, based on the rather thin scriptural evidence of 1 Kings 4:33. See *Advancement of Learning* in *Major Works*, pp. 151–152.

42 Bacon, *New Atlantis*, in *Major Works*, p. 471.

43 Ibid., p. 480. Appended to the *New Atlantis* since its very first printing along with Bacon's *Sylva Sylvarum: or A Natural Historie* (not by Bacon itself, who had died a year earlier, but by those responsible for publication) was a short list of goals at which a real College of the Six Days' Works should aim. Included in the list are the following: "The prolongation of life," "The restitution of youth in some degree," "The retardation of age," "The curing of diseases counted incurable," "The mitigation of pain," "The increasing and exalting of the intellectual parts," "Versions [i.e., conversions or transformations] of bodies into other bodies," "Making new species," "Transplanting of one species into another," "Instruments of destruction, as of war and poison," "Exhilaration of the spirits, and putting them in good disposition," "Deceptions of the senses," and "Greater pleasures of the senses." Ibid., pp. 488–489.

Obviously Bacon was telling a morality tale to his own England. In Bensalem, as in Bacon's England, the priesthood was subordinate to the state, a situation that kept doctrinal disputes, at best, under precarious control. What England lacked to give it respite from continual theological turmoil, so it seemed, was the addition of a Salomon's House, a situation that would be remedied soon enough after Bacon's death with the founding of the Royal Society. By the addition of Salomon's House to England, Bacon hoped to shift the passions for theological controversy to the task of mastering nature.

Taking up Bacon's cause, Boyle argued for a kind of Protestant empire, built upon the mastery of nature, and therefore fueled simultaneously by the very human desire for material comfort and wealth *and* the Protestant desire to displace Catholicism internationally in the new age of commerce, expansion, and missionary endeavor. This focus on industry through the mastery of nature had the added benefit, hinted at by Bacon, that theological differences, which divide, would be set aside in the task of mastering nature, which promotes everyone's common material interest.[44] Broad-based religious consensus—or at least, a regard for theological diversity as merely a private matter—would bring the peace that promotes commerce and industry; commerce and industry bring prosperity and power; prosperity and power would not only aid in the international struggle against Catholicism, but would reinforce through its very success the importance of maintaining broad-based religious consensus.

The influence of Bacon's imagined peaceful island of Bensalem—where religious differences are entirely submerged and all happily bend their efforts toward the mastery of nature in Salomon's House—on Boyle's and the Royal Society's vision could not be more pronounced. Looking back, one may well shudder at this "aggressive, acquisitive, mercantilist ideology justified in the name of both Restoration and Reformation," and assume that "those who put it forward were insincere about religion, or that even if they were sincere, theirs was a religion solely of greed and self-aggrandizement." But as James Jacob points out, that would be a mistake.

> Given the circumstances of the Restoration, it seemed the best alternative. England was divided by deep religious and political cleavages and challenged by Catholic Europe. The ideology of the Royal Society would compose internal differences by committing every group and individual in the nation to experimental science and its material fruits. Both internal order and the pursuit of science, trade, and empire, would make England strong enough to face and ultimately overcome the external threat posed by her Catholic enemies.[45]

Yet, that having been said, one must recognize the effect that the attempt to ground this vision in Scripture would have. It would demand an exegesis that supported both Latitudinarianism theologically and mercantilism practically, a minimalist Christology with a focus on morality for the sake of public order coupled with a release

44 On this, see especially Thomas Sprat's formulation in his *History of the Royal Society* (1667) as summarized by James Jacob, "Restoration, Reformation and the Origins of the Royal Society," *History of Science,* 13 (1975), pp. 155–176, especially pp. 169–170.

45 Ibid., p. 171.

of acquisitiveness and worldliness from the ignominy that the Scriptures and Christian tradition had for all previous centuries bestowed upon them. This need for such an exegesis is the context for understanding Locke's treatment of Scripture.

Putting on Whigs

Locke remained a friend of Boyle until the latter's death in 1691, and Locke himself was elected a fellow of the Royal Society in 1668. Although Locke was certainly influenced by Boyle's vision, this vision—and Locke's, as well—would face rocky political shoals between the Restoration of 1660 and the Glorious Revolution of 1688–1689. The return of the Anglican state church brought with it a return of Anglican hegemony at Oxford, but no purgings at first. Locke was elected lecturer in Greek on Christmas Eve 1660. His father would die the following February, leaving Locke a small estate. Locke's mother had died in 1654, and his only remaining brother would die in 1663. Locke would thereafter be the lone survivor of his family (and, as it turns out, a bachelor for life).

In 1665, Locke accepted an offer as secretary on a diplomatic mission to the Elector of Brandenburg, his first trip to the continent. Returning to Oxford the following year, 1666, he met Anthony Ashley Cooper (who would become the Earl of Shaftesbury in 1672). Locke's fortunes would soon become tied to Shaftesbury's.

Locke, who had decided to take a degree in medicine, would leave Oxford to be Shaftesbury's personal physician in 1667, and Shaftesbury would become especially endeared to him after he successfully saw him through on operation on his liver in 1668. Shaftesbury was a champion of religious toleration. For this and other reasons, Locke would soon follow suit, a change in direction that would mark the rest of his work, especially that on Scripture. What brought about the change?

To back up a bit, Anthony Ashley Cooper (or Lord Ashley) had actually been one of the conspirators (along with Locke's patron, Alexander Popham) involved in inviting Charles II to take the crown (and indeed was arrested on this charge by Cromwell's successors). As a consequence of his support, Lord Ashley's political fortunes rose dramatically with Charles's return.[46] Although Charles had originally promised limited toleration of dissenters at Breda before his arrival, soon the staunch Anglicans in Parliament passed a series of laws enforcing Anglican conformity and greater restrictions against non-Anglicans (usually referred to as the Clarendon Code, after the Earl of Clarendon). In Parliament, Ashley fought them for the sake of toleration, especially (recalling Boyle) insofar as religious persecution distracted the nation from trade. Locke himself drafted an essay on toleration in 1667, as sign that he was now considering toleration both plausible and practical.[47]

But there were further religious-political complexities. The restoration of monarchy with Charles II meant the restoration of divine right monarchy with the king

46 Cranston, *John Locke*, pp. 105–107.

47 Ibid., pp. 111–112.

as head of the church—the Anglican Church. But rooting all political and religious authority in the king assumed, from Henry VIII, that the king would be Anglican. Charles II had definite Catholic leanings, and indeed in the famous secret Treaty of Dover (1670) made with the great champion of Catholic royal absolutism, King Louis XIV of France, Charles promised (for a generous subsidy) to return England to the Catholic fold at the earliest opportunity. That opportunity was lost when, in February 1685, Charles II died (but not without declaring himself a papist in the end).

Although Charles II had been more circumspect, his brother James II was quite ardent and public about his Catholicism. That, of course, made even more trouble for the notion of divine right monarchy, which had been designed for the support of the Anglican state church. Sensing the danger during Charles II's reign, some members of Parliament attempted to bar James II from the throne through the Exclusion Bill, which they tried to push through between 1678 and 1681, and which would have designated Charles II's illegitimate son, the Duke of Monmouth, as the next legitimate heir.

Although the Exclusion Bill did not pass, it did create lasting political parties, the Whigs (who wanted to exclude James II and tolerate Protestant dissenters from Anglicanism) and the Tories (who supported James II's accession because they supported divine right monarchy, even though they were generally high-church Anglicans who disliked his Catholicism).[48]

To Whigs, the looming accession of the Catholic James II seemed to be the unwinding of the Protestant religious revolution that had begun a century and a half earlier with Henry VIII (a revolution that many wished to continue beyond Anglicanism to Presbyterianism or something even more radical). To Tories, the Exclusion Act seemed to be a lapse back into the Radical Reformation and the republican chaos of the Cromwellian years from which England had just (barely) escaped.

Upon taking the throne in 1685, James II immediately set about re-Catholicizing the highest levels of government in open defiance of the Test Act (1673), which specified that only Anglicans could hold either military or civil offices. Ironically, in order to move ahead with his Catholic ambitions against entrenched Anglicanism, James had to make use of political alliances with the other dissenters from the official state religion, the radical reformationists who had had such power under Cromwell (and as radical republicans, had definite regicidal leanings). Thus, James's bids for religious toleration seemed to be letting papists in through the back door, and sectarian chaos in the front.

But James was old, and both moderate Whigs and Anglican Tories thought they could bide their time, given that James's two daughters by his first wife, Mary and Anne, were both Protestant. But the birth on June 10, 1688, of Prince James Edward immediately changed the future landscape, since he would certainly be designated the Catholic heir

---

48 The original names of those who would become the Whigs and Tories were the Petitioners and Abhorrers. The threat of the Exclusion Bill brought Charles to dismiss (or prorogue) Parliament in 1681. Those in favor of exclusion petitioned against dissolution (future Whigs); those who were horrified at exclusion, abhorred the petition (future Tories). See Christopher Hill, *The Century of Revolution, 1603–1714* (New York: W. W. Norton, 1980), pp. 168–169.

to the English throne. In July 1688 Prince William of Orange of the Netherlands with his wife, Mary (daughter of James), were invited to invade England, and gladly accepted the invitation. William finally sailed with a fleet of four hundred ships in November.

Since 1672, William had been trying to convert his stadholderate in the Netherlands to a hereditary monarchy for the House of Orange, a transformation stoutly resisted by the republican forces in the Netherlands. Through his wife, Mary, he was provided the monarchical opportunity in England. In the face of William's imposing invasion from abroad and crumbling support at home, James II, the queen, and James III fled to France, and William and Mary became king and queen of England in 1688, a so-called Glorious Revolution.

Locke, the Radical Revolutionary

What was Locke doing during this period? Quite a lot. Both Ashley and Locke had pushed Charles II for religious toleration—except for Catholics, whom Locke argued could never be trusted since their loyalty was to Rome. About two years after his secret treaty, Charles issued a royal Declaration of Indulgence, tolerating both Protestant nonconformists loosely under the Anglican fold *and* (much to the chagrin of Locke) Roman Catholics. In the meantime, the English were at war with the Dutch over trade, and Ashley, now the Earl of Shaftesbury, was shunted out of power by staunch Anglicans in Parliament.

Soon Shaftesbury, Locke, and other Whigs began political plotting. Shaftesbury was arrested in 1667 and sent to the Tower for a year, but emerged to rise up in government once again. During that same year, the Green Ribbon Club was formed, a political association based on the most radical opposition to Charles's government, an association that traced its pedigree to the Levellers of the Civil War years. They were fervently anti-papal. Shaftesbury was the leading member, and that meant Locke was privy to its machinations. Shaftesbury's argument that "popery never can nor will grow but by absolute government,"[49] summarizes the connection Whigs drew between Henry VIII-style absolutism and the danger of a monarch reinstituting Catholicism in England.

Locke was in France during the latter 1670s—being trailed, interestingly enough, by a young clergyman, Denis Grenville, a spy for Charles II.[50] While in France, he met and was influenced by several prominent followers of the Epicurean atomist Gassendi. By the time of his return, England was in a froth over notions of a popish plot, exacerbated by the rumors of one Titus Oates in 1678, who claimed that Catholics planned to kill Charles and place the Duke of York (the future James II), his Catholic brother, on the throne. A purge of Catholics was on, a development that fit the plans of the Whigs, and hence a cause taken up zealously by Shaftesbury. Shaftesbury also pushed for exclusion, and then for the accession of the illegitimate but Protestant Duke of

49 Quoted in Richard Ashcraft, *Revolutionary Politics & Locke's Two Treatises of Government* (Princeton: Princeton University Press, 1986), p. 203.

50 Ibid., pp. 135–136.

Monmouth. As opposition mounted, King Charles dissolved Parliament twice in 1681. After the second time, Shaftesbury, Locke, and other radical Whigs began to plan for armed rebellion in earnest. In the summer of 1681, Shaftesbury was arrested again and sent to the Tower on charges of treason, but soon enough released.

Charles II became more determined to crush Whig rebellion. In mid-1682, a warrant was issued for Shaftesbury's arrest, and he went into hiding. At the end of November, disguised as a Presbyterian minister, Shaftesbury stole away to Holland, only to die there at the end of the first month of 1683. Midsummer of that same year, a Whig plot was uncovered to kidnap and kill the king and his brother at Rye House, on their return from Newmarket. Locke was one of the inner circle of radical Whigs embroiled in the Rye House Plot.[51]

Among the Radicals in the Netherlands

By September of 1683—a mere six years after the death of Spinoza—Locke was in the Netherlands, a radical Whig in exile with other fellow exiles from England. He would not return until February 1689. Locke and these fellow exiles were integral to the failed Monmouth rebellion in 1685, aimed at James II.[52] The English government tried to get Locke extradited, but he went into hiding, taking the false name Dr. van der Linden.

To say the least, Locke's years in the Netherlands were intellectually formative, especially in regard to his later treatment of Scripture. He spent considerable time both among exiled political radicals from England and the most radical of early Enlightenment circles. Not long after arriving, Locke met and became friends with the liberal Remonstrant (i.e., Arminian) theologian Philip van Limborch (1633–1712), who professed a minimalist creed of Christianity based upon reason, a perfect cross-channel match to English Latitudinarianism.[53] He soon read the works of another even more liberal theologian, Jean Le Clerc, whom he would also come to know quite well. In 1687, after moving about from place to place, Locke was invited to join the household of Benjamin Furly, where he would live for the next two years (although Locke had known Furly since 1683), and they would remain friends until Locke's death.[54] We shall look at each figure in turn.

51 Many historians over many years have denied that there was an actual Rye House conspiracy, and since Locke himself was later hailed as a bastion of respectability, biographers have tried to distance Locke from any political intrigue. On the historicity of the conspiracy, and the evidence that Locke himself was one of the conspirators, see ibid., Ch. 8.

52 See ibid., Ch. 9.

53 On the connection between English Latitudinarianism and Dutch Arminianism see Rosalie Colie, *Light and Enlightenment. A Study of the Cambridge Platonists and the Dutch Arminians* (Cambridge: Cambridge University Press, 1957).

54 On Locke and Furly see William Hull, *Benjamin Furly and Quakerism in Rotterdam* (Lancaster, PA: Lancaster Press, Inc., 1941), pp. 82–100.

Locke's interest in toleration (again, except for Catholics) received affirmation with Limborch.[55] Limborch was a prominent spokesman for those Dutch Protestants who rejected the rigors, and especially the predestination, of Calvinism, and argued for the toleration of wide disagreement among Christians (or put the other way around, argued for agreement upon a very thin account of Christianity and freedom to disagree about the rest). Locke spent a considerable amount of time in exile reading Remonstrant theology, not only that of Limborch (especially his *Theologia Christiana*) but also the works of Simon Bischop (1584–1643), better known as Episcopius, who had earlier tried to systematize Arminianism. As Limborch wrote to Lady Masham a few months after Locke's death, upon reading the Remonstrants, Locke "was surprised to find how closely they agreed with many of his own opinions."[56] Limborch and Locke were fast friends, bound by the more liberal strain of the Remonstrants. While Locke himself tended toward Socinianism, Limborch shied away.[57]

Jean Le Clerc (1657–1736) was a liberal Protestant refugee from France—but "Dutch in everything but name and place of birth"[58]—and a correspondent and friend of Limborch. Le Clerc was early on attracted to Arminianism against Calvinism, an attraction that brought him into contact with Limborch. He came to Amsterdam in 1683 and began a long career teaching at the Remonstrant university. Le Clerc became famous with *Sentimens de Quelques Théologiens de Hollande sur L'Histoire Critique du Vieux Testament* (1685), an "attack" upon Richard Simon. The *Sentimens* contained a section, *Five Letters Concerning the Inspiration of the Holy Scriptures*, that appeared in English translation in 1690 (the translation, by some, being attributed to Locke himself). While some of the *Five Letters* were dedicated to radicalizing scriptural scholarship, others were bent on rebutting deism. In regard to the former, Le Clerc argued that reason, not inspiration, must be the ground for the historical assessment of Scripture, and further introduced doubt about the actual inspiration of the Apostles, given that they were merely acting as historians and must be judged accordingly. St. Luke, for example, "learn'd not that which he told us by Inspiration, but by Information from those who knew it," and more generally, "The Apostles did not pass in their own time for Persons, every word of whose was an Oracle."[59]

---

55 Locke was instrumental in getting Limborch's *Historia Inquisitionis* published, a work that advanced the cause for toleration by examining the history of religious inquisition from the Middle Ages on. The book was dedicated to the Latitudinarian archbishop of Canterbury, John Tillotson, whose promotion evidences the victory of Latitudinarianism as Anglican orthodoxy after the Glorious Revolution of 1688. See Luisa Simonutti, "Limborch's *Historia Inquisitionis* and the Pursuit of Toleration," in Coudert, et al, *Judaeo-Christian Intellectual Culture in the Seventeenth Century*, pp. 237–255.

56 Limborch to Damaris Cudworth, Lady Masham, March 24, 1705. Quoted in Luisa Simonutti, "Religion, Philosophy, and Science: John Locke and Limborch's Circle in Amsterdam," in James Force and David Katz, *Everything Connects: In Conference with Richard H. Popkin* (Leiden: Brill, 1999), pp. 295–324, p. 304.

57 On the important relationship between Socinianism and the rise of the modern historical-critical method, see Klaus Scholder, *The Birth of Modern Critical Theology: Origins and Problems of Biblical Criticism*, translated by John Bowden (London: SCM Press, 1990), Ch. 2.

58 Samuel Golden, *Jean LeClerc* (New York: Twayne Publishers, Inc., 1972), p. 26.

59 Ibid., p. 135–137.

In Britain, at least, the reception of Le Clerc's arguments was hostile, one divine complaining that, "I know nobody that has more formally assail'd the Inspiration of the Sacred Books of the New Testament. *Spinoza* led the way. . . . But . . . [Le Clerc] has given a more subtle and more dangerous Air to *Spinoza*'s Notions and has digested them into a System."[60] However much Le Clerc truly was influenced by or in sympathy with Spinoza, his critics believed that he had the same ill effects on the authority of Scripture. The *Sentimens* caused even Locke consternation, as he wrote to Limborch, because Le Clerc's own philological analysis seemed to undermine the divine inspiration of the biblical texts.

> If everything in holy writ is to be considered without distinction as equally inspired by God, then this surely provides philosophers with a great opportunity for casting doubt on our faith and sincerity. If on the contrary, certain parts are to be considered as purely human writings, then where in the Scriptures will there be found the certainty of divine authority, without which the Christian religion will fall to the ground? What criterion will there be, or what measure?[61]

At Locke's own request, Limborch introduced Locke to Le Clerc in the winter of 1685–1686. Despite his original worries or perhaps because of them, Locke soon became a collaborator and life-long friend of Le Clerc, writing for Le Clerc's *Bibliothèque universelle et historique*, a journal begun in 1686 and dedicated to abridgments of the latest writings, especially those from Britain (one of the most famous being an abridgment of Locke's *Essay* in 1688). As noted, it may even have been Locke who translated the controversial *Five Letters*. Le Clerc continued to promote Locke's works as they came out, and was also instrumental in popularizing Newton on the continent with a review of the *Principia* in 1688. Needless to say, theological liberalism was well represented.

Between 1693 and 1695, Le Clerc focused on biblical studies, producing commentaries on the Pentateuch, and a paraphrase of the beginning of St. John's Gospel (in which he defended himself against the persistent charge of Socinianism). He continued to write, producing an extraordinary amount, and became a renowned controversialist, writing theological works "so inflammatory that they drew long replies from some of the most eminent theologians in England."[62] He attempted a *Harmony of the Evangelists*, translated into English in 1701, that treated the Gospels as historical accounts that the historian could reconcile. Locke was quite taken with it, and ordered a specially bound copy, remarking to a correspondent wanting to know the best way to understand Scripture that "Mr. LeClerc's edition of his *Harmony* in Greek and Latin will be the best."[63]

---

60 The churchman was Claude Grosteste Lamothe, as quoted in ibid., p. 136.

61 Letter of Locke to Limborch, September 26, 1685. Quoted in Simonutti, "Religion, Philosophy, and Science," p. 311.

62 Golden, *Jean LeClerc*, p. 133.

63 Ibid., p. 152.

In 1703, Le Clerc began another literary journal, this one aimed at popularizing the latest intellectual controversies, the *Bibliothèque Choisie* (later continued as the *Bibliothèque Ancienne et Moderne*). As with the first, these two journals were designed for the intelligent reader who had no time to read the originals, and therefore acted as important disseminators of the latest controversies. All three had a heavy concentration of British works, and consequently helped set the stage for eighteenth-century Anglophilia on the Continent; all three journals (along with Le Clerc's other works) were also bent on stripping Christianity of "unreasonable" elements of myth, superstition, and credulity.

Benjamin Furly (1636–1714) was another radical with whom Locke became intimately connected while in exile. The Furly family had actually been Protestant refugee immigrants to Colchester, England, from the Netherlands. In England, Furly had become (along with his father) a Quaker in 1655, a conversion that brought immediate persecution. As a result, Benjamin Furly emigrated to Holland in 1658, both to avoid persecution in England but also for the substantial economic opportunities it would provide a merchant. Furly was quite learned, knowing (at least) Latin, Greek, Dutch, English, German, French, and Italian, and both wrote and translated many works. Importantly, "Furly maintained a salon in Rotterdam, kept a splendid library of heretical books, and established his home as the *entrepôt* between English republicans, Dutch Dissenters, and French refugees."[64] Furly's notorious library contained an enormous collection of the most subversive literature available, and it therefore became a kind of meetinghouse for many of Europe's radical thinkers.

It was at Furly's that Locke met with others in a private "society" they called "The Lantern Club"—set up by Locke himself[65]—and so called either after the inner light of the Quakers, or, even more scandalously, after a tract of 1662 written by one of Spinoza's circle, Pieter Balling, entitled *Het Licht op den Kandelaar* (in Latin, *Lucerna super Candelabrum*; in English, *The Light on the Candlestick*). In Balling's work, the Quaker inner light is made all but synonymous with Cartesian-Spinozan natural reason.[66] Locke studied many of the radical works, including those of the Dutch deist Isaac Vossius (1618–1698), Anthonie van Dale (1638–1708), and of course, Spinoza (Locke owning his own copy of the *Tractatus*).[67] In the next chapter we will see in more detail just how radical Furly's circle was, but suffice it to say here that it was even more so than the circle that had gathered around Spinoza.

While an exile in Holland, Locke wrote, or at least finished, some of his most famous and influential works, the *Epistola de Tolerantia*, the *Essay Concerning Human*

---

64 Margaret Jacobs, *The Radical Enlightenment: Pantheists, Freemasons, and Republicans* (London: George Allen & Unwin, 1981), p. 149, 161. On Furly's library, see William Hull, *Benjamin Furly and Quakerism in Rotterdam*, pp. 137–155.

65 Cranston, *John Locke*, pp. 282–283. William Hull maintains that it was Furly that set it up. Hull, *Benjamin Furly and Quakerism in Rotterdam*, p. 87–88.

66 See Hull, *Benjamin Furly and Quakerism in Rotterdam*, p. 87; Jonathan I. Israel, *Radical Enlightenment: Philosophy and the Making of Modernity 1650–1750* (Oxford: Oxford University Press, 2001), pp. 60–61 (fn. 60), 314, 343–344.

67 Simonutti, "Religion, Philosophy, and Science," pp. 305.

Understanding, and the *Two Treatises on Government*. Although it is beyond the concerns of the present work to examine each in detail, it is necessary to gain a general understanding of how each relates to Locke's treatment of Scripture.

Locke's Plea for Toleration

Locke's *Epistola de Tolerantia* was written (according to the popular literary form) as a "private" letter to Limborch, himself a champion of toleration. Locke wrote the *Epistola* in 1685 after the failed Monmouth rebellion, and published it anonymously in May 1689, after William and Mary had displaced James II and Locke himself had returned to England. It was translated into English by radical Whig William Popple in 1689 (again, published anonymously) as *A Letter Concerning Toleration*. Such anonymity was not modesty on Locke's part. Locke was a known revolutionary, and (as Richard Ashcraft points out) "the association of toleration with faction and rebellion had always constituted one of the strongest and most frequently cited grounds for its denial. . . ."[68] Yet even after rebellion, in 1686 James II was willing to pursue a policy of toleration, not that he had any love for Quakers and other Protestant dissenters, but as a means to end restrictions upon Catholics.[69] But by the time of the Glorious Revolution of 1688, the question was what religious leeway William and Parliament would allow. Locke's *Letter* is, therefore, not an abstract treatise, but a plea for toleration to an as-yet-unstable government in England. It is not, however, a merely commonsense and socially respectable document. As Ashcraft rightly states:

> Toleration has so often been viewed as the logical outcome of a rational or enlightened liberal position, that it has been forgotten by commentators what a distinctly political act it was in the period from 1686 to 1688 to offer a defense of the Dissenters. They were, after all, a very small minority of the total religious population; they had repeatedly been perceived as being political subversives; and enough of them had been prominently involved in various conspiracies and rebellions during the previous twenty-five years to make the charge stick. It was not a popular undertaking for one to speak openly in their defense.[70]

The *Letter* is also significant for our purposes because in pursuit of political toleration it duplicated, in many respects, the political Averroism we have seen in Marsilius's *Defensor Pacis*, and in doing so, relied upon a particular mode of exegetical defense. Since toleration must be rooted in Scripture (at least, to make it politically effective among the intended Protestant audience), then Scripture must be molded to fit the end of toleration.

68 Ashcraft, *Revolutionary Politics & Locke's Two Treatises of Government*, p. 477.

69 Ibid., pp. 484–485.

70 Ibid., p. 501.

Locke began by asserting "Toleration to be the chief Characteristical Mark of the True Church,"[71] providing two related reasons for this claim. First, all attempts throughout history of imposing orthodoxy were really only "rather Marks of Men striving for Power and Empire over one another, than of the Church of Christ." Providing a variation of Spinoza's assertions about the relativity of religious belief, Locke maintained that orthodoxy cannot be concerned with truth rather than power, because claims of orthodoxy are merely expressions of one's subjective desires: "for every one is Orthodox to himself. . . ." Second, toleration is actually demanded by "Charity, Meekness, and Good-will in general towards all Mankind, even to those that are not Christians. . . ." Rather than lord it over others—Locke quoted as evidence Luke 22:25–26—true Christians should leave others alone, and focus on correcting each "his own Lusts and Vices."[72] Again in parallel to Spinoza, Locke elevated morality over doctrine: "*Whoredom, Fraud, Malice, and such like enormities* . . . are certainly more contrary to the Glory of God, to the Purity of the Church, and to the Salvation of Souls, than any conscientious Dissent from Ecclesiastical Decisions, or Separation from Publick Worship, whilst accompanied with Innocency of Life."[73] As an antidote to the charge that toleration breeds civil rebellion, Locke turned the charge on its head (providing a neat defense of himself and his fellow revolutionaries): "if men enter into Seditious Conspiracies, 'tis not Religion that inspires them to it in their Meetings; but their Sufferings and Oppressions . . . [which] raise Ferments, and makes men struggle to cast off an uneasie and tyrannical Yoke."[74] Thus, in a complete about-face of his earlier Hobbesian position, Locke asserted that "It is not the diversity of Opinions, (which cannot be avoided) but the refusal of Toleration to those that are of different Opinions, (which might have been granted) that has produced all the Bustles and Wars, that have been in the Christian World, upon account of Religion."[75] One cannot help but see the influence that Spinoza had on Locke while in the Netherlands.

This type of argument—that what matters is "Innocency of Life" (which we can all agree upon), rather than the niceties of particular forms of worship (which no one will ever agree upon)—may appear quite ordinary to us, but was quite radical at the time. It was most famously associated with the skeptic Pierre Bayle's account of Spinoza, wherein Bayle argued that an atheist could be quite moral, and in fact more moral than most Christians.[76] Locke provided a somewhat tamer version of Bayle's argument: a dissenter can be more moral than an orthodox believer; and since Christianity really

71 John Locke, *A Letter Concerning Toleration*, translated by William Popple (London, 1689), reprinted and edited by James Tully (Indianapolis, IN: Hackett Publishing Company, 1983), p. 23.

72 Ibid.

73 Ibid., p. 24.

74 Ibid., p. 52. This results in a right to rebellion: "What else can be expected, but that these men, growing weary of the Evils under which they labour, should in the end think it lawful for them to resist Force with Force, and to defend their natural rights (which are not forfeitable upon account of Religion) with Arms as well as they can?", p. 55.

75 Ibid.

76 This argument occurs first in Bayle's *Pensées diverses sur la comète* (1682) and then in his famous article on Spinoza in his *Dictionnaire* (1697).

is about being moral, then as it turns out dissenters make better Christians than the so-called orthodox.

Whatever the merits of this type of argument, it's crucial that (following Spinoza) it shifted the focus of exegesis significantly from faith to works, or more accurately, from questions of doctrine to the verities of public morality. The former may then be treated as matters of indifference, or *adiaphora*; the latter as fundamental. That is no small shift. Since morality, as Locke understood it, was rationally knowable and universal, special revelation lost its significance.

The results were significant. Rather than Scripture taking believers into the heart of profound mystery, where the actual *events* of sacred history reveal, as types, eternal and supernatural truths, the Bible became a kind of morality manual that, at its best, illustrated merely rational moral truths. Since these moral truths become the single focus, all else in the text became inconsequential, and hence could be treated as accidental historical material. (In fact, Locke jettisons much of the Old Testament as "not obligatory to us Christians" precisely because in the Mosaic Law the ceremonial, judicial, and moral aspects are inextricably intertwined in a theocracy.[77]) To put matters bluntly, for Locke sacred history was important only insofar as it provided a typology of the decent English Latitudinarian gentleman and man of business.

Given that Locke did indeed wish to appeal to that type of emerging utilitarian man, he quickly turned from a justification by Scripture for toleration, to an argument of "Necessity and Advantage." In sum, Locke's argument was that toleration is necessary because intolerance is the real cause of civil war, and it is advantageous, because civil war obviously destroys the peace that allows for commerce and the accumulation of property.

According to Locke, toleration, properly speaking, was a mean between two extremes, the "Spirit of Persecution" (as found especially in Tory Anglican zeal) and "Libertinism and Licentiousness" (as found among the Quakers, Levellers, Diggers, and Ranters).[78] Toleration is moderation, and the best way to establish such moderation was through a kind of political Averroism wherein civil law dealt only with the body, and religion dealt only with the soul (an arrangement that would appear to duplicate Luther's two kingdoms, but rested on a different foundation and was aimed at a much different goal). Accordingly, Locke defined the "Commonwealth . . . to be a Society of Men constituted only for the procuring, preserving, and advancing of their own *Civil Interests*," where civil interests were limited to "Life, Liberty, Health, and Indolency of Body; and the Possession of outward things, such as Money, Lands, Houses, Furniture, and the like." For Locke, "true and saving Religion" consisted in "the inward perswasion of the Mind, without which nothing can be acceptable to God."[79] No one can compel "inward perswasion," so "the Magistrate's Power extends not to the establishing of any Articles of Faith, or Forms of Worship, by the force of

77 Locke, *A Letter Concerning Toleration*, p. 44.

78 Ibid., pp. 25–26.

79 Ibid., pp. 26–27. Locke calls this "the *principal Consideration* . . . which absolutely determines this Controversie," p. 38.

Laws."[80] The "power of Civil Government relates only to Mens Civil Interests," that is, it "is confined to the care of the things of this World, and hath nothing to do with the World to come."[81] Again, this is only a slight variation on Spinoza.

Toleration therefore demanded an entirely secularized government, and the way to ensure that it stayed secular, was by making faith entirely privatized. In regard to the substance of faith, "Every man . . . has the supreme and absolute Authority of judging for himself."[82] Since faith was defined in terms of "inward perswasion," then as each is inwardly persuaded, so also he may define "church." Or, there are as many churches as there are inner persuasions. Consequently, there can be no established state church—indeed, "there is absolutely no such thing, under the Gospel, as a Christian Commonwealth"[83]—rather, each church existing within the secularized commonwealth is "a free and voluntary society"[84] and no church may compel the members of another.

Again, the ultimate reason to deny compulsion seemed to be a kind of intractable subjectivism inherent in defining faith as inner persuasion: "For every Church is Orthodox to it self; to others, Erroneous or Heretical."[85] Although each church may establish doctrine and discipline, no church can force any member in regard to those matters touching the body, which come under what Locke has defined as "civil interests."[86] "No body therefore, in fine, neither single Persons, nor Churches, nay, nor even the Commonwealths, have any just Title to invade the Civil Rights and Worldly Goods of each other, upon pretence of Religion."[87] The only time civil force could be used against some sect was when it fell into the extreme of libertinism and license, as the radicals had done during the Civil Wars.[88] Excluded from toleration were also those whose beliefs render them "under the Protection and Service of another Prince," Roman Catholics and Muslims (although elsewhere in the *Letter* Locke affirms toleration for "*Pagan* . . . *Mahumetan* . . . [and] *Jew*[89]), and finally, atheists, since the "taking away of God, tho but even in thought, dissolves all."[90]

Although Locke did not violate his own terms by demanding that Christian faith should take one particular positive form, he did suggest something akin to Hobbes's Least Common Denomination as the "true Church," one that made "the Conditions of her Communion consist in such things, and such things only, as the Holy Spirit has in the Holy Scriptures declared, in express Words, to be necessary to Salvation. . . ."

80 Ibid., p. 27.
81 Ibid., p. 28.
82 Ibid., p. 47.
83 Ibid., p. 44.
84 Ibid., p. 28.
85 Ibid., p. 32.
86 Ibid., pp. 30–31.
87 Ibid., p. 33.
88 Ibid., pp. 41–42, 49–50.
89 Ibid., p. 54.
90 Ibid., pp. 50–51.

Of course, there lay implicit in his notion of the "true Church" an entire exegetical program, one directed not at searching the fullness of Scripture for the fullness of mystery, but at parsing "express Words . . . necessary to Salvation" from "such things as the Holy Scriptures do either not mention, or at least not expressly command."[91] Furthermore, in regard to the Word preached, since charity understood as toleration was, for Locke, the only foundation of civil peace, those who professed to teach their flocks must admonish their "Hearers of the Duties of Peace, and Good-will towards all men," that is, "Charity, Meekness, and Toleration."[92]

As should be clear, the *Epistola de Tolerentia* was a very political document, outlining a "moderate" path between what Locke considered to be the two extremes that had been tearing apart English political life over the last half-century, Henrician state-church Anglicanism and theological, philosophical, and political radicalism. Both Tories and radicals could quote Scripture to support their position, and did so precisely because of the indebtedness of England to the Protestant principle of *sola scriptura*. But even more interesting, both could use the new materialism for support. Henrician Tories could use Hobbes for support of divine right monarchy, even while radicals, taking Hobbes's materialism to other conclusions, could use it to undermine kingship, nobility, private property, and even scriptural authority itself. Since Locke himself accepted the new materialist physics, he was also faced with the task of providing a "moderate" materialism, one that likewise avoided both extremes.

But are these really two different tasks? Rather than treating Locke's thought as divided into neat compartments—religion and Scripture, philosophy of nature, epistemology, political philosophy—and pretend that these are unrelated to his very active political life, it is far better to understand all these pieces as parts of a coherent whole. In that full context, one can see the deep and broad significance of Locke's philosophical masterpiece, the *Essay Concerning Human Understanding*.

Locke's Essay Concerning Human Understanding

Locke had begun drafting his famous *Essay* as early as 1671, but it was during his exile in the Netherlands that the most substantial writing and editing occurred. The *Essay* is usually treated in abstraction from the political turmoil of Locke's time as one of the great documents in epistemology, a treatise on the science of knowledge and knowing. As will become apparent, such an approach is quite insufficient.

That Locke was concerned with epistemology—the self-defined purpose of his *Essay* being "to inquire into the original, certainty, and extent of human knowledge,

91 Ibid., p. 29. This leads to the following definition of "orthodoxy" through the elimination of the possibility of any heresy: "He that denies not any thing that the holy Scriptures teach in express words, nor makes a Separation upon occasion of any thing that is not manifestly contained in the Sacred Text; however he may be nick-named by any Sect of Christians, and declared by some, or all of them to be utterly void of true Christianity, yet indeed and in truth this man cannot be either a Heretick or Schismatick," p. 58.

92 Ibid., p. 34.

together with the grounds and degrees of belief, opinion, and assent"[93]—is not surprising. When Descartes turned away from being, from nature, from the *ordo essendi*, to the knowing intellect itself, the thinking I, and the *ordo cognoscendi*, the modern preoccupation, even obsession, with epistemology began (in fact, the very "science" of epistemology was invented). Locke was one of the many who attempted to solve the difficulties caused by this effort to root certainty in the knowing intellect itself.

The importance of Locke's *Essay* becomes much clearer against the backdrop of his turbulent political and theological context. Given that England was being torn apart by different religious factions, each quoting Scripture as authoritative for its beliefs and actions, one can see the importance of clearly defining what can truly be known by faith through revelation, and what by reason. Or to be more pointed, one can see the practical utility of philosophically defining the nature of reason and faith to fit the kind of moderate, quasi-Latitudinarian solution to England's turmoil offered by Locke in his *Epistola de Tolerentia*.

This is not an argument for temporal priority of the *Epistola* to the *Essay*. Rather, the *Epistola*, the *Essay*, and the *Two Treatises* as well, are all part of Locke's unified project. The goal of the *Essay*, then, was (at least in significant part) to maximize the realm of reason and minimize the realm of faith—not undermine, but minimize, since as Locke has already made clear, political order demands religious beliefs, albeit tamed and firmly circumscribed. Obviously, this project would affect how Scripture was understood and used (and given the *Essay*'s enormous influence upon the eighteenth century, it *did* influence how it was understood and used).

Locke presented human beings as having moderate reasoning capabilities, a mean between pretensions to absolute Godlike knowledge and pure skepticism. "Men have reason to be well satisfied with what God hath thought fit for them, since he has given them," asserted Locke, "whatsoever is necessary for the conveniences of life and information of virtue; and has put within the reach of their discovery, the comfortable provision for this life and the way that leads to a better."[94] Locke's epistemological moderation was strikingly similar to the practical moderation (if one may call it that) of Machiavelli and Bacon, turning men from high-flying speculation to very earthly concerns for comfortable existence—the realm of Locke's secularized civil government.

The way Locke cut off access to metaphysical speculation is of some concern, since how he trimmed humanity's wings would obviously affect the status of revealed knowledge. To be all too quick—that is, laying aside both the intricacies and well-known confusions of his argument—Locke tried to effect a union of the rationalism of Descartes and the empiricism of Boyle, based on the atomist materialism of both (as shared by Galileo, Hobbes, and Newton as well[95]). Following Descartes, Locke placed

93 John Locke, *An Essay Concerning Human Understanding*, abridged and edited by John Yolton (London: J. M. Dent, 1993), I.i.2. Yolton's is an abridgement of Locke's fifth edition, published in 1706, the last published by Locke.

94 Ibid., I.i.5.

95 One might more accurately say that Locke, with his characteristic moderation, accepts atomism as the best hypothesis. Ibid., IV.iii.3.

the locus of certainty in the human intellect's clear and distinct perception of its own ideas (as rooted in "simple ideas"), but following Boyle, these ideas (either speculative or practical) were not innate but gotten from perception, or more accurately, from sensation and reflection.

> We can have *knowledge* no further than we have *ideas* . . . no *knowledge* further than we can have perception of that agreement or disagreement [of ideas]; which perception being: (1) either by *intuition*, or the immediate comparing [of] any two *ideas*; or (2) by *reason*, examining the agreement or disagreement of two *ideas* by the intervention of some others [in a demonstration]; or (3) by *sensation*, perceiving the existence of particular things.[96]

This union "limits" human knowing in two ways. Since reason is defined in terms of *our* clear and distinct ideas, then reason must judge revelation accordingly, and since what can be sensed limits reason, then what is beyond sense is nonsense. Thus, Locke's "moderation" actually served to limit revelation by reason.

Locke then spent a very long time laying down and arguing for his epistemological position in the *Essay*, and it was only at the very end that he addressed the relationship of faith and reason. But the brevity of the chapter "Of Faith and Reason, and their Distinct Provinces" does not imply that it was simply tacked on as an afterthought. The severe limitation of faith was the culmination of his extended argument about the nature of reason. There is, in Locke's final pronouncements, a stunning bluntness.

> In all things, therefore, where we have clear evidence from our *ideas* and those principles of knowledge I above mentioned, *reason* is the proper judge; and *revelation*, though it may, in consenting with it, confirm its dictates, yet cannot in such cases invalidate its decrees; *nor can we be obliged, where we have the clear and evident sentence of reason, to quit it for the contrary opinion, under a pretence that it is a matter of faith*, which can have no authority against the plain and clear dictates of *reason*.[97]

Although Locke admitted that God may reveal something to us beyond reason ("original revelation"[98]), yet revelation that is based on the authority of others ("traditional revelation," which included both Scripture and tradition), must always bow before reason, for *"no proposition can be received for divine revelation* or obtain the assent due to all such, *if it be contradictory to our clear intuitive knowledge."*[99] Reason, defined in terms of clarity and distinction, then became the judge of revelation. Implicit in this claim—and in fact the entire modern reconstruction of reason—was the assumption that human reason is the highest mode of intellection possible, so that what is most clear and evident to human reason must exist according to our mode of reasoning, or not exist at all. More than one critic of Locke realized the implications of

96 Ibid., IV.iii.1–2.

97 Ibid., IV.xviii.6.

98 Ibid., IV.xviii.3.

99 Ibid., IV.xviii.3, 5.

this view for the doctrine of the Trinity (which is why Locke was immediately accused of Socinianism).

Locke's assertion that reason so defined must judge revelation had direct implications for judging the caliber of inspiration of the books of the Bible. Unless we have an *original* revelation that "such or such a book, is of divine inspiration," then "the believing or not believing that proposition or book to be of divine authority can never be matter of faith, but matter of reason, and such as I must come to an assent to only by the use of my reason, which can never require or enable me to believe that which is contrary to itself: it being impossible for reason ever to procure any assent to that which to itself appears unreasonable."[100] Hence, the full import of Locke's later treatise *The Reasonableness of Christianity*. The principle of *sola scriptura* was therefore transformed into the principle *sola ratio*.

> There can be no evidence that any traditional revelation is of divine original, in the words we receive it and in the sense we understand it, so clear and so certain as that of the principles of reason; and therefore *nothing that is contrary to, and inconsistent with, the clear and self-evident dictates of reason has a right to be urged or assented to as a matter of faith, wherein reason hath nothing to do.*[101]

As with Descartes, Hobbes, and Spinoza, the *ratio* of *sola ratio* was narrowly defined, restricted by the notion that what reason knows *as* clear and evident (the mathematical) should define reason as such. But Locke was more moderate a rationalist than either Descartes or Spinoza, and more moderate an empiricist than Boyle,[102] even though the moderate hybrid seemed to produce inner difficulties and contradictions that have vexed readers ever since. Whatever the ultimate merits of Locke's epistemological arguments, they are clearly essential to understanding his approach to faith.

---

100 Ibid., IV.xviii.6.

101 Ibid., IV.xviii.10.

102 Although reason knows its own clear and distinct ideas, "we cannot have an *intuitive knowledge* that shall extend itself to all our *ideas* and all that we should know about them; because we cannot examine and perceive all the relations they have one to another, by juxtaposition or an immediate comparison one with another." Furthermore, our sensitive knowledge reached "no further than the existence of things actually present to our senses," rather than to all actual, sensible things. As noted above, we do not sense substances but collections of secondary qualities, and since the primary qualities are ultimately rooted in the atomic realm far beneath our senses, these too are beyond the reach of knowledge, and so we are not really certain of the way that primary qualities exist in the atomic realm, or the way that they would relate to secondary qualities. So that "*the extent of our knowledge* comes not only short of the reality of things, but even of the extent of our own *ideas*." Ibid., IV.iii.3–16. Not coincidentally, Locke again draws a kind of Machiavellian-Baconian lesson from this moderation: "*the certainty of* things existing *in rerum natura*, when we have *the testimony of our senses* for it, is not only *as great* as our frame can attain to [i.e., given our relatively large size as compared to atomic reality], but *as our condition needs*. For our faculties [of sensation] being suited not to the full extent of being, nor to a perfect, clear, comprehensive knowledge of things free from all doubt and scruple, but to the preservation of us in whom they are, and accommodated to the use of life: they serve to our purpose well enough if they will but give us certain notice of those things which are convenient or inconvenient to us." Ibid., IV.xi.8.

Further, abstracting from the question of whether Locke's epistemological position is true, or even coherent, one can certainly grasp its import for the volatile situation of English political life of his time. As he himself made clear in his summary, "to this crying up of *faith* in opposition to *reason*, we may, I think, in good measure ascribe those absurdities that fill almost all the religions which possess and divide mankind."[103] In his political context, rival interpretations of Scripture were dividing England. Locke provided a way out of the dilemma by offering a method of subjecting the Bible as "traditional revelation" to an analysis according to his understanding of reason.

The method was offered in the context of his distinguishing between "demonstration" and "probability," the former pertaining to knowledge, the latter to faith, belief, and opinion. Again, knowledge is rooted in the intuition of one's own clear and distinct ideas, in a step-by-step demonstration by reason in comparing these clear ideas, and in sensation. Probability fails in regard to some or all of these (e.g., by using unclear ideas, or not properly comparing them, or glossing over unproven steps in the demonstration, or having no sensation of the relevant particulars). Since faith is not knowledge but belief, therefore it must be based on probability; consequently, faith must be judged by reason according to its *degree* of probability. The criteria Locke offered in regard to the "*grounds*" of probability bear immediate relation to the rational analysis of the biblical text, even though Locke himself did not explicitly set them forth in the text for that purpose.

> *First*, The conformity of anything with our own knowledge, observation, and experience.
>
> *Secondly*, The testimony of others, vouching their observation and experience. In the testimony of others is to be considered: (1) The number. (2) The integrity. (3) The skill of the witness. (4) The design of the author, where it is a testimony out of a book cited. (5) The consistency of the parts, and circumstances of the relation. (6) Contrary testimonies.[104]

One can be reasonably sure that Locke did implicitly intend these to be applied to Scripture because of the elaboration and illustrations he provided, and even more evidently, because this section (IV.xv–xvi) almost immediately preceded the above-quoted culminating chapter, "Of Faith and Reason, and their Distinct Provinces" (only one chapter on reason itself intervening).

The context of Locke's elaboration and illustration was a discussion of *tolerance*. Given that our capacities for knowledge are themselves moderate, and faith and belief are based on mere probability, "it would, methinks, become all men to maintain *peace*, and the common offices of humanity, *and friendship, in the diversity of opinions*, since we cannot reasonably expect that anyone should readily and obsequiously quit his opinion and embrace ours, with blind resignation to an authority which the understanding of man acknowledges not." The case for tolerance was even greater in regard to religious opinions, for "one who takes his opinions upon trust, how can we imagine

---

103 Ibid., IV.xx.11.

104 Ibid., IV.xv.4.

that he should renounce those tenets, which time and custom have so settled in his mind, that he thinks them self-evident and of an unquestionable certainty, or which he takes to be impressions he has received from God himself or from men sent by Him?"[105]

Locke then elaborated his principles for judging probability, whereupon it becomes quite clear that Scripture itself would provide the lowest kind of probability (and since it was the foundation of Christianity, demand the greatest tolerance among rival interpretations). In regard to matters of fact, if we do not sense something ourselves, we rely on the testimony of others. Recalling the grounds of probability listed above, if the testimony of a witness conformed to "our own knowledge, observation, and experience," it obviously had a high degree of probability, almost approaching knowledge. "The difficulty is when testimonies contradict common experience, and the reports of history and witnesses clash with the ordinary course of nature or with one another: there it is where diligence, attention, and exactness is required, to form a right judgment and to proportion the assent to the different evidence and probability of the thing. . . ."[106]

Locke provided an interesting illustration in light of the contemporary controversies in regard to multiple extant copies of biblical manuscripts, controversies of which he was well aware, given his reading of Richard Simon and his close friendship with Limborch and Le Clerc. In the law of England, remarked Locke, "though the attested copy of a record be good proof, yet the copy of a copy, never so well attested and by never so credible witnesses, will not be admitted as a proof in judicature," so that "any testimony, the further off it is from the original truth, the less force and proof it has." Consequently, in regard to "*traditional truths, each remove weakens the force of the proof;* and the more hands the tradition has successively passed through, the less strength and evidence does it receive from them."[107] Given Locke's distinction between "original revelation" and "traditional revelation," the latter including Scripture, the full force of Locke's point becomes clear.

But even more interesting, Locke seemed intent upon readers understanding the *political* dimension of textual transmission, and his comments are worth quoting at length because they sound as if they were written by a twenty-first-century exegete.

> I think nothing more valuable than the records of antiquity: I wish we had more of them and more uncorrupted. But this truth itself forces me to say that no *probability* can rise higher than its first original. What has no other evidence than the single testimony of one only witness must stand or fall by his only testimony, whether good, bad, or indifferent; and though cited afterwards by hundreds of others, one after another, is so far from receiving any strength thereby, that it is only the weaker. Passion, interest, inadvertency, mistake of his meaning, and a thousand odd reasons or capriccios men's minds

105 Ibid., IV.xvi.4.
106 Ibid., IV.xvi.9.
107 Ibid., IV.xvi.10.

> are acted by ([and which are] impossible to be discovered) may make one man quote another man's words or meaning wrong. He that has but ever so little examined the citations of writers cannot doubt how little credit the quotations deserve where the originals are wanting, and consequently how much less quotations of quotations can be relied on. This is certain, that what in one age was affirmed upon slight grounds can never after come to be more valid in future ages by being often repeated. But the further still it is from the original, the less valid it is, and has always less force in the mouth or writing of him that last made use of it than in his from whom he received it.[108]

It is hard to think that Locke had any other ancient manuscripts in mind than biblical manuscripts. How much controversy spilling over into political bloodshed occurred in regard to the manuscripts of Cicero or Plato? Or to put it another way, *since* battles of faith were built upon Scripture, the fervent searching for and sorting out of biblical manuscripts was a far greater concern, producing a comparatively greater number of manuscripts during this period than any other "records of antiquity." On Locke's account, the very multiplicity of manuscripts, the recognition that none of them were original, and the discrepancies therein would sufficiently deflate the status of the biblical text to the lowest probability, hence supporting the greatest tolerance.

There is then, a direct connection between Locke's epistemology and his Averroistic plan for political tolerance. Reducing the status of revelation to the lowest kind of probability could become a scholarly project (much akin to Spinoza's strategy of placing endless obstacles before the exegete), one that used the scholarship of those like Richard Simon to undermine the credibility of the text, thereby affirming the need for political tolerance. Yet, at the same time, these exegetical endeavors could provide at least a thin theism, largely constrained to affirming morality, so as not to remove the necessary help that religion gave to maintaining order in society. To test whether or not this was Locke's strategy, one must examine more fully the use of Scripture in Locke's political thought in the *Two Treatises,* wherein the political philosophy of the *Epistola* is spelled out in more detail.

The First Treatise of Government

Although Locke's *Two Treatises* were written in exile, they were not published until 1690, and even then, only anonymously. The extended title gives us the focus of each: in the first, *The False Principles and Foundation of Sir Robert Filmer and His Followers are Detected and Overthrown*, and in the second, *An Essay Concerning the True Original, Extent, and End of Civil Government*.

The *First Treatise* was directed against Sir Robert Filmer, who was born in 1588, the same year as Thomas Hobbes, the year that the Spanish Armada sailed against

108 Ibid., IV.xvi.11.

England. Unlike Locke, Filmer came from the prosperous gentry, the oldest son of eighteen children. As the eldest, he inherited his father's estate when he died in 1629. Although Filmer did not fight in the Civil Wars, his writings made it clear that he was an undying advocate of divine right monarchy, a royalist to the bone. His most famous work[109] was *Patriarchia: The Naturall Power of Kinges Defended against the Unnatural Liberty of the People*, a work written sometime during the 1630s (while Charles I wrestled with Parliament), but not published until 1680, nearly thirty years after Filmer's death (during the attempt by Whigs such as Shaftesbury and Locke to bar James II from the throne through the Exclusion Bill). In it, Filmer claimed that the king's power was absolute because (1) it was derived from the natural patriarchal power of fathers over families, and (2) God had given dominion to Adam, the patriarch of all humanity, and hence Adam was the origin and foundation of all patriarchal-royal power.[110] In short, Filmer offered a natural argument (paternal rule is natural; fathers are kings writ small; kings are fathers writ large), buttressed by supernatural authority (Scripture affirmed that patriarchy and kingship were originally united in Adam, and passed on, father to son, since).

Filmer's arguments were neither original nor abstract. The Frenchman Jean Bodin (1530–1596) wrote a defense of absolute monarchy, *The Six Books of the Republic* (1576), which was translated into English in 1606 and greatly influenced Filmer. The patriarchal-biblical defense of absolute monarchy was, in fact, a popular form of defense of the English crown even during the late Elizabethan period, and certainly under the first two Stuarts, James I and Charles I (as, for example, in Hadrian Saravia's *De Imperandi Authoritate*, 1593[111]). What needs especially to be understood is the anti-Catholic nature of the patriarchal-biblical defense, for it was particularly strong in Filmer, as seen by his singling out for especial censure Cardinal Bellarmine (1542–1621) and the Spanish Jesuit theologian Francisco de Suarez (1548–1617). Both Bellarmine and Suarez argued that the patriarchal rights of the fathers were indeed granted to them directly by God, but that a father's power differed fundamentally from a king's: a father received his power directly from God, but a king received his from the people. For Filmer, such "subtle schoolmen" were actually attempting "to thrust down the king below the pope," and "thought it the safest course" to achieve that goal, "to advance the people above the kings . . . so that papal power may more easily take [the] place of the regal."[112]

109 Filmer published a variety of things, including other works supporting absolute monarchy, such as *The Anarchy of a Mixed or Limited Monarchy* and *The Necessity of the Absolute Power of all Kings* (both in 1648); *Observations concerning the Originall of Government* (1652), a treatise written against Thomas Hobbes's *Leviathan* and John Milton's *Pro Populo Anglicano*; and *Observations upon Aristotles Politics concerning Forms of Government* (1652).

110 Robert Filmer, *Patriarchia*, I.3–4 in Johann Sommerville, ed., *Patriarchia and Other Writings* (Cambridge: Cambridge University Press, 1991).

111 Ibid., see Somerville's Introduction, pp. xvi–xvii.

112 Ibid., I.1.

Again, Filmer offered a biblical defense of his argument, that is, a *sola scriptura* argument against Catholic apologists, which involved him in an extended exegesis of Israelite history to prove his point:

> And indeed not only Adam but the succeeding patriarchs [of Israel] had, by right of fatherhood, royal authority over their children. . . . For as Adam was lord of his children, so his children under him had a command and power over their own children, but still with subordination to the first parent, who is lord paramount over his children's children to all generations, as being the grandfather of his people. . . . [And so] I see not then how the children of Adam, or of any man else, can be free from subjection to their parents. And this subjection of children is the only fountain of all regal authority, by the ordination of God himself. . . . This lordship which Adam by creation had over the whole world, and by right descending from him the patriarchs did enjoy, was as large and ample as the absolutest dominion of any monarch which hath been since creation.

Obviously this kind of argument involved very specific scriptural claims. For example, we know that the contemporary English king has "power of life and death" over all his subjects because Judah had the power of life and death over his daughter-in-law, Tamar (Genesis 38:24). Or, a king has absolute power over his army because Abraham had command over an army (Genesis 14:14), and absolute power to make peace by treaty, as again Abraham demonstrated in his "league with Abimelech" (Genesis 21:23–24).[113]

Or to take another kind of example, since Filmer's argument depended upon familial continuity of all generations, he had to establish such continuity in biblical history. Thus, "Not only until the Flood, but after it, this patriarchal power did continue," so that the "three sons of Noah" became the source of all nations after them, and hence the conduit of patriarchal power descended, father and son, from Adam onward. After the Tower of Babel, "God was careful to preserve the fatherly authority by distributing the diversity of languages according to the diversity of families."[114] Moses, of course, was chosen as a father-king by God to govern the Israelites, and "when God gave the Israelites kings, He re-established the ancient and prime right of lineal succession to paternal government."[115]

The foundation of Filmer's rejection of popular sovereignty was rooted in Adam as the father of all mankind—so much so, that in another work reasoned upon the same principles, Filmer stated that "a natural freedom of mankind cannot be supposed without the denial of the creation of Adam."[116] So thorough was this union of paternal to monarchical authority that Filmer simply assumed that the Decalogue's command

113 Ibid., I.4.

114 Ibid., I.5.

115 Ibid., I.7

116 Robert Filmer, *Observations Upon Aristotles Politiques*, Preface, in Sommerville, ed., *Patriarchia and Other Writings*.

to "honour thy father" was an injunction to obey the king,[117] and so absolute was paternal authority that Filmer claimed that "Adam was the father, king and lord over his family. A son, a subject and a servant or a slave, were one and the same thing at first. The father had power to dispose or sell his children or servants."[118] At the same time—and even *against* the seeming implications of absolute authority—Filmer cast the paternal nature of a monarch as being like that of a good father.

> If we compare the natural duties of a father with those of a king, we find them to be all one, without any difference at all but only in the latitude or extent of them. As the father over one family, so the king, as father over many families, extends his care to preserve, feed, clothe, instruct and defend the whole commonwealth. His wars, his peace, his courts of justice and all his acts of sovereignty tend only to preserve and distribute to every subordinate and inferior father, and to their children, their rights and privileges, so that all the duties of a king are summed up in an universal fatherly care of his people.[119]

Filmer's scriptural defense would obviously call for a scriptural counterargument; but his natural defense of paternal authority and its extension to kingship would likewise have to be answered. It was the publication of Filmer's *Patriarchia* in 1680 that brought Locke—in the midst of his behind-the-scenes attempt to exclude James II as heir to the throne—to counter each of Filmer's defenses with his *Two Treatises of Government*.

Locke's *First Treatise*, written in a rather sardonic vein, accused Filmer of providing an all-but-groundless argument based upon one very thin premise, "the darling tenet of Adam's sovereignty," a tenet that itself, Locke maintained, was "taken for granted—without proof. . . ."[120] To demonstrate this point, Locke engaged in an in-depth exegesis of Scripture, illustrating quite well how thoroughly politicized the Tory and Whig use of the Bible could become. Locke's concern throughout was not so much what the Bible did say, but what it did not—i.e., anything to support Filmer's arguments.

For example, Locke engaged in a minute analysis of Genesis 1:24–28 (including an account of the Hebrew) to show that Adam's dominion, granted by God, was only over the earth, the sea, plants, fish, reptiles, birds, and animals, and so "gave Adam no monarchical power over those of his own species. . . ." Even this dominion "was not a private dominion but a dominion in common with the rest of mankind." [121] Furthermore, as Locke stressed at great length, dominion was shared by Adam and

117 Filmer, *Patriarchia*, I.10. More clearly in his *Observations Upon Aristotles Politiques*, Preface: "The power of government is settled and fixed by the commandment of 'honour thy father'. If there were a higher power than the fatherly, then this commandment could not stand and be observed."

118 Filmer, *Observations Upon Aristotles Politiques*, Preface.

119 Filmer, *Patriarchia*, I.10.

120 Thomas Cook, ed., John Locke, *Two Treatises of Government* (New York: Hafner Press, 1947), *First Treatise*, II.11 and 14.

121 Ibid., IV.25–29.

Eve.[122] Most importantly, this grant of dominion to Adam was not political at all, but *economic*: God's granting of dominion was, insisted Locke, a grant of "the right a man has to use any of the inferior creatures for the subsistence and comfort of his life," so that Genesis 1:28 was (*contra* Filmer) the origin of the absolute right to private property, a right dear to the Whig cause.[123]

In regard to Filmer's claim that Adam's absolute dominion was passed on, father to first son, through the biblical patriarchs, Locke engaged in a detailed textual argument to prove that "under the law the privilege of birthright was nothing but a double portion [of the father's property], so that we see that before Moses, in the patriarchs' time . . . there was no knowledge, no thought, that birthright gave rule or empire, paternal or kingly authority, to any one over his brethren."[124] Note again the recasting of the lessons of Scripture by Locke in terms of property.

And so, if Filmer could justly be charged with politicizing the Bible by bending it to the service of absolute monarchy (a charge Locke made against him[125]), then Locke falls under the same indictment, for bending it to the service of social contract mercantilism favoring the Whigs against the monarchy and nobility.

Locke carried this political cause so far that he felt compelled to deny the naturalness of the family and its obvious function as the origin of all society. Locke's mode of procedure was to lampoon Filmer's excesses, and then substitute his own arguments (rather thinly rooted in the Bible) as the only alternative. Filmer obviously intended that kings "as father over many families" rule for the good of their subjects, as fathers do over their children, with "fatherly care." Yet, as we have seen, the identity of king and father brought Filmer, an advocate of monarchical absolutism, to attribute the severity of kings to fathers. Locke seized the latter excess, and ignored the former more natural and attractive aspect of fatherhood.[126]

In his zeal to undercut Filmer, Locke seemed intent on undermining the belief that fatherhood was either naturally benevolent or even naturally intentional. Against

122 Ibid., IV.29, V.44–49, VI.61–64.

123 "Property, whose original is from the right a man has to use any of the inferior creatures for the subsistence and comfort of his life, is for the benefit and sole advantage of the proprietor, so that he may even destroy the thing that he has property in by his use of it, where need requires; but government, being for the preservation of every man's right and property by preserving him from the violence or injury of others, is for the good of the governed. . . ." Ibid., IX.92.

124 Ibid., XI.115.

125 Locke asserts that Filmer's "zeal" for absolute monarchy caused him "to warp the sacred rule of the Word of God to make it comply with his present occasion—a way of proceeding not unusual to those who embrace not truths, because reason and revelation offer them, but espouse tenets and parties for ends different from truth, and then resolve at any rate to defend them, and so do with the words and sense of authors they would fit to their purpose, just as Procrustes did with his guests, lop or stretch them, as may best fit them to the size of their notions; and they always prove like those so served, [to end up] deformed, lame, and useless." Ibid., VI.60.

126 Thus, Locke sums up Filmer's "description of his father authority" as "a divine unalterable right of sovereignty whereby a father or a prince hath an absolute, arbitrary, unlimited, and unlimitable power over the lives, liberties, and estates of his children and subjects; so that he may take or alienate their estates, sell, castrate, or use their persons as he pleases—they being all his slaves, and he lord or proprietor of everything, and his unbounded will their law." Ibid., II.9.

universal and natural benevolence, Locke reported the Incas "that begot children on purpose to fatten and eat them."[127] As for the father's intentions, Locke reduced children to an accident of lust, thereby affirming the Hobbesian notion that human beings are governed by desire rather than by reason and love, and are accidentally rather than essentially social by nature: "What father of a thousand, when he begets a child, thinks farther than the satisfying his present appetite? God in his infinite wisdom has put strong desires of copulation into the constitution of men, thereby to continue the race of mankind, which he doth most commonly without the intention and often against the consent and will of the begetter."[128] To further ensure that there was no analogy between God as Creator and fathers and mothers as procreators that could serve as a basis for patriarchal-monarchical government, Locke maintained that even "those who desire and design children are but the occasions of their being and, when they design and wish to beget them, do little more towards their making than Deucalion and his wife in the fable did towards making mankind by throwing pebbles over their heads."[129]

Removing (or, at least, severely disparaging) patriarchal-familial authority as natural and good allowed Locke to put forth the Hobbesian notion that we are all endowed with *individual* natural, original freedom:

> [M]an has a *natural freedom* . . . since all that share in the same common nature, faculties, and powers are in nature equal and ought to partake in the same common rights and privileges, till the manifest appointment of God, who is "Lord over all, blessed for ever," can be produced to show any particular person's supremacy, or a man's own consent subjects him to a superior.[130]

This assertion of natural *individualism*, which served as the foundation of modern liberal political theory, obviously displaced familial authority as primary and definitive, and so became (quite literally) the governing metaphor of modernity. This displacement signaled the historical shift that Locke himself was trying to effect, from political rule by family (monarch, nobility, father), to political rule by property; more particularly, from the kind of rule that defined pre-Civil War England, to the rule by the propertied class in Parliament that came (after a significant struggle) to define post-Civil War England.

The shift from family to property, aristocratic to capitalist rule, was signaled most dramatically by Locke's elevation of the desire for individual self-preservation above all others, a move that he attempts to vindicate theologically by making God the author of this essentially Hobbesian desire: "the first and strongest desire God planted in men, and wrought into the very principles of their nature, being that of self-preservation, that is the foundation of a right to the creatures for the particular support and use of each individual person himself."[131] As we have seen above, Locke claimed scriptural

127 Ibid., VI.57.

128 Ibid., VI.54.

129 Ibid.

130 Ibid., VI.67.

131 Ibid., IX.88 and 96.

support from Genesis 1:28, in which God blessed Adam and Eve, bid them be fruitful and multiply, "and fill the earth and subdue it; and have dominion over the fish of the sea and over the birds of the air and over every living thing that moves upon the earth."[132] Interpreting "dominion" as the individual right to self-preservation[133] allowed Locke to set forth the obtaining and increasing of property as an extension of self-preservation, and make it the fundamental right defining civil society.

Second to this individual desire, "God planted in men a strong desire also of propagating their kind and continuing themselves in their posterity."[134] But Locke had already characterized this as a kind of accident of lust to ensure, against Filmer, that familial and hence monarchical rule was not natural. This caused an inversion of the biblical relationship of parents to children. The biblical account focused on the honor due by children to fathers and mothers as Godlike givers of life; Locke moved the emphasis in the parent-child relationship from natural honor to natural rights—not the natural love and care of the parents for children, or even the rights of the parents over the children, but the rights of the children to self-preservation from their parents.[135] This enabled familial rule to be characterized as entirely transitory, in effect as long as the children are not yet able to preserve themselves and all but disappearing once they can. By contrast, individual freedom and the right of self-preservation are permanent, and in fact, the elevation of individual property-seeking frees sons from economic bonds to their fathers, thereby allowing the pursuit of commerce to break apart the rule of nobility, which was maintained through primogeniture.

Since paternal-familial power is transitory, and the desire for self-preservation and hence property is permanent, then (as Locke stated famously in his *Second Treatise*) "The great and chief end . . . of men's uniting into commonwealths and putting themselves under government is the preservation of their property."[136] That is, to translate it directly into his contemporary political situation: monarchical power exists, if it exists, at the behest of Parliament, and Parliament represents the interests of the propertied class rather than the nobility, money rather than birth.

The Second Treatise of Government

In the *Second Treatise*, Locke for the most part laid Scripture aside and presented a full-blown political philosophy largely indebted to Hobbes but much more moderate in tone. To understand political power, Locke maintained, we must "derive it from its

132 Ibid., IX.84–86.

133 "And thus man's property in the creatures was founded upon the right he had to make use of those things that were necessary or useful to his being." Ibid., IX.86.

134 Ibid., IX.88.

135 "For children being by the course of nature born weak and unable to provide for themselves, they have by the appointment of God himself, who hath thus ordered the course of nature, a right to be nourished and maintained by their parents; nay, a right not only to a bare subsistence, but to the conveniences and comforts of life as far as the conditions of their parents can afford it." Ibid., IX.89.

136 John Locke, *Second Treatise*, IX.123.

original," and "consider what state all men are naturally in, and that is a state of perfect freedom to order their actions and dispose of the possessions and persons as they think fit, within the bounds of the law of nature, without asking leave or depending upon the will of any other man."[137] Although this alleged state of nature (taken over directly from Hobbes) served well the Whig notion that all rights are rooted in the right of private property, it was decidedly unbiblical, unnatural, and unhistorical. Obviously, there was no state of nature recorded in the Bible. It was also unnatural: Society could not possibly have begun with isolated individuals methodically seeking self-preservation, but with families. Since it was unnatural, it was likewise unhistorical: No recorded society ever began from a set of isolated individuals, each seeking individual self-preservation, who later banded together through a social contract.[138]

Realizing this, Locke first provided a *theological* justification that projected the Whig concern for private property back upon the Creator himself. Since all human beings are

> the workmanship of one omnipotent and infinitely wise Maker—all the servants of one sovereign master, sent into the world by his order, and about his business—they are his property whose workmanship they are, made to last during his, not one another's pleasure; and being furnished with like faculties, sharing all in one community of nature, there cannot be supposed any such subordination among us that may authorize us to destroy another. . . .[139]

Being God's *property* took the place of the biblical assumption that we were made in the *image* of God. That we are all equally God's property was the foundation in turn of the "law of nature" that "teaches all mankind who will consider it that, being all equal and independent, no one ought to harm another in his life, health, liberty, or possessions. . . ."[140]

Locke immediately transformed this curious theological assertion of equality to a Hobbesian right to preserve oneself in the state of nature and to destroy *others* who violated this right, for "the execution of the law of nature is, in that state, put into every man's hands, whereby everyone has a right to punish the transgressors of that law to such a degree as may hinder its violation."[141] Of this, Locke soberly noted, it "will seem a very strange doctrine to some men. . . ."[142] Rather than answer the objection, Locke sidestepped it, using another theological finesse: "I doubt not but it will be objected that it is unreasonable for men to be judges in their own cases, that self-love will make men partial to themselves and their friends, and, on the other side, that ill-

137 Ibid., II.4.

138 Locke took up this obvious objection only to sidestep it by arguing that (1) since the state of nature so quickly became a state of war, it was no wonder that there are no records of it, and (2) absolute monarchs had better be wary of demanding too close attention to historical origins, since a close look at their own origins would certainly undermine their own position. Ibid., VIII.101–103

139 Ibid., II.6.

140 Ibid.

141 Ibid., II.7.

142 Ibid., II.9 and 13.

nature, passion, and revenge will carry them too far in punishing others, and hence nothing but confusion and disorder will follow; *and that therefore* God hath certainly appointed government to restrain the partiality and violence of men."[143]

This last phrase allowed Locke a segue to avoid the objections and continue unhindered with his Hobbesian account of the state of nature, now denoted a "state of war,"[144] a condition that only a Whig government, based on the absolute right to private property, could cure. One cannot help but see the parallel to the English Civil Wars and Locke's solution as it would be embodied in the Glorious Revolution.

Locke then expanded his argument in the *First Treatise,* wherein God's grant of dominion in Scripture was transformed by an entirely mercantilist spirit. The influence of Bacon and Boyle is palpable. "God, who hath given the world to men in common, hath also given them reason to make use of it to the best advantage of life and convenience. The earth and all that is therein is given to men for the support and comfort of their being." One could justly call this a concise scriptural vindication of Bacon's project to conquer nature for the sake of this-worldly comfort, and a crib of Boyle's aims for the Royal Society.

The scriptural dominion argument thereby served Locke's effort to couch his political argument in terms of property. Every man, Locke asserted, "has a property in his own person. . . . The labour of his body and the work of his hands . . . are properly his." From this came Locke's labor theory of property and value: for whatever "he removes of the state that nature hath provided and left it in, he hath mixed his labour with, and joined to it something that is his own, and thereby makes it his property."[145] Property thus understood wholly in terms of the right to self-preservation included both the person and anything he deemed useful to self-preservation. This allowed Locke to include everything the mercantilist spirit could consume, and so he moved rather quickly from asserting the right to eat apples and acorns, to claiming a right to "the grass my horse has bit, the turfs my servant has cut, and the ore I have digged. . . ."[146] Soon enough, the introduction of gold permitted the right of self-preservation to be extended to the right of the industrious to unlimited wealth—another Whig victory.[147]

As in the *First Treatise,* all this was grounded in a particular reading of Scripture, one that supported the industrious mercantilist class both against the idle gentry and against the Civil War radicals like the Levellers, who called for redistribution of property without the requisite labor. "God gave the world to men in common," conceded Locke, "but since he gave it [to] them for their benefit and the greatest conveniences of life they were capable to draw from it, it cannot be supposed he meant it should always remain common and uncultivated. He gave it to the use of the industrious and

143 Ibid., II.13. Emphasis added.

144 Ibid., III.16–21.

145 Ibid., V.26–27.

146 Ibid., V.28.

147 Ibid., V.37, 46–50.

rational—and labour was to be his title to it—not to the fancy or covetousness of the quarrelsome and contentious."[148]

This Whig interpretation of Scripture left out a fundamental theological doctrine. Locke was silent about labor being a punishment (Genesis 3:17–19), and, in fact, his entire account of the state of nature failed to mention anything of the fall and sin. Instead, he presented "the ground" not as cursed by God, but almost useless *by nature*, "of so little value without labour" that, rather than the intrinsic goodness of nature, it is "labour indeed that put[s] the difference of value on everything. . . ."[149]

As with Hobbes, the absence of sin allowed Locke to assert that each in the state of nature had an unlimited right to self-preservation and accumulation of property, and furthermore, that each was the judge and executor of his own cause, a condition that led ineluctably to a state of war. The remedy was civil society, "the chief end whereof is the preservation of property," formed by a voluntary compact or contract, and defined solely by the protection of private property, and the encouragement of further industry and accumulation.[150]

At this point, Locke turned away from Hobbes. Because the only reason to quit the state of nature and accept the restraints of government was the protection of private property, then to put oneself under a Hobbesian absolute monarch was to enter a condition worse than the state of nature, which "is to think that men are so foolish that they take care to avoid what mischiefs may be done them by polecats or foxes, but are content, nay, think it safety, to be devoured by lions."[151] *Contra* Hobbes, and later Tories that used him, Locke would not allow the sovereign to be a monarch. Instead, civil society must be defined by rule of the majority through the legislative power,[152] or more concretely, by the rule of property owners in Parliament: "the legislative is the supreme power . . . and all other powers in any members or parts of the society [are] derived from and subordinate to it."[153] If a king tried to usurp that power, then the people have a right to rebel, for "the true remedy of force without authority is to oppose force to it."[154] All of which is to affirm, as quoted above, Locke's assertion that "The great and chief end . . . of men's uniting into commonwealths and putting themselves under government is the preservation of property."[155]

In the political context of the day—Locke was writing the *Two Treatises* while in exile in the Netherlands—his political theory was a palimpsest of the political situation, with the Civil Wars being the state of nature as state of war, and James II being the devouring lion, far worse than the polecats and foxes of the Civil War. The way out offered by Locke was a radical reconstruction of government, tearing away the divine

148 Ibid., V.34.
149 Ibid., V.36–37, 40, 43.
150 Ibid., VII.85, 87; VIII.95–99; IX.123–127.
151 Ibid., VI.90, 93.
152 Ibid., VI.96–97; XI.134.
153 Ibid., XIII.150.
154 Ibid., XIII.155; XVIII.199–XIX.243.
155 Ibid., IX.124.

right of kings and the rule in Parliament by Tory nobles, and placing government in the hands of the industrious and propertied Whigs.

One should recall (recalling Locke's arguments in the *Epistola de Tolerantia*) that limiting government to the protection and advance of property reinforced Locke's Averroistic political argument that the "power of Civil Government relates only to Mens Civil Interests," that is, it "is confined to the care of the things of this World, and hath nothing to do with the World to come."[156] Just as Locke's epistemology in the *Essay* reinforced the supremacy of human reason over revelation, so also Locke's account of politics in the *Two Treatises* supported his political Averroism. This represented a victory of the Spinozan argument for a "tolerant" form of government that brought with it an exegesis of Scripture that downplayed all doctrinal content and affirmed only a useful moral core.

Again, all three works were written while Locke was in exile, and would not be published until he returned to England soon after William and Mary, called upon by Parliament, would oust James II from power. In this revolution, Locke was not a mere bystander.

The Glorious Revolutionary

The failure of the Rye House Plot in 1683 and the Monmouth rebellion in 1685 were major blows to the exiled radical Whigs, and also detrimental to Locke's safety. The discovery of sedition gave the king more determination (and probably more sympathy among his subjects), in crushing rebellion and more fervently maintaining his divine right to rule. James II wrote to William of Orange after the discovery of the Rye House Plot, "if the right use be made of this conspiracy . . . that which was designed to the destruction of [the monarchy] will prove of great advantage to it."[157] Of course, the irony of confiding such thoughts to his brother-in-law, soon to usurp him, is rather stunning.

There was good cause for English suspicion of Locke, and the crown continually attempted to have him seized and returned to England. As noted above, Locke spent his time among the network of exiled English radicals and their equally radical Dutch sympathizers, radical both in regard to politics and religion. Though the English radicals were, after the failure of Monmouth

> exhausted and discouraged, hundreds of these exiles were dedicated and hardened opponents of James II, Catholicism, and what they believed was an arbitrary and illegal political regime in England. From the early days of the exclusion crisis, they had placed themselves in opposition to the Stuarts, seeking every opportunity to bring about their downfall. They were not about to give up the struggle . . . a new conspiracy was rising from the ashes of

156 Locke, *A Letter Concerning Toleration*, p. 28.

157 William Emerson, *Monmouth's Rebellion* (New Haven: Yale University Press, 1951), p. 72.

> rebellion. . . . Locke, both by his long-held convictions and by his concrete actions between 1685 and 1689, clearly placed himself in the same camp as the radicals.[158]

Locke wrote his *Epistola de Tolerantia* during the winter of 1685–1686. Obviously, given the above analysis, such a letter could not be meant to appease James II, bent as he was on reinstituting Catholicism. It was, indeed, a revolutionary document, one that called for the end to the Anglican state church and the complete exclusion of Catholicism from toleration. As we have seen, Locke provided the justification for such a revolution in both the *Epistola* and the *Second Treatise*, and that included a radical reformulation of Christianity itself (of which we have only seen the beginnings in his *Epistola* and *Essay*).

Between 1685 and 1688, while James offered the "olive branch" of toleration to radicals in the Netherlands, he was even more ardently directing his spy network to seize and drag back for trial and execution any rebels that could be found. James II repeatedly entreated William to collaborate in the roundup, but William was politely uncooperative. William's diffidence is understandable, since the plot to have him replace James was already forming. As James's re-Catholicizing policies began to alienate even the Tories and moderate Whigs, the radicals gained wider support, and the cross-channel espionage and counterespionage heated up considerably. Locke's movements became so secretive during the period from 1686 to 1688 that it is all but impossible to trace him.[159] We do know that between August and October 1687, Locke visited the Hague several times, and most likely met with William and others planning the Glorious Revolution.[160]

While Prince William had sailed with his fleet to invade England in late 1688, his wife, Princess Mary, had stayed behind. It was she who invited Locke to accompany her over the Channel, an invitation he gladly accepted. He set sail with her and her company on the *Isabella* in February 1689. Later that same year, *Two Treatises* was published anonymously, both a justification for the Revolution and a blueprint for completing it. In the Preface, Locke offered his "discourse concerning government" as "sufficient to establish the throne of our great restorer, our present King William" and "to make good his title in the consent of the people,"[161]—and, as Maurice Cranston adds, make good "the coming triumph of Lockean political philosophy."[162] The original Latin and the English translation of the *Epistola* were both published anonymously that same year, as was the *Essay* (which Locke was most enthusiastic to have come out under his name).

158 Ashcraft, *Revolutionary Politics & Locke's Two Treatises of Government*, p. 473.

159 Ibid., p. 530.

160 Ibid., p. 537.

161 Locke, *Two Treatises of Government*, Preface.

162 Cranston, *John Locke*, p. 302.

Locke was an honored member of English society upon his return. William III offered him several political opportunities, but for reasons of health and personal temperament, Locke much preferred as quiet a life as he could manage. He became acquainted with Isaac Newton (1642–1727), the new intellectual giant championing the aims of Boyle's Royal Society. Although Locke made a go at trying to understand Newton's *Principia*, published in 1687, his mathematical abilities were limited, and on the assurances of Christiaan Huyghens (1629–1695), took the entire system on faith. The surviving correspondence between Locke and Newton is, interestingly enough, mostly taken up with theological issues. Boyle himself died in 1691, but not before giving Locke the burden and honor of editing for publication his *History of the Air* (1692). Locke also started up another of his clubs, the Dry Club, almost the sole focus of which was the discussion of religious toleration (and hence, of what needed to be done to religion to make it tolerant).

Locke gained greater honor (even amidst controversy) as successive editions of his *Essay* came out, but even so he deigned to publish his *Reasonableness of Christianity* anonymously in 1695. Despite his protestations to the contrary (and there were many), "Locke's argument was plainly Unitarian or Socinian," as Cranston remarks, although we must add not so much by what he did say, but in what he did not. There was throughout a thundering silence in regard to the Trinity. Locke himself always remained a public Anglican, sheltered under the elastic definition of orthodoxy offered by the Latitudinarians, such as his good friend, the archbishop of Canterbury, John Tillotson.

Given the hostile reception of *The Reasonableness of Christianity*—led in part by John Edwards (1637–1716)—Locke was wise to attempt anonymity, but was unable to restrain himself from replying in succeeding tracts to the charges made against him. Despite the animus of Edwards and many others, Locke's *Reasonableness of Christianity* came to be one of the great documents defining the course of future scriptural scholarship, especially as it flowed forth into the eighteenth century upon the swelling tide of Locke's considerable intellectual authority. As will become clear, its arguments are the culmination of the *Epistola*, the *Two Treatises*, and the *Essay*.

Christianity Made Reasonable

In his *Epistola* Locke remarked that the "true Church" is one that made "the Conditions of her Communion consist in such things, and such things only, as the Holy Spirit has in the Holy Scriptures declared, in express Words, to be necessary to Salvation. . . ." *The Reasonableness of Christianity*, published anonymously in 1695, set forth the scriptural foundation of this "true Church" in terms of the barest *minimum* necessary to affirm salvation. It is a long and rather tedious work, precisely because it purposely claimed to say so little, but did so at such great length, much of that length taken up with endless citations from Scripture. Locke's exegetical goal was to demonstrate that according to Scripture—and contrary to the rival credal and doctrinal claims of Catholics, Anglicans, and the multitude of different Protestant sects—"all that was to be believed for justification was no more but this single proposition: that 'Jesus of Nazareth was the Christ, or the Messiah.'"[163] On top of this slim foundation, one must be moral. These two together—all warring opinions of Christians to the contrary—would get us to heaven. Of course, since nothing else was necessary, then nothing else could be demanded, and hence all else must be tolerated. Such is the sum and substance of *Reasonableness*. It all but reduced Christianity to a moral code supported by a creed that was so simple and broadly defined that it could not fail to include nearly everyone (even if, as it turns out, it pleased no one but those inclined to Latitudinarianism bordering on Socinianism or else dedicated to religious toleration at all costs).

To see the effect of this political goal upon exegesis, one must focus on Locke's assumptions and the kind of arguments he used to establish this minimalist creed. Locke began by portraying his own position as a mean between the extremes of Calvinism and deism, between those who "would have all Adam's posterity doomed to eternal infinite punishment for the transgression of Adam," and others who think "no redemption is necessary" and that "Jesus Christ [is] nothing but the restorer and preacher of pure natural religion. . . ."[164] For Locke, the sin of Adam brought with it the punishment of death—the end of his immortality—and it was this mortality that all humanity inherits. But death was not the same thing as eternal punishment in hell, which each human being merits only insofar as he himself failed to be moral.[165] To merit eternal life, however, one must believe that Jesus is the Messiah (against the deists) and perform good works (against Calvinist predestination and Lutheran justification by faith alone, and for the sake of public order).

Locke set out to demonstrate that his minimalist creed was actually in Scripture, his primary exegetical strategy being to reduce all other titles for Christ to the one title of Messiah. The title "Son of God," Locke assured the reader, "was the known title of the Messiah at that time,"[166] that is, it was an historical epithet, or "expression,"[167] rather than an ontological description: "*Messiah* and the *Son of God*, were synonymous terms at that time amongst the Jews,"[168] terms "indifferently used for the same thing."[169] Accordingly, Son of God does not imply actually being a son, for "his being 'sent by the Father,' is but another way of expressing the Messiah . . . [so] to be sent by the Father and to be the Messiah was the same thing. . . ."[170] Furthermore, "the coming of the

163 All references will be to George Ewing, ed., John Locke, *The Reasonableness of Christianity as Delivered in the Scriptures* (Washington, DC: Regnery, 1965), 50 (paragraph number in this edition).

164 Ibid., 1.

165 Ibid., 2–11.

166 Ibid., 38.

167 Ibid., 52.

168 Ibid., 52, 97.

169 Ibid., 61.

170 Ibid., 58.

Messiah, the kingdom of heaven, and the kingdom of God being the same thing,"[171] no doctrinal substance is added by the latter two. Even *euaggelion*, "good news," "is nothing but the good tidings that the Messiah and his kingdom was come. . . ."[172] Consequently, "'believing on him' signifies no more than believing him to be the Messiah."[173]

In these assertions, Locke engages in a typological contraction reminiscent of Hobbes. Typical of the Reformation, Locke asserted that "the civil [i.e., judicial] and ritual [i.e., ceremonial] part of the law delivered by Moses obliges not Christians."[174] Locke's reasoning was that the ceremonial and judicial law were given by God only as "positive commands . . . suited to particular circumstances of times, places, and persons, [and] have a limited and only temporary obligation, by virtue of God's positive injunction. . . ."[175] Excluding the ceremonial law excluded any typology that considered Christ as the new High Priest who is Himself the efficacious sacrifice.

Although such typological contraction was nothing new, Locke went further by shifting the focus to Jesus understood solely as the *political* Messiah. Whereas Christian orthodoxy had taken the Jewish understanding of the political Messiah to be a type in the Old Testament that was expanded in Jesus through His divinity, through His actually *being* the Son of God, Locke contracted the meaning of the "Son of God" to fit the Jewish understanding of Messiah, and so made Him merely political again. So that, "to believe him to be 'Him of whom Moses and the prophets did write,' or to be the 'Son of God,' or to the 'the king of Israel,' was in effect the same as to believe him to be the Messiah, and an assent to that was what our Savior received for believing."[176] Of course, this would seem to reduce Jesus to what the Jews were indeed expecting, which, as Locke remarked, was "an extraordinary man yet to come from God, who, with an extraordinary and divine power, and miracles, should evidence his mission, and work their deliverance."[177]

Needless to say, Locke's aim of reducing all doctrinal claims to mere political Messiahship involved him in some rather strained exegesis—as, for example, his treatment of the Gospel of John, where the exalted beginning was trimmed to fit a significantly deflated end. Locke pointed to the end, where it declared the Gospel was written "that ye may believe that Jesus is the Messiah, the Son of God" (John 20:31), meaning, for Locke, a merely political Messiah. Locke neatly concluded that, "it is plain that the Gospel was written to induce men into a belief of this proposition, 'That Jesus of Nazareth was the Messiah. . . .'"[178] Obviously Locke was implying that the more exalted Prologue of St. John's Gospel should be interpreted according to simple

171 Ibid., 55, 59.
172 Ibid., 99.
173 Ibid., 82.
174 Ibid., 23.
175 Ibid., 20.
176 Ibid., 52.
177 Ibid., 58.
178 Ibid., 29.

political Messiahship, a conclusion he hints at by declaring that "*word*, and the *word of God*" wherever they appear, mean only "preaching Jesus to be the Messiah."[179]

Given Locke's deep anti-Catholic animus, his interpretation of the great eucharistic passages in John 6 is not surprising, casting it as "a mixture of allegorical terms of eating, and of bread, bread of life, which came down from heaven, etc.," wherein "the true meaning of this discourse of our Savior was, the confession of St. Peter at the end, that 'Thou hast the words of eternal life': i.e., thou teachest us the way to attain eternal life; and accordingly, 'we believe, and are sure, that thou art the Messiah, the Son of the living God.' This was the eating his flesh and drinking his blood, whereby those who did so had eternal life."[180] The Eucharist was merely an affirmation of the minimalist creed.

Petrine authority was similarly dealt with. Following Hobbes, he declared that Peter's confession in Matthew 16:16, "'Thou art the Messiah, the Son of the living God,'" was *itself* the rock upon which Jesus will build the church, rather than upon Peter the Apostle.[181] The desire to cut off Catholic claims also brought Locke to maintain that of the "three great offices" among the Jews, "priests, prophets, and kings," only the office of king was carried over into the New Testament, Locke remarking that, "Though these three offices be in Holy Writ attributed to our Savior, yet I do not remember that he anywhere assumes to himself the title of a priest or mentions anything relating to his priesthood, nor does he speak of his being a prophet but very sparingly. . . ."[182] Locke skirted the detailed priestly analysis of Christ in Hebrews by asserting that the "epistles were written upon several occasions . . . to those who were in the faith, and true Christians already, and so could not be designed to teach them the fundamental articles and points necessary to salvation," so that Hebrews was merely an epistle, the occasion of which was "the setting out and confirming the Christian faith to the Hebrews . . . by allusions and arguments from the ceremonies, sacrifices, and economy of the Jews, and references to the Old Testament."[183] The particular priestly language was, then, doctrinally inconsequential since it was tailored to the Jews as the particular means of convincing them that Jesus was the Messiah.

Locke thereby introduced a complete division between the Gospels (and Acts) on one hand, and the epistles on the other, the former containing all that was necessary to salvation, and the latter written upon particular occasions and hence containing a mixture of particular expressions and arguments that could not be taken as doctrinally fundamental. "But it is not in the epistles [that] we are to learn what are the fundamental articles of faith. . . . We shall find and discern those great and necessary points best in the preaching of our Savior and his apostles to those who were yet strangers, and ignorant of the faith. . . ."[184] Obviously, this exegetical approach cut down on the

179 Ibid., 41, 62–63.
180 Ibid., 103.
181 Ibid., 104–105.
182 Ibid., 183. See also 18–23.
183 Ibid., 248.
184 Ibid., 248.

domain of theological (and hence political) controversy since "every sentence of theirs [i.e., the epistle writers] must not be taken up and looked on as a fundamental article, necessary to salvation, without an explicit belief whereof, nobody could be a member of Christ's church here, nor be admitted into his eternal kingdom hereafter."[185]

While Locke's minimalist creed did away with nearly all grounds for controversy, the confession of this creed was not enough to get into heaven (nor would it, by itself, sustain public order). Faith must be accompanied by repentance and works, or more accurately, civic morality. The union of "faith and repentance, i.e., believing Jesus to be the Messiah and a good life," defined the "reasonableness" of *The Reasonableness of Christianity*.[186] The problem is that in the sections of morality (185–246) it certainly seems as if Locke was *reducing* Christianity itself to what is reasonable (which would accord with his account of faith in the *Essay*), and furthermore, recalling Machiavelli and Spinoza, Christianity's "reasonableness" seems to consist only in its being a practical and effective way to teach morality to the vulgar, who are simply incapable of apprehending morality by reason.

Locke presented an entirely earthly morality; that is, there was no biblical transformation of an earthly mode of morality in the Old Testament, to a supernatural morality as defined by a new heaven and earth in the New Testament. The Old Testament moral code was sufficient, except that it "was shut up in a little corner of the world," given only to the Jews. Consequently, the world needed Jesus to preach the moral code to all.[187]

But as we soon find out, the Old Testament code of morality, being based upon nature, was not really "shut up," since pagan philosophers were able (with some struggle, confusion, and incompleteness) to grasp it as well by natural reason. However:

> [I]t is too hard a task for unassisted reason to establish morality in all its parts upon its true foundation with a clear and convincing light. And it is at least a surer and shorter way, to the apprehensions of the vulgar and mass of mankind, that one manifestly sent from God and coming with visible authority from him, should, as king and lawmaker, tell them their duties and require their obedience, than to leave it to the long and sometimes intricate deductions of reason, to be made out to them. Such trains of reasoning the greatest part of mankind have neither the leisure to weigh nor, for want of education and use, skill to judge of.[188]

Almost pure Spinoza. Revelation was necessary, Locke asserted, because morality "must have its authority either from reason or revelation."[189] So far, philosophy has been unable to provide an entirely coherent, compelling account of morality. Even if

---

185 Ibid.

186 Ibid., 172. This seems to be the only passage in which Locke uses the term "reasonableness" in the whole treatise.

187 Ibid., 240.

188 Ibid., 241.

189 Ibid., 242.

it would "from undeniable first principles" provide "us ethics in a science like mathematics, in every part demonstrable . . . this yet would not have been so effectual to man [as revelation] in this imperfect state, nor proper for the cure." Why?

> The greatest part of mankind want leisure or capacity for demonstration, nor can carry a train of proofs. . . . And you may as soon hope to have all the day-laborers and tradesmen, the spinsters and dairymaids, perfect mathematicians, as to have them perfect in ethics this way. Hearing plain commands is the sure and only course to bring them to obedience and practice. The greatest part cannot *know*, and therefore they must *believe*.[190]

And so, "the instruction of the people were best left to the precepts and principles of the gospel." The reason Scripture is effective is that the reader (at least the vulgar reader) takes what Christ says in regard to morality as authoritative *because* He worked miracles (thus revealing the reason why Locke, against Spinoza, the deists, and other mechanists, insisted upon the reality of the miraculous in the New Testament, as long as the miracles stayed *in* the New Testament, and did not continue down through history). While day-laborers, tradesmen, spinsters, and dairymaids may not be able to follow, say, the arguments in Spinoza's *Ethics*, the "healing of the sick, the restoring sight to the blind by a word, the raising and being raised from the dead, are matters of fact, which they can without difficulty conceive, and that he who does such things, must do them by the assistance of a divine power." Locke then made very clear why he limited doctrine to the affirmation that "Jesus is the Messiah" *and* why that minimal creed included the affirmation that Jesus performed miracles and will reward the moral with eternal life.

> These things [i.e., miracles] lie level to the ordinariest apprehension; he that can distinguish between sick and well, lame and sound, dead and alive, is capable of this doctrine. To one who is once persuaded that Jesus Christ was sent by God to be a King, and a Savior of those who do believe in him; all his commands become principles; there needs [to be] no other proof for the truth of what he says, but that he said it. And then there needs no more, but to read the inspired books to be instructed; all the duties of morality lie there clear, and plain, and easy to be understood.[191]

The entire of Locke's exegetical aim now appears more clearly. Jesus was reduced to being the Messiah so He could be a lawmaker-king, a miracle worker who confirmed the authority of morality for those incapable of philosophical demonstration. Despite Locke's hedging and pious rhetorical flourishes, one cannot help but draw the conclusion that his main interest seems to be the utility of the Bible for keeping political order. In that, Locke followed in the footsteps of Averroes, Marsilius, Machiavelli, and Spinoza.

---

190 Ibid., 243. See also 252.

191 Ibid., 243.

As with Marsilius's tracts, the attentive reader of Locke's *Reasonableness* cannot help but ask: Is this a wise philosopher who feigns belief, or is he truly a believer? Unlike Spinoza and the deists who would follow Locke, Locke himself did not deny miracles or the afterlife, or claim that reason alone, without revelation, could provide a foundation for secular public order. But the chief reason appears to be that these miracles as reported in Scripture (including the Resurrection) and the promise of heaven and threat of hell are the very things *necessary to convince the vulgar to act morally.*

Ironically, the inclusion of miracles, the Resurrection, heaven, and hell in his exegesis made Locke appear to be *moderate* by contrast to Spinoza and the deists, even though in many respects he was just as radical in his principles, as has appeared with his use of Hobbes and philosophical reliance on the new materialism. This hybridism made Locke, *as a moderate radical,* a more powerful and effective historical bearer of the radical Enlightenment (cf. John Toland). It is interesting, in this regard, that there is strong evidence to suspect that Locke's *Reasonableness of Christianity* was actually written in reaction to John Toland's much more radical *Christianity not Mysterious*. That may seem odd, given that Toland's work was published a year *after* Locke's *Reasonableness*. But evidence suggests that Locke had seen at least a significant portion of Toland's unpublished manuscript, which based its arguments explicitly upon Locke's *Essay*, and therefore threw himself into writing the more moderate *Reasonableness* so he could rush it into publication before Toland's work appeared.[192]

Reasonable Controversies Near the End

As noted above, however reasonable Locke intended his *Reasonableness* to be, it stirred up considerable controversy, bringing Locke to offer two separate "vindications" of his arguments in 1696 and 1697. Even then, he maintained his anonymity until his dying day (or the day after, given that he made arrangements for his authorship to be revealed in his will).

Almost immediately upon publication of *Reasonableness*, Locke was attacked by Anglican John Edwards in *Some Thoughts concerning the Several Causes and Occasions of Atheism* (1695). The main charge, which had considerable bite, was that Locke was a thinly disguised Socinian. Edwards pointed out the obvious, that the author (whom he suspected was Locke) "gives it [to] us over and over again in these formal words, *viz*. that *nothing is required to be believed by any Christian man but this, that Jesus is the Messiah* . . . yet this Gentleman forgot, or rather willfully omitted a plain and obvious passage in one of the Evangelists, *Go teach all nations, baptizing them in the name of the Father, and of the Son, and of the Holy Ghost, Mat*. 28.19."[193] Edwards

192 On this point see John Biddle, "Locke's Critique of Innate Principles and Toland's Deism," *Journal of the History of Ideas* (1976), 37, pp. 411–422.

193 John Edwards, *Some Thoughts concerning the Several Causes and Occasions of Atheism*, contained in Victor Nuovo, ed., *John Locke and Christianity: Contemporary Responses to The Reasonableness of Christianity* (Bristol, England: Thoemmes Press, 1997), p. 180. In regard to his suspicions it was Locke, see p. 183.

also chastised Locke for downgrading the epistles,[194] and even more trenchantly, for exegetically stripping the Gospels of all that is not easily understood so that "every thing in Christianity must be clear and intelligible, everything must be presently comprehended by the Weakest noddle, or else it is no part of *Religion*, especially of *Christianity*. . . ."[195] Edwards ended, "this Gentleman and his fellows are resolved to be *Unitarians*; they are for *One* Article of Faith, as well as *One* Person in the Godhead," and when "the Catholick Faith [here, meaning Anglican] is thus brought down to One Single Article, it will soon be reduced to none: the Unit will dwindle into a Cypher."[196] In 1696, Edwards fired another shot, *Socinianism Unmask'd. A Discourse shewing the Unreasonableness of a Late Writer's Opinion Concerning the Necessity of only One Article of Christian Faith*. Against Locke's (anonymous) complaints about Edward's treatment of *Reasonableness*, Edwards remarked, "I have only this to say, A Plain Downright Adversary might perhaps have met with another usage, but such a Stubborn Dissembler could not expect *fairer quarter*."[197]

Whether Locke could fairly be accused of Machiavellian dissembling about his true beliefs or not, others joined in attacking *Reasonableness*, including Edward Stillingfleet (1635–1699), the Latitudinarian Anglican bishop of Worcester, in his *Discourse in Vindication of the Doctrine of the Trinity* (1697), which was aimed at John Toland as well, and more obviously in *The Bishop of Worcester's Answer to Mr Locke's Letter concerning Some Passages Relating to his Essay of Humane Understanding* (1697). Stillingfleet and Locke carried on a long and famous debate, cut short by the former's death in 1699. Part of that debate centered on whether Locke's suggestion that thinking matter was possible amounted to admitting Spinozism;[198] part focused on controversies in regard to the doctrine of the Resurrection, Stillingfleet having sniffed out what he took to be Locke's annihilationism. Meanwhile, the *Essay*, which Locke did present as his own, was also being heavily criticized, the general complaint being

194 Ibid., pp. 181–182.

195 Edwards continues: "Now then the sum of all that he aims at is this, that we must not have any Point of Doctrine whatsoever in our Religion that the *Mob* doth not at the very first naming of it perfectly understand and agree to. We are come to a fine pass indeed: the Venerable *Mob* must be ask'd what we must *believe*: and nothing must be receiv'd as an Article of Faith but what those Illiterate Clubmen vote to be such. The *Rabble* are no *System-makers*, no *Creed-makers*; and therefore away with *Systems* and *Creeds*, and let us have but One Article, though it be with the defiance of all the rest, which are of equal necessity with that One." Ibid., p. 184–185.

196 Ibid., pp. 185–186.

197 John Edwards, *Socinianism Unmask'd. A Discourse shewing the Unreasonableness of a Late Writer's Opinion Concerning the Necessity of only One Article of Christian Faith*, as contained in Nuovo, ed., *John Locke and Christianity*, pp. 227–228.

198 In his *Essay* Locke had mused, "We have the *ideas* of *matter* and *thinking*, but possibly shall never be able to know whether any mere material being thinks or no: it being impossible for us, by the contemplation of our own *ideas*, without revelation, to discover whether Omnipotency has not given some systems of matter, fitly disposed, a power to perceive and think, or else joined and fixed to matter, so disposed, a thinking immaterial substance. . . ." John Locke, *An Essay Concerning Human Understanding*, IV.iii.6.

(as Cranston notes) that "Locke's philosophy was inimical to religion."[199] But even so, it was the attacks upon *Reasonableness* that concerned him more. A stinging accusation made by John Edwards in his *Brief Vindication of the Fundamental Articles of the Christian Faith* (1697) is worth quoting at length. The context is a defense by Edwards against those who disparage the universities.

> Mr. Hobbes is a modern instance, who was wont to decry the university studies and learning because he had espoused a set of notions which were destructive not only to academic but all religious principles. But a later instance we have in one Mr. Locke, who . . . hath taken the courage to tread in his old friend's [i.e., Hobbes'] steps. . . . Nor is he [i.e., Locke] pleased with our old Christianity, but hath offered a new scheme to the world, the same (the very same words, as well as to the thing) with what Mr. Hobbes propounded as the perfect and complete model of faith viz: To believe in Christ is nothing else than to believe that Jesus is the Christ: and no other faith, besides this article, is required to eternal life (*De Cive* cap. 18). . . . This is the doctrine which is revived and furbished up in the pretended *Reasonableness of Christianity*: and you see whence it was borrowed. When that Writer [i.e., Locke] was framing a New Christianity, he took Hobbes' *Leviathan* for the *New Testament*, and the Philosopher of Malmesbury for our Saviour and the Apostles.[200]

Whatever Edwards's rhetorical excesses here, he was surely right that Hobbes suggested boiling Christianity down to just one article, "that *Jesus is the Christ*,"[201] which was the only "Beleef" preached by Jesus Himself, John the Baptist, and Apostles.[202] Hobbes also had whittled down the passage in Matthew (16:18–19) to mean not that Peter himself was the rock on which the Church was built, but that his profession that Jesus was the Christ is the "onely Article" of faith necessary for salvation.[203] And finally, as Locke also stressed the need for a simple account of faith to appeal to the vulgar, so had Hobbes asserted that this single article makes "the Faith required to Salvation" to be "Easie."[204]

Being classed as a rehash of the renowned atheist Hobbes, along with the other criticisms of *Reasonableness*, was enough to goad Locke into undertaking an extensive analysis of the Pauline epistles, his *Paraphrase and Notes on the Epistles of St. Paul*, which Locke began working on in the late 1690s, but which were published posthumously over the years 1705–1707.

---

199 Cranston, *John Locke*, p. 429.

200 Quoted in ibid., p. 430.

201 Thomas Hobbes, *Leviathan, reprint of the 1651 edition of Leviathan, or The Matter, Forme, & Power of a Common-wealth Ecclesiasticall and Civill* (Oxford: Clarendon Press, 1965), III.42, p. 389 [272].

202 Ibid., III.42, p. 401 [281], p. 430 [301–302].

203 *Ibid.*, III.42, p. 430 [301–302].

204 *Ibid.*, III.43, p. 463 [325–326].

The Method of Paraphrasing St. Paul

During his years in exile, while Locke was writing three of his most important works, he also spent a surprising amount of time studying the Bible (principally the New Testament) and the latest scholarly critiques and analyses. Clearly, his intimate friendship with Limborch and Le Clerc brought him into the center of the exegetical debates. We know, for example, that during this period he studied Richard Simon's *Histoire Critique du Vieux Testament* and the many responses generated by Simon's analysis of the Old Testament. We also know that he possessed a copy of Simon's *Histoire Critique du text du Nouveau Testament*. Through these works and other commentaries, Locke was taken to the heart of the debates about manuscripts. Locke himself also owned and used Brian Walton's six-volume *Biblia Sacra Polyglotta*, and had access to many other compilations that dwelt on the reconciliation of textual variations.[205]

When Locke wrote *Reasonableness*, then, he was well acquainted with the difficulties of textual analysis that had arisen within the last half-century, and since he had spent so many years at the very hub of theological and philosophical radicalism in the Netherlands, he was cognizant of where these difficulties could lead. Despite Locke's intentions, *Reasonableness* made him appear to most as just another of the radicals, a Socinian at best, a Hobbesian at worst.

The *Paraphrase* was Locke's last effort to demonstrate that what he had begun in the *Epistola de Tolerantia* could be vindicated in Scripture, and it "stands as one of the great landmarks in the history of Biblical criticism."[206] It was expressly written according to "the driving impulse to find some rational grounds for extending the basis of Christian tolerance by reducing the number of beliefs necessary to salvation."[207]

Since *Reasonableness* purposely focused just on the Gospels and Acts, Locke now turned to the epistles of St. Paul for defense of his theology, a move that he hoped would take the sting out of the charge that he had lopped off the epistles in *Reasonableness* because they did not fit nicely into his theological minimalism. But furthermore, since his entire argument in *Reasonableness* was about justification—what man really needs to believe and to do to be saved—it was difficult to avoid dealing with the extended accounts of justification in St. Paul.

Upon publication of each separate commentary over the years 1705–1707, reviews and reactions appeared, some positive, some neutral, and some negative. Interestingly enough given their long friendship, Jean Le Clerc's review in 1707 was not entirely positive, Le Clerc pointing out Locke's lack of prowess in the biblical languages (a gentleman amateur's knowledge of Greek, Latin, and Hebrew no longer being

205 See Arthur Wainwright, ed., John Locke, *A Paraphrase and Notes on the Epistles of St. Paul to the Galatians, I and 2 Corinthians, Romans, Ephesians* (Oxford: Clarendon Press, 1987), Introduction, pp. 26–28.

206 Gretchen Graf Pahl, "John Locke as Literary Critic and Biblical Interpreter," in Members of the Department of English, *Essays Critical and Historical Dedicated to Lily B. Campbell* (New York: Russell & Russell, 1968), pp. 139–157, quote on p. 139.

207 Ibid., p. 141.

sufficient in light of the more scholarly analysis available), and even more, that Locke had depended on Le Clerc without acknowledgment.[208] Robert Jenkin (1656–1727) offered a book-length criticism in 1709, almost entirely negative; but in the same year Newton's successor at Cambridge, William Whiston (1667–1752), offered a positive assessment. The great hymn writer Isaac Watts (1674–1748), who had been favorably predisposed to Locke's philosophy, was so shocked that he penned a poetic recantation of the *Paraphrase* put into the mouth of Locke in heaven, who now from this supernatural vantage above reason hopes the "Eternal Darkness" will "veil the Lines/ Of that unhappy Book,/Where glimmering Reason with false Lustre shines,/Where the mere mortal Pen mistook/What the celestial meant."[209] During the first quarter of the eighteenth century, attacks and defenses continued to pour forth in regard to Locke's theological position, with the *Paraphrase* considered to be essential to understanding it (and, indeed, its definitive statement).

From very early on Locke's *Paraphrase* also generated a kind of "school" of imitators in biblical studies issuing their own scriptural commentaries, including John Shute Barrington (1678–1734), James Peirce (1674?–1726), Joseph Hallett (1691?–1744), George Benson (1699–1762), Nathanael Lardner (1684–1768), and John Taylor (1694–1761). Not coincidentally, all had Arian or Socinian leanings.[210] Throughout the eighteenth century, the century in which Locke's philosophy itself became the gospel of the high Enlightenment, Locke's *Paraphrase* continued to arouse both admiration and animosity. While the orthodox railed against it, deists such as Henry St. John, Viscount Bolingbroke (1678–1751), who counted Locke as a philosophical mentor, found Locke's piety, affirmations of the miraculous, and insistence upon the necessity of revelation in the *Paraphrase* cause for confusion and umbrage.

Despite the criticism from both the orthodox for going too far and unorthodox for not going far enough, Locke's *Paraphrase* "was one of the main commentaries on Paul's Epistles in eighteenth-century Britain."[211] In America of the eighteenth and early nineteenth century, Locke's prestige was high, and hence his *Paraphrase* was especially embraced by those on the outskirts of orthodoxy, such as the Unitarian William Ellery Channing (1780–1842). On the Continent, given Locke's authority, the *Paraphrase* was widely read there as well, not only by Le Clerc, but by scholars such as Johann Jakob Wettstein (1693–1754) and Jean Alphonse Turretin (1671–1737). Soon translations of parts of the work began to appear. Perhaps most important of all, in Germany it was read approvingly by Siegmund Jakob Baumgarten (1706–1757) and very heavily influenced Johann David Michaelis (1717–1791), who wrote the Preface to the German translation of the *Paraphrase* (1768–1769). Michaelis himself had already translated the paraphrases of Locke's earlier followers James Peirce and George Benson from

208 See Wainwright's Introduction to Locke, *A Paraphrase*, pp. 59–73, for an account of the book's reception; for Le Clerc's reaction, see pp. 60–61.

209 Ibid., p. 63.

210 Ibid., pp. 65–67.

211 Ibid., p. 69.

English into Latin in the latter 1740s. Another German translation of the *Paraphrase*, this time only the material on Romans, appeared in 1773.[212]

Given the immense influence of the *Paraphrase* (and the relative neglect both by scholars of Locke and historians of scriptural scholarship), Locke's final work demands consideration.

First, in his rather extensive Preface, Locke emphasized the obscurity of St. Paul (as opposed to the simplicity of the Gospels and Acts). The obscurity had several "intrinsick" causes, from being written in Greek and being written as letters that assumed contextual knowledge now lost to us, to St. Paul's own rather torrid style.[213] But there are "external Causes" as well, the first being the accepted division of the text into chapters and verses which all too easily allows "parcels and . . . scraps" of the letter to be removed from its epistolary context by readers and used independently. Taken out of context, Locke complained, they easily become weapons of doctrinal disagreement among rival sects, "every Sect being perfectly Orthodox in its own Judgment."[214] The diffraction of the epistles has become all the more pronounced as multiple commentators from each of the sects have arisen with rival interpretations.[215] Of course, such multiplicity fuels public disagreements, and acts against tolerance and peace.

Locke provided an *interpretive method* as the solution. What was needed, claimed Locke, was a "Rule" or method that helped sort out which of the commentators, "explains the Words and Phrases according to the Apostle's *Meaning*."[216] Thus, in much subtler form, Locke presented the same shift in emphasis as Spinoza, from truth to meaning, focusing on the original context of the letters, so that most of the doctrinal sharpness of St. Paul could be explained away by the particular context in which he wrote.[217]

Locke presented his method autobiographically, much as Descartes had, so that like Descartes he began in a state of confusion after "reading of the Text and Comments in the ordinary way. . . ." The first step toward clarity, Locke related, was his laying aside the commentaries and reading each of the epistles "all through at one Siting, and to observe as well as I could the Drift and Design of his writing it."[218] Several such readings were required before he "came to have a good general View of the Apostle's main Purpose in writing the Epistle, the chief Branches of his Discourse wherein he prosecuted it, the Arguments he used, and the Disposition of the whole."[219] The overriding assumption in his analysis was that in each letter St. Paul has one "Point," which, once found through multiple readings, "will conduct us with Surety through those seemingly dark Places, and imagined Intricacies in which Christians have

212 Ibid., pp. 70–73.
213 Ibid., Preface, pp. 103–105.
214 Ibid., Preface, pp. 105–107.
215 Ibid., Preface, pp. 107–108.
216 Ibid., Preface, p. 109. Emphasis added.
217 Pahl, "John Locke as Literary Critic and Biblical Interpreter," p. 142.
218 Locke, *A Paraphrase*, Preface, p. 110.
219 Ibid.

wander'd so far one from another, as to find quite contrary Senses." This "seeking in him the Coherence of a Discourse tending with close strong reasoning to a Point . . . seems not to have been much made use of, or at least [not] so throughly pursued as I am apt to think it deserves."[220]

The "Point" serves to minimize the splintering of the text that for Locke led to creating rival interpretations, and hence rival Christian sects. It also allows the historical context of the point to be emphasized, so that sectarians do not contrive grand doctrinal differences out of what amount to small pieces of very personal letters. Rather than taking up "parcels and . . . scraps," in Locke's method the exegete is forced to attend to the single point of the letter, and fit each part coherently into that single aim. This process also helped eliminate interpretations that would not fit the designated "Point" of the letter, for if "such or such an Interpretation does not give us this genuine Sense" as known from "his Design, and the Aim he proposed to himself in Writing," then that interpretation must be false.[221]

Perhaps most important of all for the history of biblical interpretation, the focus on the point of the letter, as interpreted by the tightly circumscribed historical context, opened up a "crack in that hitherto rigid assumption . . . that the essential doctrine of all the books in the Bible, Old Testament and New alike, is the same, however customs and minor points of law might vary with the times."[222] In doing so, Locke was acting at least indirectly against the traditional understanding of typological fulfillment of the Old Testament in the New by turning readers' attention away from unifying exegesis to particularizing exegesis, searching after the "Point" of each writing independently.

But unlike Spinoza, who had much the same aim, Locke did not set out an explicit methodology; rather, he led by example. Locke took the reader to the "Point" of each Epistle in a synopsis appearing before the biblical text, and then reinforced this point in his paraphrase and commentary that appeared after the text. For Galatians, the "subject and designe . . . is to dehort and hinder the Galatians from bringing themselves under the bondage of the Mosaical law," or more specifically, "to keep the Galatians from hearkening to those Judaizing Seducers who had almost perswaded them to be circumcised."[223] In I Corinthians, the "main designe of St Paul . . . is to support his own authority dignity and credit with that part of the church which stuck to him" against "a new Instructor a Jew by nation who had raised a faction against St. Paul."[224] For II Corinthians, it is likewise "to take off the people from the new Leader they had got who was St Pauls opposer, and wholly to put an end to the faction and disorder which that false Apostle had caused in the Church of Corinth."[225] In Romans, the "principal aim . . . seems to be to perswade them [the Gentiles at Rome] to a steady perseverance in the profession of Christianity by convinceing them that god is the god

220 Ibid., p. 112.

221 Or in Locke's words, it is "nothing at all to his present purpose." Ibid.

222 Pahl, "John Locke as Literary Critic and Biblical Interpreter," p. 145.

223 Locke, *A Paraphrase, Galatians*, Synopsis (p. 119) and Ch. I.1–5, Contents (p. 120).

224 John Locke, *A Paraphrase, I Corinthians*, Synopsis, pp. 163–164.

225 Ibid., *II Corinthians*, Synopsis, p. 263.

of the Gentiles as well as the Jews, and that now under the gospel there is noe difference between Jew and Gentile," so that "they are by faith in Jesus Christ the people of god without circumcision or other observances of the Jews. . . ."[226]

One can easily see Locke's own agenda peeking through his delineation of St. Paul's "points," and even in Locke's sketching of the particular character of St. Paul himself. As Gretchen Graf Pahl deftly puts it, in Locke's paraphrases we can see the "character" of St. Paul "develop, in all its subtlety, and become a very real human being whose aims are not unlike those of Locke himself. The personality who steps out of Locke's scholarly pages is no esoteric messenger of grace to a few elect, but a great fighter for tolerance among all Christians, a leader who has devoted his life to battling the narrow Judaizing sectarians of his own day."[227] We should recall, however, the complexity of Locke's notion of tolerance. He was not only attempting to impose a political Latitudinarianism, but explicitly trying to exclude Catholicism from this political-theological compromise. As Locke very early on wrote to fellow radical Henry Stubbe in 1659:

> The only scruple I have [in regard to Stubbe's argument for complete tolerance] is how the liberty you grant the Papists can consist with the security of the nation . . . since I cannot see how they can at the same time obey two different authorities carrying on contrary interest, especially where that which is destructive to ours is backed with an opinion of infallibility and holiness supposed by them to be immediately derived from God, founded in Scripture and their own equally sacred traditions, not limited by any [political] contract and therefore not accountable to anybody. . . .[228]

Obviously, Locke shared this scruple with Hobbes, or inherited it from him. Given the Catholic Church's claims to be carrying forth the Old Testament priesthood and sacrificial system, casting St. Paul as the enemy of the Judaizers allowed for direct biblical support for his fundamentally anti-Catholic political stance.

And so, upon inspection, Locke's sketch of St. Paul seems to look surprisingly like Locke himself. One cannot help but be reminded of Albert Schweitzer's quip about exegetes looking down the well and seeing their own reflection. But in sharply dividing the universalist party from the Judaizing party, Locke was also preparing the way for the later exegetical emphasis—not altogether devoid of anti-Catholic animus—on understanding the New Testament primarily as a witness to an early split between Judaizing and non-Judaizing factions. As Pahl notes, Locke was one of the first "to approach all the Epistles from the standpoint of this basic Apostolic cleavage, and the first to realize how many of Paul's seemingly obscure statements could be rendered clear by interpreting them as Paul's defenses against 'Judaizing' Christians, or as his

---

226 Ibid., *Romans*, Synopsis pp. 483–484.

227 Pahl, "John Locke as Literary Critic and Biblical Interpreter," p. 145.

228 Locke's letter to Henry Stubbe, mid-September 1659, in David Wootton, ed., John Locke, *Political Writings* (New York: Penguin, 1993), pp. 137–139.

indirect attacks upon them."[229] So, while wide toleration coupled with exclusion of Catholics may have been Locke's aim, this goal in turn spawned an important exegetical emphasis that would have ramifications far beyond Locke's immediate intentions.

In reading his paraphrases, also note the importance of structure. The very structure of Locke's approach supported his aims. In Locke's surrounding the text of the epistles by his explanation and illumination of the "Point," he was leaving as little as room as possible for rival interpretations and giving the widest authoritative scope to his own.

But Locke also had to deal with particular passages that would not seem to support the Whig agenda. For example, Locke kneaded St. Paul's rather severe contrast between flesh and Spirit to allow for a respectable mercantilist spirit. St. Paul's text in Galatians 6:8, as provided by Locke, reads: "For he that soweth to his flesh, shall of the flesh reap corruption: but he that soweth to the Spirit, shall of the Spirit reap life everlasting." Locke's paraphrase was significantly less threatening, rounding the sharp edges for the man of commerce. "He that lays out the stock of good things he has, onely for the satisfaction of his own bodily necessitys, conveniencys or pleasures, shall at the harvest find the fruit and product of such husbandry to be corruption and perishing: But he that lays out his worldly substance according to the rules dictated by the spirit of god in the gospel shall of the spirit reap life everlasting."[230]

Likewise, Locke was loathe to give a straight reading to St. Paul's admonition to be "subject unto the higher powers" (Romans 13:1), given that it was a favorite text of those arguing for divine right monarchy. While Locke admitted "This section conteins the duty of Christians to the civil magistrate," he argued that, in St. Paul speaking of "higher powers," he meant:

> the supreme civil power, which is in every common-wealth derived from God, and is of the same extent every where. i e is absolute and unlimited by any thing but the end for which god gave it (viz) the good of the people sincerely pursued according to the best of the skill of those who share that power, and so not to be resisted. But how men come by a rightfull title to this power; or who has that title, he is wholy silent, and says noe thing of it. To have medled with that would have been to decide of civil rights, contrary to the designe and business of the gospel, and the example of our Saviour, who refused medleing in such cases with this decisive question. *Who made me a Judg or Divider over you?* Luk. XII.14.[231]

Whereas St. Paul did not distinguish between legitimate and illegitimate civil power, Locke did, pointing us toward a secular standard in which (as with the *Epistola*) civil rights were made wholly distinct from faith. As for the right to revolution, Locke provided some wiggle room in a footnote, asserting that "Christians by virtue of being

229 Pahl, "John Locke as Literary Critic and Biblical Interpreter," p. 147.

230 Locke, *A Paraphrase, Galatians*, text and paraphrase VI.8, p. 157.

231 Ibid., *Romans*, contents XIII.1–7, pp. 586–587.

Christians are not any way exempt from obedience to the civil magistrates, nor ought by any means to resist them, though by what is said [in] ver. 3 it seems that St Paul meant here magistrates having and exerciseing a lawfull power."[232]

Other aspects of Locke's philosophy show through. Given Locke's ambiguity in regard to human beings having an immaterial soul, it is not surprising that Locke is rather circumspect in regard to I Corinthians 15. St. Paul's text of I Corinthians 15:44 (as quoted by Locke) on the Resurrection of the body read: "It is sown a natural body, it is raised a spiritual body. There is a natural body, and there is a spiritual body." Locke's paraphrase betrays his materialist bent: "The body we have here surpasses not the animal nature, at the resurrection it shall be spiritual. There are both animal and spiritual bodys."[233] Locke's footnote on "animal" explained that:

> Σωμα ψυχικον which in our bibles is translated *natural body* should I think more suitably to the propriety of the Greek and more conformable to the Apostles meaning be translated *Animal body*. For that which St Paul is doeing here is to shew that as we have animal bodys now (which we derived from Adam) endowed with an animal life which unless supported with a constant supply of food and air will fail and perish and at last, doe what we can, will dissolve and come to an end.

And so, as the paraphrase continued, St. Paul's contention that the "first man Adam was made a living soul" really meant that he was "made of an animal constitution indowed with an animal life. . . ."[234] Locke's spin implies that he was (with Hobbes) a mortalist, i.e., he held that there was no immaterial soul, but that human beings, just like animals, simply disintegrate at death. In a paper written by Locke, "*Resurrectio et quae sequuntur*," he made it clear that he was (again with Hobbes) an annihilationist, believing that the damned were recreated *ex nihilo*, punished with fire, and completely destroyed (rather than eternally punished), a position consistent with mortalism. In defending annihilationism, Locke used almost exactly the same arguments as Hobbes, asserting in addition that "everlasting in a true scripture sense may be said of that which endures as long as the subject it affects endures. Soe everlasting priesthood XL Exod 15 was a priesthood that lasted as long as the people lasted in an estate capable of the Mosaical worship," so also everlasting in regard to "hell fire" must be understood to be like "Gehenna . . . where the fire never was quenched yet it does not follow nor is it said that the bodys that were burnt in it were never consumed. . . ."[235] Both the everlasting priesthood and everlasting fire were thereby removed in one exegetical blow.

One final example. Twice in footnotes Locke called attention to St. Paul's expectation of the coming of Jesus again as imminent in a way that certainly implied it to be

232 Ibid., paraphrase XIII.1, footnote, p. 588.

233 Ibid., *2 Corinthians*, text and paraphrase XV.44, pp. 248, 253–254.

234 Ibid., footnote to XV.44, p. 254, and paraphrase XV.45, p. 254.

235 John Locke, "*Resurrectio et quae sequuntur*," contained in Appendix VI to Wainwright, ed., Locke, *A Paraphrase*; quotes on p. 683.

evidence that St. Paul himself was simply wrong. In a footnote to his paraphrase of I Corinthians 5:3,[236] Locke remarked "That the Apostle lookd on the comeing of Christ as not far off appears by what he says I Thess. IV.15–V.6 which Epistle was written some years before this. See also to the same purpose I Cor. I.7. VII.29.32. X.11 Rom XIII.11.12 Heb X.37."[237] Similarly, in the footnote to his paraphrase of Romans 13.11–12,[238] Locke stated that "It seems by these two verses as if St Paul lookd upon Christs comeing as not far off; to which there are several other concurrent passages in his Epistles. See I Cor I.7."[239]

In general, Locke's exegesis does sound surprisingly orthodox, at least to modern ears. To the orthodox of his time, however, it was little more than Spinozism. Looking backward, we cannot help comparing Locke to the radicals to come. Such company makes Locke the picture of moderation, the self-portrait Locke no doubt wished to have painted. But it is worth noting that the orthodox of the early eighteenth century, comparing him to their traditional exegesis, saw him as providing a deceptively contrived form of moderation that masked his radicalism. We see his moderation as compared to what was to come; they saw his radicalism in light of where it would lead. In regard to the *Paraphrase*, Locke was slippery in regard to the divinity of Christ and the Holy Trinity (committing sins of omission), yet unlike the more radical of his circle Locke was quite willing to affirm Christ's miracles and His Resurrection. But if one reads the *Paraphrase* in the light of his *Epistola*, the *Essay*, and especially *Reasonableness*—as it certainly was by those who followed him—the *Paraphrase* seemed designed to function as an exegetical filter that dampened the fires of scriptural controversy, even while it supported the use of Scripture as a moral prop for the vulgar. In short, he offered a refined form of Spinoza's Moral Vulgate.

The End of Locke

Locke spent the last few years of his life "in rest, study and religious meditations,"[240] the fruit of which was the posthumously published *Paraphrase*. Unfortunately, Locke, who was never very healthy, was ill for extended periods, even becoming deaf for a time. Yet from his bed he kept watch with great interest on the political scene through papers and friends, and was understandably distressed at the increase in Tory power after the turn of the century. King William had died in 1702, and with the accession of Queen Anne, Tory power rose and with it the desire for political revenge

236 "If soe be the comeing of Christ shall overtake me in this life before I put off this body."

237 Locke, *A Paraphrase, 2 Corinthians*, paraphrase V.3, footnote, p. 284.

238 "And all this doe considering that it is now high time that we rouse our selves up, shake off sleep, and betake our selves with vigilancy and vigor to the dutys of a Christian life. For the time of your removal out of this place of exercise and probationership is nearer that when you first enterd into the profession of Christianity."

239 Locke, *A Paraphrase, Romans*, paraphrase XIII.11–12 footnote, p. 590.

240 Cranston, *John Locke*, p. 449, the words describing Locke coming from a July 20, 1700, letter of Limborch to Locke.

and restitution of the old order. Unsurprisingly, the changing political winds brought new criticism of Locke and the Whigs, and along with it, an attempt to suppress his *Essay* at Oxford, along with two works by Le Clerc.

In the midst of controversy, Locke continued his work on the *Paraphrase*, sending his unpublished manuscript to friends for comment, one of the most notable being Isaac Newton. Locke was well aware that he had little time, writing to Peter King in the spring of 1704 that, "the dissolution of this cottage is not far off."[241] Yet Locke would recover his health enough to live until October, when on the twenty-eighth he expired in an armchair, having just listened to Psalms read to him by Lady Masham. The previous night he had remarked to those surrounding him, "My work here is almost at an end, and thank God for it. I may perhaps die tonight; but I cannot live above three or four days. Remember me in your evening prayers."[242] Locke's work was not almost at an end, however. He became, after his death, the most renowned and influential philosopher of the eighteenth century, in both England and on the Continent. He was *the* philosopher of the Enlightenment—or more accurately the moderate Enlightenment—and that prestige carried over into his treatment of Scripture.

Conclusion: Locke and Scripture

Clearly, Locke's approach to Scripture must be understood in the context of his corpus of philosophical-political arguments, and just as important, in the political circumstances of his time. While not discounting his personal piety, it is fair to say that, with Marsilius, Machiavelli, and others, Locke treated Christianity largely in terms of its political utility in governing the unreasonable masses. And like Spinoza in particular, there was not much left after his exegesis but a morality upheld by a rather thin theism. It is certainly true that Locke, unlike his more radical contemporaries among whom he circulated, was unwilling to jettison Christ's miracles and Resurrection, but his reason seems to have been that the unwashed masses need miracles to take the place of reason in providing authority for the moral commands in the Gospel.

Given that the goal of exegesis was to provide a "reasonable" form of Christianity suited to Locke's characteristic political views, it is not surprising that Locke tended to find that the Whig political platform was supported by his reading of the Old and especially the New Testament. Locke's treatment of God's granting of dominion to Adam in Genesis both served to undermine his monarchist political enemies and to provide support for his own preferred Whig mercantilism. His jettisoning of God the Father for a God who claims us as His property likewise undermined patriarchal claims to political power, and affirmed the claims of the industrious propertied Whigs to political power. His theological minimalism at once provided the foundation for religious toleration, and also destroyed the foundation of Anglican and Catholic notions of sacraments and priesthood. His political Averroism, where the civil realm is entirely

241 Quoted in ibid., p. 471.

242 Quoted in ibid., pp. 479–480.

secular and religion is entirely private, has become an established and unquestionable political fact for the West. It is so completely beyond question that reading it today, we must remind ourselves that its establishment demanded a particular philosophy and mode of exegesis to support it. Whether or not succeeding generations influenced by Locke's *Essay*, *Reasonableness*, and the *Paraphrase* were aware of these very political sources of Locke's treatment of faith, religion, and Scripture, it is undeniable that they guided Locke in writing them.

In Locke one discovers some critical seeds that will grow over the next two centuries and become established aspects of historical-critical scholars. Locke's jettisoning of God the Father for God the property-owner was part of the larger philosophical-scientific movement initiated by Boyle and culminating in Newton, which replaced the personal God intimately working with His creatures in history, with a distant and impersonal God, a watchmaker deity, who set the world up and let it go, to wind toward its own internal mechanical principles. Although Locke, and even Newton, allowed for miracles, soon enough the miraculous foundered upon the mechanism, and Hobbes's and Spinoza's elimination of the miraculous from Scripture would be mainstreamed.

From the vantage of hindsight, that would make Locke appear quite conservative by comparison with what came after. But in sober fact he was a *moderate radical*. If Locke was a moderate, it was in providing a moderation of Hobbes and Spinoza, rather than a liberalization of the *via antiqua*. Locke moderated Hobbes's state of nature, but only to ensure that the industrious propertied class in Parliament could rule over the king; Locke moderated Spinoza's rejection of the miraculous, but only to better support political order among the "vulgar." Locke moderated Hobbes's claim that the king was *the* interpreter of Scripture and doctrine, but did so by making each individual himself the sovereign interpreter, provided he keep within the bounds of a reasonable Christianity; Locke moderated Spinoza's regime of complete tolerance, by a less tolerant but more stable Latitudinarianism.

Locke made other important contributions to the development of the historical-critical method. In his *Essay*, he outlined the principles by which Scripture could be judged historically. Although he himself left the application to others, it is clear from the context of his discussion that Locke intended such an application to take place. Further, he was not only well versed in the problem of sorting out multiple biblical texts in regard to authenticity, but let the reader know how the transmission of texts through tradition must undoubtedly corrupt them over time, making retrieval of the original Christianity, through exegesis, an impossible task. Again, he let history draw the conclusions.

Also of note: Locke's defining his minimalist creed in accordance with political Messiahship, and comments about St. Paul's errors in regard to the imminent second coming, certainly helped prepare the way for the nineteenth-century claim that Jesus Himself was merely a political Messiah, but a failed one. Obviously, Locke's Socinianism—an implicit denial by silence of Christ's divinity—made this conclusion all the more demanded. Locke tended not to draw the conclusions himself; rather, he planted the seed. Another sign of his moderation.

In regard to exegetical method, Locke also seems moderate as compared to Spinoza, but his moderate presentation contained much more of Spinozism than might appear at first. His concentration on St. Paul as a writer of very particular letters that must not be taken out of the context of their time and place duplicated Spinoza's focus on the contextual meaning of the biblical figure rather than the truth of what he said. Locke's conclusion that St. Paul's main emphasis consisted in his universalist antagonism to Judaizers served to reinforce a Spinozan minimalist creed and eliminate Catholicism from the political compromise. Locke was therefore highly influential in carrying forth the notion that the New Testament itself does not represent a unified view but rather a church in conflict, a notion that will be carried over in later exegetical attempts to take apart the text in accordance with the alleged factions.

Locke is best understood as a moderate radical. As a moderate radical, he was the bearer of the very radicalism at the heart of his thought. At the same time he pulled away from it, he drew attention to it and allowed it to enter the mainstream of respectable thought. To understand this more fully, one must turn from Locke the cryptically moderate to John Toland, the openly radical.

CHAPTER 12

REVOLUTION, RADICALS, REPUBLICANS, AND JOHN TOLAND

The Real John Toland

Now it is time to trace the radical developments adumbrated earlier in considerations of Spinoza and Locke, through an analysis of one of the most colorful of early Enlightenment figures, John Toland. Here as before, the starting point must be biography.

Such an approach is necessary because the development of modern scriptural scholarship is all too often seen as issuing from a mild deism, itself the result of the gradual liberalizing of Christianity that grew into an ever more detached, autonomous critical method. As the story goes, this method, through its purely objective efforts, culminated in a scientific study of the Old and New Testaments. The culmination of this study was the flowering in the nineteenth century, the great century of Teutonic biblical scholarship, of a purely naturalized account of Judaism and Christianity at odds with the outmoded and even puerile supernaturalism that previously defined the faith of unenlightened, precritical ages. Seen in this way, Toland's most famous work, *Christianity not Mysterious* (1696), is understood as a good example of mild deism, a representation of the early phase of the transition.

It is necessary to challenge this characterization of Toland, and indeed, the usual story into which this characterization fits. Toland was no mild deist. In studying his wider body of writings and in investigating his radical milieu, one finds the usual story turned on its head. The nineteenth and twentieth century culmination of the historical-critical method is, generally speaking, readily available in the radical, anti-Christian circles of the late seventeenth and early eighteenth century. In these circles, the secular assumptions *form* and *guide* the infancy of modern critical scholarship, the birth of which was already witnessed in Hobbes and Spinoza.

More than any other figure of this period, John Toland illustrates the importance of understanding the radical undercurrents of the late seventeenth and early eighteenth centuries that will come to full flower in the nineteenth and twentieth. As will become clear, the radical conclusions of the historical-critical method were built into the method itself. To demonstrate this, one must stand back and take a much wider view of his entire life and writings. A good place to begin is at the end, with an assessment by a contemporary that reveals a fundamental ambiguity in Toland and his writings.

The Ambiguous John Toland

"As for religion . . . it is more easy to guess what he was not, than to tell what he was. 'Tis certain, he was neither Jew nor Mahometan: But whether he was a Christian, a Deist, a Pantheist, an Hobbist, or a Spinozist, is the Question."[1] That's a fitting epitaph for John Toland, one of the most controversial and ambiguous figures of the late seventeenth and early eighteenth centuries. That this text belongs among the early classics of modern scriptural scholarship is beyond dispute,[2] but getting to the heart of what Toland actually intended is much more difficult for precisely the reasons the epitaph suggests. To do so, one must have recourse to some later writings in which Toland revealed the reasons for his notorious ambiguity.

Letters to Serena

In his *Letters to Serena* (1704), amid a section describing how the belief in the immortality of the soul arose, Toland remarked that while the Epicurean philosophers in particular most famously denied the existence of the soul, in all other philosophical schools there were always

> particular Persons who really oppos'd the Soul's Immortality, tho they might accommodate their ordinary Language to the Belief of the People: for most of the Philosophers . . . had two sorts of Doctrins, the one internal and the other external, or the one private and the other publick; the latter to be indifferently communicated to all the World, and the former only very cautiously to their best Friends, or to some few others capable of receiving it, and that wou'd not make ill use of the same.[3]

The two sorts of doctrine created a kind of double-speak, a method of equivocation that allowed philosophers to speak on two levels at once. Such equivocation was

1 A. Boyer, *The political state of Great Britain* XXIII (1722), p. 342, quoted in Justin Champion, *Republican Learning: John Toland and the Crisis of Christian Culture, 1696–1722* (Manchester and New York: Manchester University Press, 2003), p. 69.

2 William Baird, *History of New Testament Research, Vol. I: From Deism to Tübingen*, pp. 39–41; Henning Graf Reventlow, "English Deism and the Anti-Deist Apologetic," in Magne Sæbø, ed., *Hebrew Bible/ Old Testament: The History of Its Interpretation*: Vol. II, *From the Renaissance to the Enlightenment* (Göttingen: Vandenhoeck & Ruprecht, 2008), Ch. 35, pp. 859–862. See also Reventlow's much more thorough treatment in *The Authority of the Bible and the Rise of the Modern World*, translated by John Bowden (Philadelphia, PA: Fortress Press, 1985), pp. 294–308.

3 John Toland, *Letters to Serena* (Stuttgart-Bad Connstatt: F. Frommann, 1964, facsimile of the 1704 edition printed in London by Bernard Lintot), II.14, pp. 56–57.

necessary for a reason familiar from the accounts of Marsilius, Machiavelli, Descartes, Hobbes, and Spinoza (if not Locke): The mob was incapable of understanding philosophy and hence needed to be controlled by religion. Using the Pythagoreans as an example, Toland noted that while they spoke publicly of transmigration of souls, they really "meant no more than the eternal Revolution of Forms in Matter. . . . But in the external or popular Doctrin he [Pythagoras] impos'd on the Mob by an equivocal Expression, that *they shou'd become various kinds of Beasts after Death,* thereby to deter 'em the more effectively from Wickedness."[4] The unphilosophic many were incapable of receiving truth, for if they learned that there was actually no soul, and hence no afterlife with the threat of punishment for misdeeds, there would be no end to their wickedness.

But it is especially important that the multitude do not receive an out-and-out lie; rather, they receive a kind of half-truth, an "equivocal Expression": the soul is immortal, not as an individual immaterial entity that survives physical death, but insofar as the material substrate of someone's body is taken up into other things after death. Such equivocation allowed the philosopher to tell only a half-lie in public, using the very irrationality of the many to control them. The full truth was spoken by such philosophers "only very cautiously to their best Friends, or to some few others capable of receiving it."

Pantheisticon

This same distinction between the philosopher and the many was repeated in Toland's *Pantheisticon* (1720).[5] As the title suggests, this work aimed to give an account of Toland's philosophical system, pantheism (a more detailed analysis of which will follow). The *Pantheisticon* is a rather curious document, as its subtitle suggests: *the Form of Celebrating the Socratic-Society*. Following Toland's distinction, it would appear to be an esoteric text meant for the few (and, in fact, only a relative few were published anonymously). It purported to be a "New Fellowship *and* New Regulation" for a private quasi-religious (perhaps even Masonic) philosophical association rooted in a kind of materialism seemingly even more radical than Spinoza's, and hence clearly at odds with Christianity. The proposed Socratic society must be private precisely because "*the Generality of Mankind is averse from Knowledge, and vents Invectives against its Partizans. . . .*"[6] For this reason, "Philosophy . . . designedly shuns the Multitude. . . ." We need to "separate ourselves from the Multitude," Toland confided to his philosophic readers, "for the Multitude . . . is a Proof of what is worst."[7]

4 Ibid., p. 57.

5 John Toland, *Pantheisticon: or, the Form of Celebrating the Socratic-Society*, originally in Latin in 1720 (English translation, London, 1751, Samuel Paterson; facsimile, New York: Garland Publishing, Inc., 1976).

6 Ibid., "Preface to the Reader," pp. 3–4.

7 Ibid., pp. 4–5.

Not surprisingly, Toland repeated the esoteric/exoteric distinction as essential to the pantheist creed because, even though the philosopher should shun the multitude, he must still live among them. "Philosophy is divided by the *Pantheists*, as well as other antient Sages, into *External*, or popular and depraved; and *Internal*, or pure and genuine. . . ." Although the internal philosophy is the same, the external is relative, depending upon the established or accepted religion that governs the place each pantheist happens to live. Like a good Machiavellian, each philosopher "professes [in public] the Heresy [i.e., the particular religion] he sucked in with his Milk, (so it be not entirely false) or that, which has been anywhere established." The result is a particular version of the Averroistic double or twofold truth, for "nothing is more prudent than the old Saying, *We must talk with the People, and think with Philosophers*."[8] Toland then defended the "Two-fold Philosophy of the Pantheists."[9]

> But perhaps it may be imputed as a Fault to the PANTHEISTS for embracing two Doctrines, the one *External* or popular, adjusted in some Measure to the Prejudices of the People, or to Doctrines publickly authorized for true; the other *Internal* or philosophical, altogether conformable to the Nature of Things, and therefore to Truth itself: And moreover for proposing this secret Philosophy, naked and entire, unmasked, and without any tedious Circumstance of Words, in the Recesses of a private Chamber, to Men only of consummate Probity and Prudence.[10]

Toland deflected blame from the pantheists, however. The problem was not in the philosophers but in the people who are governed not by "Truth itself" but by their prejudices and the particular sanctioned religion that supported them. Truth was forever at odds with mere prejudice, and truth unjustly suffered. While the philosophers behave toward the prejudiced multitude with all due condescension "as fond Nurses do towards their babbling Minions," the "babbling Minions" strike back at all those "who do adhere not by Line and Level to the Opinions of the Ignorant." Therefore the philosophers are "ill used" and persecuted. For his own protection, the wise man cannot remain passive, but must "use his Endeavours to do all that can be done, that is, by plucking out the Teeth and paring the Nails of the worst and most pernicious of Monsters. . . ."[11]

This plucking and paring forms the pantheist's external doctrine "adjusted in some Measure to the Prejudices of the People, or to Doctrines publickly authorized for true." Since in his particular historical setting this adjustment must obviously be

---

8 Toland goes on to offer the further advice if the philosopher finds the public religion utterly vicious: "But should the Religion derived from one's Father, or enforced by the Laws, be wholly, or in some respects, wicked, villainous, obscene, tyrannical, or depriving Men of their Liberty, in such Case the *Brethren* may, with all the Legality in the World, betake themselves immediately to one more mild, more pure, and more free." This occurs in a short essay Toland inserts before the actual *Pantheisticon*, entitled, "Of the Antients and Modern Societies of the Learned," XVI, pp. 56–57.

9 Ibid., "Of a Two-fold Philosophy of the Pantheists," I.93. This essay was appended by Toland after the actual *Pantheisticon*.

10 Ibid., II.96.

11 Ibid., II.97–99.

made to Christianity, we must face the obvious possibility that Toland's *Christianity not Mysterious*—so influential in the early development of modern scriptural scholarship—was just such an exercise of plucking and paring. Before doing so, we must inquire more deeply about the mode of adjustment because that will form the foundation of the requisite method of approaching Scripture.

Toland asserted that the adjustment should be such that it brings no danger to the philosopher: "the PANTHEIST . . . shall not, in the first Place, to his Prejudice [i.e., his safety], run counter to the received *Theology*, that in philosophical Matters swerves from Truth; neither shall he be altogether Silent, when a proper Occasion presents itself; yet he shall never run the Risque of his Life, but in Defence of his Country and Friends."[12] This quasi-patriotic statement should not mislead us; as with many other later Enlightenment figures, Toland considered the philosopher not to be "the Native of any circumscribed Place, but a Citizen of the whole World, as one City. . . ."[13] That is, his ultimate patriotic allegiance was to the international or cosmopolitan community of like-minded philosophers.

To return to *Letters to Serena*, the threat of persecution by the superstitious and ignorant brings philosophers, as an act of prudence, to hide their true opinions in their exoteric writings. While the philosophers are "undeceiv'd" by popular prejudice, "yet the prevailing Power of Interest will make us hypocritically (or, if you please, prudently) to pretend the contrary, for fear of losing our Fortunes, Quiet, Reputation, or Lives."[14] That hypocrisy or prudence results in "equivocal Expression." "I am conscious to myself," Toland remarked by way of apology, "that this Silence, and prudent Reservedness of Mind, will not be agreeable to all Persons; however the PANTHEISTS shall not be more open, 'till they are at full Liberty to think as they please, and speak as they think."[15]

Clidophorus

In 1720 Toland published *Clidophorus, or Of the Exoteric and Esoteric Philosophy*, which, as its title proclaimed, dealt once again with this all-important distinction. In it, Toland was even more clear that he wished this distinction to be applied as a kind of key to his own writings—*Clidophorus* itself meaning in Greek "key" (*kleis*) "bearer" (*phoreus*).[16] Toland pointed straightaway to his contemporary situation, wherein "there

12 Ibid., V.106–107.

13 Ibid., IV.104–105.

14 Toland, *Letters to Serena*, I.9, p. 9.

15 Toland, *Pantheisticon*, "Of a Two-fold Philosophy of the Pantheists," V.108.

16 Toland alluded to this distinction as a *key* several times: in regard to the proper reading of Plato (V, p. 75); in regard to Heraclitus (V, p. 76); in regard to the Egyptians and Pythagoras (VIII, p. 85). In veiled self-allusion, he remarked in regard to Heraclitus: "The readers wanted a key, that might open 'em a passage into his secret meaning: and such a key, that I may hint it *en passant*, is to be, for the most part, borrow'd by the skilful from the writers themselves" (V, p. 76). To understand more fully what the skilful Toland "borrow'd" one would first have to read the ancients mentioned by him as teaching the

is no discovering, at least no declaring of TRUTH in most places, but at the hazard of a man's reputation, imployment, or life."[17] This situation "must of necessity produce shiftings, ambiguities, equivocations, and hypocrisy in all its shapes. . . ."[18] The possibility of persecution brings it about that "the same Philosophers *do not always seem to say the same thing*, tho they continu'd of the same opinion; which is as true as Truth it self, of many writers in our own time."[19] That the "*same men do not always seem to say the same things on the same subjects*" was a hermeneutical problem facing readers of such philosophers' writings, a problem that "can onely be solv'd by the distinction of *the External and Internal Doctrine*," that is, a "double Philosophy, or Theology, if you'd rather have it so!" This double philosophy was the "true key" for unlocking their ambiguity.[20]

As he declared in his other works, the exoteric-esoteric distinction had a pedigree reaching back to ancient philosophy,[21] which for Toland was almost invariably rooted in esoteric pantheism that looked suspiciously Spinozan. For example, the Egyptians, "who were the wisest of mortals, had a twofold doctrine; the one secret, and in that respect sacred; the other popular, and consequently vulgar."[22] The goddess Isis, popularly understood as a queen, was in fact the "*Nature of all things*, according to the Philosophers, *who held the* UNIVERSE *to be the principal* GOD, or the supreme being. . . ." In support, Toland offered the inscription (which sounds eerily like the name God revealed to Moses in Exodus 3:14) from a statue of Isis at Sais—"I AM ALL THAT WAS, IS, AND SHALL BE."[23] The same statue and inscription meant different things to the philosophers and to the vulgar.

Again, the contrived ambiguity of the philosophers was made necessary, first of all, by the incapacities of the vulgar. Toland supplied some quite interesting illustrations, including Moses, among those who had recourse to exoteric discourse in his dealings with the vulgar Israelites, the hidden assumption being that he must have had his apprenticeship in true philosophy from the Egyptians. "MOSES, the most illustrious Lawgiver of the Jews . . . is not disown'd by his followers, to have departed sometimes from the accurate truth of divine and natural matters; and frequently to accommodate his words, when speaking of GOD himself, to the capacity and preconceiv'd opinions of the vulgar."[24]

Toland was quite familiar with Machiavelli, and his treatment of Moses was considerably similar, shot through with the same kind of ambiguity. When discussing

doctrine.

17 John Toland, *Clidophorus* in *The Theological and Philological Works of the Late John Toland* (London: W. Mears, 1732; facsimile, Elibron Classics, 2005), II, p. 67.

18 Ibid., II, p. 68.

19 Ibid., VI, p. 77.

20 Ibid., VIII, p. 85. The specific context is Toland's discussion of the Egyptians and Pythagoreans.

21 Again, the esoteric-exoteric distinction was ubiquitous among the ancients. In the *Clidophorus* he lists, among others, Zoroaster, Pythagoras, Zamolxis, Epimenides, Numa (ibid., I, pp. 64–65), Parmenides (III, pp. 69–70), the Druids, Aristotle, Plato, the Stoics, and Heraclitus (IV–V, pp. 72–76).

22 Ibid., III, p. 70.

23 Ibid., III, p. 71.

24 Ibid., VI, p. 78.

those ancients who maintained that "it was lawful to ly for the public good" because "the common people . . . being incapable of reflection, ought to be manag'd by guile, and to be deluded by agreable fables into obedience to their Governors," Toland mentioned that "DIODORUS SICULUS, and other antient writers, were not afraid to rank MOSES in this class, tho his laws be truly divine, without any mixture of weakness or folly."[25] Just above this point in the text, Toland had referred to the Roman lawgiver Numa, the very one Machiavelli had classed with Moses as pretending divine sanction for his laws. But not only Moses, "JESUS CHRIST himself taught for the most part in parables," thereby indicating that he distinguished between His esoteric "true doctrine" and the popular one, speaking in parables so as "*not to cast . . . pearls before swine. . . .*" The same was also true, Toland declared, for St. Paul and the Apostles.[26]

There was a second cause of the twofold doctrine, for the philosophers had to deal both with the vulgar and with conniving and vindictive priests. "Priests were every where the cause, why the Philosophers invented those occult ways of speaking and writing." Priests prey upon the ignorance of the vulgar, spinning the people's superstition into gold to put in their own pockets, and concealing their ruses by declaring them "Mysteries." [27] In so doing, they are, in one sense, following the wisdom of the ancient philosophers, "who declar'd it their opinion, that FRAUD *and* SUPERSTITION *were necessary means, to keep the common people in good order*."[28] Toland's problem with the priests was not so much that they manipulated the people, but that they dominated the philosophers who could expose their fraud, so that the philosophers are ever fearful of "being accus'd of impiety by the Priests" and hence "expos'd in their turn to the hatred, if not to the fury of the Vulgar."[29]

One cannot help but see Toland's own situation peering through the pages here, Toland, the implacable foe of all things priestly, the bearer of the true philosophy of pantheism so at odds with the cosmology of Christianity and unjustly attacked by the obscurantist priests. It was no accident that his first book, *Christianity not Mysterious*, was an attack on mystery, and consequently on the priesthood. Whatever good the use of superstition has done in making it easier for philosophers to control the many, "it must necessarily happen, that Superstition shou'd occasion more evil than good in the world" precisely because it turned out not to be "advantageous to any, excepting PRIESTS or PRINCES, who dexterously turn it to their own interest. . . ."[30] Toland would count priests and princes his two lifelong foes.

There is perhaps some insight into Toland's proposed remedy for this situation in his discussion of Plato, Demophilus the Pythagorean, and Varro. Plato, who "spoke divinely," declared that "*to discover the creator and parent of the Universe, was difficult: but to explain his nature to the Vulgar, impossible*; which is not the less true," added Toland, "were this

25 Ibid., I, p. 65.
26 Ibid., VI, pp. 78–79.
27 Ibid., XII, p. 94.
28 Ibid., VII, p. 81. In the context, Toland mentioned, in particular, Strabo.
29 Ibid., XII, p. 94.
30 Ibid., VII, p. 82.

Vulgar ever so willing to understand."[31] Demophilus likewise maintained that "*to begin any discourse about* God *among men of prejudic'd opinions, is by no means safe: for whether truth is told to such or falshood, tis equally dangerous*." A solution to the dilemma was outlined by Varro, who offered a "*threefold Theology*, the Mythical, Physical, and Political; or the Fabulous, Philosophical, and Civil: wherof the first and the last sort are certain masks of Truth, or rather ingenious subterfuges from telling it."[32]

If one might draw an inference in regard to the threefold theology, it seems likely that Toland regarded Christianity itself as mythical or fabulous (i.e., rooted in fables); the many particular instantiations of Christianity, especially since the Reformation, as political or civil; and, of course, his own pantheism as providing true physical or natural theology. Again, there appears a variation of the Averroistic hierarchy.

The problem was that the political instantiations of Christianity were not designed by philosophers but by clerics, and would therefore have to be replaced by a philosophically based political or civil theology. Toland's proposed cure follows that path of "the Stoics, who reduc'd all the fabulous and popular Theology to the natural, or so explain'd all the fables of the Poets and the Vulgar, as to have been originally meant of natural causes and effects." The Stoic situation would match Toland's, since popular, superstitious religion run by clerics was in both instances already in place and so could not simply be rejected. Toland's revolution demanded that, as with the Stoics, the truth be told circumspectly.

> They [the Stoics] were too sagacious to admit the truth of such things in the literal sense, and too prudent to reject them all as nonsense: which led them of course, by the principle of self-preservation, to impose upon them a tolerable sense of their own; *that they might not be deem'd wholly to deny the Religion in vogue, but to differ onely from others about the design and interpretation of it.*[33]

"This artifice," remarked Toland, "I fancy has not perish'd with the Stoics. . . ."[34] Significantly, Toland's account of Varro comes from St. Augustine's *City of God*, in which (reports Augustine) Varro claimed that "the things which the poets write are beneath what the peoples ought to follow, while the things which the philosophers write are above what is expedient for the multitude to investigate." Consequently, Varro argued that, "These two theologies [i.e., the mythical and the philosophical] are inconsistent with each other, but nevertheless not a few things from each of them may be appropriated for the principles of the civil theology."[35] Civil theology, then, was a mean between two irreconcilable extremes, poetry and philosophy, imagination and rationality, irremediable ignorance and pure truth.

To apply Varro's account to Toland, one would infer that Toland's project was to construct a "tolerable" civil theology, a mixture of mythical Christianity and panthe-

31 Ibid., XI, p. 90.

32 Ibid., XI, p. 91.

33 Ibid., XI, p. 91. Emphasis added.

34 Ibid.

35 Ibid., and St. Augustine, *City of God*, VI.6, translation from Augustine, *Political Writings*, translated by Michael Tkacz and Douglas Kries (Indianapolis, IN: Hackett Publishing Company, Inc., 1994).

ism, of a particular historical religion and universal philosophic truth. As with the Stoics, it would demand a rewriting of the myths, leaning toward a reduction of "all the fabulous and popular Theology to the natural," so that "all the fables" in the Old and New Testament could be explained according to "natural causes and effects." The project would therefore demand a politicizing of the Bible insofar as its aim was the production of a civil theology.

Of course, one must test this hypothesis against Toland's life and other works. But given what Toland clearly maintained in the above-cited works, there is good reason to suspect that the esoteric-exoteric distinction is essential for interpretation of the rest of his work. That would mean that Toland's public writings do not fully represent his private views, but are adjusted to the prevailing beliefs of his time. If that is in fact the case, then one should find in them much "equivocal Expression," existing as a kind of bridge between his true beliefs and the accepted religious beliefs of his time. This would be nowhere more true than in his writings concerning scriptural interpretation and civil theology.

This is an ambitious argument, and given that it goes against the grain of the current "orthodox" manner of interpreting the history of scriptural scholarship and Toland's place in it, every effort must be made to render it plausible.

To begin to vindicate it, one must first examine Toland's life. This will reveal his private beliefs (both political and philosophical), and what effect they would have upon his understanding of Judaism and Christianity. As with Spinoza, it will become clear that Toland's circle of friends formed a kind of underground for the dissemination of the most radical ideas that were so strikingly at odds with Christian orthodoxy. Finally, a comparison of *Christianity not Mysterious* with Toland's other biblical exegetical works will show how these works fit into his radical political-philosophical revolution.

Toland's Early Life and Education

Comparatively little is known for certain of Toland's early life. Rumored to be the illegitimate offspring of an Irish Roman Catholic priest and his concubine, John Toland—baptized Joannes Eugenius or Janus Junius—was born on the northern Irish peninsula on November 30, 1670, and was raised a Roman Catholic until he converted to Protestantism in his mid-teens.[36] Proving himself academically, he was able to win a full scholarship to Glasgow, studying there from 1687 to 1689. During this period came the ominous year of 1688, which witnessed England's "Glorious Revolution." Understanding this political

36 Toland declared in his *Apology for Mr. Toland* (speaking in the third person) that he "was not sixteen Years old, when he became as zealous against *Popery* as he has ever since continu'd, and by God's Assistance always will do." John Toland, *Apology for Mr. Toland* (1697) contained in Philip McGuinness, Alan Harrison, and Richard Kearney, eds., *John Toland's Christianity not Mysterious: Text, Associated Works and Critical Essays* (Dublin: The Lilliput Press, 1997), p. 117. On his life, along with the biographies listed below, one should consult the account given soon after his death, "The Life of Mr. Toland," in John Toland, *A Collection of Several Pieces of Mr. John Toland* (London: J. Peele, 1726; facsimile, New York: Garland Publishing, Inc., 1977).

context more thoroughly is essential for understanding the inextricable intertwining of Toland's political, philosophical, and theological concerns.

Against the background of the English Civil Wars and the Restoration, the 1688 Revolution certainly did seem "glorious" to some. But it contained significant ambiguity that exceeded the boundaries of Locke's particular spin on it. Was it a Tory affirmation of divine right monarchy? Was it a Whig affirmation of the powers of Parliament to define who could be a legitimate king? Was it a republican affirmation of the power of the people through Parliament, even over the monarchy—not for the execution of a king, but perhaps even better, the power to make and unmake him? In some senses, it was all three, combined in a calculatingly vague way to keep the Glorious Revolution from turning into a bloody one. Most certainly, it was a revolution that entailed a most definite shift toward parliamentary power. But that shift was conservative insofar as it in effect made Parliament the guarantor of Henry VIII's Act of Supremacy and as it ensured that the voice of property owners would rule Parliament, rather than radical republicans.

Given that the Glorious Revolution was actually a compromise, those who bristled at compromise were far less inclined to think it glorious. At one end were the many supporters of James II, who were quite willing to nurse ambitions to bring back James III. These were the Jacobites (after the Latin form of "James"), who yearned for the restoration of the Stuart monarchy, which had come to the throne after the death of Elizabeth with James I (1603–1625). But more important and influential were the radical republicans, whose hopes had risen so high with the abolition of monarchy in 1649. It was to this loose-knit group that John Toland belonged, and he was far more radical than most.

The influence of Machiavelli on radical republican thought (especially through his *Discourses on Livy*) was quite pronounced, and has been duly noted by many scholarly works.[37] On the surface, the connection is not difficult to see. The *Discourses* lifted up the ancient Roman republican virtues, virtues that were built upon the solid base of a politically involved citizenry rather than a monarchy. Given that Machiavelli was already quite well known by the time of the English Civil Wars, it is not surprising that with the beheading of Charles I in 1649 and the declaration that England would now be a republic or commonwealth, Machiavelli's thoughts on republicanism would come to the fore, being championed in one form or another by such men as Algernon Sidney (1623–1683), Marchamont Nedham (1620–1678), Henry Neville (1620–1694), and James Harrington (1611–1677).[38]

37 As mentioned in our chapter on Machiavelli, see especially J.G.A. Pocock, *The Machiavellian Moment: Florentine Political Thought and the Atlantic Republican Tradition*; Gisela Bock, Quentin Skinner, and Maurizio Viroli, *Machiavelli and Republicanism* (Cambridge: Cambridge University Press, 1990); Paul Rahe, ed., *Machiavelli's Liberal Republican Legacy* (Cambridge: Cambridge University Press, 2005); and Vickie Sullivan, *Machiavelli, Hobbes, and the Formation of a Liberal Republicanism in England* (Cambridge: Cambridge University Press, 2004).

38 For an overview of the influence of Machiavelli in regard to these figures see especially Rahe, "Machiavelli in the English Revolution," in Rahe, ed., *Machiavelli's Liberal Republican Legacy*, pp. 9–35, or in more expanded form, Rahe, *Republics Ancient & Modern: New Modes & Orders in Early*

Two things are worth mentioning at this point. First, Machiavelli was lifting up Roman republicanism *against* Christianity, implicitly arguing for the superiority of the former over the latter. Hence, Machiavelli's republicanism is inseparable from his scriptural exegesis undermining the authority of Scripture by reinterpreting Moses as a merely political figure. Second and related, Machiavelli's political thought entailed a self-conscious rejection of otherworldly goals that could determine political life, and in this secular schema, religion had to be relegated to a useful tool to keep public order.

Essential to John Toland's radical republicanism was the destruction of any notion of divine right monarchy, even that which would support the Anglican Church. To be more exact, he believed that true republicanism could only be maintained if the support of Scripture and history (i.e., Tradition) for a monarchical-priestly nexus of rule could be completely undermined and a new civil theology put in its place. Toland's republicanism was not, like some of his fellow political outsiders, rooted in the radical Reformation, but as will become apparent, in the radical Enlightenment. This separates his exegetical endeavors from the Reformation, links him firmly to Machiavelli's project, and places him at the fountainhead of modern scriptural scholarship.

Toland went from Glasgow to the University of Edinburgh in 1689. It was during this period, biographer Robert Sullivan maintains, that Toland "first cultivated his enduring esoteric interests," earning him the reputation of having dabbled in Rosicrucianism,[39] and certainly preparing him for his later immersion in the Masonic movement.[40] He was also tutored by one David Gregory, who ensured that each one of his students worked in Newton's physics in completion of his degree.[41] "Then he came into *England*," from Edinburgh in 1690, as Toland himself narrated in the third person, "and liv'd in as good *Protestant* Families as any in the Kingdom, till he went to the famous University of *Leyden* in *HOLLAND* to perfect his studies; and upon his return from thence lodg'd in a private House at *Oxford*, till about two Years ago he came to *London*. . . ."[42]

In reality, the good Protestant families were Presbyterian of the looser Dutch Arminian kind, rather than stricter Puritan Calvinist, dissenters from the Church of England and hence the church-state alliance. It was arranged by them for Toland to go study in fall of 1692 for the Presbyterian ministry at the University of Leiden and Utrecht, the intellectual homes of Dutch Arminianism.[43] Although Toland did study with

Modern Political Thought (Chapel Hill, NC: University of North Carolina Press, 1994).

39 The charge was made by Edmund Gibson (1669–1748). Robert Sullivan, *John Toland and the Deist Controversy: A Study in Adaptations* (Cambridge: Harvard University Press, 1982), p. 3. Margaret Jacob argues that, although it is significant that the charge is made against Toland, the charge is unlikely to be true. Margaret Jacob, *The Newtonians and the English Revolution, 1689–1720* (Hassocks, Sussex: The Harvester Press, 1976), p. 217.

40 The Masonic connections of John Toland and the radical enlightenment are discussed in Margaret Jacob, *The Radical Enlightenment: Pantheists, Freemasons and Republicans* (London: George Allen & Unwin, 1981), especially Ch. 5.

41 Jacob, *The Newtonians and the English Revolution, 1689–1720*, pp. 210–211.

42 Toland, *Apology for Mr. Toland*, p. 117.

43 Sullivan, *John Toland and the Deist Controversy*, pp. 3–4.

Frederick Spanheim (the Younger) at Leiden, he seems to have slipped comfortably into the radical intellectual circles in the Netherlands rather than having spent his time in formal education. He would return to England in 1693, interestingly enough, as a carrier of clandestine literature, smuggling in a book by Jean Le Clerc and also the works of Philip van Limborch (1633–1712) for none other than John Locke. Recall that Le Clerc had been accused of both Socinianism and Spinozism, and Limborch was a champion of religious toleration and rational religion along the lines of Le Clerc.[44] Although associated with Limborch, Le Clerc, and now Toland, Locke himself was far more circumspect.

Reading and Trafficking in Clandestine Texts

Beyond a doubt, Toland's stay in Holland was formative, and like Locke's, his formation took place in the most radical of intellectual circles.[45] We know that he gravitated quickly to the library of Locke's friend, the Quaker Benjamin Furly of Rotterdam. As we noted in the chapter on Locke, Furly was the proud owner of one of Europe's most complete collections of subversive literature, and it was Furly who had engaged Toland as a smuggler of heterodox books. Toland also had ready access to other great heterodox libraries, both in England and on the Continent: in England, the libraries of Anthony Collins and Anthony Ashley (the Third Earl of Shaftesbury), and on the Continent, the infamous libraries of Prince Eugene of Savoy and Eugene's associate, the Baron d'Hohendorf.[46]

In the late seventeenth and early eighteenth centuries, these libraries were enclaves harboring devotees of the most heterodox opinions; and they did not merely house unorthodox literature, but (along with coffeehouses) provided a location for discussion and dissemination of ideas. Toland became a bearer of heterodoxy in every sense of the word, not just carrying and sending books (his own and others), but also bearing ideas back and forth from England and the continent. As Justin Champion remarks, the traffic of clandestine books was international; in the "European-wide republic of letters . . . one of Toland's supreme skills was to be able to broker intellectual resources from a variety of cultural capitals—London, Hanover, Leiden, Dublin and Vienna being the most obvious."[47] In this trafficking,

> Toland . . . certainly acted as a broker and maker of such a radical milieu by his transmission of books and "clandestine" texts. Just as the circulation and exchange of manuscripts made communities, so did libraries. The exchange of news about books, gleaned from literary journals, or on the recommendation

44 For the intricacies of Limborch's position, see Jonathan I. Israel, *Radical Enlightenment: Philosophy and the Making of Modernity 1650–1750* (Oxford: Oxford University Press, 2001), pp. 354–358.

45 See Jacob, *The Newtonians and the English Revolution, 1689–1720*, pp. 212–213.

46 For a discussion of the importance of these libraries as a source of heterodoxy, and their role in Toland's radicalism, see Justin Champion, *Republican Learning: John Toland and the Crisis of Christian Culture, 1696–1722*, Ch. 1.

47 Ibid., p. 39.

> of a helpful bookseller, meant that any one individual had potential access to a network of information across Europe. . . . Toland not only contributed many works that became the subject of this literary exchange, but also was responsible for circulating other texts for communal discussion.[48]

Two of the most important texts with which Toland was involved, indirectly and directly, reveal the depth of the heterodoxy disseminated: the anonymous *Traité des trois imposteurs* and Giordano Bruno's *Spaccio de la bestia trionfante*. The first gives a very clear idea of the depth of heterodoxy among Toland's closest friends and intellectual companions; the second offers an important glimpse, in the context of the history of ideas, of Toland's own heterodoxy. Each will be considered in due course.

Toland's Character and Reputation

While the stay in Holland was definitely formative, it is clear that even before going to Holland Toland was, to say the least, colorful and strong-headed. As he himself reports in the third person, rumor had it that "about the fourteenth Year of his Age he gravely declar'd he would be the *Head of a Sect* e'er he was Thirty; and before he was forty he should make as great a stir in the Commonwealth as *Cromwel* ever did."[49] His activities soon fulfilled the prophecies. After returning from Holland to Oxford (three years *before* publication of *Christianity not Mysterious*) Toland became notorious as a "Mocker," reportedly burning a copy of the *Book of Common Prayer*, and (in the words of a contemporary) "talking against the Scriptures, commending Commonwealths, justifying the murder of K. C. 1st [i.e., King Charles I], railing against Priests in general, with a Thousand other Extravagancys."[50] It was reported that one time, in the midst of reading a Greek New Testament, Toland suddenly cast it angrily away, and "in a great rage cried Damn the Galatians, which was the place where he was reading."[51]

In 1695, while Toland was at Oxford, a tract entitled *Two Essays Sent in a Letter from Oxford, to a Nobleman in London* was published in London by "L. P. Master of Arts."[52] Toland was rumored to be its author. *Two Essays* championed pantheism (implying it even of Moses), denied the universality of the Noachian flood, set out the distinction between esoteric and exoteric truth (notably, in a discussion of the Egyptian "mythologick theology"), defended Hobbes, undermined the Genesis

48 Ibid., p. 36.

49 Toland, *An Apology for Mr Toland*, p. 115. Of this rumor, Toland states ambiguously, "whether true or false God knows; for Mr. *Toland* remembers nothing of the matter." Ibid.

50 Sullivan, *John Toland and the Deist Controversy*, p. 5.

51 Quoted in Justin Champion's Introduction to John Toland, *Nazarenus* (Oxford: Voltaire Foundation, 1999), p. 9.

52 The full title is *Two essays sent in a letter from Oxford to a nobleman in London: the first concerning some errors about the creation, general flood, and the peopling of the world: in two parts : the second concerning the rise, progress, and destruction of fables and romances, with the state of learning.*

account of Creation, quoted Lucretius approvingly, and ended with a pantheistic tag from Virgil, *Jovis omnia plena* (All things are full of god).[53]

Although Toland's authorship is conjecture,[54] *that* it was a contemporary rumor is important enough, showing that Toland's reputation was such that he was immediately taken to be a natural candidate. Toland, if he had not imbibed Spinoza's pantheism before going to Holland in 1692, was certainly introduced to his writings in the circle of Benjamin Furly; he certainly read the pantheist Bruno in 1698, if not before. In short, there are very good reasons to be suspicious that Toland's views were already quite radical, both philosophically and politically, *before* he published his most famous text, *Christianity not Mysterious*, and so one is justified in examining whether it might be an exoteric text.

Christianity not Mysterious was first published anonymously in December of 1695. Soon after, Toland let his name appear as the author (hence the usual publication date of 1696). It occasioned a strong and immediate negative reaction, and Toland was lifted from obscurity to celebrity through charges of heresy. Toland both reveled in the notoriety and disdained the mounting acidic attacks. John Locke soon cut off all relations with him, a move made necessary for the judicious and moderate Locke, precisely because the noted heretic Toland kept boasting of his connection to the famed philosopher. Toland returned to his native Ireland in 1697, only to be run out again after *Christianity not Mysterious* was publicly condemned and ordered to be consigned to the flames by the hangman. Toland fled back to England in September 1697 to avoid jail.

Rewriting History

During this period of Toland's formation, the 1690s, England lived under William. During William's reign, Toland edited—or more accurately, rewrote—a number of important pro-republican works of the mid-century Commonwealth years, to address an England that was solidly monarchist. This was a tricky business, given that the republicans resurrected by Toland were regicides. In rapid succession, Toland produced *The Life of John Milton* (1698), *Memoirs of Lieutenant General Ludlow* (1699), and *The Oceana of James Harrington* (1700). Characteristic of all three is Toland's suppression of the regicidal aspects, or more accurately, his rewriting of the complete republican denial of monarchy found in the originals so that they affirmed instead a qualified affirmation of constitutional monarchy. In addition, Toland all but erased the original fervent religious foundation of Milton's and Ludlow's republicanism and replaced it with radical Whig notions, secular in foundation and therefore amenable

53 See the discussions of the *Two Essays* in Sullivan, *John Toland and the Deist Controversy*, pp. 6, 114–115, and 174–176; and David Berman, "Disclaimers as Offence Mechanisms in Charles Blount and John Toland," in Michael Hunter and David Wootton, *Atheism from the Reformation to the Enlightenment* (Oxford: Oxford University Press, 1992), pp. 268–272.

54 For the status of this conjecture, see Rhoda Rappaport, "Questions of Evidence: An Anonymous Tract Attributed to John Toland," *Journal of the History of Ideas* 58.2 (1997): 339–348.

to Toland's aims.[55] This proclivity for rewriting texts to support his purposes must be taken into account in his works dealing with Scripture.

Also worthy of note is that Toland could hardly help but pick up the Machiavellian influence in Harrington, even if he had not already read Machiavelli himself. Some scholars have also made the case that it was John Toland who edited Algernon Sidney's *Discourses Concerning Government*, and if such is the case, again he would have been exposed to another strain of Machiavellian republican influence.[56]

The Life of John Milton

Toland was a master not just of rewriting but (like Machiavelli) of insinuation, casting out seeds of doubt as seeming asides that revealed his hidden thoughts. His *Life of John Milton* contains an important example that bears directly on modern scriptural scholarship.

Milton had attacked the *Eikon Basilike*, a hagiographical work published immediately after Charles I's execution but allegedly written by him beforehand. The *Eikon* supported divine right monarchy with ample scriptural texts, and vividly presented Charles as a Christlike martyr. It became wildly popular among monarchists. At the behest of the short-lived Republic itself, Milton attacked it in his *Eikonoklastes* (1649), showing it to be a forgery.

Toland's revival of Milton's attack was itself a subversive religio-political act. In Justin Champion's words, "To attack the authority of *Eikon Basilike*, as Toland was to make clear, was to attack the authority of Scripture; literary deconstruction or assault also implied political and religious subversion."[57] An example illustrates Toland's subversive tendencies. In *The Life of John Milton*, Toland not only happily dwelt on Milton's deconstruction of the *Eikon Basilike*, but mused upon how such a forgery could come to be accepted as authentic.

> When I seriously consider how all this happen'd among our selves within the compass of forty years, in a time of great learning and politeness, when both parties [republicans and monarchists] so narrowly watch'd over one another's actions, and what a great revolution in civil and religious affairs was partly occasion'd by the credit of that book [the *Eikon Basilike*] I cease to wonder any longer how so many suppositious pieces under the name of CHRIST, apostles, and other great persons, should be publish'd and approv'd in those primitive times, when it was of so much importance to have 'em believ'd; when the cheats were too

55 On Toland's rewriting of republican works, see Blair Worden, "Whig history and Puritan politics: the *Memoirs* of Edmund Ludlow revisited," *Historical Research*, vol. 75, no. 188, pp. 209–237, and Champion, *Republican Learning*, Ch. 4.

56 On the connection between Machiavelli, Sydney, and Toland, see Vickie Sullivan, "Muted and Manifest English Machiavellianism," in Rahe, ed., *Machiavelli's Liberal Republican Legacy* (Cambridge: Cambridge University Press, 2006), pp. 58–86.

57 Champion, Introduction to Toland, *Nazarenus*, p. 19.

> many on all sides for them to reproach one another, which yet they often did when commerce was not near so general as now, and the whole earth intirely overspread with the darkness of superstition. I doubt rather the spuriousness of several more such books is yet undiscover'd, thro the remoteness of those ages, the death of the persons concern'd, and the decay of other monuments which might give us true information; especially when we consider how dangerous it was always for the weaker side to lay open the tricks of their adversaries, tho never so gross: and that the prevailing party did strictly order all those books which offended them to be burnt, or otherwise suppress, which was accordingly perform'd, as well in obedience to the laws by som, as out of conscientious obligations by others, which made the execution more effectual than usually happens in cases of an ordinary nature. Of this we are furnish'd with numberless examples by church-historians, who have preserv'd intire several laws and orders enacted to this purpose.[58]

By a seemingly offhand remark, Toland turned questions regarding a contemporary forgery in the service of monarchy to implications regarding the authenticity of the books of the existing New Testament canon, hinting that the outcome of this ancient struggle was just as politically motivated.

The hint was not lost on the readers of *The Life of John Milton,* who expressed immediate outrage. As the anonymous author of *Remarks on the Life of Mr Milton, as published by J. T.* (1699) stated, Toland "seems to question the whole of the New Testament as a forgery like that of . . . [the] Eicon Basilike."[59] Rather than deflect such criticism, in his follow-up work, *Amyntor; Or a Defense of Milton's Life* (1699), Toland provided "*A Catalogue of Books mentioned by the Fathers and other Ancient Writers, as truly or falsely ascrib'd to* JESUS CHRIST, *his Apostles, and other eminent Persons,*"[60] a Richard Simon-like list put to the service of deconstructing *traditio* and the canon rather than affirming it. The effect of the long list was to reinforce Toland's original musing, that the sifting of true from spurious texts was really a political power struggle over Scripture not unlike that occurring in his own time among rival Christian parties. He was therefore able to take Richard Simon's scholarship and, by insinuation, use it as a means to undermine the credibility of the canon, setting history *against* Tradition.[61]

Two-Edged Critical Sword

Toland's inversion of Simon illustrates well the two-edged sword of historical scholarship as it was to develop. As Justin Champion argues, "Toland was explicitly adopting a form of public polemic that at one and the same time appropriated and distorted the infrastructure of orthodox cultural authorities." He took the patristic

58 John Toland, *The Life of John Milton with Amyntor; or a defense of Milton's life* (London: John Darby, 1699; reprinted by The Folcroft Press, Inc., 1969), pp. 77–78.

59 Quoted in Champion's Introduction to Toland, *Nazarenus*, p. 28.

60 Toland, *The Life of John Milton with Amyntor*, pp. 165–177.

61 On Toland's extensive use of Simon see Champion, Introduction to Toland, *Nazarenus*, pp. 87–89.

scholarship compiled by orthodox divines (Catholic and Anglican) and cited all the orthodox Church Fathers, but did so to magnify any and all differences and disagreements. Further, "Toland invariably used the great patristic heresiographical sources [i.e., lengthy reports by the orthodox of condemned heresies] to provide himself with testimonies in favour of theological deviance rather than to condemn it."[62] In short, Toland always used the "other edge" of the sword.

It is of the utmost importance to understanding the development of historical-*critical* scholarship that Toland's polemical works were not written polemically, for "Toland adopted the tone of scholarship rather than polemic, writing as a critic rather than a theologian," and his "critical corrosion of sacred authorities was not merely a means to an end, but part of the objective of the work." As Champion notes:

> This is a point that needs careful understanding: the role of textual criticism was neither a neutral scholarly discourse nor the sole achievement of modernising rationalists. Although some historical accounts of the birth of textual criticism tend to adopt a whiggish narrative of the forces of progress unshackling themselves from the twilight shadows of religion, the context of late-seventeenth-century debates between men such as [Henry] Dodwell and Toland, or Richard Bentley and Anthony Collins, suggests that "criticism" was the product of a battle over rival processes of cultural authentification. "Criticism" was not a discourse used solely by the heterodox against the status quo, but a resource constructed and competed for by different interests.[63]

Courting Philosopher of the House of Hanover

Such was Toland's activity as the reign of William drew to a close at the end of the seventeenth century. William ruled until his death in 1702, but died without heir, and Anne, the Stuart daughter of James II, was therefore crowned queen. Anne married Prince George of Denmark and ruled until 1714. Although Anne had eighteen pregnancies, all ended either in miscarriage or early death, so that she too died without an heir. The Act of Settlement in 1701 had already designated for succession the Protestant House of Hanover if Anne produced no heirs; Sophia of Hanover was the granddaughter of James I. But a few weeks before Queen Anne's death, Sophia herself died. Her son, George I, was then crowned king of England (1714–1727) even though he spoke no English. This change from the House of Stuart to the House of Hanover is known as the Hanoverian succession, and Toland wanted to play an important part in it.

Toland wrote a number of treatises supporting the Hanoverian succession: *Anglia libera: or the limitation and succession of the Crown of England explained and asserted* (1701); *Reasons for addressing his Majesty to invite into England their highnesses, the*

62 Ibid., pp. 35–37.

63 Ibid., p. 49.

Electoral Dowager and the Electoral Prince of Hanover (1702); and *Account of the courts of Prussia and Hannover* [sic] (1705) with John Darby. As Champion notes, Toland "promoted his vision of a republican monarchy by acting, almost single-handedly, as a publicist for Sophia of Hanover."[64] But this promotion had its esoteric side, for Toland took it upon himself personally to educate the House of Hanover in his most radical ideas, as a kind of Platonic philosopher educating a future king or queen in the new civil theology. It was Toland's defense of the Act of Settlement in *Anglia libera* that got him invited to join the embassy to present the Electress Sophia of Hanover with the news of her good fortune, and hence began his intimate (if short-lived) relationship with Sophia and her daughter, Sophie, the queen of Prussia.

Both Sophia and Sophie were happily inclined to heterodoxy, at least in private. In October 1701 in Berlin, for example, Queen Sophie presented Toland for debate to her chaplain, Isaac Beausobre, and Toland jubilantly and thoroughly undermined every aspect of the faith, beginning with a bold declaration of his doubts about the authenticity of the accepted books of the New Testament canon, and about the doctrine of the Resurrection in particular.[65] Given Toland's skeptical attack, the chaplain soon charged him to declare what he *did* hold. Rather than answer, Toland drew Beausobre into the skeptical *method* itself, using Richard Simon as his main critical source and method to undermine the historical credibility of the texts and hence the doctrines supported by the texts. As Toland biographer Stephen Daniel remarks, "to raise doubts about an issue that normally goes unquestioned so that he could expand on the *method* whereby such doubts become plausible" was Toland's characteristic modus operandi both in debate and writing.[66] Toland's *Letters to Serena*—Serena being Queen Sophie of Prussia—was fashioned upon Toland's private conversations and debates, which the queen found so intriguing. It contained an account of his esoteric/exoteric distinction.

Toland returned to England later in 1702, now quite notorious on both sides of the Channel. In the next years, he attempted to wend his way directly and indirectly into politics and among the politically powerful, not only because he desired to affect the political order, but also out of financial desperation. Unlike Sophia and Sophie, Queen Anne was quite pious, and Toland found it expedient to declare himself publicly (that is, exoterically) to be a good and faithful member of the Church of England.

Yet, even while declaring himself to be orthodox, he was biding his time until the House of Hanover would be enthroned, and privately penning his most heterodox works, disseminating the most heterodox ideas, and frequenting the most heterodox circles both in England and the Continent. During this time Toland published (among others) *Letters to Serena* (1704), *Origines Judaicae* (1709), and *Adeisidaemon* (1709).

The Electress Sophia died in June 1714, and Toland's hope for a philosopher-queen and a comfortable place at court for himself died with her. "Lord! How near

64 Champion, *Republican Learning*, p. 125.

65 See Champion's account in his Introduction to Toland, *Nazarenus*, pp. 10–13.

66 Stephen Daniel, *John Toland: His Methods, Manners, and Mind* (Kingston and Montreal: McGill-Queen's University Press, 1984), pp. 157–158.

was my old woman being a Queen! and your humble servant being at his ease!"[67] The House of Hanover would succeed with the coronation of George I that same year, but Toland would not succeed with it.

Toland's Earthly End

For his remaining years, Toland was able to combine notoriety with penury. He published more public and more heterodox works, including *Nazarenus* (1718), *Pantheisticon* (1720), and *Tetradymus* (1720, the four works being *Hodegus, Clidophorus, Hypatia,* and *Mangoneutes*). Sales of these and his other books yielded very little, and Toland's reputation as a heretic frustrated his attempts at begging patronage. A desperate shot at speculating on the South Sea Company in 1720 ended disastrously, and Toland's situation and his health began declining rapidly, soon bringing him to lie bedridden in someone else's house by Christmas 1721. He was buried on March 13, 1722.

Such was the life, at least in outline, of John Toland. It is necessary to look in more detail at certain aspects of his life and especially of his writings to understand the full import of Toland upon subsequent scriptural scholarship. Precisely because he is most often classed as a nondescript deist, it is worth spending the effort to elucidate his radical esoteric side. Then it will become clear that Toland was himself not merely another moderate English divine continually blurring Christianity's sharp doctrinal edges with Latitudinarianism until it shaded into the gentleman's religion of deism—but rather part of a larger, radical international intellectual movement that had rejected Christianity. This very fact might even lead one to wonder how much deism was merely the public, exoteric face of esoteric radicals. However that may be, looking at the esoteric movement in some detail allows us to understand that much that is considered radical in the nineteenth and twentieth centuries was already present in the late seventeenth.

Toland's Radical Circle and The Treatise of the Three Impostors

When Toland went to Holland in 1692, he found himself in the center of Europe's clandestine radical Enlightenment, in which Spinoza played such a major part. One of the most notorious and influential of its intellectual products was *Le traité des trois imposteurs*, first published in 1719 as the latter half of *La Vie et L'Esprit de Spinosa* by Charles Levier at the Hague, but circulating in manuscript for quite some time prior.[68] *La Vie et L'Esprit de Spinosa* illustrates with great clarity the kind of ideas circulating

67 Quoted in Sullivan, *John Toland and the Deist Controversy*, p. 34.

68 For the history and background of *Le traité des trois imposteurs*, including the history of subsequent scholarship, see Silvia Berti, "The First Edition of the *Traité des trois imposteurs*, and its Debt to Spinoza's *Ethics*," in Michael Hunter and David Wootton, *Atheism from the Reformation to the Enlightenment* (Oxford: Clarendon Press, 1992), Ch. 7; and Richard Popkin, "Spinoza and the Three Imposters" in his *The Third Force in Seventeenth-Century Thought* (Leiden: Brill, 1992), Ch. 8, pp. 135–148.

in Toland's newfound esoteric coterie, ideas in obvious indebtedness to Spinoza, but far sharper and hence far more deeply cutting to orthodoxy.

La Vie was the first biography of Spinoza. Written about 1678, most probably by his avid disciple Jean Maximilien Lucas, it presented Spinoza as a paragon of virtue, a view later to be made more famous in Pierre Bayle's famous *Dictionnaire* portrait of Spinoza as the virtuous atheist. *L'Esprit de Spinosa*, the second part, appeared throughout the eighteenth century under the title *Le traité des trois imposteurs*. The *Traité* was one of the most widely read of the radical, anti-Christian works of the early Enlightenment. Its publisher, Charles Levier (himself a disciple of Spinoza[69]), was part of the same radical underground as Toland, Furly, Eugene of Savoy, and Baron d'Hohendorf, which also included Prosper Marchland, Thomas Johnson, Jean Rousset de Missy, and Jean Aymon (the latter three, along with Levier, most likely the actual editors of *Le Traité des trois imposteurs*, although the original writer of the edited text seems to have been one Jan Vroesen, a young Dutch diplomat and member of the Furly circle[70]).

The *Traité* is best described as a compendium of heterodox arguments bound together in one well-calculated missile aimed at all three revealed religions—or better at their founders Moses, Jesus, and Mahomet (or, Mohammed, as we spell it today). It contains both the arguments of Spinoza himself—Richard Popkin commenting that, "If Spinoza had lived in the world of the literary agent, he or his heirs could have collected money in the form of royalties," and offering the conjecture that Spinoza himself may have been directly involved in its writing[71]—and also (in a Who's Who of those who had been accused of heterodoxy, libertinism, and atheism) the arguments of Lucretius, Hobbes, Giulio Vanini, François de La Mothe le Vayer, Guillaume Lamy, Pierre Charron, Gabriel Naudé, and Machiavelli.

Ironically, *Le traité des trois imposteurs* was itself an impostor, masquerading as an ancient manuscript, *De tribus impostoribus*.[72] The latter had been much discussed over the previous few centuries, a mysterious clandestine text attacking orthodoxy that allegedly circulated in rumor but oddly enough could not be found in fact. In 1712 Bernard de La Monnoye published a short account of the legendary work in

---

69 As identified by Marchland. See Berti, "The First Edition of the *Traité des trois imposteurs*," pp. 195–196.

70 Ibid., pp. 204–209.

71 Popkin notes that a "sizeable part" of the *The Three Imposters* is "either word for word, or obvious paraphrase, from the French translation of the *Tractatus*, which appeared in 1678." Popkin, "Spinoza and the Three Imposters," pp. 145–147.

72 De La Monnoye examined the claims for authorship for (among others) Frederick I and II, Averroes, Simon de Tournay, Giannino de Solcia, Herman Ristwyck, Fausto da Longiano, Claude Beauregard, Giordano Bruno, Michael Servetus, Arnauld de Villeneuve, John Milton, Pietro Arretino, Poggio, Boccaccio, Machiavelli, Rabelais, Pomponazzi, Cardano, and Vanini. For an extract of de La Monnoye's letter, see "Sentiments Concerning the *Treatise of the Three Impostors*: Extract of a Letter or Dissertation of Mr. de La Monnoye on this Subject," in Abraham Anderson, *The Treatise of the Three Impostors and the Problem of Enlightenment: A New Translation of the* Traité des trois Imposteurs *(1777 Edition), with Three Essays in Commentary* (Lanham: Rowman & Littlefield, 1997), pp. 43–53. See also Berti, "The First Edition of the *Traité des trois imposteurs*," p. 197.

Menagiana, but concluded that, although there were countless well-documented alleged sightings of *De tribus impostoribus*, its existence was no more than a rumor.

There is evidence of a thesis at least like *De tribus impostoribus* circulating in England during much of the latter half of the 1600s, and it is quite conceivable that Toland would have encountered it. That such evidence exists reveals how early extreme heterodoxy appeared in England.[73] Clearly, by the time Toland wrote *Christianity not Mysterious* in the mid 1690s, the theme of religious imposture was well known in England, and certainly well known to Toland. In France, de La Monnoye's public denial of the reality of the infamous *De tribus impostoribus*, whatever its accuracy, provided a platform for Jean Rousset de Missy to arouse interest in a new version of the *Traité* that was, at that very time, under construction by radicals in the library of Furly. Their plan was to pass off their newly edited attack upon orthodoxy as the more famous, semilegendary *De tribus impostoribus*.

In January 1716 Rousset (writing anonymously as J.L.R.L.) claimed he could destroy de La Monnoye's argument simply because "I have seen *meis oculis* [with my own eyes] the famous little Treatise *de Tribus Impostoribus*, & have it in my Cabinet."[74] He then gave an entirely fictitious account of how he came upon the manuscript, and claimed to

---

73 Thomas Browne claimed to have seen a copy of the "miscreant piece of the Three Impostors" in his *Religio medici* of 1643, as did one Richard Smith about 1670. In the spring of 1656, Henry Oldenburg of the Royal Society wrote to Adam Boreel about a heretical work circulating at the time that declared Moses, Christ, and Mohammed to be religious imposters, and in the summer of 1672 John Baptista Damascene was tried and acquitted of the charge of proclaiming that "Jesus Christ, Moyses and Mahomet were three greate rogues." Religious and political radical Henry Stubbe (1631–1676), a friend of Hobbes and Locke, wrote his *Account of the rise of progress of Mahometanism* about 1670, a work that presented an entirely political reading of Christ and Mohammed. Stubbe did not take them to be imposters, but wise legislators who knew how to reform corrupt religion for the sake of political order (Stubbe siding with Islam as a better version of political religion). Stubbe also undermined the authority and unity of the Old and New Testaments. Charles Blount's translation of Philostratus's *Life of Apollonius* (1680) contained many of the same subversive texts that were later combined in the *Traité des trois imposteurs* from the works of Spinoza, Vanini, Hobbes, and Averroes, and his *Oracles of Reason* (1693) shows direct evidence of having been written with knowledge of a manuscript Latin version of the *Three Impostors* at hand. Richard Popkin, *The History of Scepticism from Savonarola to Bayle*, revised and expanded edition (Oxford: Oxford University Press, 2003), p. 198, and Popkin, "Spinoza and the Three Imposters" pp. 136–141; Justin Champion, "Legislators, impostors, and the politic origin of religion: English theories of 'imposture' from Stubbe to Toland," in Silvia Berti, Françoise Charles-Daubert, and Richard Popkin, *Heterodoxy, Spinozism, and Free Thought in the Early-Eighteenth-Century Europe: Studies on the Traité des Trois Imposteurs* (Dordrecht: Kluwer Academic Publishers, 1996), pp. 333–356 (Damascene's quote on p. 333); on Stubbe, see Champion, "Legislators, impostors, and the politic origin of religion," pp. 342–349. See also James Jacob, *Henry Stubbe: Radical Protestantism and the Early Enlightenment* (Cambridge: Cambridge University Press, 1983). According to Champion, Bount may have had the Latin version *De tribus impostoribus* published at Wittenberg in 1640. Ibid, p. 335. Alcofribas Nasier asserts that a Latin version printed at Rackau in Germany is dated 1598, and which was subsequently published by Emil Weller in 1846. *The Three Impostors*, translated by Alcofribas Nasier (privately printed, 1904; reprint, Kessinger, n.d.), pp. 4–5, 7.

74 Rousset's "Response to the Dissertation of Mr. de La Monnoye, on the *Treatise of the Three Impostors*" is included in Anderson, *The Treatise of the Three Impostors and the Problem of Enlightenment*, pp. 55–60, quoted passage on p. 55.

prove that "the book is found to have been composed by a savant of the first order of the court of this emperor [Frederick II, the Hohenstaufen Holy Roman Emperor, 1220–1250] & by his order."[75] It is of no small consequence that in Rousset's fictitious account of the discovery of the book, the German officer Trausendorff, who happens to bring it into a bookshop in "Frankfurt on Main in 1706," also carries with him two other books, "*Spascio della bestia trionfante*, whose publication did not seem to me very ancient: I think that it is the same one of which *Toland* had an English translation printed, a few years ago, & which the copies were sold so dear" and "Cicero's . . . *de natura Deorum*."[76]

Toland did indeed translate Bruno's *Spascio* or *Spaccio* anonymously as *Spaccio della bestia trionfante, or the Expulsion of the Triumphant Beast, translated from the Italian of Giordano Bruno* (London, 1713), about which more later. As for Cicero's *On the Nature of the Gods*, it was a treasure trove for the unorthodox, which "came into its own" in the skeptical eighteenth century, going through twenty editions.[77] Book III of *de natura Deorum* contains an acidic criticism of all religion put in the mouth of the first century BC Academic skeptic Gaius Aurelius Cotta. The fictitious Trausendorff (possibly a play on the name of Baron d'Hohendorf) therefore bore three potent heterodox texts of the radical Enlightenment underground, all of which Toland knew quite well.

Rousset's attempt to pass off the newly written *Traité* as the legendary *de Tribus Impostoribus* was itself a sly and ironical masquerade, given that he himself stated in his presentation of its contents that the "fifth chapter treats of the soul" in which not only the opinions of "the philosophers of antiquity" are reported, but also "the sentiment of Descartes," a knowing anachronism if ever there was one. To add to the tongue-in-cheek ruse, the *Traité* also contained much of Spinoza, and even footnotes Hobbes several times, making it a self-revealing, "transparently fraudulent" imposture on impostors.[78] Clearly, the authors and editors of the *Traité* wanted readers to understand it as a thoroughly modernized attack on orthodoxy, one that could ride upon the fame of the legendary *de Tribus Impostoribus*, but take it further.

This mode of reconstructing an existing text to make it a bearer of revolutionary ideas was one of the most widely used and successful strategies of the radicals, one of which Toland himself was the master. Some attention to the arguments of the *Traité* will provide great insight into how early, historically, the direct attack on biblical

75 Ibid., p. 58. Frederick, known as the *Stupor mundi*, Wonder of the World, was an inveterate foe of the papacy, and was even declared to be the anti-Christ by Pope Gregory IX. He was known for his religious skepticism, thereby making him a likely candidate for *de Tribus Impostoribus*, but even more, a hero of skepticism against revealed religion.

76 Ibid., p. 55–56.

77 John M. Ross, Introduction to Cicero's *The Nature of the Gods*, translated by Horace McGregor (New York: Penguin Books, 1972), p. 56. As Ross notes, whereas Cicero's presentation of Stoicism most endeared Christians up until the Renaissance, Cicero's Academic skepticism was embraced by the Enlightenment as a foil against Christianity: "Cicero's principal appeal . . . in the seventeenth and eighteenth centuries, was to the skeptics and savants," p. 61.

78 The phrase is from Abraham Anderson. See his insightful essay, "Sallnegre, La Monnoye, and the *Traité des trios Imposteurs*," in Anderson, *The Treatise of the Three Impostors and the Problem of Enlightenment*, pp. 89–126.

revelation occurred, how important Machiavelli, Hobbes, and Spinoza were in its formulation, and further, how thoroughly Toland was immersed in it.

The opening salvos of the *Traité* offer a collage from Spinoza's *Ethics* (Part I, Appendix) and Hobbes's *Leviathan* (I.12, the famous chapter "Of Religion"). In it, we learn that religion is caused by ignorance and fear, and that certain crafty imposters (priests, prophets, and princes) have learned to use religion to secure and advance their secular power.[79] In short, the *Traité* gives a Machiavellian account, but condemns such imposture rather than commending it. This represents a monumental shift in modern thought: Revealed religion moves from an imposture to be *used* politically (Machiavelli and Hobbes), to an obstacle that must be both *exposed* and then *destroyed* (Voltaire's *écrasez l'infâme*, the high Enlightenment, and later Marx). The *Traité* is an important transition document, to say the least.

According to the *Traité,* the genesis of humanity's downfall is as follows. Originally, human beings followed the natural law, conforming themselves to "right reason." But soon fear of imaginary invisible powers caused them to raise "altars to these imaginary beings," thereby "shaking off the yoke of nature & of reason." They then "bound themselves by vain ceremonies & by a superstitious cult of the vain phantoms of the imagination." After exalting these invisible powers, benighted humanity

> imagined that nature was a being subordinated to these [invisible] Powers. From then on they imagined it [i.e., nature] as a dead mass, or as a slave which acted only following the order of these Powers. As soon as this false idea had struck their mind, they no longer had anything but contempt for nature, & respect only for those pretended beings, which they named their Gods. Thence came the ignorance in which so many peoples are plunged. . . .[80]

A vicious circle: ignorance of nature causes religion; religion, in causing contempt of nature, raises ignorance of nature to a theological virtue. This circle is even more vicious because religion causes war by breeding diverse sects according to the peculiarities of its devotees. "This germ of Religion (I mean hope & fear) seconded by the different passions & opinions of men, produced that great number of bizarre beliefs which are the causes of so many evils & of so many revolutions which happen in States."[81]

---

79 *The Three Impostors*, III.i–viii [IV.i–viii]. Unless otherwise noted, we will be using the translation in Anderson, *The Treatise of the Three Impostors and the Problem of Enlightenment,* since it is superior, and closer to the original French edition than Alcofribas Nasier's. As the chapter and section headings sometimes differ from the earlier version, we offer in brackets any variations as checked against Nasier's translation of *The Three Impostors* (noted as "From a French manuscript of the work written in the year 1716"), and more importantly, Silvia Berti's authoritative French 1719 edition (with Italian translation), *Trattato dei tre Impostori: La vita e lo spirito del Signor Benedetto de Spinoza* (Torino: Giulio Einaudi, 1994). When Nasier's and Berti's chapter and section numbers differ, we will indicate them separately. Where important textual variations occur, we will rely either on Nasier's translation as checked against the French in Berti's edition, or on Anderson as modified to the original 1719 edition.

80 III.i [IV.i].

81 III.v [IV.v].

Breaking this vicious circle means turning away from revealed religion and back to nature. That is not an irreligious act, because (following Spinoza) nature and God are the same thing: "Until now we have fought the popular idea [*Préjugez populaires*] concerning the Divinity, but we have not yet said what God is, and if we were asked, we should say that the word represents to us an Infinite Being, of whom one of his attributes is to be a substance eternal and infinite," and this infinity is material, for "neither matter or quantity have anything unworthy of God. . . ."[82]

Although the *Traité* quotes Scripture here for its own purposes, its deeper contempt for Scripture is undisguised. The "Prophets . . . were nothing more among the Hebrews than what the augurs & diviners were among the Pagans." Foolish believers, taking the Prophets as real

> consult the Bible as if God & nature were explained there in some particular fashion; although this book is only a tissue of fragments stitched together at different times, collected by different persons, & published on the authority of the Rabbis who decided according to their fancy what should be approved or rejected, as they found it in conformity or opposed to the Law of Moses. Such is the malice & the stupidity of Christians.[83] They pass their lives in quibbling & persist in respecting a book in which there is no more order than in the Alcoran [Koran] of Mahomet; a book, I say, which no one understands, it is so obscure & ill conceived; a book which serves only to foment divisions.[84]

The spell that holds ignorant believers is cast "by the cleverness [*l'adresse*] of Princes & of Ecclesiastics,"[85] who themselves being impostors, use the credulity of the masses to control them for their own profit. "The ambitious who have always been great masters in the art of deceiving, have followed this route when they gave laws; & to oblige the People to submit itself voluntarily they have persuaded it that they had received them from a God or a Goddess."[86]

Turning immediately to the "founders of Religions," the *Traité* offers a Machiavellian account of Moses, Jesus Christ, and Mahomet, the "three impostors" of the book's title. In it, we see the complete politicizing of the Bible; it is Machiavelli without disguise. Not only is revelation cast as the result of the political schemes of its original Machiavellian founders and perpetrators, but it is then politically recast for the sake of establishing a new secular state that relies on a Spinozan natural religion rather than Christian revelation.

The "celebrated Moses" was "the grandson of a great Magician." As there "was never any people more ignorant than the Hebrews, and consequently, more credulous,"

82 Nasier's translation as corrected by Berti, III.i. Anderson, II.x.

83 Although Anderson's translation of the later edition has "Such is the malice & the stupidity of men," Berti's 1719 edition has "*Oui, telle est la Folie & la stupidité des Chrêtiens . . .*" Hence, our correction. Berti, III.i, lines 91–92.

84 II.xi. [III.i].

85 Here, we use the original French instead of Anderson's "by the Politics of Princes & of Priests." Berti, III.ii; Anderson, II.xi.

86 III.ix [V.i]

Moses' conjuring easily convinced the Jews that he had direct contact with God.[87] "Thus, these poor unfortunates, dazzled by his Illusions, & ravished by their being adopted by the Master of God, having emerged from hard servitude, applauded Moses, & swore to obey him."[88] Of course, as Machiavelli argued, only armed prophets succeed, so that mere clever prestidigitation by Moses was not enough. "However clever Moses was, he would have had great difficulty in making himself obeyed, if he had not had force in hand. Trickery without arms rarely succeeds." Anyone who questioned his rule, Moses simply eliminated, so that he "reigned as an absolute Despot. . . ."[89]

Whereas Machiavelli was far more circumspect in criticizing Christ, the *Traité* is open and savage in its denunciation.

> Jesus Christ who was ignorant neither of the maxims nor of the science of the Egyptians, gave currency to this opinion [that he was divine when] he thought it suited his designs. Considering how much Moses had made himself famous, although he had commanded but a people of ignoramuses, he [i.e., Jesus] undertook to build on this foundation, & got himself followed by some imbeciles whom he persuaded that the Holy Spirit was his Father; & his Mother a Virgin: these good people, accustomed to indulge themselves in dreams & fancies, adopted his notions & believed all that he wanted . . . As the number of fools is infinite, Jesus Christ found Subjects everywhere. . . .[90]

Following again Machiavelli's sly comment that unarmed prophets fail, the *Traité* noted that "having neither money nor army, he [i.e., Jesus] could not fail to perish: if he had had these two instruments, he would have succeeded no less than Moses or Mahomet . . . [for] the greatest defect of his politics was not to have provided enough for his safety."[91]

Yet the politics of Jesus Christ was in some respects ingenious. Christ, "seeing the extreme corruption of the Republic of the Jews, judged it near its end, & believed that another ought to be reborn from its ashes." Just as with Moses, and "in imitation of

87 Translation directly from Berti, V.ii, 24–25. Although not in the 1719 version, in Nasier and Anderson we then have added the following about Moses. After leading them out of Egypt, Moses employed his "grossest piece of trickery," telling the Hebrews that "a brazier whose flame they followed [by night], & by day by smoke of this same brazier"—a simple method guides of the region used—was actually "a miracle, & a mark of the protection of God." Rather than God leading them, it was simply Moses' "brother-in-law Hobad [Hobab]" carrying the torch, but the "poor wretches, delighted to find themselves adopted by the Master of the Gods upon leaving a cruel servitude, applauded Moses & swore to obey him blindly." III.x [V.ii, Nasier]. As we'll see below, this section shows the unmistakable influence of Toland, as it was actually lifted from his *Hodegus* written sometime about 1708 in Holland (and hence circulating among friends in manuscript), but not published until 1720. Champion, "Legislators, impostors, and the politic origin of religion," pp. 352–353. In the Preface (p. iv) to the *Tetradymus,* Toland mentions that, "I show'd my Manuscript at the Hague in the year 1708 . . .," *The Theological and Philological Works of the Late John Toland.*

88 Our translation from Berti, V.ii, 33–35.

89 III.x [V.ii], Nasier; V.iii. Berti.

90 III.xii [VII.i].

91 III.xii [VII.i].

the other innovators," Christ "had recourse to miracles which have always been the shipwreck of the ignorant, & the refuge of the adroitly ambitious." Yet, to displace Moses, He had to oppose him directly, replacing Moses' temporal claims and promises with "the hope of the advantages of another life which one would obtain, he said, by believing in him. . . ."[92]

To those who are reasonable, the claim of a Kingdom of Heaven based upon magic tricks makes for "a Religion established on foundations" that are "feeble," but we must remember that "the most absurd opinions" are given "currency" by "women & fools." Indeed, that is why "Jesus Christ had no Learned men among his followers" and instead admitted "none but the poor in spirit, the simple & the imbeciles." By contrast, "Reasonable minds [*Esprits raisonnables*] should console themselves that they have no business with madmen."[93]

Nor is the morality proclaimed by Christ exemplary, as some later deists would claim. In fact, all that is good in the Bible came from pagan sources, or at least is presented more sublimely in pagan sources. In particular, the Stoic Epictetus, who smiled as the guards of Nero broke his leg, is by far preferable to Jesus Christ, "who wept & sweated with fear at the least alarm he was given, & who gave evidence, just before dying of a pusillanimity altogether contemptible, & which one did not see among his Martyrs."[94]

But whereas its founder perished, Christianity succeeded. The disciples after the Crucifixion were in despair, but "on the report of some women they retailed his resurrection, his Divine sonship & the rest of the fables of which the Gospels are so full."[95] The Jews rejected them, but the Gentiles were won over largely due to the efforts of St. Paul, "a young man of a lively & active mind, a bit better taught than illiterate fishermen."[96]

As for Mahomet, he too "made miracles, & knew how to profit from the passions of the people," an "ignorant populace, to which he explicated the new Oracles of Heaven." At first, Mahomet duped the "wretches" by having some of his companions hide in a well to deliver the "Oracles" in a booming voice as if from heaven; to cover his imposture, he incited the "imbecile crowd" to throw stones in the well, thereby killing the colleagues who could have exposed his impostor.[97] Mahomet "raised himself up & was happier than Jesus, insofar as he saw before his death the progress of his law," and he "was happier than Moses" for he "died in peace & with all his wishes gratified. . . ."[98]

And so, "Moses, Jesus & Mahomet being such as we have just painted them, it is evident that it is not in their writings that one must search for a true idea of the Divinity."[99]

92 III.xiv [V.iv].
93 III.xvi [VIII.vi].
94 III.xviii [IX.ii, Nasier; IX,i, Berti].
95 III..xx [X.ii, Nasier; X.i, Berti].
96 III.xx [X.ii, Nasier; X.i, Berti].
97 III.xxii [XI.i–ii].
98 III.xxiii [XI.iii].
99 IV.i ["Sensible and Obvious Truths, I in Nasier; XVIII.i, Berti].

As it turns out, one must go to Spinoza: "God is a simple Being, or an infinite Extension, who resembles what he contains, which is to say that he is material. . . ."[100] Since we can have a clear and distinct idea of nature (as understood through mathematics), we can therefore have "a clear & distinct idea" of God-as-nature.[101] Since God is nature, everything in nature manifests the perfection of God, so that "there is nothing for it [i.e., God] beautiful or ugly, good or bad, perfect of imperfect," and we therefore cannot believe that "the universal Being commonly called *God* cares more for a man than for an ant, for a lion than for a stone. . . ."[102] God-as-nature does not care for human beings, and further, since our souls are not immaterial, there is no heaven or hell to fear.[103]

The *Traité* therefore put forth a refined paganism as a substitute for the religion of "three impostors," wherein "there is in the universe a very subtle spirit [*Esprit très subtil*][104] or a matter very loose & always in movement whose source is the sun. . . . This then *is* what the soul of the world is; this is that which governs & vivifies it. . . . the purest fire there is in the universe." This fire brings life to that "which it enters," and "is what men call *soul*, or what they name *animal spirits*, which spread through all the parts of the body."[105] Descartes's animal spirits were transformed into the *spiritus mundi*.

A more politicized account of the Bible would be hard to imagine. In fact, it is on the basis of the *Traité*'s politicized reading that Judaism, Christianity, and Islam are rejected and replaced by a Spinozan nature religion. It is not surprising that the work was published and circulated clandestinely, but that does not mean it lacked influence. The radical underground movement was widespread and very effective during the eighteenth century in undermining belief in Christianity among the intelligentsia, thereby ever broadening the radical circle until what was underground at the beginning of the eighteenth century surfaced and became more public and more bold by the end.

It is not clear exactly what relationship Toland had with the production and dissemination of the *Traité*. It seems almost impossible that he was not involved in the ongoing discussions as the *Traité* took shape, given that his close associates Furly, Eugene of Savoy, and d'Hohendorf were all intimately involved, and Toland also knew the editor, Jean Aymon, well. Further, as we shall see, there are so many parallels to the *Traité* in Toland's writings that it is unreasonable not to infer a shared community of discourse. On the other hand, it seems unlikely that he was directly involved in the *entire* production of the text, except as an active member in the ongoing exchange of ideas in Furly's circle that informed its production.[106] Although the *Traité* gives us much insight into Toland's intellectual milieu and the kind of radical ideas freely circulating at the turn of the century, to get a clearer picture of Toland himself, one must consult another radical work

100 Our translation from Berti, XVIII.ii.

101 IV.ii ["Sensible and Obvious Truths, II in Nasier; XVIII.ii, Berti].

102 IV.iii ["Sensible and Obvious Truths, III in Nasier; XVIII.iii, Berti].

103 IV.v–V.vii ["Sensible and Obvious Truths," V to "Of the Soul," VII in Nasier; XVIII.v–XX.iii in Berti]. One can hardly miss the connection to ancient Epicureanism here.

104 Anderson corrected by Berti.

105 V.vii ["Of the Soul," VII in Nasier; XX.i].

106 For a discussion, see Champion, *Republican Learning*, pp. 170–173.

whose dissemination was explicitly due to Toland's efforts, Giordano Bruno's *Spaccio de la bestia trionfante*.

Toland and The Expulsion of the Triumphant Beast

As we know from Rousset's "Response to the Dissertation of Mr. de La Monnoye, on the *Treatise of the Three Impostors*" cited above, Toland was known for his publication of an English version of Bruno's *Spaccio de la bestia trionfante* in 1713.[107] Indeed, Toland was actually engaged in trying to pass off Bruno's *Spaccio* as the *de Tribus Impostoribus*,[108] an endeavor that might seem quite peculiar until we recall that the *de Tribus Impostoribus* itself had a centuries old legendary existence prior to its fabrication in the Furly circle as the *Traité*.

A look at Bruno's work and Bruno himself reveals why Toland found him attractive, and a figure worth propagating. Bruno's *Spaccio de la bestia trionfante*, or *Expulsion of the Triumphant Beast*, is part of a trilogy of works written by Bruno between 1584 and 1585, the other two being *La cabala del cavallo Pegaseo* (*The Cabala of the Pegasean Horse*) and *De gli eroici furori* (*The Heroic Furors*).[109] A common theme of all three is that the rational understanding of nature must replace ignorance. In the *Spaccio*, reason is set against the "beast" of ignorance, expelling it by expelling orthodox Christian theology and Aristotelianism, both of which stand in the way of the intellect's grasp of nature.[110]

---

107 It has been argued that William Morehead was the actual translator of the *Spaccio* into English. For the case against Morehead, and for Toland, see J.A.I. Champion, *The Pillars of Priestcraft Shaken: The Church of England and its Enemies, 1660–1730* (Cambridge: Cambridge University Press, 1992), pp. 151–152.

108 Champion, *Republican Learning*, pp. 172–173.

109 For a short introduction with biography of Bruno see Arthur Imerti's Introduction to his translation of Giordano Bruno, *The Expulsion of the Triumphant Beast* (Lincoln, NE: University of Nebraska Press, 2004), pp. 3–65. Imerti's introduction was written for the original edition of the translation in 1964. For the details of the life of Bruno see Dorothy Singer, *Giordano Bruno: His Life and Thought* (New York: Henry Schuman, 1950), and Francis Yates, *Giordano Bruno and the Hermetic Tradition* (Chicago: University of Chicago Press, 1964).

110 Like Toland later, Bruno had doubts about orthodoxy early on, and gravitated toward the reading of heterodox authors. Upon entering the Dominican monastery when he was about seventeen, he already doubted the Trinity. On Bruno's doubt, see Imerti's Introduction to *The Expulsion of the Triumphant Beast*, p. 4. Again like Toland after him, Bruno had trouble staying in one place because his fiery temper and indiscretion inevitably brought him to proclaim his unorthodox views. He was driven out of his order, then out of Italy, Calvinist Geneva, and the University of Toulouse (where he received his doctorate in theology, and then a chair in philosophy), out of France (because of religious war), and then out of Oxford University. In Imerti's words, Bruno's experiences prepared him as the author of the heretical *Spaccio*. "The religious and philosophical doubts engendered by Bruno's reading of heretical authors during his early years in Naples, his unhappy experiences with the Neapolitan and Roman Inquisitions, his humiliation at the hands of the Aristotelian Calvinists in Geneva, his witnessing of the horrors wrought by the religious civil wars in France, his bitter controversy with the advocates of Aristotle at Oxford—all contributed to the making of the heretical author of *Lo spaccio*. Henceforth, the iconoclast resolved to carry on a merciless war against pedants and pedantry, against the reformed sects (particularly Calvinists), and finally against Christianity itself." Ibid., p. 9.

The *Spaccio*, like the *Traité*, condemns all revealed religions in the name of reason, but does so under the guise of condemning pagan religion. As Domenico Berti remarks, "Bruno lumps together paganism, Judaism, Christianity, and Mohammedanism. He convokes all of these religions to the syndicate of reason, and censures all, accuses, condemns, and repudiates all," his aim being "the proclamation of natural religion and the negation of all positive religions." [111]

At the heart of Bruno's natural religion was pantheism, or one might say protopantheism, since it was Toland himself who later coined the term. Yet in declaring God to be immanent in nature—"Nature . . . is none other than God in things . . . *natura est deus in rebus*"[112]—"Bruno was not only a true pantheist but also the direct ancestor of Spinoza."[113] Sounding eerily like Spinoza's later distinction of *natura naturans* and *natura naturata*, Bruno (through the character of Sophia) states, "God, as absolute, has nothing to do with us except insofar as he communicates with the effects of Nature and is more intimate with them than Nature herself. There fore, if he is not Nature herself, he is certainly the nature of Nature, and is the soul of the Soul of the world, if he is not the Soul herself."[114] Like Toland after him, Bruno believed that the Egyptians had first and most thoroughly grasped pantheist principles.[115]

For Bruno that established a primacy of Egyptian over Judaic religion "because the Jews have been proved to be the excrement of Egypt, and there is no one who could have imagined with any verisimilitude that the Egyptians have taken some worthy or unworthy principle from them."[116] In fact, it was the Jews who depended upon the Egyptians, for "the leader and lawgiver of the Jewish people . . . Moses . . .

---

111 Quoted in Bruno, *The Expulsion of the Triumphant Beast*, p. 284, endnote 8 and p. 32.

112 In Bruno's dialogue these words are spoken by Momus, as commented upon, in Latin, by Saulino. We use Imerti, *The Expulsion of the Triumphant Beast*, Third Dialogue, Second Part, p. 235.

113 Ibid., p. 45. See also Ernst Cassirer, *The Philosophy of the Enlightenment*, translated by Fritz Koelln and James Pettegrove (Princeton: Princeton University Press, 1951), pp. 40–41. J. Lewis McIntyre claimed, with the accord of other scholars, that Spinoza must have had Bruno in front of him when he composed his *Short Treatise*. See McIntyre, *Giordano Bruno* (New York: Macmillan, 1903), pp. 337–343.

114 Bruno, *The Expulsion of the Triumphant Beast*, Third Dialogue, Second Part, p. 240. Indeed, Spinoza's distinction between *natura naturans* and *natura naturata* seems to be a duplication of Bruno's distinction between "eternal incorporeal substance" which does not change but causes change and "eternal corporeal substance" which does change. Ibid., Explanatory Epistle, pp. 75–76.

115 "Those wise men knew God to be in things, and Divinity to be latent in Nature, working and glowing differently in different subjects and succeeding through diverse physical forms, in certain arrangements, in making them [i.e., the forms] participants in her, I say, in her being, in her life and intellect. . . ." There is "one simple Divinity found in all things, one fecund Nature, preserving mother of the universe insofar as she diversely communicates herself, casts her light into diverse subjects and assumes various names." Since God was in things, therefore the Egyptians rightly "worshiped not only the earth, the moon, the sun, and other stars of the heaven but also crocodiles, lizards, serpents, [and] onions." And the "Egyptians, as wise men know, from these external natural forms of beasts and live plants used to ascend and (as their successes demonstrate) used to penetrate Divinity." In its worship of God in and through nature, "Egypt is the image of heaven or, better said, the colony of all things that are governed and practiced in heaven. To speak the truth, [Egypt] . . . is the temple of the world." Bruno, *The Expulsion of the Triumphant Beast*, Third Dialogue, Second Part, pp. 236–238, 241, 247–248

116 Ibid., p. 251.

departed from the court of Pharaoh learned in all the sciences of the Egyptians, who in the multitude of his manifestations [i.e. miracles] surpassed all of those who were experts in magic," and therefore he "demonstrate[d] his excellence so as to be a divine emissary to that people and a representative of the authority of the god of the Jews."[117]

And what of Christianity? The effect of Bruno's pantheism, as one can easily imagine, was that since the Divine was immediately present in Creation, accessible through nature rather than through revelation, Christ understood as Logos and Mediator was displaced by the deity understood as a natural principle of Creation. Therefore, Christ (represented as Orion) is subjected to bitter satire. In a satirical tone, the character Momus suggests to the council of gods:

> [Orion] knows how to perform miracles, and . . . can walk over the waves of the sea without sinking, without wetting his feet, and with this, consequently, will be able to perform many other fine acts of kindness. Let us send him [Orion] among men, and let us see to it that he give them to understand all that I want and like them to understand: that white is black, that the human intellect, through which they seem to see best, is blindness, and that that which according to reason seems excellent, good, and very good, is vile, criminal, and extremely bad. I want them to understand that Nature and Divinity cannot concur in one and the same end, and that the justice of the one is not subordinate to the justice of the other, but that they [Nature and Divinity] are contraries, as are shadows and light.[118]

Needless to say, Bruno's pantheism did not endear him to the Inquisition, and his satire of Christ certainly contributed to his sad end. His wanderings from orthodoxy did not end with expulsion from Oxford and the *Spaccio*. Consequently, neither did his physical peregrinations. He continued to settle in various places around Europe, moving on each time because of his controversial views. Eventually, he was yielded into the hands of the Venetian and Roman Inquisitions and burned at the stake on February 16, 1600, a martyr of heterodoxy and a model for Toland. In this regard, Margaret Jacob writes: "What must be emphasized is the inspiration Toland received for his activities from his reading of Bruno, whose works were constantly at his side during many of his forays onto the Continent. Indeed over a century after Bruno's death in 1600 how much Toland resembles him in spirit as he wanders about the courts of Europe teaching what he has culled from Bruno's *Spaccio*."[119]

Toland had no wish for martyrdom, but in championing Bruno's *Spaccio* he obviously considered it to be, like the *Traité*, a kind of weapon of reason against the orthodoxy he likewise disdained. While Toland may have read Bruno earlier, we know that he purchased a copy of the *Spaccio* in 1698.[120] On both the Continent and England,

117 Ibid., Third Dialogue, Second Part, p. 245.

118 Ibid., Third Dialogue, Third Part, p. 255.

119 Jacob, *The Newtonians and the English Revolution, 1689–1720*, p. 228.

120 From the library of Francis Bernard, and bound together with Bruno's *De la causa, principio et Uno*; *De l'infinito universo et mondi*; and *Dialogi la Cena de la Ceneri*. See ibid., p. 228–229, and Champion, *The Pillars of Priestcraft Shaken*, p. 150.

Toland read the *Spaccio* in private with his like-minded radical friends, "culled this radical philosophy [of pantheism] from the writings of Giordano Bruno," and "transformed it into a philosophical justification for republican politics."[121] He considered it a seminal work to be preached among his fellow esoteric revolutionaries: "concerning the *Spaccio*" he wrote to philosopher Georg Leibniz, "it is not a secret to be communicated to everybody."[122] The "secret" was to remain esoteric, even while it informed exoteric writings and political actions. Toland's championing of Bruno, in fact, had far-reaching effects in the history of philosophy, his efforts helping to initiate many translations of Bruno's works in the eighteenth century.

Toland's attempt to pass off the *Spaccio* as the legendary *de Tribus Impostoribus* was no more dishonest than the attempt by others of his radical circle to put forth the *Traité des trois imposteurs*. Both had the very same aim—the displacement of Christianity by a new religion of reason rooted in the collapse of God and nature in pantheism. As with Bruno, the cosmological revolution could not help but have political ramifications. After all, the society in which both lived was literally built upon Christian cosmology, and the control of the state by Christianity (in whatever form), meant the domination of all aspects of life—from art to literature, from education to science, from societal structure to civil law—by ignorance, error, and superstition. For this reason, one needs a more thorough grasp of Toland's pantheism as the counter-cosmology for his hoped-for new world order.

Toland's Cosmological Revolution: Pantheism

In regard to Toland's indebtedness both to Bruno and to Spinoza for his pantheism, it might not be too off the mark to say that Toland "corrects" Spinozism by radicalizing it through a return to Bruno. In the *Letters to Serena* (Queen Sophie of Prussia), the fourth letter is entitled "To a Gentleman in Holland, showing Spinosa's System of Philosophy to be without any Principle or Foundation." Under the pretence of attacking Spinoza as erroneous—"I am persuaded the whole System of SPINOSA is not only false, but also precarious and without any sort of Foundation"[123]—Toland made Spinozism even more corrosive of orthodoxy. That is, Toland pretended to rebut Spinoza in order to present a more radical version of Spinozism that owed much to Bruno. In so doing, he perhaps wanted to prove that there "was only one real 'Spinozist' in the world and that was Toland himself."[124]

The problem with Spinoza, so we are told, is that he fell into the common error of considering matter to be "a dull and heavy Lump,"[125] that, being entirely inert,

121 Jacob, *The Newtonians and the English Revolution, 1689–1720*, p. 227.

122 The letter was, apparently, written some time after 1710. Quoted in Champion, *The Pillars of Priestcraft Shaken*, p. 152.

123 Toland, *Letters to Serena*, IV.4.135.

124 Rienk Vermij, "Matter and Motion: Toland and Spinoza," in Wiep Van Bunge and Wim Klever, *Disguised and Overt Spinozism around 1700* (Leiden: E. J. Brill, 1996), pp. 275–288. Quote on p. 288.

125 Toland expresses the words in relation to Anaxagoras, but further applies them to Spinoza. Toland,

must receive motion from outside. But Spinoza allowed for "no Being separate or different from the Substance of the Universe, no Being to give it Motion, to continue or to preserve it, if it has none of its own." The problem was not that Spinoza identified God with nature (a problem Toland conveniently fails to mention), but that Spinoza believed that "Matter was naturally inactive"[126] yet didn't give an account of *how* God, whom he identified with nature, moved it.

By contrast, Descartes did: He posited God *outside* of nature, and then "suppos'd God at the beginning to have given a shake to the lazy Lump [of matter]"[127] to get it moving. The problem with Descartes's solution, and hence also Newton's, is that "they are forc'd at last to have recourse to God, and to maintain that as he communicated Motion to Matter at the beginning, so he still begets and continues it whenever, and as long as there's occasion for it, and that he actually concurs to every Motion in the Universe."[128]

Toland's solution? "I hold then that *Motion is essential to Matter*, that is to say, as inseparable from its Nature as Impenetrability or Extension, and that it ought to make a part of its Definition."[129] In the fifth letter, Spinoza went on to maintain that "matter being defin'd active as well as extended (to which you may add Solidity, with the incomparable Mr. LOCK) then all the motive effects follow very naturally, and need not be explain'd by any other Cause, no more than the Consequences of Extension."[130] In confirming Spinoza's pantheism and making motion intrinsic to matter, Toland eliminated the "recourse to God" as the external cause of nature's motion. Nature deified had its own internal cause of motion.

If it had been immediately accepted, Toland's pantheism would have undermined the entire basis of the eighteenth-century Newtonian proof of the existence of God (which did require an external force because it considered matter to be inert) *before* it had even gathered steam. Indeed, as Rienk Vermij points out, "The Newtonians seem more to have developed their ideas in reaction to Toland's, rather than vice versa."[131] As of the early 1800s, the Newtonians had not fully and carefully made

---

Letters to Serena, IV.10.142.

126 Ibid., IV.10.143. In this, Toland is for some reason not being quite fair to Spinoza, given Spinoza's important assertion that each composite natural thing has a "*conatus*," a kind of impulse to preservation. See Spinoza's *Ethics*, III, Propositions 6–7.

127 Toland, *Letters to Serena*, IV.13.152.

128 Ibid., IV.15.156–157.

129 The "Motion of the Whole" is called "*Action*" and all local motions of whatever kind are "still call'd *Motion*, being only the several changeable *Determinations* of the *Action* which is always in the Whole, and in every Part of the same, and without which it cou'd not receive any Modifications. I deny that Matter is or ever was an inactive dead Lump in absolute Repose, a lazy and unweildy [sic] thing . . . [and] this Notion alone accounts for the same Quantity of Motion in the Universe . . . that Matter cannot be truly defin'd without it, that it solves all the Difficultys about the moving Force, and all the rest which we have mention'd before." Ibid., IV.16.158–160. This shows, as Vermij notes, that "Toland is not attacking what people called Spinozism: that clearly would entail proving the reverse position, that motion is *not* essential to matter. If anything, he is upholding Spinozism. He recognized that Spinoza was a philosopher close to his own position, an ally in the struggle against priestcraft and superstition." Rienk Vermij, "Matter and Motion: Toland and Spinoza," p. 287.

130 Toland, *Letters to Serena*, V.2.166.

131 Vermij, "Matter and Motion: Toland and Spinoza," p. 285.

out the relationship of God to motion of the world, so that Toland's *Serena* acted as a catalyst and counterpoint, representing the ever-present danger that their pious mechanism would lapse into pantheism and then into atheism, and with it, would come the collapse of public order upheld by Whig Anglicanism. Given the connection of pantheism to radical politics during the English Civil Wars, the fear that the public order would collapse if pantheism were accepted was well founded in fact. Politics and the most abstruse philosophical physics were intimately intertwined.

It is now clearer why the moderate party—Boyle, Locke, and the Newtonians—which allied religion with a maintenance of privilege and property, had reason to fear the implications and associations of pantheism. Toland's *Pantheisticon* showed exactly how much of an abyss lay between publicly respectable Christianity and the full implications of Spinozism in the revolutionary cosmos Toland advocated.

The *Pantheisticon* was published by Toland, and meant as an esoteric treatise only for a very small audience of the like-minded (not for the ragged multitude or the orthodox).[132] For Toland, the only item of the pantheist creed is "*All Things are from the Whole, and the Whole is from all Things*."[133] In almost an exact duplication of Spinoza and even more of Bruno, Toland declared that the "Force and Energy of the Whole, the Creator and Ruler of All, and always tending to the best End, is GOD, whom you may call the *Mind*, if you please, and *Soul* of the Universe; and hence it is, that the *Socratic Brethren*, by a peculiar Term . . . are called PANTHEISTS; this Force, according to them, being not separated from the *Universe* itself, but by a Distinction of Reason alone."[134]

Calling it a distinction of reason alone meant, of course, that in the identifying of God and nature, "God" could safely be dropped and nature could run on its own steam. Rather than having a Creator God outside of nature, the impersonal "Force and Energy" bring about the creation of all individual creatures in a quasi-evolutionary manner. "From that Motion and Intellect that constitute the Force and Harmony of the infinite Whole, innumerable Species of Things arise, every Individual of which is both a Matter and Form to itself, Form being nothing else than a disposition of Parts in each Body."[135] Indeed, somewhat like Heraclitus, Toland seems to identify fire (and hence the sun) as the creative "Force and Energy."[136] As Toland's pantheism is necessarily materialist, this fire explains even thought.[137]

132 Toland, *Pantheisticon*.

133 Ibid., III.15.

134 Ibid., IV.17–18.

135 Ibid., IV.16.

136 "The Ethereal Fire environing all Things, and therefore supreme; permeating all Things, and therefore intimate, of which a Kitchen Fire is a certain analogical and imperfect Similitude; the Ether, I say . . . this Fire alone, more fleet than Thought itself, and by far more subtil than any other Kind of Matter . . . *rules all Things . . . it disposes of all Things, according to Nature, without Noise, and imperceptible, either to the Sight or Touch. In it is Soul, Mind, Prudence, Encrease, Motion, Diminution, Alteration, Sleep, Watching, it governs All in all Things, and never suffers* celestial *and terrestrial Beings to be at Rest*. This Fire is *Horace's Particle of divine Breath*, and *Virgil's inwardly nourishing Spirit, heavenly Origin, fiery Vigour . . . The Animal Spirits* of the Moderns, and their *Liquidity of Nerves*, are but empty Titles, unless they denote this Fire." Ibid., "Of the Antients and Modern Societies of the Learned," VI.22–24.

137 "Thought . . . is a peculiar Motion of the Brain, the proper Organ of this Faculty; or rather a certain

Such pantheism, since it is entirely irreconcilable with Christianity, demands its own religious ritual, and Toland provides a quasi-liturgical ceremony in the *Pantheisticon*, set in the form of recitation and response between the President and societal members as Responders. Needless to say, the ceremony is meant to occur behind closed doors:

Pres: Keep off the prophane People.
Resp: The Coast is clear, the Doors are shut,
All's safe
Pres: All Things in the World are one,
And one is All in all Things
Resp: What's All in all Things is God,
Eternal and Immense,
Neither begotten, nor ever to perish.
Pres. In him we live, we move, and exist.
Resp: Every Thing is sprung from him,
And shall be reunited to him,
He himself being the Beginning, and
End of all Things.[138]

The Cosmological-Political Project

Although pantheism is the esoteric religion of the few, yet pantheists must live among the unenlightened many. Esoterics therefore do not destroy the religion of the many, but transform it by remolding it, insofar as they are able, without "superstition." Thus Toland offered an appropriate quote from Cicero's *On the Nature of the Gods*:

> Not that it should be understood, that by destroying Superstition, Religion is also destroyed, for it is a wise Man's Business to uphold the Institutions of his Ancestors, and retain their Rites and Ceremonies; but what I intimate is, that the Beauty of the World, and Order of heavenly Things, force us to confess, that there exists an excellent and *Eternal Nature*, which should be the Object of the Contemplation and Admiration of all Mankind. Wherefore, as the *Religion* is

---

Part of the Brain . . . constitutes the principal Seat of the Soul, and performs the Motion both of Thought and Sensation . . . The Ethereal Fire . . . by a wonderful Structure of the Brain thereunto adjusted, and by exterior Objects that act on the Brain, through the Means of the Nerves of the Sense, and excite therein various Imaginations, duly executes all the Machinery of Conception, Imagination, Remembrance, Amplification, and Diminution of Ideas. It is this Fire alone, more fleet than Thought itself, and by far more subtil than any other Kind of Matter, which can with so quick a Motion run over the tended Cords and Ligaments of the Nerves, and variously agitate them, according to the different Impressions of Objects upon the Nerves." Ibid., VI.22–23.

138 Ibid., "The Second Part [of the Form of Celebrating the Socratic-Society] Containing The Deity and Philosophy of the Society," pp. 70–71.

> to be propagated, that's joined to the Knowledge of *Nature*, so all the Roots of *Superstition* are to be plucked out, and cast away.[139]

The wise man will "use his Endeavours to do all that can be done, that is, by plucking out the Teeth and paring the Nails of the worst and most pernicious of Monsters. . . ."[140] The wise man knows that this will entail not only keeping the esoteric philosophy hidden, but also the adroit use of political power, or at least, the direct influence of political power against the "Monsters" of popular superstition. In this way, philosophy must become political in order to re-form the reigning superstition into a new civil theology.

> It is to Men in Power, and Politicians actuated with this noble Disposition of Mind, that we are indebted for all the *religious Liberty*, that is any where now a Days with, which has redounded not a little to the great Advancement of Letters, Commerce, and Civil Concord. Whereas, on the contrary, to the Superstitious, or pretended Worshippers of Supreme Powers, I mean, to spirit-haunted Enthusiasts, or scruplously [sic] Pious, are owing all Feuds, Animosities, Mutinies, Mulcts, Rapines, Stigmates, Imprisonments, Banishments, and Deaths. Thus it necessarily must happen, *That one Thing should be in the Heart, and in a private Meeting; and another Thing Abroad, and in public Assemblies.*[141]

Pantheism was already "in the Heart" of Toland in the 1690s, both from Spinoza and Bruno, and it formed an integral part of his political machinations in regard to the Hanoverian succession. Toland took a copy of Bruno's *Spaccio* with him to the continent in 1702, and it was during this sojourn that he conceived of *Letters to Serena*,[142] wherein he presented his radicalization of Spinoza through Bruno. A year prior to this, we recall, he had been over on a diplomatic mission with others to bring to Sophia, the Electress of Hanover, the Act of Settlement (1701) ensuring the Hanoverian succession. In 1702, Toland went to Prussia to visit Queen Sophie Charlotte, the daughter of Sophia, and presented her a copy of the *Spaccio* for her inspection.[143] Toland's preaching of Bruno's *Spaccio de la bestia trionfante* in Europe, his presentation of the *Spaccio* to Sophia, and his *Letters to Serena* (dedicated to Sophie) must then be understood as supremely philosophical-political acts, well planned and assiduously executed. Toland was a missionary to the intelligentsia and to the powerful. As Justin Champion argues:

> From the very moment Toland managed to intrude himself into the diplomatic mission charged with presenting the *Act of Settlement* to Sophia, he used his intimacy with her as a theatre for the display of his arguments. This relationship with Sophia (and her daughter) was both public and private: the series of public defences and *eloges* of her political legitimacy and rational

139 Ibid., "The Third Part: Containing the Liberty of the Society; and a Law, neither deceiving, nor to be deceived," p. 87.

140 Ibid., II.98–99.

141 Ibid., II.99.

142 Vermij, "Matter and Motion: Toland and Spinoza," p. 276.

143 Jacob, *The Newtonians and the English Revolution, 1689–1720*, p. 231.

> character were matched by a private liaison manifest in a series of profoundly erudite and heterodox conversations about the nature of the soul, the sacred status of Scripture and political theory. . . . So, just as Toland was engaged in advancing a political defence of the Hanoverian succession in public, he was also discussing heterodox accounts of key metaphysical problems with the next successor. This convergence of public and private discourse was made more manifest by the publication of the substance of these discussions in 1704 in *Letters to Serena*, a work closely associated with the Hanoverian interest, which established the connections between such metaphysical speculation and more mainstream political thought.[144]

It is not too much to suggest that Toland conceived the Hanoverian succession as the political means by which a new civic religion could be instantiated in England, one rerooted in pantheism but wearing the public face of a radically reformed Christianity. This political act would obviously demand a theological reconstruction of the existing Christianity of the realm. To achieve this, Toland would take an entirely new tack on scriptural interpretation, one that will eventually eliminate or depreciate everything "priestly" as a "fall" from the original natural religion, a move that would support his secular republicanism by removing scriptural support for the royal-priestly nexus of power manifested in the Anglican Church.

One of Toland's most ingenious productions, in this regard, was his reconstruction of Moses as a republican legislator rather than a divine prophet. "Toland's applause for Moses was part of a public strategy for rendering republican institutions more readily accommodated to the dominant Christian discourses of his time," argues Justin Champion. "If Moses could be shown to be a republican pantheist who designed a rational religion for political purposes then Toland's arguments were less exposed to vilification as irreligious. Toland's [arguments] took the radical arguments of the *Traité* right into the heart of the British establishment."[145]

Adjusting Moses: The Respublica Mosaica

The strategy of rewriting as a mode of intellectual revolution had already appeared with the *Traité des trois imposteurs*. As is clear from his use of Milton, Harrington, and Ludlow, Toland himself was a master of this method, appropriating texts from the past by rewriting or representing them according to the revolutionary ideas he wished to form the future. Toland, the radical republican, and probably quite warm to notions of regicide, understood that with the Glorious Revolution English monarchy was there to stay. Although the monarchy could not be replaced by pure republican government, let alone a secular-based republican government, it could be redirected and reformed according to republican ideas precisely because

144 Champion, *Republican Learning*, pp. 167 and 169.

145 Ibid., p. 185.

the monarchy had been reestablished by parliament. If Toland could likewise intellectually form the royal family of the Hanoverian succession, providing them with his exoteric philosophy *and* a new civic religion, then enlightened philosophers would rule enlightened kings. Since Christianity was, like monarchy, firmly reinstituted with the Glorious Revolution precisely as a bulwark against radical political thought, for Toland's plan to work, he would have to rewrite sacred as well as English political history.

The place to begin this rewriting was the biblical account of Moses. In 1709 Toland published *Origines Judaicae*. In this short work, as Jan Assmann points out, "Toland's portrait of Moses is very much the same as that to be found in [the] blasphemous pamphlet that circulated in the late seventeenth and eighteenth centuries under the title of *L'esprit de Monsieur Benoit de Spinosa: Traité des trois imposteurs. . . .*"[146] but with a *very* important difference. Rather than presenting Moses as an impostor, Toland presented him as a wise legislator who used religion in Polybian-Machiavellian fashion.

In the *Origines Judaicae,* Toland, following Machiavelli, placed Moses *among* the pagan lawgivers, those who used religion to support their political aims even though they knew it to be false. In a very real sense, Moses stands for Toland. And again like Machiavelli, Toland used pagan sources (Diodorus, Tacitus, and especially Strabo) against the Bible to draw his portrait of Moses. The importance of Strabo for Toland's designs is clear from the following account (which Toland reproduced in full) of Moses from Strabo's *Geography*:

> Moses . . . was one of the Aegyptian priests, and held a part of Lower Aegypt [i.e., Goshen], as it is called, but he went away from there to Judaea, since he was displeased with the state of affairs there, and was accompanied by many people who worshipped the Divine Being. For he said, and taught, that the Aegyptians were mistaken in representing the Divine Being by the images of beasts and cattle, as were the Libyans; and that the Greeks were also wrong in modeling gods in human form; for, according to him, God is this one thing alone that encompasses us all and encompasses land and sea—the thing which we call heaven, or universe, or the nature of all that exists [*tēn tōn ontōn phusin*].[147]

This "Moses Strabonicus,"[148] Toland claimed rather boldly, was the *real* Moses, revealed by a pagan, and obscured by the biblical text itself: "Mosem enivero fuisse

---

146 Jan Assmann, *Moses the Egyptian: The Memory of Egypt in Western Monotheism* (Cambridge: Harvard University Press, 1997), p. 93.

147 Strabo, *The Geography of Strabo*, translated by Horace Jones, *The Loeb Classical Library* (Cambridge: Harvard University Press, 1966), Vol. VII, Book XVI.ii.35. Diodorus also says of Moses that his rejecting any anthropomorphizing in images was due to his holding that "the heaven surrounding the earth alone is God, and the Lord of the Whole" (*ton periechonta tēn gēn ouranon monon einai theon, kai tōn holōn kurion*). *Diodorus of Sicily*, translated by C. H. Oldfather, *The Loeb Classical Library* (Cambridge: Harvard University Press, 1960), Vol. XII, Book XL.3.4, our translation.

148 Assmann's felicitous phrase, *Moses the Egyptian*, p. 95.

Pantheistam, sive, ut cum recentioribus loquar, Spinosistam, incunctanter affirmat in isto Loco Strabo," "Moses was truly a Pantheist, or, as is it said more recently, a Spinozist, [which is] unhesitatingly affirmed in this Place in Strabo."[149] Moses Strabonicus prohibited idolatry for precisely the opposite reason than the real Moses: Nature *is* God, and therefore, to represent God as one thing in nature, one form, is to present God as less than He is.

Moses (Strabo asserted) put forth a very simple worship, so that the people should "worship God without an image" and "live self-restrained and righteous lives."[150] Taking followers out of Egypt and to Jerusalem was neither a miraculous nor a military act: "Moses, instead of using arms, put forward as defence his sacrifices and his Divine Being [*to theion*], being resolved to seek a seat of worship for Him and promising to deliver to the people a kind of worship and a kind of ritual which would not oppress those who adopted them either with expenses or with divine obsessions or with other absurd troubles."[151] Strabo, like Machiavelli after him, compared Moses with a number of other ancient lawgivers who consulted their gods to make their particular laws, or at least pretended to do so—Strabo himself introducing a note of skepticism: "For these things, whatever truth there may be in them, have at least been believed and sanctioned among men."[152]

From this purely natural *prisca theologia*—rooted in philosophical pantheism and devoid of miracle, supernatural revelation, and ceremony—the later Jews fell, Strabo claimed: "His successors for some time abided by the same course, acting righteously and being truly pious toward God; but afterwards . . . first superstitious and then tyrannical men [*to men prōton deisidaimonōn, epeita turannikōn anthrōpōn*] were appointed to the priesthood. . . ." As a result of this "fall" from original purity, the Jews embraced circumcision, dietary restrictions, and "other observances of the kind." [153]

In using Strabo to class Moses as one of a number of pagan legislators, Toland was aligning himself with the Machiavellian treatment of Moses as a manipulator of divine things for political purposes that Machiavelli had put within his republican arguments

149 Latin quoted in Champion, *The Pillars of Priestcraft Shaken*, p. 131, our translation. Although it may seem outlandish to ascribe pantheism to Moses, it should be remembered that the modern revival of ancient Epicurean atomism brought with it various attempts to prove that Moses had been the first atomist, and the ancient Greeks had inherited the idea from him, the most famous and thorough penned by Ralph Cudworth, *The True Intellectual System of the Universe* (1678), but also pushed by Robert Boyle and hinted at by Isaac Newton. See Danton Sailor, "Moses and Atomism," *Journal of the History of Ideas*, Vol. 25, No. 1 (1964): 3–16.

150 Strabo, *The Geography of Strabo*, Vol. VII, Book XVI.ii.35.

151 Ibid., Vol. VII, Book XVI.ii.36.

152 Ibid., Vol. VII, Book XVI.ii.39. Strabo compares Moses to (among others) Minos, Lycurgus, the Gymnosophists in India, and the Magi of the Persians: "Moses was such a person as these. . . ." Ibid., Vol. VII, Book XVI. ii.38–39. Diodorus too classes Moses as one of the great lawgivers, along with Minos, Lycurgus, Zoroaster (Zathraustes), and Zalmoxis (Zamolxis), who claimed divine origins for their laws, either because they thought the laws truly marvelous and divine, *or* because such a claim would be more likely to make the many obey. *Diodorus of Sicily*, Vol. I, Book I, 94.1–2.

153 Strabo, *The Geography of Strabo*, Vol. VII, Book XVI.ii.37. We have slightly modified the translation.

in the *Discourse*. The connection between Machiavelli, republicanism, and the use of pagan figures and sources for clarification was not lost on Toland's contemporaries. As Justin Champion notes:

> To many late-seventeenth-century readers the tradition of Solon, Lycurgus and Numa was fundamentally problematic because their politics were non-Christian. Certainly the accounts of their use of "politic religion" found in Machiavelli's *Discourses* tended to underscore the impiety of the republican tradition against the *de jure divino* models of government. By the 1690s and 1700s the transformation of "political legislators" into "political impostors" had been made by the various clandestine works of European *libertines erudits*: [Toland's] describing Moses as a legislator was not therefore only a politically deviant act, but fundamentally an irreligious one too.[154]

Certainly, Toland did little to allay readers' fears in his opening of the *Origines Judaicae,* declaring (upon authority of Cicero) that religion was "a mere ingine of state policy . . . that a belief in the immortal Gods was an invention contrived by wise and profound legislators for the general benefit of the commonwealth, in order that those whom reason could not influence, might be trained to their duty by a sense of religion."[155] But again, in contrast to the *Traité des trois imposteurs*, Toland did not, in the quasi-exoteric work of his *Origines Judaicae,*[156] present Moses as merely a duplicitous manipulator or impostor. Rather, Moses was presented as a wise pantheist, who had learned the lessons of the Egyptians well, and legislated accordingly.

To fill out our understanding of Toland's use of Moses, we may turn to his *Tetradymus*, which contains the four essays *Hodegus*, *Clidopherous*, *Hypatia*, and *Mangoneutes*. Toland's *Hodegus* was written about 1708 in Holland, circulating among friends in manuscript before being published in 1720. He made clear several times throughout *Hodegus* that he was setting forth only a "short Specimen" of a larger work, the "COMMONWEALTH OF MOSES" or "REPUBLIC OF MOSES" or "MOSAIC REPUBLIC,"[157] as he variously called it. As Toland admitted in the promised larger work, "I shall give

154 Champion, *Republican Learning*, pp. 106–107. Toland had used this motif before in his *The Oceana of James Harrington* (1700). He had resurrected the regicide Harrington's republican writings against monarchy, made in the turbulent years of revolution at mid-seventeenth century, by rewriting them to support a republican-leaning understanding of constitutional monarchy. On the iconography on the frontpiece, there was (among other things) five portraits of Moses, Solon, Confucius, Lycurgus and Numa—the inclusion of Confucius added beyond that of Machiavelli's republican pantheon, even further demoting the special status of Moses. Ibid.

155 This is from an English translation, according to Champion, "located in John Ryland's Library call mark 3 f. 38," rather than from a publicly available version. See Champion, *Republican Learning*, p. 175 and p. 187, n. 42.

156 As it was published in Latin, its readership was thereby more restricted. Although given the rather incendiary content, learned English divines soon made the content known to a wider audience.

157 John Toland, *Hodegus*, in *The Theological and Philological Works of the Late John Toland*, III.6, X.16, and XIV.25.

so new a turn and face . . . not onely to the whole political System [of Moses], as well as to several of the particular Laws of this incomparable Legislator . . . that I find it highly necessary to publish before-hand some short Specimen of my undertaking . . . to prevent surprise, and to accustom my readers to such sort of explications."[158]

The *Hodegus*, as the full title reveals, focuses on the *Pillar of Cloud and Fire, that Guided the Israelites in the Wilderness, not Miraculous: But a Thing equally practis'd by other nations, and in those places not only useful but necessary*. The title itself reveals even more. The word *hodēgos* is Greek means guide, and focuses attention not on the pillar and fire itself, but on the "*Angel of the* LORD, which carry'd the Pillar" who, Toland claimed, was actually not an angel but "a mere mortal man, the overseer or director of the portable fire, and the guide of the Israelites in the wilderness," whom Toland declared to be "no other than HOBAB, the brother-in-law of MOSES. . . ."[159] The substitution of Hobab for the angel represents an example of Toland's entire exegetical approach of substituting natural for supernatural interpretations. Indeed, Toland himself was the *hodēgos*, the new "mere mortal" guide, leading readers through the exegetical wilderness. Since the *Hodegus* was just a "Specimen" of a larger work that Toland promised to be new and shocking—a work he either did not complete or destroyed—one must distill his method of the whole from this part.

All but duplicating Spinoza, the overriding principle governing Toland's exegesis was that "*that thing ought not to be reputed a Miracle, which can be explain'd by the laws of Nature or ordinary means, and where a perfect account is given of all appearances*."[160] This principle allowed Toland to explain away any alleged miracle as merely natural so long as *any* natural explanation could account for the same phenomenon. The focus was not on *what* happened, but on *whether* a parallel natural account can be given. The problem with, or virtue of, this principle (depending on how one is looking at it) is that there is no limit on the possible number of counterexplanations, given that the events under consideration occurred thousands of years ago. It is difficult to think of *any* event, natural or supernatural, that could not be explained as occurring by a nearly unlimited number of other means or causes.

A related exegetical principle used by Toland: "Where things . . . seem in all respects alike [in several different works], they ought to be deem'd of the like nature, tho one author be more particular in relating circumstances than another. . . ."[161] This principle allowed Toland to interpret what *really* happened in sacred history according to pagan historical accounts that bear some resemblance, rather than according to the internal demands of the faith, *traditio*, or the whole of Scripture itself. The best way to understand these two principles is, of course, in exegetical action.

Toland began by asserting that in the Old Testament, "Miracles no doubt are there related, yet comparatively very few." In fact, less than "one third" (how much

158 Ibid., III.6.

159 Ibid., XXV.46, XXVII.51. That Hobab is the focus is affirmed by Toland, who states that he was originally going "to intitle this *Dissertation* HOBAB . . ." Ibid., XXVII.52).

160 Ibid., XVI.27.

161 Ibid.

less, he does not say) of the alleged miracles are truly miraculous, and in fact (echoing Spinoza), "the writers of those books have neither recorded such things for Miracles themselves, nor intended they shou'd be so understood by others."[162] The pillar of cloud and fire, Toland argued, was one such thing, for in desert countries torches are used to guide large numbers of travelers, those marching behind able to see the cloud or smoke of the burning torch by day and the fire by night. This was confirmed by classical sources such as Silius Italicus, Lucan, Pliny, Quintus Curtius, Herodotus, and others.[163] As Quintus Curtius reported, when Alexander led his vast armies, the normal trumpet signal to decamp was "*not sufficiently heard*" so "*he order'd a Pole, which might be seen from all parts, to be set on the top of the General's tent, on which a signal hung visible to all alike; namely* FIRE *was observ'd by night, and* SMOKE *by day*."[164] In accord with the two above-mentioned principles, we must assume the same purely natural explanation in regard to the Jews and in regard to "MOSES their General . . . and soon after their Legislator. . . ."[165] Since there is a natural explanation of the pillar of cloud and fire available from extra-biblical sources; therefore, we can presume that "there was no more of miracle in the one than in the other."[166] Furthermore, since the classical sources reveal that the signal fire was "suppos'd to have been manag'd by proper Officers: the same supposition ought as naturally to be made concerning the fire over the tent of JEHOVAH. . . ."[167] And so, the "*Angel of GOD* mention'd" as going before the Israelites must actually be "no other, than a mere mortal man, the Guide of the Israelites in the Wilderness; and the overseer or director of the portable Fire, as part of his peculiar office and province."[168] That is, the "angel" was really only Hobab, the confusion resulting from the translation of the word for messenger as angel, "the Hebrew word" being "not less general than the Greec word, from which we have form'd *Angel*. It signifies any *Messenger* whatsoever, mortal or immortal; so that circumstances alone can determine, what kind of messenger is meant."[169] Toland concludes that, "the *Angel of the* LORD, who directed the *Pillar*, was a mere man; because all that he did might be done by man, and has been actually done by many men."[170] The *Hodegus* was obviously meant to complete the picture of Moses presented in the *Origines Judaicae* as merely a wise legislator, *not* a prophet.

What was Toland really up to in his treatment of Moses? It is reasonable to suppose that the "key" to unlock his aims lies in the *Clidopherous*, which Toland published side by side with the *Hodegus* in his *Tetradymus*. As mentioned above, the *Clidopherous* focused explicitly on the esoteric-exoteric distinction, the double philosophy, made necessary by the unbridgeable divide separating the true philosophers and the vulgar.

162 Ibid., II.5.
163 Ibid., IV.7–9, XI.18–19.
164 Ibid., X.17.
165 Ibid., VIII.14.
166 Ibid., X.17.
167 Ibid., XIII.23.
168 Ibid., XVII.29.
169 Ibid., XXV.47.
170 Ibid., XXVI.48.

But since the vulgar cannot be enlightened, therefore (following Strabo) "FRAUD *and* SUPERSTITION *were necessary means, to keep the common people in good order*." But rather than simply resorting to complete duplicity, Toland desired a semirational reconstruction of "superstition," based upon Varro's distinction of a "*threefold Theology*, the Mythical, Physical, and Political; or the Fabulous, Philosophical, and Civil: wherof the first and the last sort are certain masks of Truth, or rather ingenious subterfuges from telling it." The story of Moses as presented in the Bible is an example of the Mythical or Fabulous Theology. In order for the true philosophers, the pantheists like Toland, to live among the unenlightened, the Mythical must be transformed by the Philosophical Theology into a new exoteric civil religion, a kind of midway point between rational theology and irrational superstition. In so doing, Toland believed that he had to follow "the Stoics, who reduc'd all the fabulous and popular Theology to the natural, or so explain'd all the fables of the Poets and the Vulgar, as to have been originally meant of natural causes and effects." Hence Moses was a pantheist who performed no miracles, and who was merely a legislator handing down what amounted to a deist code of ethics compatible with a new secular political order. "Demythologizing" and rationalizing the Bible, therefore, were specifically political acts for Toland, ones that exactly paralleled the ancient Stoic exercise of rationalizing religious fables.

To summarize Toland's portrait of Moses, it was of a man whose real views were quite as radical as those of his companions in the circle around Benjamin Furly that produced the esoteric and anonymous *Traité des trois imposteurs*. But Toland believed that these esoteric views, although true, would be destructive of society, since most people cannot be "enlightened" and hence need religion. Therefore, simply attacking Moses as the *Traité* did (however theoretically satisfying that might be) would be politically disastrous. Thus, in his exoteric works, Toland reformulated Judaism rather than destroying it. His portrait of Moses as a clever legislator in *Hodegus* and the *Origines Judaicae*, rather than a contemptible impostor, was part of that reformulation, one that allowed Moses to be used in the service of Toland's republicanism.[171] What one must understand—and there is hardly a more important point in relation to the subject at hand—is that Toland's exegesis was, in its very method, *designed for that politicized aim*. Having seen Toland's treatment of the Old Testament, we may now turn to his treatment of the New.

Plucking out the Teeth and Paring the Nails: Christianity not Mysterious *and* Nazarenus

"In the mask of a Christian," wrote Phillip Skelton in his *Deism Revealed* (1749), Toland "gets admittance into the minds of his readers, in order to steal away their principles of religion and honesty, not to enrich his own, but only to disfurnish their

171 On this point, see Champion, "Legislators, impostors, and the politic origin of religion," pp. 340–342, 355–356.

minds."[172] As noted, *Christianity not Mysterious* was Toland's first published work (or at least the first he put his name to), but it came out *after* his nearly two-year stay in the most radical circles of Holland (1692–1693). Against the usual treatment of scholars, it should be clear by now that we cannot understand the arguments in this, his most famous treatise, without consideration of the larger context of his life and other writings.

The full title is quite significant: *Christianity not Mysterious: or, a Treatise Shewing, That there is nothing in the Gospel Contrary to Reason, Nor Above it: And that no Christian Doctrine can be properly call'd a Mystery*. To declare that Christianity was *not* mysterious was loaded both politically and theologically. Politically, it meant that mediation of theological mysteries through a priesthood was unnecessary, therefore, political mediation by a state-sponsored priesthood was tyrannical; theologically, it meant that there was nothing incomprehensible about the deity, implying (as his enemies immediately picked up) that Toland was rejecting the Trinity—not in the name of Socinianism, as his critics charged, but in the name of a materialism on its way to developing into pantheism.[173]

As Toland's Preface indicated, the work was written with the esoteric-exoteric distinction in mind. The current political-theological climate was not friendly to his views, so that "the deplorable Condition of our age" was such that "a Man dares not openly and directly own what he thinks of Divine Matters . . . but he is either forc'd to keep perpetual Silence, or to propose his Sentiments to the World by way of Paradox under a borrow'd or fictitious name."[174]

As his Preface indicates, *Christianity not Mysterious* was indeed published anonymously (although Toland very soon owned up publicly); but even more crucial, Toland was admittedly not writing "openly and directly" but "by way of Paradox," thus

172 Quoted in Champion's Introduction to Toland, *Nazarenus*, p. 1.

173 Scholars who treat Toland's larger corpus, rather than merely focusing on *Christianity not Mysterious*, generally assume that there was an intellectual development toward pantheism very soon after the publication of *Christianity not Mysterious* in 1696, but that Toland was not a pantheist while writing it. Supporting this denial of any pantheism at this point is Toland's explicit affirmation of John Locke's philosophy (Section Three, Ch. 2), rather than Spinoza's. Against this, we believe that Toland was already quite familiar with pantheism, and well on his way on the short path from materialism to pantheism proper, if he had not already arrived. In support, we submit that (1) Proto-pantheism was already well-established in radical republican circles during the Cromwellian years, and Toland entered early among those who carried forth this intellectual tradition after the restoration of the monarchy; (2) Toland had already been immersed in the very center of Spinozism in Holland 1692–1693, and so would have been well versed in Spinoza's brand of pantheist materialism; (3) the arguments against Toland being the author of the anonymous pantheist tract of 1695, *Two Essays sent in a Letter from Oxford, to a Nobleman in London*, are unconvincing,; and (4) if Toland was not already (at least) strongly disposed toward pantheism before writing *Christianity not Mysterious*, one would have great difficulty in explaining his sudden "conversion" to Bruno so soon after its publication. That *Christianity not Mysterious* only shows direct, unambiguous affirmation of Locke does not, in and of itself, preclude him holding or tending toward a more radical materialism than Locke's at the time, since Locke's materialism is ambiguous enough. We also suggest that it was in Toland's best interest to ally himself publicly with a much less radical philosophy.

174 John Toland, *Christianity not Mysterious*, Preface, p. 5.

we must beware (recalling his esoteric-exoteric distinction) of the use of "equivocal Expression," wherein he "accommodate[s]" his "Language to the Belief of the People."[175] We have good reason to suspect, then, that *Christianity not Mysterious* does not represent Toland's own views. Rather, it is an "*External* or popular" work "adjusted in some Measure to the Prejudices of the People, or to Doctrines publickly authorized for true" rather than an "*Internal* or philosophical" work that Toland considered "altogether conformable to the Nature of Things, and therefore to Truth itself." To recall the above conclusions in regard to Moses, we submit that it is a piece of civil theology, a politicized account of Christianity.

Another confirming signal of this interpretation is that Toland explicitly stated that he was writing for "the Advantage of the Vulgar."[176] One may approach this statement from two angles. First, recall that during the Cromwellian years, the most radical religious and political views circulated especially among the lower classes—views antithetical to the priesthood, sacraments, kingship, and friendly to materialism and pantheism, republicanism, Socinianism, and reaching even to the rejection of Scripture itself as authoritative—then it becomes apparent how revolutionary the "Advantage of the Vulgar" might be. Second, recalling Toland's account of exoteric writing being made necessary by the vulgar, one may assume that his esoteric philosophic beliefs are behind the design of *Christianity not Mysterious*, reshaping Christianity so that it is more friendly to his philosophy yet remains a moral force to control the unphilosophic multitude.

At the heart of Toland's argument is the assertion that "*Reason* is the only Foundation of all Certitude; and that nothing reveal'd, whether as to its *Manner* or *Existence*, is more exempted from its Disquisitions, than the ordinary Phenomena of Nature."[177] In not raising revelation above reason, but instead asserting its identity (or merely the superfluity or even inferiority of revelation), Toland was obviously following Spinoza's radicalization of Descartes, which, argues Richard Popkin, he likely imbibed while in Holland "from Locke's friend, Jean Le Clerc."[178] In line with Spinoza's

175 We note that, paradoxically, Toland himself calls attention to this charge just two pages hence (p. 7): "That the well-meaning Christian may not suspect, as it falls out very ordinarily, that I aim at more than I declare, and cunningly disguise some bad Principles under the fair Pretence of defending the true Religion; I assure him that I write with all the Sincerity and Simplicity imaginable, being as thoroughly convinc'd of what I maintain, as I can be of any thing." As a careful reading of this well-crafted sentence reveals, Toland is only affirming that he is "thoroughly convinc'd" of his own opinions, not that he is not aiming "at more than I declare." The degree of "Sincerity and Simplicity imaginable" is, as he has already pointed out, calibrated by the difference between his own views and the "deplorable Condition of our age." This kind of ambiguous disclaimer at the beginning of a heterodox work was quite common at the time. See Berman, "Disclaimers as Offence Mechanisms in Charles Blount and John Toland," and also Berman, "Deism, Immortality, and the Art of Theological Lying" in J. A. Leo Lemay, ed., *Deism, Masonry, and the Enlightenment* (Newark: University of Delaware Press, 1987), pp. 61–78.

176 Toland, *Christianity not Mysterious*, Preface, p. 10.

177 Ibid., "The State of the Question," p. 17.

178 Richard Popkin, "Cartesianism and Biblical Criticism," in Thomas Lennon, John Nicholas, and John Davis, eds., *Problems of Cartesianism* (Kingston and Montreal: McGill-Queen's University Press, 1982), pp. 61–81, quote on p. 70.

Cartesianism, Toland defined knowledge in terms of "simple and distinct Ideas,"[179] so that "*what is evidently repugnant to clear and distinct Ideas, or to our common Notions, is contrary to Reason*" and "*the Doctrines of the Gospel*, if it be the Word of God, *cannot be so*."[180]

This was not a commonsense position, but a revolutionary one. As with Descartes and Spinoza, Toland was collapsing the *ordo essendi*, including the Being of God, into mathematically defined nature, so that the most certain mode of the human *ordo cognoscendi*, deductive mathematical knowledge, defined both reason and nature. Pantheism is the natural effect of this collapse, and supports it in turn. Hence, even if Toland were not a full-fledged pantheist at this point, in order to eliminate suprarational revelation in the way that he did, he would soon be led logically to this position.

Obviously Toland rejected any notion that sin has distorted reason[181] or that divine wisdom could be above human wisdom. "As for acquiescing in what a Man understands not, or cannot reconcile to his Reason, they know the best fruits of it that practise it. For my part, I'm a Stranger to it, and cannot reconcile my self to such a Principle." At the heart of his refusal of this "Principle" is the assumed Spinozan identity between the creature's and Creator's (and hence revealer's) mind, an identity that allowed Toland to declare confidently that "he that comprehends a thing, is as sure of it as if he were himself the Author."[182] Because of this, Toland also rejected any notion of the need for an infused power (the virtue of faith) to know revelation as truth above reason: "Now since by *Revelation* Men are not endu'd with any new Faculties, it follows that God should lose his end in speaking to them, if what he said did not agree with their common Notions."[183] One can then see why Toland redefined faith as "a most firm Perswasion built upon substantial Reasons."[184] Faith was built from human reason upward, if upward it rose at all, for Toland would allow no mystery, nothing above human reason, nothing that would seem to contradict reason. "*Contradiction* and *Mystery* are but two emphatick ways of saying Nothing. *Contradiction* expresses Nothing by way of Ideas that destroy one another, and *Mystery* expresses Nothing by Words that have no Ideas at all."[185]

Even more important, for our purposes, is the politicized explanation Toland offered as to why anyone would assert that the Creator's mind is qualitatively distinct from the creature's, that is, why some believe that Christianity *is* mysterious. This "blameable Credulity" and "temerarious Opinion" is "ordinarily grounded

179 Toland, *Christianity not Mysterious*, Section One, Ch. 2, p. 23.

180 Ibid., Section Two, "That the Doctrines of the Gospel are not contrary to Reason," p. 31.

181 Ibid., Section Two, Ch. 4 which argues at length against the orthodox notion of the "*Pravity of Humane Reason*."

182 Ibid., Section Two, Ch. 1, p. 37. This is the source of Toland's assertion that "*Revelation*" is "a *Mean of Information*," that is, simply another way that rational information can reach us. Ibid., Section Two, Ch. 2, p. 39.

183 Ibid., ch. 4, p. 81.

184 Ibid., Section Three, Ch. 4, p. 83. All of chapter four is pertinent in Toland's reduction of faith to reason.

185 Ibid., Section Three, Ch. 4, p. 84.

upon an ignorant and wilful Disposition; but more generally maintain'd out of a gainful Prospect. For we frequently embrace certain Doctrines not from any convincing Evidence in them, but because *they serve our Designs better than the Truth*; and because other Contradictions we are not willing to quit, are better defended by their means."[186] In short, all or nearly all affirmations of mystery, of truth above reason, are actually—if we might borrow from Nietzsche's later formulation—manifestations of the political will to power. This is a rather ironical assertion, given that Toland's own reformulation of Christianity *without* mystery is made in the service of his republican aims.

This led Toland to affirm what has become a sacrosanct rule of biblical exegesis, a rule at odds with the entire history of exegesis leading up to the modern period, and, in fact, one of the definitive marks of the historical-critical method. Since the infused suprarational power of faith is not needed, then no rule of faith governs interpretation: "Nor is there any different Rule to be follow'd in the Interpretation of *Scripture* from what is common to all other Books."[187] There is no different rule to be followed precisely because "*Christianity was intended* [to be] *a Rational and Intelligible Religion*," and this, interestingly enough, is "*prov'd from the Miracles, Method, and Stile of the New Testament*."[188] Toland's curious affirmation of the miraculous amounts to a rhetorical slight of hand: "Now to what Purpose serv'd all these Miracles," asked Toland, "if the Doctrines of Christ were incomprehensible? or were we oblig'd to believe reveal'd Nonsense?"[189] Since Christianity is therefore "*a Rational and Intelligible Religion*," then, as we have just seen, the method of interpretation is the *same* as we would use with "all other Books." As for the "*Stile of the New Testament*," Toland declared that it is "most easy, most natural, and in the common Dialect of those to whom it was immediately consign'd," meaning that it contained nothing above reason, nothing mysterious that would require an interpretive priesthood.[190]

This last point was essential to Toland's republican efforts to displace the priestly-monarchical political alliance. For this reason, he gave a purely political interpretation of mystery. There are only two senses of mystery, declared Toland: things "designedly kept secret or accidently obscure" or things "*inconceivable in themselves however clearly reveal'd*." Importantly, the first sense of mystery has political implications, bringing to mind Toland's later account of priests in his writings on the esoteric/exoteric distinction: "cunning *Priests*" invent "ridiculous, obscene, or inhumane Rites"

186 Ibid., Section Two, Ch. 1, p. 38. Emphasis added.

187 Ibid., Section Two, Ch. 3, p. 44.

188 Ibid., Section Two, Ch. 3, p. 43, chapter title.

189 Ibid., Section Two, Ch. 3, p. 44. Toland defines a miracle as "*some Action exceeding all humane Power, and which the Laws of Nature cannot perform by their ordinary operations*." Although he does not deny miracles, he does assert that "whatever is contrary to *Reason* can be no *Miracle*," for reason defines what it is possible to do, even for the Deity. Further, "God is not . . . prodigal of *Miracles*," so that they are bent to confirming Christ's non-mysterious, simple religion. Finally, miracles are not "above Reason," because "Miracles are produc'd according to the Laws of Nature, tho above its ordinary Operations, which are therefore supernaturally assisted." Ibid., Section Three, Ch. 4, pp. 88–91.

190 Ibid., Section Two, Ch. 3, p. 45–7.

to "*vail*" their secret "mysterious" goings-on from the multitude so as to manipulate them better.

As it turns out, in the New Testament "*Mystery* is always us'd in the first Sense of the Word. . . ."[191] so that a mystery merely means "Matters of Fact only known to God and lodg'd in his Decree . . . call'd *Mysteries*, not from any present Inconceivableness or Obscurity" in themselves, but merely "*by reason of the Vail under which they were formerly hid.*" Since "*under the Gospel this Vail is wholly remov'd*" then "*such Doctrines cannot now properly deserve the Name of Mysteries.*" [192] God does not reveal anything above reason, but only what is reasonable but hitherto unknown.

Of course, the implication is that since mystery in this sense means rational but momentarily secret information, once the information is openly stated in the Gospel, reason alone can grasp it without the mediation of a priesthood. Thus the continuing existence of a priesthood always implies the chicanery of "cunning Priests" manipulating the multitude for their own "by-Interest,"[193] and their appeal to mystery serves only "*to stop the Mouths of such as demand a Reason where none can be given, and to keep as many in Ignorance as Interest shall think convenient.*"[194]

These assumptions allowed Toland to reformulate history in terms of degeneration from rational religion to priestly superstition, a reformulation that would have direct implications for scriptural exegesis among the deists and all whom they influenced. Jesus Christ came to preach "the purest Morals," and teach "reasonable Worship." That is, he "stripp'd the Truth of all those external Types and Ceremonies" that prevailed among the Jews and that were recorded in the Old Testament," and "rendered it [the Truth] easy and obvious to the meanest Capacities." While "His Disciples and Followers kept to this Simplicity for some considerable time," the "converted *Jews*," who were "mighty fond of their *Levitical* Rites and Feasts," were at first tolerated out of deference to their weakness, but soon "what at the Beginning was but only tolerated in weaker Brethren, became afterwards a part of *Christianity* it self, under the Pretence of *Apostolick* Prescription or Tradition." Later, pagan converts and then heathen philosopher converts further degraded the simple Gospel, and as Christianity spread, it soon became politically ensconced in the empire, and hence advantageous to all who "profess'd themselves of the Emperor's Perswasion" and "embrac'd" Christianity solely "out of Politick Considerations. . . ."[195] The history of Christianity, as told by Toland, is a history of decay by politicization, a movement from rational religion to irrational mystery.

With this background, Toland claimed, we can therefore understand, "*how Christianity became mysterious*, and how so divine an Institution did, through the Craft and Ambition of *Priests* and *Philosophers*, degenerate into mere *Paganism*." There was

191 Ibid., Section Three, Ch. 1, p. 57.

192 Ibid., Section Three, Ch. 3, pp. 65–67.

193 Ibid., Section Three, Ch. 3, p. 74. Toland provides a short dialogue parody of the "interest" driven priest, cleverly manipulating his parishioners by appeal to mystery.

194 Ibid., Section Three, Ch. 4, p. 79.

195 Ibid., Section Three, Ch. 5, pp. 92–94.

little "mystery" for the first hundred and fifty years, but gradually the corruption entailed in Judaizing coupled with the corruptions of pagan notions of priesthood and superstition displaced non-mysterious Christianity with mysterious Christianity. Signs of this degeneration, declared Toland, were the development of priesthood itself, the changing of baptism and the Lord's Supper into mysterious sacraments that demanded that same priesthood, and dietary and sexual abstinence.[196] In sum, the degeneration was from an entirely rational religion to Catholicism, the extreme form of politicized mystery-mongering, according to Toland's historical schema.

We pause to note how neatly Toland's view maps onto Luther's, but with an entirely different aim, thereby repeating a pattern we have seen with Marsilius and Ockham, where secularizing and reforming strands coincide, the latter reinforcing the former even while they are fundamentally at odds.

The implications for scriptural exegesis of Toland's historical account of degradation are immensely important. Given these assumptions, Toland would have to treat Judaism with its sacrificial priesthood itself as corrupt (which seems to be his drift in *Christianity not Mysterious*), or more particularly, treat the Judaic priesthood as a corruption of some original, simple Mosaic religion (which, as we have seen, he does in *Origines Judaicae* and *Hodegus*). As a consequence, the Levitical priesthood and sacrificial system cannot be treated as types fulfilled in the New Testament. Certainly, his animus against mystery precluded any mystagogical interpretation, that is, typological interpretation focusing on prefigurements of Christian sacraments present in the Old Testament. All such attempts at mystagogy must be the result of Judaizing or paganizing corruptions.[197]

Thus, in regard to "Plucking out the Teeth and Paring the Nails," it is clear that, even in this early work, *Christianity not Mysterious*, there is not much left of Christianity once Toland rendered it non-mysterious. But this was by no means Toland's only or his most "mature" assessment of the New Testament. In 1718, he published the much more radical *Nazarenus*, which finished what *Christianity not Mysterious* had started.

Interestingly enough, both the esoteric and exoteric versions of this treatise are extant, the former, a private manuscript written in French (c. 1709–1710) and entitled *Christianisme, Judaique et Mahometan, ou Relation de L'ancien Evangile de Barnabas, et de la l'Evangile moderne des Mahometans*, and the latter, published in English in 1718, and entitled *Nazarenus: or, Jewish, Gentile, and Mahometan Christianity*.[198] The focus of both was the Gospel of Barnabas, which Toland wished to pass off as illuminating the beliefs of the earliest Christians, but which was actually a medieval forgery. His goal was the insinuation that the Gospel of Barnabas, which treated Jesus as merely human, predated the canonical Gospels, and therefore authenticated the Islamic denial of Christ's divinity.

196 Ibid., Section Three, Ch. 5, pp. 94–98.

197 Ibid. See especially Section Three, Ch. 5, pp. 94–95.

198 Happily, both are contained in Champion's edition of Toland, *Nazarenus* cited above.

Toland conceived of *Nazarenus* perhaps as early as 1698.[199] In contrast to *Christianity not Mysterious*, in which Toland focused on stating a theological position, *Nazarenus* carried out its subversive intent entirely through textual criticism. The criticism focused on the Gospel of Barnabas, which Toland alleged to have discovered in Amsterdam in 1709.[200] Again, the earlier French version of *Nazarenus* was written, as Champion notes, "for a private and heterodox audience (Eugène [of Savoy] and his circle)." As an esoteric work, it offers a much better grasp of what Toland really thought in the earlier version, and hence it provides an interpretive touchstone for the later exoteric version.

In the earlier version, "there are no rhetorical strategies deployed to hide or obscure his opinion," whereas in the later version, by contrast, Toland "mollifies the clarity of the argument and makes identifying the position of the author much more difficult and ambiguous." In moving from esoteric to exoteric, "from public to private, we move from a lucid authorial voice, to muffled equivocation."[201] Yet the point of the later work was as subversive as the earlier, and, in fact, the effect was all the more so because of its equivocation, or, we might say, moderation.

As should by now be apparent, Toland's aim was to undermine orthodox Christianity, and refound it upon moorings amenable to his esoteric views and political goals. In Champion's words, "*Nazarenus* was an attempt to reform the established church in England. Following the Harringtonian insistence upon the compatibility of a national church and the toleration of religious diversity, *Nazarenus* was a strategic attempt to advance a pluralistic civil religion." The most important figures defining Toland's approach were Spinoza, Simon, and Hobbes,[202] and part of Toland's strategy for public transformation of belief was bringing their corrosive arguments to a wider audience so as "to achieve a relativistic understanding of religion."[203]

In *Nazarenus,* Toland acknowledges that the Gospel of Barnabas as he found it was not original, but "certainly the performance of a Mahometan Scribe," in that it purported to give a life of Jesus amenable to Islam (including not only the denial of Christ's divinity, but that Judas was crucified in His stead). But rather than disregard it as a medieval forgery, Toland claimed it to be a window opening upon the earliest Christians: "Tis, in short, the ancient Ebionite or Nazaren System [hence the title *Nazarenus*], as to the making of JESUS a mere man (tho not with them the Son of JOSEPH, but divinely conceiv'd by the Virgin MARY) and agrees in every thing almost with the scheme of our modern Unitarians. . . ."[204] The Gospel of Barnabas demonstrated that "the fundamental doctrines of Mahometanism . . . have their rise . . . from the earliest monuments of the Christian religion."[205]

199 See Toland's letter in the appendix to Champion's edition of Toland, *Nazarenus*, pp. 300–301.

200 Toland was shown the manuscript by a diplomat, who later (1713) donated it to Eugène of Savoy. See ibid., p. 65, and Toland's own account in *Nazarenus*, I.v, p. 143.

201 Ibid., p. 71.

202 Ibid., pp. 85–89.

203 Ibid., pp. 97, 102.

204 Toland, *Nazarenus*, I.v, pp. 143–144.

205 Ibid., I.i, p. 135.

As a sign of the ancient origin of the denial of Christ's divinity and the Islamic affirmation that Jesus was not crucified, Toland noted a number of early Christian groups (considered as heterodox) that held much the same position, including the "Basilidians" (who "in the very beginning of Christianity, deny'd that CHRIST himself suffer'd, but that SIMON *of Cyrene* was crucify'd in his place"), and the "Cerinthians" and "Carpocratians" (who "affirmed JESUS to have been a mere Man"). Rather than openly assert that the labels of orthodox and heterodox should be reversed, Toland chose to advance his agenda by rhetorical insinuation: "Tis a strange thing, one wou'd think, they shou'd differ about a fact of this nature [whether it was Judas or Jesus who was actually crucified] so early; and that CERINTHUS, who was contemporary, a countryman, and a Christian, shou'd with all those of his Sect, deny the resurrection of CHRIST from the dead. . . ."[206]

Through the strategy of presenting heterodox sources as one of a number of competing voices among early Christians, Toland prepared for the undoing of the scriptural canon by the claim that the formation of the canon was entirely politicized. The presence of so much heterodoxy implied that orthodoxy was simply the voice that won out, not on its own merits, but through political machination.

Toland's softening up of contemporary notions of heterodox and orthodox allowed him to assert the primacy of the sect of the Nazarenes. That "Nazarens" or "Ebionites," Toland declared, "were the first converts among the Jews to Christianity; that is to say, the first Christians, and consequently the only Christians for some time."[207] Almost identically to "the Socinianism of our times," the Nazarens

> *affirm'd* JESUS *to have been a mere man, as well by the father as the mothers side, namely the Son of* JOSEPH *and* MARY; *but that he was just, and wise, and excellent, above all other persons, meriting to be peculiarly call'd* THE SON OF GOD, *by reason of his most virtuous life and extraordinary endowments: and that they join'd with their Christian profession, the necessity of circumcision, of the observation of the Sabbath, and of the other Jewish ceremonies*; which necessity must be understood only of the Jewish Christians. . . ."[208]

Toland was thereby able to put a different exegetical spin on the Jewish-Gentile division than Locke, but with the same aim: the celebration of tolerance as the central Christian doctrine, or better, the central doctrine of Toland's new civil theology. According to Toland, the Nazarenes "were mortal enemies to PAUL," the Apostle to the Gentiles, rejecting his epistles as well as the canonical Acts of the Apostles, which put St. Paul in a good light.[209] This "split" between the original Jewish converts and Paul's later Gentile version explains the tension evident in even the canonical Gospels between Jew and Gentile, circumcision and uncircumcision, works and faith, Law and Gospel.[210] This

206 Ibid., I.vi, p. 145.
207 Ibid., I.ix, p. 151.
208 Ibid., I.ix, pp. 152–153.
209 Ibid., I.ix, p. 153 and I.xi, p. 157.
210 Ibid., I.ix–xi, xvi.

tension provided an opportunity for Toland to draw the lesson of tolerance, for (unlike Paul) "the Apostles were farr from condemning the Nazarens, that they confirm'd their doctrine by their own practice," so that "*Toleration* . . . is no less plainly a duty of the *Gospel*, than it is self-evident according to the Law of Nature: so that they who persecute others in their reputations, rights, properties, or persons, for merely speculative opinions, or for things in their own nature indifferent, are so farr equally devested both of Humanity and Christianity." This two-fold "scheme," as Toland called it, represented "the TRUE ORIGINAL PLAN OF CHRISTIANITY," and was directly applicable to the present day, allowing Judaizers to exist alongside those professing justification by faith alone. In fact, "no other scheme can reconcile Christianity. . . ."[211]

While Toland presented his "live and let live" scheme as the original plan of Christianity, he also made clear (as we have seen above) that the Nazarens held to the original form of Christianity, and by implication, that the latter-day Socinians were closest to the mark of "true" Christians. He asked rhetorically:

> Since the Nazarens or Ebionites are by all Church-historians unanimously acknowledg'd to have been the first Christians, or those who believ'd in CHRIST among the Jews, with which his own people he liv'd and dy'd, they having been the witness of his actions, and of whom were all the Apostles: considering this, I say, how it was possible for them to be the first of all others (for they are made to be the first Heretics) who shou'd form wrong conceptions of the doctrine and designs of JESUS? and how came the Gentiles, who believ'd on him after his death, by the preaching of persons that never knew him, to have truer notions of these things; or whence they cou'd have their information, but from the believing Jews?[212]

It might seem that Toland could therefore justly be called a Socinian, a modern-day Nazarene, and indeed, Socinianism was the charge leveled against him even as early as *Christianity not Mysterious*. Toland himself noted (rather cagily) in *Nazarenus*, in regard to his own beliefs, "I own that, for more than one reason, I have less exception to the name of NAZAREN than to any other."[213] But against this, recall that by this time Toland had thoroughly embraced, through Bruno and Spinoza, an even more radical form of pantheism than Spinoza's. Socinianism was a heresy of Christianity, resting on an acceptance of the reality of revelation in Scripture even while deviating from orthodox interpretation, denying Christ's essential divinity even while holding to His virgin birth, divine adoption, and even Resurrection. Pantheism was forged in an entirely different cosmos, one in which God and nature were one and the same, and supernatural revelation was therefore impossible. For the radical pantheism of Toland's circle, Christ was not less than Divine, but (with Moses and Mohammed,) an impostor, a Machiavellian manipulator. Therefore, the gap between Toland's pantheism and Socinianism is far, far wider, than the gap between Socinianism and orthodox

211 Ibid., I.xii, p. 161; I.xiv, p. 170; I.xvi, p. 178; I.xviii, p. 181; I.xx, p. 193.

212 Ibid., I.xix, p. 186.

213 Ibid., I.xviii, p. 183.

Christianity. In light of Toland's distinction between esoteric and exoteric, and philosophical and civil theology, Toland's qualified endorsement of Socinianism should be understood as an affirmation of an exoteric civil theology, not his own esoteric views.

Drawing it all together, it is clear that *Nazarenus* was simply one of Toland's later attempts to ground his civil theology through a scholarly deconstruction of orthodox-heterodox distinction, using the tools provided by Richard Simon and others to further the Spinozan project.

Conclusion

As we have tried to show at great length, there is much more to John Toland than *Christianity not Mysterious*, and much more to *Christianity not Mysterious* than has generally been presumed in the "Whiggish narrative" of the history of scriptural scholarship. Rather than a gradual transition from uncritical to critical, a close look at Toland's wider body of writings and his radical milieu reveals a quite different history, one of purposeful subversion. If Toland is representative of the actual intellectual and cultural dynamics of the late seventeenth and early eighteenth century, then the standard assessment of deism must undergo significant revision, from being a moderate form of Christianity as it faded into rationalism, to being (at least for some) the exoteric face of an esoteric philosophical worldview radically at odds with Christianity.

Understanding this critical period in terms of purposeful subversion rather than gradual enlightenment would entail a much different historical narrative, a much richer, certainly much more ambiguous story than the "Whig history" of linear progress as told by those scriptural scholars looking back with satisfaction from the twentieth and twenty-first century, seeing history leading triumphantly up to their academic doorsteps.

An essential component of this new, more ambiguous history is the presence of a twofold philosophy, a kind of Averroism, which arose because of the essential antagonism existing between the ever more radical materialist cosmology and the Judeo-Christian cosmology. With Descartes, the antagonism was muted because he judiciously avoided the clash between rival worldviews by polite and patronizing fideism. But when Spinoza cast away the dualism and embraced materialist pantheism, the antagonism became acute. Toland set the antagonism into his esoteric-exoteric structure, so that Christianity could be reformulated as a civil religion.

This civil religion was obviously a politicized form of Christianity. Since the unphilosophic multitude can never become enlightened by true philosophy, they must be controlled by religion, at least for the time being. The control takes the form of a carefully rewritten version of Christianity that removes all doctrinal divisions. We say "rewritten" because reformulation had to be done by exegetical reconstruction of the biblical text. As we have seen, Toland attempted to remove doctrinal divisions by an historical-exegetical deconstruction of the orthodox-heterodox, canonical-non-canonical distinctions, so that Christianity could be pared down to a kind of minimal moralism that would assure public peace rather than disturb it. Both Toland's picture of Moses the republican legislator and of the first Christians as doctrinally minimal Nazarenes indistinguishable from good Jews, Muslims, and Unitarians, were carefully crafted for that political purpose. Toland's attempt to portray Moses as a philosopher-pantheist, however clumsy and contrived, was meant to reduce the friction between the new civil religion and true philosophy.

The esoteric-exoteric structure allows us to see that motives and methods must be assessed together. In Toland, we have shown how comprehensively his motives determined his method of exegesis, and how easily scriptural scholarship was co-opted for political purposes.

An undeniably important example is Toland's use of Richard Simon to undermine the canon so that he could present orthodoxy as defined by the politically victorious, designed to pluck the teeth and pare the nails of Christianity, thereby making it a suitable civil religion to support his secular republicanism.

But since the method is defined by the motive, the method carries the motive hidden within it. If we might overstate it somewhat, the critical method applied by the exegete recreates Toland within the soul of the exegete. To take a pertinent example, working through Bart Ehrman's *Lost Christianities: The Battles for Scripture and the Faiths We Never Knew* (2003), the reader feels as if he is perusing Toland's *Nazarenus* redivivus. While the scholarship is more refined after three hundred years, Ehrman's mode of approach and the conclusions are almost exactly the same. It is worth mentioning that Ehrman himself went through the transformation in graduate school in biblical studies, which Wilfred Cantwell Smith aptly noted "are on the whole calculated to turn a fundamentalist into a liberal."[214] That Ehrman came out thinking much like John Toland tells us that Toland calculated well in launching his exegetical method.

Ehrman is not, of course, the only later exegete who manifests ideas found in Toland. To take another, far more influential example, D. F. Strauss's finale to his *Life of Jesus Critically Examined* included a stunning example of the purposeful use of equivocal speech, wherein the enlightened pastor, like Toland, says one thing but means another, the two levels of speech corresponding to Strauss's enlightened esoteric Hegelianism and (to quote Toland again) "the external or popular Doctrin . . . impos'd on the Mob by an equivocal Expression." "In his discourses to the church," Strauss says of the enlightened theologian that

> he will indeed adhere to the forms of the popular conception, but on every opportunity he will exhibit their spiritual significance, which to him constitutes their sole truth, and thus prepare—though such a result is only to be thought of as an unending progress—the resolution of those forms into their original ideas in the consciousness of the church also. Thus . . . at the festival of Easter, he will indeed set out from the sensible fact of the resurrection of

214 See Ehrman's autobiographical sketch in the Introduction to his *Misquoting Jesus: The Story Behind Who Changed the Bible and Why* (New York: HarperCollins, 2005).

> Christ, but he will dwell chiefly on the being buried and rising again with Christ, which the Apostle himself has strenuously inculcated.[215]

For Strauss, the spiritual truth was the esoteric truth of scientific materialism, the truth that had slowly to displace the literal but unhistorical and unphilosophic "truth" of Scripture by a double process of demythologizing the Bible and equivocally restating its doctrines according to a philosophical framework not much different than Toland's dynamic pantheism, a kind of Hegelianism mixed with Baconian mastery of nature and evolutionary theory, wherein history is driven toward its culmination in a this-worldly divinization of humanity itself. Strauss's mixture was, if anything, more politicized than Toland's because the divinization manifests itself in the concrete race and nation.

> In an individual, a God-man, the properties and functions which the church ascribes to Christ contradict themselves; in the idea of the race, they perfectly agree. Humanity is the union of the two natures—God become man, the infinite manifesting itself in the finite, and the finite spirit remembering its infinitude; it is the child of the visible Mother and the invisible Father, Nature and Spirit; it is the worker of miracles, in so far as in the course of human history the spirit more and more completely subjugates nature [via technology], both within and around man, until it lies before him as the inert matter on which he exercises his active power; it is the sinless existence, for the course of its development is a blameless one, pollution cleaves to the individual only, and does not touch the race or its history. It is Humanity that dies, rises, and ascends to heaven, for from the negation of its phenomenal life there ever proceeds a higher spiritual life; from the suppression of its mortality as a personal, national, and terrestrial spirit, arises its union with the infinite spirit of the heavens. By faith in this Christ, especially in his death and resurrection, man is justified before God; that is, by the kindling within him of the idea of Humanity, the individual man participates in the divinely human life of the species.[216]

With Strauss, we can see quite vividly the effect of Toland's revival of the Stoic practice of rewriting "all the fabulous and popular Theology" so that it conforms "to the natural," but in this case, the natural philosophy of the Stoics has been replaced by the philosophical materialism of the nineteenth century as spiritualized through Hegel.

But we do not need to look so far for a confirming pattern, nor do we need to seek far for a connection between Toland's efforts and those of the Hegelians who would so influence the later development of the historical-critical method. In the eighteenth century the natural philosophy that defined exegetical efforts was that of

215 Peter Hodgson, ed., D. F. Strauss, *The Life of Jesus Critically Examined* (Philadelphia, PA: Fortress Press, 1972), Section 152, p. 783.

216 Ibid., p. 780.

Newton. The Newtonian "Whig" cosmology entailed a mechanical world that needed a deity to initiate its movements from without, and periodically readjust them when they got out of alignment—a deity already far removed from the biblical God who was a Father continually and intimately involved with His creation and especially with those creatures made in His image. But in tribute to Toland's prescient critique of Newton, all that was needed to displace the watchmaker deity was the supposition that nature had a principal of motion within, a principal that itself could be equivocally divinized, resulting in a deification of both humanity and nature in something called "history," the incarnation of the God become man in the person of the state. The rediscovery of dynamic pantheism in the nineteenth century, of an inner force that drives nature and history to its destined culmination—not in God or a kingdom not of this world, but in the concrete nation—represents a victory for Toland over Newton, of radicals over moderate radicals, of radical political liberalism over moderate political liberalism.

CHAPTER 13

CONCLUSION

We have tried to demonstrate that root assumptions of the modern approach to Scripture are only properly understood in terms of the larger secular revolution that takes place on all levels, from the cosmological to the political, and that each level reinforces all the others. Marsilius's and Machiavelli's desire to turn attention from the next world to this entailed a fundamental shift to a secular worldview that, in elevating this world over the next, lifted politics above theology. The consequent subordination of Scripture to secularism was the first phase in its modern politicization. Adumbrations of the modern approach to Scripture arose as part of the process of subordination, as in, for example, Machiavelli's exegetical habit of correcting sacred by secular or pagan history.

It should be clear that the politicization of Scripture took place through a new approach to politics itself, one that placed political desires or the necessities of the political situation above theological truths. In part, this new approach was a reaction to hypocrisy and corruption on the part of the Church. No one can doubt that the crass use of biblical authority made by corrupt Italian popes leading up to the time of Machiavelli provided an all too clear example of politicizing Scripture that gave Machiavelli the lesson that religion was mere hypocritical pretense masking political ambition. It also gave Luther the impetus to jettison *traditio* as hopelessly mired in and by sin, so that Christian faith would need to be built upon Scripture alone.

Machiavelli's approach led to direct and Luther's to indirect politicization of Scripture, and both informed the future development of the modern approach to the Bible. The new secular approach to politics, seen first in Henry VIII, whose policies were so thoroughly defined by Marsilius, Wycliffe, and Machiavelli, as well as his own political situation and ambitions, was further refined and deepened by the great fathers of modern political philosophy, and hence modern political liberalism, the Englishmen Hobbes and Locke, who both made signal contributions to the development of the modern approach to Scripture.

Luther aided these developments indirectly by placing sole emphasis on the authority of Scripture alone, for as we have seen, within a matter of a decade, *sola scriptura* resulted in an intractable set of rival interpretations that soon became embedded in rival political entities. The divide in regard to scriptural interpretation between Catholic and Protestant, and Protestant and Protestant, thereby became politicized. This in turn led to the desire for a solution, one provided by Spinoza, in which doctrinal differences were neutralized through a self-consciously designed *method* of exegesis. As we have seen with Richard Simon, these methods could be advanced quite apart from the original politicizing intention, but as our analysis of Locke and Toland make clear, the method thus advanced could all the more easily and powerfully be reunited to the original secularizing intention.

Perhaps most important of all, the politicization of Scripture took place within a radically redefined cosmos, a mathematical-mechanical view of nature that was in continual antagonism to the Judeo-Christian cosmology. We are not, here, focusing on whether the earth or the sun was at the center of things, but on much more profound philosophical assumptions. Descartes, Hobbes, and Spinoza defined nature so that it was ontologically mathematical and mechanical. It soon became apparent that, since this universe was an entirely law-governed, self-contained, and self-sustaining machine, that the active, living, creating, and redeeming God of the Old and New Testament would either have to be redefined (by being subsumed into nature via pantheism), relieved of the power to control and sustain His creation (thereupon standing outside of nature as an entirely dispassionate and detached watchmaker), or simply rejected (by the more radical of the radical Enlightenment).

The understanding of and approach to the biblical text followed suit; or to put it in a more precise form, the mathematical-mechanical approach to nature was duplicated in the new exegetical approach to Scripture, the new understanding of nature completely defining the new understanding to the interpretation of the Bible. Since miracles had been excised from nature, they had to be removed from the text. Since nature was entirely defined by mathematics, knowledge of mathematical-mechanical laws displaced prophecy, and so prophecy had to be removed from the text. In fact, since there was, with pantheism, assumed to be an identity of the logos of nature with the Logos of God, scientists who studied the logos of nature provided the highest revelation possible, thereby demoting the revelation contained in the Bible as at best puerile. All that was left, so it seemed, was the moral message of the text, and the focus on the Bible as merely moral reinforced its politicization.

By the time we get to John Toland, all the most radical elements of the new secularized worldview are in place, and so all the most radical—yet familiar—claims about biblical revelation are present. As our consideration of Toland and the radical Enlightenment made quite evident, in regard to the content and method of scriptural scholarship, there is not all that much to be found in the most vociferous and seemingly "radical" twentieth- and twenty-first-century biblical scholars that is not found in the Netherlands and England of the late seventeenth and early eighteenth century.

We have thereby arrived at a central insight of the essential connection between content and method. In regard to the development of the historical-critical method, neither the content of Scripture nor the proper method of its interpretation were neutral. Rather, what Scripture seemed to contain, and the method appropriate to its interpretation, came to be entirely defined by the mutually reinforcing combination of the new secularized political aims and the new secularized cosmos. The new this-worldly aim of politics had to be shorn of divine influence so that it could work independently of otherworldly influence; it demanded a cosmology free of otherworldly goals, divine manipulation, or divine threat. Its focus was man, earthly peace, and earthly power and glory. The new mathematical-mechanical world, with nature defined according to human mathematical knowledge as the highest wisdom and human technical control as the highest power, was man-centered in every sense, as opposed to God-centered.

To repeat, this shift in focus is far more important than whether the ruling cosmology was earth-centered or sun-centered. In a God-centered cosmology, both nature and Scripture were understood as manifesting a wisdom higher than that which human beings could fully grasp, albeit a wisdom that condescended to human capacities. The notion that faith exceeded human capacities was simply an obvious corollary to the fact that divine wisdom and power exceeded human wisdom and power. The methods appropriate to the interpretation of Scripture reflected both this distance and God's loving condescension. The use of allegory in interpretation of the biblical text, for example, was ultimately based on a recognition that the providential power and wisdom of the Creator and Redeemer God could use things in nature and events in history as guides—simultaneously real and symbolic—leading humanity towards an ever deeper penetration of (and by) the Divine Mystery of the Most Holy Trinity. The content of both nature and revelation were ultimately mysterious—supprarational, not irrational—because God was mysterious, and creation and Scripture both reflected the ultimately impenetrable depths of the Triune God, both Creator and Redeemer, even while they radiated His wisdom and love.

In the man-centered cosmology, the gap between divine and human wisdom, divine and human creation were closed. The content of the mathematical-mechanical universe defined what method was appropriate to its illumination. If the universe is fundamentally mathematical and mechanical, then of course the method of illumination must be mathematical and mechanical. If biblical exegesis were to become "scientific," it would then have to follow and conform to the content and method appropriate to the man-centered universe. The anti-Trinitarianism of deism, Unitarianism, and pantheism were all the result of adopting a man-centered universe that, being entirely in accord with our human capacities, is entirely without mystery. Anti-sacramental interpretations of the content of Scripture as well as the removal of miracle from the biblical text were both entailed in the elimination of mystery. In a mathematically defined cosmos, God's wisdom did not exceed ours. We, too, are mathematicians. If God created a merely mechanical cosmos, we too are makers of machines. In theory, and given enough time, we can both fully understand and fully re-create what God has made—and, perhaps, improve upon it.

We stress again the very particular political causes and goals reinforcing the redefinition of content and method in scriptural interpretation. The use of excommunication by a string of frankly political popes did as much to bring about the desire for an anti-sacramental view of nature and scriptural interpretation as did the new modern Epicurean vision of a purely secular world devoid of the perturbations of religious conflict. Given that hypocrisy provides the seeds of skepticism, and skepticism of unbelief, the machinations of late medieval and Renaissance popes may well be considered the seed-plot of secularism. But as we have shown, the lines of influence are more complex. Luther's interpretation of the primacy of justification by faith alone also contributed to desacramentalizing the interpretation of Scripture, especially as it lent itself to a more radical reading, where sacraments were taken to be mere symbols. This view was reinforced by, and reinforced in turn, the new anti-sacramental, mathematical-mechanical picture of nature, creating a certain unintended symbiosis between certain kinds of Protestantism and the revolutionary secular cosmos.

Ultimately, however, it was the entirely self-conscious fathers of modernity—Machiavelli, Descartes, Hobbes, Spinoza, Locke, and Toland—who used the various religious conflicts and forces to forge the *via moderna* in its largest sense, both cosmological and political, and therefore helped to determine the roots of what is "modern" in the modern historical-critical method. Their combined efforts were thereby pivotal in defining what it means to be "critical" and to engage in a legitimate "method." Whatever the sins and confusions of Christians that form a backdrop to the development of the new politicizing exegesis, the "Enlightenment project" was itself a positive project with identifiable assumptions and aims that can be recognized, delineated, and judged.

As our study should make evident, this task of recognition, delineation, and judgment goes far beyond the confines generally associated with the history of modern biblical scholarship. If our work has made an important contribution to the task of critically assessing modern historical-critical scholarship, we hope it has opened readers up to the immense philosophical, political, and historical complexity that formed the matrix of such acknowledged seminal figures and texts as Spinoza and his *Theologico-Political Treatise*, Locke and his *Reasonableness of Christianity*, and John Toland and his *Christianity not Mysterious*. We also hope that it puts an end to cursory "Whig History" treatments of such figures as Thomas Hobbes, where the only thing of importance is whether or not he denied Mosaic authorship of the Pentateuch. The issue is not whether or not someone denied Mosaic authorship, but how and why. That takes us into a host of complexities in regard to England's particular history, Hobbes's philosophical materialism, the adequacy of his political philosophy—all of which bear upon how and why Hobbes cast doubt on Mosaic authorship.

It should now be clear that merely picking out from earlier centuries adumbrations of the positions of nineteenth-century German scholars overlooks the far broader and deeper extrabiblical influences that shaped key assumptions of latter-day scholars. For example, Spinoza's entire philosophical approach, which undergirds his exegetical method, is based upon a radicalization of Descartes's project, one that itself rests on a presumed identity of being (nature) and the mathematical mode of human knowing. Can one then judge the exegetical method of Spinoza without thinking long and hard about all the philosophical issues and ambiguities involved in Descartes's project?

Finally, since this work was written to dovetail with existing treatments of the history of modern scriptural scholarship that normally begin in earnest where ours ends, we hope that we have set some kind of standard for the kind of complexity of approach that should be taken to later figures such as Matthew Tindal, Johann Salomo Semler, Johann David Michaelis, W.M.L. de Wette, Hermann Reimarus, Johann Griesbach, Johann Eichhorn, Friedrich Schleiermacher, D. F. Strauss, F. C. Baur, Johannes Weiss, Heinrich Ewald, Bruno Bauer, Julius Wellhausen, Rudolph Bultmann, and Hermann Gunkel.

Examples of work in this area are less numerous than one would like. The late J. C. O'Neill's *The Bible's Authority: A Portrait Gallery of Thinkers from Lessing to Bultmann* is one of the most insightful attempts at telling a far more complex history of the later centuries of biblical criticism. Another worthy volume is *Biblical Studies and the Shifting of Paradigms: 1850–1914,* edited by Henning Graf Reventlow and William Farmer.[1] Such treatments are far too rare. We hope that our study will contribute to making them less so, and will therefore also aid the overall task of the critical analysis of the assumptions that (in union with the scholarly tools) formed the historical-critical method.

We end with a short foray into the later time period that we hope future histories will treat more critically, the centuries of scriptural scholarship which are usually treated with great thoroughness by histories of the subject, the eighteenth and nineteenth centuries. As we mentioned in the Introduction, we intend our study to dovetail with such histories, but as should be clear from our analysis of the fourteenth to the early eighteenth century, we believe that our approach provides needed illumination of even those figures like Hermann Reimarus, Gotthold Lessing, D. F. Strauss, and other later figures who have been treated so many times in so many histories. In providing a very brief analysis, we hope to indicate how the various themes and movements we have treated in *The Secularization of Scripture* could play out in future treatments of the better-known Old and New Testament scholars.

We begin with Lessing, a figure often taken in histories of scriptural scholarship as the originator of the radical critique of Scripture. It is hard for readers today to imagine the shock caused by the publication (between 1774 and 1778) of the Wolfenbüttel Fragments by Gotthold Lessing. Lessing himself was not the author, but one Hermann Samuel Reimarus (1694–1768). Reimarus lived a dual life, so to speak. He was an expert in Hebrew, but was actually admitted to the University of Wittenberg's Faculty of Philosophy based on his dissertation of 1532 on Machiavelli, *Abhandlung über Machiavellismus vor Machiavell.* Christoph Bultmann rightly wonders "how far this study of Machiavellianism may have influenced his understanding of history generally, and, more particularly, his later characterizations of the moral corruption of Israelite and Judean rulers as well as the political intentions of Jesus and the Apostles."[2]

Reimarus had read Toland's works, taking from him not only the implications of his treatment of Christianity, but also Toland's advice for "philosophers" to avoid bringing persecution upon themselves by stating openly what they really believe (an additional reason for Reimarus's caution in this regard, as his father-in-law, Johann Albrecht Fabricius, was a famous defender of orthodoxy). Rather than speaking equivocally in public, Reimarus set down his true thoughts only in private. Publically, he was

1 Henning Graf Reventlow and William Farmer, *Biblical Studies and the Shifting of Paradigms: 1850–1914* (Sheffield, England: Sheffield Academic Press, 1995).

2 Christoph Bultmann, "Early Rationalism and Biblical Criticism on the Continent," in Magne Sæbø, ed., *Hebrew Bible/Old Testament: The History of Its Interpretation:* Vol. II, *From the Renaissance to the Enlightenment* (Göttingen: Vandenhoeck & Ruprecht, 2008), Ch. 36, p. 879.

an orthodox apologist, supporting the moderate system of Christian Wolff, in which reason supported revelation (Wolff being significantly influenced by the "moderate" Locke); privately, the radical Enlightenment had fairly well shattered his faith, and he believed that reason contradicted revelation. The Wolfenbüttel Fragments represented his private thoughts as taken from a secret work, *Apologie oder Schutzschschrift für die vernünftigen Verehrer Gottes.*

Looking back, however shocking the Fragments were to pious Christians in Germany, they certainly contained nothing any more novel than we found in the radical Enlightenment figures of Spinoza's Netherlands or Toland's England nearly a century prior. That unorthodox thought had penetrated Germany and helped to form the German Enlightenment, which therefore had its own radical underside, as Spinozism and English Deism both made their way into the German intelligentsia.[3] Reimarus was not a lone rebel.

Long before Reimarus, Spinozism had been spread both by its detractors and by its admirers. In regard to its detractors, two important sources for early knowledge of Spinoza in Germany were Christian Kortholt's *De tribus impostoribus magnis liber* (1680)—the three imposters being Herbert of Cherbury, Hobbes, and Spinoza—and Pierre Bayle's *Dictionnaire historique et critique* (1697), appearing in German between 1741–1744. Obviously Kortholt's book, even though antagonistic to Spinoza, evidenced in the title a common knowledge in Germany of some form of the heterodox treatise *De tribus impostoribus*, a sign of how early heterodoxy had entered its borders. As for Bayle's portrait of Spinoza, as David Bell notes, "It enjoyed tremendous success and influence and was virtually standard reading among students at German universities."[4]

Sometimes detractors turned into advocates, like Johann Georg Wachter (1673–1757).[5] In 1699, a more popular work, critical of Spinoza, was printed by Wachter, *Der Spinozismus im Jüdenthumb, oder, die von dem heütigen Jüdenthumb, und dessen Geheimen Kabbala Vergötterte Welt*, in which he argued for a negative identity of

3 On the radical Enlightenment in Germany see Jonathan I. Israel, *Radical Enlightenment: Philosophy and the Making of Modernity 1650–1750* (Oxford: Oxford University Press, 2001), Ch. 34; Jean-Marie Vaysse, "*Spinoza dans la problématique de l'idéalisme allemande: Historicité et manifestation*," in André Tosel, Pierre-François Moreau, and Jean Salem, eds., *Spinoza au XIXe siècle* (Paris: Sorbonne, 2007), pp. 65–74; Martin Mulsow, "Libertinismus in Deutschland? Stile der Subversion in Politik, Religion und Literatur des 17. Jahrhunderts," *Zeitschrift für historische Forschung* 31 (2004), pp. 37–71; Martin Mulsow, *Moderne aus dem Untergrund. Radikale Frühaufklärung in Deutschland 1680–1720* (Hamburg: Meiner, 2002, *Habilitationsschrift*); Frederick C. Beiser, *The Fate of Reason: German Philosophy from Kant to Fichte* (Harvard: Harvard University Press, 2006); Siegfried Wollgast, "*Spinoza und die deutsche Frühaufklärung*," *Studia Spinozana* 9 (1992), pp. 163–179; Winfried Schroder, *Spinoza in der deutschen Frühaufklärung* (Wurzburg : Konigshausen + Neumann 1987); Thomas P. Saine, *The Problem of Being Modern, or, The German Pursuit of Enlightenment from Leibniz to the French Revolution* (Detroit, MI: Wayne State University Press, 1997).

4 David Bell, *Spinoza in Germany from 1670 to the Age of Goethe* (Leeds, England: Maney & Sons, 1984), p. 3.

5 On Wachter, see Israel, *Radical Enlightenment*, pp. 645–652, and Bell, *Spinoza in Germany from 1670 to the Age of Goethe*, pp. 16–17.

Judaism, the cabbala, and Spinozism, but did so on the basis of the superiority of natural religion to Judaism. The cabbalists had perverted natural religion precisely as had Spinoza, by identifying God and nature. Wachter later published a reversal, *Elucidarius Cabalisticus* (1706), in which the radical nature of his thought became clear. In it, Wachter argued (much like Toland) that true natural religion was known only by the philosophic few who controlled the vulgar by fantastic stories and feigned miracles.[6] The intense reaction to *Elucidarius* convinced Wachter that he had better take Tolandesque measures of self-protection, and work out his true views in private. As Jonathan Israel reports, Wachter worked on a manuscript (*De Primordiis Christianae religionis*) between 1703 and 1717 that, although not published, was destined to have a great effect via its clandestine manuscript circulation.

> Wachter seems indeed to have been the first to advance the idea which began to circulate with his manuscript and was later taken up by Voltaire and others, that Christianity originated in the Jewish sect of the Essenes and that Jesus, who "often reprehended the Pharisees and Sadducees but never the Essenes," was actually an Essene, a theory resurrected in the twentieth century with the discovery of the Dead Sea Scrolls. The Essenes, however, according to Wachter, were merely a link in the chain, their core teachings proclaiming love of God, of virtue, and of men, reaching back to the early Greek thinkers, who first glimpsed the truths of "natural religion" and passed on this priceless treasure camouflaged under diverse theological and philosophical terminologies until it could be more effectively spread through the esoteric, cabbalistic techniques of the Jews and finally reach its fullest and most majestic expression in Spinoza.[7]

One cannot help but call to mind the parallel effort on behalf of the Nazarenes undertaken by Toland in his *Nazarenus* (1718). Interestingly enough, Frederick the Great, king of Prussia (1740–1786), was convinced by Wachter's thesis.[8]

There were also, early on, fervent advocates of Spinoza in Germany. Matthew Knutzen (1646–74?), an avowed atheist, was influenced by Spinozism. Knutzen wrote three pamphlets, a Latin epistle, and two dialogues. Spinoza's biblical criticism "provided material for Knutzen's onslaught on the biblical canon, which occurs in all three pamphlets."[9]

Friedrich Wilhelm Stosch (1646–1704), "the first to use expressly Spinozistic terms and concepts positively"[10] in Germany, published clandestinely his *Concordia Rationis & Fidei Sive Harmonia Philosophiae Moralis & Religionis Christianae* in 1692. In it, Stosch showed clear evidence of firsthand knowledge of both Spinoza's *Ethics* and

6 Israel, *Radical Enlightenment*, p. 649.
7 Ibid., p. 651.
8 Ibid.
9 Bell, *Spinoza in Germany from 1670 to the Age of Goethe*, pp. 13–14.
10 Israel, *Radical Enlightenment*, p. 641.

Tractatus.[11] The same goes for Theodor Ludwig Lau (1670–1740) and his *Meditationes philosophicae de Deo, mundo et homine* (1717). Lau affirmed the identity of God and nature, and also set forth a thesis recalling the "three imposters" theme, implicating not only Moses, Mohammed, and Christ, but also Luther and Calvin, whom he considered to be frauds who used religion for social control.[12] Christian Gabriel Fischer (1683–1751), professor of natural philosophy at the University of Königsberg, was dependent on Spinoza's *Tractatus* for his biblical exegesis in his *Vernünftige Gedanken von der Natur* (1743).[13]

A most interesting and instructive example is Johann Christian Edelmann (1698–1767), "certainly the most audacious and notorious freethinker of the period."[14] Edelmann wrote an autobiography describing how he lost his faith. He had been quite willing to defend the infallibility of the Bible until he received a package from a friend in June 1740 that contained Spinoza's *Tractatus*. After reading it, Edelmann did an about-face, and went on the attack against orthodoxy, using the arguments of Spinoza. That same year he wrote *Moses mit Aufgedeckten Angesichte, Moses with his face unveiled*, in which he denied Mosaic authorship, pointed out a multitude of contradictions, and cited Ezra as the real, first editor of the biblical text. To drive home the radical critique, he included all three of Knutzen's acerbic atheistic pamphlets in full.[15]

Spinoza's *Ethics*, which provided the pantheistic philosophical framework undergirding the *Tractatus*, was not available in German until the publication of Johann Lorenz Schmidt's translation in 1744, which appeared along with a translation of Christian Wolff's refutation of Spinoza from his *Theologia naturalis* of 1737 "to get it past the censor."[16] Given all this, we can see that Reimarus's radicalism, however shocking, is understandable given the inroads made by Spinozism into Germany during the first half of the 1700s. Of course, Germany was also influenced by Deism. Deism entered Germany in much the same way as Spinozism, both as summarized by detractors and as propagated by enthusiasts. Reimarus read John Toland, Anthony Collins, Thomas Woolston, Thomas Chubb, and Matthew Tindal. There are exact parallels in the rationalistic argument of Reimarus and those that occur in Toland's *Christianity not Mysterious*.[17]

---

11 Bell, *Spinoza in Germany from 1670 to the Age of Goethe*, pp. 15–16.

12 See Israel, *Radical Enlightenment*, pp. 652–654, and Bell, *Spinoza in Germany from 1670 to the Age of Goethe*, p. 16.

13 Bell, *Spinoza in Germany from 1670 to the Age of Goethe*, p. 13.

14 Ibid., p. 17.

15 Ibid., pp. 17–18.

16 J. C. O'Neill, *The Bible's Authority: A Portrait Gallery of Thinkers from Lessing to Bultmann* (Edinburgh: T. & T. Clark, 1991), p. 14. On Schmidt's role here, see Jonathan I. Israel, *Enlightenment Contested: Philosophy, Modernity, and the Emancipation of Man 1670–1752* (Oxford: Oxford University Press, 2006), pp. 188–194; and Jonathan Sheehan, *The Enlightenment Bible: Translation, Scholarship, Culture* (Princeton: Princeton University Press, 2005), pp. 120–131.

17 See the Introduction to Charles Talbert, ed., *Reimarus: Fragments*, translated by Ralph Fraser (Chico, CA: Scholars Press, 1985), pp. 16–17.

The same Johann Lorenz Schmidt (1702–1749) who smuggled Spinoza's *Ethics* into Germany in translation as appended to Wolff's attack, also published a translation in 1741 of the English Deist Matthew Tindal's *Christianity as Old as the Creation* (1730). Schmidt well exhibited the complex, integral relationship between Deism and Spinozism, and that makes it worth treating him in a little more detail (along with the fact that his own fate as a radical would influence Reimarus).

Schmidt, a preacher's son, was turned to Deism through his devotion to Wolff. Much like Locke's, Wolff's moderate Christianity contained a kind of radical core that, whatever his intentions, led adherents to Deism and Spinozism, Schmidt himself being an obvious case in point.[18] Prior to publishing translations of Spinoza and Tindal, Schmidt had already created a furor in 1735 with the publication of the so-called Werthheim Bible, a German translation of the Pentateuch with his commentary. As Jonathan Israel notes, the Werthheim Bible "provoked a furious outcry all over Germany. For his text was obviously a systematic attempt to dilute, or explain away, everything miraculous in the Five Books, substituting uncompromisingly naturalistic explanations. Especially offensive . . . was his deliberate erasing of every (traditionally alleged) Old Testament reference to the future coming of Christ, and dismissal of the doctrine of the Holy Trinity, as unfounded and bogus."[19] In January 1737, the emperor and Imperial Chancery banned the book, and Schmidt was arrested in July, but then inadvertently released, after which he fled to Holland.

The lesson was not lost on Reimarus. As Christoph Bultmann maintains, "The fate of Johann Lorenz Schmidt . . . who suffered persecution in Germany after the publication of his annotated translation of the Pentateuch . . . may have been one reason why Reimarus began to write an apology for a purely rational form of worship of God."[20] Certainly it served as a warning, and contributed to Reimarus's dual existence as a public moderate and private radical. As with Toland, this dual existence had political implications relating directly to Reimarus's treatment of Scripture. Before penning his *Apology*, Reimarus had planned a six-part work, *Gedanken von der Freiheit eines vernünftigen Gottesdienstes*, outlining a natural religion, setting out a rationalist approach to exegesis of Scripture, and (just like Spinoza) ending with a plea for political toleration. According to Christoph Bultmann, "The work was obviously intended to function as an appeal for toleration and equal rights for those who were and those who were not able to overcome their doubts regarding the truth of biblical revelation. *In a study of Reimarus's biblical criticism this wider framework should not be neglected.*"[21] No one doubts the extraordinary influence of Reimarus on the history of scriptural scholarship and on the solidifying of the historical-critical method in the

18 On the ambiguous effect of Wolff see Israel, *Radical Enlightenment*, pp. 552–558.

19 Ibid., p. 553. For a more extensive account see Israel, *Enlightenment Contested*, pp. 188–194; Sheehan, *The Enlightenment Bible*, pp. 120–131; and Paul Spalding, *Seize the Book, Jail the Author: Johann Lorenz Schmidt and Censorship in Eighteenth-Century Germany* (West Lafayette, IN: Purdue University Press, 1998).

20 Bultmann, "Early Rationalism and Biblical Criticism on the Continent," p. 880.

21 Ibid., p. 880–881. Emphasis added.

nineteenth century. What is almost invariably overlooked, however, is that Reimarus's exegetical approach had woven into its method Spinoza's goal of political liberalism.

It was, to repeat, Gotthold Lessing who brought the radical Reimarus to light. Lessing imbibed Spinoza from Schmidt's translation of the *Ethics*, and was himself suspected of being yet another secret Spinozist.[22] We might get at Lessing's contribution to modern critical scholarship by saying that that he turned Spinoza, not on his head, but on his side. To be less cryptic, Lessing took the Averroistic vertical hierarchy stretching from the vulgar to the philosophic, which Spinoza took to be ineradicable, and set it horizontally, so that the hierarchy was stretched through history, the vulgar gradually becoming enlightened as they moved from needing wondrous events and imaginative metaphors (i.e., biblical stories) in order to grasp philosophical truths indirectly, to the more advanced stage of embracing the truths of reason directly.

That historical schema, spelled out in his "The Education of the Human Race," reveals the exact meaning of his famous words, the "*accidental truths of history can never become the proof of necessary truths of reason*."[23] The prescientific, the vulgar, can only appropriate rational truths through imaginative portrayals envisioned in a cosmos in which God intrudes to make His will and power known. Once humanity moves beyond this vulgar stage historically, they not only do not need the stories, but they realize that a cosmos with miracles is itself a vulgar, unphilosophical belief. As he puts it quite succinctly in "On the Proof of the Spirit and of Power," "I live in the eighteenth century, in which miracles no longer happen."[24] The cosmos has not changed; rather, humanity has accepted a "rational" cosmos, one that works machine-like according to the mathematical-mechanical laws of nature. There never could be any supernatural irruption, either of miracle or prophecy. The historical reports of miracles and prophecies we get in the Bible are therefore "accidental." Such "reports of fulfilled prophecies are not fulfilled prophecies . . . reports of miracles are not miracles." They are both *reports* of the vulgar. It is *historically* true that they *believed* they had witnessed miracles and prophetic utterances, but that is an accidental truth of history, not a necessary truth as known by philosophy. The unbridgeable gap between the vulgar and philosophic in Spinoza's vertical hierarchy thereby becomes "the ugly, broad ditch" between past and present of which Lessing famously declared, "I cannot get across, however often and however earnestly I have tried to make the leap."[25] At best the revelation in Scripture becomes something like "a very useful mathematical truth [that] had been reached by the discoverer through an obvious fallacy."[26]

Lessing's publication of Reimarus's Fragments caused an enormous uproar, making it clear to Lessing that his fellow Germans and other Europeans were not yet ready to dispense with the "historical truths" of the Gospel, that is, they were not yet

22 See Gérard Vallée, *The Spinoza Conversations between Lessing and Jacobi: Text with Excerpts from the Ensuing Controversy* (Lanham, MD: University Press of America, 1988).

23 Gotthold Lessing, "On the Proof of the Spirit and of Power," in Henry Chadwick, ed. and translator, *Lessing's Theological Writings* (Stanford, CA: Stanford University Press, 1956), p. 53.

24 Ibid., p. 52.

25 Ibid., p. 55.

26 Ibid., p. 56.

enlightened. For this reason—and here we cannot help but recall Spinoza's political finale to the *Tractatus*—Lessing affirmed the necessity of toleration, substituting as central to the new gospel the "Testament of John" ("Little children, love one another") for the doctrinally rich (and hence divisive) Gospel of John.[27] This allowed the intellectually advanced to live among the retrograde in political peace according to a merely moral creed.

Lessing therefore advanced a direct rationalistic attack on Scripture through the publication of Reimarus's Fragments, even while he seemed to set out a somewhat softer position. We say "softer" insofar as Lessing allowed "positive religions," i.e., particular religions defined by revelation in a precritical age, to play a tutorial position, educating humanity in its infancy. Revelation is not above reason, for "revelation gives nothing to the human race which human reason could not arrive at on its own," so that history is the "development of revealed truths into truths of reason" in three stages, the childhood (as evidenced in the Old Testament), the young adult (as evidenced in the New Testament), and finally the "third age," the philosophic age.[28] Rather than what is prior presenting a type for later fulfillment, Lessing assumes that each stage leaves the others behind: in the second age, the Old Testament is jettisoned, then in the third, the New likewise becomes superfluous.

It is a small leap from Lessing's view of history to the Hegelian dialectic, and yet another small step brings us to D. F. Strauss. Reimarus's entire *Apology* was not published. Interestingly, our knowledge both of Reimarus's life and the contents of the *Apology* come from a summary and biography written by the Hegelian David Friedrich Strauss (1808–1874) in 1861–1862, about a quarter century after Strauss published his *Life of Jesus Critically Examined* (1835). Strauss's *Life* is an acknowledged seminal text in the history of modern historical scholarship that (as we noted before) self-consciously embodied the mechanistic cosmology. This cosmology by definition denied the possibility of miracles, and so Strauss confidently (and influentially) relegated miracles to myths.

We repeat Strauss's words from the *Life of Jesus* that we have already quoted in our chapter on Descartes: an "account is not historical," and hence "the matter related could not have taken place in the manner described," wherein "the narration is irreconcilable with the known and universal laws which govern the course of events. Now according to these laws, agreeing with all just philosophical conceptions and all credible experience, the absolute cause never disturbs the chain of secondary causes by single arbitrary actions of interposition."[29] If it is not historical, then an account is mythical. By now, we recognize this as an effect of the radicalizing of Descartes by

27 Ibid., p. 56, and in the same edition, "The Testament of John," pp. 57–61. See also O'Neill's discussion of Lessing, *The Bible's Authority*, pp. 13–27; and Henning Graf Reventlow, *History of Biblical Interpretation: Volume 4: From the Enlightenment to the Twentieth Century* (Atlanta, GA: Society of Biblical Literature, 2010), pp. 165–175.

28 Gotthold Lessing, "The Education of the Human Race," in Chadwick, *Lessing's Theological Writings*, pp. 82–98; quotes, p. 83 (para. 4), p. 95 (para. 76), p. 97 (paras. 88–89).

29 Peter Hodgson, ed., David Friedrich Strauss, *The Life of Jesus Critically Examined*, fourth edition, (Philadelphia, PA: Fortress, 1972), Section 16, Introduction, pp. 87–88.

Spinoza. We also recognize its authority for Ernst Troeltsch's later essay, written at the close of the century, that Strauss so heavily influenced, "On Historical and Dogmatic Method in Theology." In it, (as we noted in the first chapter) Troeltsch cogently summarizes the assumption of the historical-critical method that miracles cannot occur and so must have other explanations.

But "mythical" had a particular meaning for Strauss, an undeveloped truth rather than a falsehood. Strauss embraced, via Hegel, the union of Spinoza's pantheistic immanentizing of the Divine and a spiritualized version of Bacon's salvific project of mastering nature through human technology, so that human technical-political progress in this world became the focus of a new secular salvation history as the realization of spirit's power over matter.[30] This secularization, since it finds its fulfillment in human political institutions and in the advance of human technical power over nature in the creation of a this-worldly new Eden, entails a deep politicization of the Bible. It also offers a kind of rarifying of Toland's cure of the essential tension between the vulgar and the philosophers, which Toland had himself borrowed from the Stoics (who, we recall, had "reduc'd all the fabulous and popular Theology to the natural, or so explain'd all the fables of the Poets and the Vulgar, as to have been originally meant of natural causes and effects"). For Toland, Stoic philosophers had protected themselves from the vulgar by refashioning myths according to philosophical truths that the vulgar could not possibly grasp. For Strauss (following Lessing and Hegel), the dialectic of history itself forges philosophical truths out of myths. And so, Jesus was not really resurrected. But His disciples truly and sincerely *came to believe* that He was, a psychological effect of their intense grief working on their desire that He be alive, a kind of wish fulfillment soon embellished by supportive passages from the Old Testament.[31] Christ therefore became not the fulfillment of Old Testament typology, but a kind of type Himself of the newly exalted divine-like power of humanity over nature that (to the nineteenth century) seemed so miraculous (even hinting at the promise of a kind of temporal immortality, if not for the individual, at least for the state).

From the perspective of our study, Strauss himself is the fulfillment of the "type" of Descartes and his project of mastering nature as laid out in the *Discourse*.

For the purposes of understanding the history of scriptural scholarship, we emphasize that Strauss gives us what Descartes lacked: a detailed exegesis of Scripture bent to the service of an entirely this-worldly, secular project, one where, as a consequence, Christian dogma as derived from Scripture is redefined accordingly, and humanity and human life in this world are divinized. Thus, for Strauss, what must be denied to Jesus Christ as a person is affirmed of the human race, as Spinoza's pantheism comes to be concentrated in humanity itself.

Nearer the end of his life, Strauss jettisoned any attempt to salvage Scripture, and embraced instead a purely secular Darwinian worldview. Or, to put it in the context of our study, Strauss dropped as entirely unnecessary the spiritual aspect of the Hegelian historical dialectic, and embraced the remainder, the historical development of matter

30 Ibid., Section 151, p. 779.

31 Ibid., 3.4.140, pp. 735–736, 742–743.

as culminating in the evolution of humanity, and the consequent human mastery of nature in turn. As we mentioned in regard to Toland, it was that thinker's pantheistic assumption that (contrary to Newton) nature itself had an inner dynamic energetic drive, thereby making it entirely unnecessary to posit an external, Newtonian-Deistic God as cause of nature's motions. Newtonian Deism, through the mediation of the Hegelian immanentizing of Spirit in matter, thereby gave way to purely material Darwinian evolutionism. At that point, Strauss realized, there was nothing left of the Old Religion that was salvageable, and so one must devote oneself to the New Religion of scientific materialism (as he outlined in his *Der alte und der neue Glaube* in 1872).[32]

So went Strauss. Let us step back again to the previous century and pick up another strand, beginning with Johann Salomo Semler (1725–1791). Recalling the first chapter, Semler's importance for the development of modern historical-critical scholarship is universally attested, but as we noted in treating Spinoza, Semler also published Lodewijk Meyer's *Philosophia S. Scripturae Interpres* in 1776. That introduces us to considerable ambiguity concerning Semler's contribution to the development of the historical-critical method.

Semler was a devoted pupil of Sigmund Jacob Baumgarten (1706–1757), who, somewhat like Reimarus, had a public and private religion, and who in the service of the latter provided a conduit of Deist thought to Germany.[33] As O'Neill points out, this duality was experienced directly by Semler, who often dined with Baumgarten. "Baumgarten at table in his own house revealed to his pupil something not easily discoverable from his public lectures: the complete distinction he made between public state religion and technical theology on the one hand, and private religion, the divine teaching leading to salvation, on the other hand. He also initiated Semler into English theology of the latitudinarian kind, with leanings toward socinianism. . . ."[34]

Semler exhibited the same kind of duality wherein the inner light of his father's pietism was (as had occurred with so many others) transformed into the inner light of reason. When the unorthodox Carl Friedrich Bahrdt was denied a theological chair, Semler "showed himself a strict upholder of the right of the Prussian state and the state's theological faculties to censor anti-Lutheran and unorthodox teaching," even though Semler "in fact shared most of Bahrdt's positions (as Bahrdt tartly remarked.)" It was, for Semler, "the duty of university theologians," who were servants of the state, "to maintain and uphold the local beliefs of the state they happened to serve."[35] As with our other figures, this duality must be taken into account when we assess his patrimony as one of the fathers of modern biblical scholarship.[36]

32 On Strauss's biblical interpretation see Reventlow, *History of Biblical Interpretation*, pp. 245–262.

33 See John Hayes, "Historical Criticism of the Old Testament Canon," in Magne Sæbø, ed., *Hebrew Bible/Old Testament: The History of Its Interpretation*, Vol. II, *From the Renaissance to the Enlightenment*, Ch. 42, p. 999.

34 O'Neill, *The Bible's Authority*, p. 39.

35 Ibid., pp. 41–42.

36 On Semler's place in the history of modern biblical criticism, see Reventlow, *History of Biblical Interpretation*, pp. 175–190; Anders Gerdmar, *Roots of Theological Anti-Semitism: German Biblical Interpretation and the Jews, from Herder and Semler to Kittel and Bultmann* (Leiden: Brill, 2008), pp. 39–50; Eric Carlsson,

Following Spinoza, Meyer, Locke, and the Deists, Semler declared that reason must adjudicate revelation. Part of this adjudication, for Semler, consisted in a form of Spinoza's hermeneutic of condescension as modified by Toland's distinction between esoteric and exoteric teaching.[37] Jesus only wished to teach the pure moral truth, but given the ignorance of his hearers, he needed (in Semler's words) to practice "a sort of *condescension*" in regard to the "many mistakes in the thinking of the hearers and readers. . . ." For Semler, this gap between inner moral truth and outward conformity to ignorance was itself evidence of a fundamental exegetical distinction between esoteric truth and accommodating exoteric beliefs—a distinction he found in Scripture. "Right at the beginning it is expressly noted in Mark 4:2 that Jesus taught the people only in parables . . . whereas when he was again *alone* and with his disciples he said, To you it is given to know and understand the mystery of the Kingdom of God, which I concede has been very unclearly presented in parables." And so, although Jesus did not believe in demons, he spoke as if he did for the sake of the vulgar.[38] (Like Hobbes, Semler was particularly emphatic about removing the demonic as irrational.)[39] The same was true, asserted Semler, for the Apostles, and in fact, the earliest "division" of Christians occurred between St. Paul, who preached the pure, spiritual religion, and the Judaizers, who tried to drag the esoteric message back to exoteric roots in the Old Testament (or who, like St. Peter, let it be dragged).[40] Little familiarity with the consequent history of modern biblical scholarship is necessary to recognize the importance of Semler's exegetical division between Judaizers and Gnostic philosophers. This division received support from Luther's long-standing and hence influential dialectical antagonism of New against the Old Testament (although the doctrine of "faith alone" was now transformed into "reason alone"), and also from the Spinozist Wachter (Semler maintaining that the tension preexisted Christ in the Hellenic and Hebraic Jews, the former sprouting the Essenes and coming to full flower in St. Paul[41]). It also anticipated the arguments of F. C. Baur.

Given that the fundamental truths of the spiritual religion are actually rational moral truths, the "accidental truths" of accommodation as contained in Scripture (if we may borrow from his contemporary Lessing) were not definitive for the revelation

---

"Johann Salomo Semler, the German Enlightenment and Protestant Theology's Historical Turn" (Ph.D. diss., University of Wisconsin-Madison, 2006); Sheehan, *The Enlightenment Bible*, pp. 114–115; and Gottfried Hornig, *Johann Salomo Semler. Studien zu Leben und Werk des Hallenser Aufklärungstheologen* (Tübingen: Niemeyer, 1996).

37 On accommodation in both Spinoza and Semler, see Peter G. Bietenholz, *Historia and Fabula: Myths and Legends in Historical Thought from Antiquity to the Modern Age* (Leiden: Brill, 1994), Ch. 6, and in Semler, see also William Baird, *History of New Testament Research, Vol. I: From Deism to Tübingen* (Minneapolis, MN: Fortress Press, 1992), pp. 123–124.

38 Quotes from Semler's *Versuch einer biblischen Dämonologie* (1776) in O'Neill, *The Bible's Authority*, p. 45.

39 See J. Blackwell, "Controlling the Demonic: Johann Salomo Semler and the Possession of Anna Elisabeth Lohmann (1759)," in W. Daniel Wilson and Robert C. Holub, *Impure Reason: Dialectic of Enlightenment in Germany* (Detroit, MI: Wayne State University Press, 1993), pp. 425–442.

40 O'Neill, *The Bible's Authority*, pp. 50–51.

41 Hayes, "Historical Criticism of the Old Testament Canon," pp. 1002–1003.

of the true, inner spiritual and rational religion (the real "Word of God").[42] There can be little doubt that Semler distinguishes between "Scripture" and the "Word of God," the latter being purely rational (in the Enlightenment sense, that is).

Since the esoteric truths can be had independently of Scripture, and, moreover, are not expressed everywhere in Scripture (because Scripture is shot through with accommodation to unenlightened beliefs of previous ages), then the very notion of a canon must be called into question. So declared Semler. Ironically, the historical impetus of Luther's canon within the canon undoubtedly helped prepare for Semler's reappropriation, albeit according to a much different spirit. Semler's spirit was entirely rationalist, and his aim was both to historicize the canon and to define a new canon according to moral works, not dogmatic faith.[43] In William Baird's apt words, "According to Semler, there is one primary test of canonicity: does the document convey universal, moral truth?"[44] As Semler remarks, in reading early church history

> one finally discovers that the canonical books . . . as little contain the universal unalterable complete sum of the Christian religion as those other books not in the canon: the Epistle of Barnabas, the writings of Hermas and of Clement in Rome. They are very good treatises for the first teachers in the then-prevailing circumstances; but any further decision, whether of the church or of many private Christians, that such-and-such a divinity attaches to these *canonical* writings has no part in the *universal content* of the Christian religion.[45]

Semler's rationale for questioning the whole notion of a canon recalls Spinoza's assertions about the very particular and peculiar way that the preenlightened are moved to moral belief. That particularity and peculiarity are what defined the "canon," not the Holy Spirit or reason. The result is that "such a judgment" of canonicity "is part of the local particular history of Christians." At best it instructs us about what moved *them* to believe, a merely historical fact—one that in turn forms an exegetical, winnowing *method* of approaching the biblical text. It is not difficult to see that the method is not neutral, but in fact merely reinforces Semler's assumption of particularity (which should make us skeptical of his hermeneutical dictum that an interpreter "should carry nothing into a text . . . out of his own thoughts"[46]).

Even more important for our purposes, Semler argued that the problem of particularity is not merely exegetical but political. Since these books are now taken to be canonical and entirely inspired—the particular and historical elevated to universality—they become the occasion for abuse and discord because believers "now use or misuse these books for their own cognition, for their own ends; and . . . now employ

42 Ibid., p. 1003.

43 Ibid., p. 1004.

44 Baird, *History of New Testament Research, Vol. I: From Deism to Tübingen*, p. 122.

45 Quote from Semler's *Neue Versuche die Kirchenhistorie der ersten Jahrhunderte mehr aufzuklären* (1788) in O'Neill, *The Bible's Authority*, p. 46.

46 From volume I of Semler's *Vorbereitung zur theologischen Hermeneutik* (1760–1761), as quoted in Baird, *History of New Testament Research, Vol. I: From Deism to Tübingen*, p. 125.

them against one another in order to present, once and for all, an exclusive summary of the Christian religion—namely, their own—; [and so] use them to put themselves over one another." This exegetical confusion causes serious political discord that can be cleared up *if* we understand the true esoteric moral teaching encased within the accidental exoteric shell, embracing the former and discarding the latter, for "it is quite certain that these Gospel narratives were all written only with the purpose of bringing those (who up till then were Jews) to the point where they could let go their traditions and opinions about a Messiah and follow their own moral judgment, concerning the God-pleasing destiny of his Son."[47]

In order to undo the damage, the exegete must reverse history by turning to history, and reduce what appear to be the "essential" dogmas of theology to the accidental truths of history (i.e., historicize them). A happy result of this procedure is that it will return individual believers to the original condition of toleration, of each being free to pick from the Scriptures what happens to move him theologically, as long as it serves only to inspire him to moral probity. One can hear the echo of Spinoza's liberalism in Semler's description of the original freedom of the first Christians and in his take-home lesson for his contemporaries.

> All readers were [originally] left free, according to their ability, to attach themselves to every one of these narratives, but this dependence of individual readers could not then become part of the universal and external new religion, in so far as this new religion itself had only just begun to take small steps upwards. The fact that the Church or the official teachers have made this a part of the essence or main content of the Christian religion on which should hang even the everlasting blessedness of all Christians: that belongs on the contrary to the history of the Church. . . . Of course individual Christians are free to affirm in their own mind the whole content, every line and every paragraph, however little they understand them, and thereby to make this the additional content of their own religion. But no Church, no teacher can elevate this to the genuine main content of the whole Christian religion of all time. From the nature of the case it is impossible. At the very least, all Christians who see this must remain utterly and completely free to distinguish between their present Christian knowledge and practice and what was once the knowledge and practice of those Christians who lived in Galatia, in Rome, etc.[48]

Of course, in arguing for complete toleration *and* in supporting the right of the Prussian state to define doctrine and the duty of state theologians to affirm the *religio* of the state, Semler was caught in a considerably ambiguous position—the very same position of both Hobbes and Spinoza. However, it was not a contradiction that undermined their position, but an ambiguity inherent in the gap between the enlightened few and the unenlightened many. The bid for toleration, and the consequent privatization of religion, were ways to move the state more toward the philosopher and away from the vulgar.

---

47 Quote from Semler's *Neue Versuche die Kirchenhistorie der ersten Jahrhunderte mehr aufzuklären* from O'Neill, *The Bible's Authority*, pp. 46–47.

48 Ibid., p. 47.

One of Semler's most famous and influential followers was Johann Gottfried Eichhorn (1752–1827), who is, of course, famous for laying the foundations (along with Jean Astruc before him) of the Documentary Hypothesis, dividing Genesis into J and E (which would later be subdivided into the more famous JEDP of Julius Wellhausen). But as with the question of Mosaic authorship, our focus is not solely on *how* he divided, but *why*.

Eichhorn studied at the University of Göttingen under Johann David Michaelis and the historian and philologist Christian Gottlob Heyne.[49] From Heyne he got an appreciation of the classical science of authenticating texts, especially the uncovering of different source layers, and also the notion that myth represents a prerational stage appropriate to primitive humanity. For Eichhorn, this allowed the enlightened exegete both to search out layers in the biblical text according to stages of intellectual development, and to offer rational reconstructions of the original events that later had become shrouded in mythical language. Our second stream is flowing toward D. F. Strauss as well.

As John Rogerson notes, this was an extension of Semler's notion of accommodation.[50] It is certainly reminiscent of Toland's account of providing a Stoic finesse to irrational religious myths, which "saved" the myths only by reinterpreting them in accordance with one's own philosophical predilections. And as O'Neill argues, it is reasonable to assume that Eichhorn's underlying philosophical assumptions were very close to Stoicism.[51] While this may seem an odd assessment, we must recall how close Toland's and the radical Enlightenment's pantheism was to classical Stoicism. As with Stoicism, the fundamental, life-giving, energizing element was fire, a philosophical position we saw duplicated both in Toland and the *Traité des trois Imposteurs*. The point is not that Eichhorn was a pantheist, but that as part of one philosophical framework, the Stoics were equally well known for making the esoteric-exoteric distinction championed centuries later by Toland, and, moreover, for affirming the need for philosophers to provide a rational retelling of irrational myths.

To cite one example of Eichhorn's Stoic finesse, he asserted that the story of the Fall, itself a myth, contains a germ of philosophic truth, one of the "basic principles of the highest wisdom" that "longing for another state of affairs which appears to be better is the final principle of human unhappiness."[52] The strange events of the Fall itself were not real, but (as Spinoza and Toland would have it) prescientific attempts to express something about purely natural events. So, for example, behind the Adam and Eve story, there was, suggested Eichhorn, a couple who had become aware of their sexuality after eating slightly poisoned fruit, and who had been consequently fright-

49 On Michaelis's important role in the history of biblical criticism, see Michael C. Legaspi, *The Death of Scripture and the Rise of Biblical Studies* (Oxford: Oxford University Press, 2010), especially Chs. 4–6; Rudolf Smend, *From Astruc to Zimmerli* (Tübingen: Mohr Siebeck, 2007), pp. 30–42; and Sheehan, *The Enlightenment Bible*, pp. 185–217.

50 John Rogerson, *Old Testament Criticism in the Nineteenth Century: England and Germany* (Philadelphia, PA: Fortress Press, 1985), p. 17.

51 O'Neill, *The Bible's Authority*, pp. 89–94.

52 Ibid., pp. 89–90.

ened away from their garden oasis by a thunderstorm that they interpreted as divine displeasure.[53] Prophecy was not itself divinely inspired, but simply the result of reason following out the lines of cause and effect, especially in regard to the usual consequences of moral actions. The hearers of the prophets took this reasoning power to be divine, because they were unaccustomed "to penetrate into the real causes of things" and so "believed [themselves] to perceive in those utterances the co-operation of a divinity."[54] Surely this was a more respectful treatment of the prophets than Spinoza's, but it was an entirely secular one nonetheless, one that sets the prophets as proto-rationalists against the liturgical-priestly ceremonialists. The prophets, as successors of Moses, were thereby cast by Eichhorn as deliverers from superstition, revealing how Israel, following the lead of the prophets, "could throw them [the "heavy burden of external rituals . . . and offerings"] away, and by an improved mind could make all offerings . . . superfluous." Prophecy becomes the vehicle for replacing revelation with entirely secular philosophy. We repeat Reventlow's incisive comment, one that speaks volumes: "Eichhorn [here] presents himself again as a genuine representative of Enlightenment!"[55]

For our purposes, it is important that this kind of rationalizing approach allowed Eichhorn to posit historical layers in the biblical text accordingly, from mythical to rational. In order to provide some kind of deeper textual unity to these layers, Eichhorn assumed that there were enlightened thinkers in the past (i.e., biblical writers or editors) who, realizing the immaturity of their hearers, accommodated their speech and writing to the vulgar. The task of the enlightened exegete was to ferret out the philosophical kernel that underlay the unenlightened layers. Against the alleged neutrality of the exegete, we are rightly suspicious of the pedigree of Eichhorn's philosophy after tracing it back through Semler, Toland, Spinoza, and so on. It would seem to be a philosophy with an agenda that defines the method.

If this kind of accommodation was used in the past, reasoned Eichhorn, it was just as necessary in his own time, for he himself held much more radical notions than he let on publicly. In O'Neill's words, Eichhorn thought that, "The task of enlightened men is to say as much of the truth as can be received at the time." He could speak publicly about the Garden of Eden as actual, but, "As Eichhorn later confessed, he did not really believe this was an historical sequence of events; he simply thought this sort of statement was the only way to lead his contemporaries a step towards the actual truth. The truth was that the story was a saga or myth; the only way primitive people could express philosophical truth was in mythical language." Since the people of his own

53 See Rogerson, *Old Testament Criticism in the Nineteenth Century: England and Germany*, pp. 17–18.

54 Quoted in Henning Graf Reventlow, "Towards the End of the 'Century of Enlightenment': Established Shift from *Sacra Scriptura* to Literary Documents and Religion of the People of Israel," in Magne Sæbø, ed., *Hebrew Bible/Old Testament: The History of Its Interpretation:* Vol. II, *From the Renaissance to the Enlightenment*, ch. 44, p. 1055.

55 Ibid.

time were as yet unready to give up their mythical beliefs, Eichhorn would condescend to bend his speech accordingly.[56]

With Eichhorn's affirmation of the mythical, we are heading once again to D. F. Strauss. There should be little doubt that in Strauss the various streams we have been following in this chapter, and indeed the entire book, come together; equally clear is that the contours of the streams are not neutral, but defined by the long-developing secular outlook we have traced. That makes the following words of Julius Wellhausen rather curious.

> Philosophy does not precede, but follows [biblical criticism], in that it seeks to evaluate and systematise that which it has not itself discovered. The authors of the two great theological works of 1835 [Strauss's *Life of Jesus* and Vatke's *Biblical Theology*] were Hegelians, it is true. But that which is of scholarly significance in them does not come from Hegel. Just as Vatke continues and completes the work of de Wette, so Strauss continues and completes that of the old rationalists. The particular value of the *Life of Jesus* lies not in the philosophical introduction and conclusion, but in the middle part, which is by far the largest section of the book.[57]

On Wellhausen's view, the philosophically heavy-laden beginning and end have no effect on Strauss's detailed exegetical procedure and conclusions. Given the anti-supernaturalist assumption that defines how Strauss wielded his method, one can be rightly skeptical of Wellhausen's easy dismissal of the charge that philosophical presuppositions define Strauss's exegetical method. If our own lengthy analysis has established anything, it is that philosophy *did* precede biblical criticism, and that is no less true in the time leading up to Wellhausen.

Eichhorn himself, who had helped birth the two-source hypothesis of Genesis that Wellhausen would bring to fruition, was professor of philosophy at Göttingen (1788–1827), where Wellhausen would later study theology and teach Old Testament. One can assume the spirit of Eichhorn still lingered. Moreover, as Reventlow states, Wellhausen's "arrangement of Israel's religious history into the three epochs of early religious freedom, the advance of the law with the appearance of Deuteronomy and the late hierocracy as the end of true religious life," was "itself a product of the prevailing intellectual climate. . . ."[58] He continues, "The three stage model of the history of Israel's religion that Wellhausen had made popular,

56 O'Neill, *The Bible's Authority*, p. 86. On the important place Eichhorn plays in the history of modern biblical criticism, see Reventlow, *History of Biblical Interpretation*, pp. 211–218 and 221–228; Pierre Gibert, *L'invention critique de la Bible: XVe–XVIIIe siècle* (Paris: Éditions Gallimard, 2010), pp. 305–306, 322–325, 327–331, 340–343, and 346–348; and Michael C. Legaspi, *The Death of Scripture*, p. 156.

57 Quoted in J. W. Rogerson, "Philosophy and the Rise of Biblical Criticism: England and Germany," in S. W. Sykes, ed., *England and Germany: Studies in Theological Diplomacy* (Frankfurt am Main: Verlag Peter D. Lang, 1982), pp. 63–79; quote on p. 63.

58 Henning Graf Reventlow, "The Role of the Old Testament in the German Liberal Protestant Theology of the Nineteenth Century," in Reventlow and Farmer, eds., *Biblical Studies and the Shifting of Paradigms: 1850–1914*, pp. 132–148; quote on p. 142.

in which the earliest period fitted to the Protestant ideal of religious freedom and the latest, post-exilic period was the stage of Jewish torpid legalism, formed the common picture of the Old Testament for a long time."[59] Reventlow obviously intends the Lutheran dialectical antithesis of Gospel versus Law as the remote background, but even more, he is calling attention to the influence of *liberal* Protestantism that had, for complex reasons, made peace with modern political liberalism (at least of a particular sort—as O'Neill points out, Wellhausen "thoroughly approved of the Prussian annexation of the Kingdom of Hannover and of Bismarck's aggressive policy to establish a great German nation").[60]

In regard to political liberalism, as we recall, a common feature running from Marsilius through Hobbes, Spinoza, and Toland was the denigration of the priesthood because the primacy of the priesthood implied a primacy of the sacred over the secular, the priest over the king. Whatever Wellhausen's intentions, dividing the Old Testament up into four sources, JEDP, and casting the Priestly as a later, artificial constriction and deformation of an earlier, better form of worship, accomplished the very result, exegetically, aimed at by the most adamantly secular thinkers we have covered. In so doing, it would appear that Wellhausen functioned like Ockham and Luther, unintentionally aiding a purely secular reconstruction of religion.

Yet one wonders about Wellhausen's innocence. His picture of the earliest worship found in the Old Testament seems more natural than supernatural, more Deist than Protestant. In his *Prolegomena to the History of Ancient Israel* (1883), Wellhausen asserted:

> In the early days, worship arose out of the midst of ordinary life, and was in most intimate manifold connection with it. A sacrifice was a meal, a fact showing how remote was the idea of antithesis between spiritual earnestness and secular joyousness. . . . Religious worship was a natural thing in Hebrew antiquity; it was the blossom of life, the heights and depths of which it was its business to transfigure and glorify.[61]

The assumption of the simplicity of the ancient cult came from W.M.L. de Wette (1780–1849). De Wette's *Contributions to Old Testament Introduction* (1806–1807) "is the first work of Old Testament scholarship to use the critical method in order to present a view of the history of Israelite religion that is radically at variance with the view implied in the Old Testament itself." As with Wellhausen after him, de Wette maintained that the priesthood was a late, post-exilic institution, one that attempted

59 Ibid., pp. 147–148.

60 O'Neill, *The Bible's Authority*, p. 199. On Wellhausen's political commitments and his importance for biblical criticism, see also Reventlow, *History of Biblical Interpretation*, pp. 311–325; Smend, *From Astruc to Zimmerli*, pp. 91–102; James Pasto, "Who Owns the Jewish Past? Judaism, Judaisms, and the Writing of Jewish History" (Ph.D. diss., Cornell University, 1999), pp. 151–260; and Arnaldo Momigliano, "Religious History without Frontiers: J. Wellhausen, U. Wilamowitz, and E. Schwartz," *History and Theory* 21.4 (1982), pp. 49–64.

61 Julius Wellhausen, *Prolegomena to the History of Ancient Israel* (Cleveland, OH: Meridian Books, 1957), Ch. II.iii, pp. 76–77.

to vindicate its existence through the re-editing of Israel's more ancient documents. De Wette sought to peel back the priestly editorial layers to get at the original religion before it was overlaid with later accretions. In almost the exact words Wellhausen would later use, de Wette maintained that no developed priesthood existed in the earliest times. In the early period, "There is a complete freedom of worship. As among the Patriarchs and the Homeric Greeks, God's open heaven was his temple, each meal a sacrifice, each festive and important event a festival, and each prophet, king and father of household was without further qualification a priest."[62]

Again, denigration of the priesthood, or rather, the assertion of a priesthood of believers, was certainly Luther's hallmark. But we also recall that Spinoza presented the initiation of the Levitical priesthood as the downfall of the Israelites from the original condition where fathers were the priests of the family. Was de Wette's assertion, then, theological or philosophical, indebted to Luther or to Spinoza?

It was philosophical, as de Wette's quasi-autobiographical novel, *Theodore, or the Doubter's Ordination* (1821) makes clear. In it, Theodore hears the lectures of a Kantian—in real life, the lectures de Wette heard at the University of Jena by the Kantian Jakob Friedrich Fries—and he undergoes a "conversion." The "lectures on morals from a Kantian philosopher" opened up a "new world . . . to him."

> The notions of the self-sufficiency of reason in its lawgiving, of the freedom of the will through which he was elevated above nature and fate, of the altruism of virtue which was its own justification and sought no reward, of pure obedience to the self-given moral law: all these notions gripped him powerfully, and filled him with a high self-awareness. Those shadowy ideas about love of God and of Christ, about the new birth, about the rule of God's grace in the human mind, all of which he still carried from the instruction of his schoolmaster, these he translated into this new philosophical language, and so they appeared to him clearer and more certain.[63]

In short, de Wette's conversion was a kind of Stoic-Kantian reinterpretation of traditional Lutheran theology that made it compatible with fundamentally philosophical conceptions even while appearing under the guise of the old theological language. De Wette's religious raptures owe more, ultimately, to Kant's *Critique of Judgement* than a real recovery of ancient religion. We do not have to retrace the historical connections between Hobbes, Spinoza, Locke, through the eighteenth century to Hume and finally to Kant to make the quite simple point (against Wellhausen) that a particular philosophy *preceded* de Wette's biblical criticism and significantly determined its outcome; that is, the "history" of Israel as he understood it depended upon what de Wette himself considered more philosophically pristine, or perhaps better (given the indebtedness to Kant through Fries), more *sublime*. As with the Deists, it was an essentially moral vision of religion, but given that in Kant de Wette

62 From de Wette's *Beiträge zur Einleitung in das Alte Testament*, Vol. I, as quoted in John Rogerson, *Old Testament Criticism in the Nineteenth Century: England and Germany*, pp. 32–33.

63 Quoted in ibid., pp. 36–37.

allows sublimity to act as a kind of aesthetic attractant to morality, drawing us to the cold rigor of duty.

Whatever de Wette's intentions, his philosophical presuppositions aided the already existing tendency (birthed in Hobbes and Spinoza) to reverse a forward-moving Divine Economy—one that created, in turn, an inversion of typology. If priestly aspects came later, then God was not moving history to a fulfillment in the Church; therefore, forward-looking typological considerations of the text must give way to backward-looking critical analysis of the layers of editing in which each is marked according to a preestablished view of what must be earlier and what must be a contaminant.[64] As Rogerson asserts, "it must be observed that his *philosophical* position did not permit him to see history as a process in which divine purpose was being unfolded," that is, "it was the unwillingness of the Friesian system to allow that history is a purposive process that enabled de Wette to make such radical proposals about the history of Israel; to suggest that there was a radical divergence between the Old Testament story and what could be known about the actual facts."[65] Again, Wellhausen's easy assurance that philosophy did not impinge upon exegetical methods in his predecessors does not stand up to scrutiny.

One might well ask what this all has to do with politicizing the text. While the analysis of politicization would be as complex in nineteenth-century Germany as we found it in late seventeenth-century Britain, we may at least point out some important aspects. The latter half of the nineteenth century is marked by the task, managed by Bismarck, of unifying Germany, a largely Protestant country but with a significant Catholic majority. Of obvious importance in this regard is the *Kulturkampf*, the struggle between Bismarck and the Catholic hierarchy (1870–1880). Obviously a kind of liberal Protestant notion of a pure, original Judaism that was only later contaminated by an elaborate centralized priesthood would be an exegetical support for a repudiation of Catholicism and an affirmation of Protestantism.

In the same political light, we may view the development of the historical-critical affirmation of the priority of Mark over Matthew. As William Farmer notes, German universities, including the theological faculties, were under control of the state, a situation we saw developing under Luther. It must be understood that it was "the German

64 On de Wette's significance within the history of biblical criticism, the anti-Jewish animus, and philosophical background to his work, see Reventlow, *History of Biblical Interpretation*, pp. 231–245; Gerdmar, *Roots of Theological Anti-Semitism*, pp. 77–94; J. W. Rogerson, "Setting the Scene: A Brief Outline of Histories of Israel," *Proceedings of the British Academy* 143 (2007), pp. 3–14, especially pp. 5–7; Smend, *From Astruc to Zimmerli*, pp. 43–56; Thomas Albert Howard, *Religion and the Rise of Historicism: W.M.L. de Wette, Jacob Burckhardt, and the Theological Origins of Nineteenth-Century Historical Consciousness* (Cambridge: Cambridge University Press, 2000); James Pasto, "Islam's 'Strange Secret Sharer': Orientalism, Judaism, and the Jewish Question," *Comparative Studies in Society and History*, 40.3 (1998), pp. 437–474, esp. pp. 442–446 and 448; and John W. Rogerson, *W.M.L. de Wette: Founder of Modern Biblical Criticism: An Intellectual Biography* (Sheffield: Sheffield Academic Press, 1992).

65 Rogerson, *Old Testament Criticism in the Nineteenth Century: England and Germany*, pp. 48–49. Emphasis added.

university system and more precisely German science or *Deutsche Wissenschaft* that was to provide the *magisterium* (that is the final court of appeal) in the ideological struggle for the salvation of the German nation."[66] We must therefore take into account the "influence of the ideological needs of society upon literary interpretation," even though biblical scholars routinely ignore this aspect of the history of biblical scholarship.

What were, then, Germany's needs? Biblical faith was still considered necessary to the maintenance of public order, but how could it be made credible, and hence still effective, in an age of science? The first need was to make biblical exegesis seem more scientific. "In the nineteenth century, one science that provided some ruling models was biology. Since life appeared to develop from simpler forms into ever more complicated forms, it became credible to think of literary forms as developed from simple to the complex." That is, Darwinism (which was itself indebted philosophically to Spinozism as modified by Toland) had scientific authority; biblical science could then imitate the evolutionary model for credibility, where one moves from simple to complex, J to P, Mark to Matthew.[67] The second ideological need was theological. In order to be of service to "a Protestant dominated Empire led by a Protestant Kaiser," where papal power had to be curtailed, biblical studies had to support an anti-Catholic notion of development—or better, devolution—from pristine purity to decadence. Third, and seemingly at odds with the second need, was that even after external influence by the papacy was eliminated, scholarship had to support a broad-based political regime consisting of Protestant, Catholic, and Jewish elements on liberal terms, ones that minimized doctrinal differences so that "following the Enlightenment . . . all [were] recognized as citizens of the Second Reich."[68] This allowed a kind of liberalism that, to its merit, also helped blunt anti-Semitism (by, for example, demoting Matthew's harsh words against his fellow Jews[69]). Yet, even with this benefit, we cannot avoid the fact that the aim of this kind of exegesis was, in Farmer's words, a kind of *political accommodation*. "Nineteenth-century Biblical criticism served German society well in enabling it to meet these pressing ideological needs. The state supported universities facilitated the inevitable process of intellectual accommodation and/or assimilation. . . . Enlightenment Biblical criticism which became state supported Biblical scholarship smoothed the way for this accommodation."[70]

Does that then mean that the JEDP hypothesis, along with the notion of the historical primacy of the Gospel of Mark—and all the scholarship that supports them—are hopelessly mired in nineteenth-century political ideology? This would certainly be too hasty a conclusion. But at least we can say this: Given what we have uncovered about the complexity of the history of scriptural scholarship up to the early eighteenth century, and our short synopsis of the development since then, we have every

66 William Farmer, "State *Interesse* and Markan Primacy: 1870–1914," in Reventlow and Farmer, eds., *Biblical Studies and the Shifting of Paradigms: 1850–1914*, pp. 15–49; quote on p. 21.

67 Ibid., p. 22.

68 Ibid., p. 23.

69 Ibid., p. 24.

70 Ibid.

reason to believe that significantly more detailed studies of the politicizing aspects of nineteenth-century scriptural scholarship are called for, and only such studies can hope to disentangle the legitimate tools of the historical-critical method from the various political and secular aims. We hope that this work of ours, focusing on the six oft-neglected centuries leading up to the nineteenth, will help prepare scholars to undertake just such studies.

BIBLIOGRAPHY

Adams, Marilyn McCord. *William Ockham*, Volume I. Notre Dame: University of Notre Dame Press, 1987.

Anderson, Abraham. *The Treatise of the Three Impostors and the Problem of Enlightenment: A New Translation of the* Traité des trois Imposteurs *(1777 Edition), with Three Essays in Commentary*. Lanham: Rowman & Littlefield, 1997.

Anonymous. *True Effigies of the Monster of Malmesbury: or, Thomas Hobbes in His Proper Colours*. 1680.

Aquinas, St. Thomas. *The Division and Methods of the Sciences*. Toronto, Ontario: Pontifical Institute of Mediaeval Studies, 1986, fourth revised edition.

———. *Summa Theologiae*. Five volumes. Westminster, MD: Christian Classics, 1981.

Aristotle. *Eudemian Ethics*. In *Athenian Constitution. Eudemian Ethics. Virtues and Vices*. Translated by H. Rackham. Loeb Classical Library. Cambridge: Harvard University Press, 1935.

———. *Aristotle's Nicomachean Ethics*. Translated by Hippocrates G. Apostle. Grinnell, IA: The Peripatetic Press, 1984.

———. *Politics*. Translated by Carnes Lord. Chicago: University of Chicago Press, 1984.

Ashcraft, Richard. *Revolutionary Politics & Locke's Two Treatises of Government*. Princeton: Princeton University Press, 1986.

Ashley, Maurice. *The Greatness of Oliver Cromwell*. New York: Collier Books, 1962.

Assmann, Jan. *Moses the Egyptian: The Memory of Egypt in Western Monotheism*. Cambridge: Harvard University Press, 1997.

Aubrey, John. *Aubrey's Brief Lives*. Edited by Oliver Lawson Dick. Ann Arbor, MI: University of Michigan Press, 1957.

Augustine, *Political Writings*. Translated by Michael Tkacz and Douglas Kries. Indianapolis, IN: Hackett Publishing Company, Inc., 1994.

Averroes. *Averroes' Tahafut Al-Tahafut*, Volumes I and III. Translated by Simon Van Den Bergh. Cambridge: Cambridge University Press, 1987.

———. *The Book of the Decisive Treatise: Determining the Connection Between the Law and Wisdom*. Translated by Charles Butterworth. Provo, UT: Brigham Young University Press, 2001.

Bacon, Francis. *The Advancement of Learning*. In *The Major Works*. Edited by Brian Vickers. Oxford: University of Oxford Press, 1996.

———. *The Great Instauration*. In *The New Organon and Related Writings*. Edited by Fulton Anderson. New York: Macmillan Publishing Company, 1988.

———. *The Major Works*. Oxford: University of Oxford Press, 1996.

Baillie, Robert. *Letters and Journals of Robert Baillie*. Edited by David Laing. Edinburgh: A. Lawrie, 1841–42.

Baird, William. *History of New Testament Research, Volume I: From Deism to Tübingen*. Minneapolis, MN: Fortress Press, 1992.

Barr, James. *History and Ideology in the Old Testament: Biblical Studies at the End of a Millennium*. Oxford: Oxford University Press, 2000.

———. "Interpretation, History of Modern Biblical Criticism." In *The Oxford Companion to the Bible*. Edited by Bruce M. Metzger and Michael D. Coogan. Oxford: Oxford University Press, 1993.

Bartholomew, Craig G. "Uncharted Waters: Philosophy, Theology and the Crisis in Biblical Interpretation." In *Biblical Interpretation*. Edited by Craig Bartholomew, Colin Greene, and Karl Möller. Grand Rapids, MI: Zondervan, 2000.

Barton, John. *The Old Testament: Canon, Literature and Theology*. Aldershot: Ashgate, 2007.

———. *The Nature of Biblical Criticism*. Louisville: Westminster/John Knox Press, 2007.

Bartuschat, Wolfgang. "The Ontological Basis of Spinoza's Theory of Politics." In *Spinoza's Political and Theological Thought*. Edited by C. De Deugd. Amsterdam, Oxford: North-Holland, 1984.

Bayle, Pierre. *Historical and Critical Dictionary, Selections*. Translated by Richard Popkin. Indianapolis, IN: Hackett Publishing, 1991.

Beiser, Frederick C. *The Fate of Reason: German Philosophy from Kant to Fichte*. Harvard: Harvard University Press, 2006.

Bell, David. *Spinoza in Germany from 1670 to the Age of Goethe*. Leeds, England: Maney & Sons, 1984.

Benin, Stephen. *The Footprints of God: Divine Accommodation in Jewish and Christian Thought*. Albany, NY: SUNY Press, 1993.

Bentley, Jerry. "Biblical Philology and Christian Humanism: Lorenzo Valla and Erasmus as Scholars of the Gospel." *Sixteenth Century Journal* 8, no. 2 (1977).

———. *Humanists and Holy Writ: New Testament Scholarship in the Renaissance*. Princeton: Princeton University Press, 1983.

Berman, David. "Disclaimers as Offence Mechanisms in Charles Blount and John Toland." In Michael Hunter and David Wootton, *Atheism from the Reformation to the Enlightenment*. Oxford: Oxford University Press, 1992.

Berti, Silvia. "The First Edition of the *Traité des trois imposteurs*, and its Debt to Spinoza's *Ethics*." In Michael Hunter and David Wootton, *Atheism from the Reformation to the Enlightenment*. Oxford: Clarendon Press, 1992.

———. *Trattato dei tre Impostori: La vita e lo spirito del Signor Benedetto de Spinoza*. Torino: Giulio Einaudi, 1994.

Biddle, John. "Locke's Critique of Innate Principles and Toland's Deism." *Journal of the History of Ideas* 37 (1976).

Bietenholz, Peter G. *Historia and Fabula: Myths and Legends in Historical Thought from Antiquity to the Modern Age*. Leiden: Brill, 1994.

Black, Ladbroke. *The Love Letters of Henry the Eighth*. London: Blandford Press, Ltd., 1933.

Blackwell, J. "Controlling the Demonic: Johann Salomo Semler and the Possession of Anna Elisabeth Lohmann (1759)." In W. Daniel Wilson and Robert C. Holub, *Impure Reason: Dialectic of Enlightenment in Germany*. Detroit, MI: Wayne State University Press, 1993.

Blenkinsopp, Joseph. *The Pentateuch: An Introduction to the First Five Books of the Bible*. New York: Doubleday, 1992.

Bloch, Marc. *The Royal Touch: Sacred Monarchy and Scrofula in England and France*. London: Routledge, 1973.

Bobrick, Benson. *Wide as the Waters: The Story of the English Bible and the Revolution It Inspired*. New York: Simon & Schuster, 2001.

Bock, Gisela, Quentin Skinner, and Maurizio Viroli. *Machiavelli and Republicanism*. Cambridge: Cambridge University Press, 1990.

Boehner, Philotheus, O.F.M. *Ockham: Philosophical Writings*. Indianapolis, IN: Hackett, 1990.

———. "The Realistic Conceptualism of William Ockham." In E. M. Buytaert, *Philotheus Boehner, O.F.M., Ph.D.: Collected Articles on Ockham*. St. Bonaventure, NY: The Franciscan Institute, 1958.

Bonney, Richard. *The Thirty Years' War 1618–1648*. Oxford: Osprey Publishing, 2002.

Bossy, John. "Met on the *Via Moderna*." In Peter Biller and Barrie Dobson, *The Medieval Church: Universities, Heresy, and the Religious Life: Essays in Honour of Gordon Leff*. Woodbridge, Suffolk: The Boydell Press, 1999.

Bowle, John. *Hobbes and His Critics: A Study in Seventeenth Century Constitutionalism*. New York: Barnes & Noble, 1969.

Boyer, A. *The political state of Great Britain* XXIII (1722). In Justin Champion, *Republican Learning: John Toland and the Crisis of Christian Culture, 1696–1722*. Manchester and New York: Manchester University Press, 2003.

Boyer, Carl. *A History of Mathematics*, second ed. New York: John Wiley & Sons, Inc., 1991.

Bramhall, John. *Castigations of Mr. Hobbes*. New York & London: Garland Publishing, 1977.

Bray, Gerald, ed. *Documents of the English Reformation*. Minneapolis, MN: Fortress Press, 1994.

Brecht, Martin. *Martin Luther: His Road to Reformation, 1483–1521*. Translated by James Schaaf. Philadelphia, PA: Fortress Press, 1985.

———. *Martin Luther: The Preservation of the Church, 1532–1546*. Translated by James Schaaf. Minneapolis, MN: Fortress Press, 1993.

Brown, Alison. "Savonarola, Machiavelli and Moses." In *The Medici in Florence: The Exercise and Language of Power*. Perth: University of W. Australia, 1992.

Bruno, Giordano. *The Expulsion of the Triumphant Beast*. Translated by Arthur Imerti. Lincoln, NE: University of Nebraska Press, 2004.

Bruns, Gerald. *Hermeneutics Ancient and Modern*. New Haven: Yale University Press, 1992.

Bultmann, Christoph. "Early Rationalism and Biblical Criticism on the Continent." In *Hebrew Bible/Old Testament: The History of Its Interpretation:* Volume II, *From the Renaissance to the Enlightenment*. Edited by Magne Sæbø. Göttingen: Vandenhoeck & Ruprecht, 2008.

Burns, Norman. *Christian Mortalism from Tyndale to Milton*. Cambridge: Harvard University Press, 1972.

Calvin, John. *Institute of the Christian Religion*. Translated by Ford Lewis Battles. Philadelphia, PA: Westminster Press, 1960.

Carlsson, Eric. "Johann Salomo Semler, the German Enlightenment and Protestant Theology's Historical Turn." Ph.D. diss., University of Wisconsin-Madison, 2006.

Carraud, V. "Les références scripturaires du corpus cartésien." *Bulletin Cartésien* XVIII, Liminaire II, *Archives de Philosophie* 53.1 (1990).

Cassirer, Ernst. *The Philosophy of the Enlightenment*. Translated by Fritz Koelln and James Pettegrove. Princeton: Princeton University Press, 1951.

Catto, J. I. "John Wyclif and the Cult of the Eucharist." In *The Bible in the Medieval World: Essays in Memory of Beryl Smalley*. Oxford: Basil Blackwell, 1985.

————. "Wyclif and Wycliffism at Oxford, 1356–1430." In *The History of the University of Oxford: Vol II, Late Medieval Oxford*. Edited by J. I. Catto and Ralph Evans. Oxford: Clarendon Press, 1992.

Cavanaugh, William T. "'A Fire Strong Enough to Consume the House': The Wars of Religion and the Rise of the State." *Modern Theology* 11 (1995).

————. *The Myth of Religious Violence: Secular Ideology and the Roots of Modern Conflict*. Oxford: Oxford University Press, 2009.

Champion, Justin A. I. "Apocrypha, Canon and Criticism from Samuel Fisher to John Toland, 1650–1718." In *Judaeo-Christian Intellectual Culture in the Seventeenth Century*. Edited by Allison Coudert, et al. Dordrecht: Kluwer Academic Publishers, 1999.

————. "Legislators, impostors, and the politic origin of religion: English theories of 'imposture' from Stubbe to Toland." In Silvia Berti, Françoise Charles-Daubert, and Richard Popkin, *Heterodoxy, Spinozism, and Free Thought in the Early-Eighteenth-Century Europe: Studies on the* Traité des Trois Imposteurs. Dordrecht: Kluwer Academic Publishers, 1996.

————. "Pere Richard Simon and English Biblical Criticism, 1680–1700." In James Force and David Katz, *Everything Connects: In Conference with Richard Popkin*. Leiden: E. J. Brill, 1999.

————. *The Pillars of Priestcraft Shaken: The Church of England and its Enemies, 1660–1730*. Cambridge: Cambridge University Press, 1992.

————. *Republican Learning: John Toland and the Crisis of Christian Culture, 1696–1722*. Manchester and New York: Manchester University Press, 2003.

Cicero. *De Natura Deorum*. In *On the Nature of the Gods* (*De Natura Deorum*), *Academica*. Translated by H. Rackham. Loeb Classical Library. Cambridge: Harvard University Press, 1933.

Cohn, Norman. *The Pursuit of the Millennium: Revolutionary Millenarians and Mystical Anarchists of the Middle Ages*, revised ed. New York: Oxford University Press, 1970.

Cole, John R. *The Olympian Dreams and Youthful Rebellion of René Descartes*. Urbana and Chicago: University of Illinois Press, 1992.

Colie, Rosalie. *Light and Enlightenment: A Study of the Cambridge Platonists and the Dutch Arminians*. Cambridge: Cambridge University Press, 1957.

Cooke, Paul. *Hobbes and Christianity: Reassessing the Bible in Leviathan*. Lanham, MD: Rowan & Littlefield, 1996.

Copeland, Rita. "Rhetoric and the Politics of the Literal Sense in Medieval Literary Theory: Aquinas, Wyclif, and the Lollards." In *Interpretation: Medieval and Modern*. Edited by Piero Boitani and Anna Torti. Cambridge: D. S. Brewer, 1993.

Cottingham, John, ed. *The Cambridge Companion to Descartes*. Cambridge: Cambridge University Press, 1992.

Courtenay, William."The Academic and Intellectual Worlds of Ockham." In *The Cambridge Companion to Ockham*. Edited by Paul Vincent Spade. Cambridge: Cambridge University Press, 1999.

———. "Nominalism and Late Medieval Religion." In Charles Trinkaus and Heiko Oberman, *The Pursuit of Holiness in Late Medieval and Renaissance Religion*. Leiden: Brill, 1974.

———. "The Role of English Thought in the Transformation of University Education in the Late Middle Ages." In James Kittelson and Pamela Transue, *Rebirth, Reform and Resilience: Universities in Transition, 1300–1700*. Columbus, OH: Ohio State University Press, 1984.

———. "University Masters and Political Power: The Parisian Years of Marsilius of Padua." In *Politische Reflexion in Der Welt Des Späten Mittelalters/Political Thought in the Age of Scholasticism*. Edited by Martin Kaufhold. Leiden: Brill, 2004.

———. "Was There an Ockhamist School?" In *Philosophy and Learning: Universities in the Middle Ages*. Edited by Maarten Hoenen, J. J. Josef Schneider, and Georg Wieland. Leiden: Brill, 1995.

Cranston, Maurice. *John Locke: A Biography*. Oxford: Oxford University Press, 1985.

Curley, Edwin. "Kissinger, Spinoza, and Genghis Kahn." In *The Cambridge Companion to Spinoza*. Edited by Don Garrett. Cambridge: Cambridge University Press, 1996.

———. "Notes on a Neglected Masterpiece: Spinoza and the Science of Hermeneutics." In *Spinoza: The Enduring Questions*. Edited by Graeme Hunter. Toronto: University of Toronto Press, 1994.

———. "The State of Nature and Its Law in Hobbes and Spinoza." *Philosophical Topics* 19 (1991). Reprinted in *Spinoza: Critical Assessments. Volume III: The Political Writings*. Edited by Genevieve Lloyd. London and New York: Routledge, 2001.

Dahmus, Joseph. *The Prosecution of John Wyclyf*. New Haven: Yale University Press, 1952.

Daly, Lowrie J. *The Political Theory of John Wyclif*. Chicago, IL: Loyola University Press, 1962.

D'Amico, John. "Ulrich von Hutten and Beatus Rhenanus as Medieval Historians and Religious Propagandists in the Early Reformation." In *Roman and German Humanism, 1450–1550*. Brookfield, VT: Variorum, 1993.

Daniel, Stephen. *John Toland: His Methods, Manners, and Mind*. Kingston and Montreal: McGill-Queen's University Press, 1984.

Davies, Alan. *Infected Christianity: A Study of Modern Racism*. Kingston and Montreal: McGill-Queen's University Press, 1988.

Davis, Charles T. "Ockham and the Zeitgeist." In Charles Trinkaus and Heiko Oberman, *The Pursuit of Holiness in Late Medieval and Renaissance Religion*. Leiden: Brill, 1974.

De Deugd, C., ed. *Spinoza's Political and Theological Thought*. Amsterdam, Oxford: North-Holland, 1984.

de Grazia, Sebastian. *Machiavelli in Hell*. New York: Vintage, 1994.

de La Monnoye, Bernard. "Sentiments Concerning the *Treatise of the Three Impostors*: Extract of a Letter or Dissertation of Mr. de La Monnoye on this Subject." In Abraham Anderson, *The Treatise of the Three Impostors and the Problem of Enlightenment: A New Translation of the* Traité des trois Imposteurs *(1777 Edition), with Three Essays in Commentary*. Lanham: Rowman & Littlefield, 1997.

Descartes, René. *Discourse on Method* and *Meditations on First Philosophy*. Indianapolis, IN: Hackett Publishing Company, 1980.

———. *Discourse on Method*. Translated with an interpretive essay by Richard Kennington. Newburyport, MA: R. Pullins Company, 2007.

———. *Philosophical Essays: Discourse on Method; Meditations; Rules for the Direction of the Mind*. Translated by Laurence Lafleur. New York: Macmillan Publishing Company, 1964.

Desharnais, Richard. "Scholasticism, Nominalism, and Martin Luther." In *Studies in Philosophy and the History of Philosophy*. Edited by John Ryan. Washington, DC: Catholic University of America Press, 1969.

Dickens, A. G. *The English Reformation*, second ed. University Park, PA: Pennsylvania State University Press, 1991.

———, *The German Nation and Martin Luther*. London: Edward Arnold, 1974.

Dillenberger, John, ed. *Martin Luther: Selections from His Writings*. New York: Doubleday, 1961.

Dolcini, C. "Marsilio da Padova e Giovanni di Jandun." *Storia della chiesa* v. 9: *La crisi del Trecento e il papato avignonese (1274–1378)*. Edited by D. Quaglioni. Cinisello Balsamo: San Paolo, 1994.

———. *Introduzione a Marsilio da Padova, I filosofi*. Bari: Laterza, 1995.

Donaldson, Peter. *Machiavelli and Mystery of State*. Cambridge: Cambridge University Press, 1988.

Dowel, John. *The Leviathan Heretical*. 1683.

Dungan, David Laird. *A History of the Synoptic Problem: The Canon, the Text, the Composition, and the Interpretation of the Gospels*. New Haven: Yale University Press, 1999.

Dunn, Richard. *The Age of Religious Wars: 1559–1689*. New York: W. W. Norton, 1970.

Dupré, Louis. *Passage to Modernity: An Essay in the Hermeneutics of Nature and Culture*. New Haven: Yale University Press, 1993.

Eachard, Rev. John. *Mr Hobbs's State of Nature Considered in a dialogue between Philautus and Timothy*. 1672.

Ebeling, Gerhard. "The Significance of the Critical Historical Method for Church and Theology in Protestantism." In *Word and Faith*. Translated by James Leitch. Philadelphia: Fortress Press, 1969.

Edwards, John. *Socinianism Unmask'd. A Discourse shewing the Unreasonableness of a Late Writer's Opinion Concerning the Necessity of only One Article of Christian Faith*. In *John Locke and Christianity: Contemporary Responses to The Reasonableness of Christianity*. Edited by Victor Nuovo. Bristol, England: Thoemmes Press, 1997.

———. *Some Thoughts concerning the Several Causes and Occasions of Atheism*. In *John Locke and Christianity: Contemporary Responses to The Reasonableness of Christianity*. Edited by Victor Nuovo. Bristol, England: Thoemmes Press, 1997.

Edwards, Mark. *Luther and the False Brethren*. Stanford, CA: Stanford University Press, 1975.

Eells, Hastings. *The Attitude of Martin Bucer toward the Bigamy of Philip of Hesse*. New Haven: Yale University Press, 1924.

Ehrman, Bart. Introduction to *Misquoting Jesus: The Story Behind Who Changed the Bible and Why*. New York: HarperCollins, 2005.

Elton, G. R. *Policy and Police: The Enforcement of the Reformation in the Age of Thomas Cromwell*. Cambridge: Cambridge University Press, 1972.

Emerson, William. *Monmouth's Rebellion*. New Haven: Yale University Press, 1951.

Evans, G. R. *John Wyclif: Myth & Reality*. Downers Grove, IL: InterVarsity Press, 2005.

———. "Wyclif's *Logic* and Wyclif's Exegesis: the Context." In *The Bible in the Medieval World: Essays in Memory of Beryl Smalley*. Edited by Katherine Walsh and Diana Wood. Oxford: Basil Blackwell, 1985.

Farmer, William. "State *Interesse* and Markan Primacy: 1870–1914." In *Biblical Studies and the Shifting of Paradigms: 1850–1914*. Edited by Henning Graf Reventlow and William Farmer. Sheffield, England: Sheffield Academic Press, 1995.

Faur, José. *In the Shadow of History: Jews and* Conversos *at the Dawn of Modernity*. Albany, NY: SUNY Press, 1992.

Filmer, Robert. *Patriarchia*, I.3–4. In *Patriarchia and Other Writings*. Edited by Johann Sommerville. Cambridge: Cambridge University Press, 1991.

———. *Observations Upon Aristotles Politiques*, Preface. In *Patriarchia and Other Writings*. Edited by Johann Sommerville. Cambridge: Cambridge University Press, 1991.

Fix, Andrew. *Prophecy and Reason: The Dutch Collegiants in the Early Enlightenment*. Princeton: Princeton University Press, 1991.

Forrester, Duncan. "Martin Luther and John Calvin." In *History of Political Philosophy*, second ed. Edited by Leo Strauss and Joseph Cropsey. Chicago: University of Chicago Press, 1981.

Forshall, J., and F. Madden, eds. *The Holy Bible . . . Made from the Latin Vulgate by John Wycliffe and His Followers*. Oxford: Oxford University Press, 1850.

Frampton, Travis L. *Spinoza and the Rise of Historical Criticism of the Bible*. London: T. & T. Clark, 2006.

Frend, W.H.C. *The Rise of Christianity*. Philadelphia, PA: Fortress Press, 1984.

Fudge, Thomas *The Magnificent Ride: The First Reformation in Hussite Bohemia*. Aldershot, England: Ashgate, 1998.

Furcha, E. J., ed. *The Essential Carlstadt*. Waterloo, Ontario: Herald Press, 1995.

Gabriel, Astrik. "'*Via Antiqua*' and '*Via Moderna*' in the Fifteenth Century." In *Antiqui und Moderni: Traditionsbewußtsein und Fortschrittsbewußtsein im späten Mittelalter.* Edited by Albert Zimmermann. Berlin: Walter De Gruyter, 1974.

Galilei, Galileo. *Opere Complete di Galileo Galilei,* Volume IV. Firenze: 1842. Quoted in E. A. Burtt, *The Metaphysical Foundations of Modern Physical Science*. New York: Doubleday, 1932.

Garnett, George. *Marsilius of Padua and "The Truth of History."* Oxford: Oxford University Press, 2006.

Pierre, Gassendi. *Animadversiones in Decimum Libri Diogenis Laertii, qui est de Vita, Moribus Placitisque Epicuri*. 1649.

———. *De Vita et Moribus Epicuri*. 1647.

———. *Syntagma Philosophiae Epicuri, cum Refutationibus Dogmatum, Quae Contra Fidem Christianum ab eo Asserta Sunt*. 1649.

Genequand, Charles. *Ibn Rushd's Metaphysics: A Translation with Introduction of Ibn Rushd's Commentary on Aristotle's Metaphysics, Book L m*. Leiden: Brill, 1986.

Gerdmar, Anders. *Roots of Theological Anti-Semitism: German Biblical Interpretation and the Jews, from Herder and Semler to Kittel and Bultmann*. Leiden: Brill, 2008.

Gewirth, Alan. "John of Jandun and the *Defensor Pacis*." *Speculum* XXIII (1948).

———. *Marsilius of Padua and Medieval Political Philosophy,* Volume 1. New York and London: Columbia University Press, 1951.

Ghosh, Kantik. *The Wycliffite Heresy: Authority and the Interpretation of Texts*. Cambridge: Cambridge University Press, 2002.

Gibert, Pierre. "The Catholic Counterpart to the Protestant Orthodoxy." In *Hebrew Bible/Old Testament: The History of Its Interpretation*: Volume II, *From the Renaissance to the Enlightenment*. Edited by Magne Sæbø. Göttingen: Vandenhoeck & Ruprecht, 2008.

———. *L'invention critique de la Bible: XVe-XVIIIe*. Paris: Éditions Gallimard, 2010.

Gilbert, Neal Ward. "Ockham, Wyclif, and the 'Via Moderna,'" In *Antiqui und Moderni: Traditionsbewußtsein und Fortschrittsbewußtsein im späten Mittelalter.* Edited by Albert Zimmermann. Berlin: Walter De Gruyter, 1974.

Gillespie, Michael Allen. *The Theological Origins of Modernity*. Chicago: University of Chicago Press, 2008.

Gilson, Etienne. *History of Christian Philosophy in the Middle Ages*. New York: Random House, 1955.

Goddu, André. "Ockham's Philosophy of Nature." In Paul Vincent Spade, *The Cambridge Companion to Ockham*. Cambridge: Cambridge University Press, 1999.

Godthardt, Frank. "The Philosopher as Political Actor—Marsilius of Padua at the Court of Ludwig the Bavarian: The Sources Revisited." In *The World of Marsilius of Padua*. Edited by Gerson Moreno-Riaño Turnhout: Brepols, 2006.

Golden, Samuel. *Jean LeClerc*. New York: Twayne Publishers, Inc., 1972.

Grant, E. "Science and Theology in the Midle Ages." In *God and Nature: Historical Essays on the Encounter between Christianity and Science*. Edited by D. C. Lindberg and R. L. Numbers. Berkeley and Los Angeles: University of California Press, 1986.

———. "The Condemnation of 1277: God's Absolute Power and Physical Thought in the Late Middle Ages." *Viator* 10 (1979).

Gullan-Whur, Margaret. *Within Reason: A Life of Spinoza*. New York: St. Martin's Press, 1998

Hagen, Kenneth. *The Theology of Testament in the Young Luther: The Lectures on Hebrews*. Leiden: Brill, 1974.

Hahn, Scott. *Letter and Spirit: From Written Text to Living Word in the Liturgy*. New York: Doubleday, 2005.

Haldane, Elizabeth and G.R.T. Ross, *The Philosophical Works of Descartes*. New York: Dover, 1955.

Hall, Louis Brewer. *The Perilous Vision of John Wyclif*. Chicago, IL: Nelson-Hall, 1983.

Haller, J. "Zur Lebensgeschichte des Marsilius von Padua." *ZKG* 48 (1929). In Johannes Haller, *Abhandlungen zur Geschichte des Mittelalters*. Stuttgart: Verlag, 1944.

Hargreaves, H. "Popularizing Biblical Scholarship: The Role of the Wycliffite Glossed Gospels." In *The Bible in Medieval Culture*. Edited by W. Lourdaux and D. Verhulst. Louvain, 1979.

———. "The Wycliffite Versions." In *The Cambridge History of the Bible*. Cambridge: Cambridge University Press, 1969.

Harrison, Peter. "The Bible and the Emergence of Modern Science." *Science & Christian Belief* 18, No. 2 (2006).

———. "Fixing the Meaning of Scripture: The Renaissance Bible and the Origins of Modernity." *Concilium* 294 (2002).

———. "Voluntarism and Early Modern Science." *History of Science* 40 (2002).

Harrison, R. K. *Introduction to the Old Testament*. Grand Rapids: Eerdmans, 1969.

Harrisville, Roy, and Walter Sundberg, *The Bible in Modern Culture: Baruch Spinoza to Brevard Childs,* second ed. Grand Rapids, MI: Eerdmans, 2002.

Harvey, Margaret. "Adam Easton and the Condemnation of John Wyclif." *English Historical Review* 118, April 1998.

Harvey, Warren. "A Portrait of Spinoza as a Maimonidean." *Journal of the History of Philosophy* 19 (1981).

Hayden-Roy, Patrick. *The Inner Word and the Outer World: A Biography of Sebastian Franck*. New York: Peter Lang, 1994.

Hayes, John. "Historical Criticism of the Old Testament Canon." In *Hebrew Bible/Old Testament: The History of Its Interpretation*: Volume II, *From the Renaissance to the Enlightenment*. Edited by Magne Sæbø. Göttingen: Vandenhoeck & Ruprecht, 2008.

Hayes, John H. "The History of the Study of Israelite and Judaean History." In *Israelite and Judaean History*. Edited by John H. Hayes and J. Maxwell Miller. London: SCM Press, 1977.

Hendrix, Scott. "Luther against the Backdrop of the History of Biblical Interpretation." In *Tradition and Authority in the Reformation*. Brookfield, VT: Variorum, 1996.

Henry VIII, King of England. *Assertio Septem Sacramentorum or Defence of the Seven Sacraments*. Translated by Rev. Louis O'Donovan. New York: Benziger Brothers, 1908.

Herde, Peter. "From Adolf of Nassau to Lewis of Bavaria, 1292–1347." In *The New Cambridge Medieval History*, Volume VI. Edited by Michael Jones Cambridge: Cambridge University Press, 2000.

Hibbert, Christopher. *The Rise and Fall of the House of Medici*. New York: Penguin, 1979.

Hill, Christopher. *The Century of Revolution, 1603–1714*. New York: W. W. Norton, 1980.

———. *The English Bible and the Seventeenth-Century Revolution*. New York: Penguin Books, 1994.

———. "Freethinking and Libertinism: the Legacy of the English Revolution." In *The Margins of Orthodoxy: Heterodox Writing and Cultural Response, 1660–1750*. Edited by Roger Lund. Cambridge: Cambridge University Press, 1995.

———. *The World Turned Upside Down: Radical Ideas During the English Revolution*. London: Penguin Books; reprint 1991.

Hillerbrand, Hans J. *Landgrave Philipp of Hesse, 1504–1567: Religion and Politics in the Reformation*. Saint Louis, MO: Foundation for Reformation Research, 1967.

———, ed. *The Protestant Reformation*. New York: Harper & Row, 1968.

Hobbes, Thomas *De Corpore,* translation from the English version, *Elements of Philosophy Concerning Body,* in Thomas Hobbes, *Metaphysical Writings*. Edited by Mary Whiton Calkins. La Salle, IL: Open Court, 1905.

———. *The Elements of Law Natural and Politic*. Edited and translated by J.C.A. Gaskin. Oxford and New York: Oxford University Press, 1994.

———. *Hobbes's Leviathan*. Reprint of the 1651 edition of *Leviathan, or The Matter, Forme, & Power of a Common-wealth Ecclesiasticall and Civill*. Oxford: Clarendon Press, 1965.

Hoenen, Maarten J.F.M. "*Via Antiqua* and *Via Moderna* in the Fifteenth Century: Doctrinal, Institutional, and Church Political Factors in the *Wegestreit*." In Russell Friedman and Lauge Nielsen, *The Medieval Heritage in Early Modern Metaphysics and Modal Theory, 1400–1700*. Dordrecht: Kluwer Academic Publishers, 2003.

Hoffmeier, James K. *Israel in Egypt: The Evidence for the Authenticity of the Exodus Tradition*. Oxford: Oxford University Press, 1996.

Holborn, Hajo. *Ulrich von Hutten and the German Reformation*. Translated by Roland Bainton. Westport, CT: Greenwood Press, 1965.

Hornig, Gottfried. *Johann Salomo Semler. Studien zu Leben und Werk des Hallenser Aufklärungstheologen*. Tübingen: Niemeyer, 1996.

Horowitz, Irving L. "Averroism and the Politics of Philosophy." *The Journal of Politics* 22, No. 4 (November 1960).

Howard, Thomas Albert. *Religion and the Rise of Historicism: W.M.L. de Wette, Jacob Burckhardt, and the Theological Origins of Nineteenth-Century Historical Consciousness.* Cambridge: Cambridge University Press, 2000.

Hudson, Anne. *Lollards and Their Books* London: The Hambledon Press, 1985.

————. *The Premature Reformation: Wycliffite Texts and Lollard History.* Oxford: Clarendon Press, 1988.

Hull, William. *Benjamin Furly and Quakerism in Rotterdam.* Lancaster, PA: Lancaster Press, Inc., 1941.

Hume, David. *A Treatise of Human Nature,* second ed. Edited by L. A. Selby-Bigge, Oxford: Clarendon Press, 1978.

Hunt, John. *Religious Thought in England.* London: Strahan & Co, 1870; reprint AMS Press, 1973.

Hyde, Edward, Earl of Clarendon. *A Brief View and Survey of the Dangerous and Pernicious Errors to Church and State, In Mr. Hobbes's Book, Entitled Leviathan.* 1676.

Israel, Jonathan I. "The Banning of Spinoza's Works in the Dutch Republic (1670–1678)." In Wiep Van Bunge and Wim Klever, *Disguised and Overt Spinozism Around 1700.* Leiden: E. J. Brill, 1996.

————. *Enlightenment Contested: Philosophy, Modernity, and the Emancipation of Man 1670–1752.* Oxford: Oxford University Press, 2006.

————. *Radical Enlightenment: Philosophy and the Making of Modernity 1650–1750.* Oxford: Oxford University Press, 2001.

————. "Spinoza, King Solomon, and Frederik van Leenhof's Spinozistic Republicanism." In H. De Dijn, F. Mignini, and P. van Rooden, "Spinoza's Philosophy of Religion." *Studia Spinozana* 11 (1995).

Jacob, James. "The Anglican Origins of Modern Science: The Metaphysical Foundations of the Whig Constitution." *Isis* 71 (1980).

————. "Boyle's Atomism and the Restoration Assault on Pagan Naturalism." *Social Studies of Science* 8 (1978).

————. *Henry Stubbe, Radical Protestantism and the Early Enlightenment.* Cambridge: Cambridge University Press, 2002).

————. "Restoration, Reformation and the Origins of the Royal Society." *History of Science* 13 (1975).

————. *Robert Boyle and the English Revolution: A Study in Social and Intellectual Change.* New York: Burt Franklin & Co., Inc., 1977.

————. "Robert Boyle and Subversive Religion in the Early Restoration." *Albion* 6 (1974).

Jacob, Margaret. *The Newtonians and the English Revolution, 1689–1720.* Hassocks, Sussex: The Harvester Press, 1976.

————. *The Radical Enlightenment: Pantheists, Freemasons, and Republicans.* London: George Allen & Unwin, 1981.

Jacquot, Jean. "Thomas Harriot's Reputation for Impiety." *Notes and Records of the Royal Society of London* IX (1952).

John, Eric. *The Popes: A Concise Biographical History*. New York: Hawthorn Books, Inc., 1964.

Johnson, Marion. *The Borgias*. New York: Holt, Rinehart and Winston, 1981.

Kahn, Victoria. *Machiavellian Rhetoric from the Counter-Reformation to Milton*. Princeton: Princeton University Press, 1994.

Karant-Nunn, Susan. *Germania Illustrata: Essays on Early Modern Germany Presented to Gerald Strauss*. Ann Arbor, MI: Edwards Brothers, 1992.

———, *Zwickau in Transition, 1500–1547*. Columbus: Ohio State University Press, 1987.

Kargon, Robert. *Atomism in England from Hariot to Newton*. Oxford: Clarendon Press, 1966.

Kasher, Asa, and Shlomo Biderman. "Why Was Baruch De Spinoza Excommunicated." In David Katz and Jonathan I. Israel, *Sceptics, Millenarians and Jews*. Leiden: E. J. Brill, 1990.

Katz, David. *God's Last Words: Reading the English Bible from the Reformation to Fundamentalism*. New Haven: Yale University Press, 2004.

Keen, Maurice. "Wyclif, the Bible, and Transubstantiation." In Anthony Kenny, *Wyclif in His Times*. Oxford: Clarendon Press, 1986.

Kelley, Donald."*Tacitus Noster*: The *Germania* in the Renaissance and Reformation." In *Tacitus and the Tacitean Tradition*. Edited by T. J. Luce and A. J. Woodman. Princeton: Princeton University Press, 1993.

Kennington, Richard. *On Modern Origins: Essays in Early Modern Philosophy*. Lanham, MD: Lexington Books, 2004.

Kenny, Anthony. "The Realism of the *De Universalibus*." In *Wyclif in His Times*. Oxford: Clarendon Press, 1986.

Klein, Jacob. *Greek Mathematical Thought and the Origin of Algebra*. New York: Dover Publications, 1992.

Klever, Wim. "A New Source of Spinozism: Franciscus van den Enden." *Journal of the History of Philosophy* 29 (October 1991).

Knauth, Wolfgang, and Sejfoddin Nadjmabadi, *Das altiranische Fürstenideal von Xenophon bis Ferdousi*. Wiesbaden: Steiner, 1975.

Knight, Douglas. *Rediscovering the Traditions of Israel: The Development of the Traditio-Historical Research of the Old Testament, with Special Consideration of Scandinavian Contributions*, revised ed. Missoula, MT: Scholars Press, 1975.

Kolakowski, Leszek. "Dutch Seventeenth-Century Non-Denominationalism and *Religio Rationalis*: Mennonites, Collegiants and the Spinoza Connection." In *The Two Eyes of Spinoza & Other Essays on Philosophers*. Edited by Zbigniew Janowski. South Bend, IN: St. Augustine's Press, 2004.

———. "The Tragic Career of Uriel da Costa" In *The Two Eyes of Spinoza & Other Essays on Philosophers*. Edited by Zbigniew Janowski. South Bend, IN: St. Augustine's Press, 2004.

Korvela, Paul-Erik. *The Machiavellian Reformation: An Essay in Political Theory*. Jyväskylä: University of Jyväskylä, 2006.

Kraus, Hans-Joachim. *Geschichte der historisch-kritischen Erforschung des Alten Testaments*. Neukirchen: Kreis Moers, 1956.

Krentz, Edgar. *The Historical-Critical Method*. Philadelphia, PA: Fortress Press, 1975.

Kümmel, Werner. *The New Testament: The History of the Investigation of Its Problems*. Translated by S. McLean Gilmour and Howard C. Kee. Nashville, TN: Abingdon Press, 1972.

Lachterman, David. *The Ethics of Geometry: A Genealogy of Modernity*. New York: Routledge, 1989.

————. "Laying Down the Law: The Theological-Political Matrix of Spinoza's Physics." In *Leo Strauss's Thought: Toward a Critical Engagement*. Edited by Alan Udoff. Boulder & London: Lynne Rienner Publishers, 1991.

————. "The Physics of Spinoza's *Ethics*. In *Spinoza: New Perspectives*. Edited by Robert Shahan and J. I. Biro. Norman, OK: University of Oklahoma Press, 1978.

Lacy, T. A., ed. *The King's Book, or A Necessary Doctrine and Erudition for Any Christian Man*. London: Society for Promoting Christian Knowledge, 1932.

Laertius, Diogenes. *Lives of Eminent Philosophers*. Translated by R. D. Hicks. Volumes I–II. Loeb Classical Library. Cambridge: Harvard University Press, 1925.

Lambe, Patrick. "Biblical Criticism and Censorship in Ancien Régime France: The Case of Richard Simon." *Harvard Theological Review* 78:1–2 (1985).

Leff, Gordon. "The Place of Metaphysics in Wyclif's Theology." In Anne Hudson and Michael Wilks, *From Ockham to Wyclif*. Oxford: Basil Blackwell, 1987.

Legaspi, Michael C. *The Death of Scripture and the Rise of Biblical Studies*. Oxford: Oxford University Press, 2010.

Lemay, J. A. Leo, ed., *Deism, Masonry, and the Enlightenment*. Newark: University of Delaware Press, 1987.

Lessing, Gotthold. "The Education of the Human Race." In *Lessing's Theological Writings*. Edited and translated by Henry Chadwick. Stanford, CA: Stanford University Press, 1956.

————. "On the Proof of the Spirit and of Power." In *Lessing's Theological Writings*. Edited and translated by Henry Chadwick. Stanford, CA: Stanford University Press, 1956.

Levenson, Jon D. *The Hebrew Bible, the Old Testament, and Historical Criticism*. Louisville, KY: Westminster/John Knox Press, 1993.

Levy, Ian Christopher. *John Wyclif: Scriptural Logic, Real Presence, and the Parameters of Orthodoxy*. Marquette, WI: Marquette University Press, 2003.

Lloyd, Genevieve, ed. *Spinoza: Critical Assessments. Volume III: The Political Writings*. London and New York: Routledge, 2001.

Locke, John. *A Letter Concerning Toleration*. Translated by William Popple. London, 1689; reprinted and edited by James Tully. Indianapolis, IN: Hackett Publishing Company, 1983.

————. *An Essay Concerning Human Understanding*. Abridged and edited by John Yolton. London: J. M. Dent, 1993.

———. *The Reasonableness of Christianity as Delivered in the Scriptures.* Edited by George Ewing. Washington, DC: Regnery, 1965.

———. "*Resurrectio et quae sequuntur.*" In Appendix VI, John Locke, *A Paraphrase and Notes on the Epistles of St. Paul to the Galatians, I and 2 Corinthians, Romans, Ephesians.* Edited by Arthur W. Wainwright. Oxford: Clarendon Press, 1987.

———. *Two Tracts on Government.* Edited by Philip Abrams. Cambridge: Cambridge University Press, 1967.

———. *Two Treatises of Government.* Edited by Thomas Cook. New York: Hafner Press, 1947.

Loeb, Louis. "Is There Radical Dissimulation in Descartes's *Meditations*?" In *Essays on Descartes's Meditations.* Edited by Amélie Oksenberg Rorty. Berkeley, CA: University of California Press, 1986.

Lucretius. *On the Nature of Things* (*De Rerum Natura*). Translated by W.H.D. Rouse. Loeb Classical Library. Cambridge: Harvard University Press, 1924.

Lucy, William. *Observations, Censures and Confutations of Notorious Errors in Mr Hobbes His Leviathan.* 1663.

Lundin, Roger. "Interpreting Orphans: Hermeneutics in the Cartesian Tradition." In Lundin, Roger, Clarence Walhout, and Anthony Thiselton, *The Promise of Hermeneutics.* Grand Rapids, MI: Eerdmans Publishing Company, 1999.

Lundin, Roger, Clarence Walhout, and Anthony Thiselton, *The Promise of Hermeneutics.* Grand Rapids, MI: Eerdmans Publishing Company, 1999.

Luther, Martin. *Against the Heavenly Prophets in the Matter of Images and Sacraments.* In *Karlstadt's Battle with Luther.* Edited by Ronald J. Sider. Philadelphia: Fortress Press, 1978.

———. *Commentary on Psalm 101.* In *Luther's Works*, Volume 13, *Selected Psalms II.* Edited by Jaroslav Pelikan. Saint Louis: Concordia Publishing House, 1956.

———. *Disputation against Scholastic Theology.* In *Luther's Works*, Volume 31, *Career of the Reformer I.* Edited by Helmut Lehmann. Philadelphia, PA: Muhlenberg Press, 1957.

———. *The Freedom of a Christian.* In *Martin Luther: Selections from His Writings.* Edited by John Dillenberger. New York: Doubleday, 1961.

———. *Lectures on Romans.* Edited and translated by Wilhelm Pauck. Philadelphia: Westminster Press, 1961.

———. *Martin Luther: Selections from His Writings.* Edited by John Dillenberger. Preface to the Complete Edition of Luther's Latin Writings. New York: Doubleday, 1961.

———. *The Pagan Servitude of the Church.* In *Martin Luther: Selections from His Writings.* Edited by John Dillenberger. New York: Doubleday, 1961.

———. *Whether Soldiers, Too, Can Be Saved* (1526). In *Works of Martin Luther.* Philadelphia, PA: Muhlenberg Press, 1931.

Marsiglio of Padua. *Defensor Minor.* In *Writings on the Empire:* Defensor minor *and* De Translatione Imperii. Edited by Cary Nederman. Cambridge: Cambridge University Press, 1993.

———. *Defensor Pacis*. Translated by Alan Gewirth. Toronto: University of Toronto Press, 1980.

Martin, Craig. "Rethinking Renaissance Averroism." *Intellectual History Review* 17, Issue 1 (March 2007).

Martines, Lauro. *April Blood: Florence and the Plot against the Medici*. Oxford: Oxford University Press, 2004.

Martinich, A. P. *Hobbes: A Biography*. Cambridge: Cambridge University Press, 1999.

———. *The Two Gods of Leviathan*. Cambridge: Cambridge University Press, 1992.

Maurer, Armand. *The Philosophy of William of Ockham in the Light of Its Principles*. Toronto: Pontifical Institute of Mediaeval Studies, 1999.

Machiavelli, Niccolò. *Discourses on Livy*. Translated by Harvey Mansfield and Nathan Tarcov. Chicago, IL: University of Chicago Press, 1996.

———. *Florentine Histories*. Translated by Laura Banfield and Harvey Mansfield. Princeton: Princeton University Press, 1990.

———. *The Prince*. Translated by Harvey Mansfield. Chicago: University of Chicago Press, 1985.

Malcolm, Noel. "A Summary Biography of Hobbes." In *The Cambridge Companion to Hobbes*. Edited by Tom Sorell. Cambridge: Cambridge University Press, 1996.

Marius, Richard. *Martin Luther: The Christian between God and Death*. Cambridge, MA: Belknap Press, 1999.

Massil, Stephen W. "Immigrant Librarians in Britain: Huguenots and Some Others." Available online at http://www.ifla.org/IV/ifla69/papers/058e-Massil.pdf.

Mayer, Thomas. *Thomas Starkey and the Commonweal: Humanist Politics and Religion in the Reign of Henry VIII*. Cambridge: Cambridge University Press, 1989.

McCarthy, John, ed. *Modern Enlightenment and the Rule of Reason, Studies in Philosophy and the History of Philosophy*, Volume 32. Washington, DC: Catholic University of America Press, 1998.

McGrath, Alister. *The Intellectual Origins of the European Reformation*. Grand Rapids, MI: Baker, 1993.

McIntyre, J. Lewis *Giordano Bruno*. New York: Macmillan, 1903.

McKenna, J. W. "How God became an Englishman." In *Tudor Rule and Revolution: Essays for G. R. Elton*. Edited by D. J. Guth and J. W. McKenna. Cambridge: Cambridge University Press, 1982.

McShea, Robert. *The Political Philosophy of Spinoza*. New York: Columbia University Press, 1968.

Meinecke, Friedrich. *Machiavellianism: The Doctrine of* Raison d'Etat *and Its Place in Modern History*. Translated by Douglas Scott. New York: Frederick A. Praeger Publishers, 1965.

Meyer, Lodewijk. *Philosophy as the Interpreter of Holy Scripture*. Translated by Samuel Shirley. Marquette, WI: Marquette University Press, 2005.

Miethke, J. *De potestate papae. Die päpstliche Amtskompetenz im Widerstreit der politischen Theorie von Thomas von Aquin bis Wilhelm von Ockham, Spätmittelalter und Reformation*. Tübingen: Mohr Siebeck, 2000.

———. "*Marsilius von Padua. Die politische Philosophie eines lateinischen Aristotelikers des 14. Jahrhunderts.*" In *Lebenslehren und Weltentwürfe im Übergang vom Mittelalter zur Neuzeit: Politik–Naturkunde–Theologie*. Edited by H. Boockmann, B. Moeller, and K. Stackmann. Göttingen: 1989.

Milton, J. R. "Locke's Life and Times." In *The Cambridge Companion to Locke*. Edited by Vere Chappell. Cambridge: Cambridge University Press, 1994.

Mintz, Samuel. *The Hunting of Leviathan: Seventeenth-Century Reactions to the Materialism and Moral Philosophy of Thomas Hobbes*. Cambridge: Cambridge University Press, 1962.

Momigliano, Arnaldo. "Religious History without Frontiers." J. Wellhausen, U. Wilamowitz, and E. Schwartz." *History and Theory* 21.4 (1982).

More, Henry. *An Antidote Against Atheism*. 1653.

Mosse, George L. "Puritan Radicalism and the Enlightenment." *Church History* 29 (1960).

Mulier, Eco. *The Myth of Venice and Dutch Republican Thought in the Seventeenth Century*. Assen, Netherlands: Van Gorcum, 1980.

Mulsow, Martin. "*Libertinismus in Deutschland? Stile der Subversion in Politik, Religion und Literatur des 17. Jahrhunderts.*" *Zeitschrift für historische Forschung* 31 (2004).

———. *Moderne aus dem Untergrund. Radikale Frühaufklärung in Deutschland 1680–1720*. Hamburg: Meiner, 2002, *Habilitationsschrift*.

Nadler, Steven. "The Bible Hermeneutics of Baruch de Spinoza." In *Hebrew Bible/Old Testament: The History of Its Interpretation*: Volume II, *From the Renaissance to the Enlightenment*. Edited by Magne Sæbø. Göttingen: Vandenhoeck & Ruprecht, 2008.

———. *Spinoza: A Life*. Cambridge: Cambridge University Press, 1999.

Nederman, Cary. "Marsiglio of Padua Studies Today—and Tomorrow." In *The World of Marsilius of Padua*. Edited by Moreno-Riaño. Turnhout: Brepols, 2006.

Nellen, H.J.M. "Growing Tension between Church Doctrines and Critical Exegesis of the Old Testament." In *Hebrew Bible/Old Testament: The History of Its Interpretation*: Volume II, *From the Renaissance to the Enlightenment*. Edited by Magne Sæbø. Göttingen: Vandenhoeck & Ruprecht, 2008.

Nelson, Eric. *The Hebrew Republic: Jewish Sources and the Transformation of European Political Thought*. Cambridge: Harvard University Press, 2010.

Niewöhner, F. "*Die Religion Noahs bei Uriel da Costa und Baruch de Spinoza. Eine historische Miniature zur Genese des Deismus.*" In *Spinoza's Political and Theological Thought*. Edited by C. De Deugd. Amsterdam, Oxford: North-Holland, 1984.

Novick, Peter. *That Noble Dream: The "Objectivity Question" and the American Historical Profession*. Cambridge: Cambridge University Press, 1988.

Nyden-Bullock, Tammy. *Spinoza's Radical Cartesian Mind*. London: Continuum, 2007.

Oakley, Francis. "Christian Theology and the Newtonian Science: The Rise of the Concept of the Laws of Nature." *Church History* 30 (1961).

———. "Conciliarism in England: St. German, Starkey, and the Marsiglian Myth." In Thomas M. Izbicki and Christopher M. Bellitto, *Reform and Renewal in the Middle Ages and the Renaissance*. Leiden: Brill, 2000.

———. *Natural Law, Laws of Nature, Natural Rights: Continuity and Discontinuity in the History of Ideas*. New York: Continuum, 2005.

Oberman, Heiko. "*Facientibus Quod in se Est Deus non Denegat Gratiam*: Robert Holcot O. P. and the Beginnings of Luther's Theology." In Steven E. Ozment, *The Reformation in Medieval Perspective*. Chicago: Quadrangle Books, 1971.

———. "Luther and the *Via Moderna*: The Philosophical Backdrop of the Reformation Breakthrough." In *The Two Reformations: The Journey from the Last Days to the New World*. New Haven: Yale University Press, 2003.

———. *Luther: Man between God and the Devil*. Translated by Eileen Walliser-Schwarzbart. New Haven: Yale University Press, 1989.

———. *The Two Reformations: The Journey from the Last Days to the New World*. New Haven: Yale University Press, 2003.

———. "*Via Antiqua* and *Via Moderna*: Late Medieval Prolegomena to Early Reformation Thought." In *The Impact of the Reformation*. Grand Rapids, MI: William B. Eerdmans Publishing Company, 1994.

Offler, H. S. "Empire and Papacy: the Last Struggle." In *Church and Crown in the Fourteenth Century*. Edited by A. I. Doyle. Aldershot: Ashgate, 2000.

O'Grady, Paul. *Henry VIII and the Conforming Catholics*. Collegeville, MN: The Liturgical Press, 1990.

O'Malley, John, Thomas Izbicki, and Gerald Christianson, *Humanity and Divinity in Renaissance and Reformation: Essays in Honor of Charles Trinkaus*. Leiden: Brill, 1993.

O'Neill, J. C. *The Bible's Authority: A Portrait Gallery of Thinkers from Lessing to Bultmann*. Edinburgh: T. & T. Clark, 1991.

Oyer, John. *Lutheran Reformers against Anabaptists*. Hague: Martinus Nijhoff, 1964.

Pahl, Gretchen Graf. "John Locke as Literary Critic and Biblical Interpreter." In University of California Department of English, *Essays Critical and Historical Dedicated to Lily B. Campbell*. New York: Russell & Russell, 1968.

Parker, Geoffrey. *The Thirty Years' War*. London and New York: Routledge & Kegan Paul, 1984.

Parsons, Robert. *A Sermon Preached at the Funeral of the Rt Honorable John Earl of Rochester*. 1680.

Pasto, James. "Islam's 'Strange Secret Sharer': Orientalism, Judaism, and the Jewish Question." *Comparative Studies in Society and History* 40.3 (1998).

———. "Who Owns the Jewish Past? Judaism, Judaisms, and the Writing of Jewish History." Ph.D. diss., Cornell University, 1999.

Pastor, Ludwig. *The History of the Popes*. St. Louis, MO: Herder, 1902.

Perler, D., and U. Rudolph, *Occasionalismus: Theorien der Kausalität im arabisch-islamischen und im europäischen Denken*. Göttingen: 2000.

Piaia, Gregorio. "*Averroisme politique: Anatomie d'un mythe historiographique*." In *Orientalische Kultur und europäisches Mittelalter*. Edited by Albert Zimmermann and Ingrid Craemer-Ruegenberg. Berlin/New York: de Gruyter, 1985.

———. "*L'averroismo politico e Marsilio da Padova*." In *Saggi e ricerche su Aristotele, Marsilio da Padova, M. Eckhart, Rosmini, Spaventa, Marty, Tilgher,*

Omodeo, metafisica, fenomenologia ed estetica. Edited by Carlo Giacon. Padua: Antenore, 1971.

Pincin, C. *Marsilio,* Pubblicazioni dell'Istituto di Scienze Politiche dell'Università di Torino, 17 Turin (1967).

Pines, Shlomo. "Spinoza's 'Tractatus Theologico-Politicus,' Maimonides, and Kant." *Scripta Hierosolymitana* 20 (1968).

Plato. *The Republic of Plato,* second ed. Translated by Allan Bloom. New York: Basic Books, 1968.

Plutarch. *Lives.* Translated by Bernadotte Perrin. Volumes I–XI. Loeb Classical Library. Cambridge: Harvard University Press, 1914–1926.

Pocock, J.G.A. *The Machiavellian Moment: Florentine Political Thought and the Atlantic Republican Tradition*. Princeton: Princeton University Press, 1975.

Polybius. *Histories.*

Popkin, Richard. "Bible Criticism and Social Science." In *Methodological and Historical Essays in the Natural and Social Sciences*. Edited by Robert S. Cohen and Marx W. Wartofsky. Dordrecht: D. Reidel Publishing, 1974.

————. "Cartesianism and Biblical Criticism." In *Problems of Cartesianism*. Edited by Thomas Lennon, John Nicholas, and John Davis. Kingston and Montreal: McGill-Queen's University Press, 1982.

————. "The Hebrew Translation of Margaret Fell's 'Loving Salutation.' The first publication of Spinoza?" *Studia Rosenthalia* 21 (1987).

————. *The History of Scepticism from Savonarola to Bayle*, revised and expanded ed. Oxford: Oxford University Press, 2003.

————. *Isaac La Peyrère (1596–1676): His Life, Work and Influence*. Leiden: E. J. Brill, 1987.

————. "Spinoza and Bible Scholarship." In *The Books of Nature and Scripture: Recent Essays on Natural Philosophy, Theology, and Biblical Criticism in the Netherlands of Spinoza's Time and the British Isles of Newton's Time*. Edited by James Force and Richard Popkin. Dordrecht: Kluwer Academic Publishers, 1994.

————. "Spinoza and La Peyrère." In *Spinoza: New Perspectives*. Edited by Robert Shahan and J. I. Biro. Norman, OK: University of Oklahoma Press, 1978.

————. "Spinoza and the Three Imposters." In *The Third Force in Seventeenth-Century Thought*. Leiden: Brill, 1992.

Preus, James. *From Shadow to Promise: Old Testament Interpretation from Augustine to the Young Luther.* Cambridge: Harvard University Press, 1969.

Preus, Samuel. "The Bible and Religion in the Century of Genius: Part II: The Rise and Fall of the Bible." *Religion* 28 (1998).

Pullman, Bernard. *The Atom in the History of Human Thought*. Oxford: Oxford University Press, 1998.

Raab, Felix. *The English Face of Machiavelli*. London: Routledge & Kegan Paul, 1964.

Rahe, Paul, ed. *Machiavelli's Liberal Republican Legacy.* Cambridge: Cambridge University Press, 2005.

———. *Republics Ancient & Modern: New Modes & Orders in Early Modern Political Thought*. Chapel Hill, NC: University of North Carolina Press, 1994.

Rappaport, Rhoda. "Questions of Evidence: An Anonymous Tract Attributed to John Toland." *Journal of the History of Ideas* 58.2 (1997).

Rattansi, P. M. "The Social Interpretation of Science in the Seventeenth Century." In *Science and Society 1600–1900*. Edited by Peter Mathias. Cambridge: Cambridge University Press, 1972.

Ratzinger, Joseph Cardinal. "Biblical Interpretation in Crisis: On the Question of the Foundations and Approaches of Exegesis Today." In *Biblical Interpretation in Crisis: The Ratzinger Conference on Bible and Church*. Edited by Richard John Neuhaus. Grand Rapids, MI: Eerdmans, 1989.

Reedy, Gerald, S.J. *The Bible and Reason: Anglicans and Scripture in Late Seventeenth-Century England*. Philadelphia, PA: University of Pennsylvania Press, 1985.

Rees, E. A. *Political Thought from Machiavelli to Stalin*. New York: Palgrave Macmillan, 2004.

Renna, Thomas. "Wyclif's Attacks on the Monks." In Anne Hudson and Michael Wilks, *From Ockham to Wyclif*. Oxford: Basil Blackwell, 1987.

Reventlow, Henning Graf. *The Authority of the Bible and the Rise of the Modern World*. Translated by John Bowden. Philadelphia: Fortress Press, 1985.

———. *History of Biblical Interpretation*, four volumes. Translated by Leo G. Perdue. Atlanta, GA: Society of Biblical Literature, 2009–2010.

———. "The Role of the Old Testament in the German Liberal Protestant Theology of the Nineteenth Century." In *Biblical Studies and the Shifting of Paradigms: 1850–1914*. Edited by Henning Graf Reventlow and William Farmer. Sheffield: Sheffield Academic Press, 1995.

———. "Towards the End of the 'Century of Enlightenment': Established Shift from *Sacra Scriptura* to Literary Documents and Religion of the People of Israel." In *Hebrew Bible/Old Testament: The History of Its Interpretation:* Volume II, *From the Renaissance to the Enlightenment*. Edited by Magne Sæbø. Göttingen: Vandenhoeck & Ruprecht, 2008.

Reventlow, Henning Graf, and William Farmer, eds. *Biblical Studies and the Shifting of Paradigms: 1850–1914*. Sheffield, England: Sheffield Academic Press, 1995.

Rodis-Lewis, Geneviève. *Descartes: His Life and Thought*. Translated by Jane Marie Todd. Ithaca and London: Cornell University Press, 1995,1998.

Rogers, G.A.J. and Alan Ryan, eds. *Perspectives on Thomas Hobbes*. Oxford: Clarendon Press, 1988.

Rogerson, John. "Early Old Testament Critics in the Roman Catholic Church—Focusing on the Pentateuch." In *Hebrew Bible/Old Testament: The History of Its Interpretation*: Volume II, *From the Renaissance to the Enlightenment*. Edited by Magne Sæbø. Göttingen: Vandenhoeck & Ruprecht, 2008.

———. *Old Testament Criticism in the Nineteenth Century: England and Germany*. Philadelphia, PA: Fortress Press, 1985.

———. "Philosophy and the Rise of Biblical Criticism: England and Germany." In *England and Germany: Studies in Theological Diplomacy*. Edited by S. W. Sykes. Frankfurt am Main: Verlag Peter D. Lang, 1982.

———. "Setting the Scene: A Brief Outline of Histories of Israel." *Proceedings of the British Academy* 143 (2007).

———. *W.M.L. de Wette: Founder of Modern Biblical Criticism: An Intellectual Biography*. Sheffield: Sheffield Academic Press, 1992.

Rosenthal, Michael. "Why Spinoza Chose the Hebrews: The Exemplary Function of Prophecy in the *Theological-Political Treatise*." *History of Political Thought* 18 (1997). Reprinted in *Spinoza: Critical Assessments. Volume III: The Political Writings*. Edited by Lloyd. London and New York: Routledge, 2001.

Ross, Alexander. *Leviathan drawn out with a Hook*. 1653.

Ross, John M. Introduction to Cicero's *The Nature of the Gods*. Translated by Horace McGregor. New York: Penguin Books, 1972.

Rublack, Hans-Christoph. "Success and Failure of the Reformation: Popular 'Apologies' from the Seventeenth and Eighteenth Centuries." In Susan Karant-Nunn, *Germania Illustrata: Essays on Early Modern Germany Presented to Gerald Strauss*. Ann Arbor, MI: Edwards Brothers, 1992.

Sæbø, Magne, ed. *Hebrew Bible/Old Testament: The History of Its Interpretation*: Volume II, *From the Renaissance to the Enlightenment*. Göttingen: Vandenhoeck & Ruprecht, 2008.

Sailor, Danton. "Moses and Atomism." *Journal of the History of Ideas* 25, No. 1 (1964).

Saine, Thomas P. *The Problem of Being Modern, or, The German Pursuit of Enlightenment from Leibniz to the French Revolution*. Detroit, MI: Wayne State University Press, 1997.

Sandmel, Samuel. *The Hebrew Scriptures: An Introduction to Their Literature and Religious Ideas*. New York: Alfred A. Knopf, 1963.

Sandys-Wunsch, John. *What Have They Done to the Bible? A History of Modern Biblical Interpretation*. Collegeville, MN: Liturgical Press, 2005.

Scarisbrick, J. J. *Henry VIII*. Berkeley and Los Angeles: University of California Press, 1968.

Scholder, Klaus. *The Birth of Modern Critical Theology: Origins and Problems of Biblical Criticism*. Translated by John Bowden. London: SCM Press, 1990.

Schroder, Winfried. *Spinoza in der deutschen Frühaufklärung*. Wurzburg: Konigshausen + Neumann 1987.

Scribner, R. W., and C. Scott Dixon. *The German Reformation*, second ed. New York: Palgrave Macmillan, 2003.

Scribner, Robert, Roy Porter, and Mikuláš Teich, *The Reformation in National Context*. Cambridge: Cambridge University Press, 1994.

Sheehan, Jonathan. *The Enlightenment Bible: Translation, Scholarship, Culture*. Princeton: Princeton University Press, 2005.

Sider, Ronald. *Andreas Bodenstein von Karlstadt: The Development of His Thought, 1517–1525*. Leiden: E. J. Brill, 1974.

Ronald Sider, ed., *Karlstadt's Battle with Luther: Documents in a Liberal-Radical Debate*. Philadelphia, PA: Fortress Press, 1978

Siebrand, H. "On the Early Reception of Spinoza's Tractatus Theologico-Politicus in the Context of Cartesianism." In *Spinoza's Political and Theological Thought*. Edited by C. De Deugd. Amsterdam: North-Holland Publishing, 1984.

Simon, Richard. *A Critical History of the Old Testament*. 1682 English translation by "a Person of Quality." Printed by Walter Davis; reprinted by Classic Reprints No. 61; Pensacola, FL: Vance Publications, 2002.

Simonutti, Luisa. "Limborch's *Historia Inquisitionis* and the Pursuit of Toleration." In *Judaeo-Christian Intellectual Culture in the Seventeenth Century*. Edited by Allison Coudert, et al. Dordrecht: Kluwer Academic Publishers, 1999.

———. "Religion, Philosophy, and Science: John Locke and Limborch's Circle in Amsterdam." In James Force and David Katz, *Everything Connects: In Conference with Richard H. Popkin*. Leiden: Brill, 1999.

Singer, Dorothy. *Giordano Bruno: His Life and Thought*. New York: Henry Schuman, 1950.

Smalley, Beryl. "The Bible and Eternity: John Wyclif's Dilemma." In *Studies in Medieval Thought and Learning from Abelard to Wyclif*. London: Hambledon Press, 1981

———. "John Wyclif's *Postilla super totam bibliam*." *Bodleian Library Record* iv (1953).

———. *The Study of the Bible in the Middle Ages* Notre Dame, IN: University of Notre Dame Press, 1964.

———. "Wyclif's *Postilla* on the Old Testament and his *Principium*." *Oxford Studies Presented to Daniel Callus* (1964).

Smend, Rudolph. *From Astruc to Zimmerli: Old Testament Scholarship in Three Centuries*. Translated by Margaret Kohl. Tübingen: Mohr Siebeck, 2007.

Smith, Christian. *The Secular Revolution: Power, Interests, and Conflict in the Secularization of American Public Life*. Berkeley, CA: University of California Press, 2003.

Smith, Steven. *Spinoza, Liberalism, and the Question of Jewish Identity*. New Haven: Yale University Press, 1997.

Smith, W. Bradford. "Germanic Pagan Antiquity in Lutheran Historical Thought." *Journal of the Historical Society* IV: 3 (2004).

Smith, Wilfred Cantwell. "The Study of Religion and the Study of the Bible." *Journal of the American Academy of Religion* 39 (1971).

Sorkin, David. *The Religious Enlightenment: Protestants, Jews, and Catholics from London to Vienna*. Princeton: Princeton University Press, 2008.

Spalding, Paul. *Seize the Book, Jail the Author: Johann Lorenz Schmidt and Censorship in Eighteenth-Century Germany*. West Lafayette, IN: Purdue University Press, 1998.

Spinoza, Baruch. *Ethics; Treatise on the Emendation of the Intellect; and Selected Letters*. Indianapolis, IN: Hackett Publishing, 1992.

Spinoza, Benedict. *A Political Treatise*. In *A Theologico-Political Treatise* and *A Political Treatise*. Translated by R.H.M. Elwes. New York: Dover, 1951.

———. *Principles of Cartesian Philosophy*. Translated by Samuel Shirley Indianapolis, IN: Hackett Publishing Company, Inc., 1998.

———. *Theologico-Political Treatise*. Translated by Martin Yaffe. Newburyport, MA: R. Pullins & Company, 2004.

Spitz, Lewis. "Luther as Scholar and Thinker." In *Luther and German Humanism*. Brookfield, VT: Variorum, 1996.

Lewis Spitz, *Conrad Celtis: The German Arch-Humanist*. Cambridge: Harvard University Press, 1957.

Steinberg, S. H. *The Thirty Years' War and the Conflict for European Hegemony, 1600–1660*. New York: W. W. Norton, 1966.

Steinmann, Jean. *Richard Simon et les origins de l'exégèse biblique* Paris: Desclée de Brouwer, 1960. In *Christianity and the Stranger*. Edited by Francis Nichols. Atlanta, GA: Scholars Press, 1995.

Steinmetz, David. *Reformers in the Wings: From Geiler von Kayserberg to Theodore Beza*, second ed. Oxford: Oxford University Press, 2001.

Stout, Harry S. "Marsilius of Padua and the Henrician Reformation." *Church History* (1974).

Strabo. *The Geography of Strabo*. Volumes I–VIII. Translated by Horace Jones. Loeb Classical Library. Cambridge: Harvard University, 1917–1932.

Strand, Kenneth. *Reformation Bibles in the Crossfire: The Story of Jerome Emser, His Anti-Lutheran Critique and His Catholic Bible Version*. Ann Arbor, MI: Ann Arbor, Publishers, 1961.

Strauss, David Friedrich. *The Life of Jesus Critically Examined*, fourth ed. Edited by Peter Hodgson. Philadelphia, PA: Fortress, 1972.

Strauss, Gerald. "Success and Failure in the German Reformation." *Past and Present* (May 1975).

———. "Protestant Dogma and the City Government: The Case of Nuremberg." *Past and Present* (April 1967).

Strauss, Gerald. *Manifestations of Discontent in Germany on the Eve of the Reformation*. Bloomington: Indiana University Press, 1971.

Strauss, Leo. *Spinoza's Critique of Religion*. Translated by E. M. Sinclair. Chicago: University of Chicago Press, 1997.

———. "Three Waves of Modernity." In *An Introduction to Political Philosophy: Ten Essays by Leo Strauss*. Edited by Hilail Gildin. Detroit, MI: Wayne State University Press, 1989.

Strayer, Joseph R. "France: The Holy Land, the Chosen People, and the Most Christian King." In *Medieval Statecraft and the Perspectives of History*. Princeton: Princeton University Press, 1971.

Sullivan, Robert. *John Toland and the Deist Controversy: A Study in Adaptations*. Cambridge: Harvard University Press, 1982.

Sullivan, Vickie. *Machiavelli, Hobbes, and the Formation of a Liberal Republicanism in England*. Cambridge: Cambridge University Press, 2004.

———. "Muted and Manifest English Machiavellianism." In *Machiavelli's Liberal Republican Legacy*. Edited by Paul Rahe. Cambridge: Cambridge University Press, 2006.

———. *Machiavelli's Three Romes*. DeKalb, IL: Northern Illinois University Press, 1996.

Syros, Vasileios. "Did the Physician from Padua Concur with the Rabbi from Cordoba? Marsilius of Padua and Moses Maimonides on the Political Utility of Religion." Forthcoming.

———. *Die Rezeption der aristotelischen politischen Philosophie bei Marsilius von Padua: Eine Untersuchung zur ersten Diktion des* Defensor pacis, *Studies in Medieval and Reformation Traditions*. Leiden/Boston: Brill, 2007

———. "Marsilius of Padua's Classical Sources." In *The Life and Thought of Marsilius of Padua*. Edited by Cary J. Nederman and Gerson Moreno–Riaño. Leiden/Boston: Brill, in press.

———. "Simone Luzzatto's Image of the Ideal Prince and the Italian Tradition of Reason of State." In *Redescriptions: Yearbook of Political Thought and Conceptual History*. Münster: Verlag, 2005.

Tacitus. *The Annals of Imperial Rome,* revised ed. Translated by Michael Grant. New York: Penguin, 1989.

Talbert, Charles, ed. *Reimarus: Fragments*. Translated by Ralph Fraser. Chico, CA: Scholars Press, 1985.

Tatnall, Edith C. "John Wyclif and *Ecclesia Anglicana*." *Journal of Ecclesiastical History* 20, No. 1 (April 1969).

Taylor, A. E. "The Ethical Doctrine of Hobbes." In K. C. Brown, *Hobbes Studies*. Cambridge: Harvard University Press, 1965.

Taylor, Charles. *A Secular Age*. Cambridge: Harvard University Press, 2007.

Taylor, Richard C. "Averroes: God and the Noble Lie." In *Laudemus viros gloriosos: Essays in Honor of Armand Maurer, CSB*. Edited by R. E. Houser. Notre Dame: University of Notre Dame Press, 2007.

Tenison, Thomas. *The Creed of Mr Hobbes Examined*. 1670.

The Three Impostors. Translated by Alcofribas Nasier. Privately printed, 1904; reprint, Kessinger, n.d.

Thompson, W.D.J. Cargill. *The Political Thought of Martin Luther*. Totowa, NJ: Barnes & Noble Books, 1984.

Tierney, Brian. *The Crisis of Church & State, 1050–1300*. Englewood Cliffs, NJ: Prentice-Hall, Inc., 1964

Toland, John. *Apology for Mr. Toland* (1697). In *John Toland's Christianity not Mysterious: Text, Associated Works and Critical Essays*. Edited by Philip McGuinness, Alan Harrison, and Richard Kearney. Dublin: The Lilliput Press, 1997.

———. *Christianity not Mysterious: Text, Associated Works and Critical Essays*. Edited by Philip McGuinness, Alan Harrison, and Richard Kearney. Dublin: The Lilliput Press, 1997.

———. *Clidophorus,* in *The Theological and Philological Works of the Late John Toland*. London: W. Mears, 1732; facsimile, Elibron Classics, 2005.

———. *Hodegus,* in *The Theological and Philological Works of the Late John Toland*. London: W. Mears, 1732; facsimile, Elibron Classics, 2005.

———. *The Life of John Milton with Amyntor; or a defense of Milton's life*. London: John Darby, 1699; reprinted by The Folcroft Press, Inc., 1969.

———. "The Life of Mr. Toland." In *A Collection of Several Pieces of Mr. John Toland*. London: J. Peele, 1726; facsimile, New York: Garland Publishing, Inc., 1977.

———. *Letters to Serena*. Stuttgart-Bad Connstatt: F. Frommann, 1964, facsimile of the 1704 edition printed in London by Bernard Lintot.

———. *Pantheisticon: or, the Form of Celebrating the Socratic-Society*. Originally published in Latin in 1720. English translation, London, 1751, Samuel Paterson; facsimile, New York: Garland Publishing, Inc., 1976.

Tornay, Stephen Chak. "Averroes' Doctrine of the Mind." *The Philosophical Review* 52, No. 3 (May 1943).

Treasure, Geoffrey. "'That great and knowing virtuoso': The French background and English refuge of Henri Justel." In Randolph Vigne and Charles Littleton, *From Strangers to Citizens: The Integration of Immigrant Communities in Britain, Ireland and Colonial America, 1550–1750*. Brighton: Sussex Academic Press, 2001.

Troeltsch, Ernst. "On Historical and Dogmatic Method in Theology." In *Religion in History*. Translated by James Adams and Walter Bense. Minneapolis, MN: Fortress Press, 1991.

Tuchman, Barbara. *The March of Folly: From Troy to Vietnam*. New York: Alfred A. Knopf, 1984.

Tyndale, William. *The Obedience of a Christian Man*. Edited by David Daniell. London: Penguin Books, 2000.

———. *Tyndale's New Testament (1534)*. Edited by David Daniell. Modern spelling edition. New Haven: Yale University Press, 1992.

———. *Tyndale's Old Testament, Being the Pentateuch of 1530, Joshua to 2 Chronicles of 1537, and Jonah*. Edited by David Daniell. Modern spelling edition. New Haven: Yale University Press, 1992.

Vallée, Gérard. *The Spinoza Conversations between Lessing and Jacobi: Text with Excerpts from the Ensuing Controversy*. Lanham, MD: University Press of America, 1988.

Valois, N. "Jean de Jandun et Marsile de Padoue auteurs du *Defensor pacis*." *Histoire littéraire de France* XXXIII (Paris 1906).

Van Bunge, Wiep, ed. *The Early Enlightenment in the Dutch Republic, 1650–1750*. Leiden: Brill, 2003.

Van Bunge, Wiep, and Wim Klever. *Disguised and Overt Spinozism Around 1700*. Leiden: E. J. Brill, 1996.

van der Wall, Ernestine. "Orthodoxy and Scepticism in the Early Dutch Enlightenment." In *Scepticism and Irreligion in the Seventeenth and Eighteenth Centuries*. Edited by Richard Popkin and Arjo Vanderjagt. Leiden: Brill, 1993.

Van Melsen, Andrew G. *From Atomos to Atom: The History of the Concept Atom*. New York: Harper & Brothers, 1960.

Vaysse, Jean-Marie. "*Spinoza dans la problématique de l'idéalisme allemande: Historicité et manifestation*." In *Spinoza au XIXe siècle*. Edited by André Tosel, Pierre-François Moreau, and Jean Salem. Paris: Sorbonne, 2007.

Verbeek, Theo. *Descartes and the Dutch: Early Reactions to Cartesian Philosophy*. Carbondale, IL: Southern Illinois University Press, 1992.

Vermij, Rienk. "Matter and Motion: Toland and Spinoza." In Wiep Van Bunge and Wim Klever, *Disguised and Overt Spinozism around 1700*. Leiden: E. J. Brill, 1996.

Vickers, Brian, ed. Francis Bacon, *The Major Works*. Oxford: University of Oxford Press, 1996.

Vignaux, Paul. "On Luther and Ockham." In Steven E. Ozment, *The Reformation in Medieval Perspective*. Chicago: Quadrangle Books, 1971.

Viroli, Maurizio. *From Politics to Reason of State: The Acquisition and Transformation of the Language of Politics, 1250–1600*. Cambridge: Cambridge University Press, 1992.

———. *Niccolò's Smile: A Biography of Machivelli*. Translated by Antony Shugaar. New York: Hill and Wang, 2000.

Wainwright, Arthur W., ed. John Locke, *A Paraphrase and Notes on the Epistles of St. Paul to the Galatians, I and 2 Corinthians, Romans, Ephesians*. Oxford: Clarendon Press, 1987.

Warrender, Howard. *The Political Philosophy of Hobbes*. Oxford: Clarendon Press, 1957.

Wellhausen, Julius. *Prolegomena to the History of Ancient Israel*. Cleveland, OH: Meridian Books, 1957.

Westfall, Richard. *Science and Religion in Seventeenth-Century England*. Ann Arbor, MI: The University of Michigan Press, 1973.

Whitehall, John. *The Leviathan Found Out; or the Answer to Mr. Hobbes's Leviathan, In that which my Lord Clarendon hath past over*. 1679.

Wiker, Benjamin. *Moral Darwinism: How We Became Hedonists*. Downers Grove, IL: InterVarsity Press, 2002.

Wiker, Benjamin, and Jonathan Witt. *A Meaningful World: How the Arts and Sciences Reveal the Genius of Nature*. Downers Grove, IL: InterVarsity Press, 2006.

Wilhelmsen, Frederick. *Man's Knowledge of Reality: An Introduction to Thomistic Epistemology*. Englewood Cliffs, NJ: Prentice-Hall, 1956.

Wilks, Michael. "Royal Patronage and Anti-Papalism from Ockham to Wyclif." In Anne Hudson and Michael Wilks, *From Ockham to Wyclif*. Oxford: Basil Blackwell, 1987.

William of Ockham. *A Letter to the Friars Minor*. In William of Ockham, *A Letter to the Friars Minor and Other Writings*. Edited by Arthur McGrade and John Kilcullen. Translated by John Kilcullen. Cambridge: Cambridge University Press, 1995.

———. *The Work of Ninety Days,* two volumes. Translated by John Kilcullen and John Scott. Lewiston, NY: Edwin Mellen Press, 2001.

Williams, Neville. *Henry VIII and His Court*. New York: Macmillan Company, 1971.

Wilson, Derek. *In the Lion's Court: Power, Ambition, and Sudden Death in the Reign of Henry VIII*. New York: St. Martin's Press, 2001.

Wolf, A. *The Correspondence of Spinoza*. New York: Russell & Russell, Inc., 1966.

Wolfson, Harry. *The Philosophy of Spinoza*. New York: Meridian Books, 1934.

Wollgast, Siegfried. "*Spinoza und die deutsche Frühaufklärung*." *Studia Spinozana* 9 (1992).

Wolseley, Sir Charles. *The Unreasonablenesse of Atheism made manifest*, second ed. 1669.

Woodbridge, John. "German Reponses to the Biblical Critic Richard Simon: from Leibniz to J. S. Semler." In *Historische Kritik und biblischer Kanon in der deutschen Aufklärung*. Edited by Henning Graf Reventlow, Walter Sparn, and John Woodbridge. Wiesbaden: Otto Harrassowitz, 1988. *Wolfenbütteler Forschungen* (41).

Wootton, David, ed. John Locke, *Political Writings*. New York: Penguin, 1993.

Worden, Blair. "Whig history and Puritan politics: The *Memoirs* of Edmund Ludlow revisited." *Historical Research* 75, no. 188.

Wyclif, John. *On the Truth of Holy Scripture*. Translated by Ian Christopher Levy. Kalamazoo, MI: Medieval Institute Publications, 2001.

————. *On Universals*. Translated by Anthony Kenny. Oxford: Clarendon Press, 1985.

Wycliffe, John. *De Civili Dominio*. Volumes I–IV. Critical and historical notes by Dr. Iohann Loserth. London: Trübner & Co., 1885–1904.

————. *Tractatus de Officio Regis*. Edited by A. W. Pollard and C. Sayle. London, 1887.

Xenophon. *Cyropaedia*. Volumes I–II. Translated by Walter Miller. Loeb Classical Library. Cambridge: Harvard University Press, 1914.

Yates, Francis. *Giordano Bruno and the Hermetic Tradition*. Chicago: University of Chicago Press, 1964.

Yovel, Yirmiyahu. *Spinoza and Other Heretics: The Marrano of Reason*. Princeton: Princeton University Press, 1989.

Zeeveld, W. Gordon. *Foundations of Tudor Policy*. London: Methuen & Co., Ltd., 1969.

ACKNOWLEDGEMENT

Research for this book was made possible, in part, by grants from the St. Paul Center for Biblical Theology.

INDEX

C

D

E

F

G

H

I

J

K

L

Q

R

Z

Related Reading

THE YES OF JESUS CHRIST
Spiritual Exercises in Faith, Hope, and Love
Pope Benedict XVI (Joseph Ratzinger)
ISBN 978-08245-23749

Pope Benedict XVI, with the help of Jesus and the Saints, shows us how to live guided by a definitive affirmation that God exists and a conscious acknowledgment that our efforts and goals only have meaning when contextualized by divine grace.

Secular thought and optimism have failed to answer the great questions of human existence. We are not wise enough to understand all the workings of the world but Pope Benedict XVI (Joseph Ratzinger) reminds us that we can call on the knowledge of Jesus and the saints. Ratzinger explains that although we may not know that God exists, we can rely on others' experience, and indeed that reliance is fundamental to the functioning and spiritual health of humankind.

Ratzinger helps us distinguish between an optimism that is a denial of reality and hope that rests in the faith of what God can do. He invites us to rediscover that our ability to say yes to ourselves and to one another comes from the gift of God's yes in Christ.

Support your local bookstore or order
directly from the publisher by calling
1-800-888-4741.

To request a catalog or inquire about
Quantity orders, please e-mail
info@CrossroadPublishing.com

Related Reading

I BELIEVE IN THE HOLY SPIRIT
The Complete Three-Volume Work In One Volume
Yves Congar
ISBN 978-08245-16963

A rare and comprehensive treatment of the Church's understanding of the Spirit and the working of the Spirit in the life of the Church, by one of the great Roman Catholic theologians of the 20th century.

Yves Congar, the influential theologian who made major contributions to Vatican II and the ecumenical movement in the Catholic Church, follows the notion of the Holy Spirit through scripture and history to reveal the profound meaning of this often-overlooked element of the Trinity.

Translated from the French by David Smith, Congar's work is accessible and stimulating, and addresses both biblical and historical sources with an unmatched authority and specificity. An articulate and scholarly investigation of the idea and power of Spirit—in the life of the Church and the world.

Support your local bookstore or order directly from the publisher by calling 1-800-888-4741.

To request a catalog or inquire about Quantity orders, please e-mail info@CrossroadPublishing.com

Related Reading

THE DOCTORS OF THE CHURCH
Thirty-Three Men and Women Who Shaped Christianity
Bernard McGinn
ISBN 978-08245-25491

Written by one of the world's top authorities on the history of Christianity, this user-friendly resource is an introduction to 33 remarkable individuals who shaped our understanding of the Catholic faith.

"McGinn's portrayal of each doctor is rich, as the brief life narrative of each doctor sketches out the interplay between inspiration, institution, and context that each doctor within him- or herself. It is the product of this interplay that becomes the means through which the doctors relate to God and their world and institution. The information McGinn imparts about the doctors is understandably succinct yet substantive, teasing the reader to plunge more fully in the doctor's life and thought. For those readers who seek brief 'pearls of wisdom,' this book delivers, liberally quoting from their writings, whether they are tomes, treatises, sermons, or letters." —Oswald John Nira, *Spiritual Life*.

A fascinating look at the men and women who have made major contributions to Christianity, this work also tells the story of the development of Christian theology—one doctor at a time.

Support your local bookstore or order directly from the publisher by calling 1-800-888-4741.

To request a catalog or inquire about Quantity orders, please e-mail info@CrossroadPublishing.com